GLEIM®

2021 EDITION

EA REVIEW

PART 1: INDIVIDUALS

by

Irvin N. Gleim, Ph.D., CPA, CIA, CMA, CFM

and

James R. Hasselback, Ph.D.

Gleim EA Review for the
IRS Special Enrollment Exam
5/1/2021 - 2/28/2022

Gleim Publications, Inc.
PO Box 12848
Gainesville, Florida 32604
(800) 87-GLEIM or (800) 874-5346
(352) 375-0772
www.gleimEA.com
GleimEA@gleim.com

For updates to this 2021 edition of *EA Review: Part 1, Individuals*

Go To: www.gleim.com/EAupdate

Or: Email update@gleim.com with **EA 1 2021-1** in the subject line. You will receive our current update as a reply.

Updates are available until the next edition is published.

ISSN: 1523-6722

ISBN: 978-1-61854-408-7   *EA 1: Individuals*
ISBN: 978-1-61854-409-4   *EA 2: Businesses*
ISBN: 978-1-61854-410-0   *EA 3: Representation, Practices & Procedures*
ISBN: 978-1-61854-418-6   *Enrolled Agent Exam Guide: A System for Success*

First Printing: February 2021

ACKNOWLEDGMENTS

The authors appreciate and thank the Internal Revenue Service and Prometric for their cooperation. Questions have been used from the 1978-2020 Special Enrollment Examinations.

Environmental Statement -- This book is printed on recycled paper sourced from suppliers certified using sustainable forestry management processes and is produced either TCF (Totally Chlorine-Free) or ECF (Elementally Chlorine-Free).

ABOUT THE AUTHORS

Irvin N. Gleim is Professor Emeritus in the Fisher School of Accounting at the University of Florida and is a member of the American Accounting Association, Academy of Legal Studies in Business, American Institute of Certified Public Accountants, Association of Government Accountants, Florida Institute of Certified Public Accountants, The Institute of Internal Auditors, and the Institute of Management Accountants. He has had articles published in the *Journal of Accountancy*, *The Accounting Review*, and the *American Business Law Journal* and is author/coauthor of numerous accounting books, aviation books, and CPE courses. Other exam prep and textbook titles from Dr. Gleim include

- Gleim CPA Review
- Gleim CMA Review
- Gleim CIA Review
- Gleim Exam Questions and Explanations Series

James R. Hasselback is an Adjunct Professor at Louisiana State University. He has previously taught at Florida State University, Eastern Michigan University, the University of Florida, and Texas A&M University. A member of the American Accounting Association and the American Taxation Association, he has published over 160 papers in professional and academic journals, including *The Accounting Review*, *The Tax Adviser*, *Financial Management*, *Journal of Real Estate Taxation*, and the *American Business Law Journal*. Dr. Hasselback has presented papers at many national and regional professional meetings and has served as chairman at tax sessions of professional conferences. He regularly presents continuing education seminars for certified public accountants. In addition, he has been coauthor and technical editor of a two-volume introductory taxation series published by CCH, Inc., for the past 30 years and has served as technical editor of several publications by CCH and Harper-Collins. Dr. Hasselback has compiled over 40 editions of the *Accounting Faculty Directory*.

A PERSONAL THANKS

This manual would not have been possible without the extraordinary effort and dedication of Jacob Bennett, Julie Cutlip, Ethan Good, Doug Green, Fernanda Martinez, Bree Rodriguez, Veronica Rodriguez, Teresa Soard, Justin Stephenson, Joanne Strong, Elmer Tucker, Candace Van Doren, and Ryan Van Tress, who typed the entire manuscript and all revisions and drafted and laid out the diagrams, illustrations, and cover for this book.

The authors also appreciate the production and editorial assistance of Sirene Dagher, Michaela Giampaolo, Jessica Hatker, Sonora Hospital-Medina, Katie Larson, Michael Lupi, Bryce Owen, Shane Rapp, and Alyssa Thomas.

The authors also appreciate the critical reading assistance of Ali Band, Corey Connell, Adrianna Cuevas, Kimberly Haft, Melissa Leonard, Allen Lin, Nicola Martens, Martin Salazar, Maris Silvestri, and Miranda Valcarcel.

The authors also appreciate the video production expertise of Gary Brook, Philip Brubaker, Matthew Church, Andrew Johnson, Mackenzie O'Connell, and Michaela Wallace, who helped produce and edit our Gleim Instruct Video Series.

Finally, we appreciate the encouragement, support, and tolerance of our families throughout this project.

iv

REVIEWERS AND CONTRIBUTORS

Garrett W. Gleim, CPA, CGMA, leads production of the Gleim CPA, CMA, CIA, and EA exam review systems. He is a member of the American Institute of Certified Public Accountants and the Florida Institute of Certified Public Accountants and holds a Bachelor of Science in Economics with a Concentration in Accounting from The Wharton School, University of Pennsylvania. Mr. Gleim is coauthor of numerous accounting and aviation books and the inventor of multiple patents with educational applications. He is also an avid pilot who holds a commercial pilot rating and is a certified flight instructor. In addition, as an active supporter of the local business community, Mr. Gleim serves as an advisor to several start-ups.

Matthew Hutchens, J.D., CPA, EA, is a Lecturer of Accountancy at the University of Illinois Gies College of Business. Prior to joining the University of Illinois, he was a Staff Attorney at a Low Income Taxpayer Clinic and a Senior Staff Accountant in the National Tax Office of Crowe LLP. He received a law degree from the Indiana University Maurer School of Law and a bachelor's degree in Accounting and Finance from the Indiana University Kelley School of Business. Mr. Hutchens provided substantial editorial assistance throughout the project.

D. Scott Lawton, B.S., is a graduate of Brigham Young University-Idaho and Utah Valley University, and he has passed the EA exam. He has worked as an auditor for the Utah State Tax Commission. Mr. Lawton provided substantial editorial assistance throughout the project.

LouAnn M. Lutter, M.S. Acc., CPA, received a Master of Science in Accounting from the University of Colorado, Boulder. Previously, she was an Accounting Manager in Corporate Accounting and Shared Business Services at Caesars Entertainment. Ms. Lutter provided substantial editorial assistance throughout the project.

Mark S. Modas, M.S.T., CPA, holds a Bachelor of Arts in Accounting from Florida Atlantic University and a Master of Science in Taxation from Nova Southeastern University. Prior to joining Gleim, he worked in internal auditing, accounting and financial reporting, and corporate tax compliance in the public and private sectors. Mr. Modas provided substantial editorial assistance throughout the project.

Nate Wadlinger, J.D., LL.M., EA, CPA, is a Lecturer of Taxation at Florida State University, where he teaches tax courses in the Bachelor and Master of Accounting programs. Mr. Wadlinger received his Bachelor of Science in Accounting, Master of Accounting, and Juris Doctor from the University of Florida and his LL.M. in Taxation from Boston University. In addition, he is an EA, a CPA licensed by the State of Florida, and a member of the Florida Bar. Mr. Wadlinger is the EA Gleim Instruct lecturer.

Chun Nam Wo, M.S. Acc., CPA, received a Master of Science in Accountancy with a concentration in Data Analytics from the University of Illinois at Urbana-Champaign. Mr. Wo provided substantial editorial assistance throughout the project.

TABLE OF CONTENTS

DETAILED TABLE OF CONTENTS

PREFACE

The purpose of this book is to help **you** prepare to pass Part 1, Individuals, of the IRS Special Enrollment Exam, which is commonly referred to as the EA (enrolled agent) exam. Our goal is to provide an affordable, effective, and easy-to-use study program. Our course

1. Explains how to maximize your score through learning strategies and exam-taking techniques perfected by Gleim EA.

2. Outlines all of the content topics described in the IRS Exam Content Outlines and tested on Part 1 of the EA exam.

3. Organizes all of the subject matter tested on Part 1 in 14 easy-to-use study units, reflecting 2020 tax law (which is what will be tested on the 2021 EA exam).

4. Presents multiple-choice questions taken or modeled from past EA examinations to prepare you for the types of questions you will find on your EA exams.

    a. In our book, the answer explanations are presented to the immediate right of each question for your convenience. Use a piece of paper to cover our detailed answer explanations as you answer the question and then review all answer choices to learn why the correct one is correct and why the other choices are incorrect.

    b. You should also practice answering these questions through our online platform, which mimics Prometric's user interface, so you are comfortable answering questions online like you will do on test day. Our adaptive course will focus and target your weak areas.

5. Provides the tax rate schedules with inflation-adjusted amounts as a detachable bookmark in the book and as an additional resource PDF in the online course for your convenience.

The outline format, spacing, and question and answer formats in this book are designed to increase readability, learning, understanding, and success on the EA exam. Our most successful candidates use the Gleim Premium EA Review System*, which includes Gleim Instruct videos; our Access Until You Pass Guarantee; our innovative SmartAdapt technology; expertly authored books; the largest test bank of multiple-choice questions; audio lectures; flashcards; and the support of our team of accounting experts. Candidates' success is based on the Gleim system of teaching not only the topics tested, but also what you can expect on exam day. We want you to feel confident and in control when you sit for the exam.

We want your feedback immediately after you take the exam and receive your exam score. Please go to www.gleim.com/feedbackEA1 to share suggestions on how we can improve this edition. The EA exam is a **nondisclosed** exam, which means you must maintain the confidentiality of the exam by not divulging the nature or content of any EA question or answer under any circumstances. We ask only for information about our materials and any improvements that can be made regarding topics that need to be added or expanded or need more emphasis.

Good Luck on the Exam,

Irvin N. Gleim
James R. Hasselback

February 2021

PREPARING FOR AND TAKING
THE IRS ENROLLED AGENT EXAMINATION

READ THE *ENROLLED AGENT EXAM GUIDE: A SYSTEM FOR SUCCESS*

Obtain a free copy of the Gleim *Enrolled Agent Exam Guide* by visiting www.gleim.com/PassEA. Then, continue to reference it throughout your studies for a deeper understanding of the EA exam and exam-taking strategies.

OVERVIEW OF THE EA EXAMINATION

The **exam consists of three parts, with 3.5 hours for each part** (4 hours total seat time to include tutorial, survey, and optional 15-minute break). The total exam for all three parts is 10.5 hours of testing (12 hours total seat time to include tutorials, surveys, and optional 15-minute breaks). It covers **federal taxation; tax accounting; and the use of tax return forms for individuals, partnerships, corporations, trusts, estates, and gifts**. It also covers **ethical considerations and procedural requirements**.

The questions on the examination are directed toward the tasks that enrolled agents must perform to complete and file forms and tax returns and to represent taxpayers before the Internal Revenue Service. Each part of the examination consists of **100 multiple-choice questions** and covers the following tax topics:

Part 1 - Individuals
Part 2 - Businesses
Part 3 - Representation, Practices and Procedures

Based on the experience of our customers who have taken all three parts of the exam, Gleim recommends that candidates sit for Parts 1 and 2 before taking Part 3. Feedback indicates that Part 3 candidates should be knowledgeable about topics covered in Parts 1 and 2 as they relate to the topics that Part 3 tests.

IRS's NONDISCLOSURE AGREEMENT

The EA exam is nondisclosed. The following is taken from the IRS's *Candidate Information Bulletin*. It is reproduced here to remind all EA candidates about the IRS's strict policy of nondisclosure, which Gleim consistently supports and upholds.

> *This exam is confidential and proprietary. It is made available to you, the examinee, solely for the purpose of assessing your proficiency level in the skill area referenced in the title of this exam. You are expressly prohibited from disclosing, publishing, reproducing, or transmitting this exam, in whole or in part, in any form or by any means, verbal or written, electronic or mechanical, for any purpose, without the prior express written permission of the IRS.*

DATES OF THE EXAMINATION/TAX LAW COVERED

The 2021 examination test window will begin May 1, 2021, and examinations will be offered continuously through February 28, 2022.

Each testing year's EA exam (through February of the following year) covers the tax law in effect the previous December 31. For example, the May 1, 2021-February 28, 2022, testing window will test tax law in effect December 31, 2020.

Gleim consistently monitors any changes the IRS makes to the exam. The 2021 exam incorporates tax law changes due to the Coronavirus Aid, Relief, and Economic Security (CARES) Act effective March 27, 2020, and the Consolidated Appropriations Act, 2021, which went into effect in December 2020. Additionally, the IRS released updated Exam Content Outlines in January 2021, effective May 1, 2021. Stay up to date on any EA exam changes at www.gleim.com/EAexamchanges.

GLEIM PREMIUM EA REVIEW WITH SMARTADAPT

Gleim Premium EA Review features the most comprehensive coverage of exam content and employs the most efficient learning techniques to help you study smarter and most effectively. The Gleim Premium EA Review System is powered by SmartAdapt technology, an innovative platform that identifies where you should focus (and where you should not) as you move through the following steps for optimized EA review:

Step 1:

Complete a Diagnostic Study Quiz. As you work through this quiz, you will get immediate feedback on your answer choices. This allows you to learn as you study the detailed answer explanations. Meanwhile, your quiz results set a baseline that our SmartAdapt technology will use to create a custom learning track for each bite-sized module.

Step 2:

Solidify your knowledge by studying the suggested Knowledge Transfer Outline(s) or watching the suggested Gleim Instruct video(s). You will also be able to take notes within your online course while reviewing either of these learning tools.

Step 3:

Focus on weak areas and perfect your question-answering techniques by taking the adaptive quizzes that SmartAdapt directs you to.

Final Review:

After completing all study units, take the first Exam Rehearsal, a full-length mock exam. Then, SmartAdapt will guide you through a Final Review based on your results, which will help pinpoint where you need to focus. Finally, a few days before your exam date, take the second Exam Rehearsal. SmartAdapt will tell you when you are ready to pass with confidence.

To facilitate your studies, the Gleim Premium EA Review System uses the largest bank of multiple-choice questions on the market. Our system's content and presentation precisely mimic the whole exam environment so you feel completely at ease on test day.

TIME-BUDGETING AND QUESTION-ANSWERING TECHNIQUES FOR THE EXAM

The following suggestions are to assist you in maximizing your score on Part 1 of the EA exam. Remember, knowing how to take the exam and how to answer individual questions is as important as studying/reviewing the subject matter tested on the exam.

1. **Budget your time.** We make this point with emphasis–**finish your exam before time expires**.

   a. You will have 3 hours and 30 minutes (210 minutes) to answer 100 multiple-choice questions. On your Prometric computer screen, the time remaining (starting with 03:30:00) appears in the top middle of the screen.

   b. As you work through the individual multiple-choice questions, monitor your time. If you allocate 1.5-2 minutes per question, you will require 150-200 minutes to finish all 100 questions, leaving 10-60 minutes to review your answers and "flagged" questions (see item 2.b. below). Spending 2 minutes should be reserved for only the most difficult questions. You should complete 10 questions every 15-20 minutes. If you pace yourself during the exam, you will have adequate time.

   c. The exam is broken into two halves of 50 questions each with an optional 15-minute break. The first half should take 75-100 minutes. You should finish answering and reviewing by the time you are 105 minutes through your exam. The remaining time will be spent on the second half.

2. **Answer the questions in consecutive order.**

   a. Do **not** agonize over any one question. Stay within your time budget: 1.5-2 minutes per question.

   b. Note any items you are unsure of by clicking the button with the flag icon and return to them later if time allows. Plan on going back to all flagged questions.

   c. Never leave a question unanswered. Make your best guess within your budgeted time. Your score is based on the number of correct responses. You will not be penalized for guessing incorrectly. You can always flag the question and return to it later.

3. **For each multiple-choice question,**

   a. **Try to ignore the answer choices as you determine the answer.** Do not allow the answer choices to affect your reading of the question.

      1) If four answer choices are presented, three of them are incorrect. These incorrect answers are called **distractors** for good reason. Often, distractors are written to appear correct at first glance until further analysis.

      2) In computational items, distractors are carefully calculated so that they are the result of making common mistakes. Be careful, and double-check your computations if time permits.

   b. **Read the question** carefully to determine the precise requirement.

      1) Focusing on what is required enables you to ignore extraneous information and proceed directly to determining the correct answer. This will save you valuable time.

         a) Be especially careful to note when the requirement is an **exception**; e.g., "Which of the following is **not** includible in gross income?"

c.   **Determine the correct answer** before looking at the answer choices.

    1)   However, some multiple-choice items are structured so that the answer cannot be determined from the stem alone. See the stem in 3.b.1)a) on the previous page.

c.   **Then read the answer choices carefully.**

    1)   Even if the first answer appears to be the correct choice, do not skip the remaining answer choices. Questions often ask for the "best" of the choices provided. Thus, each choice requires your consideration.

    2)   Treat each answer choice as a true/false question as you analyze it.

e.   **Click on the best answer.**

    1)   If you are uncertain, you have a 25% chance of answering the question correctly by guessing blindly. Improve your odds with educated guessing.

    2)   For many of the multiple-choice questions, two answer choices can be eliminated with minimal effort, thereby increasing your educated guess to a 50-50 proposition.

4.   After you have answered all 100 questions, return to the questions that you flagged. Then, verify that all questions have been answered.

5.   **If you don't know the answer:**

a.   Again, guess but make it an educated guess. First, rule out answers you think are incorrect. Second, speculate on what the IRS is looking for and/or the rationale behind the question. Third, select the best answer or guess between equally appealing answers. Your first guess is usually the most intuitive. If you cannot make an educated guess, read the stem and each answer, and pick the most intuitive answer.

b.   Make sure you accomplish this step within the predetermined time budget.

LEARNING FROM YOUR MISTAKES

Learning from questions you answer incorrectly is very important. Each question you answer incorrectly is an **opportunity** to avoid missing actual test questions on your EA exam. Thus, you should carefully study the answer explanations provided until you understand why the original answer you chose is wrong, as well as why the correct answer indicated is correct. This learning technique is clearly the difference between passing and failing for many EA candidates.

Also, you must determine why you answered questions incorrectly and learn how to avoid the same error in the future. Reasons for missing questions include

1.   Misreading the requirement (stem)
2.   Not understanding what is required
3.   Making a mathematical error
4.   Applying the wrong rule or concept
5.   Being distracted by one or more of the answers
6.   Incorrectly eliminating answers from consideration
7.   Not having knowledge of the topic tested
8.   Employing poor intuition when guessing

HOW TO BE IN CONTROL WHILE TAKING THE EXAM

You have to be in control to be successful during exam preparation and execution. Control can also contribute greatly to your personal and other professional goals. Control is a process whereby you

1. Develop expectations, standards, budgets, and plans.
2. Undertake activity, production, study, and learning.
3. Measure the activity, production, output, and knowledge.
4. Compare actual activity with expected and budgeted activity.
5. Modify the activity to better achieve the desired outcome.
6. Revise expectations and standards in light of actual experience.
7. Continue the process or restart the process in the future.

Exercising control will ultimately develop the confidence you need to outperform most other EA candidates and PASS the EA exam!

Learn more about these strategies and other helpful tips in our free *Enrolled Agent Exam Guide: A System for Success*. You can view this booklet online at www.gleim.com/PassEA.

IF YOU HAVE QUESTIONS ABOUT GLEIM MATERIALS

Gleim has an efficient and effective way for candidates who have purchased the Premium EA Review System to submit an inquiry and receive a response regarding Gleim materials directly through their course. This system also allows you to view your Q&A session in your Gleim Personal Classroom.

Questions regarding the information in this introduction and/or the *Enrolled Agent Exam Guide* (study suggestions, studying plans, exam specifics) should be emailed to personalcounselor@gleim.com.

Questions concerning orders, prices, shipments, or payments should be sent via email to customerservice@gleim.com and will be promptly handled by our competent and courteous customer service staff.

For technical support, you may use our automated technical support service at www.gleim.com/support, email us at support@gleim.com, or call us at (800) 874-5346.

FEEDBACK

Please fill out our online feedback form www.gleim.com/feedbackEA immediately after you take the EA exam so we can adapt to changes on the exam. Our approach has been approved by the IRS.

STUDY UNIT ONE

FILING REQUIREMENTS

(25 pages of outline)

To determine the proper tax liability, the taxpayer must claim the appropriate filing status, elect the available deductions, and comply with the necessary filing requirements.

1.1 PRELIMINARY WORK TO PREPARE TAX RETURNS

Prior-Year Return

1. Use of the prior year's returns for comparison helps prevent gross mathematical errors and identify significant changes.

   a. If the comparison shows that there were no significant changes, the current-year return should result in similar amounts and tax liability or refund.

   b. Comparison of the prior year's returns helps to identify applicable items that are not common to all individuals (retirement pay, sale of principal residence, itemized deductions, applicable taxes, etc.).

EXAMPLE 1-1 Prior-Year Return
The taxpayer's prior-year Form 1040 shows repayment of the First-Time Homebuyer Credit.
The preparer should ask questions such as

1. Did the house cease to be the main home, either by change in use or disposal/sale?
     2. What was the total amount of the original credit received?
     3. How much of the credit has already been repaid?

2. The accuracy of the prior year's return affects the accuracy of the current year's return in areas in which the prior year is relied upon (state taxes paid or refunded). It also increases efficiency in completing the current return.

Previous IRS Correspondence

3. A taxpayer's previous correspondence (e.g., letters, notices) with the IRS is likely to provide insight to issues still affecting a current return. It should be reviewed to ensure, among other things, compliance with prior audits, adjustments, or judgments.

Personal Information

4. Taxpayer personal information (e.g., date of birth, age, marital status, dependents, etc.) is used to verify the identity of the taxpayer and related dependents.

    a. The age of an individual determines if (s)he qualifies for additional deductions (65 and over), retirement distributions, dependency, etc.

    b. Married filing jointly status often increases beneficial dollar limits for deductions and credits.

    c. A state-issued photo ID from the taxpayer is a good source for obtaining personal information.

Nationality

5. Immigration status and/or citizenship (e.g., citizen, resident alien, or nonresident alien).

    a. If a taxpayer is an alien (not a U.S. citizen), (s)he is considered a nonresident alien unless either the green card test or the substantial presence test for the calendar year is met.

    b. Even if a taxpayer does not meet either of these tests, (s)he may be able to choose to be treated as a U.S. resident for part of the year (dual-status aliens). This usually occurs in the year of arrival in or departure from the United States.

    c. A non-U.S. citizen typically is denied a Social Security number (SSN). Any individual required to have a U.S. taxpayer identification number but not eligible for a SSN obtains an Individual Taxpayer Identification Number (ITIN) from the IRS. The ITIN is used to comply with U.S. tax laws and to process and account for tax returns and payments. ITINs are issued regardless of immigration status (e.g., for both resident and nonresident aliens).

6. The following table lists the key forms to file and the applicable due dates:

IF you are liable for . . .	THEN use . . .	DUE by . . .
Income tax	Form 1040 and Schedule C	15th day of 4th month after end of tax year
Self-employment tax	Schedule SE	File with Form 1040
Estimated tax	Form 1040-ES	15th day of 4th*, 6th*, and 9th months of tax year, and 15th day of 1st month after the end of tax year
Social Security and Medicare taxes and income tax withholding	Form 941 or 944	April 30*, July 31, October 31, and January 31 See Publication 15
Providing information on Social Security and Medicare taxes and income tax withholding	Form W-2 (to employee) Forms W-2 and W-3 (to the Social Security Administration)	January 31 January 31
Federal unemployment (FUTA) tax	Form 940	January 31 April 30*, July 31, October 31, and January 31, but only if the liability for unpaid tax is more than $500

* For 2020 only, April 1 through pre-July 15 due dates are automatically extended to July 15.

Information Returns

7. The following information returns provide potential sources of taxpayer gross income:

W-2 – Wage and Tax Statement
W-2G – Certain Gambling Winnings
Form 1099-B – Proceeds from Broker and Barter Exchange Transactions
Form 1099-C – Cancellation of Debt
Form 1099-DIV – Dividends and Distributions
Form 1099-G – Certain Government Payments
Form 1099-INT – Interest Income
Form 1099-K – Payment Card and Third Party Network Transactions
Form 1099-MISC – Miscellaneous Income
Form 1099-NEC – Nonemployee Compensation
Form 1099-OID – Original Issue Discount
Form 1099-PATR – Taxable Distributions Received From Cooperatives
Form 1099-Q – Payments From Qualified Education Programs (Under Sections 529 and 530)
Form 1099-R – Distributions From Pensions, Annuities, Retirement or Profit-Sharing Plans, IRAs, Insurance Contracts, etc.
Form 1099-S – Proceeds From Real Estate Transactions
Form 1099-SA – Distributions From an HSA, Archer MSA, or Medicare Advantage MSA

Individual or Business

8. Determine if an individual and/or a business entity is involved.

   a. A personal, living, or family expense is not deductible unless the Code specifically provides otherwise. Nondeductible expenses include

      1) Rent and insurance premiums paid for the taxpayer's own dwelling;
      2) Life insurance premiums paid by the insured;
      3) Upkeep of a personal automobile;
      4) Personal interest; and
      5) Payments for food, clothing, or domestic help.

Items Affecting Future Returns

9. Certain items from the prior-year return may be needed to complete the current-year return (state income tax refund, AMT for credit, gain or loss carryover, charitable gift carryover, Schedule D, Form 8801, etc.).

All Required Taxes Filed

10. A determination should be made as to which taxes apply to the taxpayer, e.g., income tax, withholding (estimated tax), FICA (self-employment tax) and FUTA, AMT, estate tax, gift tax, GST tax.

Special Filing Requirements

11. Foreign income. For purposes of determining whether a taxpayer must file a return, gross income includes any income that can be excluded as foreign-earned income or as a foreign housing amount.

12. If a taxpayer is a U.S. citizen or resident alien, the rules for filing income, estate, and gift tax returns and for paying estimated tax are generally the same whether the taxpayer is in the United States or abroad.

    a.   A taxpayer's income, filing status, and age generally determine whether a taxpayer's income tax return must be filed.

    b.   In general, U.S. citizens and resident aliens are taxed on their worldwide income. Generally, nonresident aliens are only taxed on U.S. source income. An exception to this general rule is if a nonresident elects to be treated as a U.S. resident, e.g., in order to file a joint return with the spouse who is a citizen or resident alien.

Reporting Foreign Financial Accounts and Specified Foreign Assets

13. Generally, any U.S. citizen, resident, or person doing business in the United States who has an ownership interest in, or signatory authority or other authority over, a financial account (or several accounts) in a foreign country with an aggregate value in excess of $10,000 at any time during the calendar year must file a Form FinCEN Report 114, *Report of Foreign Bank and Financial Accounts* (commonly referred to as an FBAR), reporting certain information with respect to that account by April 15 of the subsequent year or the extension due date of October 15. Failure to file an FBAR is subject to both civil and criminal penalties.

EXAMPLE 1-2   Required FBAR Filing

On January 1, a U.S. taxpayer deposits $5,000 in an account in foreign country X. On July 1, the taxpayer deposits $5,001 in an account in foreign country Y. On July 2, the taxpayer withdraws the $5,000 from X to make a purchase. Because the taxpayer had a total of more than $10,000 (in this case $10,001) in foreign accounts (in this case a combined total of two separate countries/accounts) at any time during the year (i.e., July 1), the taxpayer must file an FBAR for the year.

---

    a.   Individuals living in the U.S. must use Form 8938 to report specified foreign financial assets with an aggregate value greater than $50,000 at the last day of the year or more than $75,000 at any time during the tax year (these thresholds double for married individuals filing jointly). For single individuals and married individuals filing separately who are living outside the U.S., the thresholds are $200,000 at the last day of the year or more than $300,000 at any time during the tax year (like those living in the U.S., these thresholds double for married individuals filing jointly who are living outside the U.S.). Form 8938 is required to be filed with an individual's annual income tax return. Individuals not required to file an annual income tax return are not required to file Form 8938.

b.   The purposes of Form 8938 and the FBAR are similar, and there is significant overlap. Yet filing Form 8938 does not relieve an individual of the requirement to file the FBAR. Many individuals will be required to file both Form 8938 and the FBAR to report substantially the same information.

   1)   Despite the similarities, there are some differences between the FBAR and Form 8938.

      a)   The FBAR is not filed with an individual's federal income tax return and must be filed online with the Financial Crimes Enforcement Network by April 15 each year.

      b)   In contrast, Form 8938 is filed with any annual return, whether it is an income tax return or an information return, listed as follows: Form 1040, Form 1040-NR, Form 1040-SR, Form 1041, Form 1041-N, Form 1065, Form 1120, and Form 1120-S.

      c)   In addition, the filing thresholds for Form 8938 and the FBAR are different, and the foreign financial assets that must be reported on Form 8938 are not limited to bank and financial accounts.

c.   Form 5471 is used by certain U.S. citizens and residents who are officers, directors, or shareholders in certain foreign corporations. The forms and schedules are used to satisfy the reporting requirements of Secs. 6038, 6046, and 965 (transition tax) and the related regulations. This form is filed with the tax return.

Transactions with Foreign Trusts

14.   U.S. persons and executors of estates of U.S. decedents file Form 3520 to report certain transactions with foreign trusts, ownership of foreign trusts under the rules of Secs. 671 through 679, and receipts of certain large gifts or bequests from certain foreign persons.

Interest in Foreign Partnerships

15.   U.S. persons qualifying, based on interest in a foreign partnership, under one or more of the following four categories of filers must complete and file Form 8865 with the tax return.

   a.   Category 1: 50% or greater ownership

   b.   Category 2: 10% or greater ownership of U.S.-controlled partnership

   c.   Category 3: Contributed property (1) resulting in at least a 10% interest or (2) with a value of more than $100,000

   d.   Category 4: Had a reportable event (acquisition, disposition, or change in proportional interest)

16. The following table is a basic listing of changes to be discussed as part of the preliminary work to prepare a tax return:

Personal and Financial Changes

Factor	Examples
Lifestyle change	Marriage Divorce Birth or adoption of child Loss of right to claim a dependent Purchase of a new home Retirement Filing Chapter 11 bankruptcy
Wage income	Either spouse starts or stops working or starts or stops a second job
Change in the amount of taxable income not subject to withholding	Interest income Dividends Capital gains Self-employment income IRA (including certain Roth IRA) distributions
Change in the amount of adjustments to income	IRA deduction Student loan interest deduction Alimony expense (pre-2019 divorces)
Change in the amount of itemized deductions or tax credits	Medical expenses Taxes Interest expense Gifts to charity Dependent care expenses Education credit Child Tax Credit Earned Income Credit

17. The return is due the 15th day of the 4th month after the end of the tax year (this includes when filed with respect to a decedent or filed by the estate).

   a. A taxpayer is allowed an automatic 2-month extension to file if, on the regular due date of the return, (s)he is living outside of the U.S. and Puerto Rico due to (1) his or her main place of business or post of duty or (2) on-duty military service.

18. A publicly traded partnership (PTP) is any partnership an interest in which is regularly traded on an established securities market regardless of the number of its partners.

    a. A PTP that has effectively connected income, gain, or loss must pay withholding tax on any distributions of that income made to its foreign partners.

        1) In this situation, a PTP must use Form 1042, *Annual Withholding Tax Return for U.S. Source Income of Foreign Persons*, and Form 1042-S, *Foreign Person's U.S. Source Income Subject to Withholding*, to report withholding from distributions.

    b. A taxpayer's net income from a PTP may not be used to offset net losses from other PTPs or net losses from other passive activities. A disallowed loss from a PTP is carried forward and allowed as a deduction in a tax year when the PTP has net income or when the taxpayer disposes his or her entire interest in the PTP.

STOP AND REVIEW! You have completed the outline for this subunit. Study multiple-choice questions 1 and 2 on page 32.

1.2 FILING STATUS

The standard deduction amount and applicable tax rates vary with filing status.

Married Filing a Joint Return

1. Taxpayers can choose married filing jointly as their filing status if they are considered married and both spouses agree to file a joint return. On a joint return, both spouses report combined income and deduct combined allowable expenses. Taxpayers can file a joint return even if one of the spouses had no income or deductions.

    a. Two individuals are treated as legally married for the entire tax year if, on the last day of the tax year, they are

        1) Legally married and cohabiting as spouses

        2) Legally married and living apart but not separated pursuant to a valid divorce decree or separate maintenance agreement

        3) Separated under a valid divorce decree that is not yet final

        NOTE: If a spouse dies, status for each spouse is determined when the spouse dies, unless the surviving spouse remarries before the end of the tax year (in which case the decedent files married filing separate).

    b. A joint return is not allowed if one spouse was a nonresident alien (NRA) at any time during the tax year, unless the U.S. citizen and the NRA spouse so elect and agree to be taxed on their worldwide income.

    c. Generally, if one spouse files separately, so must the other. An exception to this is if the other spouse qualifies for head of household while married. Then one spouse may file separately and the other may file as head of household.

    d. Once a joint return has been filed for the year and the time for filing the return of either spouse has expired, the spouses may not amend the return to file separate returns.

    e. Married individuals who file separate returns may later file a joint (amended) return. Payment of the entire joint tax liability is not required at the time the amended return is filed.

f.   If an individual obtains a marriage annulment (no valid marriage ever existed), the individuals must file amended returns claiming a filing status of single or head of household, whichever applies.

   1)   All prior tax years not closed by the statute of limitations must be amended.

g.   A joint return is signed by both spouses. Generally, the spouses are jointly and severally liable for the tax due and any interest and penalties.

   1)   One spouse may be relieved of joint and several liability under the "innocent spouse" provisions in very limited circumstances.

h.   Married individuals who file a joint return account for their items of income, deduction, and credit in the aggregate.

   1)   A joint return is allowed when spouses use different accounting methods.
   2)   Spouses with different tax years may not file a joint return.

i.   **Same-Sex Spouses**

   1)   Since 2013, same-sex couples have qualified for married filing status. The related Supreme Court rulings from 2015 have little effect on federal taxes, other than an expected increase in the volume of married same-sex taxpayers filing joint or separate returns.

      a)   This ruling only applies to married individuals, not to those in domestic partnerships or civil unions.

j.   **Injured Spouse**

   1)   When a joint return is filed and only one spouse owes a past-due amount, the other spouse can be considered an injured spouse.

      a)   An injured spouse can get a refund for his or her share of the joint overpayment that would otherwise be used to pay the past-due amount.

   2)   To be considered an injured spouse, the taxpayer must

      a)   File a joint return,
      b)   Have reported income (such as wages, interest, etc.),
      c)   Have made and reported tax payments (such as federal income tax withheld from wages or estimated tax payments) or claimed the Earned Income Credit or other refundable credit,
      d)   Not be required to pay a past-due amount, and
      e)   File Form 8379.

k. **Innocent Spouse Relief**

  1) Generally, both spouses are responsible for paying the full amount of tax, interest, and penalties due on a joint return. However, if qualified for innocent spouse relief, a taxpayer may be relieved of part or all of the joint liability.

  2) Qualifying events include

   a) An understatement of tax because the spouse omitted income or claimed false deductions or credits, and the innocent taxpayer was not aware of the understatement;

   b) An understatement of tax, and the innocent taxpayer is divorced or otherwise no longer living with the spouse; or

   c) Given all the facts and circumstances, it is not fair to hold the innocent taxpayer liable for the tax.

  3) Related types of relief include separation of liability relief, equitable relief, and relief from liability arising from community property law.

Married Filing Separate Returns

2. Each spouse accounts separately for items of income, deduction, and credit. A spouse who uses his or her own funds to pay expenses of jointly owned property is entitled to any deduction attributable to the payments.

Qualifying Widow(er)

3. This status is available for 2 years following the year of death of a spouse and may be elected if

  a. The surviving spouse did not remarry during the tax year.

  b. The surviving spouse qualified (with the deceased spouse) for married filing joint return status for the tax year of the death of the spouse.

  c. The surviving spouse maintained a household for the taxable year. Household maintenance means the spouse furnishes more than 50% of the costs to maintain the household for the tax year.

   1) The household must be the principal place of abode of a qualifying dependent of the surviving spouse.

   2) The dependent must be a son or daughter, a stepson or stepdaughter, or an adopted child. This does not include a foster child. (This is an exception to the general dependent rules covered in Subunit 1.4.)

   NOTE: An adopted child is always treated as the taxpayer's own child; i.e., the term "child" includes "adopted child."

  d. The surviving spouse can file a joint return in the tax year of the death of the spouse.

   1) The surviving spouse must not have remarried prior to the end of the year.

Head of Household

4.   An individual qualifies for head of household status if (s)he satisfies conditions with respect to filing status, marital status, and household maintenance.

   a.   Filing status. The individual may not file as a surviving spouse.

   b.   Marital status. Generally, the taxpayer must be unmarried on the last day of the year. A married person may qualify for head of household status if the conditions in item d. on page 17 are satisfied, i.e., considered unmarried. An individual is not treated as married for head of household status if the spouse is a nonresident alien at any time during the tax year.

Household Maintenance

   c.   An individual must maintain a household that is the principal place of abode for a qualifying individual.

   1)   To maintain a household for federal filing status purposes, an individual must furnish more than 50% of the costs, of mutual benefit, of maintaining the household during the tax year.

Qualifying Expenditures	Nonqualifying Costs
Property tax	Clothing
Mortgage interest	Education
Rent	Medical treatment
Utilities	Life insurance
Upkeep	Transportation
Repair	Vacations
Property insurance	Services by the taxpayer
Food consumed in-home	Services by the dependent

Qualifying Person and Time

   2)   The taxpayer must maintain a household that constitutes the principal place of abode for more than half of the taxable year for at least one qualified individual who is

   a)   A qualifying child or
   b)   A qualifying relative. (Both of these are defined in Subunit 1.4.)

   3)   Note that there are two special rules concerning a qualifying person:

   a)   First, the taxpayer with a dependent parent qualifies even if the parent does not live with the taxpayer.

   b)   Second, if a qualifying child lives with the taxpayer, the qualifying child need not be the taxpayer's dependent. For example, if all regular requirements are met but the custodial parent releases claim to the child as his or her dependent to the noncustodial parent per Form 8332.

   Otherwise, the IRS maintains that the qualifying individual must occupy the same household (except for temporary absences).

4) The following table is an additional guide for qualifying children and relatives:

IF the person is a . . .	AND . . .	THEN that person is . . .
qualifying child (such as a son, daughter, or grandchild who lived with the taxpayer more than half the year and meets certain other tests)	(s)he is single	a qualifying person, whether or not the taxpayer can claim the person as a dependent.
	(s)he is married **and** the taxpayer can claim him or her as a dependent	a qualifying person.
	(s)he is married **and** the taxpayer cannot claim him or her as a dependent	not a qualifying person.
qualifying relative who is the taxpayer's father or mother	the taxpayer can claim him or her as a dependent	a qualifying person.
	the taxpayer cannot claim him or her as a dependent	not a qualifying person.
qualifying relative other than the taxpayer's father or mother (such as a grandparent, brother, or sister who meets certain tests)	(s)he lived with the taxpayer more than half the year, **and** (s)he is related to the taxpayer in one of the ways listed under immediate relationships in Subunit 1.4, **and** the taxpayer can claim him or her as a dependent	a qualifying person.
	(s)he did not live with the taxpayer more than half the year	not a qualifying person.
	(s)he is not related to the taxpayer in one of the ways listed under immediate relationships in Subunit 1.4 **and** is the taxpayer's qualifying relative only because (s)he lived with the taxpayer all year as a member of the taxpayer's household	not a qualifying person.
	the taxpayer cannot claim him or her as a dependent	not a qualifying person.

d. A married individual who lives with a dependent apart from the spouse will be considered unmarried and qualify for head of household status if, for the tax year,

1) The individual files separately;

2) The individual pays more than 50% toward maintaining the household;

3) The spouse is not a member of the household for the last 6 months;

4) The household is the principal home of the individual's child, stepchild, or qualified foster child for more than half the year; and

5) The individual can claim the child as a dependent.

EXAMPLE 1-3   Head of Household Filing Status

Hector and Maria are married with one child. Hector moves out of the residence in May. They are not divorced by the end of the year. Maria maintains the household for the remainder of the year and claims the child on her individual tax return. Maria may claim head of household status. Hector would then be required to file as married filing separately.

Single

5. An individual must file as an unmarried individual if (s)he neither is married nor qualifies for surviving spouse or head of household status.

EXAMPLE 1-4   Filing Status -- Year of Separation

George and Rebecca married 5 years ago. At the end of the current year, they were legally separated under a final decree of separate maintenance. They are considered unmarried for the year and, if neither has a qualified dependent, they will each file as single individuals.

The Standard Deduction

6. Taxable income (TI) is adjusted gross income (AGI) minus the greater of itemized deductions or the standard deduction.

$$\text{Taxable income} = \frac{\text{Adjusted}}{\text{gross income}} - \frac{\text{Greater of allowable itemized deductions}}{\text{on Schedule A or the standard deduction}}$$

   a. The taxpayer itemizes deductions if the total allowable itemized deductions is greater than the standard deduction. Otherwise, the taxpayer claims the standard deduction. A person must elect to itemize, or no itemized deductions will be allowed.

      1) Election is made by filing Schedule A of Form 1040.
      2) Election in any other taxable year is not relevant.
      3) Election may be changed by filing an amended return (Form 1040-X).

Ineligible

   b. The following persons are **not allowed the standard deduction**:

      1) Persons who itemize deductions
      2) Nonresident alien individuals
      3) Individuals who file a "short period" return
      4) A married individual who files a separate return and whose spouse itemizes
      5) Partnerships, estates, and trusts

   c. The standard deduction is the sum of the basic standard deduction and additional standard deductions.

EXAMPLE 1-5   Ineligible Standard Deduction

Gary and Sara Beers are married but file separately. Gary has AGI of $40,000 and $8,200 of itemized deductions. Sara has $30,000 of AGI and $17,000 of itemized deductions. Gary and Sara can elect to take the standard deduction of $12,400 each. If they elect to itemize, Gary will have itemized deductions of $8,200 and Sara will have itemized deductions of $17,000. If either Gary or Sara choose to itemize, the other is required to itemize.

Basic Standard Deduction

   d. The basic standard deduction amount depends on filing status and dependency status on another's return. The table on the next page lists the amount per filing status.

      1) The basic standard deduction amount of a child under age 19 or a student under age 24 who can be claimed as a dependent on another individual's income tax return is limited to the greater of either

         a) $1,100 or
         b) Earned income for the year plus $350 up to $12,400 (i.e., the applicable single standard deduction).

      2) Earned income does not include dividends or capital gains from the sale of stock.

Additional Standard Deduction

e. Additional standard deduction amounts, indexed for inflation, appear in the table below.

    1) An individual who has attained the age of 65 or is blind is entitled to the amount.

        a) "Blind" in this context means no better than 20/200 vision in the better eye even with corrective lenses.

    2) The individual is entitled to the amount if (s)he attains age 65 before the end of the tax year

        a) Even if (s)he dies before the end of the year

        b) But not if (s)he dies before attaining age 65, even if (s)he would have otherwise reached age 65 before year's end.

    3) A person who becomes blind on or before the last day of the taxable year is entitled to the amount.

    4) Once qualified, the standard deduction is allowed in full.

        a) It is not prorated if a person dies during a tax year.

2020 Standard Deduction Amounts		
Filing Status	Basic	Additional
Married Filing Jointly	$24,800	$1,300
Qualifying Widow(er)	24,800	1,300
Head of Household	18,650	1,650
Single (other than above)	12,400	1,650
Married Filing Separately	12,400	1,300

    5) An individual who has both reached age 65 and is blind is entitled to twice the amount.

EXAMPLE 1-6   **Standard Deduction -- Head of Household**

Toni Mills, 52 qualifies as head of household. Her basic standard deduction is $18,650. She does not qualify for an additional standard deduction.

EXAMPLE 1-7   **Additional Standard Deduction -- Head of Household**

Mike Forth is 68, legally blind, and qualifies as head of household. His basic standard deduction is $18,650. He also qualifies for two additional standard deductions of $3,300 ($1,650 for being 65 or older + $1,650 for being blind). His total standard deduction is $21,950.

EXAMPLE 1-8   **Additional Standard Deduction -- Married Filing Jointly**

Adam and Betty Washington are both over 65 and legally blind. They are married and file a joint return. They qualify for four additional standard deductions (one each for being over 65 and one each for being blind). Their total standard deduction for the year is $30,000 [$24,800 basic standard deduction + ($1,300 × 4 additional standard deductions)].

EXAMPLE 1-9   **Standard Deduction -- Head of Household**

Joni Woodson is unmarried and fully supports her 72-year-old mother. Joni qualifies as head of household. Joni's basic standard deduction is $18,650. Joni may not claim the additional standard deduction for her dependent mother.

STOP AND REVIEW! You have completed the outline for this subunit. Study multiple-choice questions 3 through 9 beginning on page 32.

1.3 FILING REQUIREMENTS

An individual must file a federal income tax return if gross income is above a threshold, net earnings from self-employment is $400 or more, or (s)he is a dependent (i.e., listed on another person's tax return) with more gross income than the standard deduction or with unearned income over $1,100.

Gross Income Filing Threshold

1. Until 2026, the gross income filing threshold amount generally is the standard deduction (excluding any amount for being blind).

    a. The first exception to the general rule is the $5 filing threshold for married filing separately taxpayers.

    b. The second exception is that, except for married filing separately, the filing requirement limitations are increased for taxpayers by the additional standard deductions for being over 65, but not for being blind.

    NOTE: Gross income does not include any Social Security benefits unless (1) the taxpayer(s) is (are) married filing a separate return and lived with the spouse at any time during the year or (2) one-half of the Social Security benefits plus other gross income and any tax-exempt interest is more than $25,000 ($32,000 if married filing jointly).

    c. Married individuals filing separately are not allowed to include the standard deduction in the threshold computation because if one taxpayer itemizes his or her deductions, the other is required to itemize.

    d. Each individual who is over age 65 is entitled to an additional standard deduction when calculating the gross income threshold.

Additional Standard Deduction	
Married Filing Jointly Qualifying Widow(er) Married Filing Separately	$1,300
Head of Household Single	$1,650

    e. Any personal residence disposition gain that was excluded and any foreign-earned income that was excluded must be added back to gross income for purposes of this filing requirement.

EXAMPLE 1-10   Gross Income Filing Requirements

Josie is retired and receives only $2,500 in interest income for the year. She sold her residence, which she has lived in for over 10 years, for $180,000 with a gain of $40,000. Even though any gain on the sale of the residence is excluded from income, Josie is required to file an income tax return because the gain is added to gross income for filing purposes.

---

    f. Special conditions may also require filing, e.g., liability for a special tax, such as AMT or receipt of wages from a church.

    g. Even if not required, an individual should file to obtain a refund and possibly to establish a record and trigger running of statutes of limitation.

Signature Requirement

2. The taxpayer, the taxpayer's spouse, and the paid return preparer all must sign the completed return, declaring under penalty of perjury that they have examined the return and the accompanying schedules and statements and, to the best of their knowledge and belief, the return and schedules are true, correct, and complete.

   a. The penalty of perjury means if the taxpayer willfully makes and subscribes any return, statement, or other document that the taxpayer does not believe to be true and correct as to every material matter, the taxpayer has committed a felony and could be penalized up to $250,000 (for an individual).

Due Date

3. Generally, the income tax return must be filed (postmarked) not later than the 15th day of the 4th month following the close of the tax year. This is April 15 for calendar-year taxpayers. If the 15th day is a Saturday, a Sunday, or a legal holiday, the due date is the next day that is not a Saturday, a Sunday, or a legal holiday.

   a. An **automatic extension** of 6 months is provided for an individual who files Form 4868 or uses a credit card to make the required tax payment on or before the initial due date.

   b. A U.S. citizen or resident who is on **military or naval duty outside the U.S.** (or Puerto Rico) on April 15 is given an automatic 2-month extension without the necessity of filing Form 4868.

      1) Filing of Form 4868 during the 2 months will allow another 4-month extension.

   c. The due date for a decedent's final return is the date on which the return would have been due if death had not occurred.

   d. A Form 1040-NR **nonresident alien's** tax return (when not subject to wage withholding) must be filed by the 15th day of the 6th month after the close of the tax year (unless extended).

      1) A nonresident alien must file his or her tax return on the 15th day of the 4th month after the close of the tax year (unless extended) if his or her wages are subject to withholding.

Liability Payment

4. Tax liability must be paid when the return must be filed. Automatic extension for filing the return does not extend time for payment.

   a. Interest will be charged from the original due date.

   b. A penalty of 5% per month up to 25% of unpaid liability is assessed for failure to file a return.

   c. In general, a failure to pay penalty is imposed from the due date for taxes (other than the estimated taxes) shown on the return.

      1) The penalty is 0.5% per month of the tax not paid, up to 25%.

      2) A failure to pay penalty may offset a failure to file penalty.

      3) When an extension to file is timely requested, a failure to pay penalty may be avoided by paying an estimate of unpaid tax in conjunction with the extension request.

         a) The payment may not be less than 90% of the actual tax liability due, and the balance must be paid when the return is filed.

         b) Exceptions and adjustments to these rules do apply in unique situations.

Recordkeeping

5. Books of account or records sufficient to establish the amount of gross income, deductions, credit, or other matters required to be shown in any tax or information return must be kept.

    a. Records must be maintained as long as the contents may be material in administration of any internal revenue law.

    b. Employers are required to keep records on employment taxes until at least 4 years after the due date of the return or payment of the tax.

6. If an individual is required to report employment taxes or give tax statements to employees, (s)he must have an employer identification number (EIN).

    a. The EIN is a 9-digit number the IRS issues to identify the tax accounts of employers.

7. Penalties are applied when an employer fails to make a required deposit of taxes on time.

    a. The penalties do not apply if any failure to make a proper and timely deposit was due to reasonable cause and not to willful neglect.

    b. For amounts not properly or timely deposited, the penalty rates are

        1) 2% for deposits made 1 to 5 days late
        2) 5% for deposits made 6 to 15 days late
        3) 10% for deposits made 16 or more days late

    NOTE: Although many due dates were delayed for 2020, these penalty rates and rules still apply to the new/delayed due dates.

Identity Protection Personal Identification Number (IP PIN)

8. The IRS IP PIN is a 6-digit number assigned to eligible taxpayers to help prevent the misuse of their Social Security numbers on fraudulent federal income tax returns. The IP PIN helps the IRS verify a taxpayer's identity and accept their electronic or paper tax return.

    a. If a return is e-filed with the taxpayer's SSN and an incorrect or missing IP PIN, the IRS system will reject it until the return is submitted with the correct IP PIN or filed on paper. If the same conditions occur on a paper-filed return, the IRS will delay its processing and any refund that may be due for taxpayer protection while the IRS determines if the return is the taxpayer's.

STOP AND REVIEW! **You have completed the outline for this subunit. Study multiple-choice questions 10 through 15 beginning on page 35.**

1.4 DEPENDENTS

Overview

1. Until 2018, taxpayers were allowed personal exemptions reducing their adjusted gross income for themselves and any of their qualified dependents. From 2018 through 2025, the exemption amount is $0; in essence, the personal exemption is eliminated for these years. For that reason, this review course has removed all coverage of personal exemptions.

    a. However, the rules pertaining to qualified dependents still apply because dependency status affects more than just the exemption. For example, as discussed in Subunit 1.2, having dependents is required for qualifying for Head of Household. It is also required to qualify for the Child Tax Credit and certain Earned Income Credit amounts. Therefore, it is important to learn the rules qualifying someone as a dependent of the taxpayer.

Dependent Status

2. To qualify as a dependent, the individual must be a qualifying child or a qualifying relative. A spouse is never considered a dependent.

Qualifying Child

    a. To be a qualifying child, four tests must be met:

        1) Relationship – The child must be the taxpayer's son, daughter, stepson, stepdaughter, brother, sister, stepbrother, stepsister, or any descendant of any such relative. Adopted individuals and eligible foster children meet the relationship test.

        NOTE: An adopted child is always treated as the taxpayer's own child; i.e., the term "child" includes "adopted child."

        2) Age – The child must be under the age of 19 or a full-time student under the age of 24. Full-time student status requires 5 months of enrollment/registration at a school or in an on-farm training course.

        3) Principal Residence – The child must have the same principal place of abode as the taxpayer for more than half of the year.

        4) Not Self-Supporting – The child must not have provided over half of his or her own support.

Qualifying Relative

    b.   To be a qualifying relative, the following tests [1)-4)] must be met:

        1)   Relationship or residence. An individual must satisfy either a relationship or a residence requirement to qualify as a dependent.

            a)   Residence. The residence requirement is satisfied for any individual who merely resides with a potential claimant (of the dependent) for the entire tax year.

            b)   Relationship. The relationship requirement is satisfied by existence of an extended (by blood) or immediate (by blood, adoption, or marriage) relationship. The relationship need be present to only one of the two married persons who file a joint return. Any relationship established by marriage is not treated as ended by divorce or by death.

                i)   Extended relationships: grandparents and ancestors; grandchildren and descendants; uncles or aunts; nephews or nieces

                ii)   Immediate relationships

- Parent: natural, adoptive, stepparent; father or mother-in-law
- Child: natural, adoptive, stepchild; son or daughter-in-law; foster child
- Sibling: full or half brother or sister; adoptive brother or sister; stepbrother or sister; brother or sister-in-law

              NOTE: A cousin can only be claimed as a dependent if (s)he lived with the taxpayer all year.

        2)   Gross income of the individual (to be claimed as a dependent) must be less than $4,300 for 2020.

            a)   Gross income for the gross income dependency test is all income that is received but not exempt from tax.

                i)   Any expenses from rental property do not reduce rental income.

                ii)   Gross income from a business is the total net sales minus the cost of goods sold, plus any miscellaneous income from the business.

                iii)   Gross income includes all unemployment compensation.

                iv)   Social Security benefits are generally excluded from gross income unless additional income is received.

                v)   Municipal bond interest is exempt from tax.

EXAMPLE 1-11   **Qualifying Relative**

Allan Cripes, 22, earned $4,400 working part time while attending school full time. Allan lives with Doris, his cousin, the entire year. Doris pays more than one-half of Allan's support. Allan will not be a dependent of Doris since Allan exceeds $4,300 of gross income.

---

        3)   Support. The person who may claim an individual as a dependent must provide more than 50% of the (economic) support of the individual for the year.

            a)   Support includes welfare benefits, Social Security benefits, and any support provided by the dependency exemption claimant, the dependent, and any other person.

b) Only amounts provided during the calendar year qualify as support. However, amounts paid in arrears (i.e., payment for child support for a previous year) are not considered as support for the current year.

c) Support includes money and items, or amounts spent on items, such as

    i) Food, clothing, shelter, utilities

    ii) Medical and dental care and insurance

    iii) Education

    iv) Child care, vacations, etc.

d) Excluded. Certain items (or amounts spent on them) have not been treated as support, e.g., scholarship received by a dependent, taxes, and life insurance premiums.

    i) The purchase of capital items (e.g., furniture, appliances, and cars) cannot be included in total support if they are purchased for personal and family reasons and benefit the entire household.

e) The amount of an item of support provided in a form other than cash is usually its cost, if purchased, or FMV, if otherwise obtained.

f) Support received as a single amount is prorated among more than one possible dependent, e.g., three children.

g) A divorced or separated individual need not meet the support test if (s)he and the (ex-)spouse meet (or have met) the following conditions:

    i) Provided more than 50% of the support

    ii) Had (between them) custody for more than 50% of the year

    iii) Lived apart for the last half of the year

    iv) Did not have a multiple support agreement in effect

NOTE: The parent having custody for more than 50% of the year is entitled to the dependency exemption, but the dependency exemption may be allocated to the noncustodial parent if there is an agreement signed by the custodial parent and attached to the noncustodial parent's return.

h) Multiple support agreement (Form 2120). One person of a group that together provides more than 50% of the support of an individual may, pursuant to agreement, be allowed the dependency exemption.

    i) The person must be otherwise eligible to claim the dependency exemption and must provide more than 10% of the support.

    ii) No other person may provide more than 50% of the support.

    iii) Each other person in the group who provided more than 10% of the support must sign a written consent filed with the return of the taxpayer who claims the dependency exemption.

4) The individual must not be a qualifying child of the taxpayer or any other taxpayer.

a) A child being adopted is eligible to be claimed as a dependent by the adopting parents if an identifying number for the child is obtained. Initially, an adoption taxpayer identification number (ATIN) is assigned.

b) Both a dependent who dies before the end of the calendar year and a child born during the year may be claimed as dependents.

Qualifying as a Dependent

c. There are special rules that apply to individuals qualifying as a dependent:

   1) Dependent taxpayer test. If an individual meets the requirements to be classified as a dependent on another person's tax return, the individual (dependent) will be treated as having no dependents for the tax year.

   2) Filing status (occasionally referred to as the joint return test). An individual does not qualify as a dependent on another's return if the individual is married and files a joint return.

      a) However, such an individual can qualify as a dependent if (s)he files a joint return solely to claim a refund of withheld tax without regard to the citizenship test.

EXAMPLE 1-12	Filing by Dependents to Obtain a Refund

Mr. and Mrs. Kind provided more than half the support for their married daughter and son-in-law who lived with the Kinds all year. Neither the daughter nor the son-in-law is required to file a 2020 tax return. They do so only to get a refund of withheld taxes. The Kinds may claim the daughter and the son-in-law as dependents on their 2020 joint return.

   3) Citizenship or resident. To qualify as a dependent, an individual must be, for any part of the year, a U.S. citizen, resident, or national, or a Canadian or Mexican resident.

EXAMPLE 1-13	Citizenship of Dependents

Resident aliens living in the U.S. provide all the support for their four minor children even though they all live with various relatives in other countries. One is in Mexico, two others are in Canada, and the fourth is in Chile. All family members are citizens of Chile. The resident aliens may claim dependent exemptions for only the three children residing in Mexico and Canada.

   4) Taxpayer identification number. The taxpayer must provide the correct taxpayer identification number (TIN) of a dependent on the income tax return.

Overview of the Rules for Claiming a Dependent

    d.   This table is only an overview of the rules.

- A taxpayer cannot claim any dependents if the taxpayer, or the spouse if filing jointly, could be claimed as a dependent by another taxpayer.
- A taxpayer cannot claim a married person who files a joint return as a dependent unless that joint return is only a claim for refund and there would be no tax liability for either spouse on separate returns.
- A taxpayer cannot claim a person as a dependent unless that person is a U.S. citizen, U.S. resident alien, U.S. national, or a resident of Canada or Mexico.
- A taxpayer cannot claim a person as a dependent unless that person is the taxpayer's **qualifying child** or **qualifying relative**.

Tests To Be a Qualifying Child	Tests To Be a Qualifying Relative
1. The child must be a son, daughter, stepchild, foster child, brother, sister, half brother, half sister, stepbrother, stepsister, or a descendant of any of them. 2. The child must be (a) under age 19 at the end of the year and younger than the taxpayer (or the spouse if filing jointly); (b) under age 24 at the end of the year, a student, and younger than the taxpayer (or the spouse if filing jointly); or (c) any age if permanently and total disabled. 3. The child must have lived with the taxpayer for more than half of the year. 4. The child must not have provided more than half of his or her own support for the year. 5. The child is not filing a joint return for the year (unless that joint return is filed only as a claim for refund of withheld income tax or estimated tax paid). If the child meets the rules to be a qualifying child of more than one person, only one person can actually treat the child as a qualifying child.	1. The person cannot be the taxpayer's qualifying child or the qualifying child of anyone else. 2. The person either (a) must be related to the taxpayer in one of the ways listed previously under Immediate relationships or (b) must live with the taxpayer all year as a member of the taxpayer's household (and the taxpayer's relationship must not violate local law). 3. The person's gross income for the year must be less than $4,300. 4. The taxpayer must provide more than half of the person's total support for the year.

STOP AND REVIEW! **You have completed the outline for this subunit. Study multiple-choice questions 16 through 26 beginning on page 38.**

1.5 DEPENDENT'S UNEARNED INCOME

1. The standard deduction for a dependent with unearned income is limited to the greater of $1,100 or the amount of earned income plus $350.

EXAMPLE 1-14	Standard Deduction of Dependent

If a dependent has $1,100 or less of earned income, the standard deduction is $1,100. If a dependent has more than $1,100 and less than $12,050 of earned income, the standard deduction is earned income plus $350. If a dependent has $12,050 or more of earned income, the standard deduction is $12,400.

Kiddie Tax

2. For 2020, net unearned income (NUI) of a dependent under 19 (under 24 for full-time students) at the close of the tax year is taxed to the dependent at the parent's marginal rate. This is referred to as the "kiddie" tax.

    a. Net unearned income is unearned income minus the sum of

        1) $1,100 (first $1,100 clause) and

        2) The greater of (a) $1,100 of the standard deduction or $1,100 of itemized deductions or (b) the amount of allowable deductions that are directly connected with the production of unearned income.

EXAMPLE 1-15	Taxable Income of a Dependent Child

Chris, dependent child age 5, has $4,600 of unearned income and no earned income. How much of his income may be taxed at the parent's marginal rate?

Unearned income	$4,600
First $1,100 clause	(1,100)
Standard deduction	(1,100)
Net unearned income	$2,400

EXAMPLE 1-16	Kiddie Tax

Melvin, an unmarried individual age 15, is claimed as a dependent by his parents. He received income of $6,450 from earnings and had taxable interest of $2,300 on a savings account. Melvin's taxable income is $1,950 [$8,750 gross income ($6,450 + $2,300) – $6,800 standard deduction ($6,450 + $350)]. The amount taxed at the parents' marginal rate is $100 ($2,300 unearned income – $1,100 – $1,100). The amount taxed at Melvin's tax rate is $1,850 ($1,950 taxable income – $100 taxed at his parents' marginal tax rate).

    b. A dependent is allowed at least a $2,200 ($1,100 + $1,100) reduction in unearned income.

    c. **Unearned** income is all taxable income other than earned income. Earned income is payment received for performance of personal services and is usually reported on Form W-2.

Examples of Child Income

Earned	Unearned
Salaries	Interest
Wages	Dividends
Tips	Capital gains
	Trusts distributions
	Debt cancellation
	Pension/Annuities
	Social Security
	Royalties
	Taxable scholarships

    d.   The "kiddie" tax does not apply to an 18-year-old dependent (under 24 for full-time students) if the dependent has earned income that exceeds one-half of the dependent's support.

3.   The tax on a dependent is the greater of

TI -- dependent	$X,XXX
Times: Rate	.XX
Total tax	$X,XXX

OR

TI -- dependent	$X,XXX
Less: NUI	(XX)
Total	$X,XXX
Times: Rate (child)	.XX
Total (1)	$X,XXX

TI -- parent	$X,XXX
Plus: NUI	XX
Total	$X,XXX
Times: Rate (parent)	.XX
Total (2)	$X,XXX

Total (1)	$X,XXX
Plus: Total (2)	X,XXX
Total	$X,XXX
Less: Tax on parent's TI	(X,XXX)
Total tax	$X,XXX

4.   If more than one child has NUI, the parents' total NUI must be proportioned among the children to determine the amount taxed to each child.

STOP AND REVIEW! **You have completed the outline for this subunit. Study multiple-choice question 27 on page 43.**

1.6 NONRESIDENT AND DUAL-STATUS ALIENS

1. A taxpayer is considered a dual-status alien if the taxpayer was both a nonresident and resident alien during the year.

2. Generally, a taxpayer is considered a resident alien if either the green card test or the substantial presence test is met. Even if the taxpayer does not meet either of these tests, (s)he may be able to choose to be treated as a U.S. resident for part of the year.

Green Card Test

3. A taxpayer is a resident for tax purposes if (s)he was a lawful permanent resident (immigrant) of the United States at any time during the year.

Nonresident Alien

4. A nonresident alien may file a joint return if (s)he is married to a U.S. citizen or resident at the end of the year.

    a. If the couple files a joint return, both spouses are treated as U.S. residents for the entire tax year.

5. If a taxpayer chooses to be treated as a U.S. resident, both spouses are taxed on worldwide income.

6. A taxpayer is considered unmarried for head of household purposes if the taxpayer's spouse was a nonresident alien at any time during the year and the taxpayer does not choose to treat his or her nonresident spouse as a resident alien.

    a. A taxpayer's spouse is not a qualifying person for head of household purposes.

    b. A taxpayer must have another person qualifying as a dependent and meet the other tests to be eligible to file as a head of household.

7. Even if a taxpayer is considered unmarried for head of household purposes because the taxpayer is married to a nonresident alien, the taxpayer is still considered married for purposes of the Earned Income Credit.

    a. A taxpayer is not entitled to the Earned Income Credit unless a joint return is filed and other qualifications are met.

8. Nonresident aliens can deduct certain itemized deductions if income is received that is effectively connected with a U.S. trade or business.

    a. These deductions include state and local income taxes, charitable contributions to U.S. organizations, casualty and theft losses, and other itemized deductions.

9. If a taxpayer is a nonresident alien who is married to a U.S. citizen or resident at the end of the year and chooses to be treated as a U.S. resident, (s)he can take the standard deduction.

10. A nonresident alien is not eligible for the credit for the elderly and the education credits unless (s)he elects to be treated as a U.S. resident.

11. Nonresident aliens are required to file a return if they earn any wages effectively connected with a U.S. trade or business.

12. Most types of U.S. source income received by a foreign taxpayer are subject to a tax rate of 30%.

13. A scholarship, fellowship, grant, etc., received by a nonresident alien for activities conducted outside the U.S. is treated as foreign source income and therefore is not subject to U.S. taxation.

Substantial Presence Test

14. A taxpayer is considered a U.S. resident if (s)he was physically present in the United States for at least

    a. 31 days during 2020 and

    b. 183 days during 2020, 2019, and 2018, counting all days of physical presence in 2020 but only 1/3 the number of days of presence in 2019 and only 1/6 the number of days in 2018.

Ending Resident Status

15. Either spouse may choose to revoke resident status of the nonresident alien spouse. Other means by which the status is ended include death, divorce or legal separation, and inadequate records. The following table breaks down the details of each:

Revocation	**Either spouse can revoke the choice for any tax year.** ● The revocation must be made by the due date for filing the tax return for that tax year. ● The spouse who revokes the choice must attach a signed statement declaring that the choice is being revoked. The statement revoking the choice must include the following: ▪ The name, address, and Social Security number (or taxpayer identification number) of each spouse ▪ The name and address of any person who is revoking the choice for a deceased spouse ▪ A list of any states, foreign countries, and possessions that have community property laws in which either spouse is domiciled or where real property is located from which either spouse receives income ● If the spouse revoking the choice does not have to file a return and does not file a claim for refund, send the statement to the Internal Revenue Service Center where the last joint return was filed.
Death	**The death of either spouse ends the choice, beginning with the first tax year following the year in which the spouse died.** ● If the surviving spouse is a U.S. citizen or resident alien and is entitled to the joint tax rates as a surviving spouse, the choice will not end until the close of the last year for which these joint rates may be used. ● If both spouses die in the same tax year, the choice ends on the first day after the close of the tax year in which the spouses died.
Divorce or legal separation	**A divorce or legal separation ends the choice as of the beginning of the tax year in which the legal separation occurs.**
Inadequate records	**The Internal Revenue Service can end the choice for any tax year that either spouse has failed to keep adequate books, records, and other information necessary to determine the correct income tax liability, or to provide adequate access to those records.**

STOP AND REVIEW! **You have completed the outline for this subunit. Study multiple-choice questions 28 and 29 on page 44.**

QUESTIONS

1.1 Preliminary Work to Prepare Tax Returns

1. When preparing a current-year tax return, which of the following benefits are derived from the use of the previous year's return?

I.   Prevents gross mathematical errors
II. Identifies significant changes
III. Increases efficiency

    A. I and II only.

    B. I and III only.

    C. II and III only.

    D. I, II, and III.

Answer (D) is correct.
    REQUIRED: The benefits of having the previous year's return available when preparing the return of the current year.
    DISCUSSION: Use of the prior-year return helps to prevent gross mathematical errors or identify significant changes. The accuracy of the prior-year return increases efficiency in completing the current-year return. These are just a few of the benefits of obtaining a copy of the previous year's return (Publication 17).

2. Which taxpayer information is necessary to have before preparing a tax return?

    A. Immigration status.

    B. Age of an individual.

    C. Marital status.

    D. All of the information is needed.

Answer (D) is correct.
    REQUIRED: The information that is necessary to have before preparing a tax return.
    DISCUSSION: Taxpayer personal information (e.g., date of birth, age, marital status, dependents, etc.) is used to verify the identity of the taxpayer and related dependents. The age of an individual determines if (s)he qualifies for additional deductions (65 and over), retirement distributions, dependency, etc. MFJ status often increases beneficial dollar limits for deductions and credits. If a taxpayer is an alien (not a U.S. citizen), (s)he is considered a nonresident alien, unless either the green card test or the substantial presence test for the calendar year is met.

1.2 Filing Status

3. John and Linda Smith are a childless married couple with no other dependents who lived apart for all of the current year. On December 31 of the current year, they were legally separated under a decree of separate maintenance. Based on the facts, which of the following is the only filing-status choice available to them for the current year?

    A. Married filing joint return.

    B. Married filing separate return.

    C. Head of household.

    D. Single.

Answer (D) is correct.
    REQUIRED: The proper filing status for the taxpayer.
    DISCUSSION: The determination of whether an individual is married is made as of the close of the taxable year, so John and Linda are both single for the current year (Publication 17). Couples under a separate maintenance agreement are not considered married.
    Answer (A) is incorrect. They are unmarried at year end. **Answer (B) is incorrect.** They are unmarried at year end. **Answer (C) is incorrect.** They are not maintaining a home as a principal place of abode for a child or other dependent.

4. Which of the following is NOT a requirement that must be met in determining whether a taxpayer is considered unmarried for head of household filing-status purposes?

A. An individual must file a separate return.

B. An individual must pay more than one-half the cost of keeping up a home for the tax year.

C. An individual's home must be, for the entire year, the main home of his or her child, stepchild, or qualified foster child whom (s)he or the noncustodial parent can properly claim as a dependent.

D. An individual's spouse must not have lived in their home for the last 6 months of the tax year.

5. Joe is 37 years old. His wife died during the tax year, and he has not remarried. His deceased wife had no income. He has two minor children living with him. Joe paid all of the costs for keeping up his home for the tax year, and he has paid for all of the support of his wife and these children. The filing status with the lowest tax rate for which Joe qualifies is

A. Qualifying widower with dependent child.

B. Married filing separately.

C. Head of household.

D. Married filing jointly.

Answer (C) is correct.
  REQUIRED: The item that is not a requirement in determining if a taxpayer is unmarried for head of household filing-status purposes.
  DISCUSSION: In determining if a taxpayer qualifies for head of household filing status, the taxpayer is considered unmarried if all the following requirements are met:

1. The taxpayer filed a separate return.
2. The taxpayer paid more than half the cost of keeping up the home for the tax year.
3. The taxpayer's spouse did not live in the home during the last 6 months of the tax year.
4. The home was, for more than half the year, the main home of the taxpayer's child, stepchild, or adopted child whom the taxpayer or the noncustodial parent can properly claim as a dependent.
5. The taxpayer must be able to claim the child as a dependent.

Therefore, this answer is correct because the requirement is that the home be the main home of the child, stepchild, or qualified foster child for **more than half the year**, not the entire year [Publication 17 and Sec. 2(b)].

Answer (D) is correct.
  REQUIRED: The filing status with the lowest rate for the taxpayer.
  DISCUSSION: Publication 501 states, "If your spouse died during the year, you are considered married for the whole year for filing status purposes. If you didn't remarry before the end of the tax year, you can file a joint return for yourself and your deceased spouse. For the next 2 years, you may be entitled to the special benefits described later under *Qualifying Widow(er)*" (Publication 17).
  Answer (A) is incorrect. Qualifying widower with dependent child, or surviving spouse, status is only available for 2 years following the year of death of spouse. **Answer (B) is incorrect.** Joe qualifies for married filing jointly status in the year of his wife's death. **Answer (C) is incorrect.** Joe qualifies for married filing jointly status in the year of his wife's death.

6. For 2020, Jane is unmarried and paid more than half the cost of keeping up her home. All of the following dependents would qualify Jane to file as head of household EXCEPT

    A. Jane's grandson, who lived with her but was absent from her home for 9 months in 2020 while attending boarding school.

    B. Jane's father, whom she can claim as a dependent and whose main home for 2020 was a home for the elderly for which Jane paid more than one-half the cost.

    C. Jane's married son, who could properly be claimed as a dependent on his father's return only.

    D. Jane's sister, whom Jane can claim as a dependent and who lived with Jane until she died in May 2020.

Answer (C) is correct.
    REQUIRED: The person who does not qualify as the taxpayer's dependent for head of household filing-status purposes.
    DISCUSSION: A taxpayer qualifies for head of household filing status if (s)he is not married or is considered unmarried at the close of the tax year, is not a surviving spouse, and maintains a household that is also the principal place of abode for more than half of the year for any one of certain qualifying individuals.
    A married son, stepson, daughter, or stepdaughter is a qualifying individual only if the taxpayer is entitled to claim the person as a dependent or the taxpayer by written declaration allows the noncustodial parent to claim the person as a dependent.
    Jane must have been able to claim the married son as a dependent in order to qualify as head of household.
    Answer (A) is incorrect. Time spent at school is deemed temporary and does not apply to the 6-month test. **Answer (B) is incorrect.** A taxpayer can maintain a separate household for a parent, such as a rest home, and still qualify as a head of household. **Answer (D) is incorrect.** Brothers and sisters are qualifying relatives for head of household status.

7. Ms. N, who is married, wants to file as head of household for the current year. Which of the following will prevent her from filing as head of household?

    A. Her spouse lived in her home for the final 6 months of the current year.

    B. She and her husband did not commingle funds for support purposes.

    C. She paid more than half the cost of keeping up her home for the tax year.

    D. Her home was, for more than 6 months of the year, the principal home of her son, whom she can claim as a dependent.

Answer (A) is correct.
    REQUIRED: The item that will prevent the taxpayer from filing as head of household.
    DISCUSSION: A married person may qualify for head of household status if the conditions for "considered unmarried" are met. A married individual who lives with a dependent apart from the spouse will be considered unmarried and qualify for head of household status if, for the tax year, (1) the individual files separately; (2) the individual pays more than 50% toward maintaining the household; (3) the spouse is not a member of the household for the last 6 months; (4) the household is the principal home of the individual's child, stepchild, or qualified foster child for more than half the year; **and** (5) the individual can claim the child as a dependent.
    Answer (B) is incorrect. The fact that she and her husband did not commingle funds for support purposes will not prevent her from filing as head of household. **Answer (C) is incorrect.** This is a requirement that must be met in order to file as head of household. **Answer (D) is incorrect.** This is a requirement that must be met in order to file as head of household.

8. Which of the following is NOT a requirement you must meet to claim head of household filing status?

A. Your spouse did not live in your home during the last 6 months of the tax year.

B. You paid more than half of the cost of keeping up your home for the entire year.

C. Your home was the main home of your foster child for the entire year.

D. You are unmarried or considered unmarried on the last day of the year.

Answer (C) is correct.
    REQUIRED: The item that is not a requirement in determining if a taxpayer is unmarried for head of household filing-status purposes.
    DISCUSSION: In determining if a taxpayer qualifies for head of household filing status, the taxpayer is considered unmarried if all the following requirements are met:

1. The taxpayer filed a separate return.
2. The taxpayer paid more than half the cost of keeping up the home for the tax year.
3. The taxpayer's spouse did not live in the home during the last 6 months of the tax year.
4. The home was, for more than half the year, the main home of the taxpayer's child, stepchild, or eligible foster child.
5. The taxpayer must be able to claim the child as a dependent.

The requirement is that the home be the main home of the child, stepchild, or eligible foster child for **more than half the year** [Publication 17 and Sec. 2(b)].

9. Which dependent relative does NOT have to live in the same household as the taxpayer claiming head of household filing status?

A. Daughter.

B. Mother.

C. Uncle.

D. Sister or brother.

Answer (B) is correct.
    REQUIRED: The relative who does not have to live in the same household as the taxpayer claiming head of household filing status.
    DISCUSSION: Section 2(b) provides head of household status for an unmarried taxpayer who maintains a household that constitutes the principal place of abode of the taxpayer's father or mother, but only if the taxpayer is entitled to claim the parent as a dependent. The taxpayer is considered as maintaining a household only if (s)he furnishes over half of the cost of maintaining it. In the case of anyone other than the taxpayer's father or mother, such person(s) must actually occupy the taxpayer's own household for the taxpayer to be considered a head of household (Publication 17).

1.3 Filing Requirements

10. Mr. Todd, who is 43 years old, has lived apart from his wife since May 2020. For 2020, his two children, whom he can claim as dependents, lived with him the entire year, and he paid the entire cost of maintaining the household. Assuming that Mr. Todd cannot qualify to file a joint return for 2020, he must, nevertheless, file a return if his gross income is at least

A. $5

B. $24,800

C. $12,400

D. $18,650

Answer (D) is correct.
    REQUIRED: The minimum amount of gross income a taxpayer must earn to be required to file a return.
    DISCUSSION: Generally, a taxpayer must file a tax return if the taxpayer's gross income equals or exceeds his or her standard deduction [Sec. 6012(a)]. Standard deductions in 2020 are $24,800 for married filing jointly, $18,650 for heads of household, and $12,400 for single individuals (Publication 501). A taxpayer who has two children and files as head of household must file a return if his or her gross income equals or exceeds $18,650.
    Answer (A) is incorrect. The amount of $5 is the special threshold for MFS taxpayers. **Answer (B) is incorrect.** The amount of $24,800 is the standard deduction for MFJ taxpayers. **Answer (C) is incorrect.** The amount of $12,400 is the standard deduction for single individuals.

11. Ms. Maple, a single woman age 65, retired in 2020. Prior to her retirement, she received a $6,000 bonus plus $5,050 in wages. After her retirement, she received $9,000 in Social Security benefits. Which of the following is true?

A. Ms. Maple does not have to file a 2020 income tax return.

B. Ms. Maple has to file a 2020 income tax return.

C. Ms. Maple has to file a 2020 income tax return but may exclude the $6,000.

D. Ms. Maple has to file a 2020 income tax return but may exclude the $9,000 in Social Security benefits from income.

Answer (A) is correct.
REQUIRED: The true statement concerning filing an income tax return.
DISCUSSION: In general, a taxpayer does not have to file a return if his or her gross income is less than his or her standard deduction [Publication 501 and Sec. 6012(a)]. For single individuals who are 65 or over, the standard deduction increases by $1,650. Therefore, the filing threshold will be $14,050 ($12,400 basic standard deduction + $1,650 additional standard deduction). Ms. Maple's income does not qualify her Social Security benefits for gross income inclusion in determining her filing requirement.

12. John Stith, whose father died June 15, 2020, is the executor of his father's estate. John is required to file a final income tax return for his father. When is this return due if he does not file for an extension (ignoring Saturdays, Sundays, and holidays)?

A. October 15, 2020.

B. March 15, 2021.

C. April 15, 2021.

D. June 15, 2021.

Answer (C) is correct.
REQUIRED: The due date for a decedent's final return.
DISCUSSION: The final return of a decedent is due by the date on which the return would have been due had death not occurred. Thus, the final return is generally due by April 15 (Publication 17).

13. Which of the following is true regarding the filing of Form 4868, *Application for Automatic Extension of Time to File U.S. Individual Income Tax Return*?

A. Filing Form 4868 provides an automatic 2-month extension of time to file and pay income tax.

B. Any U.S. citizen who is out of the country on April 15, 2021, is allowed an automatic 6-month extension of time to file his or her 2020 return and pay any federal income tax due.

C. Interest is charged on tax not paid by the due date of the return even if an extension is obtained.

D. Electronic filing cannot be used to get an extension of time to file.

Answer (C) is correct.
REQUIRED: The true statement regarding Form 4868.
DISCUSSION: An automatic extension of 6 months is provided for an individual who files Form 4868 or uses a credit card to make the required tax payment on or before the initial due date. Tax liability must be paid on the original due date of the tax return. Automatic extension for filing the return does not extend time for payment. Interest will be charged from the original due date. If the required payment is made by the regular due date for the return, the return can be filed anytime before the 6-month extension period ends.
Answer (A) is incorrect. Filing Form 4868 provides a 6-month extension of time to file the individual tax return, but it does not provide an extension of time for the payment of tax due. **Answer (B) is incorrect.** A U.S. citizen or resident who is on military or naval duty outside the U.S. on April 15 is only given a 2-month extension for time to file. **Answer (D) is incorrect.** An extension request using Form 4868 may be filed electronically.

14. Which of the following statements is true regarding the filing of a Form 4868, *Application for Automatic Extension of Time to File U.S. Individual Income Tax Return*, for your 2020 tax return?

    A. Interest is not assessed on any income tax due if a Form 4868 is filed.

    B. Form 4868 provides the taxpayer with an automatic additional 8-month extension to file.

    C. Even though you file Form 4868, you will owe interest and may be charged a late payment penalty on the amount you owe if you do not pay the tax due by the regular due date.

    D. A U.S. citizen who is out of the country on April 15 will be allowed an additional 12 months to file as long as "Out of the Country" is written across the top of Form 4868.

Answer (C) is correct.
    REQUIRED: The true statement regarding filing Form 4868.
    DISCUSSION: An automatic extension of 6 months is provided for an individual who files Form 4868 or uses a credit card to make a required tax payment on or before the initial due date. The tax liability, however, must be paid when the return must be filed. Automatic extension for filing the return does not extend time for payment. Interest will be charged from the original due date, and penalties may accrue (Publication 17).
    Answer (A) is incorrect. Interest will accrue from the original due date. **Answer (B) is incorrect.** Form 4868 provides a 6-month extension, not an 8-month extension. **Answer (D) is incorrect.** No such exception applies. Form 4868 provides for a 6-month extension. A longer extension is only available for those serving in military or naval duty outside of the U.S.

15. All of the following concerning extension of time to file are correct EXCEPT

    A. An automatic 6-month extension can be requested by filing Form 4868.

    B. If the required payment is made by credit card by the regular due date for the return, the return can be filed any time before the 6-month extension period ends.

    C. Requesting an automatic 6-month extension before the regular due date for the return postpones the requirement to make payment of any tax due.

    D. A U.S. citizen or resident who is on military or naval duty outside the U.S. (or Puerto Rico) on April 15 is given an automatic 2-month extension without the necessity of filing Form 4868.

Answer (C) is correct.
    REQUIRED: The incorrect statement regarding the extension of time to file.
    DISCUSSION: An individual who is required to file an income tax return is allowed an automatic 6-month extension of time to file the return by filing Form 4868. However, no extension of time is allowed for payment of the tax due. A taxpayer desiring an extension of time to file his or her tax return and avoid the failure to pay penalty must file Form 4868, accompanied by the payment of tax estimated to be owed for the year and not yet paid, by the normal due date of the tax return (Publication 17).
    Answer (A) is incorrect. An automatic extension is available by either filing Form 4868 or using a credit card to make the required tax payment by the due date of the return. The taxpayer may file the return any time before the 6-month extension period ends. **Answer (B) is incorrect.** It is a correct statement concerning extension of time to file. **Answer (D) is incorrect.** It is a true statement concerning citizens or residents outside the U.S. or Puerto Rico who are on military or naval duty. Additionally, filing Form 4868 during the 2 months will allow another 4-month extension.

1.4 Dependents

16. All of the following are true EXCEPT

A. A brother-in-law must live with the taxpayer the entire year to be claimed as a dependent even if the other tests are met.

B. A son, age 21, was a full-time student who earned $4,400 from his part-time job. The money was used to buy a car. Even though he earned $4,400, his parents can claim him as a dependent if the other dependency tests were met.

C. For each person claimed as a dependent, the Social Security number, adoption taxpayer identification number, or individual taxpayer identification number must be listed.

D. If a married person files a separate return, (s)he cannot claim his or her spouse as a dependent even if the spouse had no gross income and was not the dependent of another taxpayer.

Answer (A) is correct.
REQUIRED: The false statement regarding the relationship requirement.
DISCUSSION: The relationship requirement is satisfied by existence of an extended (by blood) or immediate (by blood, adoption, or marriage) relationship. The relationship need be present to only one of the two married persons who file a joint return. Any relationship established by marriage is not treated as ended by divorce or by death. An individual must satisfy either a relationship or a residence requirement but does not have to satisfy both (Publication 501).
Answer (B) is incorrect. Gross income of the individual (to be claimed as a dependent) must be less than $4,300 for 2020. However, this test does not apply to a child of the claimant who is either under 19 years of age or a student under 24 years of age. **Answer (C) is incorrect.** For each person claimed as a dependent, the Social Security number, adoption taxpayer identification number, or individual taxpayer identification number must be listed. **Answer (D) is incorrect.** A married person cannot claim a spouse as a dependent.

17. Section 152 of the Code contains two sets of tests, "qualifying child" and "qualifying relative," either of which may be applied to determine whether an individual has dependency status and may therefore be claimed as a dependent by a taxpayer. Which of the following is NOT a test under both classifications?

A. Citizenship test.

B. Residence test.

C. Joint return test.

D. Gross income test.

Answer (D) is correct.
REQUIRED: The test that is not a criterion for determining dependency.
DISCUSSION: The four tests under the "qualifying child" classification are (1) relationship, (2) age, (3) principal residence, and (4) support. The four tests under the "qualifying relative" classification are (1) relationship or residence, (2) gross income, (3) support, and (4) dependency. Both the qualifying child and qualifying relative tests require that the dependent not file a joint return, meet the citizenship requirement, and provide his or her taxpayer identification number. The gross income test only applies to the qualifying relative (Publication 501).

18. Jill and John, married filing jointly, have provided more than 50% of the support for two minor children and Jill's mother. The children each had interest income of less than $700. Jill's mother received a taxable pension of $2,850, dividends of $1,500, and interest of $1,000. How many dependents can the taxpayers claim on their 2020 tax return?

A. 1

B. 3

C. 2

D. 0

Answer (C) is correct.
REQUIRED: The correct number of dependents.
DISCUSSION: Jill and John's children meet the definition of "qualifying child." There are five requirements that a qualifying relative must meet to be classified as a dependent of the taxpayer.

1. The taxpayer must provide more than 50% of the dependent's support.
2. The dependent must earn less than $4,300 or be the taxpayer's child that meets one of the following requirements:

   a. Is under age 19
   b. Is under age 24 and full-time student

3. The dependent must be related to or reside with the taxpayer.
4. If the dependent is married, (s)he must not file a joint return.
5. The dependent must be a U.S. citizen, national, resident, or must reside in Canada or Mexico (Publication 17).

Answer (A) is incorrect. One dependent excludes one of the eligible children. Jill's mother should not be included because she earned more than the $4,300 applicable amount. **Answer (B) is incorrect.** Three dependents includes all the members of the household except the taxpayers. Jill's mother should not be included because she earned more than the $4,300 applicable amount. **Answer (D) is incorrect.** Both of the children qualify as dependents.

19. In meeting the gross income test for claiming his father as a dependent, Doug considered the income received by his father. This income included gross rents of $4,000 (expenses were $2,000), municipal bond interest of $1,200, dividends of $1,400, and Social Security of $4,000. What is Doug's father's gross income for dependency test purposes?

A. $3,400

B. $5,400

C. $9,400

D. $8,600

Answer (B) is correct.
REQUIRED: The income included in the computation of gross income for the purposes of meeting the gross income dependency test.
DISCUSSION: Gross income defined for the purposes of the gross income dependency test is all income that is received but is not exempt from tax. In addition, any expenses from rental property should not be deducted for the purposes of this computation. Any tax-exempt income, such as Social Security, is not included in gross income for this purpose (Publication 501). Doug should only consider the gross rents and the dividends in the computation of gross income from his father for the purposes of the gross income for dependency test. Thus, the total income of Doug's father is $5,400 ($4,000 gross rents + $1,400 dividends).
Answer (A) is incorrect. Expenses from the rental income should not be deducted for the purposes of the gross income for dependency test. **Answer (C) is incorrect.** Social Security is considered tax-exempt income and should not be included in gross income for dependency test purposes. **Answer (D) is incorrect.** Municipal bond interest and Social Security are considered tax-exempt income and should not be included in gross income for dependency test purposes. In addition, the expenses from rental activity should not be deducted from the gross rents.

20. John and Joanne are the sole support of the following individuals, all U.S. citizens, none of whom lives with them. None of these individuals files a joint return or has any gross income.

Jennie, John's mother
Julie, Joanne's stepmother
Jonathan, father of John's first wife

How many dependents may John and Joanne claim on their joint return?

A. 3
B. 2
C. 1
D. 0

Answer (A) is correct.
REQUIRED: The number of dependents to which the taxpayer is entitled.
DISCUSSION: To qualify for dependency, the taxpayer must provide over 50% of the support of a U.S. citizen who meets certain relationship tests stated in Sec. 152(a). Section 152 allows dependency for fathers, mothers, stepfathers, and stepmothers. Relationships established by marriage are not ended by death or divorce (Publication 501). Thus, each of the individuals listed qualifies under the relationship test of Sec. 152.

21. Holly and Harp Oaks were divorced in 2019. The divorce decree was silent regarding dependency for their 12-year-old daughter, June, for 2020. Holly has legal custody of her daughter and did not sign a statement releasing the dependent claim. Holly earned $8,250, and Harp earned $80,000. June had a paper route and earned $5,250. June lived with Harp 4 months of the year and with Holly 8 months. Who may claim the dependent for June in 2020?

A. June may, since she had gross income over $4,300 and files her own return.

B. Since June lived with both Holly and Harp during the year, they both may claim her as a dependent.

C. Holly may, since she has legal custody and physical custody for more than half the year.

D. Harp may, since he earned more than Holly and therefore is presumed to have provided more than 50% of June's support.

Answer (C) is correct.
REQUIRED: The taxpayer who may claim the child of divorced parents as a dependent.
DISCUSSION: A divorced or separated individual need not meet the support test if (s)he and the (ex-)spouse met the following conditions:

1. Provided more than 50% of the support
2. Had (between them) custody for more than 50% of the year
3. Lived apart for the last half of the year
4. Did not have a multiple support agreement in effect

The parent having custody for more than 50% of the year is entitled to claim the dependent. But the dependent may be claimed by the noncustodial parent if there is an agreement signed by both parents and attached to the noncustodial parent's return. Since there was no agreement or statement that would allow Harp to claim the dependent and Holly has custody for the majority of the year, Holly may claim June as a dependent (Publication 501).
Answer (A) is incorrect. Since June is under 19, she qualifies as a dependent of her parents regardless of her income. **Answer (B) is incorrect.** Only one parent may claim June as a dependent. **Answer (D) is incorrect.** Without an agreement giving Harp the right to claim his daughter, he may not do so because he did not have custody of her for the majority of the year.

22. Under Pete's divorce decree, he must pay $500 a month to Laura, his former spouse, for the support of their two children. In 2019, he paid $5,500 instead of the $6,000 he was required to pay. In 2020, he paid $6,000 child support for 2020 and $500 towards child support he neglected to pay in 2019. For purposes of determining whether Pete may claim his children as dependents, which of the following statements accurately represents the amount of support attributable to each year?

   A. $5,500 for 2019; $6,500 for 2020.

   B. $6,000 for 2019; $6,000 for 2020.

   C. $5,500 for 2019; $6,000 for 2020.

   D. $5,500 for 2019; $6,000 for 2020; $500 for 2018.

Answer (C) is correct.
   REQUIRED: The amount Pete can claim as support to pass the dependency support test.
   DISCUSSION: A taxpayer must furnish one-half of the total support provided during the calendar year before claiming a dependent under the qualifying relative rules. Amounts received as arrearages in payment for support of a child for a previous year are not considered contributions in the current year in determining whether the husband furnished more than half of the support for the taxable year. There are three exceptions to the rule about claiming the dependent: first, when there is a multiple support agreement; second, when a parent releases his or her right to the dependent with Form 8332; and finally, when the exception applies to certain pre-1985 divorce decrees (Publication 501).
   Authors' note: The amount Pete pays each year is irrelevant if the children are qualifying children of the former spouse and he has Form 8332 signed by his former spouse.
   Answer (A) is incorrect. Pete cannot include prior-period child support payments to determine the amount of dependency support. **Answer (B) is incorrect.** Pete did not provide $6,000 of support in the prior year. **Answer (D) is incorrect.** Pete cannot include prior-period child support payments to determine the amount of dependency support.

23. Mrs. Brown had taxable income of $600, Social Security benefits of $1,800, and tax-exempt interest of $200. She used all of these amounts for her own support. Her son paid the rest of her support. Which of the following amounts of support paid by her son would meet the support test to allow him to claim Mrs. Brown as a dependent?

   A. $900

   B. $1,800

   C. $2,100

   D. $2,700

Answer (D) is correct.
   REQUIRED: The amount of support required to claim someone as a dependent.
   DISCUSSION: A dependent under the qualifying relative rules is defined in Sec. 152(a), which requires the taxpayer to provide over one-half of the support of the individual. Mrs. Brown's son must give her more than $2,600 ($600 taxable income + $1,800 Social Security benefits + $200 tax-exempt interest) of support in order to satisfy this requirement (Publication 501).

24. With regard to claiming a dependent, all of the following statements are true EXCEPT

    A. A person does not meet the member-of-the-household test if at any time during the tax year the relationship between the taxpayer and that person violates local law.

    B. A person who died during the year, but was a member of your household until death, will meet the member-of-the-household test.

    C. To meet the citizenship test, a person must be a U.S. citizen or resident, or a resident of Canada or Mexico.

    D. In calculating a person's total support, do not include tax-exempt income used to support that person.

25. All of the following are included in calculating the total support of a dependent EXCEPT

    A. Child care even if the taxpayer is claiming the credit for the expense.

    B. Amounts veterans receive under the GI bill for tuition and allowances while in school.

    C. Medical insurance benefits, including basic and supplementary Medicare benefits received.

    D. Tax-exempt income, savings, or borrowed money used to support a person.

Answer (D) is correct.
    REQUIRED: The statement regarding dependents that is false.
    DISCUSSION: A taxpayer must furnish more than one-half of the total support provided during the calendar year before claiming the person as a dependent. The support may come from taxable income, tax-exempt receipts, or loans (Publication 501).
    Answer (A) is incorrect. The relationship test is failed if the relationship is in violation of local law. **Answer (B) is incorrect.** A dependent is allowed to be claimed in the year of death. **Answer (C) is incorrect.** Residents of Canada and Mexico qualify as dependents regardless of their citizenships.

Answer (C) is correct.
    REQUIRED: The item not taken into account in determining total support of a dependent.
    DISCUSSION: A taxpayer must provide over one-half of the support for a person to be considered a dependent [Sec. 152(a)]. The term support includes food, shelter, clothing, medical and dental care, education, and other items contributing to the individual's maintenance and livelihood [Reg. 1.152-1(a)(2)]. Although medical care is an item of support, medical insurance benefits are not included. Medical insurance premiums are included (Publication 501).
    Answer (A) is incorrect. Child care contributes to the maintenance and livelihood of the individual and is considered support. **Answer (B) is incorrect.** Education contributes to the maintenance and livelihood of the individual and is considered support. **Answer (D) is incorrect.** All funds used to support a person, whether tax exempt, borrowed, or from savings, contribute to the maintenance and livelihood of the individual and are considered support.

26. In the current year, Sam Dunn provided more than half the support for his wife, his father's brother, and his cousin. Sam's wife was the only relative who was a member of Sam's household. None of the relatives had any income, nor did any of them file an individual or a joint return. All of these relatives are U.S. citizens. Which of these relatives should be claimed as a dependent or dependents on Sam's current-year joint return?

   A. Only his wife.

   B. Only his father's brother.

   C. Only his cousin.

   D. His wife, his father's brother, and his cousin.

Answer (B) is correct.
   REQUIRED: The relative(s) who could be claimed as a dependent on the taxpayer's return.
   DISCUSSION: Section 152(a) lists those relatives who may be claimed as dependents if they receive over half of their support from the taxpayer. The taxpayer's uncle is included in this list, so Sam's father's brother may be claimed by him as a dependent (Publication 501).
   Answer (A) is incorrect. Sam's wife is not classified as a dependent. **Answer (C) is incorrect.** Section 152(a) does not include cousins in its list of relatives, and Sam's cousin was not a member of the household. **Answer (D) is incorrect.** Sam's wife is not classified as a dependent. Also, Sec. 152(a) does not include cousins in its list of relatives, and Sam's cousin was not a member of the household.

1.5 Dependent's Unearned Income

27. When can a minor's income be taxed at his or her parent's marginal rate?

   A. When a child has any income and is under age 18.

   B. When a child has net unearned income regardless of his or her age.

   C. When a child has unearned income and is under age 18.

   D. When a child has net unearned income and is under age 18 with at least one living parent.

Answer (D) is correct.
   REQUIRED: The circumstances that require a minor's parent's marginal rate to be used to tax the minor's income.
   DISCUSSION: Net unearned income of a child is taxed at the parent's marginal rate. For this purpose, a minor is any child under 18 years of age at the end of the tax year, or 18 (under 24 and a full-time student) and not having earned income in excess of one-half of his or her support. The provision applies to net unearned income, which is specially defined (Publication 17).
   Answer (A) is incorrect. The child must have net unearned income. **Answer (B) is incorrect.** Income is taxed at the parent's marginal rate only if the child (1) is under 18 or (2) is 18 or a full-time student under 24 and does not have earned income in excess of one-half of his or her support. **Answer (C) is incorrect.** The child must have net unearned income, not just unearned income.

1.6   Nonresident and Dual-Status Aliens

28. Jean Blanc, a citizen and resident of Canada, is a professional hockey player with a U.S. hockey club. Under Jean's contract, he received $68,500 for 165 days of play during the current year. Of the 165 days, 132 days were spent performing services in the United States and 33 playing hockey in Canada. What is the amount to be included in Jean's gross income on his Form 1040-NR?

A. $0

B. $34,250

C. $54,800

D. $68,500

Answer (C) is correct.
   REQUIRED: The U.S gross income of a nonresident alien who performs services in the U.S. for part of the year.
   DISCUSSION: A nonresident alien must include in U.S. gross income that income from U.S. sources effectively connected with the conduct of a trade or business in the United States (Sec. 871). Under Sec. 864, the performance of personal services in the U.S. constitutes a trade or business in the United States. If income is derived therefrom, it is considered to be from a U.S. source (Publication 17). According to the IRS and the courts, services of a professional hockey player are allocable to U.S. and non-U.S. time periods during the preseason training camp, the regular season, and post-season playoffs, but not the off-season. Therefore, Jean must include the portion of his income that is attributable to the performance of personal services in the U.S., i.e., 80% (132 ÷ 165 days). Eighty percent of $68,500 is $54,800, which must be reported as U.S. income.

29. Mr. H is a foreign student studying for a degree in the United States. There is no income tax treaty between his country and the United States. During the 9 months of the school year, Mr. H is employed part-time by a corporation incorporated in his home country doing business in the United States. During summer vacation, Mr. H returns home, where he is employed by the same company. Which of the following statements is true regarding U.S. taxes?

A. All income is taxable on a U.S. tax return.

B. All income is excludable, and filing a U.S. tax return is not required.

C. Only income earned for services in the United States is taxable.

D. All income is taxable on a U.S. tax return, and credit is allowed for foreign taxes paid on his summer income.

Answer (C) is correct.
   REQUIRED: The U.S. taxation of compensation earned both in the U.S. and abroad by a foreign student in the United States.
   DISCUSSION: Under Sec. 871, income from U.S. sources effectively connected with a U.S. trade or business must be included in a nonresident alien's U.S. gross income. The performance of personal services in the United States constitutes a trade or business in the United States (Publication 17 and Sec. 864). Therefore, the income earned by Mr. H while employed part-time in the United States is taxable.
   Answer (A) is incorrect. A nonresident alien has no U.S. income when the personal services income is earned outside the United States and is not connected with the conduct of a U.S. trade or business. **Answer (B) is incorrect.** The income earned in the United States is taxable. **Answer (D) is incorrect.** A nonresident alien has no U.S. income when the personal services income is earned outside the United States and is not connected with the conduct of a U.S. trade or business.

Access the **Gleim EA Premium Review System** featuring our SmartAdapt technology from your Gleim Personal Classroom to continue your studies. You will experience a personalized study environment with exam-emulating multiple-choice questions.

STUDY UNIT TWO

GROSS INCOME I

(23 pages of outline)

This study unit is the first of two that presents items that are included in gross income, income items that are excluded from gross income, and income items for which the Internal Revenue Code provides a partial exclusion from gross income. The following formula is an overview of the steps to compute federal income tax liability for individual taxpayers.

Individual Income Tax FORMULA
GROSS INCOME
− Section 62 Adjustments/Deductions (above the line)
= **ADJUSTED GROSS INCOME**
− Greater of Itemized Deductions or Standard Deduction
− Qualified Business Income Deduction
= **TAXABLE INCOME**
× Tax Rate
= **GROSS TAX Liability**
− Credits
= **NET TAX Liability or Refund Receivable**

2.1 GROSS INCOME

The IRC (Internal Revenue Code) defines gross income as all income from whatever source derived except as otherwise provided.

1. Section 61(a) enumerates types of income that constitute gross income. The list is not exhaustive.
   a. Compensation for services, including fees, commissions, and fringe benefits
   b. Gross income derived from business
   c. Gains derived from dealings in property
   d. Interest
   e. Rents
   f. Royalties
   g. Dividends
   h. Alimony and separate maintenance payments (executed before 2019)
   i. Annuities
   j. Income from life insurance and endowment contracts (This is a broader application than the general exclusion for proceeds due to death.)
   k. Pensions
   l. Income from discharge of indebtedness
   m. Distributive share of partnership gross income
   n. Income in respect of a decedent (income earned but not received before death)
   o. Income from an interest in an estate or trust

2.   Other types of income also constitute gross income unless a statute specifically excludes them.

   a.   This specifically includes income derived from all sources regardless of whether the taxpayer receives a Form W-2 or Form 1099.

   b.   Form 1099-MISC is used for reporting a variety of types of income not reported on a W-2 or other specific Form 1099s. Any errors on this form should be reported to the payor. If the payor will not correct and reissue the new form, the taxpayer must attach an explanation and report the correct amount.

Domestic vs. Foreign Source Income

3.   There are several factors that determine the source (domestic or foreign) of a specific type of income. The following table explains the general rules:

Item of Income	Factor Determining Source
Salaries, wages, other compensation	Where services performed

Business income:
  Personal services
  Sale of inventory—purchased
  Sale of inventory—produced
	
	Where services performed
	Where sold
	Allocation

Interest	Residence of payor
Dividends	Whether a U.S. or foreign corporation
Rents	Location of property

Royalties:
  Natural resources
  Patents, copyrights, etc.
	
	Location of property
	Where property is used

Sale of real property	Location of property
Sale of personal property	Seller's tax home
Pension distributions attributable to contributions	When services were performed that earned the pension
Investment earnings on pension contributions	Location of pension trust
Sale of natural resources	Allocation based on fair market value of product at export terminal

4.   Items are included in income based on the method of accounting used by the taxpayer.

   a.   The cash method of accounting includes income when constructively received.

   b.   The accrual method of accounting reports income when

      1)   All events have occurred fixing the right to receive the income.
      2)   The amount can be determined with reasonable accuracy.

   c.   The accrual method of accounting is required when there are inventories.

   d.   The hybrid method allows a business to use the cash method for the portion of the business that is not required to be on the accrual method.

   e.   Income is reported when it can be estimated with reasonable accuracy. Adjustments are made in a later year for any differences between the actual amount and the previously reported amounts.

EXAMPLE 2-1   **Cash vs. Accrual-Method Income**

Lucy is a calendar-year accrual-method taxpayer. She provided services on December 21, Year 1. She billed the customer in the first week of January Year 2 but did not receive payment until February Year 2. She must include the amount received for the services in her Year 1 income. If she were on the cash basis, she would report the income in Year 2.

Constructive Receipt

5. Income, although not actually in a taxpayer's possession, is constructively received in the taxable year during which it is credited to his or her account, set apart for him or her, or otherwise made available so that (s)he may draw upon it at any time, or so that (s)he could have drawn upon it during the taxable year if notice of intention to withdraw had been given.

    a. A check received in the mail is considered to be income on the date received, whether or not it is cashed.

    b. To determine receipt of income from securities trades, the trade date, rather than the settlement date, should be used.

    c. However, income is not constructively received if the taxpayer's control of its receipt is subject to substantial limitations or restrictions.

    d. Constructive receipt applies to the cash method of accounting. Under the accrual method, income is reported in the year earned.

Claim-of-Right Doctrine

6. A taxpayer receiving payments under a claim of right and without restrictions on its use or disposition includes the payment in income in the year received even though the right to retain the payment is not yet fixed or the taxpayer may later be required to return it.

    a. If payment is not received, then the payment is not included in income.

Compensation for Services

7. All compensation for personal services is gross income. The form of payment is irrelevant.

    a. If services are paid for in property, its fair market value at the time of receipt is gross income.

    b. The amount included in income becomes the basis in the property.

    c. If services were performed for a price agreed on beforehand, the price will be accepted as the FMV of the property only if there is no evidence to the contrary.

    d. Gross income of an employee includes any amount paid by an employer for a liability (including taxes) or expense of the employee.

    e. Income from self-employment is included in gross income. The director of a corporation is considered self-employed, and all fees are included in gross income.

    f. Reported and unreported compensation (e.g., tips) is gross income.

        1) Food service employers required to allocate tip income use 8% of food and drink sales to determine the allocable amount.

    (Food/drink sales × 8%) – All employee's reported tips = Amount to be allocated

Business Income from Electronic Payments

8. Taxpayers who receive payments in either of the following forms will receive a Form 1099-K, *Payments Card and Third Party Network Transactions*, from the payment settlement entity:

   a. From payment cards (e.g., credit/debit/stored-valued cards), or

   b. Through a third-party network when the total transactions exceed both $20,000 in value and 200 in volume for the year.

Virtual Currency

9. In some environments, virtual currency, e.g., Bitcoin, operates like "real" currency (i.e., the coin and paper money of the United States or of any other country that is designated as legal tender, circulates, and is customarily used and accepted as a medium of exchange in the country of issuance), but it does not have legal tender status in any jurisdiction.

   a. Virtual currency is treated as property for U.S. federal tax purposes. General tax principles that apply to property transactions apply to transactions using virtual currency. Among other things, this means that

      1) Wages paid to employees using virtual currency are taxable to the employee, must be reported by an employer on a Form W-2, and are subject to federal income tax withholding and payroll taxes.

      2) Payments using virtual currency made to independent contractors and other service providers are taxable and self-employment tax rules generally apply. Normally, payors must issue Form 1099.

      3) The character of gain or loss from the sale or exchange of virtual currency depends on whether the virtual currency is a capital asset in the hands of the taxpayer.

      4) A payment made using virtual currency is subject to information reporting to the same extent as any other payment made in property.

   b. A taxpayer who receives virtual currency as payment for goods or services must, in computing gross income, include the fair market value of the virtual currency, measured in U.S. dollars, as of the date the virtual currency was received.

Prepaid Income

10. Generally, prepaid income is taxable in the year received whether the taxpayer is on the cash or accrual method of accounting.

    a. Prepayments for merchandise inventory are not income until the merchandise is shipped.

Bartering

11. Bartered services or goods are included in gross income at the fair market value of the item(s) received in exchange for the services.

Assignment of Income

12. Gross income includes income attributable to a person even though the income is received by other persons. This doctrine imposes the tax on income on those who earn it, produce the right to receive it, enjoy the benefit of it when paid, or control property that is its source.

EXAMPLE 2-2   Assignment of Income
Swift, a life insurance salesperson, directs his employer to pay his commissions to his daughter. The commissions paid to Swift's daughter are gross income to Swift.

   a. The doctrine applies to income earned by personal services or derived from property.

EXAMPLE 2-3   **Assignment of Income Derived from Property**

Taxpayer makes a gift of interest earned on securities to her 20-year-old daughter who attends college. The interest is gross income to Taxpayer.

---

    b.   Assignment of an income-producing asset is effective to shift the gross income to the assignee.

EXAMPLE 2-4   **Assignment of Income-Producing Asset**

Taxpayer gives the underlying securities to her 20-year-old daughter. Interest earned after the transfer is gross income to the daughter.

---

    c.   Effective assignment requires that the transfer of property be complete and bona fide, with no control retained over either the property or the income it produces, and that the transfer take place before the income is actually earned.

Royalties

13.   Royalties are payments to an owner from people who use a right belonging to that owner. Royalties constitute ordinary gross income and are not a return of capital.

Personal Rental Income

14.   Cash or the FMV of property or services received for the use of personal property is taxable as rental income.

    a.   Schedule C (not Schedule E, which is for rental of real estate) is used if the taxpayer is in the business of renting personal property. A taxpayer is in the business of renting personal property if the primary purpose for renting the property is income or profit and the taxpayer is involved in the rental activity with continuity and regularity. If rental of personal property is not a business, any income belongs on Form 1040 (Schedule 1), line 8, and any deductions from the rental of personal property for profit on line 22.

Not-for-Profit Rental Income

15.   If property is not rented to make a profit, taxpayers can deduct their rental expenses only up to the amount of their rental income. A taxpayer cannot deduct a loss or carry it forward to the next year if rental expenses are more than rental income for the year.

    a.   Not-for-profit rental income is reported on Form 1040 or 1040-NR. Taxpayers can include their casualty losses on the appropriate lines of Schedule A if they itemize their deductions.

    b.   If rental income is more than rental expenses for at least 3 years out of a period of 5 consecutive years, taxpayers are presumed to be renting property to make a profit.

    c.   If taxpayers are starting a rental activity and do not have 3 years showing a profit, they can elect to have the presumption made after they have the 5 years of experience required by the test. They may choose to postpone the decision of whether the rental is for profit by filing Form 5213.

        1)   Form 5213 must be filed within 3 years after the due date of the return (determined without extensions) for the year in which the taxpayer first carried on the activity or, if earlier, within 60 days after receiving written notice from the Internal Revenue Service proposing to disallow deductions attributable to the activity.

Alimony

16. **Alimony** and separate maintenance payments are included in the gross income of the recipient (payee) and are deducted from the gross income of the payor for divorce decrees executed (i.e., established) prior to 2019. Alimony is not deductible by the payor and is not included in the gross income of the recipient if (a) the divorce is finalized after 2018 or (b) a pre-2019 divorce is modified after 2018 and that modification expressly provides for exclusion from income.

    a.   A payment is considered to be alimony (even if paid to a third party, e.g., home mortgage) when it is

        1)   Paid in cash
        2)   Paid pursuant to a written divorce or separation instrument
        3)   Not designated as other than alimony
        4)   Terminated at death of recipient
        5)   Not paid to a member of the same household
        6)   Not paid to a spouse with whom the taxpayer is filing a joint return

Child Support

    b.   Child support payments are an exclusion from the gross income of the recipient and are not deductible by the payor. These payments are not alimony.

        1)   If the divorce or separation instrument specifies payments of both alimony and child support, and only partial payments are made, then the partial payments are considered to be child support until this obligation is fully paid, and any excess is then treated as alimony.

        2)   If the payment amount is to be reduced based on a contingency relating to a child (e.g., attaining a certain age, marrying), the amount of the reduction will be treated as child support.

Property Settlement

    c.   Property settlements, which are simply a division of property, are not treated as alimony.

        1)   Property transferred to a spouse or former spouse incident to a divorce is treated as a transfer by gift, which is specifically excluded from gross income.

            a)   "Incident to a divorce" means a transfer of property within 1 year after the date the marriage ceases or a transfer of property related to the cessation of the marriage.

            b)   This exclusion does not apply if the spouse or former spouse is a nonresident alien.

Alimony Recapture

    d.   Current tax law includes a recapture provision, which is intended to prevent large property settlements from being treated as alimony. Recapture occurs if payments significantly decrease in the second or third year after a divorce. The following steps show how to calculate the final amount of recapture:

        1)   Second-year alimony recapture is equal to

            2nd-year alimony – ($15,000 + 3rd-year alimony)

        2)   First-year alimony recapture is equal to

$$\text{1st-year alimony} - \left[\frac{\substack{\text{(2nd-year alimony} \\ \text{– 2nd-year recapture)} \\ \text{+ 3rd-year alimony}}}{2} + \$15{,}000 \right]$$

3) Both the first-year and second-year recapture amounts are included in the payor's gross income and deducted from the payee's gross income in Year 3.

EXAMPLE 2-5   Alimony Recapture

After Lisa divorced Jed in Year 1, she paid him $60,000 of alimony in Year 1, $40,000 in Year 2, and $10,000 in Year 3. Excess alimony in Year 2 was $15,000 [$40,000 − ($15,000 + $10,000)]. Excess alimony in Year 1 was $60,000 − {[($40,000 − $15,000 + $10,000) ÷ 2] + $15,000}, or $27,500. In Year 3, Lisa must include in gross income the total of Year 1 and Year 2 excess alimony, or $42,500. Jed is also allowed a deduction of the same amount.

Annuity Contracts

17. The portion of amounts received under an annuity contract for which a statute does not provide an exclusion is gross income. Taxpayers are permitted to recover the cost of the annuity (the price paid) tax-free.

EXAMPLE 2-6   Annuity Contracts

Donna paid $1,200 for an annuity that pays $200 per month for an entire year, for a total of $2,400 ($200 × 12 months). The percentage of each payment that can be excluded is 50% ($1,200 price of annuity ÷ $2,400 total payments). Therefore, Donna may exclude $100 ($200 × 50%) of each payment from income for a total of $1,200 ($100 × 12 months).

401(k) Plans

18. Employer contributions generally are not included in the income of the participant.

Income from Life Insurance and Endowment Contracts

19. Proceeds received due to the death of the insured are generally excluded from gross income.

   a. Interest paid on the proceeds of a policy that is paid out over time is gross income to the beneficiary.

   b. The amount excluded from gross income of an applicable policy holder with respect to an employer-owned life insurance contract is not to exceed the premiums and other amounts paid by the policyholder for the life insurance policy.

      1) The income inclusion rule does not apply to a member of the insured's family, to any individual who is the designated beneficiary of the insured under the contract (other than an applicable policy holder), to a trust established for the benefit of the insured's family or a designated beneficiary, or to the estate of the insured.

Debt Discharge

20. Discharge of indebtedness can result in gross income.

   a. Gross income includes the cancellation of indebtedness when a debt is canceled in whole or in part for consideration.

      1) If a creditor cancels a debt (Form 1099-C) in consideration for services performed by the debtor, the debtor must recognize income in the amount of the debt as compensation for his or her services.

      2) Income from discharge of indebtedness is reported on the same form as for any other income (i.e., Schedule C for a sole proprietor).

   b. Generally, a corporation has gross income from discharge of indebtedness when it satisfies a debt by transferring its own corporate stock to the creditor.

      1) The amount of gross income is the amount by which the principal of the debt exceeds the value of the transferred stock, plus the value of any other property transferred.

c.   If a creditor gratuitously cancels a debt, the amount forgiven is treated as a gift (the IRC generally provides for exclusion of gifts from gross income).

d.   Exceptions. Gross income does not include discharges that

1)   Occur in bankruptcy, except the stock for debt transfer as described in item 20.b. on the previous page.

2)   Occur when the debtor is insolvent but not in bankruptcy.

a)   The amount excluded is the smaller of the debt canceled or the amount of insolvency, based on the excess of liabilities over the FMV of assets on the date of debt cancellation.

3)   Are related to qualified farm indebtedness.

4)   Are a discharge of qualified real property business indebtedness.

5)   Are related to principal residence indebtedness. (Item i. below has more information on this exception.)

e.   When a taxpayer excludes discharge of indebtedness under d.1), 2), or 3) above, the taxpayer must reduce his or her tax attributes in the following order:

1)   NOLs
2)   General business credit
3)   Minimum tax credit
4)   Capital loss carryovers
5)   Basis reductions

NOTE: The taxpayer may first elect to decrease the basis of depreciable property.

f.   When there is a debt discharge involving real property, there are typically two separate transactions:

1)   The property is sold to the lender. Form 1099-A may be issued. A gain or loss may be required to be reported on the transaction.

2)   The lender cancels the debt. Form 1099-C may be issued. Income may have to be reported as discussed above.

g.   The sale of the property and the cancellation of the debt do not have to occur in the same year. If they occur in the same year, the lender will issue only a Form 1099-C.

h.   When a canceled debt is a nonbusiness debt (e.g., discount for early payment of a mortgage loan), it is to be reported as other income on line 8 of Form 1040 (Schedule 1).

EXAMPLE 2-7	Debt Cancellation

The amount of debt cancellation as a reward for early payoff of a home mortgage is other income reported on line 8 of Schedule 1, Form 1040.

i.   The Mortgage Forgiveness Debt Relief Act excludes discharges of up to $2 million ($1 million if married filing separately) of indebtedness, which is secured by a principal residence and which is incurred in the acquisition, construction, or substantial improvement of the principal residence.

1)   This exclusion applies to discharge of debt occurring after 2006.

2)   The amount excluded from gross income reduces the basis of the residence, but not below zero, and only when the taxpayer retains the residence.

3)   Principal residence has the same meaning as when used in Sec. 121.

4)   The exclusion does not apply if the discharge is due to any reason not directly related to a decline in the home's value or the taxpayer's financial condition.

Student Loan Cancellation

    j.   Federal, state, and/or local government student loan indebtedness may be discharged and excluded from income if the former student engages in certain employment (e.g., in a specified location, for a specified period, for a specified employer) or the discharge is due to the death or total and permanent disability.

Social Security Benefits

21.   Social Security benefits are generally not taxable unless additional income is received. The gross income inclusion is dependent upon the relation of provisional income (PI) to the base amount (BA) and the adjusted base amount (ABA).

    a.   PI = Adjusted gross income (AGI) + Tax-exempt interest + Excluded foreign income + 50% of Social Security benefits. In other words, tax-exempt interest is included or taken into account but the exclusion of foreign income is not, resulting in all foreign income being included in AGI.

    b.   BA means $32,000 if married filing jointly (MFJ), $0 if married filing separately and having lived with the spouse at any time during the tax year (MFSLT), or $25,000 for all others.

    c.   ABA is the BA plus $12,000 if MFJ, $0 if MFSLT, or $9,000 for all others.

If . . .	PI ≤ BA	BA < PI ≤ ABA	PI > ABA
Then SS benefit inclusion equals . . .	0%	50%	85%

EXAMPLE 2-8	Taxable Social Security Benefits

Mr. and Mrs. Slom, both over 65 and filing jointly, received $20,000 in Social Security benefits. Additionally, they reported $30,000 of taxable interest, $15,000 of tax-exempt interest, $18,000 in dividends, and a taxable pension of $16,000. Therefore, their AGI excluding Social Security benefits is $64,000 ($30,000 taxable interest + $18,000 dividends + $16,000 taxable pension payments).

- PI is $89,000 [$64,000 AGI + $15,000 tax-exempt interest + 50% of Social Security benefits ($10,000)].

- The adjusted base amount is $44,000.

- Gross income will include $17,000 (85% of Social Security benefits) since this amount is less than 85% of the excess of PI over the ABA plus the lesser of 50% of the incremental BA ($6,000) or 50% of Social Security benefits.

- Calculation of included Social Security benefits:

1)	AGI, excluding Social Security benefits	$64,000
2)	+ Tax-exempt interest/excluded foreign income	+ 15,000
3)	= Modified AGI	= $79,000
4)	+ 50% of Social Security benefits	+ 10,000
5)	= PI	= $89,000
6)	− BA ($32,000, $25,000, or $0)	− 32,000
7)	= Excess PI (If < $0, then $0 inclusion)	= $57,000
8)	− Incremental base amount ($12,000, $9,000, or $0)	− 12,000
9)	= Excess PI	= $45,000
10)	Smaller of amount in line 7 or 8	$12,000
11)	50% of line 10	6,000
12)	Smaller of amount in line 4 or 11	6,000
13)	Multiply line 9 by 85%	38,250
14)	Add lines 12 and 13	44,250
15)	Social Security benefits × 85%	17,000
16)	Taxable benefits = Smaller of amount in line 14 or 15	17,000

Railroad Retirement

22. The Railroad Retirement Board allows for participants to receive retirement annuities at age 60 with 30 or more years of service. Social Security beneficiaries are not eligible until age 62, regardless of how long they have been paying into the system.

    a. The Social Security Benefits Worksheet is used to determine whether any of the benefits are taxable.

Illegal Activities

23. Income from illegal activities is gross income.

Scholarships

24. Amounts received by an individual as scholarships or fellowships are excluded from gross income to the extent that the individual is a candidate for a degree from a qualified educational institution and the amounts are used for required tuition or fees, books, supplies, or equipment (not personal expenses, such as room and board).

    a. Gross income includes any amount received, e.g., as tuition reduction, in exchange for the performance of services, such as teaching or research.

    b. Generally, a reduction in undergraduate tuition for an employee of a qualified educational organization does not constitute gross income.

    c. Subsistence payments administered by Veteran Affairs are excluded from gross income.

EXAMPLE 2-9   Scholarships

Laura received a scholarship of $2,500, and as a condition for receiving the scholarship, Laura must serve as a part-time teaching assistant. Of the $2,500 scholarship, $1,000 represents payment for teaching. Assuming Laura only uses her scholarship for qualified education expenses, Laura will be able to exclude $1,500 from income. The $1,000 she received for teaching is taxable and must be included in income.

Prizes and Awards

25. If the prize or award is in a form other than money, the amount of gross income is the FMV of the property. The honoree may avoid inclusion by rejecting the prize or award. Some prizes and awards are excludable.

    a. Certain employee achievement awards may qualify for exclusion from the employee's gross income as a de minimis fringe benefit.

        1) An award recipient may exclude the FMV of the prize or award from his or her gross income if

            a) The amount received is in recognition of religious, scientific, charitable, or similar meritorious achievement;

            b) The recipient is selected without action on his or her part;

            c) The receipt of the award is not conditioned on substantial future services; and

            d) The amount is paid by the organization making the award to a tax-exempt organization (including a governmental unit) designated by the recipient.

2) A prize or award may qualify for exclusion as a scholarship.

3) Employee achievement awards may qualify for exclusion from the recipient employee's gross income if they are awarded as part of a meaningful presentation for safety achievement or length of service and

a) The awards do not exceed $400 (cost to employer) for all nonqualified plan awards,

b) The awards do not exceed $1,600 (cost to employer) for all qualified plan awards, and

c) The awards are tangible personal property. Cash and cash equivalents, including gift cards, are not tangible personal property.

4) Awards in excess of limitations

a) If the employer exceeds the cost limitations for the award, the employee's exclusion from income is only preserved in part. In this case, the employee must include in his or her gross income, as compensation, the greater of

i) An amount equal to the portion of the cost to the employer of the award that was not allowable as a deduction to the employer (as opposed to the excess of the fair market value of the award) or

ii) The amount by which the fair market value of the award exceeds the maximum dollar amount allowable as a deduction to the employer.

EXAMPLE 2-10   Award in Excess of Limitations

Assume that an award cost the employer $500, rather than $400, and its fair market value is $475. In this case, the employer's deduction is limited to $400, and the amount includible by the employee in his or her income is $100, i.e., the greater of

- The difference between the item's cost and the deduction limitation ($100) or
- The amount by which the item's fair market value exceeds the deduction limitation ($75).

If the fair market value was $600, the amount includible in the employee's income would be $200.

The remaining portion of the fair market value of the award, $375 ($475 – $100), is not included in the employee's gross income.

---

5) A qualified plan award is an employee achievement award provided under an established written program that does not discriminate in favor of highly compensated employees.

Unemployment Benefits

26. Unemployment benefits received under a federal or state program, as well as company-financed supplemental plans, are gross income.

a. Strike benefits received from a union are also included in income.

Compensation for Injury or Sickness

27. Gross income does not include benefits specified that might be received in the form of disability pay, health or accident insurance proceeds, workers' compensation awards, or other "damages" for personal physical injury or physical sickness.

    a. Specifically excluded from gross income are amounts received

        1) Under workers' compensation acts as compensation for personal injuries or sickness

        2) Under an accident and health insurance policy purchased by the taxpayer even if the benefits are a substitute for lost income

        3) By employees as reimbursement for medical care and payments for permanent injury or loss of bodily function under an employer-financed accident or health plan

        4) As a pension, annuity, or similar allowance for personal injuries or sickness resulting from active service in the armed forces of any country

    b. The following are excluded from gross income regardless of whether the damages are received by lawsuits or agreements or as lump sums or periodic payments:

        1) Damages received for personal physical injury or physical sickness

        2) Payments received for emotional distress if an injury has its origin in a physical injury or physical sickness

    c. Compensation for slander of personal, professional, or business reputation is included in gross income.

    d. An in- or out-of-court settlement for lost profits in a business or court-awarded damages is included in gross income.

    e. Punitive damages received are included in gross income, even if in connection with a physical injury or physical sickness.

        1) An amount for both actual and punitive damages must be allocated.

    f. Wrongful death damages can be excluded to the extent they were received on account of a personal injury or sickness.

    g. Damages received solely for emotional distress are included in gross income. These damages include amounts received for claims, such as employment or age discrimination.

    h. Interest earned on an award for personal injuries is included in gross income.

Recovery of Medical Deductions

    i. If the taxpayer incurred medical expenses in Year 1, deducted these expenses on his or her Year 1 tax return, and received reimbursement for the same medical expenses in Year 2, the reimbursement is included in gross income on the Year 2 return to the extent of the previous deduction that was allowed on the return.

Accident and Health Plans

28. Benefits received by an employee under an accident and health plan under which the employer paid the premiums or contributed to an independent fund are excluded from gross income of the employee.

   a. The benefits must be either

      1) Payments made due to permanent injury or loss of bodily functions or

      2) Reimbursement paid to the employee for medical expenses of the employee, spouse, or dependents.

         a) Any reimbursement in excess of medical expenses is included in income.

   b. The plan must not discriminate in favor of highly compensated executives, shareholders, or officers.

   c. Any excess reimbursement over the actual cost of medical expenses may be excluded only to the extent the taxpayer contributed to the plan.

Disability Policies

29. Proceeds from disability insurance policies are tax-free if paid for by the employee.

   a. If the employer contributed to the coverage (employer contributions are excluded from the employee's income), then the amount received must be prorated into taxable and nontaxable amounts.

   b. Payments made from a qualified trust on behalf of a self-employed person are considered employer contributions.

   c. For example, if the employer pays 75% of the insurance premiums of a disability policy, 75% of the proceeds are includible in income.

Employer-Provided Dependent Care

30. Up to $5,000 of dependent care provided by an employer is excluded from income. This includes

   a. Amounts paid directly to the taxpayer or the taxpayer's care provider for the care of the dependent

   b. FMV of employer-provided daycare facility

   c. Pre-tax contributions under a flexible spending plan

Employer-Provided Life Insurance

31. Proceeds of a life insurance policy for which the employer paid the premiums are excluded from the employee's gross income. Certain premiums paid by the employer are, however, included in the employee's gross income.

   a. The cost of group term life insurance up to a coverage amount of $50,000 is excluded from the employee's gross income.

      1) The amount included is the premiums representing excess coverage (over $50,000) less any amounts paid by the employee on the insurance policy.

Long-Term Care Coverage

32. Contributions by an employer to an employee's long-term care coverage are nontaxable employee benefits.

Pensions

33. Pensions are most often paid in the form of an annuity. Therefore, the rules for pensions are similar to the rules for annuities. Employees are able to recover their cost tax-free.

    a. The investment in the contract is the amount contributed by the employee in after-tax dollars.

    b. Amounts withdrawn early are treated as a recovery of the employee's contributions (excluded from gross income) and of the employer's contributions (included in gross income).

        1) After all of the employee's contributions are recovered, additional withdrawals are included in gross income.

    c. Persons retired on disability before they reach minimum retirement age must report their taxable disability payments as wages (this is further explained in Publication 575).

    d. A foreign pension or annuity distribution is a payment from a pension plan or retirement annuity received from a source outside the United States. They are received from a

        1) Foreign employer,

        2) Trust established by a foreign employer,

        3) Foreign government or one of its agencies (including a foreign social security pension),

        4) Foreign insurance company, or

        5) Foreign trust or other foreign entity designated to pay the annuity.

        As with domestic pensions or annuities, the taxable amount generally is the gross distribution minus the cost (investment in the contract). Income received from foreign pensions or annuities may be fully or partly taxable, even if the taxpayer did not receive a Form 1099 or the foreign equivalent reporting the amount of the income.

Death Benefits

34. All death benefits received by the beneficiaries or the estate of an employee from, or on behalf of, an employer are included in gross income.

    a. This is for employer-paid death benefits, not to be confused with the death benefits of a life insurance plan provided by an employer.

Rental Value of Parsonage

35. Ministers may exclude from gross income the rental value of a home or a rental allowance to the extent the allowance is used to provide a home, even if deductions are taken for home expenses paid with the allowance. The exclusion is the smaller of

    a. The actual expenditures of the minister for the home,
    b. The amount designated with the employer as a rental allowance, or
    c. The fair rental value of the housing, plus the cost of utilities.

    The parsonage allowance is subject to self-employment taxes. A minister should include any offerings given directly to him or her for church-related functions (e.g., marriages).

Combat Zone Compensation

36. Military officers may exclude compensation up to an amount equal to the highest rate of basic pay at the highest pay grade that enlisted personnel may receive (plus any hostile fire/imminent danger pay).

    a. The exclusion applies only to compensation received while serving in a combat zone or while hospitalized as a result of wounds, disease, or injury incurred in a combat zone.

    b. Military personnel below officer level (i.e., enlisted) are allowed the same exclusion without the cap.

Gifts or Inheritance

37. The IRC provides for exclusion from the gross income of the recipient the value of property acquired by gift or inheritance. A gift is a transfer for less than full or adequate consideration that results from the detached and disinterested generosity of the transferor.

    a. Gift transfers include inter vivos (between the living) gifts and gifts by bequest (of personal property by a will), devise (of real property by a will), and inheritance (under state intestacy law).

    b. Voluntary transfers from employer to employee are presumed to be compensation, not gifts.

Treasure Trove

38. Treasure trove is gross income for the tax year in which it is undisputedly in the taxpayer's possession.

EXAMPLE 2-11	Reporting of a Treasure Trove
Rich purchased an old piano for $500 15 years ago. In the current year, Rich finds $10,000 hidden in the piano. Rich must report the $10,000 as gross income in the current year.	

Gambling

39. All gambling winnings are gross income and may require reporting by the payor on Form W-2G.

    a. Gambling losses, e.g., nonwinning lottery tickets, are deductible only to the extent of winnings as an other itemized deduction.

    b. Gambling losses over winnings for the taxable year cannot be used as a carryover or carryback to reduce gambling income from other years.

Recovery of Tax Benefit Item

40. The tax benefit rule includes, in gross income, items received for which the taxpayer received a tax benefit in a prior year.

EXAMPLE 2-12	Recovery of Tax Benefit -- Bad Debt
Taxpayer writes off bad debt 5 years ago. In the current year, the debtor pays Taxpayer the principal of the debt written off, which must be included in gross income since the deduction 5 years ago reduced the tax liability.	

    a. Section 111 provides for exclusion of amounts recovered during the tax year that were deducted in a prior year to the extent the amount did not reduce income tax.

EXAMPLE 2-13	Recovery Not Providing a Tax Benefit
Taxpayer pays $2,000 state income tax and itemizes deductions. Subsequent refunds must be included. However, if Taxpayer used the standard deduction, the refund would not be included because no tax benefit from payment of state income tax was realized.	

Reimbursements for Moving Expenses

41. Qualified reimbursements incurred by members of the military on active duty are excluded from gross income. If the reimbursement is not for qualified moving expenses, or if the taxpayer is not a member of the military, it is included in gross income.

Adoption Assistance Programs

42. Qualified adoption expenses paid to a third party or reimbursed to an employee by an employer under a written adoption assistance program are excludable from the employee's gross income.

    a. An adoption assistance program is a written plan that

        1) Benefits employees who qualify under rules set up by the employer that do not favor highly compensated employees or their dependents,

        2) Does not pay more than 5% of its payments each year to shareholders or owners of more than 5% of the stock,

        3) Provides for adequate notice to employees of their eligibility, and

        4) Requires employees to provide reasonable substantiation of qualified expenses that are to be paid or reimbursed.

Adoption Exclusion

    b. The maximum exclusion for 2020 is $14,300.

        1) The phase-out range for upper-income taxpayers is $214,520 to $254,520 for 2020.

        2) Adoption expenses must be reduced by an amount used in determining the adoption credit.

    c. For a child who is a U.S. citizen or resident, the exclusion is taken in the year the payments were made whether or not the adoption became final.

        1) For the adoption of a foreign child, the exclusion cannot be taken until the adoption becomes final.

    d. The excluded amount is not subject to income tax withholding. However, the payments are subject to Social Security, Medicare, and federal unemployment taxes.

    e. An eligible child must be under 18 years of age or must be physically or mentally incapable of self care.

    f. Qualified adoption expenses are reasonable and necessary adoption expenses, including adoption fees, court costs, attorney fees, and other directly related expenses.

        1) Expenses that are not eligible for the adoption exclusion include

            a) Costs associated with a surrogate parenting arrangement,

            b) Expenses incurred in violation of state or federal law, and

            c) Expenses incurred in connection with the adoption of a child of the taxpayer's spouse.

Reimbursement for Living Expenses

43. Insurance payments received by a taxpayer whose residence is damaged or destroyed and who must temporarily occupy another residence are excluded. This includes taxpayers with an undamaged residence who are required not to occupy the home due to a disaster.

    a. The exclusion is limited to the excess of actual living expenses over normal living expenses.

Reimbursed Employee Expenses

44. If reimbursements equal expenses and the employee makes an accounting of expenses to the employer, the reimbursements are excluded from the employee's gross income, and the employee may not deduct the expenses (accountable plan).

    a. This rule also applies if reimbursements exceeding expenses are returned to the employer and the employee substantiates the expenses.

    b. If excess reimbursements are not returned or if the employee does not substantiate them, the reimbursements are included in the employee's gross income.

Employee Housing at an Educational Institution

45. Employee housing at an educational institution (including an academic health center) is excluded from income if the rent paid by the employee exceeds 5% of the fair market value of the housing.

Fringe Benefits

46. An employee's gross income does not include the cost of any fringe benefit supplied or paid for by the employer that qualifies as a(n)

    - No-additional-cost service
    - Qualified employee discount
    - Working condition fringe
    - De minimis fringe
    - Qualified transportation fringe
    - Qualified moving expense reimbursement (active military only)
    - Employer-provided educational assistance

No-Additional-Cost Service

    a. The value of a no-additional-cost fringe benefit provided to employees, their spouses, or their dependent children by employers is excluded from gross income.

        1) A no-additional-cost fringe is a service or product that the employer offers for sale to customers in the ordinary course of business in which the employee performs substantial services.

            a) The employer must not incur any substantial additional costs in providing the service to the employee.

            b) An example is free telephone service to a phone company employee.

        2) The fringe benefits must be available to employees on a nondiscriminatory basis; e.g., benefits available only to executives are included in their gross income.

Employee Discount

    b. Certain employee discounts on the selling price of qualified property or services of their employer are excluded from gross income. "Qualified property or services" are offered in the ordinary course of business in which the employee is performing services and are purchased by the employee for his or her own use.

        1) The employee discount may not exceed

            a) The gross profit percentage in normal offers by the employer to customers or
            b) 20% of the price offered to customers in the case of qualified services.

        2) The discounts must be available to employees on a nondiscriminatory basis.

Working Condition Fringe

   c.   The FMV of property or services provided to an employee by an employer as a working condition fringe benefit is **excludable** by the employee to the extent the employer can deduct the costs as an ordinary and necessary business expense.

       1)   Property or services provided to an employee qualify as a working condition fringe benefit only if

           a)   The employee's use of the property or services relates to the employer's trade or business,

           b)   The employee would have been entitled to a business expense deduction if the property or services that were provided by the employer had been purchased by the employee, and

           c)   The employee maintains the required records, if any, with respect to the business use of the property or services provided by the employer.

       2)   The maximum value of employer-provided vehicles first made available to employees for personal use in 2020 for which the cents-per-mile valuation may be used is $50,400.

De Minimis Fringe

   d.   The value of property or services provided to an employee is excludable as a de minimis fringe benefit if the value is so minimal that accounting for it would be unreasonable or impracticable.

       1)   The following are examples of de minimis fringes:

           a)   Occasional use of company copy machines

           b)   Typing of personal letters by a company secretary

           c)   Occasional company parties or picnics

           d)   Tickets to entertainment events, if only distributed occasionally

           e)   Occasional taxi fare or meal money due to overtime work

           f)   Coffee and doughnuts

           g)   Traditional noncash holiday gifts with a small FMV

           h)   Tokens, vouchers, and reimbursements to cover the costs of commuting by public transit as long as the amount of reimbursement provided by the employer does not exceed $270 a month for any month (2020).

       NOTE: Any cash benefit or its equivalent (e.g., use of a credit card or gift certificate) cannot be excluded as a de minimis fringe benefit under any circumstances. Season tickets to sporting events, commuting use of an employer-provided car more than once a month, or membership to a private country club or athletic facility are never excludable as de minimis fringe benefits.

2) An eating facility for employees is treated as a de minimis fringe benefit if

   a) It is located on or near the business premises of the employer and

   b) The revenue derived from the facility normally equals or exceeds its direct operating costs. *otherwise includable in GI*

EXAMPLE 2-14   De Minimis Fringe Benefit

An employer provides meals at its own eating facility, and the direct operating costs of the facility exceed the annual revenue from the facility. Because the costs exceed revenue, the benefit is taxable to employees.

NOTE: The excess value of the meals over the fees charged to employees is excluded from employees' income.

3) The value of an on-premises athletic facility provided by an employer is generally excluded from gross income of employees.

Transportation Fringe

e. Qualified transportation fringe benefits of up to $270 per month (2020) may be excluded for the value of employer-provided parking (except residential), transit passes, and transportation in an employer-provided "commuter highway vehicle" (must seat six adults with 80% of mileage used for employee commuting when the vehicle is at least 1/2 full) between the employee's residence and place of employment.

   1) Employers may offer the cash equivalent of the benefit without the loss of the $270 employee exclusion for the benefit.

   2) If an employee chooses the cash option, cash amounts received are included in gross income.

   3) Employees may use any combination of these exclusions (i.e., qualified parking at a subway terminal).

Employer-Provided Educational Assistance

f. Up to $5,250 may be excluded by the employee for employer-provided educational assistance.

   1) This rule does not apply to graduate teaching or research assistants who receive tuition reduction under Sec. 117(d).

   2) Excludable assistance payments may not include tools or supplies that the employee retains after the course or the cost of meals, lodging, or transportation.

g. Under the CARES Act, payments made by an employer to an employee or lender (up to $5,250 per employee) between March 27, 2020, and January 1, 2021, on any qualified educational loan incurred by the employee for his or her education may be excluded by the employer from the employee's taxable wages.

Foreign-Earned Income Exclusion

47. U.S. citizens and qualifying resident aliens may exclude up to $107,600 of foreign-earned income and a statutory housing cost allowance from gross income.

    a.   To qualify for exclusion, the taxpayer must have foreign-earned income, a tax home in a foreign country, and be one of the following:

        1)   A U.S. citizen who is a bona fide resident of a foreign country or countries for an uninterrupted period that includes an entire tax year,

        2)   A U.S. resident alien who is a citizen or national of a country with which the United States has an income tax treaty in effect and who is a bona fide resident of a foreign country or countries for an uninterrupted period that includes an entire tax year, or

        3)   A U.S. citizen or a U.S. resident alien who is physically present in a foreign country or countries for at least 330 full days during any period of 12 consecutive months.

    b.   The $107,600 limitation must be prorated if the taxpayer is not present in (or a resident of) the foreign country for the entire year (Form 2555).

    c.   This exclusion is in lieu of the foreign tax credit.

    d.   Deductions attributed to the foreign-earned income (which is excluded) are disallowed.

    e.   The following table clarifies the types of income for the purposes of the foreign-earned income exclusion:

Earned Income	Unearned Income	Variable Income
Salaries and wages	Dividends	Business profits
Commissions	Interest	Royalties
Bonuses	Capital gains	Rents
Professional fees	Gambling winnings	Scholarships and fellowships
Tips	Alimony	
	Social Security benefits	
	Pensions	
	Annuities	

Foreign Housing Allowance

48. The inflation-adjusted standard cost-allowance for 2020 is $32,280 ($107,600 × 30%) for those locations not on the IRS's list of high-cost locations.

    a.   Foreign housing allowances are broken into three categories:

        1)   The first $17,216 ($107,600 × 16%) of any foreign housing reimbursement is includible in income,

        2)   The next portion of any reimbursement up to the greater of $32,280 or the amount listed for the city on the IRS's list of high-cost locations is excludable from income, and

        3)   Any reimbursement exceeding the amount in item 2) above is includible in income.

    b.   The chart on the following page can help you determine whether a taxpayer can claim either the foreign-earned income exclusion or the foreign housing exclusion.

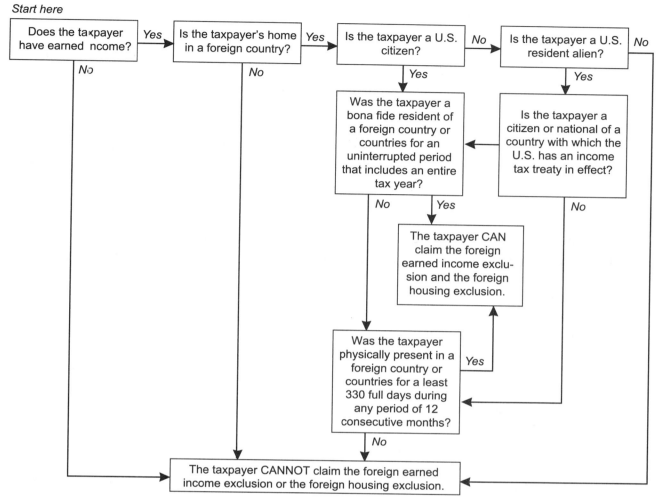

Figure 2-1

Rebate

49. A rebate to the purchaser is treated as a reduction of the purchase price. It is not included in gross income.

Community Property Income

50. The question of tax liability for married persons filing separate returns arises frequently during discussions concerning to whom income is taxable. Several states have community property laws. These states require significantly different treatment of tax liability than in states without such laws.

    a. In the nine community property states of Arizona, California, Idaho, Louisiana, Nevada, New Mexico, Texas, Washington, and Wisconsin, all property acquired by spouses **after** marriage is considered as owned by them in community, and as such, is referred to as community property.

       1) Any income from these properties is automatically considered joint or community income, and if taxpayers are filing separate tax returns, the income would be shared equally between them on their separate returns.

       2) Wisconsin has implemented a marital property act; therefore, for federal income tax purposes, it is considered a community property state.

       3) Alaska adopted an optional system whereby a couple can choose to opt in to the community property system.

b. Property acquired **before** marriage or inherited by one spouse during marriage is considered to be that spouse's separate property.

   1) In California, Arizona, Nevada, New Mexico, and Washington, any income from these separate properties is considered separate income; thus, if the spouses are filing separately, the income would not be shared and would be reported on that spouse's separate return.

   2) Conversely, in Texas, Idaho, Louisiana, and Wisconsin, income from these separate properties is considered community income; thus, if the spouses are filing separately, the income would be shared between them on their separate returns.

c. Section 66 of the IRC sets forth a specific rule for treatment of community income when the spouses live apart. The need for this section arose because, in community property states, each spouse is liable for one-half of the tax on income. Generally, when spouses are living apart, the spouse that earns the income will keep it.

d. If two individuals are married to each other at some time during a calendar year but live apart for the **entire** tax year, do not file a joint return, and one or both have earned income, none of which is transferred between them, the following rules cover the reporting of income on their separate tax returns:

   1) Earned income (other than trade or business income and partnership income) is treated as income of the spouse who rendered the personal services.

   2) Trade or business income shall be treated as the gross income and deductions of the spouse carrying on such trade or business or, if such trade or business is jointly operated, treated as the gross income and deductions of each spouse on the basis of their respective distributive share of the gross income and deductions.

   3) Community income derived from the separate property of one spouse is treated as the income of such spouse.

   4) All other community income is taxed in accordance with the applicable community property law.

Statutory Employees

51. Business taxpayers must determine the correct classification for each worker.

   a. A statutory employee is a worker who straddles the divide between being self-employed and being considered a regular employee.

      1) A statutory employee is a person who is in business for himself or herself, but who works primarily or wholly for a specific company.

   b. If workers are independent contractors under the common law rules, such workers may nevertheless be treated as employees by statute (statutory employees) for certain employment tax purposes if they fall within any one of the following four categories and meet the three conditions described under Social Security and Medicare taxes (listed in item d. on the next page):

      1) A driver who distributes beverages (other than milk) or meat, vegetable, fruit, or bakery products, or who picks up and delivers laundry or dry cleaning, if the driver is the business agent or is paid on commission.

      2) A full-time life insurance sales agent whose principal business activity is selling life insurance or annuity contracts, or both, primarily for one life insurance company.

3) An individual who works at home on materials or goods that the taxpayer/employer supplies and that must be returned to the taxpayer or to a person the taxpayer names if the taxpayer also furnishes specifications for the work to be done.

4) A full-time traveling or city salesperson who works on the taxpayer's/employer's behalf and turns in orders to the taxpayer from wholesalers; retailers; contractors; or operators of hotels, restaurants, or other similar establishments. The goods sold must be merchandise for resale or supplies for use in the buyer's business operation. The work performed for the taxpayer must be the salesperson's principal business activity.

   c. Officers of exempt organizations are considered statutory employees.

   d. The employer withholds Social Security and Medicare taxes from the wages of statutory employees if all three of the following conditions apply:

      1) The service contract states or implies that substantially all the services are to be performed by them.

      2) They do not have a substantial investment in the equipment and property used to perform the services (other than an investment in transportation facilities).

      3) The services are performed on a continuing basis for the same payer.

   e. Companies report their payments to statutory employees on Form W-2, but they must check Box 13 on the W-2 for "Statutory employee."

      1) Federal income tax is not withheld from the wages of statutory employees.

      2) Federal unemployment (FUTA) taxes are paid by employers on the first and fourth categories [b.1) and b.4) above and on the previous page] of statutory employees but not on categories b.2) and b.3).

   f. Statutory employee earnings are reported on line 1 of Schedule C, *Profit or Loss From Business.*

      1) Employees check the box on line 1 of Schedule C.

         a) The employee does not have to fill out a Schedule SE.

      2) The employee is permitted to deduct work-related expenses on Schedule C instead of Schedule A.

      3) The employee does not combine statutory employee income and other income from a business on a single Schedule C.

         a) Two Schedule Cs must be filed, and only the income from the non-statutory-employee business will flow through to Schedule SE.

   g. Statutory employees are not eligible to participate in retirement plans sponsored by the company that employs them.

      1) Statutory employees are regarded as "self-employed individuals" under Sec. 401(c)(1) and allowed to set up their own retirement plans.

      2) Full-time life insurance salespersons are deemed to be employed by the insurance company whose policies the salespersons sell for the purposes of retirement and health plans and can be covered under the insurance company retirement plan.

STOP AND REVIEW! You have completed the outline for this subunit. Study multiple-choice questions 1 through 30 beginning on page 68.

QUESTIONS

2.1 Gross Income

1. Jean is a U.S. citizen living and working in France for all of 2020. She received wages of $150,000, dividends of $10,000, and alimony (from a pre-2019 divorce) of $20,000 in 2020. She decides to use the foreign earned income exclusion available to her and file Form 2555. What is the amount of Jean's foreign earned income before any limitations are applied?

A. $0

B. $107,600

C. $150,000

D. $180,000

Answer (C) is correct.
  REQUIRED: The amount of foreign earned income before any limitations.
  DISCUSSION: Earned income is income that is received from a job for payment of services performed as a self-employed individual or as an employee of a business. Income that is otherwise received due to investments or alimony is not considered earned. Thus, Jean's foreign earned income is only the amount of income that she earned through wages of $150,000 (Publication 54).
  Answer (A) is incorrect. Jean's wages of $150,000 are considered foreign earned income. **Answer (B) is incorrect.** The exclusion is $107,600, not the total foreign-earned amount. **Answer (D) is incorrect.** The dividends and the alimony received are not earned income; thus, they are not included in the computation for foreign earned income.

2. When Joe's financial institution offered a substantial discount of $5,000 for early payment of his home mortgage, he borrowed from a family member to take advantage of this offer. How should Joe treat this discount transaction?

A. No actions or reporting required.

B. Report $5,000 on line 8, Other Income, on Form 1040 (Schedule 1).

C. Reduce his home mortgage interest deduction by $5,000.

D. Report $5,000 original issue discount as interest income.

Answer (B) is correct.
  REQUIRED: The appropriate treatment of a discount on a home mortgage.
  DISCUSSION: According to Publication 17, if a financial institution offers a discount for the early payment of a mortgage loan, the amount of the discount is canceled debt. When the canceled debt is a nonbusiness debt, it is to be reported as other income on line 8 of Form 1040 (Schedule 1).
  Answer (A) is incorrect. When a discount is offered for the early payment of a mortgage loan by a financial institution, it is treated as a canceled debt. Canceled debt must be reported as income. **Answer (C) is incorrect.** A canceled debt has no effect on the amount of interest deduction to be taken. **Answer (D) is incorrect.** Canceled debt has no effect on the amount of original issue discount interest income to be reported.

3. Generally, which of the following should be included in gross income?

A. Life insurance proceeds.

B. Child support payments.

C. Cash rebate from a dealer when a car is purchased.

D. Reimbursements from the U.S. military of a moving expense the military member/ taxpayer properly deducted on last year's tax return.

Answer (D) is correct.
  REQUIRED: The item that must be included in gross income.
  DISCUSSION: Section 82 specifically provides that, except as provided in Sec. 132(a)(6), gross income includes amounts received as reimbursement of moving expenses that are attributable to employment. Under Sec. 132(a)(6), the reimbursement is excluded if the expense would be deductible under Sec. 217 if paid by the employee. It may not be excluded, however, if the expense was actually deducted on the individual's return for any prior tax year (Publication 521).
  Answer (A) is incorrect. Life insurance proceeds are specifically excluded under Sec. 101(a). **Answer (B) is incorrect.** Section 71(c) excludes payments for the support of children. **Answer (C) is incorrect.** A rebate on a new automobile is merely a reduction of the purchase price of the automobile, not income.

4. Mr. Hines received a $6,200 grant from a local university for the fall of the current year. Mr. Hines was a candidate for a degree and was required to be a research assistant, for which services he received payment under the grant. The $6,200 grant provided the following:

Tuition	$3,600
Books and supplies	500
Pay for services as research assistant	2,100

Mr. Hines spent the entire $6,200 on tuition, books, and supplies. What amount must Mr. Hines include in his income for the current year?

- A. $2,100
- B. $2,600
- C. $3,600
- D. $6,200

Answer (A) is correct.
  REQUIRED: The amount required to be included in income.
  DISCUSSION: Although Sec. 117 excludes from gross income amounts received as qualified scholarships and tuition reduction to be used for tuition and related expenses, this exclusion does not apply to amounts representing payments for teaching, research, or other services performed by the student that are required as a condition for receiving the qualified scholarship or tuition reduction (Publication 17).
  Answer (B) is incorrect. Books and supplies qualify as a Sec. 117 exclusion. **Answer (C) is incorrect.** Tuition qualifies as a Sec. 117 exclusion. **Answer (D) is incorrect.** Only payments for services are included in gross income.

5. If your Social Security benefits are considered taxable, the maximum percent of net benefits received that can be included in income is

- A. 0%
- B. 50%
- C. 85%
- D. 100%

Answer (C) is correct.
  REQUIRED: The maximum percentage of Social Security benefits includible in gross income.
  DISCUSSION: The taxable portion of Social Security benefits will depend upon the amount of provisional income in relation to the base amount and the adjusted base amount. If provisional income exceeds the adjusted base amount, up to 85% of Social Security benefits may be taxable (Publication 17).

6. All of the following are considered "constructive receipt" of income EXCEPT

- A. Lori was informed her check for services rendered was available, but she did not pick it up.
- B. Pierre earned income that was received by his agent but was not received by Pierre.
- C. Jacque bought a 9-month certificate of deposit in November of the current year. It earned $200 interest in the current year. She can withdraw the principal and interest in the current year if she pays a penalty of one month's interest ($100).
- D. A payment on a sale of real property was placed in escrow pending settlement, at which time title would be conveyed.

Answer (D) is correct.
  REQUIRED: The occurrence that is not considered "constructive receipt" of income.
  DISCUSSION: Income, although not actually in a taxpayer's possession, is constructively received in the taxable year during which it is credited to his or her account, set apart for him or her, or otherwise made available so that (s)he may draw upon it at any time or so that (s)he could have drawn upon it during the taxable year if notice of intention to withdraw had been given (Reg. 1.451-2). However, income is not constructively received if the taxpayer's control of its receipt is subject to substantial limitations or restrictions (Publication 538). Since the taxpayer's control of the receipt of the funds in the escrow account is substantially limited until the transaction has closed, the taxpayer has not constructively received the income until the closing of the transaction in the following year.
  Answer (A) is incorrect. The check for services rendered was made available to the taxpayer during the current year. **Answer (B) is incorrect.** The receipt of income by the taxpayer's agent makes it available to the taxpayer; therefore, it is constructively received. **Answer (C) is incorrect.** The funds are available regardless of whether a penalty would be imposed.

7. Kelley's employer gave her stock in the current year for services performed with the condition that she would have to return the stock unless she completed 3 years of service. At the time of the transfer, her employer's basis in the stock was $6,000, and its fair market value was $8,000. Kelley did not make the Sec. 83(b) election. How much should she include in her income for the current year, and what would be her basis in the stock?

A. Income of $8,000; basis of $8,000.

B. Income of $6,000; basis of $6,000.

C. Income of $8,000; basis of $3,000.

D. Kelley would not report any income or have any basis in the stock until she has completed 3 years of service.

Answer (D) is correct.
   REQUIRED: The basis in stock received as compensation but subject to a substantial limitation on alienability.
   DISCUSSION: Under the claim-of-right doctrine, a taxpayer receiving income under a claim of right and without restrictions on its use or disposition is taxed on that income in the year received even though the right to retain the income is not yet fixed or the taxpayer may later be required to return it (Publication 538). In this case, however, there is a substantial limitation on the stock's use and/or disposition because Kelley must return the stock if she does not complete 3 years of service. Therefore, Kelley will not report any income or have any basis in the stock until she has completed 3 years of service.

8. During the current year, Mr. French received state unemployment benefits of $2,500 and $700 of supplemental unemployment benefits from a company-financed fund. The union paid Mr. French an additional $2,000 as strike benefits. What amount must Mr. French include in income for the current year?

A. $2,500

B. $3,200

C. $4,500

D. $5,200

Answer (D) is correct.
   REQUIRED: The amount of the items listed that must be included in gross income.
   DISCUSSION: Gross income is defined under Sec. 61 as all income from whatever source derived that is not specifically excluded. Unemployment benefits received under a federal or state program are gross income [Sec. 85(a)].
   Regulation 1.85-1(b)1(i) provides that amounts paid pursuant to private nongovernmental unemployment compensation plans are includible in income without regard to Sec. 85. Thus, the $700 from the company-financed fund and the $2,000 from the union must also be included in gross income (Publication 17).
   Answer (A) is incorrect. The $700 from the company-financed fund and the $2,000 from the union also must be included in gross income. **Answer (B) is incorrect.** The $2,000 from the union must be included in gross income. **Answer (C) is incorrect.** The $700 from the company-financed fund must be included in gross income.

9. Trish Durwood works for a small retail clothing store. She earned $26,000 in wages during the year. Because of a cash flow problem in April, Trish did not receive her $500 weekly check but instead was given a credit of $500 on the purchased clothing for her family. How much income should be shown on her Form W-2 and reported on her Form 1040?

A. $26,000

B. $25,500

C. $26,500

D. $25,000

Answer (A) is correct.
   REQUIRED: The amount of income reported on Form W-2 and Form 1040 for compensation of services.
   DISCUSSION: Compensation for services must be included in gross income [IRC Sec. 61(a)(1)]. Due to the relationship between an employee and an employer, almost everything received by the employee from the employer is included in gross income as compensation.
   Answer (B) is incorrect. The $500 applied to Trish's account should also be included as income. **Answer (C) is incorrect.** The $500 applied to Trish's account is not additional compensation. It is compensation in lieu of receiving her paycheck. **Answer (D) is incorrect.** The $500 applied to Trish's account is income in lieu of her receiving a check. This event does not reduce her income.

10. Ms. Miller set up a computer system for Mr. Town's business. In return, Mr. Town gave Ms. Miller a storage facility. Ms. Miller plans to use this facility for business purposes and plans to depreciate it. The fair market value of Ms. Miller's services and the storage facility was $50,000. Mr. Town's basis in the storage facility was $30,000. How should Ms. Miller treat the transaction, and what is her depreciable basis for the property?

A. Ms. Miller should include the $50,000 in income and use $30,000 as the depreciable basis for the storage facility she received.

B. Mr. Town should include the $30,000 in his income and use the $50,000 as the depreciable basis for the storage facility.

C. Ms. Miller should include $30,000 in income and $50,000 as the depreciable basis for the storage facility.

D. Ms. Miller should include $50,000 in income and use $50,000 as the basis for the storage facility.

Answer (D) is correct.
 REQUIRED: The income and basis for property received in exchange for a service performed.
 DISCUSSION: All compensation for personal services is gross income. The form of payment is irrelevant. If services are paid for in property, its fair market value at the time of receipt is gross income. The amount included in income becomes the basis in the property. Since the building's FMV at the time of the exchange is $50,000, the amount of income recognized and Ms. Miller's basis in the property is equal to $50,000 (Publication 17).
 Answer (A) is incorrect. The depreciable basis in the property is also equal to $50,000. **Answer (B) is incorrect.** Mr. Town is giving the building to Ms. Miller in payment for her services and should only recognize the gain on the sale of the building of $20,000. Also, he will not be able to depreciate the building because it belongs to Ms. Miller. **Answer (C) is incorrect.** Ms. Miller must include the FMV of the building received ($50,000) in income.

11. Gene Wingo had the following potentially taxable transactions in the current year. How much, if any, should be included on his current-year return?

- $200 credited to his savings account on December 31 of the current year. He did not withdraw any money from the account during the entire year.

- $2,000 withheld from his paycheck by his employer to satisfy a garnishment by his doctor.

- $1,000 discount given by his bank when he paid off his home mortgage 5 years early.

- $500 check received December 31 of the current year from an individual for one of Gene's original drawings. Gene did not cash or deposit the check until the next year.

A. $1,700

B. $2,700

C. $3,700

D. $3,200

Answer (C) is correct.
 REQUIRED: The amount includible in gross income.
 DISCUSSION: Gross income includes compensation for services ($2,000 + $500), interest ($200), and income from discharge of indebtedness ($1,000), among other items. Gene should include all $3,700 in gross income on his current year return (Publication 17).
 Answer (A) is incorrect. The $2,000 withheld from his paycheck is still attributable to him as compensation for services, even though Gene does not receive the income and it is used to pay his doctor. **Answer (B) is incorrect.** Gross income includes the cancellation of indebtedness when a debt is canceled in whole or part for consideration. If a creditor cancels a debt in consideration for services performed by the debtor, the debtor must recognize income in the amount of the debt as compensation for his or her services. **Answer (D) is incorrect.** The $500 check is received on December 31 of the current year; thus, it is in Gene's possession. The income is realized even though he does not cash or deposit the check until the next year.

12. Ruby Diaz is a commissioned salesperson. She is a cash-method taxpayer. At the end of the current year, her earnings for the year were $75,000. During the year, she also received $10,000 in advances on future commissions and repaid $8,000. How much income should Ruby report for the current year?

    A. $77,000

    B. $75,000

    C. $87,000

    D. $85,000

Answer (A) is correct.
    REQUIRED: The income reported for a cash-basis taxpayer.
    DISCUSSION: Both cash- and accrual-basis taxpayers must include amounts in gross income upon actual or constructive receipt if the taxpayer has an unrestricted claim to such amounts under Reg. 1.61-8(b). All commissions received should be included in the current year's gross income. The $8,000 repaid reduces gross income [Publication 17 and IRC Reg. 1.61-8(b)]. Ruby should report $77,000 ($75,000 + $10,000 – $8,000).
    Answer (B) is incorrect. Ruby must include the amount of advances on future commissions that she did not repay as income on her current year return. **Answer (C) is incorrect.** The amount of advanced future commissions is not included in income to the extent that it has been repaid. **Answer (D) is incorrect.** The $8,000 repaid reduces gross income.

13. Gordon, age 70, is retired and works part-time as a security guard earning $8,000. He received $5,000 interest from a savings account and $2,500 interest from tax-exempt municipal bonds. His Social Security benefits were $12,000 and his taxable pension was $6,000. To determine if any of his Social Security is taxable, Gordon should compare how much of his income to the $25,000 base amount?

    A. $27,500

    B. $21,500

    C. $19,000

    D. $25,000

Answer (A) is correct.
    REQUIRED: The amount of taxable Social Security income.
    DISCUSSION: Under Sec. 86, if the sum of the "modified" adjusted gross income plus one-half of Social Security benefits exceeds $25,000 on a single return but does not exceed $34,000, part of the Social Security benefits will be included in gross income. Modified adjusted gross income equals adjusted gross income plus tax-exempt interest (modified AGI = $8,000 + $6,000 + $5,000 + $2,500 = $21,500). The sum of the taxpayer's modified AGI of $21,500 and one-half of their $12,000 in Social Security is equal to $27,500, which should then be compared to the $25,000 minimum (Publication 17).
    Answer (B) is incorrect. The taxpayer's $6,000 pension should be included in modified AGI. **Answer (C) is incorrect.** The $2,500 in tax-exempt interest and $6,000 in pension income should be included in modified AGI. **Answer (D) is incorrect.** The $2,500 in tax-exempt interest should be included in modified AGI.

14. Which of the following does NOT have to be included in gross income?

    A. Unemployment compensation.

    B. Damages from personal injury suit involving back injuries.

    C. Prize from church raffle.

    D. Free tour from travel agency for organizing a group of tourists.

Answer (B) is correct.
    REQUIRED: The item that does not have to be included in gross income.
    DISCUSSION: Gross income means all income from whatever source derived unless specifically excluded (Sec. 61). This is an intentionally broad and all-encompassing definition. Section 104(a)(2) includes punitive damages in gross income, even in connection with a physical injury or physical sickness. However, Sec. 104(a)(2) excludes nonpunitive damages awarded for personal injuries involving physical injury or physical sickness (Publication 17).
    Answer (A) is incorrect. Unemployment compensation is included in gross income under Sec. 85. **Answer (C) is incorrect.** A prize received in a raffle (whether from a church or any other organization) is included in gross income under Sec. 74. **Answer (D) is incorrect.** The fair market value of a free tour is the receipt of an economic benefit, which is included in gross income as compensation since no provision excludes it.

15. Pastor Green received an annual salary of $20,000 as a full-time minister. The church also paid him $1,000 designated as a housing allowance to pay for his utilities. His church owns a parsonage that has a fair rental value of $6,000 in which he lives rent free. Neither the rental allowance nor the rental value of the parsonage is included in his W-2. All amounts are considered provided for services he renders as a licensed pastor. He is not exempt from self-employment tax. Compute the amount of Pastor Green's income that is subject to income tax on his return.

A. $19,000

B. $20,000

C. $27,000

D. $26,000

Answer (B) is correct.
  REQUIRED: The income included in gross income for a minister who lives in a parsonage for free and receives a rental allowance.
  DISCUSSION: Ministers may exclude from gross income the rental value of a home or a rental allowance to the extent the allowance is used to provide a home, even if deductions are taken for home expenses paid with the allowance. However, a minister should include any offerings given directly to him or her for church-related functions (Publication 517). Accordingly, Pastor Green may exclude the rental value ($6,000) of the parsonage in which he lives and the $1,000 rental allowance given to him by the church. He should claim $20,000 of income on his income tax return.
  Answer (A) is incorrect. The amount of $19,000 assumes that the $1,000 was included in the $20,000, when it was not. **Answer (C) is incorrect.** Pastor Green may exclude the rental value ($6,000) of the parsonage in which he lives and the $1,000 rental allowance given to him by the church. **Answer (D) is incorrect.** Pastor Green may exclude the rental value of the parsonage ($6,000) from his income.

16. Susan is a waitress and earned $15,000 in wages, not including any tips she received in 2020. She received tips of $17 in January, which she did not report to her employer. Because she became ill in February and did not return to work until late March, she also forgot to report the $58 for tips that she received in February. She did report the $7,000 she received as tips for the rest of the year. How much income must she report as wages, tips, and other compensation on her tax return?

A. $22,185

B. $22,075

C. $15,260

D. $15,183

Answer (B) is correct.
  REQUIRED: The income to report as wages, tips, and other compensation for 2020.
  DISCUSSION: Gross income, as defined in Sec. 61(a) of the IRC and Publication 17, is all sources of income unless excluded in the tax code. Wages and tips are not excluded in the tax code. Thus, wages, tips, and other compensation for 2020 should be $22,075 ($15,000 + $17 + $58 + $7,000).
  Answer (A) is incorrect. The amount of $22,185 includes $90 more than should be included in wages, tips, and other compensation. **Answer (C) is incorrect.** The amount of $15,260 only adds $260 in tips, instead of the total $7,075 in tips earned, to the wages. **Answer (D) is incorrect.** The amount of $15,183 only includes $183 in tips, instead of the total $7,075 in tips earned, to the wages.

17. Due to Mr. Sandburg's poor financial situation, Mr. Bond canceled the $4,000 debt that was due Mr. Bond on June 24 of the current year, with the understanding that the cancellation was not a gift. Mr. Sandburg was not insolvent or bankrupt at that time. As a result, Mr. Sandburg

A. Must still pay the debt.

B. Does not have to include the $4,000 in income.

C. Must now file for bankruptcy.

D. Must include $4,000 in his gross income.

Answer (D) is correct.
  REQUIRED: The true statement about income recognized from a cancellation of a debt.
  DISCUSSION: Under Sec. 61(a)(12), gross income includes income from the discharge of indebtedness unless it is excluded under Sec. 108. The cancellation will be excluded if the debt is canceled due to a bankruptcy action or if the taxpayer is insolvent outside bankruptcy (Publication 17). Because Mr. Sandburg was not insolvent or bankrupt, he must include the $4,000 in gross income.
  Answer (A) is incorrect. There is no longer an obligation to pay the debt. **Answer (B) is incorrect.** Mr. Sandburg does not meet the Sec. 108 exclusion provisions. **Answer (C) is incorrect.** There is no requirement to file for bankruptcy.

18. On February 10 of the current year, Rose was in an automobile accident while she was going to work. The doctor advised her to stay home for 6 months because of her injuries. On February 25 of the current year, she filed a lawsuit. On July 20 of the current year, Rose returned to work. On December 15 of the current year, the lawsuit was settled and Rose received the following amounts:

Compensation for lost wages $25,000
Personal injury damages awarded
  (none of which was for punitive
  damages) 40,000

How much of the settlement must Rose include in ordinary income on her current-year tax return?

A. $0

B. $25,000

C. $40,000

D. $65,000

Answer (A) is correct.
    REQUIRED: The amount of gross income from the payments received as a result of the injury.
    DISCUSSION: In 1996, Sec. 104(a)(2) was amended to exclude from gross income damages received on account of personal physical injury or physical sickness only. The House Committee Report for the 1996 changes states, "If an action has its origin in a physical injury or physical sickness, then all damages (other than punitive) that flow therefrom are treated as payments received on account of physical injury or physical sickness . . ." Therefore, Rose's compensation for lost wages is excluded from gross income (Publication 17).
    Answer (B) is incorrect. Compensation for lost wages is excluded from gross income. **Answer (C) is incorrect.** Personal injury damages are excluded from gross income by Sec. 104(a). **Answer (D) is incorrect.** Damages received on account of personal physical injury or physical sickness are excluded from gross income.

19. Kevin is a candidate for a master's degree at a local university. During the current year, he was granted a fellowship that provided the following:

Tuition $18,000
Books and supplies 2,000
Room and board 14,800

What is the maximum amount Kevin can exclude from gross income in the current year?

A. $20,000

B. $18,000

C. $16,800

D. $34,800

Answer (A) is correct.
    REQUIRED: The amount of a scholarship a candidate for a degree may exclude.
    DISCUSSION: A candidate for a degree may exclude from gross income amounts received as a scholarship or fellowship grant. But only amounts provided and actually used for tuition, fees, books, supplies, and equipment required for instruction qualify for this exclusion (Publication 17 and IRC Sec. 117). Room and board does not qualify.
    Answer (B) is incorrect. Books and supplies also qualify for the Sec. 117 exclusion. **Answer (C) is incorrect.** The amount used for room and board is not excluded from gross income. **Answer (D) is incorrect.** The amount used for room and board is not excluded from gross income.

20. Ms. Red, age 28, is single and received $10,000 in unemployment benefits from the state for 2020. She also received $3,000 from the state to reduce the costs of her winter fuel bill. What amount of income should Ms. Red report for 2020?

A. $10,000

B. $13,000

C. $7,600

D. $0

Answer (A) is correct.
    REQUIRED: The income that should be reported as gross income.
    DISCUSSION: Unemployment benefits received under a federal or state program are gross income. When the state provides funds specifically to help with utility bills, they may be excluded from income (Publication 17). Thus, Ms. Red must include the $10,000 in unemployment benefits that she received, but may exclude the $3,000 she received from the state to reduce the costs of her winter fuel bill.
    Answer (B) is incorrect. Ms. Red may exclude the $3,000 she received from the state to reduce the costs of her winter fuel bill. **Answer (C) is incorrect.** The $2,400 exclusion of unemployment compensation was only for 2009. **Answer (D) is incorrect.** Ms. Red must include the $10,000 of unemployment benefits in income.

21. Mr. and Mrs. Garden filed a joint return for the year. Mr. Garden received $8,000 in Social Security benefts and Mrs. Garden received $4,000. Their income also included $10,000 taxable pension income and interest income of $2,000. What part of their Social Security benefits will be taxable? (The base amount for married filing jointly is $32,000 for the year.)

A. $0

B. $6,000

C. $24,000

D. $12,000

Answer (A) is correct.

REQUIRED: The amount of Social Security benefits that are taxable.

DISCUSSION: Social Security benefits are generally not taxable unless additional income is received. The gross income inclusion is dependent on the relation of provisional income (PI) to the base amount (BA) and the adjusted base amount (ABA). If PI < BA, there is no inclusion. If PI falls between BA and ABA, up to 50% of Social Security benefits will be included. If PI > ABA, up to 85% of Social Security benefits will be included (Publication 17). The Gardens' provisional income is calculated below.

AGI, excluding Social Security benefits	$12,000
50% of Social Security benefits	6,000
Provisional income	$18,000

Since the Gardens' provisional income is less than their base amount of $32,000, none of their Social Security benefits will be taxed.

Answer (B) is incorrect. The amount of $6,000 is the portion of the Social Security benefits that must be added to the Gardens' AGI to determine provisional income. **Answer (C) is incorrect.** The amount of $24,000 is the total amount of income the Gardens received, not the Social Security benefits that must be included in gross income. **Answer (D) is incorrect.** None of the Social Security benefits are taxable.

22. An ordained minister cannot exclude the following from gross income:

A. Rental allowance.

B. Fees for marriages, baptisms, and funerals.

C. Fair rental value of parsonage.

D. Actual cost to provide a home.

Answer (B) is correct.

REQUIRED: The income an ordained minister cannot exclude.

DISCUSSION: Under Sec. 61, salaries and fees for personal services are always included in gross income. A minister should include his or her salary; the offerings given directly to him or her for marriages, baptisms, funerals, etc.; and the other outside earnings donated by him or her to the organization in his or her gross income. Regulation 1.107-1 excludes from gross income the rental value of a home, or a rental allowance to the extent it is used to rent or provide a home, furnished to a minister as a part of his or her compensation. A minister is entitled to deduct mortgage interest and real property taxes paid on a personal residence even if the amounts are derived from an allowance that is excluded from gross income (Publication 517).

Answer (A) is incorrect. Rental allowance is specifically excluded under Reg. 1.107-1 from the gross income of an ordained minister. **Answer (C) is incorrect.** Fair rental value of parsonage is specifically excluded under Reg. 1.107-1 from the gross income of an ordained minister. **Answer (D) is incorrect.** The actual cost to provide a home is specifically excluded under Reg. 1.107-1 from the gross income of an ordained minister.

23. Bill, a tax preparer, agreed to prepare the corporate tax return for EZ Interior Decorating Co. It was agreed that Bill's fee would be $4,500. EZ was experiencing cash flow problems and offered Bill a computer with a fair market value (FMV) of $3,500, a printer valued at $400, and a monitor worth $250 instead of the agreed upon $4,500. EZ had paid $6,000 for these items. Bill accepted the equipment in lieu of cash. What is Bill's basis in the property received?

A. $0

B. $4,150

C. $6,000

D. $4,500

Answer (B) is correct.
REQUIRED: The basis of property received in exchange for services rendered.
DISCUSSION: Section 83(a) provides that the receipt of property for services provided is a taxable transaction. Accordingly, the fair market value of the property must be included in gross income as compensation, and the basis of the property will be its fair market value. Publication 17 states that if services were performed for a price agreed on beforehand, the price will be accepted as the FMV of the property only if there is no evidence to the contrary.
Answer (A) is incorrect. Bill does have a basis in the property received. Answer (C) is incorrect. Bill's basis is the FMV of the property received, not the basis to EZ. Answer (D) is incorrect. Only the FMV of property received is the basis, not the agreed-upon fee.

24. Optimistic borrowed $20,000 to buy a machine for his printing business. Shortly thereafter, the economy went into a deep recession and Optimistic was not able to repay the debt although he was not insolvent. In the current year, the creditor reduced the debt by $10,000 so Optimistic could afford to pay it. The creditor was not the seller of the machine. As a result of this reduction of debt,

A. The purchase price of the machine is adjusted to reduce Optimistic's basis in the machine.

B. Optimistic has $10,000 of income.

C. The debt is a qualified business indebtedness and the basis of the machine must be reduced.

D. Any tax effect from the reduction of the debt is deferred until final payment by Optimistic.

Answer (B) is correct.
REQUIRED: The tax effect of a reduction of a debt from the purchase of business property.
DISCUSSION: The cancellation of indebtedness is included in gross income under Sec. 61(a)(12). Under Sec. 108, the discharge of indebtedness is excluded from gross income if the debtor is insolvent, in bankruptcy reorganizations, a farmer, or a taxpayer other than a C corporation that has invested in real property. The canceled debt can also be excluded if it relates to a purchase-money debt reduction. Since none of these apply, the $10,000 reduction of debt is included in Optimistic's income (Publication 17).
Answer (A) is incorrect. A reduction of purchase-money debt is treated as a purchase price adjustment only if the creditor is the seller of the property. Answer (C) is incorrect. The reduction of basis for qualified business indebtedness is not available after 1986. Answer (D) is incorrect. The discharge of indebtedness causes immediate recognition of income by a solvent taxpayer who is not a farmer or a taxpayer other than a C corporation that has invested in real property.

25. During the current year, Mr. Lamply received state unemployment benefits of $1,600. The union paid Mr. Lamply an additional $1,600 out of regular union dues. What amount must Mr. Lamply include in income?

A. $0

B. $1,600

C. $800

D. $3,200

Answer (D) is correct.
REQUIRED: The amount of the items listed that must be included in gross income.
DISCUSSION: Gross income is defined under Sec. 61 as all income from whatever source derived which is not specifically excluded. There is no exclusion for unemployment compensation benefits [Sec. 85(a)].
Regulation 1.85-1(b)1(i) provides that amounts paid pursuant to private nongovernmental unemployment compensation plans are also includible in income without regard to Sec. 85.
Answer (A) is incorrect. The amounts received from the state unemployment program and the union plan are gross income. Answer (B) is incorrect. The amount of $1,600 is incorrect for the current tax year. Answer (C) is incorrect. There was a $2,400 exclusion of unemployment income in 2009, but that exclusion has expired.

26. Randi, a flight attendant, received wages of $30,000 in the current year. The airline provided transportation on a stand-by basis, at no charge, from her home in Detroit to the airline's hub in Chicago. The fair market value of the commuting flights was $5,000. Also in the current year, Randi received reimbursements under an accountable plan of $10,000 for overnight travel, but only spent $6,000. The excess was returned. Randi became disabled in November of the current year and received workers' compensation of $4,000. What amount must Randi include in gross income on her current-year tax return?

   A. $30,000

   B. $34,000

   C. $35,000

   D. $37,000

Answer (A) is correct.
   REQUIRED: The amount includible in gross income.
   DISCUSSION: The commuting flights paid for by the employer are excluded from gross income since they are no-additional-cost fringe benefits. The reimbursed overnight travel expenses are not included in gross income because they could have been deducted by Randi as qualified business expenses and the excess reimbursements were returned. Workers' compensation is excluded from gross income under Sec. 104(a) (Publications 17 and 463). Therefore, only Randi's salary of $30,000 is included in gross income as compensation for services rendered (Sec. 61).
   Answer (B) is incorrect. Worker's compensation is excluded from gross income. **Answer (C) is incorrect.** The value of the commuting flight is excluded from gross income. **Answer (D) is incorrect.** Only the salary should be considered part of gross income.

27. Donald, an accountant, was falsely accused of fraud by a local newspaper. He sued the newspaper for libel, claiming damages both to his personal reputation in the community and to his business. In December of the current year, the jury awarded Donald the following:

$10,000 for his personal reputation
$70,000 for his business loss
$70,000 as punitive damages (to punish the
   newspaper)

How much can Donald exclude from gross income?

   A. $0

   B. $10,000

   C. $70,000

   D. $80,000

Answer (A) is correct.
   REQUIRED: The amount of a recovery from a libel lawsuit that may be excluded from gross income.
   DISCUSSION: Section 104(a)(2) excludes from gross income "the amount of any damages received (whether by suit or agreement and whether as a lump sum or periodic payments) on account of personal injuries or sickness." Section 104(a)(2) makes punitive damages that are otherwise excludable under Sec. 104(a)(2) includible in gross income (Publication 17). These rules generally apply to amounts received after August 20, 1996. Damages received on account of a nonphysical injury or sickness (e.g., injury to reputation) are also not excludable from gross income. The $70,000 of punitive damages are not generally excludable under Sec. 104(a)(2). The $70,000 for business loss is taxable to Donald as a substitute for compensation he would have otherwise earned.

28. Rev. Jones, an ordained minister, received $8,400 designated as a housing allowance. Rev. Jones used the full amount to pay his mortgage principal of $1,000, mortgage interest of $6,300, and property taxes of $1,200. Rev. Jones itemized his deductions and deducted the home mortgage interest and property taxes. What is the amount Rev. Jones may exclude from income?

   A. $0

   B. $1,000

   C. $7,300

   D. $8,400

Answer (D) is correct.
   REQUIRED: The amount of clergy housing allowance excludable from income.
   DISCUSSION: A housing allowance, to the extent that the allowance is used to rent or provide a home, is excluded from gross income. A minister is also entitled to deduct mortgage interest and real property taxes paid on a personal residence even if the amounts expended are derived from a rental allowance that is excludable from the minister's gross income [Publication 517 and IRC Sec. 265(a)(b)].
   Answer (A) is incorrect. Rev. Jones used $8,500 to provide a home. **Answer (B) is incorrect.** The entire amount of the housing allowance was used to provide a home. **Answer (C) is incorrect.** The entire amount of the housing allowance was used to provide a home.

29. Mr. Brown is a college student working on a degree in accounting. He received the following in 2020:

I.   A $4,000 scholarship used for tuition at State University

II.   A $1,000 scholarship used for fees and books

III. An $8,000 fellowship used for his room and board

Compute the amount Mr. Brown must include in income for 2020.

A. $8,000

B. $5,000

C. $13,000

D. $9,000

Answer (A) is correct.
   REQUIRED: The amount of scholarships that should be included on the 2020 tax return.
   DISCUSSION: Publication 17 states that amounts received by an individual as scholarships or fellowships are excluded from gross income to the extent that the individual is a candidate for a degree from a qualified education institution and the amounts are used for required tuition or fees, books, supplies or equipment (not personal expenses, such as room and board). Accordingly, Mr. Brown is able to exclude $5,000 from income since it was used for tuition, fees, and books, and the $8,000 must be included in gross income since it was used for room and board.
   Answer (B) is incorrect. The amount of $5,000 is excluded from income because it was used on tuition, fees, and books. In addition, $8,000 must be included in income because it was used for room and board. **Answer (C) is incorrect.** The $5,000 used for tuition, fees, and books is excluded from income. **Answer (D) is incorrect.** The $1,000 used to pay for fees and books is excluded from income.

30. For the current year, which of the following is a taxable fringe benefit?

A. Employer pays for subscriptions for professional journals delivered to employees' home addresses.

B. Employer provides meals at its own eating facility and the direct operating costs of the facility exceed the annual revenue from the facility.

C. Employer pays up to $5,250 from a qualified educational assistance program for classes that are not work related.

D. Employer reimburses employees for deductible travel expenses.

Answer (B) is correct.
   REQUIRED: The item that is a taxable fringe benefit.
   DISCUSSION: Section 132 provides an exclusion for meals furnished in an eating facility on or near the business premises of the employer if the revenue derived from the facility normally equals or exceeds the direct operating costs of the facility. Here, the costs exceed revenue, thus the employee must include the excess of FMV over the price paid for the meal in gross income (Publication 15-B).
   Answer (A) is incorrect. Section 132 provides an exclusion from the gross income of an employee for working condition fringe benefits provided by an employer. A subscription to a professional journal is considered a working condition fringe benefit. **Answer (C) is incorrect.** Payments from a qualified educational assistance program need not be for job-related classes. **Answer (D) is incorrect.** Under Sec. 132, the reimbursement of travel expenses is excluded from gross income as a working condition fringe, i.e., the expense is deductible by the employer as an ordinary and necessary business expense.

STUDY UNIT THREE

GROSS INCOME II: INTEREST, SECURITIES, AND DECEDENT

(12 pages of outline)

This study unit is the second of two that presents items that are included in gross income, income items that are excluded from gross income, and income items for which the Internal Revenue Code provides a partial exclusion from gross income.

3.1 INTEREST INCOME

1. Interest is value received or accrued for the use of money.

   a. Interest is reported under the doctrine of "constructive receipt" when the taxpayer's account is credited with the interest.

   b. Accrued interest on a deposit that may not be withdrawn at the close of an individual's tax year because of an institution's actual or threatened bankruptcy or insolvency is not includible until the year in which such interest is withdrawable.

   c. All interest is gross income for tax purposes unless an exclusion applies.

   d. Examples of taxable interest include

      1) A merchandise premium, e.g., a toaster given to a depositor for opening an interest-bearing account

         a) Under Rev. Proc. 2000-30, a noncash de minimis gift is tax-free if it does not have a value of more than $10 for a deposit of less than $5,000 or $20 for a deposit of $5,000 or more.

      2) Imputed interest on a below-market term loan

Imputed Interest

2. Loans at below-market interest rates may be the economic equivalent of a receipt of income in the amount of forgone interest. Thus, interest is imputed on below-market loans.

Below-Market Loan

3.   Below-market loans (BMLs) are categorized as demand loans or term loans.

a.   Demand loans are payable in full on demand or have indefinite maturity dates. A term loan is any loan other than a demand loan.

b.   A below-market demand loan is a loan on which interest is payable at a rate lower than the applicable federal rate. The excess of the interest that would have been payable in that year under the applicable federal rate over the actual interest payable is treated as imputed interest.

1)   The imputed interest is deemed transferred by the borrower to the lender on the last day of each year. It may be deductible by the borrower. The imputed interest is then deemed to be retransferred to the borrower by the lender. It could be either a gift, compensation (employment relationship), or a dividend (corporation/shareholder relationship) to the borrower.

c.   A below-market term loan is a loan in which the amount lent exceeds the present value of all payments due under the loan.

1)   Gift term loans. The lender is treated as transferring the excess of the amount of the loan over the present value of all principal and interest payments due under the loan, at one time, when the loan is first made. The retransfer, however, is computed at the end of each year.

2)   Non-gift term loans are treated as original issue discount. Thus, the lender has interest income over the course of the loan, and the borrower has interest expense.

d.   The imputed interest rules apply to any below-market loan that is a

1)   Gift loan

2)   Loan between a corporation and a shareholder

3)   Compensation-related loan between an employer and an employee or between an independent contractor and a person for whom the independent contractor provides services

4)   Loan that has tax avoidance as one of its principal purposes

BML Exceptions

e.   No interest is imputed for any day on which the total loans between borrower and lender are below certain amounts.

1)   If the BML (gift loan) between individuals is $10,000 or less, then there is no interest imputation unless the loan was made to acquire income-producing assets.

a)   In the case of gift loans between individuals, if the total debt is less than $100,000, the amount deemed as transferred is limited to the borrower's net investment income, and such net investment income is treated as $0 unless it exceeds $1,000.

i)   This exception allows family gift loans without penalizing the lender.

2)   If the BML between a corporation and its shareholder is $10,000 or less, there is no interest imputation unless the loan's principal purpose was tax avoidance.

3)   Certain loans without a significant tax effect are excluded from the BML rules.

Original Issue Discount (OID)

4. OID is the excess, if any, of the stated redemption price at maturity over the issue price and is included in income based on the effective interest rate method of amortization.

   a. If there is OID of at least $10 for the calendar year and the term of the obligation exceeds 1 year, the interest income must be reported on Form 1099-OID.

EXAMPLE 3-1   Original Issue Discount

Cathy purchases a 20-year 7% bond at original issue for $10,000. The stated redemption price is $12,400, and interest is paid annually. The ratable monthly portion of OID is $10. Assume that the effective rate of interest is 10%. During the first year held, interest income is $1,000 ($10,000 × 10%) and interest received is $868 ($12,400 × 7%). The difference of $132 ($1,000 − $868) is included in income under the effective interest rate method. This amount increases the investor's book value from $10,000 to $10,132. The second year's interest is $1,013.20, and the discount amortization is $145.20.

Redemption of U.S. Savings Bonds to Pay Educational Expenses

5. If a taxpayer pays qualified higher education expenses during the year, all or a part of the interest received on redemption of a Series EE, or I, U.S. Savings Bond may be excluded.

   a. To qualify,

      1) The taxpayer, the taxpayer's spouse, or a dependent incurs tuition and fees to attend an eligible educational institution.

      2) The taxpayer's modified adjusted gross income must not exceed a certain limit. The exclusion is phased out when certain levels of modified adjusted gross income are reached.

         a) The phaseout is inflation-adjusted each year.

         b) The exclusion is reduced when AGI exceeds a threshold of $82,350 ($123,550 if a joint return) for tax years beginning in 2020. The amount at which the benefit is completely phased out is $97,350 ($153,550 if a joint return) for tax years beginning in 2020.

      3) The purchaser of the bonds must be the sole owner of the bonds (or joint owner with his or her spouse).

      4) The issue date of the bonds must follow the 24th birthday(s) of the owner(s).

      5) Married taxpayers must file a joint return.

   b. If the qualified expenses are less than the total amount of principal and interest redeemed, the interest is multiplied by the exclusion rate to determine the amount excludable. The exclusion rate is qualified expenses divided by the total of principal and interest.

   — otherwise qualified expenses must be reduced by scholarships not included in gross income

Interest on State and Local Government Obligations

6. Payments to a holder of a debt obligation incurred by a state or local governmental entity (e.g., municipal or "muni" bonds) are generally exempt from federal income tax.

   a. Exclusion of interest received is allowable even if the obligation is not evidenced by a bond, is in the form of an installment purchase agreement, or is an ordinary commercial debt.

   b. These obligations must be in registered form.

   c. The exclusion applies to obligations of states, the District of Columbia, U.S. possessions, and political subdivisions of each of them.

   d. The interest on private activity bonds, which are not qualified bonds, and arbitrage bonds is not excluded from gross income.

      1) Private activity bonds are bonds of which more than 10% of the proceeds are to be used in a private business and more than 10% of the principal or interest is secured or will be paid by private business property, or more than 5% or $5,000,000 of the proceeds are to be used for private loans, whichever is lesser.

      2) Interest on qualified private activity bonds can still be excluded if the bond is for residential rental housing developments or public facilities (such as airports or waste removal), or for a qualified mortgage or VA bond, qualified small issue bond, qualified student loan bond, qualified redevelopment bond, or qualified exempt organization bond.

   e. Interest on state, local, and federal tax refunds is includible in income.

   f. Tax-exempt interest is still reported on the taxpayer's federal income tax return.

7. Recall that Form 1099-INT is the standard form used for reporting interest income. A nominee distribution is a special distribution that generally occurs when several taxpayers are entitled to interest while only one taxpayer has his or her name on the account. When interest on a single form is intended to be awarded to more than one taxpayer in this manner, the taxpayer receiving the Form 1099-INT has additional reporting responsibilities.

   a. The taxpayer must first report all interest listed on the 1099-INT, regardless of its rightful owner, on his or her Schedule B.

   b. Next, the taxpayer may subtract the interest belonging to other owners from the amount above to arrive at the total interest allocable to the taxpayer.

   c. Finally, for each other recipient of interest, the taxpayer must file two copies of Form 1099-INT: one to be furnished to the IRS, and the other to be furnished to the recipient. The taxpayer must also send a Form 1096 to the IRS with the 1099-INT indicating that the taxpayer is the "filer."

STOP AND REVIEW! **You have completed the outline for this subunit. Study multiple-choice questions 1 through 13 beginning on page 91.**

3.2 INCOME FROM SECURITIES

Dividends

1. Amounts received as dividends are ordinary gross income.

   a. **Qualified dividends** are dividends from domestic corporations or a qualified foreign corporation and are taxed at a 0%, 15%, or 20% rate depending on filing status and taxable income. Thresholds for capital gains rates are discussed in Study Unit 9, Subunit 8. The dividends must be held for more than 60 days (90 days for preferred stock).

   b. A dividend for purposes of taxable income is, generally, any distribution of money or other property made by a corporation to its shareholders, with respect to their stock, out of earnings and profits.

   c. Any distribution in excess of earnings and profits (both current and accumulated) is considered a recovery of capital and therefore is not taxable but does reduce basis.

   d. Once basis is reduced to zero, any additional distributions are capital gain and are taxed as such.

   e. Dividends paid or credited by a credit union or savings and loan are not qualified dividends.

Mutual Funds

2. Mutual fund distributions depend upon the character of the income source.

   a. Distributions or dividends from a fund investing in tax-exempt securities will be tax-exempt interest.

   b. Capital gain distributions are treated as long term regardless of the actual period the mutual fund investment is held.

   c. If the capital gain remains undistributed, the taxpayer still must report the amount as gross income (i.e., as if the capital gain were actually received).

   d. The tax rates for long-term capital gains are 0%, 15%, 20%, 25%, and 28%.

   e. Mutual funds and REITs may retain their long-term capital gains and pay tax on them instead of distributing them.

      1) A taxpayer must treat his or her portion of these long-term capital gains as a distribution even though the taxpayer did not actually receive a distribution.

Dividend Reinvestment Plans

3.   A dividend reinvestment plan allows a taxpayer to use his or her dividends to buy more shares of stock in the corporation instead of receiving the dividends in cash.

a.   The basis of stock received as a result of a dividend reinvestment plan is fair market value, even if purchased at a discounted price.

b.   A member of a dividend reinvestment plan that lets the member buy more stock at a price equal to its fair market value must report the dividends as income.

c.   A member of a dividend reinvestment plan that lets the member buy more stock at a price of less than fair market value must report as income the fair market value of the additional stock on the dividend payment date.

d.   If the dividend reinvestment plan allows members to invest more cash to buy shares of stock at a price of less than fair market value, the member must report as income the difference between the cash the member invests and the fair market value of the stock purchased. Fair market value of the stock is determined on the dividend payment date.

e.   Any service charge subtracted from the cash dividends before the dividends are used to buy additional stock is considered dividend income. – and added to dividend

---

EXAMPLE 3-2   Dividend Reinvestment Plan

A taxpayer at a company with a dividend reinvestment plan has 100 shares of stock and opts to use the cash dividend to purchase 10 more shares at a total price of $1 when the total FMV of 10 shares is $20. The transaction cost $0.50, which is deducted from the cash dividends prior to the purchase of the stock. The taxpayer's dividend income is $20.50 [(10 shares × $2 per share) + $0.50 charge].

---

f.   Reinvested dividends are taxable in the year paid.

g.   Reinvested dividends are added to the basis of the stock or mutual fund.

h.   Reinvested dividends are treated as ordinary dividends.

Stock Dividends

4.   Generally, a shareholder does not include in gross income the value of a stock dividend (or right to acquire stock) declared on its own shares unless one of five exceptions applies:

a.   If any shareholder can elect to receive cash or other property, none of the stock dividends are excluded (shareholders may, however, receive cash for fractional shares, which is included in gross income).

b.   Some shareholders receive cash or other property, and other shareholders receive stock, which increases their proportionate interest in earnings.

c.   Some common stock shareholders receive preferred stock, while other common stock shareholders receive common stock.

d.   The distribution is on preferred stock (but a distribution on preferred stock merely to adjust conversion ratios as a result of a stock split or dividend is excluded).

e.   If a shareholder receives common stock and cash for a fractional portion of stock, only the cash received for the fractional portion is included in gross income.

Constructive Dividends

5.   Payments of personal expenses by a corporation may be considered taxable constructive dividends.

Nonstatutory Stock Option Plans

6.   The term "nonstatutory stock options" refers to those options that do not qualify for the favorable tax treatment accorded options that are covered by a specific Code provision, as are qualified stock options, incentive stock options, employee stock purchase plans, and restricted stock options.

   a.   Nonstatutory stock options usually are taxed at ordinary income rates at the time they are granted, the options being considered compensation for services rendered by the employee. Generally, if an option is acquired under a nonstatutory program, the employee may be taxed when

   1)   The option is granted,
   2)   The option is exercised,
   3)   The option is sold, or
   4)   The restrictions on the disposition of the option-acquired stock lapse.

   b.   If an option has a readily ascertainable fair market value at the time it is granted in connection with the performance of services, the person who performed the services realizes compensation either (1) when the rights of the option become transferable or (2) when the right in the option is not subject to a substantial risk of forfeiture.

   1)   If the option does not have an ascertainable fair market value at the time when it is granted, taxation occurs when the right to receive the stock is unconditional.

   2)   The difference between the option cost and the fair market value of the stock at the time the optionee has a right to receive it is taxed as compensation.

EXAMPLE 3-3   Nonstatutory Stock Options

Mary Martin is granted a nonstatutory option to buy 5,000 shares of her employer's stock at $50 per share for 5 years at the time the stock is selling for $45 per share. Three years later, Mary exercises the option when the stock is selling for $55 per share. Mary has no income, and her employer receives no deduction at the time the option is granted. Upon exercise of the option, Mary has ordinary compensation of $25,000, the bargain element, and her employer receives a corresponding deduction. Mary's basis in the stock is $275,000. Upon a later sale, Mary generates a short- or long-term capital gain or loss with the holding period starting at the time the option is exercised.

Incentive Stock Options

7.   An employee may not recognize income when an incentive stock option is granted or exercised depending upon certain restrictions.

    a.   The employee recognizes long-term capital gain if the stock is sold 2 years or more after the option was granted and 1 year or more after the option was exercised.

        1)   The employer is not allowed a deduction.

    b.   Otherwise, the excess of the stock's FMV on the date of exercise over the option price is ordinary income to the employee when the stock is sold.

        1)   The employer may deduct this amount.
        2)   The gain realized is short-term or long-term capital gain.

    c.   Nonqualified stock option

        1)   An employee stock option is not qualified if it does not meet numerous technical requirements to be an incentive stock option.

        2)   If the option's FMV is ascertainable on the grant date,

            a)   The employee has gross income equal to the FMV of the option,
            b)   The employer is allowed a deduction,
            c)   There are no tax consequences when the option is exercised, and
            d)   Capital gain or loss is reported when the stock is sold.

        3)   If the option's FMV is not ascertainable on the grant date,

            a)   The excess of FMV over the option price is gross income to the employee when the option is exercised.

            b)   The employer is allowed a corresponding compensation deduction.

            c)   The employee's basis in the stock is the exercise price plus the amount taken into ordinary income.

EXAMPLE 3-4   **Incentive Stock Option**

On July 1, Year 1, Mighty, Inc., granted Henry an incentive stock option to purchase 2,000 shares of its stock for $40 a share (its FMV) for the next 5 years. On September 18, Year 2, Henry exercised the option and paid $80,000 when the stock's FMV was $53 a share. On November 23, Year 3, Henry sold the stock for $124,000. Mighty, Inc., receives no deduction upon grant, exercise, or sale. Henry reports a long-term capital gain of $44,000.

If Henry had sold the stock for $124,000 on April 15, Year 3, the special 2-year holding period would not have been met. As a result, Henry would have had $26,000 of ordinary income and $18,000 of long-term capital gain in Year 3, and Mighty, Inc., would have had compensation expense of $26,000.

Employee Stock Purchase Plans

8. An employee stock option plan is, generally, one permitting employees to buy stock in the employer corporation at a discount. Options issued under an employee stock purchase plan qualify for special tax treatment. No income is recognized under such a plan at the time the option is granted; the recognition is deferred until stock acquired under the plan is disposed of.

   a. If stock acquired under such a plan is disposed of after being held for the required period, the employee will realize ordinary income to the extent of the excess of the fair market value of the stock at the time that option was granted over the option price. Any further gain is a capital gain.

      1) If the stock is disposed of when its value is less than its value at the time the option was granted, the amount of ordinary income will be limited to the excess of current value over the option price.

   b. An employee stock purchase plan must provide that only employees may be granted options and must be approved by the stockholders of the granting corporation within 12 months before or after the date the plan is adopted. Other conditions that must be met either by the plan or in the stock offering are

      1) The option price may not be less than the smaller of

         a) 85% of the fair market value of the stock when the option is granted or
         b) 85% of the fair market value at exercise.

      2) The option must be exercisable within 5 years from the date of grant, where the option price is not less than 85% of the fair market value of the stock at exercise.

         a) If the option price is stated in any other terms, the option must not be exercisable after 27 months from the date of the grant.

      3) No options may be granted to owners of 5% or more of the value or voting power of all classes of stock of the employer or its parent or subsidiary.

      4) No employee may be able to purchase more than $25,000 of stock in any 1 calendar year.

      5) The option may not be transferable (other than by will or laws of inheritance) and may be exercisable only by the employee to whom it is granted.

      6) If the exercise price was less than the value of the stock upon grant and the option was exercised, the employee may have compensation income (with an offsetting deduction by the employer) upon disposition, including a transfer at death.

         a) The compensation equals the lesser of fair market value at grant or at exercise, less the exercise price, and is added to the stock basis.
         b) There is no offsetting deduction by the employer.

EXAMPLE 3-5   Employee Stock Purchase Plans -- Calculation

Alice Nichel was given an option to buy 200 shares of Delta, Inc., stock for $55 a share when it was selling for $62. She exercised the option 2 years later when the stock was selling for $68 and sold the stock after another 3 years for $81 a share. The lesser of $68 or $62, less $55 a share, which is $7 a share, is compensation in the year of sale, i.e., $1,400. Alice's basis is increased by $7 a share to $62. Thus, her long-term capital gain is $19 per share ($81 − $62), or $3,800.

STOP AND REVIEW! You have completed the outline for this subunit. Study multiple-choice questions 14 through 22 beginning on page 97.

3.3 INCOME IN RESPECT OF A DECEDENT (IRD)

NOTE: The following outline is duplicated in EA Part 2, Study Unit 18, Subunit 2.

The filer of a decedent's income tax and estate tax returns is required to make the appropriate allocation of income related to the decedent during the year of death. IRD is all amounts to which a decedent was entitled as gross income but that were not includible in computing taxable income on the final return. The person had a right to receive it prior to death, e.g., salary was earned or sale contract was entered into.

1. Not includible on the final income tax return of a cash-method (CM) taxpayer are amounts not received. Not includible on the final income tax return of an accrual-method (AM) taxpayer are amounts not properly accrued.

EXAMPLE 3-6	Items of Income in Respect of a Decedent
IRD	**Not IRD**
Salary earned prior to, but not received before, death of a CM taxpayer	**Salary** earned and accrued by AM taxpayer
Collection after death of A/R of CM taxpayer	**Collection** of A/R by AM taxpayer
Gain on sale of property by CM taxpayer received not before death	**Gain** on sale of property received before death
Rent accrued but not received before death by CM taxpayer	**Rent** received before death
Interest on installment debt accrued before death by CM taxpayer	**Interest** on installment debt accrued after death by AM taxpayer
Installment income recognized after death on contract entered into before death	**Installment** contract income recognized before death

2. IRD is reported by the person receiving the income when it is received.

    a. The cash method applies to income once designated IRD.
    b. IRD received by a trust or estate is fiduciary income.

3. A right to receive IRD has a transferred basis. The basis is not stepped-up to FMV on the date of death, as is generally the case for property acquired from a decedent.

EXAMPLE 3-7	Right to Receive IRD -- Transferred Basis

Mrs. Hart had earned 2 weeks' salary of $2,000 that had not been paid when she died. As a cash-method taxpayer, her basis in the right to receive the $2,000 was $0. When her estate received the income, it had $2,000 of ordinary income because its basis in the right to receive it was also $0. Note that the $2,000 is not reported on Mrs. Hart's final return.

4. IRD has the same character it would have had in the hands of the decedent.

5. IRD is taxable as income to the recipient and is includible in the gross estate. Double tax is mitigated by deductions.

    a. Deductions in respect of a decedent.

        1) Expenses accrued before death, but not deductible on the final return because the decedent used the cash method, are deductible when paid if otherwise deductible.

            a) They are deductible on the return of the taxpayer reporting the IRD.

            b) They are also deductible on the estate tax return.

    b. Deduction for estate tax. Estate taxes attributable to IRD included in the gross estate are deductible on the recipient's income tax return.

        1) Administrative expenses and debts of a decedent are deductible on the estate tax return [Form 706, *United States Estate (and Generation-Skipping Transfer) Tax Return*]. Some of them may also be deductible on the estate's income tax return (Form 1041, *U.S. Income Tax Return for Estates and Trusts*).

            a) Double deductions are disallowed.

            b) The right to deduct the expenses on Form 706 must be waived in order to claim them on Form 1041.

        2) Deduction (on Form 1041) is allowed for any excess of the federal estate tax over the amount of the federal estate tax if the IRD had been excluded from the gross estate.

    c. The tax returns that would report IRD include, but are not limited to, the following:

        1) The decedent's estate, Form 1041, if the decedent's estate receives right to the income.

        2) The beneficiary's Form 1040, if the right to income arising out of the decedent's death is passed directly to the beneficiary and is never acquired by the decedent's estate.

        3) The Form 1040 of any person to whom the decedent's estate properly distributes the income.

    NOTE: The decedent's final Form 1040 would not include IRD.

EXAMPLE 3-8	IRD -- Return Presentation

Frank Johnson owned and operated an apple orchard. He used the cash method of accounting. He sold and delivered 1,000 bushels of apples to a canning factory for $2,000, but did not receive payment before his death. The proceeds from the sale are income in respect of a decedent. When the estate was settled, payment had not been made and the estate transferred the right to the payment to his widow. When Frank's widow collects the $2,000, she must include that amount in her return. The amount is not reported on the final return of the decedent or on the return of the estate.

EXAMPLE 3-9	IRD -- Recognized Income

Assume the same facts as in Example 3-8, except that Frank used the accrual method of accounting. The amount accrued from the sale of the apples would be included on his final return. Neither the estate nor the widow would realize income in respect of a decedent when the money is later paid.

EXAMPLE 3-10	IRD -- Recognized Gain

On February 1, George High, a cash-method taxpayer, sold his tractor for $3,000, payable March 1 of the same year. His adjusted basis in the tractor was $2,000. George died on February 15, before receiving payment. The gain to be reported as income in respect of a decedent is the $1,000 difference between the decedent's basis in the property and the sale proceeds. In other words, the income in respect of a decedent is the gain the decedent would have realized had he lived.

EXAMPLE 3-11	IRD -- Recognized Income Assignment

Cathy O'Neil was entitled to a large salary payment at the date of her death. The amount was to be paid in five annual installments. The estate, after collecting two installments, distributed the right to the remaining installments to the beneficiary. The payments are income in respect of a decedent. None of the payments were includible on Cathy's final return. The estate must include in its income the two installments it received, and the beneficiary must include in income each of the three installments as the installments are received.

EXAMPLE 3-12	IRD -- Recognized Income Assignment

Paige inherited the right to receive renewal commissions on life insurance sold by her father before his death. Paige inherited the right from her mother, who acquired it by bequest from Paige's father. Paige's mother died before she received all the commissions she had the right to receive, so Paige received the rest. The commissions are income in respect of a decedent. None of these commissions were includible on Paige's father's final return. The commissions received by Paige's mother were included in her income. The commissions Paige received are not includible in Paige's mother's income, even on her final return. Paige must include them in her income.

STOP AND REVIEW! You have completed the outline for this subunit. Study multiple-choice questions 23 through 29 beginning on page 101.

QUESTIONS

3.1 Interest Income

1. Ms. Guy's books and records reflect the following for 2020:

Salary	$57,000
Interest on money market account (credited to her account in 2020, withdrawn in 2021)	1,865
Deposit from the pending sale of her rental property	4,000
Interest on savings account (credited to her account in 2019, withdrawn in 2020)	200

What is the amount Ms. Guy should include in her gross income for 2020?

    A. $45,865

    B. $58,865

    C. $62,865

    D. $63,065

Answer (B) is correct.

REQUIRED: The amount recorded in gross income for the current year.

DISCUSSION: Ms. Guy's gross income will include the $57,000 of salary as compensation for services. Interest on money market accounts earned in the current year but not withdrawn is still taxed in the current year under the doctrine of constructive receipt. Therefore, the $1,865 from interest credited in 2020 should be included in gross income, but the $200 credited in 2019 should not be included in gross income. The $4,000 deposit from the pending sale of rental property is not included because the income has not constructively been received; there are still substantial limitations on the control of the receipt (Publications 17 and 538 and IRC Sec. 61).

Answer (A) is incorrect. Gross income includes salary and interest credited during the current year. **Answer (C) is incorrect.** The deposit from the pending sale is not constructively received. **Answer (D) is incorrect.** Neither the deposit from a pending sale nor interest earned in a prior year is included in current-year income.

2. Mr. and Mrs. Apple received the following income during 2020:

- $200 in interest credited to their bank account but not withdrawn or used by them during the year

- $2,000 in interest received as a beneficiary in a trust established by Mr. Apple's father and included on Schedule K-1 from the trust

- $100 in interest on a bond issued by the State of Georgia

- $1,000 bond interest, City of Atlanta municipal bond

How much taxable interest income must Mr. and Mrs. Apple report on their 2020 tax return?

    A. $3,300

    B. $0

    C. $2,200

    D. $1,300

Answer (C) is correct.

REQUIRED: The interest that is taxable and must be reported on the 2020 tax return.

DISCUSSION: Interest is the value received or accrued for the use of money. Interest is reported under the doctrine of "constructive receipt" when the taxpayer's account is credited with the interest. Accrued interest on a deposit that may not be withdrawn at the close of an individual's tax year because of an institution's actual or threatened bankruptcy or insolvency is not includible until the year in which such interest is withdrawable. All interest is gross income for tax purposes unless an exclusion applies. Payments to a holder of a debt obligation incurred by a state or local governmental entity (e.g., municipal or "muni" bonds) are generally exempt from federal income tax (Publications 17 and 538). Accordingly, Mr. and Mrs. Apple should report $2,200 ($2,000 + $200) on their 2020 income tax return because all interest is taxable income unless an exclusion applies and there is an exclusion for the interest earned on state and local bonds.

Answer (A) is incorrect. The interest earned on the state and local bonds are excluded from income on the 2020 tax return. **Answer (B) is incorrect.** The interest that is in their bank account and the interest received from the trust are taxable. **Answer (D) is incorrect.** The $1,000 is interest received from a local bond and is excluded from income. In addition, the $2,000 of interest received from the trust should be included in income on the 2020 tax return.

3. Maria had municipal bond interest of $6,000, certificate of deposit interest of $4,000, reinvested corporate bond interest of $2,000, mutual fund municipal bond interest of $7,000, and savings account interest of $1,000. What is Maria's taxable interest?

A. $3,000

B. $7,000

C. $20,000

D. $16,000

Answer (B) is correct.
   REQUIRED: The amount of interest income included in Maria's taxable income.
   DISCUSSION: All interest is included as income unless excluded by the tax code. Municipal bond interest and mutual fund municipal bond interest may be excluded from income (Publication 17).
   Maria's taxable interest is:

Certificate of deposit interest	$4,000
Reinvested corporate interest	2,000
Savings account interest	1,000
Total taxable interest	$7,000

   Answer (A) is incorrect. The certificate of deposit interest is also included in income. **Answer (C) is incorrect.** The municipal bond interest and the mutual fund municipal bond fund are excludable from income. **Answer (D) is incorrect.** The municipal bond interest and the mutual fund municipal bond fund are excludable from income. In addition, the certificate of deposit interest should be included in income.

4. In December of the current year, Mr. Stone cashed qualified Series EE U.S. Savings Bonds, which he had purchased 10 years ago. The proceeds were used for his son's college education. All of the following statements are true concerning the exclusion of the interest received EXCEPT

A. He cannot file as married filing separate.

B. Eligible expenses include room and board.

C. If the proceeds are more than the expenses, he will be able to exclude only part of the interest.

D. Before he figures his interest exclusion, he must reduce his qualified higher educational expenses by certain benefits.

Answer (B) is correct.
   REQUIRED: The exclusion rules concerning U.S. savings bond income used for higher education.
   DISCUSSION: An individual who redeems any qualified U.S. savings bonds in a year in which qualified higher education expenses are paid may exclude from income amounts received under such redemption, provided certain requirements are met (Sec. 135). Qualified higher education expenses include tuition and fees required for enrollment at an eligible educational institution. Room and board are not classified as qualified higher education expenses, and interest used to cover these expenses may not be excluded (Publication 17).
   Answer (A) is incorrect. The exclusion is not available to married individuals who file separate returns. **Answer (C) is incorrect.** Only part of interest may be excluded if the proceeds are more than the expenses. **Answer (D) is incorrect.** He must reduce his qualified higher educational expenses by certain benefits before he figures his interest exclusion.

5. All of the following are taxable interest income EXCEPT

  A. Original Issue Discount (OID).

  B. Interest on federal tax refunds.

  C. Fair market value of a gift received for opening a savings account.

  D. Interest income received on a municipal bond.

Answer (D) is correct.
    REQUIRED: The type of interest income that is excluded from gross income.
    DISCUSSION: Payments to holder of a debt obligation incurred by a state or local governmental entity are generally exempt from federal income tax.
    Answer (A) is incorrect. The sum of the daily portion of the original issue discount is included in taxable income. **Answer (B) is incorrect.** Interest on federal tax refunds is considered taxable interest income. **Answer (C) is incorrect.** A gift received to open an account is equivalent to interest since it is paid to induce a deposit, unless it is of de minimis value.

6. Which of the following is NOT subject to federal income tax?

  A. Interest on U.S. Treasury bills, notes, and bonds issued by an agency of the United States.

  B. Interest on federal income tax refund.

  C. Interest on New York State bonds.

  D. Discount income in installment payments received on notes bought at a discount.

Answer (C) is correct.
    REQUIRED: The item of income that is not subject to federal income tax.
    DISCUSSION: Gross income is defined under Sec. 61 as all income from whatever source derived that is not specifically excluded. Section 103 specifically excludes from gross income interest on most obligations of a state or any political subdivision thereof (Publication 17).

7. Interest from the following bonds is generally tax exempt EXCEPT

  A. Qualified private activity bonds.

  B. State government bonds.

  C. U.S. savings bonds.

  D. Local government bonds.

Answer (C) is correct.
    REQUIRED: The type of interest income that is not exempt from federal taxes.
    DISCUSSION: Although interest on U.S. savings bonds may be excluded from gross income if used for certain educational purposes, in general, interest from U.S. savings bonds is not tax exempt.

8. In the current year, Uriah Stone received the following interest payments:

Interest of $400 on refund of federal income tax for a previous year

Interest of $300 on award for personal injuries sustained in an automobile accident in a previous year

Interest of $1,500 on municipal bonds

Interest of $1,000 on United States savings bonds (Series HH)

What amount, if any, should Stone report as taxable interest income on his current-year tax return?

A. $0

B. $700

C. $1,700

D. $3,200

Answer (C) is correct.
REQUIRED: The amount the taxpayer should include as interest income on his current-year tax return.
DISCUSSION: Unless otherwise excluded in another section, Sec. 61 includes interest in gross income. Section 103 excludes from gross income interest on most obligations of states or political subdivisions of a state (e.g., municipal bonds). This exclusion does not apply to the obligations of the United States. Therefore, the taxpayer's taxable interest income includes the $400 of interest on the refund of federal income taxes, and the $1,000 of interest on the United States Series HH savings bonds which is paid by check semiannually. Although an award for personal injuries is tax-exempt under Sec. 104, the interest income earned on the award is not tax-exempt. A total of $1,700 ($400 + $1,000 + $300) is included on Form 1040 line 2b as taxable interest. Interest on municipal bonds is included on Form 1040 line 2a.
Answer (A) is incorrect. Stone should report some interest income. **Answer (B) is incorrect.** The interest on U.S. savings bonds must be included. **Answer (D) is incorrect.** The interest on municipal bonds is excluded from income.

9. Ms. Smith's books and records reflect the following for Year 2:

Salary	$35,000
Interest on money market account (credited to her account in Year 1, withdrawn in Year 2)	1,000
Interest on money from a long-term savings plan from which interest cannot be withdrawn until December 31, Year 2, but principal can be withdrawn at any time (she has principal of $5,000 and accumulated interest of $700)	500

What is the amount Ms. Smith must include in her gross income for Year 2?

A. $35,000

B. $35,500

C. $36,000

D. $36,500

Answer (B) is correct.
REQUIRED: The Year 2 gross income.
DISCUSSION: Gross income includes salary and interest that is credited in the current year (Publication 17).
Answer (A) is incorrect. The amount of $35,000 excludes the $500 of interest earned in Year 2. **Answer (C) is incorrect.** The amount of $36,000 excludes the $500 of interest earned in Year 2 and includes interest earned in Year 1. **Answer (D) is incorrect.** The amount of $36,500 includes interest earned in Year 1.

10. Ms. B received the following interest in the current year:

Luggage for purchasing a 4-year certificate of deposit (fair market value)	$ 50
Interest on passbook savings account	15
Interest on certificate of deposit	200
Dividends on share account in credit union	150
Interest on State of Mississippi bonds issued to finance state highway construction	300

What is the amount of interest income to be included in income?

   A. $265

   B. $365

   C. $415

   D. $715

Answer (C) is correct.
   REQUIRED: The amount of interest income to be included in gross income.
   DISCUSSION: Under Sec. 61, gross income includes interest, whether received in cash or property, unless specifically excluded by another section. Interest is a payment for the use of money. Luggage for purchasing a certificate of deposit is a payment to obtain the use of the taxpayer's money, so it is interest and must be included in gross income. Under Rev. Proc. 2000-30, a noncash de minimis gift is tax-free if it does not have a value of more than $10 for a deposit of less than $5,000 or $20 for a deposit of $5,000 or more. The interest on the passbook savings account and certificate of deposit are items of interest income. Dividends on a share account in a credit union are the equivalent of interest and must be included in gross income as such. The total of these amounts is $415, which must be included in Ms. B's gross income (Publication 17).
   Section 103 excludes interest on most state and local governmental obligations. The interest on the state bonds to finance highway construction is excluded from gross income.
   Answer (A) is incorrect. The dividends on the share account are also included in income. **Answer (B) is incorrect.** The luggage is also included in income. **Answer (D) is incorrect.** The interest on the state bond is excluded from income.

11. Gary and Gladys invest in bonds. In the current year, they received the following interest:

California general revenue bonds	$ 800
New York City sanitation fund bonds	1,000
Seattle School District bonds	400
AT&T 20-year bonds	600

The state and local bonds are neither private activity bonds nor arbitrage bonds. How much interest income may Gary and Gladys exclude from gross income on their joint return?

   A. $0

   B. $800

   C. $1,800

   D. $2,200

Answer (D) is correct.
   REQUIRED: The amount of interest income from bonds excludable from gross income.
   DISCUSSION: Under Sec. 103, gross income does not include interest on obligations of a state or any political subdivision thereof. The use of the proceeds of the bonds does not ordinarily change the taxation of the interest (although special rules apply in the case of private activity bonds and arbitrage bonds).
   Therefore, Gary and Gladys may exclude the interest from all the state and local bonds (as listed below) but must include the $600 of interest from the AT&T bonds in gross income (Publication 17).

California general revenue bonds	$ 800
New York City sanitation fund bonds	1,000
Seattle School District bonds	400
Total excluded interest	$2,200

   Answer (A) is incorrect. A portion of the interest received is excluded from income. **Answer (B) is incorrect.** The New York and Seattle bond interest is also excluded from income. **Answer (C) is incorrect.** The Seattle bond interest is also excluded from income.

12. In a tax year in which the taxpayer pays qualified education expenses, interest income on the redemption of qualified U.S. Series EE Bonds may be excluded from gross income. The exclusion is subject to a modified gross income limitation and a limit of aggregate bond proceeds in excess of qualified higher education expenses. Which of the following is (are) true?

I. The exclusion applies for education expenses incurred by the taxpayer, the taxpayer's spouse, or any person whom the taxpayer may claim as a dependent for the year.

II. "Otherwise qualified higher education expenses" must be reduced by qualified scholarships not includible in gross income.

    A. I only.

    B. II only.

    C. Both I and II.

    D. Neither I nor II.

Answer (C) is correct.
    REQUIRED: The correct statement concerning exclusion of interest on redemption of Series EE Bonds.
    DISCUSSION: Section 135 provides an exclusion for interest on Series EE bonds to the extent it is spent on qualified higher education expenses for the year. "Qualified higher education expenses" means tuition and fees required for the enrollment or attendance of the taxpayer, the taxpayer's spouse, or any person whom the taxpayer may claim as a dependent for the year. "Otherwise qualified higher education expenses" are reduced by scholarships (and other such benefits) not includible in gross income (Publication 17).

13. Clark bought Series EE U.S. Savings Bonds. Redemption proceeds will be used for payment of college tuition for Clark's dependent child. One of the conditions that must be met for tax exemption of accumulated interest on these bonds is that the

    A. Purchaser of the bonds must be the sole owner of the bonds (or joint owner with his or her spouse).

    B. Bonds must be bought by a parent (or both parents) and put in the name of the dependent child.

    C. Bonds must be bought by the owner of the bonds before the owner reaches the age of 24.

    D. Bonds must be transferred to the college for redemption by the college rather than by the owner of the bonds.

Answer (A) is correct.
    REQUIRED: The stated requirement for exclusion of interest on Series EE U.S. savings bonds.
    DISCUSSION: Exclusion of accumulated interest on U.S. savings bonds issued at a discount is permitted. The bonds must be issued after 1989. Exclusion of interest is conditioned on each of the following: (1) the purchaser of the bonds must be the sole owner (or joint owner with his or her spouse) of the bonds; (2) the issue date of the bonds must follow the 24th birthday(s) of the owner(s); and (3) the redemption proceeds must be used to pay tuition and fees of the taxpayer, spouse, or dependent to attend a college, a university, or certain vocational schools.
    Answer (B) is incorrect. The purchaser must be the sole owner (or joint owner with his or her spouse) of the bonds. **Answer (C) is incorrect.** The requirement is that the bond's issue date must follow the owner's 24th birthday. **Answer (D) is incorrect.** The requirement is that the proceeds be used to pay qualified higher education expenses.

3.2 Income from Securities

14. Ms. X, a cash-method taxpayer, received notice from her mutual fund that it has realized a long-term capital gain on her behalf in the amount of $2,500. It also advised her that it has paid a tax of $500 on this gain. The mutual fund indicated that it will not distribute the net amount but will credit the amount to her account. All of the following statements are true EXCEPT

    A. X must report a long-term capital gain of $2,500.

    B. X is allowed a $500 credit for the tax since it is considered paid by X.

    C. X is allowed to increase her basis in the stock by $2,000.

    D. X does not report a long-term capital gain because nothing was paid to her.

Answer (D) is correct.

    REQUIRED: The false statement concerning an undistributed long-term capital gain in a mutual fund.

    DISCUSSION: A mutual fund is a regulated investment company, the taxation of which is determined by Sec. 852. Shareholders are taxed on dividends paid by the mutual fund. If part or all of the dividend is designated as a capital gain dividend, it must be treated as such by the shareholders. Undistributed capital gains also must be included in income by shareholders, but they are allowed a credit for their proportionate share of any tax on the capital gain paid by the mutual fund (Publication 17).

    Answer (A) is incorrect. X must include the undistributed capital gain in income. **Answer (B) is incorrect.** X is allowed a credit for her share of the tax paid by the mutual fund on the capital gain. **Answer (C) is incorrect.** X does increase her basis by the difference between the amount of such includible gains and the tax deemed paid by X [Sec. 852(b)(3)(D)(iii)].

15. Emily bought 50 shares of stock in Year 1 for $500. In Year 2, she received a return of capital of $100. She received an additional return of capital of $50 in Year 3. What must Emily report as long-term capital gain on her tax return for Year 3?

    A. $150

    B. $50

    C. $100

    D. $0

Answer (D) is correct.

    REQUIRED: The character of return of capital distributions.

    DISCUSSION: A return of capital is a tax-free distribution that is not made out of a corporation's earnings and profits that reduces a stock's basis by the amount of the distribution. It is not taxed until the stock's basis has been fully recovered (Publication 17).

    Answer (A) is incorrect. The amount of $150 is the basis reduction and is not taxed until the basis is recovered. **Answer (B) is incorrect.** The amount of $50 is the basis reduction for Year 3. **Answer (C) is incorrect.** The amount of $100 is the basis reduction for Year 2.

16. Joan owned stock in W Corporation, which has a dividend reinvestment plan. Joan decided to participate in the plan, and during the current year the corporation paid dividends. The plan allowed Joan to use her $3,000 dividend to buy 30 additional shares of stock at $100 per share when the fair market value of the stock was $130 per share. How much dividend income must Joan report on her current-year income tax return?

    A. $3,900

    B. $3,000

    C. $900

    D. $0

Answer (A) is correct.

    REQUIRED: The amount of dividend income under a dividend reinvestment plan.

    DISCUSSION: Dividends are gross income [Sec. 61(a)(7)]. A shareholder who, under a dividend reinvestment plan, elects to receive shares of greater value than his or her cash dividend would otherwise receive a taxable distribution under Sec. 301(a) to the extent of the value of the shares (Publication 17). Because Joan was able to buy 30 additional shares when the fair market value of the stock was $130 per share, she must report $3,900 (30 × $130) of dividend income.

    Answer (B) is incorrect. The fair market value of the stocks purchased is included in gross income. **Answer (C) is incorrect.** The fair market value of the stocks purchased is included in gross income. **Answer (D) is incorrect.** Dividend income must be reported when shares are received that have a greater value than the cash dividend.

17. John and Mary, a married couple, have a wide variety of investments and are cash-basis taxpayers. Because their self-employment earnings are considerable, they reinvested the following: $4,000 of mutual fund dividends and $5,000 of certificate of deposit interest. They also earned dividends on corporate stock of $12,000 that they received and spent. Interest of $2,000 that had accrued on a loan to a friend was not paid until the following year. What is the amount of interest and dividends currently taxable to them?

A. $21,000

B. $14,000

C. $16,000

D. $23,000

Answer (A) is correct.
REQUIRED: The amount of interest and dividends currently taxable.
DISCUSSION: Mutual fund dividends, certificate of deposit interest, and corporate stock dividends are all taxable in the current year. All dividends and interest, even those that have been reinvested, are taxable, unless a specific provision in the tax code exempts the tax (Publication 550). None of the income earned qualifies for a tax exemption. The interest is not taxable until it is received because John and Mary are cash-basis taxpayers.
Answer (B) is incorrect. The amount of $14,000 includes the accrued interest, which is not taxable until it is received by a cash-basis taxpayer. In addition, it excludes both of the reinvested incomes from the mutual fund dividends and the certificate of deposit interest.
Answer (C) is incorrect. The amount of $16,000 excludes the taxable interest from the certificate of deposit. **Answer (D) is incorrect.** The amount of $23,000 includes the accrued interest, which is not taxable until it is received by a cash-basis taxpayer.

18. Geraldine works for a corporation with a dividend reinvestment plan. In lieu of dividends, Geraldine, who currently owns 1,500 shares of stock, bought 100 additional shares of stock at $2 a share and paid a service charge of $4.75. The FMV of the stock was $12. The service charge was deducted from the dividends prior to the purchase of the stock. What must she report on her tax return as dividend income?

A. $200

B. $1,200

C. $1,204.75

D. $1,195.25

Answer (C) is correct.
REQUIRED: The amount of dividend income under a dividend reinvestment plan.
DISCUSSION: If a taxpayer is a member of a dividend reinvestment plan and the taxpayer uses the dividends to buy more shares in the corporation, you must report the dividends as income. If the taxpayer is allowed to buy more stock at a price less than its fair market value, the taxpayer must report as dividend income the fair market value of the additional stock on the dividend payment date. The taxpayer must also include as dividend income any service charge subtracted from the cash dividends before the dividends are used to buy the additional stock (Publication 17). Geraldine must report $200 (the amount of cash dividends) plus $1,000 (the additional fair market value of the stock over the purchase price) plus $4.75 (the service charge subtracted from the dividends) for a total of $1,204.75.
Answer (A) is incorrect. The dividend recognized as income is the FMV of the stock received plus the service charge. **Answer (B) is incorrect.** The taxpayer must include as dividend income any service charge subtracted from the cash dividends before the dividends are used to buy the additional stock. **Answer (D) is incorrect.** The service charge is added to, not subtracted from, the cash dividends.

19. Joe has owned shares in a company that has a dividend reinvestment plan since 2006. The plan allows him to invest more cash to buy additional shares of stock at a price less than fair market value. In the current year, Joe took advantage of that option and purchased 100 additional shares for $30 each. On the dividend payment date, the fair market value of the shares he purchased was $32 per share. Based on this information, Joe must report

A. $0. No income must be reported until the shares are sold.

B. $200 as ordinary income, based on the difference between the amount Joe paid and the fair market value of the shares.

C. $200 of short-term capital gain income, based on the fact that Joe could not have taken advantage of the option to buy the shares at the discounted price if he had not taken part in the dividend reinvestment plan.

D. $200 of long-term capital gain income, based on the fact that Joe has owned shares in the company for more than 12 months.

Answer (B) is correct.

REQUIRED: The amount and character of income under a dividend reinvestment plan.

DISCUSSION: Dividends are gross income [Sec. 61(a)(7)]. A shareholder who, under a dividend reinvestment plan, elects to receive shares of greater value than his or her cash dividend would otherwise be, receives taxable income based on the difference between the amount (s)he paid and the fair market value of the shares (Publication 17). Joe will report $200 ordinary income [100 × ($32 − $30)].

Answer (A) is incorrect. Income must be recognized when shares are received that have a greater value than the cash dividend. **Answer (C) is incorrect.** The distribution is a form of dividends, and dividends are included in ordinary income. **Answer (D) is incorrect.** The distribution is a form of dividends, and dividends are included in ordinary income.

20. Amy bought shares in the Oppenheimer Mutual Fund for $250. She received a capital gain distribution, also known as a capital gain dividend, of $90 on Form 1099-DIV for the current year. How should Amy report the capital gain dividend on her tax return?

A. Need not report it.

B. Reduce the basis on the stock to $160.

C. Report $90 as ordinary income.

D. Report the $90 as long-term capital gain.

Answer (D) is correct.

REQUIRED: The character of capital gain dividend income.

DISCUSSION: A capital gain dividend is a distribution by a regulated investment company, or mutual fund, of capital gains realized from the sale of investments in the fund. Capital gain dividends are long-term regardless of how long the shareholder has owned the stock of the regulated investment company (Publication 17).

Answer (A) is incorrect. The capital gain dividend is reported. **Answer (B) is incorrect.** The basis of the stock is not reduced, but long-term capital gain is recognized. **Answer (C) is incorrect.** The amount of $90 is treated as long-term capital gain, not ordinary income.

21. Matthew Kennedy received a dividend from Mayflow Corporation. Matthew has elected, using Mayflow's dividend reinvestment plan, to purchase additional stock at FMV with the dividend received. The dividend was $1,500 and the FMV of the stock purchased was $1,475. A $25 service charge was applied to this transaction. What must Matthew report as dividend income on his tax return for the current year?

A. $0

B. $1,500

C. $1,525

D. $1,475

Answer (B) is correct.
REQUIRED: The amount of dividend income under a dividend reinvestment plan.
DISCUSSION: If a taxpayer is a member of a dividend reinvestment plan and the taxpayer uses the dividends to buy more shares in the corporation, you must report the dividends as income. The taxpayer must report as dividend income the fair market value of the additional stock on the dividend payment date. The taxpayer also must include as dividend income any service charge subtracted from the cash dividends before the dividends are used to buy the additional stock (Publication 17). Matthew must report $1,500 ($1,475 + $25) as dividend income.
Answer (A) is incorrect. Matthew received dividend income through a dividend reinvestment plan. **Answer (C) is incorrect.** A service charge applied to purchase more stock through a dividend reinvestment plan is added to the FMV of the stock, not to the dividend received. **Answer (D) is incorrect.** A service charge applied to purchase more stock through a dividend reinvestment plan is added to the FMV of the stock.

22. Al and Iris Oran, who are married, received $10,000 in the current year as dividends from taxable domestic corporations. In the Orans' current-year joint return, the amount of these dividends subject to tax is

A. $10,000

B. $9,900

C. $9,800

D. $7,000

Answer (A) is correct.
REQUIRED: The amount of cash dividends from domestic corporations subject to tax.
DISCUSSION: Section 61(a)(7) lists dividends as being included in gross income. They are included in their entirety unless there is a specific exclusion. There is no exclusion for dividends received by an individual from a taxable domestic corporation (provided the dividends are paid out of earnings and profits, which is the assumed case unless other information is provided in a question). Therefore, the entire $10,000 of dividends are included in their gross income (Publication 17).

3.3 Income in Respect of a Decedent (IRD)

23. Which one of the following statements concerning the consequences of income being classified as "income in respect of a decedent" is true?

A. It receives no step-up in basis upon the decedent's death.

B. It is all treated as ordinary income to recipient.

C. It is all taxable to the decedent's estate.

D. It must be included in the decedent's final return.

Answer (A) is correct.
REQUIRED: The true statement of the consequences of income in respect of a decedent.
DISCUSSION: Section 1014(a) provides that the basis of property acquired from a decedent is generally the fair market value of the property on the date of the decedent's death. Section 1014(c) provides that property that constitutes a right to receive income in respect of a decedent does not receive a step-up in basis. Therefore, it has a carryover basis.
Answer (B) is incorrect. Income in respect of a decedent is treated as having the same character it would have had in the hands of the decedent [Sec. 691(a)(3)].
Answer (C) is incorrect. Income in respect of a decedent is included when received (as if on a cash basis) by the person who receives it [Sec. 691(a)(1)].
Answer (D) is incorrect. Income in respect of a decedent is income that is earned by the taxpayer but not received prior to his or her death nor accrued prior to his or her death if on the accrual method, so it is not included in the decedent's final return.

24. Fred, a calendar-year, cash-basis taxpayer who died in June of the current year, was entitled to receive a $10,000 accounting fee that had not been collected before the date of death. The executor of Fred's estate collected the full $10,000 in July of the current year. This $10,000 should appear in

A. Only the decedent's final individual income tax return.

B. Only the estate's fiduciary income tax return.

C. Only the decedent's estate tax return.

D. Both the fiduciary income tax return and the estate tax return.

Answer (D) is correct.
REQUIRED: The true treatment of income earned before death but not received until after death.
DISCUSSION: Income that a decedent had a right to receive prior to death but that was not includible on his or her final income tax return is income in respect of a decedent. The $10,000 is properly includible in the estate's (fiduciary) income tax return because Fred was a cash-basis taxpayer and would not properly include income not yet received at the time of death in his final return. Since the money was owed to Fred (he has a right to receive it), it is an asset of the estate and must be included on the estate tax return also.
Answer (A) is incorrect. Fred was a cash-basis taxpayer and would not properly include income not received at the time of death. **Answer (B) is incorrect.** The $10,000 is an asset of the estate and must also be included on the estate tax return. **Answer (C) is incorrect.** The $10,000 is income to the estate and must also be included on its income tax return.

25. Which of the following is income in respect of a decedent?

A. Cash received from a grandmother's estate.

B. Royalties received on the deceased father's published book; the right to receive these royalties was distributed from the father's estate.

C. Certificate of deposit received as a gift.

D. Both cash received from a grandmother's estate and royalties received on the deceased father's published book; the right to receive these royalties was distributed from the father's estate.

Answer (B) is correct.
    REQUIRED: The item considered income in respect of a decedent.
    DISCUSSION: Income in respect of a decedent is the amount that is earned by the taxpayer but not received prior to his or her death nor accrued prior to his or her death if on the accrual method, so it is not included in the decedent's final return. Income in respect of a decedent is included in the recipient's (e.g., the estate's) income in the year received or accrued.

26. Which of the following statements concerning the deduction for estate taxes by individuals is true?

A. The deduction for estate tax can be claimed only for the same tax year in which the income in respect of a decedent must be included in the recipient's income.

B. Individuals may claim the deduction for estate tax whether or not they itemize deductions.

C. The estate tax deduction is subject to a 2% AGI floor.

D. None of the answers are correct.

Answer (A) is correct.
    REQUIRED: The true statement concerning the deduction for estate taxes by individuals.
    DISCUSSION: Estate taxes attributable to income in respect of decedent included in the gross estate are deductible on the fiduciary income tax return. The deduction may be claimed only for the same tax year in which the income in respect of a decedent must be included in the recipient's income.
    Answer (B) is incorrect. A taxpayer cannot take both an itemized deduction and also use the standard deduction. **Answer (C) is incorrect.** The deduction is not subject to a 2% AGI floor, which was suspended for 2018 to 2025. **Answer (D) is incorrect.** A correct answer is given.

27. Mr. A sold a tract of land and reported the sale using the installment method of accounting. The net sale price was $80,000, and the cost basis was $40,000. After A's death, the final $10,000 installment (plus interest) was collected by his personal representative. What amount (other than interest) must be reported as profit on a Form 1041, *U.S. Income Tax Return for Estates and Trusts*, for the year in which the $10,000 was received?

A. $10,000

B. $5,000

C. $2,500

D. $0

Answer (B) is correct.
    REQUIRED: The amount of the payments received after death that are income in respect of a decedent.
    DISCUSSION: Income in respect of a decedent is the amount that the decedent had a right to receive prior to death but that was not properly includible on his or her final income tax return. It retains its same character to the recipient as it would have been in the hands of the decedent. There is no step-up in basis under Sec. 1014(c), so the same gross profit margin is used on an installment receipt. The gross profit margin was 50% ($40,000 ÷ $80,000), so $5,000 ($10,000 × 50%) is income in respect of a decedent. The remaining $5,000 is merely a return of capital.
    The interest on the installment debt is not income in respect of a decedent except for the portion accrued before death. All the interest received must also be reported on Form 1041.
    Answer (A) is incorrect. The payment must be adjusted by the gross profit margin. **Answer (C) is incorrect.** The gross profit margin is 50%. **Answer (D) is incorrect.** Payments must be included when received after death.

28. Ms. Smith, a cash-method taxpayer, died on September 30 of the current year. Subsequent to her death, but prior to December 31 of the current year, her beneficiary received the following:

Rental income for September $ 1,500
Proceeds from a life insurance policy   20,000
Dividend declared on September 27
   of the current year   6,000

What amount is considered income in respect of a decedent?

   A. $1,500

   B. $7,500

   C. $3,000

   D. $27,500

Answer (B) is correct.
   REQUIRED: The amount of income considered in respect of a decedent.
   DISCUSSION: Income in respect of a decedent is that which is earned by the taxpayer but is neither received prior to his or her death nor accrued prior to his or her death if on the accrual method, so it is not included in the decedent's final return. Income in respect of a decedent is included in the recipient's (e.g., the estate's) income in the year received or accrued. It is calculated the same as if the decedent were still alive; therefore, Smith's executor will include $1,500 for the rental income and $6,000 for the dividends as income in respect of a decedent.
   Answer (A) is incorrect. Income in respect of a decedent also includes the dividends declared. **Answer (C) is incorrect.** The entire amount of dividends declared and rental income are included as income in respect of a decedent. **Answer (D) is incorrect.** Proceeds from the life insurance policy were not earned until after death.

29. Pablo died October 10 of the current year. Prior to his death, Pablo had done the following: He sold and delivered a truckload of oranges to a co-op but did not receive the $3,000 payment prior to his death. The payment was made to his executor. He sold a truck to Roscoe for $5,000, but the payment was not received until after his death. Pablo's basis in the truck was $1,000. What is the amount of income in respect of a decedent for the above two payments?

   A. No amount for either transaction.

   B. $3,000 for the oranges and $5,000 for the truck.

   C. $3,000 for the oranges and $4,000 for the truck.

   D. None of the answers are correct.

Answer (C) is correct.
   REQUIRED: The amount of income in respect of a decedent.
   DISCUSSION: Income in respect of a decedent is that which is earned by the taxpayer but is neither received prior to his or her death, nor accrued prior to his or her death if on the accrual method, so it is not included in the decedent's final return. Income in respect of a decedent is included in the recipient's (e.g., the estate's) income in the year received or accrued. It is calculated the same as if the decedent were still alive; therefore, Pablo's executor will include $3,000 for the oranges and $4,000 for the truck as income in respect of a decedent.
   Answer (A) is incorrect. Income in respect of a decedent must be recognized when the income is earned by a decedent but payment is not received until after death. **Answer (B) is incorrect.** The gain on the truck is $4,000 ($5,000 payment – $1,000 basis). **Answer (D) is incorrect.** A correct answer is given.

·

Access the **Gleim EA Premium Review System** featuring our SmartAdapt technology from your Gleim Personal Classroom to continue your studies. You will experience a personalized study environment with exam-emulating multiple-choice questions.

STUDY UNIT FOUR

BUSINESS DEDUCTIONS

(17 pages of outline)

Gross income is reduced by deductions to compute taxable income. No amount can be deducted from gross income unless allowed by the Internal Revenue Code (IRC). **Above-the-line deductions** are deducted from gross income to arrive at adjusted gross income (AGI). Several deductions and credits are limited by reference to AGI. **Below-the-line deductions** are deducted from AGI to arrive at taxable income.

Business expenses for self-employed taxpayers (i.e., those filing Schedule C) are generally deductible. However, the unreimbursed business expenses of employees are nondeductible for tax years 2018 through 2025. For the reimbursed expenses of an employee, if reimbursements equal expenses and the employee makes an accounting of expenses to the employer, the reimbursements are excluded from the employee's gross income and the employer may deduct the expenses (accountable plan).

1) This rule also applies if reimbursements exceeding expenses are returned to the employer and the employee substantiates the expenses.

2) If excess reimbursements are not returned or if the employee does not substantiate them, the reimbursements are included in the employee's gross income and none of the expenses are deductible by the employee (nonaccountable plan).

   a) The employee's old 2%-of-AGI miscellaneous itemized deduction allowance is repealed for tax years 2018 through 2025.

   b) An exception to the disallowed employee deductions for business expenses remains. The exception is the above-the-line adjustment to income for certain business expenses of reservists, performing artists, and fee-basis government officials.

      i) The qualified employee (e.g., reservist, performing artist) reports these expenses on Form 2106, *Employee Business Expenses*.

   c) An employer (e.g., sole proprietor) reports the reimbursed expenses on Schedule C.

3) Reimbursements for **transportation** not exceeding $0.575/mile for 2020 are considered adequately substantiated by a record of time, place, and business purpose.

4) The employer decides which plan to use, and this determines the employee's tax consequences.

4.1 BUSINESS EXPENSES

1. A deduction from gross income is allowed for all ordinary and necessary expenses paid or incurred during a tax year in carrying on a trade or business.

    a. A sole proprietor claims these deductions on Schedule C.

2. The reporting of many of these expenses is done on Form 1099-MISC, *Miscellaneous Income*, for each payee. The following box provides some general requirements for reporting payments on Form 1099-MISC:

Reason for Payment	Minimum Amount Paid	Form Box Reported In/On
Rents		1
Prizes & Awards		3
Other Income Pmt.		3
Medical & Health*	$600	6
Crop Insurance		9
Notional Contract	(includes payments for parts and materials)	3
Attorney*		10
Fishing Boat*		5

* Generally, payments to a corporation are not reported on a Form 1099-MISC. However, these payments to corporations generally must be reported on the form.

Trade/Business and Expenses Defined

3. A trade or business is a regular and continuous activity that is entered into with the expectation of making a profit.

    a. "Regular" means the taxpayer devotes a substantial amount of business time to the activity.

4. An activity that is not engaged in for a profit is a hobby (personal).

    a. An activity that results in a profit in any 3 of 5 consecutive tax years (2 out of 7 for the breeding and racing of horses) is presumed not to be a hobby.

    b. Expenses related to a hobby are not deductible during tax years 2018 through 2025, but any income is included in gross income.

5. An expense must be **both** ordinary and necessary to be deductible.

    a. "Ordinary" implies that the expense normally occurs or is likely to occur in connection with businesses similar to the one operated by the taxpayer claiming the deduction.

        1) The expenditures need not occur frequently. In fact, an expense occurring only once in a business's lifetime may be ordinary (e.g., major litigation).

    b. "Necessary" implies that an expenditure must be appropriate and helpful in developing or maintaining the trade or business.

c. Implicit in the "ordinary and necessary" requirement is the requirement that the expenditures be reasonable. For example, if the compensation paid to a shareholder exceeds that ordinarily paid for similar services (reasonable compensation), the excessive payment may constitute a nondeductible dividend.

1) Whether an expense is reasonable depends on each taxpayer's individual facts and circumstances. Thus, an expense may be reasonable to one taxpayer and unreasonable to another.

EXAMPLE 4-1   Ordinary and Necessary

For truck drivers, the cost of satellite radio is deductible because it provides access to weather and traffic across the country and is a standard expense in the industry.

EXAMPLE 4-2   Ordinary and Necessary

The cost for an accountant to prepare a business's financial statements is always considered an ordinary and necessary business expense.

Expense Treatment

6. **Allocation**

a. Only the portion of an expenditure that is attributable to business activity is deductible.
b. A reasonable method of allocation may be used. It must clearly reflect income.

7. **Compensation**

a. Cash and the FMV of property paid to an employee are deductible by the employer.

EXAMPLE 4-3   Employee Compensation -- Property

A company distributes game consoles as compensation to each employee. Each console costs $450 and has a FMV of $600. The company takes a compensation deduction of $600 and reports income of $150 for each console given as compensation.

EXAMPLE 4-4   Employee Compensation -- Cash and PTO

In Year 1, Charlotte, an accrual-basis taxpayer, paid her employees $150,000 in cash. As of December 31, Year 1, her employees accrued $10,000 in bonuses and $20,000 in paid time off. Charlotte paid the bonuses on January 25, Year 2, and $12,000 of the accrued paid time off was used in February and paid on March 3, Year 2. None of the employees are related to Charlotte. On her Year 1 tax return, Charlotte may deduct $172,000 in compensation paid ($150,000 + $10,000 + $12,000). The $8,000 of deferred compensation is deductible when paid.

EXAMPLE 4-5   Employee Compensation -- Wages, Bonus, and Property

Allaboard Train Company paid its conductor $1,400 in cash and a scooter with a fair market value of $300 for services performed in the previous 2 weeks. Allaboard has a $150 basis in the scooter. The conductor also received a $500 bonus for his record of on-time arrivals. Allaboard may claim a deduction for $2,200 in wages ($1,400 + $300 + $500), and the employee will recognize the same amount as wage income. Notably, Allaboard will also recognize a $150 gain on the transfer of the scooter.

---

b. Compensation expenses for nonemployees, e.g., payments to independent contractors, are reported to each payee on Form 1099-NEC, *Nonemployee Compensation*. As with Form 1099-MISC, there is a $600 minimum amount required to be paid before a Form 1099-NEC must be provided.

8. **Rent**

   a.   Advance rental payments may be deducted by the lessee only during the tax periods to which the payments apply.

   b.   Generally, even a cash-method taxpayer must amortize prepaid rent expense over the period to which it applies. The exception to this rule is if the rental contract is for 12 months or less and the payments do not extend beyond the end of the next taxable year (i.e., the 12-month rule).

EXAMPLE 4-6   **Cash-Method Prepaid Rent**

A cash-method calendar-year taxpayer leases a building at a monthly rental rate of $1,000 beginning July 1, 2020. On June 30, 2020, the taxpayer pays advance rent of $12,000 for the last 6 months of 2020 and the first 6 months of 2021. The taxpayer may deduct the entire $12,000 payment for 2020. The payment applies to the right to use the property that does not extend beyond 12 months after the date the taxpayer received this right. If the taxpayer deducts the $12,000 in 2020, there is no deduction left for 2021.

Travel

9.   While away from home **overnight** on business, travel expenses are deductible. Travel expenses include transportation, lodging, and 50% of meal expenses in an employment-related context.

   a.   No deduction is allowed for

      1)   Travel that is primarily personal in nature except for

         a)   Directly related business expenses while at the destination.

      2)   The travel expenses of the taxpayer's spouse unless

         a)   There is a bona fide business purpose for the spouse's presence,
         b)   The spouse is an employee, and
         c)   The expenses would be otherwise deductible.

      3)   Attending investment meetings

      4)   Travel as a form of education

EXAMPLE 4-7   **Deductible Travel Expenses**

John Jones takes a trip that includes 4 business days and 2 personal days. The entire $400 airfare expense is deductible. However, if the trip included 5 personal days and 1 business day, no portion of the airfare expense would be deductible. Any hotel expenses for the working days are deductible.

---

   b.   **Substantiation**

      1)   A taxpayer must substantiate the amount, time, place, and business purpose of expenses paid or incurred while traveling away from home.

Transportation while Traveling

   c.   Actual expenses for automobile use are deductible (e.g., services, repairs, gasoline, depreciation, insurance, and licenses).

      1)   Alternatively, the taxpayer may deduct the standard mileage rate ($0.575/mile for 2020), plus parking fees, tolls, etc.

      2)   If a taxpayer switches from using the standard mileage rate to actual expenses, the depreciation deduction must be computed using the straight-line method.

d.   To determine a taxpayer's principal place of business for purposes of travel expenses, the location of an individual's tax home must be determined. When a taxpayer has multiple places of business, the IRS determines the principal place of business using a three-pronged test:

1)   The total time spent at each place of business
2)   The degree of business activity at each place of business
3)   The relative income earned at each place of business

e.   Taxpayers without any regular or main place of business or living location are considered itinerants (i.e., transients), and their tax home is wherever they work. Because they are never away from home, they are not allowed any travel expense deductions.

Foreign Travel

f.   Traveling expenses of a taxpayer who travels outside of the United States away from home must be allocated between time spent on the trip for business and time spent for pleasure.

EXAMPLE 4-8	Deductible Foreign Travel Expenses

Scott's foreign trip is for more than a week, and he spends 35% of his time as a personal vacation. However, he spends the other 65% providing business-related services.

Only 65% of the expenses related to the time providing business services, including transportation, lodging, local travel, etc., may be deducted.

1)   No allocation is required for costs of getting to and from the destination when

a)   The trip is for no more than 1 week,

b)   The taxpayer can establish that a personal vacation is not the major consideration, or

c)   The personal time spent on the trip is less than 25% of the total time away from home.

2)   A deduction for travel expenses will be denied to the extent that they are not allocable to the taxpayer's business when the trip is longer than 1 week.

Conventions

g.   Convention Travel Expenses

1)   Deductible

a)   Travel expenses for attending a convention related to the taxpayer's business, even when the taxpayer is an employee

i)   The fact that an employee uses vacation or leave time or that attendance at the convention is voluntary will not necessarily negate the deduction.

2)   Not deductible

a)   Expenses for a convention or meeting in connection with investments, financial planning, or other income-producing property

3) Limited deduction

    a) Expenses for conventions on U.S. cruise ships.

    b) The deduction is limited to $2,000 with respect to all cruises beginning in any calendar year.

    c) It applies only if

        i) All ports of such cruise ship are located in the U.S. or in U.S. possessions,

        ii) The taxpayer establishes that the convention is directly related to the active conduct of his or her trade or business, and

        iii) The taxpayer includes certain specified information in the return on which the deduction is claimed.

h. The following chart summarizes expenses that can be deducted when traveling away from home for business purposes:

IF there are expenses for . . .	THEN the taxpayer can deduct the cost of . . .
transportation	travel by airplane, train, bus, or car between the home and the business destination. If the taxpayer was provided with a free ticket or the taxpayer was riding free as a result of a frequent traveler or similar program, the cost is zero. Travel by ship (e.g., cruise ships) for conventions has additional rules and limits.
taxi, commuter bus, and airport limousine	fares for these and other types of transportation that take the taxpayer between • The airport or station and the hotel, and • The hotel and the work location of the customers or clients, the business meeting place, or the temporary work location.
baggage and shipping	sending baggage and sample or display material between the regular and temporary work locations.
car	operating and maintaining the car when traveling away from home on business. The taxpayer can deduct the actual expenses or the standard mileage rate, as well as business-related tolls and parking. If the taxpayer rents a car while away from home on business, (s)he can deduct only the business-use portion of the expenses.
lodging and meals	lodging and 50% of meals if the business trip is overnight or long enough to require a stop for sleep or rest to properly perform duties. Meals include amounts spent for food, beverages, taxes, and related tips and have additional rules and limits.
cleaning	dry cleaning and laundry.
telephone	business calls while on the business trip. This includes business communication by fax machine or other communication devices.
tips	tips paid for any expenses in this chart.
other	other similar ordinary and necessary expenses related to the business travel. These expenses might include transportation to or from a business meal, public stenographer's fees, computer rental fees, and operating and maintaining a house trailer.

Transportation Expenses

10. Transportation expenses for employees include taxi fares, automobile expenses, tolls and parking fees, and airfare.

    a.   These expenses are treated as **travel expenses if the taxpayer is away from home overnight**. Otherwise, they are transportation expenses.

    b.   The following illustration summarizes the rules for transportation expense deductions:

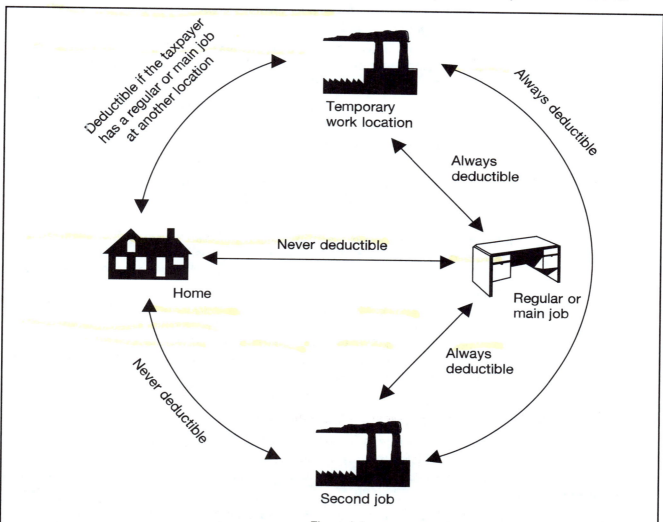

Figure 4-1

Home: The place where the taxpayer resides. Transportation expenses between the home and the main or regular place of work are personal commuting expenses.

Regular or main job: The taxpayer's principal place of business. If the taxpayer has more than one job, the taxpayer must determine which one is the regular or main job. Consider the time spent at each, the activity performed at each, and the income earned at each.

Temporary work location: A place where the work assignment is realistically expected to last (and does in fact last) 1 year or less. Unless the taxpayer has a regular place of business, the taxpayer can only deduct transportation expenses to a temporary work location **outside** of the metropolitan area.

Second job: If the taxpayer regularly works at two or more places in one day, whether or not for the same employer, the taxpayer cannot deduct the transportation costs between the home and a second job on a day off from the main job.

c.   Commuting costs are nondeductible.

1)   A self-employed individual who uses an automobile to transport tools to work will be allowed a deduction for transportation expenses only if additional costs are incurred, such as renting a trailer. A deduction is allowed only for the additional costs incurred to transport the tools to work.

2)   There are four exceptions to the commuting expense deduction disallowance.

a)   The costs of going between one business location and another business location are generally deductible.

b)   The costs of going between the taxpayer's residence and a temporary work location outside the metropolitan area where the taxpayer lives and normally works are generally deductible.

i)   A work location is considered temporary if it is expected to last less than 1 year even if it ultimately lasts more than 1 year.

ii)   A work location is considered indefinite if it is expected to last more than 1 year even if it ultimately lasts less than 1 year.

iii) A work location that is expected to be temporary but that becomes indefinite is considered to be indefinite from the point at which the employment time becomes indefinite.

c)   If the taxpayer has one or more regular work locations away from his or her residence, (s)he may deduct commuting expenses incurred in going between the residence and a temporary work location in the same trade or business, regardless of the distance.

d)   If a taxpayer's residence is the taxpayer's principal place of business within the meaning of a home office, the taxpayer may deduct commuting expenses incurred in going between the residence and another work location in the same trade or business, regardless of whether the work location is regular or temporary and regardless of the distance.

d.   Actual automobile expenses may be used for the deduction, or the taxpayer may use the standard mileage rate. —whichever is greater

1)   The standard mileage rate is $0.575/mile for 2020, plus parking fees and tolls. This rate applies to vehicles that are owned or leased.

EXAMPLE 4-9   **Standard Mileage Rate**

A self-employed taxpayer traveled 10,000 business miles in his car, paid $100 in parking fees, and $100 in tolls during the year. Using the standard mileage rate, the taxpayer may deduct $5,950 [(10,000 mi. × $0.575) + $100 parking + $100 tolls].

---

a)   This standard mileage rate cannot be used when the taxpayer owns or leases five or more cars (i.e., a fleet) that are used for business at the same time.

b)   This rate also can be used for cars used for hire (e.g., taxicabs).

2)   Actual expenses must be allocated between business use and personal use of the automobile. A deduction is allowed only for the business use.

a)   Actual automobile expenses include the following: gas and oil, lubrication and washing, repairs, garage and parking fees, insurance, tires and supplies, tolls, interest expense, leasing fees, licenses, and depreciation. Remember, depreciation is only taken on the business portion of the automobile; therefore, all depreciation is deductible.

3) Recall that the unreimbursed expenses of an employee are nondeductible.

EXAMPLE 4-10 **Mixed Use Automobile Expenses**

Carlos uses a large truck that has been fully depreciated for his business and for personal use. In 2020, he drove 20,000 miles, of which 18,000 were for business use (90%). His actual expenses were $15,000 for gas, oil, and maintenance. Carlos can deduct $13,500 ($15,000 × 90%) for business driving expenses, which exceeds the standard mileage amount of $10,350 (18,000 miles × $0.575 per mile).

---

11. The following factors are used to determine a taxpayer's tax home:

    a. The taxpayer performs part of his or her business in the area surrounding his or her main home and uses that home for lodging while doing business in the area.

    b. The taxpayer has living expenses at his or her main home that are duplicated because his or her business requires him or her to be away from that home.

    c. The taxpayer has not abandoned the area in which both his or her traditional place of lodging and his or her main home are located, members of his or her family live at his or her main home, or (s)he often uses that home for lodging.

EXAMPLE 4-11 **Tax Home**

An unmarried self-employed taxpayer lives in a rented apartment in City A and has done so for several years. The taxpayer is enrolled in a 12-month executive training program, and, after completing the course, the taxpayer will not return to City A to work. All training is away from City A. The taxpayer uses the apartment in City A frequently for personal business and socializing with friends. After completion of the course, the taxpayer moves to City B. The taxpayer does not satisfy item 11.a. above but does satisfy items 11.b. and 11.c. Therefore, for the year, the taxpayer's tax home is City A.

Insurance Expense

12. Trade or business insurance expense paid or incurred during the tax year is deductible.

    a. A cash-method taxpayer may not deduct a premium before it is paid.

    b. Prepaid insurance must be apportioned over the period of coverage.

    c. Self-employed persons may deduct from gross income 100% of amounts paid for health insurance premiums.

EXAMPLE 4-12 **Life Insurance Expenses**

Harry provides his employees with group-term life insurance equal to their salaries. In Year 1, Daniel, an employee, has a salary of $80,000. Daniel is 40 years old, so the monthly cost per $1,000 of protection is $0.10. Daniel includes in his income premiums for $30,000 ($80,000 − $50,000 excluded) of the group-term life insurance, which equal $36 ($30,000 ÷ $1,000 × $0.10 × 12 months) for the year.

Bad Debts

13. A bad-debt deduction is allowed only for a bona fide debt arising from a debtor-creditor relationship based upon a valid and enforceable obligation to pay a fixed or determinable sum of money.

14. Worthless debt is deductible only to the extent of adjusted basis in the debt.

    a. A cash-basis taxpayer has no basis in accounts receivable and generally has no deduction for bad debts.

15. A **business bad debt** is one incurred or acquired in connection with the taxpayer's trade or business.

    a. Partially worthless business debts may be deducted to the extent they are worthless and specifically written off.

    b. A business bad debt is treated as an ordinary loss.

EXAMPLE 4-13	Business Bad Debt

Peter is a cash-basis taxpayer in the lawn care business and charges clients monthly. One of his clients stopped paying and built up a $500 bill before moving out of state. Peter is not able to deduct the bad debt because he is a cash-basis taxpayer. The unpaid bill is never included in revenue, but Peter may deduct any expenses for providing the service and attempting to collect the debt. If he was an accrual-basis taxpayer, the only difference would be that gross income and bad debt would both include the unpaid $500 bill that was written off.

16. A **nonbusiness bad debt** is a debt other than one incurred or acquired in connection with the taxpayer's trade or business.

    a. Investments are not treated as a trade or business.

    b. A partially worthless nonbusiness bad debt is not deductible.

    c. A wholly worthless nonbusiness bad debt is treated as a short-term capital loss; i.e., deductible up to any capital gains plus $3,000 of ordinary income. Any excess losses can be carried forward to future tax years.

EXAMPLE 4-14	Business vs. Nonbusiness Bad Debt

Tye is a sole proprietor who designs custom skateboards. Last year, Tye discovered that he will only be able to collect $100 of a $500 loan he gave to a supplier for business reasons due to the supplier's insolvency. This is considered a business bad debt; thus, Tye may deduct the worthless portion of the debt, or $400. However, if Tye made the same loan to a friend for personal reasons, he would not be allowed a deduction. A partially worthless nonbusiness bad debt is not deductible.

17. The **specific write-off method** generally must be used for tax purposes. The reserve method generally is used only for financial accounting purposes.

Worthless Securities

18. Worthless corporate securities are not considered bad debts. They are generally treated as a capital loss.

19. The **loss on deposits** can occur when a bank, credit union, or other financial institution becomes bankrupt or insolvent.

    a. The individual may treat the nonbusiness account loss as a personal casualty loss, which is nondeductible.

    b. Alternatively, the individual can elect to treat the loss as a nonbusiness ordinary loss arising from a transaction entered into for profit.

    c. If no election is made, the default classification for the nonbusiness bad debt is a short-term capital loss subject to a $3,000 annual limit.

Business Gifts

20. Expenditures for business gifts are deductible. They must be ordinary and necessary.

    a. Deduction for business gift expenditure is disallowed unless the taxpayer substantiates, by adequate records, the following:

        1) Amount (cost) of the gift,
        2) Date of the gift,
        3) Description of the gift,
        4) Business purpose of the gift, and
        5) Business relation of the recipient to the taxpayer.

    b. Deduction is limited to $25 per recipient per year for excludable items.

        1) The $25 limit does not apply to incidental (e.g., advertising) items costing (the giver) not more than $4 each, and other promotional materials including signs and displays.

        2) Spouses are treated as one taxpayer, even if they file separate returns and have independent business relationships with the recipient.

Employee Achievement Awards

21. Up to $400 of the cost of employee achievement awards is deductible by an employer for all nonqualified plan awards.

    a. An employee achievement award is tangible personal property awarded as part of a meaningful presentation for safety achievement or length of service.

        1) Tangible personal property does not include cash, cash equivalents, gift cards/coupons/certificates, vacations, meals, lodging, event tickets (e.g., theater, sporting), stocks, bonds, and other securities.

22. Deduction of qualified plan awards is limited to $1,600 per year.

    a. A qualified plan award is an employee achievement award provided under an established written program that does not discriminate in favor of highly compensated employees.

        1) If the average cost of all employee achievement awards is greater than $400, it is not a qualified plan award.

Depreciation

23. Deduction is permitted for obsolescence or wear and tear of property used in a trade or business. Depreciation is discussed in Study Unit 9, Subunit 6.

Start-Up Costs

24. Taxpayers can deduct up to $5,000 of start-up costs and $5,000 of organizational expenditures in the taxable year in which the business begins.

    a. Examples of start-up costs include the costs of investigating the creation or acquisition of an active trade or business, to prepare to enter into the trade or business, to secure suppliers and customers, and to obtain certain supplies and equipment (noncapital).

    b. Any start-up costs or organizational expenditures in excess of the $5,000 limit are capitalized and amortized proportionally over a 15-year period beginning with the month in which the active trade or business begins. The total start-up or organizational costs deducted for the first year equal the sum total of the $5,000 limit and the amortized amount allocated to the first year.

        1) These amounts are reduced, but not below zero, by the cumulative cost of the start-up costs or organizational expenditures that exceed $50,000.

        NOTE: This phaseout is computed separately for start-up costs and organizational costs.

    c. A taxpayer is deemed to have made the election; therefore, a taxpayer is not required to attach a separate statement to the return.

Reforestation Cost

25. Amounts paid or incurred for reforestation may be expensed in the current year up to $10,000. Any remaining balance is to be amortized over a period of 7 years.

Vacant Land

26. Interest and taxes on vacant land are deductible.

Demolition

27. If a structure is demolished, demolition costs, undepreciated (remaining) basis, and losses sustained are not deductible. They are allocated to the land.

Abandoned Assets

28. A loss is deductible in the year the assets are actually abandoned with no claim for reimbursement.

    a. The loss equals the adjusted basis in the abandoned property.

COGS

29. Cost of goods sold (COGS) is deducted before arriving at gross income.

Sales – COGS = Gross income

Medical Reimbursement Plans

30. The cost of such a plan for employees is deductible by the employer.

Political Contributions

31. Contributions to a political party or candidate and, generally, lobbying expenses are not deductible.

EXAMPLE 4-15	Nondeductible Political Contributions

Craft Store pays for advertising in the program for a political party's convention. Proceeds are used for the party's activities. The expense is a political contribution, which is not deductible.

   a. Lobbying activity equates to appearances before and communications with any council or similar governing body with respect to legislation of direct interest to the taxpayer.

   b. Up to $2,000 of direct cost of lobbying activity at the state or federal level is deductible.

      1) If total direct costs exceed $2,000, this de minimis exception is entirely unavailable.

Debt of Another

32. Payment of a debt of another party is generally not ordinary for a trade or business and thus is not deductible.

   a. A legal obligation or definite business requirement renders the payment deductible, e.g., if required by suppliers to stay in business.

Intangibles

33. The cost of intangibles must generally be capitalized.

   a. Amortization is allowed if the intangible has a determinable useful life, e.g., a covenant not to compete or if a code section specifically so provides.

Tax-Exempt Income

34. An expenditure related to producing tax-exempt income is not deductible, e.g., interest on a loan used to purchase tax-exempt bonds.

Public Policy

35. A trade or business expenditure that is ordinary, necessary, and reasonable may be nondeductible if allowing the deduction would frustrate public policy.

   a. Examples are

      1) Fines and penalties paid to the government for violation of the law
      2) Illegal bribes and kickbacks
      3) Two-thirds of damages for violation of federal antitrust law
      4) Expenses of dealers in illegal drugs

         a) However, adjustment to gross receipts is permitted for the cost of merchandise.

EXAMPLE 4-16	Tax Deductible Fines

Percy signed a contract to sell Penny 100 widgets for $2,500 to be delivered on April 1. Percy must pay a $10 fine per unit for each week the shipment is late. In March, Percy received and accepted a $5,000 order from Marc for the 100 widgets that were set aside for Penny. Because Percy decided to sell the 100 widgets to Marc, he was only able to deliver 50 widgets to Penny on April 1 and delivered the remaining 50 widgets on April 5. Percy paid Penny a $500 late shipment fine. The $500 fine is tax deductible because it was a business decision and not paid to a government for violating a law.

118   *SU 4: Business Deductions*

Impairment-Related Expenses

36. Expenses of a handicapped individual for attendant care services at his or her place of employment and/or other expenses connected to his or her place of employment necessary for the individual to work are deductible expenses. The expenses are claimed under other itemized deductions for the individual's return.

Miscellaneous Expenses

37. Miscellaneous ordinary and necessary business expenses are deductible.

    a.   Examples include costs of office supplies, advertising, professional fees, and bank fees.

Withdrawal Penalties

38. Penalties on the early withdrawal of interest income are deductible as above-the-line deductions.

Business Use of Home

39. Employers (who reimburse) and the self-employed may deduct expenses incurred for the use of a person's home for business purposes but only if strict requirements are met.

    a.   The portion of the home must be used exclusively and regularly as

         1)   The principal place of business for any trade or business of the taxpayer;

         2)   A place of business that is used by patients, clients, or customers in the normal course of the taxpayer's trade or business; or

         3)   A separate structure that is not attached to the dwelling unit that is used in the taxpayer's trade or business.

    b.   The exclusive-use test is strictly applied. Any personal use of the business portion of the home by anyone results in complete disallowance of the deductions. There are two exceptions to the exclusive-use test:

         1)   Retail/wholesale. A retailer or wholesaler whose **sole** location of his or her business is his or her home need not meet the exclusive-use test.

              a)   The ordinary and necessary business expenses allocable to an identifiable space used regularly for inventory or product sample storage by a taxpayer in the active pursuit of his or her trade or business are deductible.

         2)   Day care. If the business portion of a home is used to offer qualifying day care, the exclusive-use test need not be met.

EXAMPLE 4-17	Trade or Business Requirement

A taxpayer uses part of their home exclusively and regularly to read financial periodicals and reports, clip bond coupons, and carry out similar activities related to the taxpayer's own investments. The taxpayer does not make investments as a broker or dealer. These activities do not qualify as part of a trade or business, and disqualify the home space for a deduction.

    c.   If the taxpayer has more than one business location, the primary factor in determining whether a home office is a taxpayer's principal place of business is the relative importance of the activities performed at each business location.

         1)   If the primary location cannot be determined by the relative importance test, then the amount of time spent at each location will be used.

    d.   A home office qualifies as a "principal place of business" if used by the taxpayer to conduct administrative or management activities of the taxpayer's trade or business and there is no other fixed location where the taxpayer conducts such activities.

EXAMPLE 4-18	Principal Place of Business

Brian owns Fisher Company, which does not have a physical office and has five sales people. Once a month, Brian meets with the sales team in a spare bedroom in his house that is used as a conference room. The only activities that occur in the conference room are the monthly meetings and administrative functions for Fisher Company. The conference room is treated as a home office.

    e.   Deduction for business use is limited to

        1)   Gross income derived from the use, minus

        2)   Deductions allocable to the home, allowed regardless of business or personal use, e.g., interest or taxes, minus

        3)   Deductions allocable to the trade or business for which the home office is used that are not home office expenses, e.g., employee compensation.

EXAMPLE 4-19	Home Office Deductions Allocable to the Home

Toni has $10,000 of net income from a business activity conducted in a home office. The home office makes up 30% of the square footage of the home. Toni has mortgage interest and property taxes on the home of $20,000. Toni has $5,000 in insurance and utilities on the home. The maximum amount of depreciation deduction on the home office is $2,500 {$10,000 – [30% × ($20,000 + $5,000)]}.

        NOTE: Keep in mind, the Schedule C deduction is still only the portion allocated to the business use of the home. The remaining expense, if otherwise deductible (e.g., mortgage interest), is an itemized deduction on Schedule A.

EXAMPLE 4-20	Home Office Deductions for Non-Home Office Expenses

Tammy has $32,000 of gross income from a business activity conducted in a home office. She may deduct $10,000 of mortgage interest and property taxes allocable to the home office as personal expenses. Tammy has $6,000 of home office expenses other than depreciation, $3,500 in depreciation, and $15,000 of business deductions that are not home office expenses. Only $1,000 [$32,000 – ($10,000 + $15,000 + $6,000)] of the depreciation is deductible as home office expenses.

    f.   Any currently disallowed amount is deductible in succeeding years, subject to the same limitations.

    g.   A simplified option allows taxpayers to claim $5 per square foot of home office space up to 300 ft^2, for a maximum deduction of $1,500. Individuals using this simplified method can claim all of their allowable mortgage interest and real estate taxes on Schedule A, even for the portion attributable to business use.

    h.   The deduction is not available to employees because of the repeal of the 2%-of-AGI miscellaneous itemized deductions for tax years 2018 through 2025.

EXAMPLE 4-21	Not a Qualified Home Office

Kathleen is employed as a teacher. She is required to teach and meet with students at the school and to grade papers and tests. The school provides her with a small office where she can work on her lesson plans, grade papers and tests, and meet with parents and students. The school does not require her to work at home. Kathleen prefers to use the office she has set up in her home and does not use the one provided by the school. She uses this home office exclusively and regularly for the administrative duties of her teaching job. Kathleen cannot claim a deduction for the business use of her home because (1) the home office is not for the convenience of the employer and (2) the home office deduction is not available to employees.

STOP AND REVIEW! **You have completed the outline for this subunit. Study multiple-choice questions 1 through 19 beginning on page 122.**

4.2 BUSINESS MEALS

Limit on Meals

1. The amount deductible for business meal expenses, provided to a current or potential business customer, client, consultant, or similar business contact, is 50% of the actual expense.

    a. The limit also applies to the taxpayer's own meals.

    b. Related expenses, such as taxes, tips, and parking fees, but not transportation to and from a business meal, are also subject to the 50% limit.

    c. The IRS has denied deductions for any meal expense over $75 for which the claimant did not provide substantiating evidence: documented dates, amounts, location, purpose, and business relationship.

EXAMPLE 4-22   Substantiation of a Business Meal
Lucy, an event planner, took her client Genie to dinner to discuss an upcoming art event and paid $100, including the tip. To provide sufficient documentation, Lucy saved her receipt showing the tip amount and wrote on the back of the receipt that she had dinner with Genie to discuss the art event. Later, she added the information to her business calendar and filed the receipt.

    d. For employees subject to Department of Transportation hours-of-service rules (e.g., over-the-road truck drivers), the deductible meals percentage is 80%.

    e. Additionally, the meal must not be lavish or extravagant; i.e., it must be reasonable based on facts and circumstances.

2. Meal expenses are not deductible if neither the taxpayer nor an employee of the taxpayer is present at the meal.

Entertainment

3. Most entertainment expenses are **nondeductible**.

    a. However, entertainment expenses for recreational, social, or similar activities primarily for the benefit of employees are 100% deductible. For example, the expenses for an annual company holiday party would be 100% deductible.

    b. If otherwise deductible meals occur at a nondeductible entertainment event, the meal expense must be separately stated in order to be deductible.

Ownership of Facility

4. Expenses in connection with the use of an entertainment facility that the taxpayer owns are not deductible as a business expense.

    a. Any property that a taxpayer rents, owns, or uses for entertainment purposes is considered to be an entertainment facility.

    b. Swimming pools, cars, hotel suites, and yachts are all examples of entertainment facilities.

5.   Now that most of the business deductions have been explained in Subunits 4.1 and 4.2, the
     following two tables provide guidance on how to document the deductions:

IF there are expenses for . . .	THEN records must be kept that show details of the following elements . . .			
	Amount	**Time**	**Place or Description**	**Business Purpose Business Relationship**
Travel	Cost of each separate expense for travel, lodging, and meals. Incidental expenses may be totaled in reasonable categories such as taxis, fees, tips, etc.	Dates taxpayer left and returned for each trip and number of days spent on business.	Destination or area of travel (name of city, town, or other designation).	<u>Purpose:</u> Business purpose for the expense or the business benefit gained or expected to be gained. <u>Relationship:</u> N/A
Gifts	Cost of the gift.	Date of the gift.	Description of the gift.	
Transportation	Cost of each separate expense. For car expenses, the cost of the car and any improvements, the date business use began, the mileage for each business use, and the total miles for the year.	Date of the expense. For car expenses, the date of the use of the car.	The business destination.	<u>Purpose:</u> Business purpose for the expense. <u>Relationship:</u> N/A

Date	Destination (City, Town, or Area)	Business Purpose	Odometer Readings			Expenses	
			Start	**Stop**	**Miles this trip**	**Type (Gas, oil, tolls, etc.)**	**Amount**
Weekly Total							
Total Year-to-Date							

6.   The following is a summary of the rules explained on the previous pages:

General rule	A taxpayer can deduct ordinary and necessary expenses to provide a meal to a client, customer, or employee.
Definitions	• An **<u>ordinary</u>** expense is one that is common and accepted in the taxpayer's field of business, trade, or profession. • A **necessary** expense is one that is helpful and appropriate, although not necessarily required, for the business.
Other rules	• The taxpayer cannot deduct meal expenses that are lavish or extravagant under the circumstances. • **Entertainment** expenses are nondeductible. ▪ Entertainment includes any activity generally considered to provide entertainment, amusement, or recreation and includes meals provided to a customer or client that are not separately stated.

STOP AND REVIEW! You have completed the outline for this subunit. Study multiple-choice
questions 19 through 29 beginning on page 128.

QUESTIONS

4.1 Business Expenses

1. In order to qualify as an accountable plan for reimbursement of travel expenses, the employer plan must satisfy all of the following EXCEPT

A. The expenses have a business connection.

B. The employee must make an adequate and timely accounting to the employer.

C. The employer must pay a per diem for meals.

D. The employee must timely return any excess reimbursements.

Answer (C) is correct.
  REQUIRED: The statement that is not required to satisfy requirements as an accountable plan for reimbursement of travel expenses.
  DISCUSSION: For a reimbursement plan to qualify as an accountable plan, all three of the following conditions must be met:

1. There must be a business connection to the expenses.
2. The employee must verify or be reported to have verified the expenses.
3. The employee must return any amounts that exceed the verified expenses.

  Per diem allowances for meals is a substitute plan for an accountable plan in which the company deducts a "reasonable amount" for the cost of travel expenses (Publication 463).
  Answer (A) is incorrect. It is a requirement that the expenses have a business connection for an accountable reimbursement plan. **Answer (B) is incorrect.** It is a requirement that the employee make adequate and timely accounting to the employer for an accountable reimbursement plan. **Answer (D) is incorrect.** It is a requirement that the employee timely return any excess reimbursements for an accountable reimbursement plan.

2. Thomas loaned a friend, Susan, $10,000 for a down payment on a home. Thomas and Susan signed a note in which Susan agreed to pay $100 a month with an interest rate of 4% until the loan was completely paid. Susan lost both her job and her home in 2019. In 2020, Susan filed bankruptcy and went to live with her mother. Thomas sued Susan in court for nonpayment in August 2020, but the court ruled the debt unenforceable because it had been discharged in bankruptcy. When Susan defaulted, the outstanding balance due on the note was $7,000. If Thomas had only wage income reportable during the year, how much would his deductible bad debt be in 2020, assuming that Thomas elected to treat the loss as a nonbusiness ordinary loss arising from a transaction entered into for profit?

A. $7,000

B. $6,900

C. $3,000

D. $10,000

Answer (C) is correct.
  REQUIRED: The deductibility of a loss from a nonbusiness bad debt.
  DISCUSSION: A nonbusiness bad debt is a debt other than one incurred or acquired in connection with the taxpayer's trade or business. A completely worthless nonbusiness bad debt is treated as a short-term capital loss. A short-term capital loss is subject to a $3,000 annual limit. The remaining $4,000 may be carried forward (Publication 550).
  Answer (A) is incorrect. The deduction is restricted to the $3,000 limit in 2020. **Answer (B) is incorrect.** The loss is not subject to the de minimis exclusion of $100 but is restricted to the $3,000 limit in 2020. **Answer (D) is incorrect.** Only $7,000 was written off.

3. With respect to an employer's reimbursement of employee business expenses, which of the following statements is NOT a requirement of an accountable plan?

A. The expenses incurred by the employee must have a business purpose.

B. The reimbursement of business meal expenditures is limited to 50% of the amount incurred.

C. The employee must provide an accounting to the employer within a reasonable period of time.

D. The employee must return any excess reimbursement or allowance to the employer within a reasonable period of time.

Answer (B) is correct.
   REQUIRED: The false statement regarding an employer's reimbursement of employee business expenses.
   DISCUSSION: The reimbursement of business meal expenditures is not limited except by their total amount. The employer can reimburse 100% of allowable meal expenses; however, the employer can deduct only 50% of the allowable business meal expenses on his or her tax return. Further, since the plan is an accountable one, the employer will not recognize the reimbursements as taxable wages, and the employee will exclude the reimbursement from income on his or her return (Publication 463).

4. During 2020, Ted, a self-employed taxpayer, drives his car 5,000 miles to visit clients, 10,000 miles to get to his office, and 500 miles to attend business-related seminars. He also spent $300 for airfare to another business (1-day) seminar and $200 for parking at his office. Using $.575 per mile, what is his deductible transportation expense?

A. $300

B. $3,463

C. $3,663

D. $9,213

Answer (B) is correct.
   REQUIRED: The deduction for transportation expense.
   DISCUSSION: Commuting expenses between a taxpayer's residence and a business location within the area of the taxpayer's home are generally not deductible. In addition, the cost of parking at a taxpayer's place of work is not deductible. However, transportation between home and a temporary work location in the same trade or business may be deducted. Thus, the transportation expenses to visit clients and the business-related seminars are all deductible (Publication 463).

Mileage	$3,163 (5,500 miles × $.575/mile)
Airfare	300
Deductible travel costs	$3,463

   Answer (A) is incorrect. The amount of $300 excludes the deduction for the mileage traveled to clients and the business-related seminars. **Answer (C) is incorrect.** The fee paid for parking at the office is not a deductible travel expense. **Answer (D) is incorrect.** The 10,000 miles of travel to the office is not deductible.

5. In which situation would local transportation expenses NOT be deductible for a self-employed taxpayer?

A. From the regular or main job to the second job.

B. From the regular or main job to a temporary work location.

C. From the second job to a temporary work location.

D. From home (residence) to the second job on your day off from your main job.

Answer (D) is correct.
   REQUIRED: The situation in which local transportation expenses are not deductible.
   DISCUSSION: A self-employed taxpayer is permitted a deduction for transportation expenses paid in connection with a trade or business. However, a taxpayer may not deduct the costs of commuting to and from work as a transportation expense (Publication 463).

6. In Year 1, Laura lent Pat $2,000. At that time, Pat signed an enforceable note agreeing to repay the $2,000. The loan was not made in the course of Laura's business. The loan had not been repaid in Year 3 when Pat died insolvent. For Year 3, Laura should report the nonpayment of the loan as a(n)

    A. Short-term capital loss.

    B. Long-term capital loss.

    C. Ordinary loss.

    D. Other itemized deduction.

Answer (A) is correct.
    REQUIRED: The treatment of a debt extinguished by the death of the debtor.
    DISCUSSION: A loss from a business debt is an ordinary loss, while a loss from a nonbusiness debt is treated as a short-term capital loss. A nonbusiness bad debt is a debt other than one incurred or acquired in connection with the trade or business of the taxpayer. Therefore, when Pat died in Year 3, Laura cannot be assumed to have forgiven the loan, and the amount is not considered a gift. A short-term capital loss results (Publication 550).

7. All of the following may be deducted by a self-employed taxpayer as a transportation expense EXCEPT

    A. Getting from one workplace to another in the course of your business or profession.

    B. Commuting expenses if you work during the commuting trip using your telephone to make business calls or have business associates ride with you to and from work and you have a business discussion in the car.

    C. Visiting clients or customers after going to your office.

    D. Going to a business meeting away from your regular workplace.

Answer (B) is correct.
    REQUIRED: The transportation expenses that are deductible.
    DISCUSSION: A taxpayer's costs of commuting between the taxpayer's residence and the taxpayer's place of business or employment generally are nondeductible personal expenses. However, the costs of going between one business location and another business location are generally deductible. A taxpayer may deduct daily transportation expenses incurred in going between the taxpayer's residence and a temporary work location outside the metropolitan area where the taxpayer lives and normally works. Making business calls or meeting with associates while commuting between a residence and place of business does not permit the transportation expenses to be deducted (Publication 463).

8. Sydney is an outside salesman with a sales territory covering several states. His employer's main office is in Milwaukee, but Sydney does not go there for business reasons. Sydney's work assignments are temporary, and he has no way of knowing the locations of his future assignments. He often stays with a sister in Cleveland or a brother in Chicago over some weekends during the year, but he does not work in those areas. He does not pay his sister or brother for the use of the rooms. Which location is considered Sydney's tax home?

    A. Milwaukee.

    B. Chicago.

    C. Cleveland.

    D. Sydney does not have a tax home.

Answer (D) is correct.
    REQUIRED: The determination of a tax home.
    DISCUSSION: Sydney does not have a tax home. Sydney is an itinerant since he has no established residence (Publication 463).

9. Which of the following is true regarding a nonbusiness bad debt?

    A. It is deductible as a short-term capital loss.

    B. It is not deductible.

    C. It is deductible only if you itemize.

    D. It is deductible as a long-term capital loss.

Answer (A) is correct.
    REQUIRED: The true statement regarding a nonbusiness bad debt.
    DISCUSSION: A nonbusiness bad debt is a debt other than one incurred or acquired in connection with the taxpayer's trade or business. A shareholder loan to protect his or her investment in the corporation is not treated as a business loan. A partially worthless nonbusiness bad debt is not deductible. A wholly worthless nonbusiness bad debt is treated as a short-term capital loss. This question assumes that the nonbusiness bad debt is wholly worthless. As such, it is deductible as a short-term capital loss (Publication 550).
    Answer (B) is incorrect. Only a partially worthless nonbusiness bad debt is not deductible. **Answer (C) is incorrect.** Capital losses are deductible whether you itemize or not. **Answer (D) is incorrect.** Nonbusiness bad debt is only deductible as a short-term capital loss.

10. During the year, Susan received $4,800 as interest income and also paid an early withdrawal penalty of $1,200 on a certificate of deposit she had at a local bank. Which of the following is the correct way for Susan to report these items on her tax return?

    A. Include $3,600 interest in gross income.

    B. Include $4,800 interest in gross income.

    C. Include $4,800 interest in gross income and deduct $1,200 as an itemized deduction.

    D. Include $4,800 interest in gross income and deduct $1,200 as an adjustment to income.

Answer (D) is correct.
    REQUIRED: The way to report interest earned and the penalty for its early withdrawal.
    DISCUSSION: Interest income earned must be reported in full. The $4,800 of interest must be included in gross income. The $1,200 penalty is a deduction for adjusted gross income (Publication 550).
    Answer (A) is incorrect. Penalties are not netted against interest income. **Answer (B) is incorrect.** The penalty is deductible as an above-the-line deduction. **Answer (C) is incorrect.** The penalty is deductible as an above-the-line deduction.

11. In determining which place of business constitutes an individual's tax home, all of the following factors are taken into account EXCEPT

    A. Total time spent at each place of business

    B. The degree of business activity at each place of business.

    C. The relative income earned at each place of business.

    D. The amount of expenses incurred at each place of business.

Answer (D) is correct.
    REQUIRED: The determination of an individual's home for tax purposes.
    DISCUSSION: The IRS maintains that the tax home for an individual is the location of the principal place of business for the purpose of travel expenses. When the taxpayer has two places of business, the IRS determines the principal place of business using a test based on three factors: (1) the total time spent at each place of business, (2) the degree of business activity at each place of business, and (3) the relative income earned at each place of business (Publication 463).
    Answer (A) is incorrect. Total time spent at each place of business is one of the three factors of the test employed by the IRS. **Answer (B) is incorrect.** The degree of business activity at each place of business is one of the three factors of the test employed by the IRS. **Answer (C) is incorrect.** The relative income earned at each place of business is one of the three factors of the test employed by the IRS.

12. Which of the following is a false statement concerning use of the standard mileage rate in computing deductible transportation expenses?

A. You may use up to four cars at a time in the business.

B. You must own or lease the vehicle.

C. You may use the vehicle for hire, such as a taxi.

D. You must use the vehicle over 50% of the time for business.

Answer (D) is correct.
   REQUIRED: The item not required when using the standard mileage rate.
   DISCUSSION: The standard mileage rate is allowed under the tax code. Instead of deductions for actual costs, depreciation, etc., the standard mileage rate is deductible for business miles driven. There is no required percentage of business use of the vehicle. The standard mileage rate can be used for any occasional business use of a vehicle. The standard mileage rate is adjusted (to the extent warranted) by the IRS (Publication 463).

13. Patsy lent money to Scarlett in Year 1. Scarlett signed a loan agreement and made the agreed-upon monthly payments until May of Year 3, when she stopped making payments. Patsy called Scarlett and wrote her a letter requesting payment but received no response. Then Patsy read in the newspaper that Scarlett had filed for bankruptcy with no assets. Patsy can take a deduction for a bad debt

A. Only on her timely filed Year 3 return.

B. By amending her Year 3 return within 3 years.

C. By amending her Year 1 return.

D. On her timely filed Year 3 return or by amending her Year 3 return within 7 years.

Answer (D) is correct.
   REQUIRED: The action required to take a deduction for a bad debt.
   DISCUSSION: A nonbusiness bad debt is defined as any debt other than one acquired in connection with the taxpayer's trade or business. Bad debts must be deducted in the year they become worthless (Publication 550). Furthermore, the statute of limitations to take a deduction for bad debts and worthless securities is 7 years.
   Answer (A) is incorrect. Year 3 is not the only year in which the bad debt may be deducted. Answer (B) is incorrect. The statute of limitations for bad debts and worthless securities is 7 years. Answer (C) is incorrect. The bad debt did not occur until Year 3. Thus, Patsy may not amend her Year 1 return for the bad debt.

14. Elsie, a cash-basis taxpayer, had the following nonbusiness bad debts for the current year:

Loan to sister-in-law to buy gifts, forgiven	$ 250
Loan to neighbor made in 2015, evidenced by note	1,500
Loan to son to pay college tuition	1,200
Back rent due from tenants for 3 months	600

What is the amount Elsie may claim as nonbusiness bad debts for the current year?

A. $600

B. $1,450

C. $1,500

D. $2,100

Answer (C) is correct.
   REQUIRED: The amount claimed as nonbusiness bad debts.
   DISCUSSION: A bad-debt deduction may be taken only for a bona fide debt arising from a valid debtor-creditor relationship based upon a valid and enforceable obligation to pay a fixed or determinable sum of money. Loans to family members are usually considered to be gifts unless the taxpayer can prove that a debtor-creditor relationship and a bona fide debt existed. Here, the loan to the sister-in-law was forgiven and there is no evidence supporting a bona fide debt to the sister-in-law or the son. Therefore, the loans to the sister-in-law and son do not qualify as bona fide debts. The back rent due likewise does not qualify because Elsie is a cash-basis taxpayer and does not accrue the rent owed. The loan to the neighbor, however, does constitute a nonbusiness bad debt since it was evidenced by a note (Publication 550).
   Answer (A) is incorrect. The back rent does not qualify as a nonbusiness bad debt. Answer (B) is incorrect. The loans to the sister-in-law and son do not qualify as nonbusiness bad debts. Answer (D) is incorrect. The back rent does not qualify, but the loan to the neighbor does.

15. Which of the following is NOT deductible as an "actual car expense" by a taxpayer who uses that method to figure the deductible cost of operating his or her car for business purposes?

A. Gas.

B. Depreciation.

C. Parking fines.

D. Lease fees.

16. On January 1, Ms. C lent $10,000 to her son to pay tuition expenses for college. Her son repaid $2,000 on July 1 and Ms. C forgave the balance upon her son's agreement to enter her business. What is the amount and character of the loss that Ms. C may deduct on her individual income tax return?

A. $0

B. $4,000 short-term capital loss.

C. $4,000 long-term capital loss.

D. $8,000 nonbusiness bad debt.

17. Lisa, a self-employed taxpayer, travels to various locations during her work week. Using the following data, determine the number of miles she may claim as transportation expenses for this period:

- Monday – 40 miles, round trip, from home to her full-time job

- Tuesday – 20 miles from home to her full-time job, then 10 miles from her full-time job to her part-time job, then 30 miles to her home

- Wednesday – 60 miles, round trip, from her home to her part-time job; she did not work at her full-time job

A. 160 miles.

B. 40 miles.

C. 60 miles.

D. 10 miles.

Answer (C) is correct.
REQUIRED: The item that is not allowable as an actual car expense.
DISCUSSION: Automobile expenses pertaining to a trade or business are deductible under the tax code as ordinary and necessary business expenses. A deduction is allowed for expenses for gasoline, oil, tires, repairs, insurance, depreciation, licenses, and lease fees (Publication 463). A fine or a penalty paid to a government for the violation of any law is not a deductible business expense.

Answer (A) is correct.
REQUIRED: The amount deductible for a forgiven debt owed by a related party.
DISCUSSION: A bad debt deduction may be taken only for a bona fide debt arising from a valid debtor-creditor relationship based upon a valid and enforceable obligation to pay a fixed or determinable sum of money (Publication 550). The taxpayer either made a gift to her son of the balance of the debt owed, or released the debt in consideration of her son's agreement to enter the business. Therefore, no bad debt exists, and no deduction is available.

Answer (D) is correct.
REQUIRED: The amount of miles that can be claimed as a transportation expense.
DISCUSSION: A taxpayer's costs of commuting between the taxpayer's residence and the taxpayer's place of business are generally nondeductible personal expenses. However, the costs of going between one business location and another business location are generally deductible (Publication 463). The only miles that may be deducted as a transportation expense are the miles between Lisa's two places of business, which is 10 miles.
Answer (A) is incorrect. Only the miles that were traveled between Lisa's two places of business are deductible, not the travel from her home to a place of business. **Answer (B) is incorrect.** The 40 miles round trip are not deductible since they are from Lisa's home to her place of business, while the 10 miles between her two places of business are deductible. **Answer (C) is incorrect.** The 60 miles round trip are not deductible since they are from Lisa's home to her place of business, while the 10 miles between her two places of business are deductible.

18. For 8 months of each year, George lives in Ocala, Florida, training horses for several owners as an independent contractor and earning approximately $20,000. He rents an apartment for the 8 months. He stays in motels or rented rooms at various racetracks in other states for the other 4 months of the year during horse racing season and earns approximately $10,000. What part of George's travel expenses can be deducted?

A. All meals and lodging for the entire year.

B. Only his meals and lodging for the 4 months he is away from his tax home, Ocala.

C. None of his meals or lodging because he has no tax home.

D. One-third of his total meals and lodging because he is away from his tax home one-third of the year.

Answer (B) is correct.
   REQUIRED: The portion of travel expenses that can be deducted.
   DISCUSSION: An individual's tax home can be determined by the amount of time spent in an area and the relative amount of income earned there. Since George lives in Ocala 8 months and earns more of his income there, Ocala is considered his tax home. The 4 months that he is not in Ocala, he is on temporary assignment and may deduct meals and lodging expenses associated with his business travel (Publication 463).
   Answer (A) is incorrect. He may only deduct meals and lodging expenses while away from his tax home on temporary assignment. **Answer (C) is incorrect.** Ocala is his tax home. **Answer (D) is incorrect.** The deduction is for actual expenses incurred while on temporary assignment, not a proportion of the year's expenses based on length of a temporary assignment.

4.2 Business Meals

19. James is a sole proprietor. In May, he had the following expenses:

- $500 for use of a yacht for a day's fishing with two clients

- $50 lunch with a client with whom he discusses a new product line

- $200 for dues to the country club where he plays golf with a client who provides James with 40% of his commissions

- $50 for a cheese package given to one of his clients on the client's birthday

What is the allowed expense deduction based on these May expenses?

A. $75

B. $50

C. $800

D. $600

Answer (B) is correct.
   REQUIRED: The deductible expenses.
   DISCUSSION: Entertainment expenses are not deductible. Only the business meal and gift are. The meal expense must be ordinary and necessary for the trade or business and provided to a current or potential business customer, client, consultant, or similar business contact. The taxpayer or the taxpayer's employee must be present at the meal. James is able to deduct $50 for the lunch with a client, during which he discussed a new product line, and $50 for a cheese package as a birthday present, for a total of $100 in expenses before any limitations. However, business meal expenses are only 50% deductible, and business gifts are limited to $25. The total deduction is $50 [($50 meal × 50%) + $25 gift limit].
   Answer (A) is incorrect. The deductible amount is limited to $50. **Answer (C) is incorrect.** The $500 for the yacht and the $200 in dues for the country club are not deductible expenses. In addition, the deductible items are subject to further limitations. **Answer (D) is incorrect.** The $500 for the yacht is not a deductible expense. In addition, the deductible items are subject to further limitations.

20. Generally, which of the following expenses paid by Kathy, a salesperson, are deductible expenses?

- A. Expenses incurred in obtaining municipal bonds.
- B. Cover charges for taking a client to a nightclub.
- C. Country club dues where she entertains clients.
- D. Weekly meals with business associates at local restaurants where business is conducted and a business benefit is expected.

Answer (D) is correct.
REQUIRED: The expense that is deductible.
DISCUSSION: According to Publication 463, a business meal provided to a current or potential business customer, client, consultant, or similar business contact is deductible up to 50% if the taxpayer or the taxpayer's employee is present. The meal must be ordinary and necessary for the trade or business.
Answer (A) is incorrect. Expenses incurred in obtaining tax-exempt income are not deductible. **Answer (B) is incorrect.** No business deduction is allowed for nightclub cover charges. **Answer (C) is incorrect.** No business deduction is permitted for country club dues.

21. Five elements must be proven with respect to business meal expenses. Two of the elements are the amount and business purpose of the expense. Which of the following is NOT one of the other three elements?

- A. The duration of the meal.
- B. The time/date of the meal.
- C. The place of the meal.
- D. The business relationship of the person(s) involved.

Answer (A) is correct.
REQUIRED: The information not required to substantiate a business meal expense deduction.
DISCUSSION: The tax code disallows a deduction for business meal expenses unless the taxpayer substantiates the expenditure by adequate records or corroborating evidence showing the amount, time, place, business purpose, and business relationship to the taxpayer of each person involved. The duration of the meal does not need to be disclosed (Publication 463).

22. Phillip is actively engaged in the oil business and owns numerous oil leases in the Southwest. During the current year he made several trips to inspect oil wells on the leases and to consult about future oil wells to be drilled on these sites. As a result of these overnight trips, he paid the following:

Plane fares	$4,000
Hotels	1,000
Meals	800
Entertaining lessees	500

Of the $6,300 in expenses incurred, he can claim as deductible expenses

- A. $6,300
- B. $5,800
- C. $5,400
- D. $5,000

Answer (C) is correct.
REQUIRED: The amount of expenses incurred on overnight trips that are deductible.
DISCUSSION: A deduction is allowed for travel expenses while away from home in the pursuit of a trade or business. Meals are deductible under the tax code provided they are ordinary and necessary to the active conduct of a trade or business, the expense is not lavish or extravagant under the circumstances, and the taxpayer (or an employee) is present during the meals. Entertainment expenses are nondeductible. Meal expenses are limited to 50% of their cost. Also, all these expenditures must be substantiated (Publication 463). Assuming that Phillip's expenses meet the above requirements, his total deduction is as follows:

Plane fares	$4,000
Hotels	1,000
Meals ($800 × 50%)	400
Total deduction	$5,400

Answer (A) is incorrect. Not all of the expenses may be deducted. **Answer (B) is incorrect.** Meals are limited to 50% of the expense. **Answer (D) is incorrect.** A portion of meal expenditures may be deducted.

23. The 50% limit on deductibility of business-related expenses applies to which of the following:

    A. Meals while traveling away from home on business.

    B. Employee's reimbursed expenses under an accountable plan.

    C. Meals to customers at your place of business.

    D. Meals while traveling away from home on business and meals to customers at your place of business.

Answer (D) is correct.
    REQUIRED: The item for which the 50% limit on deductibility of business-related expense applies.
    DISCUSSION: The limit applies to meal expenses while traveling away from home on business and meals to customers at your place of business (Publication 463).
    Answer (A) is incorrect. The limit also applies to meals to customers at your place of business. **Answer (B) is incorrect.** When the taxpayer is reimbursed for the meal expense, the limitation is imposed on the party making reimbursement (i.e., employer), not the employee. For employees whose expenses are not reimbursed, a deduction generally is no longer allowed. **Answer (C) is incorrect.** The limit also applies to meal expenses while traveling away from home on business.

24. With regard to business meal expenses, all of the following statements are true EXCEPT

    A. Club dues are not allowed as a deduction.

    B. A meal expense must be both ordinary and necessary to the trade or business.

    C. The deductible limit on business meal expenses is 50%.

    D. The cost of a Super Bowl ticket where a qualified business meal will be had during the game is deductible.

Answer (D) is correct.
    REQUIRED: The false statement concerning business meal expenses.
    DISCUSSION: Only the cost of the business meal is deductible, not the game ticket (Publication 463).
    Answer (A) is incorrect. A deduction is not allowed for any expense paid or incurred with respect to an entertainment, recreation, or amusement facility. **Answer (B) is incorrect.** Any allowed expense must be ordinary and necessary to the trade or business. **Answer (C) is incorrect.** The deductible limit on business meal expenses is 50%.

25. During the year, Sally Sales purchased tickets to three theater performances and two sporting events. Each event includes a meal during the event. She purchased two tickets for each event for a total of 10 tickets, each separately stating the cost of the performance/event and the meal. Sally gave these tickets away to legitimate business customers and has records to prove it. Sally did not go with these customers to the event or performance. Sally can claim

    A. The tickets as a business gift expense.

    B. The tickets as business meal expense.

    C. The tickets as either a business gift expense or as a business meal expense, whichever is to her advantage.

    D. No deduction at all since she did not attend the event with her customers.

Answer (A) is correct.
    REQUIRED: The appropriate treatment of tickets to an event.
    DISCUSSION: Sally may only claim the tickets as a business gift expense. No business meal deduction is allowed since Sally did not attend. To treat the tickets as a business gift, Sally must limit the deduction to $25 per individual donee for each year. In addition, certain other requirements, such as adequate records, must also be maintained (Publication 463).
    Answer (B) is incorrect. Sally may not claim a deduction for a business meal expense because she (or her employee) did not attend. **Answer (C) is incorrect.** Sally may not claim a deduction for a business meal expense. **Answer (D) is incorrect.** Sally is not required to attend for the business gift expense deduction.

26. Thom is sole proprietor of a small company. He recently negotiated a substantial sale. Following the signing of the contract, Thom took the clients to dinner at a cost of $150. What is Thom's deductible meal expense on his Schedule C for the current year?

A. $112.50

B. $0

C. $150

D. $75

Answer (D) is correct.
    REQUIRED: The amount and character of deductible meal expense.
    DISCUSSION: Business meals, if properly substantiated and provided to a current or potential business customer, client, consultant, or similar business contact, are deductible subject to a 50% limitation (Publication 463). The expense must be ordinary and necessary for the trade or business and attended by the taxpayer or the taxpayer's employee. Thom attended the meal with the client. The business meal is ordinary because it is common and accepted. It is also necessary because it is helpful and appropriate for the business.
    Answer (A) is incorrect. Qualifying business meal expenses are deductible. However, they are subject to a 50% limitation, not 75%. **Answer (B) is incorrect.** This dinner qualifies and the deduction is permitted to 50% of the cost of the meal. **Answer (C) is incorrect.** Qualifying business meal expenses are deductible. However, they are subject to a 50% limitation.

27. Bethany and Michael (wife and husband) are itemizing their Schedule A expenses on their 2020 return. Michael, an employee, traveled to Japan for his employer but was not reimbursed. His meal expenses totaled $500. How much can Michael deduct for meals?

A. $250

B. $500

C. $150

D. $0

Answer (D) is correct.
    REQUIRED: The amount of meal expenses deductible if not reimbursed by the employer.
    DISCUSSION: The amount deductible for meal expenses is 50% of the actual expense. The limit also applies to the taxpayer's own meals. The expense must be ordinary and necessary for the business. However, the unreimbursed expenses of employees are nondeductible. Thus, Michael's deduction is zero.

28. Charlie, who is self-employed, paid $2,000 for tickets to a baseball game, where he will entertain clients. What is the amount Charlie can deduct as entertainment expense after any limitations?

A. $0

B. $1,000

C. $1,500

D. $2,000

Answer (A) is correct.
    REQUIRED: The taxpayer's allowable deduction for entertainment.
    DISCUSSION: Entertainment expenses, even if paid in connection with a trade or business, are nondeductible (Publication 463).

29. Bob, a calendar-year, cash-basis taxpayer, owns an insurance agency. Bob has four people selling insurance for him. The salesmen incur ordinary and necessary meal and entertainment expenses for which Bob reimburses them monthly. During the current year, Bob reimbursed his agents $10,000 for meals and $26,000 for entertainment. How much of the reimbursement can Bob deduct for the meal and entertainment expenses on his current-year federal income tax return?

A. $5,000

B. $18,000

C. $36,000

D. $10,000

Answer (A) is correct.
REQUIRED: The amount an employer may deduct for meal and entertainment expenses.
DISCUSSION: Under the tax code, an employer may deduct reimbursements to an employee subject to the restrictions (Publication 463). There is a 50% limitation for meals when the employer does not treat the expenses as compensation; thus, Bob's deduction for meal expenses is $5,000 ($10,000 × 50%). The entertainment expenses are nondeductible.

Access the **Gleim EA Premium Review System** featuring our SmartAdapt technology from your Gleim Personal Classroom to continue your studies. You will experience a personalized study environment with exam-emulating multiple-choice questions.

STUDY UNIT FIVE

ABOVE-THE-LINE DEDUCTIONS AND LOSSES

(16 pages of outline)

Deductions to compute taxable income are heavily tested on the EA exam. The business expense deductions explained in this study unit are also tested in the corporate context. You should focus on classifying each deduction as an above-the-line or itemized deduction and be able to apply each deduction limit without hesitation.

Gross income is reduced by deductions to compute taxable income. No amount can be deducted from gross income unless allowed by the Internal Revenue Code (IRC). Above-the-line deductions are deducted from gross income to arrive at adjusted gross income (AGI).

Several deductions and credits are limited by reference to AGI. Below-the-line deductions are deducted from AGI to arrive at taxable income. Above-the-line deductions are also referred to as deductions to arrive at AGI and as deductions for AGI.

5.1 EDUCATOR EXPENSES

1. Primary and secondary school educators may claim an above-the-line deduction for up to $250 in 2020 in unreimbursed expenses paid or incurred for books and supplies used in the classroom. Each taxpayer (educator) on a joint return may deduct up to $250.

    a. Books, supplies, computer equipment (including related software and services) and other equipment, and supplementary materials used in the classroom qualify for the deduction.

    b. An eligible educator is an individual who, for at least 900 hours during a school year, is a kindergarten through grade 12 teacher, instructor, counselor, principal, or aide.

    c. The term "school" is defined as one that provides elementary or secondary education, as determined under state law.

EXAMPLE 5-1   Reimbursable Educator Expenses

Tommy and Lily Jones, a married couple, are both teachers in their local school system. They each spend more than $250 in unreimbursed expenses for books and supplies used in the classroom. They are allowed an above-the-line deduction of $500 on their tax return. The deduction is taken on line 10 of Schedule 1, Form 1040.

STOP AND REVIEW! You have completed the outline for this subunit. Study multiple-choice questions 1 and 2 on page 149.

5.2 HEALTH SAVINGS ACCOUNT

1. A Health Savings Account is a tax-exempt trust or custodial account set up with a U.S. financial institution in which money can be saved exclusively for future medical expenses. This account must be used in conjunction with a high-deductible health plan.

    a. The amount that may be contributed to a taxpayer's Health Savings Account depends on the nature of his or her coverage and his or her age.

        1) For self-only coverage, the taxpayer or his or her employer can contribute up to $3,550 ($4,550 for taxpayers aged 55-64).

        2) For family coverage, the taxpayer or his or her employer can contribute up to $7,100 ($8,100 for taxpayers aged 55-64).

        3) Contributions are not allowed for taxpayers aged 65 and over or for taxpayers enrolled in Medicare.

    b. The taxpayer is not required to have the insurance for the whole year to contribute the full amount.

    c. Contributions to a Health Savings Account for 2020 include contributions made until April 15, 2021.

    d. The taxpayer cannot be claimed as a dependent on another taxpayer's return.

STOP AND REVIEW! **You have completed the outline for this subunit. Study multiple-choice questions 3 and 4 on page 150.**

5.3 SELF-EMPLOYMENT DEDUCTIONS

1. **Self-Employment Tax**

    a. A self-employed person is allowed a deduction for the employer's portion of the FICA taxes paid to arrive at his or her AGI. The deduction for the employer's share is equal to 50% of the self-employment tax or

        1) 6.2% of the first $137,700 of net self-employment income (per b. below) plus
        2) 1.45% of net self-employment income (no cap).

    b. Net self-employment income is total net self-employed profits multiplied by 92.35%.

    c. The 0.9% additional Medicare tax is on the employee's portion of FICA taxes. Therefore, the 0.9% tax is not deductible.

2. **Self-Employed SEP, SIMPLE, and Qualified Plans**

    a.   A self-employed individual can deduct specified amounts paid on his or her behalf to a qualified retirement or profit-sharing plan, such as a SEP or SIMPLE plan.

    b.   The most common self-employed retirement plan used is a SEP (Keogh) plan.

        1)   The maximum annual contribution is limited to the lesser of 25% of the self-employed earnings or $57,000 (indexed for inflation).

        2)   Self-employed earnings are reduced by the deductible part of self-employment taxes.

        3)   Contributions to the plan are subtracted from net earnings to calculate self-employed earnings, creating a circular computation. For convenience, a standard rate of 20% is used to calculate the allowed deduction.

EXAMPLE 5-2	Self-Employed SEP Qualified Plan Deduction

Alice has business income of net self-employed earnings of $125,000 before the deductible part of self-employment taxes of $9,563. The maximum annual deduction is calculated as follows:

$$(\$125{,}000 - \$9{,}563) \times 20\% = \$23{,}087$$

    c.   Another option for a self-employed taxpayer is a Savings Incentive Match Plan for Employees (SIMPLE).

        1)   Self-employed taxpayers may make both employer contributions and elective employee contributions.

        2)   Employee contributions are considered deferred compensation and are limited to $13,500 in 2020.

        3)   An employer match of up to 3% of self-employed earnings may be deducted as an above-the-line deduction.

3. **Self-Employed Health Insurance Deduction**

    a.   Self-employed individuals can deduct 100% of payments made for health insurance coverage for the individual, his or her spouse, and dependents.

    b.   The deduction is limited to the taxpayer's earned income derived from the business for which the insurance plan was established.

    c.   No deduction is allowed when the taxpayer is eligible for an employer-sponsored plan by his or her employer or an employer of a spouse or dependent.

STOP AND REVIEW! **You have completed the outline for this subunit. Study multiple-choice questions 5 and 6 on page 151.**

5.4 ALIMONY

For divorces executed before 2019, alimony and separate maintenance payments are gross income to the recipient and deductible by the payor. For divorces executed after 2018, alimony is nondeductible to the payor and not included in the gross income of the recipient. Therefore, the rules explained in the rest of this subunit apply to pre-2019 divorces only.

Qualified Payments

1. Requirements for Qualified Alimony Payments

    a. Payment is made in cash or equivalent.

    b. Payment is received by or on behalf of a spouse under a divorce or separation agreement.

        1) Payments made to a third party on behalf of a spouse at the written request of the payee spouse will qualify as alimony.

            a) Common examples of payments made on behalf of the payee spouse include mortgage payments, rent, medical costs, and education.

        2) Payments may not be for upkeep of property owned by the payor, such as when the payor has retained ownership of the house and pays the mortgage.

    c. The payee spouse and payor spouse must not be members of the same household at the time of payments.

    d. The payor spouse is not liable for any payments after the death of the payee spouse.

    e. The spouses must not file joint returns with each other.

Jointly Owned Home

2. If the divorce or separation instrument states that the taxpayer must pay expenses for a home owned by the taxpayer and his or her spouse or former spouse, some of the payments may be alimony.

Mortgage Payments

    a. If required to pay all the mortgage payments (principal and interest) on a jointly owned home, and the payments otherwise qualify as alimony, a taxpayer can deduct one-half of the total payments as alimony.

        1) If deductions are itemized and the home is a qualified home, a taxpayer can claim half of the interest in figuring deductible interest.

    b. The spouse must report one-half of the payments as alimony received.

        1) If the spouse itemizes deductions and the home is a qualified home, (s)he can claim one-half of the interest on the mortgage in figuring deductible interest.

Taxes and Insurance

    c. If required to pay all the real estate taxes or insurance on a home held as tenants in common, a taxpayer can deduct one-half of these payments as alimony.

        1) The spouse must report one-half of these payments as alimony received.

        2) If a taxpayer and his or her spouse itemize deductions, each can claim one-half of the real estate taxes and none of the home insurance.

    d. If the home is held as tenants by the entirety or joint tenants, none of the payments for taxes or insurance are alimony.

        1) If a taxpayer itemizes deductions, (s)he can claim all of the real estate taxes and none of the home insurance.

e. The following table reiterates the information on the previous page for jointly owned homes:

Expenses for a Jointly Owned Home

IF the taxpayer must pay all of the . . .	AND the taxpayer's home is . . .	THEN the taxpayer can deduct and the spouse (or former spouse) must include as alimony . . .	AND the taxpayer can claim as an itemized deduction . . .
mortgage payments (principal and interest)	jointly owned	half of the total payments	half of the interest as interest expense (if the home is a qualified home).
real estate taxes and home insurance	held as tenants in common	half of the total payments	half of the real estate taxes and none of the home insurance.
	held as tenants by the entirety or in joint tenancy	none of the payments	all of the real estate taxes and none of the home insurance.

Child Support

3. Child support payments and any part of an alimony payment designated as child support are not deductible.

   a. If any amount of an alimony payment is to be reduced based on a contingency relating to a child, such as the attainment of a certain age or graduation, the amount of the specified reduction is treated as child support.

   b. If the divorce or separation instrument specifies payments of both alimony and child support, and only partial payments are made, then the partial payments are considered to be child support until this obligation is fully paid.

      1) Any excess is treated as alimony.

EXAMPLE 5-3   Child Support and Alimony

Stephen and Chelsea were divorced in 2018 and agreed that Chelsea would pay Stephen $4,500 as part of the divorce agreement. These payments are to be made in cash and discontinued upon Stephen's death. Because the two no longer live together and do not file a joint return, these amounts would typically be treated as alimony. However, an additional provision states that $1,000 of the payment will stop upon their son Daniel reaching age 18. Accordingly, this amount is presumed to be child support and only $3,500 of the payment is deductible as alimony. Additionally, for divorces after 2018, alimony payments are not deductible by the payor or includible in income of the payee. If these two taxpayers wanted to switch to the newer treatment, the modification of the pre-2019 divorce must expressly provide for non-taxability in order to be excluded from the payee's income and nondeductible by the payor.

Alimony Recapture

4. Current tax law includes a recapture provision, which is intended to prevent large property settlements from being treated as alimony. Recapture occurs if payments significantly decrease in the second or third year after a divorce. However, recapture is not required if payments decrease due to the death of either spouse or due to the fact that they vary because they represent income from a business. The following steps show how to calculate the final amount of recapture:

    a. Second-year alimony recapture is equal to

    2nd-year alimony − ($15,000 + 3rd-year alimony)

    b. First-year alimony recapture is equal to

$$\text{1st-year alimony} - \left[\frac{\begin{array}{l}\text{(2nd-year alimony} \\ - \text{ 2nd-year recapture)} \\ + \text{ 3rd-year alimony}\end{array}}{2} + \$15,000 \right]$$

    c. Both the first-year and second-year recapture amounts are included in the payor's gross income and deducted from the payee's gross income in Year 3.

EXAMPLE 5-4	Alimony Recapture

After Lisa divorced Jed in 2018, she paid him $60,000 of alimony in 2018, $40,000 in 2019, and $10,000 in 2020. Excess alimony in 2019 was $15,000 [$40,000 − ($15,000 + $10,000)]. Excess alimony in 2018 was $60,000 − {[($40,000 − $15,000 + $10,000) ÷ 2] + $15,000}, or $27,500. In 2020, Lisa must include in gross income the total of 2018 and 2019 excess alimony, or $42,500. Jed is also allowed a deduction of the same amount.

***STOP AND REVIEW!* You have completed the outline for this subunit. Study multiple-choice questions 7 through 12 beginning on page 152.**

5.5 RETIREMENT SAVINGS (IRA) CONTRIBUTIONS

Subject to certain qualifying rules and limitations, an individual who is not an active participant in an employer-maintained retirement plan may make contributions to an IRA that are fully deductible, up to the lesser of $6,000 or 100% of his or her includible compensation. Contributions must be made by the due date of the return, without regard to extensions, to qualify for return year.

1. Compensation includes earned income but not pensions, annuities, or other deferred compensation distributions.

EXAMPLE 5-5	IRA Contribution Limit

Susan occasionally performs duties as an employee of ABC Corporation but does not participate in the employer-sponsored retirement plan. Because Susan only made $4,750 in the previous year, she may not contribute more than her earnings to her IRA. In the following year, if Susan earns over $6,000, she will only be permitted to contribute $6,000.

2. An additional $6,000 may be contributed to the IRA for the taxpayer's nonworking spouse if a joint return is filed.

    a. The combined IRA contributions by both spouses may not exceed their combined compensation for the year.

Phaseout

3. If the taxpayer is an active participant in an employer-sponsored retirement plan and has modified AGI of over $104,000 in 2020 ($65,000 in 2020 for single/head of household taxpayers and $0 for taxpayers married filing separately), the IRA deduction is proportionately reduced over a phaseout range (fully phased out at $124,000).

    a. An individual is not labeled an active plan participant due to the status of that individual's spouse.

    b. If an individual's spouse is an active plan participant, that individual's deductible contribution will be phased out when modified AGI is between $196,000 and $206,000.

    c. The following table is a summary of the effect of modified AGI on deduction if covered by a retirement plan at work:

IF the taxpayer's filing status is . . .	AND the taxpayer's modified AGI is . . .	THEN the taxpayer can take . . .
single or head of household	$65,000 or less	a full deduction.
	more than $65,000 but less than $75,000	a partial deduction.
	$75,000 or more	no deduction.
married filing jointly or qualifying widow(er)	$104,000 or less	a full deduction.
	more than $104,000 but less than $124,000	a partial deduction.
	$124,000 or more	no deduction.
married filing separately	less than $10,000	a partial deduction.
	$10,000 or more	no deduction.

    d. The following table is a summary of the effect of modified AGI on deduction if **not** covered by a retirement plan at work:

IF the taxpayer's filing status is . . .	AND the taxpayer's modified AGI is . . .	THEN the taxpayer can take . . .
single, head of household, or qualifying widow(er)	any amount	a full deduction.
married filing jointly or separately with a spouse who is not covered by a plan at work	any amount	a full deduction.
married filing jointly with a spouse who is covered by a plan at work	$196,000 or less	a full deduction.
	more than $196,000 but less than $206,000	a partial deduction.
	$206,000 or more	no deduction.
married filing separately with a spouse who is covered by a plan at work	less than $10,000	a partial deduction.
	$10,000 or more	no deduction.

4. If an individual has reached age 50 before the close of the tax year, the regular contribution limit is increased by $1,000 for tax year 2020.

5. Excessive contributions (over the deductible amount) may be subject to a 6% excise tax. The distribution of excess contribution is reported on Form 1099-R in box 2a and coded in box 7.

6. The owner of an IRA must begin receiving distributions by April 1 of the calendar year following the calendar year in which the employee attains age 72 (or the calendar year in which the employee retires, if later, for active participants in an employer-sponsored plan).

    a. Under the CARES Act, all required minimum distributions in 2020 from defined contribution plans, certain annuity plans, traditional IRAs, and Roth IRAs are waived. The waiver applies regardless of whether the taxpayer has been impacted by the COVID-19 pandemic.

10% Penalty

7. IRA distributions made before age 59 1/2 for a reason other than death or disability are subject to taxation as well as a **10% penalty** tax. Some other exceptions to the penalty include distributions for

    a. Payment of medical expenses in excess of 7.5% of AGI

    b. Qualified first-time homebuyer expenses up to $10,000

EXAMPLE 5-6	Homebuyer Exception

Sonja, a 35-year-old CPA, recently withdrew $5,000 from her IRA established in 2013 in order to cover expenses related to purchasing her first home. Because this distribution qualifies as an exception to the general rules on early withdrawal, Sonja will not owe the 10% penalty tax.

    c. "Qualified higher education expenses" for the individual or his or her lineal relatives

EXAMPLE 5-7	Early Withdrawal Penalty

Jeremy withdrew $100,000 from his IRA upon reaching age 50 in order to take a vacation to Jamaica. Because this is not a special exception to the premature distribution rules, Jeremy will be subject to the 10% penalty tax of $10,000 in addition to the regular tax on the distribution.

    d. Qualified first-year birth or adoption of a child expenses up to $5,000

    e. Qualified COVID-19-related expenses up to $100,000

STOP AND REVIEW! **You have completed the outline for this subunit. Study multiple-choice questions 13 and 14 on page 154.**

5.6 HIGHER EDUCATION DEDUCTIONS

Student Loan Interest Deduction

1. Taxpayers may deduct $2,500 of interest paid on qualified educational loans in 2020.

   a. The deduction is subject to income limits.

	AGI Phaseout Range
MFJ	$140,000 to $170,000
Single, HH, QW	$70,000 to $85,000

   b. The amount of reduction in the deduction for a single filer can be calculated as follows:

   $$\$2,500 \times \frac{(AGI - \$70,000)}{\$15,000 \text{ phaseout range}}$$

EXAMPLE 5-8   Deduction Limitation

Shane, a single taxpayer, paid $4,500 in student loan interest in 2020 and made $145,000 from his job as a web designer. As a result of his high income, despite paying more than the ordinarily deductible $2,500, Shane is unable to take any deduction for the student loan interest paid due to the phaseout.

---

   c. Qualified expenses include

      1) Room and board
      2) Tuition and fees
      3) Books, supplies, and equipment
      4) Other necessary expenses (e.g., transportation)

      NOTE: This list of qualified expenses is specific for educational interest expense deduction. Other educational deductions (credits) are not as liberal (i.e., do not allow for inclusion of room and board).

Tuition and Fees Deduction

2. An above-the-line deduction is allowed for qualified higher education expenses.

   a. The deduction is limited to $4,000 and is available in full to taxpayers whose adjusted gross income does not exceed $65,000 ($130,000 for joint filers).

   b. Taxpayers whose adjusted gross income falls between $65,000 and $80,000 ($130,000 and $160,000 for joint filers) may deduct $2,000.

   c. Married individuals filing a separate return are not eligible for the qualified higher education expense deduction.

   d. Expenses eligible for the deduction include tuition and related fees (room and board are specifically excluded) required for the enrollment or attendance of the taxpayer, the taxpayer's spouse, or any dependent for whom the taxpayer is entitled to deduct a dependency exemption. Student activity fees and expenses for course-related books, supplies, and equipment are included in qualified education expenses only if the fees and expenses must be paid to the institution as a condition of enrollment or attendance.

   e. Expenses are ineligible for the deduction if they are paid with tax-free educational assistance, such as scholarships, grants, employer-provided educational assistance, or assistance for veterans.

   f. The tuition statement (Form 1098-T) provided to the taxpayer/student is required to include the name, address, and TIN (Taxpayer Identification Number) of the taxpayer/student.

STOP AND REVIEW! You have completed the outline for this subunit. Study multiple-choice questions 15 through 18 on page 155.

5.7 OTHER ABOVE-THE-LINE DEDUCTIONS

1. Performing artists qualify to deduct employee business expenses as an adjustment to gross income if all of the following requirements are met:

    a. Performing-arts services were performed as an employee for at least two employers,

    b. At least $200 was received from each of any two of these employers,

    c. Related performing-arts business expenses are more than 10% of total gross income from the services, and

    d. AGI is not more than $16,000 before deducting these expenses.

    NOTE: Married persons not living apart at all times during the year must file a joint return and figure the requirements of a., b., and c. above separately.

2. Until 2026, the deduction for job-related relocation (i.e., moving expenses) has been removed except for military service persons on active duty who move pursuant to a military order and due to a permanent change of station.

3. **Penalty on Early Withdrawal of Savings**

    a. Deduction is allowable for an early withdrawal of funds from certificates of deposit or other time savings accounts.

    b. The deduction is taken in the year the penalty is incurred.

4. **Archer MSAs** (previously called Medical Savings Accounts) allow individuals who are self-employed or employed by a small employer and who are covered by a high-deductible health insurance plan to make tax-deductible contributions to an Archer MSA and use those funds accumulated to pay medical expenses. The deduction for an Archer MSA is not included with other medical expenses and is not subject to the 7.5% limitation.

    a. Earnings generated by the plan and distributions from an Archer MSA used to pay medical expenses are nontaxable.

    b. Distributions not used for medical expenses are taxable and subject to a 20% penalty tax, unless made after age 65 or upon death or disability.

    c. Contributions to an Archer MSA are subject to an annual limitation, which is a percentage of the deductible of the required high-deductible health plan.

    d. The Archer MSA program is limited to 750,000 people.

    e. An Archer MSA can be rolled into a Health Savings Account tax-free.

5. Jury duty pay returned to an employer is deductible by the employee from gross income.

6. Expenses from the nonbusiness rental of personal property are not deductible.

7. An above-the-line charitable contribution deduction of up to $300 is allowed for individual taxpayers who do not itemize deductions. A qualified contribution is any charitable cash contribution for which a deduction is allowable that is made to a

    a. Church or association of churches;

    b. Nonprofit educational organization; or

    c. Nonprofit medical or hospital care organization, including one for medical education or medical research.

STOP AND REVIEW! **You have completed the outline for this subunit. Study multiple-choice questions 19 through 21 on page 156.**

5.8 LOSS LIMITATIONS

1. A taxpayer's deductible loss is limited to the smallest amount of the following limitations.

   a. The loss is limited

      1) To the amount of the taxpayer's basis in the activity,
      2) By the at-risk rules, and
      3) By the passive activity rules.

EXAMPLE 5-9	Business Activity Loss

A taxpayer who owns both a lumber business and a boat for personal use incurred two losses during the tax year upon selling both the boat and the lumberyard to a colleague. Though the combined loss totaled $10,000, only the portion attributable to the business is potentially deductible. Losses on sales of property held for personal use are not deductible.

At-Risk Rules

2. The amount of a loss allowable as a deduction is limited to the amount a person has at risk in the activity from which the loss arose.

   a. A loss is any excess of deductions over gross income attributable to the same activity.

   b. The rules apply to individuals, partners in partnerships, members in limited liability companies, shareholders of S corporations, trusts, estates, and closely held C corporations.

      1) Personal holding companies, foreign personal holding companies, and personal service corporations are not subject to at-risk rules.

   c. The at-risk rules are applied separately to each trade or business or income-producing activity.

   d. A person's amount at risk in an activity is determined at the close of the tax year.

      1) A person's initial at-risk amount includes money contributed, the adjusted basis (AB) of property contributed, and borrowed amounts.

      2) Recourse debt requirements include the following:

         a) A person's at-risk amount includes amounts borrowed only to the extent that, for the debt, the person has either personal liability or property pledged as security (no more than the FMV when pledged minus prior or superior claims is included).

         b) The at-risk amount does not include debt if one of the following applies:

            i) Property pledged as security is used in the activity.

            ii) Insurance, guarantees, stop-loss agreements, or similar arrangements provide protection from personal liability.

            iii) A person with an interest in the activity or one related to him or her extended the credit.

3) Nonrecourse debt is generally excluded from the amount at risk.

   a) The amount at risk in the activity of holding real property includes qualified nonrecourse financing (QNRF).

   b) In qualified nonrecourse financing, the taxpayer is not personally liable, but the financing is

      i) Used in an activity of holding real estate;

      ii) Secured by the real property;

      iii) Not convertible to an ownership interest; and

      iv) Either obtained from an unrelated third party, obtained from a related party but on commercially reasonable terms, or guaranteed by a governmental entity.

EXAMPLE 5-10   Nonrecourse Debt

Kathy purchased a small apartment building for $200,000 using $25,000 of her own money and $25,000 borrowed from her father to make the down payment. She signed a note to pay the remainder of the purchase price to the seller. The debt to the seller was nonrecourse, secured only by the apartment building. Kathy is not at-risk for the loan from the seller because the seller is a person from whom the taxpayer acquired the property.

EXAMPLE 5-11   At-Risk Rules

Mooch purchased rental real estate with some money borrowed from his mother at commercially reasonable terms and the rest of the money borrowed from the seller. Both loans were nonrecourse and only secured by the property. Mooch is at risk for the loan from his mother because of the commercially reasonable terms and the nonrecourse loan is for real property. Regardless of the terms, Mooch is not at risk for the seller's loan.

---

4) Adjustments to an at-risk amount are made for events that vary the investors' economic risk of loss.

   a) Add contributions of money and property (its AB), recourse debt increases, QNRF increases, and income from the activity.

   b) Subtract distributions (e.g., from a partnership), liability reductions (recourse or QNRF), and tax deductions allowable (at year end).

5) Disallowed losses are carried forward.

6) If the amount at risk decreases below zero, previously allowed losses must be recaptured as income.

7) If a deduction would reduce basis in property and part or all of the deduction is disallowed by the at-risk rules, the basis is reduced anyway.

Passive Activity Loss (PAL) Limitation Rules

3.   The amount of a loss attributable to a person's passive activities is allowable as a deduction or credit only against, and to the extent of, gross income or tax attributable to those passive activities (in the aggregate).

   a.   The excess is deductible or creditable in a future year, subject to the same limits.

EXAMPLE 5-12	PAL Limitation

A wealthy taxpayer invested in an architecture partnership as a passive investor. Because the taxpayer does not engage in the business outside of occasional business consulting, any income or loss derived from the business is passive in nature. Therefore, any losses derived from the partnership may only offset passive activity gains.

4.   The passive activity rules apply to individuals, estates, trusts, personal service corporations, and closely held corporations.

   a.   Although passive activity rules do not apply to grantor trusts, partnerships, and S corporations directly, they do apply to the owners of these entities.

5.   A passive activity is either rental activity or a trade or business in which the person does not materially participate.

   a.   A taxpayer materially participates in an activity during a tax year if (s)he satisfies one of the following tests:

   1)   Participates more than 500 hours

   2)   Participation constitutes substantially all of the participation in the activity

   3)   Participates for more than 100 hours and exceeds the participation of any other individual

   4)   The activity is a significant participation activity in which the taxpayer participates more than 100 hours and the taxpayer's participation in all significant participation activities exceeds 500 hours

   5)   Materially participated in the activity for any 5 years of the 10 years preceding the year in question

   6)   Materially participated in a personal service activity for any 3 years preceding the year in question

   7)   Satisfies a facts and circumstances test proving that the taxpayer participated on a "regular, continuous, and substantial" basis

   a)   A taxpayer will not be considered to have materially participated in an activity under this test if (s)he participated in the activity for 100 hours or less during the year.

EXAMPLE 5-13	Business Passive Activity Loss

For 2020, Sally realized a $10,000 net loss (sales of $95,000 less expenses of $105,000) from operating a sole proprietorship, without regard to dispositions of property other than inventory. The income tax return also showed gross income of $5,000 ($2,500 of wages, $500 interest on personal savings, and a $2,000 long-term capital gain on business property). The excess of deductions over income was $18,400 ($5,000 gross income – $10,000 loss from business operations – $1,000 nonbusiness short-term capital loss on the sale of stock – $12,400 standard deduction).

Because she does not engage in the business outside of occasional business consulting, any income or loss derived from the business is passive in nature. Therefore, any losses derived from the partnership may only offset passive activity gains.

6. Passive activity rules do not apply to

    a. Active income, loss, or credit

    b. Portfolio income, loss, or credit

    c. Casualty and theft losses, vacation home rental, qualified home mortgage interest, business use of home, or a working interest in an oil or gas well held through an entity that does not limit the person's liability

7. Rental Real Estate

    a. All rental activity is passive.

    b. Up to $25,000 of a tax year loss from rental real estate activities in excess of passive activity gross income is deductible against portfolio or active income.

EXAMPLE 5-14   PAL Limitation -- Rental Real Estate Activities

A taxpayer has wages of $30,000, $5,000 gain from a passive partnership interest, and $35,000 loss from active rental real estate activity. The taxpayer may first offset the passive gain (i.e., $5,000) with $5,000 of the passive loss. With the remaining $30,000 passive loss, $25,000 of the nonpassive gain (i.e., wages) may be offset.

---

    1) The $25,000 limit is reduced by 50% of the person's MAGI [i.e., AGI without regard to PALs, Social Security benefits, and qualified retirement contributions (e.g., IRAs)] over $100,000.

    2) Excess rental real estate PALs are suspended. They are treated as other PALs carried over.

    c. This exception to the general PAL limitation rule applies to a person who

    1) Actively participates in the activity,

    2) Owns 10% or more of the activity (by value) for the entire year, and

    3) Has MAGI of less than $150,000 [phaseout begins at $100,000; as discussed in b.1) above].

    d. Active participation is a less stringent requirement than material participation.

    1) It is met with participation in management decisions or arranging for others to provide services (such as repairs).

    2) There will not be active participation if at any time during the period there is ownership of less than 10% of the interest in the property (including the spouse's interest).

e. Real property trades or businesses rules include the following:

1) The passive activity loss rules do not apply to certain taxpayers who are involved in real property trades or businesses.

2) An individual may avoid passive activity loss limitation treatment on a rental real estate activity if two requirements are met:

a) More than 50% of the individual's personal services performed during the year are performed in the real property trades or businesses in which the individual materially participates. *including personal service corp*

b) The individual performs more than 750 hours of service in the real property trades or businesses in which the individual materially participates.

EXAMPLE 5-15   Mixed Use of Real Property

Jack owns a vacation condo on Miami Beach. He rents it out to vacationers most of the year but uses it himself a few times each year. In each of the following situations, Jack has a different ability to deduct expenses based on the amount of personal and rental use.

Situation 1: Jack uses the condo for 4 days and rents it for 200 days at fair rental value to unrelated parties. In this situation, Jack passes the rental-use and personal-use tests and is able to take all deductions applicable, subject to the passive loss rules.

Situation 2: Jack uses the condo for 24 days and rents it for 165 days at fair rental value to unrelated parties. Jack passes the rental-use test but fails the personal-use test because he personally used the rental for the greater of 14 days or 10% of the rental days. Therefore, Jack must allocate the expenses between rental use and personal use and may deduct rental expenses to the extent of rental income.

Situation 3: Jack uses the condo for 10 days and rents the condo for 10 days at fair rental value to unrelated parties. Because he fails both the personal-use test and the rental-use test, he does not need to report the rental income, but he may not deduct the related rental expenses.

---

3) This provision also applies to a closely held C corporation if 50% of gross receipts for the tax year are from real property trades or businesses in which the corporation materially participated.

4) Any deduction allowed under this rule is not taken into consideration in determining the taxpayer's AGI for purposes of the phaseout of the $25,000 deduction.

5) If 50% or less of the personal services performed are in real property trades or businesses, the individual will be subject to the passive activity limitation rules.

EXAMPLE 5-16   PAL Limitation -- Active Participation

Lynne, a single taxpayer, has $70,000 in wages, $15,000 income from a limited partnership, and a $26,000 loss from rental real estate activities in which she actively participated and is not subject to the modified adjusted gross income phase-out rule. She can use $15,000 of her $26,000 loss to offset her $15,000 passive income from the partnership. She actively participated in her rental real estate activities, so she can use the remaining $11,000 rental real estate loss to offset $11,000 of her nonpassive income (wages).

f.   Suspension of loss is allowed.

  1) A PAL not allowable in the current tax year is carried forward indefinitely and treated as a deduction in subsequent tax years.

g.   PALs continue to be treated as PALs even after the activity ceases to be passive in a subsequent tax year, except that it may also be deducted against income from that activity.

h.   Disposition of a passive activity is subject to the following rules:

  1) Suspended (and current-year) losses from a passive activity become deductible in full in the year the taxpayer completely disposes of all interest in the passive activity.

  2) The loss is deductible first against net income or gain from the taxpayer's other passive activities. The remainder of the loss, if any, is then treated as nonpassive.

Wash Sales

8.   Losses from wash sales are not deductible.

a.   A wash sale occurs when a taxpayer sells or trades an asset at a loss and, within 30 days before or after the sale, the taxpayer does one of the following:

  1) Purchases a substantially identical asset,
  2) Acquires a substantially identical asset in a fully taxable trade, or
  3) Acquires a contract or option to buy a substantially identical asset.

b.   The unrecognized loss is added to the basis of the asset that caused the wash sale.

c.   The holding periods of the original asset and the substantially identical asset are added together.

EXAMPLE 5-17   Wash Sales
On February 16, Year 1, Fred Samson purchased 100 shares of Oscar Corporation stock at $40 per share. On July 28, Year 5, he sold the 100 shares at $25 per share. On August 10, Year 5, Fred's wife, Laura, purchased 50 shares of Oscar Corporation at $30 per share. Consequently, 50 of the shares Fred sold are not eligible for the capital loss deduction because this is considered a wash sale (spouses are treated as the same taxpayer for this purpose). A capital loss deduction is available for the other 50 shares. The sale of 50 shares resulted in a $750 loss.

STOP AND REVIEW! You have completed the outline for this subunit. Study multiple-choice questions 22 through 29 beginning on page 157.

QUESTIONS

5.1 Educator Expenses

1. Caitlin served as a kindergarten aide for 1,000 hours. She incurred $350 in expenses for books and supplies used in the classroom and was not reimbursed by the school. What amount is Caitlin entitled to as the educator's expense deduction on her income tax return?

A. $175

B. $250

C. $350

D. $0

Answer (B) is correct.
  REQUIRED: The amount that may be deducted as the educator's expense deduction.
  DISCUSSION: Primary and secondary school educators may claim an above-the-line deduction for up to $250 annually in unreimbursed expenses paid or incurred for books and supplies used in the classroom. An eligible educator is an individual who, for at least 900 hours during a school year, is a kindergarten through grade 12 teacher, instructor, counselor, principal, or aide (Publication 553). Therefore, Caitlin may deduct $250 as an educator's expense.
  Answer (A) is incorrect. The deduction is not limited to 50% of Caitlin's unreimbursed expenses. **Answer (C) is incorrect.** The maximum deduction allowed for education expenses is $250. **Answer (D) is incorrect.** Caitlin qualifies for a $250 deduction.

2. Julie and Frank were married on March 10. Both are full-time third-grade teachers, and they equally incurred a total of $350 in expenses for books and supplies used in the classroom and were not reimbursed by the school. What amount are they entitled to deduct as an education expense on their joint income tax return?

A. $175

B. $250

C. $350

D. $500

Answer (C) is correct.
  REQUIRED: The allowable education deduction for classroom expenses.
  DISCUSSION: Primary and secondary school educators may claim a $250 deduction for AGI annually in unreimbursed expenses paid or incurred for books and supplies used in the classroom. For MFJ taxpayers, the deduction limit is doubled ($500) but no more than $250 each. The deduction may not exceed actual expenses of $350.
  Answer (A) is incorrect. The allowable deduction for MFJ taxpayers doubles that of other filers but may not exceed the actual expense amount. **Answer (B) is incorrect.** The limit for non-MFJ taxpayers is $250. **Answer (D) is incorrect.** Even though the general limit for MFJ taxpayers is $500, no deduction in excess of actual expenses is allowed.

5.2 Health Savings Account

3. James (33) and his wife Erica (31) established a Health Savings Account (in conjunction with a high-deductible health plan) on February 1, 2020. The annual health plan deductible is $10,000. What is the maximum amount that can be contributed to the Health Savings Account?

    A. $8,100

    B. $6,508

    C. $7,100

    D. $10,000

Answer (C) is correct.
    REQUIRED: The maximum amount that can be contributed to a Health Savings Account.
    DISCUSSION: For family coverage, the taxpayer or his or her employer can contribute up to $7,100 for 2020. Under the last-month rule, a taxpayer is eligible for the entire year if the taxpayer is eligible on the first day of the last month of the year (Publication 969).
    Answer (A) is incorrect. The maximum amount that can be contributed for family coverage for taxpayers who have reached age 55 is $8,100. **Answer (B) is incorrect.** The contribution is not reduced by one-twelfth. **Answer (D) is incorrect.** James and Erica can contribute up to the amount of the annual health plan deductible, but not more than $7,100.

4. All of the following are true about Health Savings Accounts EXCEPT

    A. A Health Savings Account can be a tax-exempt trust.

    B. A Health Savings Account can be a custodial account set up with a U.S. financial institution.

    C. The amount that may be contributed to a taxpayer's Health Savings Account does not depend on the nature of the taxpayer's coverage and age.

    D. The taxpayer need not have the insurance for the whole year to contribute the full amount.

Answer (C) is correct.
    REQUIRED: The false statement about Health Savings Accounts.
    DISCUSSION: The amount that may be contributed to a taxpayer's Health Savings Account depends on the nature of the taxpayer's coverage and age. A Health Savings Account is a tax-exempt trust or custodial account set up with a U.S. financial institution in which money can be saved exclusively for future medical expenses. The taxpayer is no longer required to have the insurance for the whole year to contribute the full amount.
    Answer (A) is incorrect. A Health Savings Account can be a tax-exempt trust. **Answer (B) is incorrect.** A Health Savings Account can be a custodial account set up with a U.S. financial institution. **Answer (D) is incorrect.** The taxpayer is no longer required to have the insurance for the whole year to contribute the full amount.

5.3 Self-Employment Deductions

5. Bernie is a self-employed accountant in 2020. He reported net income of $54,150 on his Schedule C for 2020. During the year, Bernie paid the following: $5,200 in child support, $5,000 in alimony (pre-2019 divorce), $6,000 in medical insurance premiums, self-employment tax of $7,650, and $2,000 to his IRA plan. What amounts are deductible in arriving at adjusted gross income?

A. $22,025

B. $20,025

C. $16,825

D. $25,850

Answer (C) is correct.
   REQUIRED: The deductible amounts in calculating AGI.
   DISCUSSION: Bernie is permitted to deduct certain expenses paid during the year from gross income. Alimony for pre-2019 divorces is deductible by the payor and income to the recipient. Medical insurance premiums are 100% deductible by self-employed individuals. Also, Bernie is permitted to deduct the employer's portion of self-employment taxes paid ($3,825), calculated as $7,650 self-employment tax × 50%. Bernie is allowed a deduction for his IRA contribution (Publication 17). Therefore, the total deductions to calculate AGI are $16,825 ($5,000 alimony + $6,000 medical insurance premiums + $3,825 employer's portion of self-employment taxes + $2,000 IRA contributions).
   Answer (A) is incorrect. Child support is not deductible. **Answer (B) is incorrect.** Child support is not deductible, and the IRA is deductible. Also, only a portion of self-employment taxes is deductible. **Answer (D) is incorrect.** Child support payments are not deductible. Also, only a portion of self-employment taxes is deductible.

6. For 2019 and 2020, Malcom and Julie, husband and wife, paid health insurance premiums of $3,000 each year ($1,500 for each person). Malcom was self-employed, and his net profit was $70,000 in 2019 and $80,000 in 2020. Julie was unemployed in 2019 then took a job in January 2020. She had the option to join a subsidized health plan for the family with her employer but declined. Since this expense is not deductible on Schedule C, what amount can they deduct elsewhere as a business expense on their 2019 and 2020 joint tax returns?

A. 2019: $0; 2020: $0.

B. 2019: $0; 2020: $3,000.

C. 2019: $3,000; 2020: $0.

D. 2019: $3,000; 2020: $3,000.

Answer (C) is correct.
   REQUIRED: The amount of deduction available to self-employed persons.
   DISCUSSION: Self-employed persons may deduct from gross income 100% of amounts paid during 2020 for health insurance for themselves, their spouses, and their dependents and, normally, 100% of amounts paid during 2019. However, the couple cannot take a deduction for 2020 since Julie was eligible for an employer health plan even though she declined to participate (Publication 17).
   Answer (A) is incorrect. The expense for 2019 may be deducted. **Answer (B) is incorrect.** The expense may be deducted in 2019, and nothing is deductible in 2020. **Answer (D) is incorrect.** The full payment is deductible in 2019, and nothing is deductible in 2020.

5.4 Alimony

7. Which of the following items may be considered alimony for pre-2019 divorces?

  A. Noncash property settlement.

  B. Payments you made under a written separation agreement for the mortgage and real estate taxes on a home you owned by yourself and in which your former spouse lived rent-free.

  C. Payments made to a third party on behalf of the former spouse for the former spouse's medical expenses.

  D. Payments made for the 3-month period after the death of the recipient spouse.

Answer (C) is correct.
  REQUIRED: The item that may be considered alimony.
  DISCUSSION: Payments of cash to a third party made at the written request of the payee spouse will qualify as alimony. Payments are often made on behalf of the payee spouse, such as payments for mortgages, rent, medical costs, or education (Publication 17).
  Answer (A) is incorrect. Noncash property settlements are specifically excluded from qualifying as alimony. **Answer (B) is incorrect.** Neither payment is considered alimony because you still own the house. **Answer (D) is incorrect.** Alimony payments must cease at the death of the recipient.

8. All of the following are requirements for a payment to be alimony (under instruments executed after 1984 but before 2019), EXCEPT

  A. Payments can be in cash or property.

  B. Payments cannot be a transfer of services.

  C. Payments are required by a divorce or separation instrument.

  D. Payments are not required after death of the recipient spouse.

Answer (A) is correct.
  REQUIRED: The item that is not a requirement for a payment to be alimony.
  DISCUSSION: Section 215 allows a deduction for alimony or separate maintenance payments (Sec. 71) from a pre-2019 divorce. Section 71(b) defines alimony as any payment in cash if (1) it is received under a divorce or separation instrument, (2) the instrument does not designate the payment as not includible in gross income, (3) the payee spouse and payor spouse are not members of the same household at the time the payment is made, and (4) there is no liability to make such payment for any period after the death of the payee spouse. Thus, if the payments are in services or property and not cash, they cannot be considered alimony [Publication 17 and IRC Sec. 215, Sec. 71(b)].

9. Each of the following would be one of the requirements for a payment to be alimony under instruments executed after 1984 but before 2019 EXCEPT

  A. Payments are not made to and from spouses in the same household at the date of payment.

  B. Payments are from spouses filing a joint return.

  C. Payments are not designated in the instrument as not alimony.

  D. Payments are cash equivalents.

Answer (B) is correct.
  REQUIRED: The item that is not a requirement for a payment to be alimony.
  DISCUSSION: Section 215 allows a deduction for alimony or separate maintenance payments (Sec. 71) from a pre-2019 divorce. Section 71(b) defines alimony as any payment in cash if (1) it is received under a divorce or separation instrument, (2) the instrument does not designate the payment as not includible in gross income, (3) the payee spouse and payor spouse are not members of the same household at the time the payment is made, and (4) there is no liability to make such payment for any period after the death of the payee spouse. However, the spouses cannot file a joint tax return when the payments are being made (Publication 17).

10. Which of the following is NOT a payment deductible as alimony for pre-2019 divorces?

A. Payments for life insurance premiums required by the divorce decree.

B. Payments for medical expenses of your spouse under the terms of the divorce decree.

C. Half of the mortgage payment on a home jointly owned with your ex-spouse when required by the divorce decree.

D. Payments for child support required by the divorce decree.

Answer (D) is correct.
    REQUIRED: For pre-2019 divorces, the payments that qualify as alimony.
    DISCUSSION: For pre-2019 divorces, alimony and separate maintenance payments are gross income to the recipient and deductible by the payor. The following are the requirements for qualified alimony payments.

1. The payment must be made in cash or equivalent.
2. Payment must be received on behalf of a spouse under a divorce or separation agreement.
3. Payee spouse and payor spouse must not be members of the same household at the time of payments.
4. The payor spouse is not liable for any payments after the death of the payee spouse.
5. The spouses must not file joint returns with each other.

In addition, child support payments and any part of an alimony payment designated as child support are not deductible. Since child support payments are not deductible to the payor, these payments are not considered alimony (Publication 17).
    Answer (A) is incorrect. Payments for life insurance premiums required by a divorce decree is a payment that must be received on behalf of a spouse under a divorce decree or separation agreement, so it qualifies as alimony. **Answer (B) is incorrect.** Payments for medical expenses of your spouse under the terms of a divorce decree is a payment that must be received on behalf of a spouse under a divorce decree or separation agreement, so it qualifies as alimony. **Answer (C) is incorrect.** Half of the mortgage payment on a home jointly owned with your ex-spouse when required by a divorce decree is a payment that must be received on behalf of a spouse under a divorce decree or separation agreement, so it qualifies as alimony.

11. Your divorce decree, which became final in 2018, requires that you pay $400 a month, of which $250 s specified as child support. During 2020, you pay only $4,000, although in no month did you pay less than $250. What amount may you deduct and must your former spouse report as alimony?

A. $1,000

B. $1,800

C. $2,500

D. $3,000

Answer (A) is correct.
    REQUIRED: The amount the payor may deduct and the recipient must report as alimony for a pre-2019 divorce.
    DISCUSSION: Any part of a payment which the terms of the decree specify as a sum payable for the support of minor children is not includible in the recipient's gross income and is not deductible by the payor [Sec. 71(c)]. If any payment is less than the amount specified in the decree, it will first be considered child support, until all the child support obligation is paid. The decree specified that $250 per month ($250 × 12 months = $3,000 for the year) was for child support. For a pre-2019 divorce, the remaining $1,000 ($4,000 paid − $3,000 child support) is includible in the recipient's gross income and deductible by the payor as alimony (Publication 504).

12. For a divorce executed prior to 2019, the recapture rule for alimony may apply to a taxpayer if the taxpayer's alimony payments decrease or cease during the first

A. 5 calendar years.

B. 4 calendar years.

C. 3 calendar years.

D. 2 calendar years.

Answer (C) is correct.
REQUIRED: For a divorce executed prior to 2019, the conditions for being subject to alimony recapture.
DISCUSSION: For a divorce executed prior to 2019, if the taxpayer's alimony payments decrease or cease during the first 3 calendar years, the taxpayer may be subject to the recapture rule, which reassigns portions of payments from earlier years to later years.
Answer (A) is incorrect. Five exceeds the number of years to which the recapture rules apply to alimony payments. **Answer (B) is incorrect.** Four exceeds the number of years to which the recapture rules apply to alimony payments. **Answer (D) is incorrect.** The recapture rule applies to more than just the first 2 years of alimony payments.

5.5 Retirement Savings (IRA) Contributions

13. Mrs. Domino made deductible contributions to traditional individual retirement accounts for several years. Mrs. Domino decides to withdraw $10,000 from one of her accounts in 2020. Mrs. Domino is 61 years old. How does this transaction affect Mrs. Domino's tax return for 2020?

A. Mrs. Domino must report the entire amount of $10,000.

B. Mrs. Domino does not have to report anything because she is older than 59 1/2 years.

C. Mrs. Domino does not have to report any amount because this was not withdrawn from a Roth IRA.

D. Mrs. Domino must report all of the distribution received but can elect to use the 10-year option.

Answer (A) is correct.
REQUIRED: Inclusion of IRA distributions after 59 1/2 years of age.
DISCUSSION: Traditional IRA contributions are made before-tax. Distributions made from a traditional IRA before the age of 59 1/2 years are subject to federal income tax and a 10% penalty tax. Distributions from a traditional IRA after the age of 59 1/2 years are subject to federal income tax only and must be reported. Mrs. Domino must report the distribution from her traditional IRA (Publication 17).
Answer (B) is incorrect. This distribution is from a traditional IRA. Had this distribution been from a Roth IRA, Mrs. Domino would not declare the distribution from the IRA. Distributions from a traditional IRA must be reported. **Answer (C) is incorrect.** This withdrawal is from a traditional IRA, not a Roth IRA. **Answer (D) is incorrect.** Mrs. Domino must report the distribution in the year received. The 10-year option is not available on IRA deductions.

14. Which IRA distributions made to a taxpayer before age 59 1/2 are NOT subject to the 10% penalty tax?

A. Distributions made to pay medical expenses in excess of 7.5% of AGI.

B. Distributions up to $100,000 used for qualified first-time homebuyer expenses.

C. Distributions used for qualified day care expenses for the taxpayer's child.

D. Distributions up to $10,000 used for qualified first-year adoption of a child expenses.

Answer (A) is correct.
REQUIRED: The IRA distribution not subject to the 10% penalty tax.
DISCUSSION: Most IRA distributions made to a taxpayer before age 59 1/2 are subject to taxation, as well as a 10% penalty tax. One of the exceptions is for distributions used to pay medical expenses in excess of 7.5% of AGI. These are not subject to the 10% penalty tax.
Answer (B) is incorrect. IRA distributions only up to $10,000 used for qualified first-time homebuyer expenses are not subject to the 10% penalty tax. **Answer (C) is incorrect.** IRA distributions made to a taxpayer before age 59 1/2 used to pay qualified day care expenses are subject to the 10% penalty tax. **Answer (D) is incorrect.** Qualified first-year birth or adoption of a child expenses are not subject to the 10% penalty up to $5,000, not $10,000.

5.6 Higher Education Deductions

15. In 2020, Rusty paid $5,000 of interest on a qualified education loan. Rusty is not claimed as a dependent by another taxpayer. What is the maximum deduction available to him for the education loan interest?

A. $0

B. $2,000

C. $2,500

D. $5,000

Answer (C) is correct.
REQUIRED: The maximum amount of interest from education loans that may be allowed as a for-AGI deduction in 2020.
DISCUSSION: Individuals are allowed to deduct interest paid during the tax year on any qualified education loan. The maximum amount that may be deducted is $2,500.
Answer (A) is incorrect. Qualified education loan interest is allowed as a for-AGI deduction. **Answer (B) is incorrect.** The maximum deduction available is $2,500. **Answer (D) is incorrect.** The amount available as a deduction is limited to $2,500.

16. Kathy paid $8,000 of interest on qualified education loans in 2020. Kathy is not claimed as a dependent by another taxpayer. Since she graduated from medical school 7 years ago, she has faithfully paid the minimum interest due each month. What is the maximum deduction available to her for education loan interest in 2020?

A. $0

B. $500

C. $2,500

D. $8,000

Answer (C) is correct.
REQUIRED: The amount of qualified education loan interest available for a deduction to arrive at AGI.
DISCUSSION: Individuals are allowed to deduct interest paid during the tax year on any qualified education loan. The maximum amount that may be deducted is $2,500 in 2020 (Publication 17).

17. Mr. Jones had a student loan for qualified higher education expenses on which interest was due. The loan payments were required from July 1, 2013, until December 31, 2020. The interest payments were $1,200 per year. How much may he deduct in arriving at adjusted gross income in 2020?

A. $0

B. $600

C. $1,200

D. $2,500

Answer (C) is correct.
REQUIRED: The interest expense a taxpayer may deduct in arriving at AGI
DISCUSSION: Individuals are allowed to deduct interest paid during the tax year on any qualified education loan in 2020. The maximum amount that may be deducted is $2,500 in 2020. However, the deduction for Mr. Jones is limited to the amount paid (Publication 17).
Answer (A) is incorrect. Mr. Jones may deduct the interest paid on the school loans. **Answer (B) is incorrect.** The deduction for interest on a qualified education loan is not limited to the interest paid on the loan during the first 60 months in which interest payments are required. **Answer (D) is incorrect.** Mr. Jones is limited to the interest paid.

18. Which of the following is NOT a qualified education expense for purposes of the student loan interest deduction?

A. Tuition and fees.

B. Room and board.

C. Books, supplies, and equipment.

D. All of the choices are qualified education expenses.

Answer (D) is correct.
REQUIRED: The education expense not allowed for purposes of the student loan interest deduction.
DISCUSSION: For purposes of the student loan interest deduction, these expenses are the total costs of attending an eligible educational institution, including graduate school. They include amounts paid for the following items: tuition and fees; room and board; books, supplies, and equipment; and other necessary expenses, such as transportation (Publication 17).

5.7 Other Above-the-Line Deductions

19. Which one of the following is NOT an adjustment to total income in arriving at adjusted gross income?

- A. Interest paid on student loans.
- B. Portion of health insurance of self-employed persons.
- C. Certain contributions to a medical savings account.
- D. Contributions to a Roth IRA.

Answer (D) is correct.
   REQUIRED: The item that is not an adjustment to total income in arriving at AGI.
   DISCUSSION: Section 408A(c)(1) disallows any deduction for contributions made to a Roth IRA (Publication 17).
   Answer (A) is incorrect. Interest paid on student loans is an allowed deduction in arriving at adjusted gross income under Sec. 62. **Answer (B) is incorrect.** A portion of health insurance of self-employed persons is an allowed deduction in arriving at adjusted gross income under Sec. 62. **Answer (C) is incorrect.** Certain contributions to a medical savings account are allowed as a deduction in arriving at adjusted gross income under Sec. 62.

20. Who is eligible for an Archer MSA in 2020?

- A. All individuals who elected coverage in a high-deductible health plan.
- B. A maximum of 750,000 individuals who have elected coverage in a high-deductible health plan and are only self-employed.
- C. All individuals who elected coverage in a high-deductible health plan and are only employed by a small employer with no more than 50 workers when the Archer MSA is established.
- D. A maximum of only 750,000 individuals who have elected coverage in a high-deductible health plan and are either self-employed or employed by a small employer with no more than 50 workers when the Archer MSA is established (Publication 969).

Answer (D) is correct.
   REQUIRED: The individual who is eligible for an Archer MSA.
   DISCUSSION: The Health Insurance Act of 1996 limited the availability of MSAs during the pilot period (1997-2000) to 750,000 individuals who buy a high-deductible health insurance plan and are either self-employed or employed by a small employer. The law defines a small employer as one with no more than 50 workers. The Archer MSA Program is still limited to 750,000 people (Publication 969).

21. When funds from an Archer MSA are distributed for qualified medical expenses, these funds are

- A. Generally included in the income of the taxpayer.
- B. Allocated between contributions made by the employer and the employee, and only the amount attributed to the contributions of the employee are included in income of the taxpayer.
- C. Generally excluded from the income of the taxpayer.
- D. Always included in the income of the taxpayer.

Answer (C) is correct.
   REQUIRED: The proper treatment of distributions from an Archer MSA.
   DISCUSSION: Distributions for qualified medical expenses incurred for the benefit of the individual, a spouse, or dependents are generally excluded from income. Qualified medical expenses usually are unreimbursed expenses that would be eligible for the medical expenses deduction (Publication 17).

5.8 Loss Limitations

22. Which of the following would be considered passive activity income?

A. Alaska Permanent Funds dividends.

B. State, local, and foreign income tax refunds.

C. Personal service income.

D. None of the answers are correct.

Answer (D) is correct.
REQUIRED: The income classified as passive activity income.
DISCUSSION: There are two kinds of passive activities: (1) trade or business activities in which the taxpayer does not materially participate and (2) rental activities, unless the taxpayer is a real estate professional (Publication 925).
Answer (A) is incorrect. Alaska Permanent Funds dividends are reported as "other income" on Form 1040. **Answer (B) is incorrect.** Tax refunds are not a kind of passive activity income. **Answer (C) is incorrect.** Personal service income is earned by performing personal services in fields such as law and architecture and is classified as active income.

23. Heathcliff and Gertrude file a joint income tax return for the current year. During the current year, Heathcliff received wages of $120,000 and taxable Social Security benefits of $5,000. Gertrude actively participated in a rental real estate activity in which she had a $30,000 loss. They had no other income during the current year. How much of the rental loss may they deduct on their current-year income tax return?

A. $0

B. $12,500

C. $15,000

D. $25,000

Answer (C) is correct.
REQUIRED: The amount a taxpayer may deduct for losses from active participation in rental real estate activities when adjusted gross income is in excess of $100,000.
DISCUSSION: The $25,000 allowance of losses from active participation in rental real estate activities against nonpassive income is reduced by 50% of the amount by which adjusted gross income (determined without regard to Social Security benefits, IRA contributions, and passive losses) exceeds $100,000 [Sec. 469(i)(3)]. Heathcliff and Gertrude's adjusted gross income exceeds $100,000 by $20,000 ($120,000 wages – $100,000 threshold). Therefore, the $25,000 allowance is reduced by $10,000 ($20,000 × 50%). This leaves $15,000 of losses ($25,000 allowance – $10,000 reduction) that can be deducted (Publication 925).
Answer (A) is incorrect. The taxpayer is allowed to deduct a portion of the loss. **Answer (B) is incorrect.** The amount of the allowance is $12,500 including half of the Social Security payment, which should not be included. **Answer (D) is incorrect.** The $25,000 allowance must be reduced because income exceeds the $100,000 threshold.

24. Under the rules governing the existence of a passive activity, which of the following would NOT constitute material participation in a trade or business activity for the current tax year?

A. You participated in the activity for more than 500 hours.

B. You participated in the activity for more than 100 hours during the tax year, and you participated at least as much as any other individual for the year.

C. You participated in the activity for less than 100 hours, but you participated on a regular, continuous, and substantial basis.

D. You participated in the activity for less than 50 hours during the current year, but you materially participated in the activity for 5 of the 10 preceding years.

Answer (C) is correct.
   REQUIRED: The item that does not constitute material participation.
   DISCUSSION: Generally, to be considered as materially participating in an activity during a tax year, an individual must satisfy any one of the following tests: (1) (S)he participates more than 500 hours; (2) his or her participation constitutes substantially all of the participation in the activity; (3) (s)he participates for more than 100 hours, and this participation is not less than the participation of any other individual; (4) the activity is a "significant participation activity," and his or her participation in all such activities exceeds 500 hours; (5) (s)he materially participated in the activity for any 5 years of the 10 years that preceded the year in question; (6) the activity is a "personal service activity," and (s)he materially participated in the activity for any 3 years preceding the tax year in question; or (7) (s)he satisfies a facts and circumstances test that requires him or her to show that (s)he participated on a regular, continuous, and substantial basis [Temporary Reg. Sec. 1.469-5T(a)]. The regulations state, however, that, if an individual participates in an activity for less than 100 hours, (s)he will be precluded from applying the facts and circumstances test. Thus, it does not matter that the participation was on a regular, continuous, and substantial basis since it amounted to less than 100 hours (Publication 925).

25. Bill took out a $100,000 non-recourse loan and bought an apartment building. The building is not security for the loan. Bill spent $25,000 of his own money on repairs before he rented the apartment building to the public. Bill is single, works full-time, and earns $80,000 per year. Bill's loss from the rental real estate activity, in which he actively participates, is $30,000. He has no passive income. For what amount is Bill at-risk, and how much of Bill's passive loss from his rental activity is deductible?

	At-Risk	Passive Loss
A.	$100,000	$25,000
B.	$25,000	$25,000
C.	$125,000	$30,000
D.	$125,000	$25,000

Answer (B) is correct.
   REQUIRED: The amount at risk and the passive loss deductible from a taxpayer's rental activity.
   DISCUSSION: IRS Publication 925 states that a taxpayer is not considered at risk for his or her share of any nonrecourse loan used to finance an activity or to acquire property used in the activity unless the loan is secured by property not used in the activity. Bill took out a nonrecourse loan, and the building is not security for the loan. Since Bill is deemed to actively participate in the rental real estate activity and Bill's adjusted gross income is less than $100,000, he is allowed to deduct $25,000 against other income.
   Answer (A) is incorrect. The loan is a nonrecourse loan. **Answer (C) is incorrect.** The loan is a nonrecourse loan, and Bill is limited to $25,000 of his passive loss. **Answer (D) is incorrect.** The loan is a nonrecourse loan.
   Authors' note: Based on the information given, the answer is probably $25,000 at-risk and $25,000 passive loss. You are at-risk for qualified nonrecourse financing secured by real property used in the holding of real property. Since this problem stated that the building was not security for the loan (who would lend in that manner?) and no other real property was mentioned as security, we have to consider this loan to be non-risk.

26. During the current year, Amanda, who is single, received $110,000 in salary and realized a $30,000 loss from her rental real estate activities in which she actively participates. She contributed $2,000 to an IRA. What is the amount that Amanda may claim as loss from her current-year real estate activities?

A. $20,000

B. $21,000

C. $25,000

D. $30,000

Answer (A) is correct.
REQUIRED: The amount a taxpayer may deduct for losses from active participation in rental real estate activities when adjusted gross income is in excess of $100,000.
DISCUSSION: The $25,000 allowance of losses from active participation in rental real estate activities against nonpassive income is reduced by 50% of the amount by which adjusted gross income (determined without regard to Social Security benefits, IRA contributions, and passive losses) exceeds $100,000. Amanda's adjusted gross income exceeds $100,000 by $10,000 ($110,000 salary − $100,000 threshold) [Sec. 469(i)(3)]. Therefore, the $25,000 allowance is reduced by $5,000 ($10,000 × 50%). This leaves $20,000 of losses ($25,000 allowance − $5,000 reduction) that can be deducted (Publication 925).
Answer (B) is incorrect. The $25,000 allowance is not reduced by $4,000. Answer (C) is incorrect. The $25,000 allowance must be reduced because income exceeds the $100,000 threshold. Answer (D) is incorrect. The entire loss is not deductible.

27. Larry purchased 100 shares of ABC stock on May 31, Year 1, for $100 per share. On October 28, Year 1, he sold the 100 shares for $90 per share. On November 22, Year 1, his wife, Vickie purchased 100 shares of ABC stock for $80 per share. Vickie held the stock until September 30, Year 2. On that date, she sold the stock for $110 per share. They filed married filing separately on all returns.

A. Larry has a short-term loss of $1,000 on his Year 1 tax return.

B. Vickie has short-term gain of $3,000 on her Year 2 tax return.

C. Vickie will have a short-term gain of $3,000 on her Year 2 tax return, and Larry takes the short-term loss of $1,000 on his Year 1 tax return.

D. Vickie will have a long-term gain of $2,000 on her Year 2 tax return and Larry will not have any capital loss on his Year 1 tax return.

Answer (D) is correct.
REQUIRED: The amount of gain or loss on a wash sale.
DISCUSSION: Publication 550 states, "You cannot deduct losses from sales or trades of stock or securities in a wash sale. A wash sale occurs when you sell or trade stock or securities at a loss and within 30 days before or after the sale you:

1. Buy substantially identical stock or securities,
2. Acquire substantially identical stock or securities in a fully taxable trade, or
3. Acquire a contract or option to buy substantially identical stock or securities.

If you sell stock and your spouse or a corporation you control buys substantially identical stock, you also have a wash sale." Larry's unrecognized loss can be used to reduce Vickie's gain [$11,000 selling price − ($8,000 purchase price + $1,000 Larry's unrecognized loss) = $2,000 recognized gain]. The holding periods are added together, creating a long-term capital gain.
Answer (A) is incorrect. Larry cannot deduct losses from sales of securities in a wash sale. Answer (B) is incorrect. The holding periods of Larry and Vickie's stocks are added together, creating a long-term capital gain. The amount of Vickie's $3,000 gain is reduced by Larry's $1,000 short-term capital loss. Answer (C) is incorrect. Larry cannot deduct losses from sales of securities in a wash sale. The holding periods of Larry and Vickie's stocks are added together, creating a long-term capital gain. The amount of Vickie's $3,000 gain is reduced by Larry's $1,000 short-term capital loss.

28. Barry is a lawyer. He owns 10 apartment buildings that are managed by his brother's real estate business. At the end of the year, the apartment buildings resulted in a $40,000 loss. Barry earned $80,000 in wages. His wife, Claire, earned $20,000 from her part-time job. Their other income included $5,000 in dividends from their mutual funds. They had no other income. How much of the rental loss can Barry use assuming Barry actively participates in the apartment buildings?

A. $0

B. $25,000

C. $40,000

D. $22,500

Answer (D) is correct.

REQUIRED: The amount of rent allowable as a loss.

DISCUSSION: Any rental activity is a passive activity, whether or not the taxpayer participates in the activity. An individual who actively participates in a rental real estate activity may use up to $25,000 of net losses from the rental real estate activity to offset other income. The $25,000 is reduced by 50% of the amount by which AGI (determined without regard to Social Security, IRA contributions, and passive losses) exceeds $100,000. Barry has AGI of $105,000 ($80,000 wages + $20,000 Claire's income + $5,000 dividends). Accordingly, his allowable $25,000 deduction will be reduced by $2,500 [($105,000 – $100,000) × 50%] and is therefore $22,500 ($25,000 deduction – $2,500 reduction). If Barry does not actively participate, he is not allowed a deduction (Publication 925).

Answer (A) is incorrect. Barry may use a portion of the rental loss. Answer (B) is incorrect. Barry's loss must be reduced by 50% of the excess of his AGI over $100,000. Answer (C) is incorrect. Barry may not deduct the entire loss.

29. Tom Brown, who is single, owns a rental apartment building property. This is the only rental property that Tom owns. He actively participates in this rental activity as he collects the rents and performs ordinary and necessary repairs. In 2020, Tom had a loss of $30,000 on this rental activity and had no reportable passive income. His adjusted gross income, without regard to this rental loss, is $60,000. How much of the rental loss may Tom deduct on his 2020 return?

A. $30,000

B. $25,000

C. $0

D. $6,000

Answer (B) is correct.

REQUIRED: The deductibility of passive activity losses when the taxpayer actively participates.

DISCUSSION: All rental activity is passive. A person who actively participates in rental real estate activity is entitled to deduct up to $25,000 of losses from the passive activity from other-than-passive income, provided that the individual's income does not exceed $100,000. Single individuals and married individuals filing jointly can qualify for the $25,000 amount. Married individuals who live together for the entire year and file separately cannot qualify. Thus, Tom may deduct $25,000 of the loss (Publication 925).

Answer (A) is incorrect. Tom is not allowed to deduct the entire amount of the loss. Tom may carry over the remaining $5,000. Answer (C) is incorrect. Tom can deduct $25,000 of the passive activity losses in the current tax year. Answer (D) is incorrect. There is no 10%-of-AGI limitation on the amount of losses that may be deducted.

Access the **Gleim EA Premium Review System** featuring our SmartAdapt technology from your Gleim Personal Classroom to continue your studies. You will experience a personalized study environment with exam-emulating multiple-choice questions.

STUDY UNIT SIX

ITEMIZED DEDUCTIONS

(18 pages of outline)

Below-the-line deductions are all the deductions that may be subtracted from AGI to arrive at taxable income. Each below-the-line deduction is either an itemized, standard, or qualified business income deduction.

Adjusted gross income
- Greater of allowable itemized deductions on Schedule A or the standard deduction
- Qualified business income deduction (Study Unit 7, Subunit 1)
= Taxable income

EXAMPLE 6-1	Standard vs. Itemized Deduction

David is single and has itemized deductions of $10,700. Because this amount is less than the $12,400 standard deduction, he would instead use the standard deduction and would not submit Schedule A to the IRS as part of his Form 1040 (most tax software automatically prevents the taxpayer from filing Schedule A in such a case).

6.1 MEDICAL EXPENSES

7.5% of Adjusted Gross Income (AGI)

Amounts paid for qualified medical expenses that exceed 7.5% of AGI may be deducted.

1. To qualify for a deduction, an expense must be paid during the taxable year for the taxpayer, the taxpayer's spouse, or a dependent and must not be compensated for by insurance or otherwise during the taxable year, although the service could have been rendered in a prior year.

    a. The deduction is allowed for a person who was either a spouse or a dependent at the time medical services were rendered or at the time the expenses were actually paid.

        1) Medical expenses charged on a credit card are deductible in the year the medical expenses were incurred, not when the credit card bill is paid.

        2) To qualify as a dependent, the person (dependent)

            a) Must have over half of his or her support for the year paid for by the taxpayer;

            b) Must fall within a family relationship (including adopted children or any other person who lived with the taxpayer all year as a member of the taxpayer's household); and

            c) Must be a citizen, national, or resident of the U.S., Canada, or Mexico during a portion of the tax year.

    b. However, the individual need not satisfy the gross income test or the joint return test, and a child of divorced parents is treated as a dependent of both parents.

2. Deductible medical expenses are amounts paid for

    a. Diagnosis, cure, mitigation, treatment, or prevention of disease or for the purpose of affecting any structure or function of the body (i.e., to alleviate or prevent a physical or mental disability or illness)

    b. Medical insurance

    c. Qualified long-term care premiums and services

    d. Smoking cessation programs and prescribed drugs designed to alleviate nicotine withdrawal

---

EXAMPLE 6-2   Deductible Medical Expenses

If a taxpayer undergoes facial reconstructive surgery as a result of severe burns, it is considered a deductible medical expense. However, if a taxpayer has elective facial surgery for cosmetic reasons (not related to a deformity), it is not deductible.

Professional Services

3. Deductible medical expenses include amounts paid to physicians, surgeons, dentists, chiropractors, osteopaths, chiropodists, podiatrists, psychiatrists, psychologists, etc., solely in their professional capacity.

Activity or Treatment

4. A medical expense deduction is **not allowed** for amounts paid for any activity or treatment designed merely to **improve** an individual's **general health** or sense of wellness, even if recommended by a physician.

    a. Examples include participation in a health club or a weight-loss institute.

        1) Such expenses **may be deductible** if the services are prescribed by a physician who provides a written statement that they are necessary to alleviate a physical or mental defect or illness.

Institutional Care

5. The cost of in-patient hospital care (including meals and lodging) is deductible as a medical expense.

    a. If the principal reason an individual is in an institution other than a hospital (a special school for the handicapped, a rest home, etc.) is the need for and availability of the medical care furnished by the institution, the full costs of meals, lodging, and other services necessary for furnishing the medical care are all deductible.

EXAMPLE 6-3   Inpatient Hospital Care Expenses

A parent takes a child to see a medical specialist out of state. The parent and child spend 2 nights at a hotel in the city of the specialist. They are able to deduct $200 for lodging ($50 per night × 2 nights × 2 individuals). However, if the child stays overnight under medical supervision, the full cost of inpatient care is deductible.

Prescription

6. Aside from insulin, only **medicines and drugs** that require a prescription are qualified medical expenses.

Capital Expenditures

7. The following are considered deductible medical expenses:

    a. Eyeglasses or contact lenses
    b. A guide dog
    c. Wheelchairs, crutches, or artificial limbs
    d. Special beds
    e. Air conditioning
    f. Dehumidifying equipment

8. Expenditures for new building construction or for permanent improvements to existing structures primarily for medical care may be deductible in part as a medical expense.

    a. The excess of the cost of a permanent improvement over the increase in value of the property is a deductible medical expense.

        1) Although the cost of the capital asset is not deductible, the cost of operating and maintaining the asset may be deductible when the asset is operated primarily for medical care.

    b. Construction of handicap entrance or exit ramps, installation of elevators, widening of doorways, or lowering of kitchen cabinets or equipment may each qualify.

EXAMPLE 6-4   **Medical Expenses -- Capital Expenditures**

Billy had bypass heart surgery in February 2020. At the advice of his doctor, he had an elevator installed in his home so that he would not have to climb stairs. The costs associated with this capital improvement are as follows:

Cost of elevator installed June 30, 2020	$5,000
Increase in value of home due to elevator	2,500
Maintenance and repair of elevator, September 30, 2020	500

The taxpayer may deduct the cost of the elevator installed (less any increase in FMV) plus any maintenance, repair, and operating expenses. Thus, the total allowable deduction is

Cost of Elevator Installed	$5,000
Less: Increase in FMV	(2,500)
Deductible Capital Expenditure	$2,500
Plus: Maintenance and Repair	500
Total Allowable Medical Expenses	$3,000

The maintenance and repair expenses might have qualified as medical expenses regardless of whether the elevator expenditure was deductible.

Travel

9. Amounts paid for transportation essential to (and primarily for) medical care are deductible.

    a. This includes the transportation cost of traveling to a warm climate on a doctor's order to alleviate a specific chronic ailment.

10. The taxpayer may choose between actual expenditures (e.g., taxis, airfare) or $0.17 per mile for 2020 (plus the cost of tolls and parking).

11. Expenditures for lodging are deductible up to $50 per night per individual.

12. The cost of meals is not deductible.

Insurance

13. Premiums paid for medical insurance that provides for reimbursement of medical care expenses are deductible.

    a. Premiums paid on a policy that merely pays the insured a specified amount per week, etc., are not deductible.

    b. Premiums paid for membership in an association that gives cooperative (free choice) medical service are deductible.

Medicare

14. The basic cost of Medicare insurance (Medicare Part A) is not deductible unless voluntarily paid by the taxpayer for coverage.

    a. The extra cost of Medicare (Medicare Part B) is deductible.

Payment after Death

15. If a decedent's own medical expenses are paid by his or her estate within 1 year beginning on the day after the decedent's death, the expenses may be deducted on the decedent's tax return for the year incurred.

    a. Alternatively, the estate can deduct medical expenses as a claim against the estate for federal estate tax purposes.

EXAMPLE 6-5   **Payments after Death**

George died on February 2, 2020, and his estate paid his final medical expenses on November 15, 2020. These expenses can be deducted on either George's final (2020) tax return (Form 1040) or the estate's income tax return (Form 1041), but not both.

Adopted Child

16. The amount paid by an adopting parent for medical expenses rendered directly to a child before his or her placement in the adopting parent's home constitutes a medical expense, provided that

    a. The child qualifies as a dependent of the adopting parent at the time that the medical services are rendered or at the time the fees therefore are paid,

    b. The adopting parent can clearly substantiate that any deduction claimed is directly attributable to the medical care of the child, and

    c. The medical expenses are paid by the adopting parent or his or her agent for the medical care of the particular child.

        1) Reimbursement for expenses incurred and paid by someone other than the taxpayer prior to adoption negotiations are not considered deductible medical expenses.

STOP AND REVIEW! **You have completed the outline for this subunit. Study multiple-choice questions 1 through 5 beginning on page 179.**

6.2 TAXES

A taxpayer who itemizes deductions is permitted to deduct the full amount of certain taxes that are paid and incurred during the taxable year, subject to the $10,000 ($5,000 MFS) limit on total state and local taxes.

Real Property

1. State and local real property taxes are deductible by the person upon whom they are imposed (i.e., the owner) in the year in which they were paid or accrued.

   a. If real property is bought or sold during the year, the real property tax is apportioned between the buyer and the seller on the basis of the number of days each one held the property during the real property tax year.

      1) The purchaser is presumed to own the property on the date of sale.

      2) Any taxes paid by an owner (e.g., purchaser) for a period in which someone else owned (e.g., seller) the property are not deductible but are added to the basis (e.g., cost) of the property.

   b. Taxes paid to a financial institution and held in escrow are deductible when the financial institution pays the funds over to the taxing body.

   c. Service charges for police and fire protection may be deductible if the funds are paid into a general revenue fund.

   d. Special assessments for local improvements increase the basis of the property and are not deductible. *– HOA not deductible*

EXAMPLE 6-6	Nondeductible Property Taxes

In April of Year 2, property taxes are assessed for Year 1. The taxes are paid by the due date in Year 2. The taxes are deductible on the Year 2 return. If the owner in Year 2 did not own the property in Year 1, then payment for Year 1 taxes are not deductible but are added to the basis of the property.

   e. The allowance for foreign real property taxes ended in 2017.

Ad Valorem and Personal Property

2. State and local ad valorem and personal property taxes are deductible only if the tax is

   a. Actually imposed,
   b. Imposed on an annual basis, and
   c. Substantially in proportion to the value of the property.

EXAMPLE 6-7	Deductions from Value-Based Taxes

Registration or licensing of vehicles is deductible if the tax is based on the value of the vehicle.

Income Taxes

3. State and local income taxes are deductible.

4. Foreign income taxes paid are deductible, unless the Foreign Tax Credit is claimed.

5. Individual taxpayers may claim an itemized deduction for general state and local sales taxes in lieu of state income tax. *greater of Sales or State income*

    a. Taxpayers can deduct either actual sales tax amounts or a predetermined amount from an IRS table.

Nondeductible Taxes

6. The following taxes are not deductible:

    a. Federal taxes on income, estates, gifts, inheritances, legacies, and successions.

        1) A deduction may be available on the estate tax return for income taxes paid on account of a decedent.

    b. State taxes on cigarettes and tobacco, alcoholic beverages, gasoline, licensing/ registration, estates, gifts, inheritances, legacies, and successions.

    c. Licensing/registration fees of highway motor vehicles (if based on the weight instead of the value of the vehicle).

    d. Sales tax on business property. It is added (i.e., capitalized) to the basis of the acquired property.

STOP AND REVIEW! You have completed the outline for this subunit. Study multiple-choice questions 6 through 11 beginning on page 181.

6.3 INTEREST EXPENSE

Personal Interest

1. The general rule is that no personal interest may be deducted.

2. Personal interest includes interest on credit card debt, revolving charge accounts and lines of credit, car loans, medical fees and premiums, home acquisition debt greater than the allowed deduction limit, etc. Personal interest also includes any interest on underpaid tax liabilities.

EXAMPLE 6-8   Personal Interest

Mr. Griffin paid the following in interest in the current year: $3,000 on his credit card, $1,200 on his car loan, and $500 to the IRS for failing to meet the required tax withholding. All of these interest payments are considered personal interest, so Mr. Griffin is unable to deduct any of the $4,700.

EXAMPLE 6-9   Personal Interest from Medical Expenses

Carl Wynn paid $8,000 in medical expenses related to his 5-year-old son's broken leg. In order to pay these expenses, Carl took out a loan, which incurred interest of $500. Carl may deduct medical expenses in excess of 7.5% of his AGI. However, he may not deduct the $500 of interest because it is considered personal interest.

---

3. Personal interest does not include

   a. Interest on trade or business debt
   b. Investment interest
   c. Passive activity interest
   d. Qualified residence interest
   e. Interest on the unpaid portion of certain estate taxes
   f. Student loan interest

Investment Interest

4. The IRC allows the deduction of a limited amount of investment interest as an itemized deduction.

5. Investment interest is interest paid or incurred (on debt) to purchase or carry property held for investment.

   a. Generally, investment interest includes the following:

      1) Interest allocable to portfolio income under the PAL rules

         a) Passive activity interest is includible with passive activities and deductible within the passive loss rules.

      2) Any interest derived from an activity involving a trade or business in which the taxpayer does not materially participate and which is not treated as a passive activity under the PAL rules

      3) Any deductible amount in connection with personal property used in a short sale

   b. Investment interest does **not** include qualified residence interest, interest for generating tax-exempt income, or passive activity interest.

  c. Limit.

    1) Investment interest may be deducted only to the extent of net investment income.

      a) Net investment income is any excess of investment income over investment expense(s) (other than interest expense).

    2) Investment income is

      a) Nontrade or nonbusiness income from

        i) Interest

        ii) Dividends (not subject to the capital gains tax)

        iii) Rents, royalties, and other gross income from property held for investment

      b) Net gain on the disposition of property held for investment

        i) A taxpayer may elect to treat all or a portion of long-term capital gains and qualified dividends as investment income.

      c) Income treated as gross portfolio income under the PAL rules

      d) Income from interests in activities that involve a trade or business in which the taxpayer does not materially participate if the activity is not treated as passive activity under the PAL rules

    3) Investment income does not include income from a rental real estate activity in which the taxpayer materially participates.

  d. Disallowed investment interest is carried forward indefinitely. It is deductible to the extent of investment income in subsequent tax years.

EXAMPLE 6-10   **Disallowed Investment Interest Carryforward**

Kayla borrowed money to invest. In Year 3, due to a bad market downturn, her net investment income was $4,500 before considering $15,000 of investment interest expense. In Year 3, she may deduct $4,500 of investment interest expense, and the remaining $10,500 is carried over to Year 4 to be applied against net investment income.

Residence Interest

6. Qualified residence interest (as discussed in Publication 530) is deductible on no more than $750,000 of the sum of acquisition and home equity indebtedness ($375,000 if married filing separately).

  a. Qualified residence interest is interest paid or accrued during the tax year on acquisition or home equity indebtedness that is secured by a qualified residence (Form 1098).

    1) Ministers and military personnel can deduct mortgage interest on their homes even when they receive a parsonage or military allowance that is excludable from gross income.

  b. A qualified residence is the principal residence of the taxpayer and any one other residence owned by the taxpayer and used for personal purposes for the greater of 14 days or 10% of the number of days during the year in which it is rented.

  c. A taxpayer who has more than two residences may select, each year, the residences used to determine the amount of qualified residence interest.

d.   Acquisition indebtedness is debt incurred in acquiring, constructing, or substantially improving a qualified residence. The debt must be secured by such residence.

   1)   Any debt that is refinanced is treated as acquisition debt to the extent that it does not exceed the principal amount of acquisition debt immediately before refinancing.

e.   Home equity indebtedness is all debt other than acquisition debt that is secured by the qualified residence. For tax years 2018-2025, the home equity debt must be used to buy, build, or substantially improve the qualified residence. This means the prior allowance to use the funds for other personal expenses, such as college tuition, is suspended until 2026.

EXAMPLE 6-11   Nondeductible Home Equity Interest

After 3 years of home ownership, a taxpayer's home has increased in value by $150,000. In 2020, the taxpayer took out a $100,000 home equity loan to pay for her children's college education. However, interest on a home equity loan that is not used to buy, build, or substantially improve a qualified residence is not deductible.

---

   1)   Home equity indebtedness cannot exceed the fair market value of the residence (reduced by any acquisition debt).

Maximum home equity indebtedness = Property FMV – Acquisition indebtedness

---

EXAMPLE 6-12   Itemized Deductions -- Interest

A taxpayer with AGI of $100,000 made the following transactions in Year 1:

   Paid $3,000 interest on a bank loan

   Using the loan, purchased interest-bearing bonds with interest income of $10,000 in Year 1

      No other investment income was earned in Year 1.

   Paid personal credit card interest of $650

   Paid interest in the amount of $12,000 on home mortgage for Year 1

The $15,000 total interest expense in calculating itemized deductions for Year 1 is calculated as follows:

Net investment income	$10,000	
Deductible investment expense		$ 3,000
Home mortgage interest		12,000
Total interest expense		$15,000

NOTE: Deductible investment interest is limited to net investment income. In this example, net investment income is greater than investment expense; therefore, the total expense of $3,000 is deductible. Credit card interest is a personal interest expense in this example and is not deductible.

Points Paid

    f.   Points paid by the borrower with respect to a home mortgage are prepaid interest, which is typically deductible over the term of the loan.

        1)   Amounts paid as points may be deducted in the year paid if

            a)   The loan is used to buy or improve a taxpayer's principal home and is secured by that home,

            b)   The settlement statement clearly designates the points or loan origination fees,

            c)   The points are computed as a percentage of the principal loan amount,

            d)   Payment of points is an established business practice in the area where the loan is made, and

            e)   The points paid do not exceed points generally charged in the area.

        2)   Generally, points paid to refinance a mortgage are not deductible in full in the year paid. This is true even if the new mortgage is secured by the taxpayer's main home.

    g.   Points paid by the seller are selling expenses that reduce the amount realized on the sale.

        1)   The purchaser can elect to deduct points on the acquisition indebtedness of a principal residence by reducing the basis by the amount of the points.

Mortgage Insurance Premiums

7.   Qualified mortgage insurance premiums are deductible as interest expense for 2007-2021 (Form 1098).

    a.   Applies only to policies issued from 2007-2021.

    b.   The insurance must be on acquisition indebtedness.

    c.   The deduction phases out for adjusted gross incomes exceeding $100,000 ($50,000 for married filing separately). The deduction is completely phased out for adjusted gross incomes exceeding $110,000 ($55,000 for married filing separately).

8.   To compute interest deductions, individuals must allocate interest expenditures as investment interest, personal interest, trade or business interest, portfolio interest, or interest connected to passive activities.

    a.   Interest is allocated by tracing the disbursement of the proceeds of the debt to which it relates to the expenditure for which the proceeds are used.

STOP AND REVIEW! **You have completed the outline for this subunit. Study multiple-choice questions 12 through 15 beginning on page 183.**

6.4 CHARITABLE CONTRIBUTIONS

1. Charitable contributions are deductible only if they are made to qualified organizations.
2. Donations can be made in the form of cash or noncash property.
3. All rights and interest to the donation must be transferred to the qualified organization.
4. Generally, a deduction is allowed in the year the contribution is paid, including amounts charged to a bank credit card.
5. Generally, the FMV of the property is deducted.
6. The deduction is generally limited to 50% (100% for cash contributions) of the taxpayer's AGI; however, sometimes the limit is 30% or 20%.

Qualified Organizations

7. Qualified organizations can be either public charities or private foundations.

    a. Generally, a public charity is one that derives more than one-third of its support from its members and the general public.

    b. Qualified organizations include

        1) Corporations, trusts, community chests, funds, or foundations, created or organized in the U.S. and operated exclusively for religious, charitable, scientific, literary, or educational purposes, or for the prevention of cruelty to children or animals.

        2) Posts or organizations of war veterans.

        3) Domestic fraternal societies, orders, or associations only if the contribution is to be used exclusively for religious, charitable, scientific, literary, or educational purposes, or for the prevention of cruelty to children or animals.

Receipt

8. Donations must meet the following requirements:

    a. Clothing and household items donated must be in good or better condition.

        1) The exception to this rule is that a single item donation in less than good condition with a more than $500 value is deductible with a qualified appraisal.

    b. Cash or cash equivalent donations require a bank record, or receipt, letter, etc., from the donee organization regardless of the amount. The receipt, etc., must

        1) Be written;

        2) State the name of the organization;

        3) Include the date and amount of the donation;

        4) State whether the qualified organization gave the donor any goods or services as a result of the contribution; and

        5) Be obtained on or before the earlier of

            a) The date the tax return is filed for the year of contribution or
            b) The date, including extensions, for filing the return.

    c.   Donations of $250 or more require substantiation by a contemporaneous written receipt from the organization (the bank record alone is insufficient).

EXAMPLE 6-13   **Donation of Goods**

The local chamber of commerce hosts an annual food drive for needy children (a charitable cause). While dues and other donations to the chamber of commerce are not charitable contributions (though they may be business expenses), donations of food, cash, and other property to the food drive are considered charitable donations because the donations are exclusively for a charitable purpose. These are deductible by the taxpayer as charitable contributions.

Property

9.   If a donation is in the form of property, the amount of the donation depends upon the type of property and the type of organization that receives the property.

    a.   Capital gain property is property on which a long-term capital gain would be recognized if it were sold on the date of the contribution.

    b.   Ordinary income property is property on which ordinary income or short-term capital gain would be recognized if it were sold on the date of the contribution.

    c.   The chart on page 175 has donation amounts.

    d.   If the donee organization disposes of the donated property (valued at $500 or more) within 3 years of acquisition, the donee organization must file Form 8282 within 125 days and provide a copy to the donor.

        1)   Similarly, if an organization sells a qualified donated vehicle, the donee organization must send a Form 1098-C to the donor within 30 days of sale in order for the deduction to exceed $500.

Limitations

10.   There are basically two types of charitable organizations: those classified as 50% limit organizations and all others that are classified as **non**-50% limit organizations.

50% Limit Organizations

    a.   The 50% limit organizations, which encompass the majority of qualified charitable organizations, are generally public organizations (although some private foundations are acceptable) such as the following:

        1)   Churches

        2)   Educational organizations

        3)   Hospitals and certain medical research organizations

        4)   Organizations that are operated only to receive, hold, invest, and administer property and to make expenditures to or for the benefit of state and municipal colleges and universities

        5)   The United States or any state, the District of Columbia, a U.S. possession (including Puerto Rico), a political subdivision of a state or U.S. possession, or a Native American tribal government

        6)   Private operating foundations

        7)   Private nonoperating foundations that make qualifying distributions of 100% of contributions within 2 1/2 months following the year they receive the contribution

Non-50% Limit Organizations

b.   Non-50% limit organizations encompass all other qualified charities that are not designated as 50% limit organizations.

   1)   They are primarily composed of other private organizations.
   2)   Charitable contribution deductions are subject to limitations.

      a)   The overall limitation on charitable deductions is 50% (100% for cash contributions) of AGI (applicable to the total of all charitable contributions during the year), but certain contributions may be individually limited to 30% or 20% of AGI, depending on the type of contribution given (discussed below and on page 176).

      b)   Any donations that exceed this limitation can be carried forward and deducted in the next 5 tax years.

EXAMPLE 6-14   **Charitable Contributions -- Calculation**

Celina has an AGI of $100,000. She donates $70,000 cash to her church. She also donates stock with a basis of $35,000 and held short-term to the Red Cross. She first takes a $35,000 deduction for the stock in the 50% category. She then takes $65,000 ($100,000 × 100% − $35,000) of the cash donation as a deduction in the 100% category. This leaves her with a $15,000 carryover in the 100% category to be used within the following 5 tax years.

---

c.   Further limitations

Regular 30% Limitation

   1)   This 30% limit applies to gifts to all qualified charitable organizations other than 50% limit organizations. (However, if capital gain property is donated, it may be subject to the 20% limitations discussed on page 176.) The chart on the next page summarizes all the rules.

Special 30% Limitation for Capital Gain Property

   2)   A special 30% limitation applies to gifts of capital gain property given to 50% limit organizations, but is only applicable if the donor elects **not** to reduce the fair market value of the donated property by the amount that would have been long-term capital gain if he had sold the property. If the reduction is elected, then only the 50% (100% for cash contributions) limitation applies. The chart on the next page summarizes all the rules.

Private operating foundation - 50%

other private organization - non-50% limit

50% Limit Organizations		
(Mainly Public)		
Form of Property	**Amount of Donation**	**Limitation**
Cash	Cash amount	100% AGI
Capital Gain Property	FMV (elect not to reduce FMV by potential long-term capital gain)	30% AGI (special limit)
• Tangible personal property unrelated to donee's purpose	Lower of FMV or AB	50% AGI
• Election to reduce property to adjusted basis	Lower of FMV or AB	50% AGI
Ordinary Income Property	Lower of FMV or AB	50% AGI
Services	Unreimbursed expenses	50% AGI
Non-50% Limit Organizations		
(Mainly Private)		
Cash	Cash amount	30% AGI (regular limit)
Capital Gain Property	Lower of FMV or AB	Lesser of 20% AGI or excess of 30% AGI over contributions to public charities
Ordinary Income Property	Lower of FMV or AB	30% AGI (regular limit)
Services	Unreimbursed expenses	30% AGI (regular limit)

EXAMPLE 6-15   Charitable Contribution Deduction

A single taxpayer had AGI of $80,000 in Year 6. On June 5, Year 6, the taxpayer donated land and stock to a church. The taxpayer purchased the land as an investment in Year 1 for $5,000 and purchased the stock on January 14, Year 6, for $1,500. On the day of donation, the land's fair market value was $9,000 and the stock's fair market value was $1,860.

The charitable contribution deduction for Year 6, in the amount of $10,500, is calculated as follows:

Property	Form of Property	Nature of Deduction	Deductible Amount
Land held for investment greater than 1 year	Capital gain property	FMV	$ 9,000
Stock held for investment less than 1 year	Ordinary income property	Lower of FMV or adjusted basis	1,500
Total deductible contribution			**$10,500**

20% Limitation

3) This limitation applies to capital gain property donated to non-50% limit charities. The limit is actually the lesser of 20% of AGI or 30% of AGI minus capital gain contributions to public charities.

4) In accounting for the different limitations, the order in which each is considered is as follows:

   a) 50%, then
   b) 30%, then
   c) 20%, and finally,
   d) 100% cash contributions.

5) In carrying over excess contributions to subsequent tax years, the excess must be carried over to the appropriate limitation categories.

   a) If a contribution in the 30% category is in excess of the limit, the excess is carried over and subject to the 30% limitation in the next year.

EXAMPLE 6-16   Charitable Contributions -- Calculation

Rich has an AGI of $100,000. He donates $85,000 cash to his former university (100% limitation) and $25,000 to his private foundation (30% limitation). In the current year, he can deduct $100,000, which consists of, first, all $25,000 to the 30% organization [i.e., the lesser of the $25,000 donation or the $30,000 AGI limitation ($100,000 AGI × 30%)], and second, $75,000 to the 100% organization {i.e., the lesser of the $85,000 donation or the $75,000 AGI limitation after reduction for the $25,000 donation to the 30% organization [($100,000 × 100%) − $25,000]}. The remaining $10,000 ($85,000 donation − $75,000 deduction) will be carried forward subject to the 100% AGI limitation next year.

If Rich instead donated $25,000 cash to the university and $85,000 to the private foundation, the charitable contribution that could be deducted would be calculated as follows: Only $30,000 of the $85,000 donated to the 30% organization would be deducted [i.e., the lesser of the $85,000 donation or the $30,000 AGI limitation ($100,000 × 30%)]. The full $25,000 donation to the 100% organization would be deductible {i.e., the lesser of the $25,000 donation or the $70,000 AGI limitation after reduction for the $30,000 donation to the 30% organization [($100,000 × 100%) − $30,000]}. In the current year, Rich would be able to deduct only $55,000 ($30,000 to the 30% organization + $25,000 to the 100% organization). The remaining $55,000 ($85,000 donation − $30,000 deduction) would be carried forward subject to the 30% AGI limitation.

Services

11. The value of services provided to a charitable organization is not deductible.

   a. However, out-of-pocket, unreimbursed expenses (e.g., uniforms or equipment) incurred in rendering the service are deductible.

   b. Travel expenses incurred while performing the services away from home for the charitable organization are deductible if no significant element of personal pleasure, recreation, or vacation exists.

      1) Individuals who qualify for the charitable deduction for the use of an automobile may use the statutory standard mileage rate of $0.14 per mile (plus parking fees and tolls) or actual expenses incurred.

         a) Depreciation and insurance are not deductible expenses.

Tickets

12. The value of a ticket to a charitable event is a deductible contribution to the extent the purchase price exceeds the FMV of the admission or privilege associated with the event.

Carryover

13. Generally, individuals may carry forward excess donations for 5 years.

STOP AND REVIEW! **You have completed the outline for this subunit. Study multiple-choice questions 16 through 21 beginning on page 185.**

6.5 PERSONAL CASUALTY LOSSES

Historically, taxpayers who itemize may deduct a limited amount for casualty losses to nonbusiness property that arise from theft, fire, storm, shipwreck, or other casualty. However, for tax years 2018 through 2025, this personal deduction has only been allowed for federally declared disasters.

Limitation

1. Only the amount of each loss over $100 is deductible. Only the aggregate amount of all losses over $100 each in excess of 10% of AGI is deductible.

   a. If the loss was covered by insurance, timely filing of an insurance claim is prerequisite to deduction.

      1) The portion of the loss usually not covered by insurance (i.e., a deductible) is not subject to this rule.

   b. The amount of a loss is the lesser of the decrease in FMV of the property due to the casualty or the property's adjusted basis, minus any insurance reimbursements.

   c. Regardless of the 10% AGI floor, casualty losses are deductible against casualty gains.

   d. A taxpayer may claim personal casualty losses to the extent of personal **casualty gain** even if the personal casualty losses are not attributable to qualified federally declared disasters.

EXAMPLE 6-17	Personal Casualty Losses

In 2020, Marsha incurred damages to her home from a fire that was not a qualified federally declared disaster. After insurance reimbursement, she had damage to her home in the amount of $10,000 and a $3,000 gain on an antique that was destroyed. Marsha is able to offset the $3,000 gain with the $10,000 loss. The remaining loss is not deductible.

---

2. If the net amount of all personal casualty gains and losses after applying the $100 limit (but before the 10%-of-AGI threshold) is positive, each gain or loss is treated as a capital gain or loss.

   a. If the net amount is negative, the excess over 10% of AGI is deductible as either an itemized deduction or an addition to the standard deduction.

3. The cost of appraising a casualty loss is treated as a cost to determine tax liability, for which there is no deduction.

4. The cost of insuring a personal asset is a nondeductible personal expense.

5. Additional rules for a loss in a federally declared disaster area include the following:

    a. Disaster loss treatment is available when a personal residence is rendered unsafe due to the disaster in the area and is ordered to be relocated or demolished by the state or local government.

    b. The taxpayer has the option of deducting the loss on

        1) The return for the year in which the loss actually occurred or
        2) The preceding year's return (by filing an amended return).

            a) Revocation of the election may be made before expiration of time for filing the return for the year of loss.

6. The loss is calculated on Form 4684, *Casualties and Thefts*, and carried over to Schedule A, *Itemized Deductions*.

7. Although net operating losses (NOLs) are typically associated with businesses and not individuals, items such as personal casualty losses may create an individual NOL.

STOP AND REVIEW! **You have completed the outline for this subunit. Study multiple-choice questions 22 through 25 beginning on page 188.**

6.6 OTHER ITEMIZED DEDUCTIONS

Other Itemized Deductions

1. The following expenses are deductible as other itemized deductions and are reported on line 16 of Schedule A (Form 1040):

    a. Amortizable premium on taxable bonds
    b. Casualty and theft losses from income-producing property
    c. Federal estate tax on income in respect of a decedent
    d. Gambling losses up to the amount of gambling winnings
    e. Impairment-related work expenses of persons with disabilities
    f. Repayments of more than $3,000 under a claim of right
    g. Unrecovered investment in a pension

STOP AND REVIEW! **You have completed the outline for this subunit. Study multiple-choice questions 26 through 28 beginning on page 190.**

QUESTIONS

6.1 Medical Expenses

1. To qualify for a medical expense deduction as your dependent, a person must be your dependent either at the time the medical services were provided or at the time you paid the expenses. A person generally qualifies as your dependent for purposes of the medical expense deduction if

   A. The person would qualify as a dependent except for the amount of gross income.

   B. The person was a foreign student staying briefly at your home.

   C. The person is your sibling's unmarried adult child.

   D. The person is the unrelated caregiver for your elderly parents.

Answer (A) is correct.
   REQUIRED: The person who qualifies as a dependent for the purpose of a medical expense deduction.
   DISCUSSION: For the purpose of a medical deduction, a person qualifies as a "dependent" if (s)he meets the requirements in Sec. 152 except for the following two criteria:

1.   The amount of the individual's gross income is not considered [Reg. Sec. 1.213-1(a)(3)].
2.   A child with divorced parents is treated as a dependent by both parents [Sec. 213(d)(5)].

   (Publication 502.)
   Answer (B) is incorrect. A foreign student staying briefly at the taxpayer's home does not meet the citizenship requirement. **Answer (C) is incorrect.** A taxpayer's sibling's unmarried adult child generally will not meet the support requirement of dependency. **Answer (D) is incorrect.** The unrelated caregiver of a taxpayer's elderly parents does not meet the relationship requirement of dependency.

2. John has a heart ailment. On his doctor's advice, he installed an elevator in his home so that he would not have to climb stairs. The cost of the elevator was $7,000. An appraisal shows that the elevator increased the value of his home by $5,000. John can claim a medical deduction of

   A. $2,000.

   B. $5,000.

   C. $7,000.

   D. None of the answers are correct.

Answer (A) is correct.
   REQUIRED: The medical deduction a physically handicapped taxpayer may claim when the expense increases the value of the taxpayer's home.
   DISCUSSION: Home-related capital expenditures incurred by a physically handicapped individual are deductible. An example of such an expenditure is an elevator needed for someone with a heart condition. However, the amount of any increase in value of the existing property cannot be deducted. Once a capital expense qualifies as a medical expense, amounts paid for the operation and upkeep also qualify as medical expenses. This is true even if the original capital expenditure was not entirely deductible (because it may have increased the fair market value of the residence). Therefore, $2,000 of the cost of the elevator is deductible as a medical expense ($7,000 cost – $5,000 increase in value of home). The maintenance and repair expense of the elevator is deductible, even though a portion of the cost of the elevator was not deductible (Publication 502).
   Answer (B) is incorrect. The amount by which the home increased in value is not deductible. **Answer (C) is incorrect.** The entire cost of the elevator is not deductible. **Answer (D) is incorrect.** John does qualify for a medical deduction.

3. During 2020, Mr. and Mrs. Duhon paid the following expenses for their son, Joel:

Medical insurance premiums	$1,500
Contact lenses	210
Household help recommended by a doctor	2,200

For 2020, Joel had gross income of $9,850. Because Joel had gross income of $9,850, the Duhons did not claim him as a dependent. How much of Joel's medical expenses can Mr. and Mrs. Duhon include with their deductible medical expenses?

A. $3,910

B. $1,710

C. $1,500

D. $0

Answer (B) is correct.
    REQUIRED: The amount of medical expenses deductible for an individual whose income exceeds the dependent threshold amount.
    DISCUSSION: An individual is entitled to an itemized deduction for expenses paid during the tax year for the medical care of the individual, the individual's spouse, or a dependent to the extent that such expenses exceed 7.5% of adjusted gross income. For purposes of this deduction, "dependent" is defined in Publication 502. The household help does not qualify as a medical expense. Therefore, $1,710 qualifies as deductible medical expenses. Even though Joel is not a dependent, the parents may claim the amount of qualified medical expenses.
    Answer (A) is incorrect. The household help recommended by a doctor is not a deductible medical expense. **Answer (C) is incorrect.** The contact lenses are also deductible. **Answer (D) is incorrect.** Joel is not a dependent, but only due to his gross income; therefore, the qualified medical expenses may be deducted by the parents.

4. Chris flew to Chicago for surgery. He incurred the following costs in connection with the trip:

Round-trip airfare	$ 350
Lodging ($100/night × 2 nights)	200
Restaurant meals	80
Hospital and surgeon	5,000

What is Chris's medical expense?

A. $5,490

B. $5,630

C. $5,000

D. $5,450

Answer (D) is correct.
    REQUIRED: The medical expense deduction.
    DISCUSSION: Medical expenses include amounts paid for the diagnosis, cure, mitigation, treatment, or prevention of disease or for the purpose of affecting any structure or function of the body; transportation cost of a trip primarily for and essential to medical care; qualified long-term care service; and medical insurance. A medical expense deduction is allowed for lodging, but not meals, while away from home on a trip primarily for and essential to medical care. This lodging deduction is limited to amounts that are not lavish or extravagant and cannot exceed $50 per night for each individual. The deduction may also be claimed for a person who must accompany the individual seeking medical care (Publication 17).
    Thus, Chris can deduct $350 for airfare, $100 for lodging, and $5,000 for the surgery.

5. Which of the following is deductible as medical insurance?

   A. Medical portion of auto insurance policy that provides coverage for all persons injured in or by the taxpayer's car.

   B. Insurance policy that pays you $50 a day if you are unable to work due to illness or injury.

   C. Medicare Part B.

   D. None of the answers are correct.

Answer (C) is correct.
   REQUIRED: The item deductible as medical insurance.
   DISCUSSION: To qualify for a deduction, a medical expense must be paid during the taxable year for the taxpayer, the taxpayer's spouse, or a dependent and must not be compensated for by insurance or otherwise during the taxable year. The basic cost of Medicare insurance (Medicare Part A) is not deductible unless voluntarily paid by the taxpayer for coverage. However, the extra cost of Medicare (Medicare Part B) is deductible (Publication 17).
   Answer (A) is incorrect. If an insurance contract covers both medical care and nonmedical care, none of the insurance premium is deductible unless the amount of the premium allocable to medical care insurance is separately stated. **Answer (B) is incorrect.** Premiums paid on a policy that merely pays the insured a specified amount per day are not deductible. **Answer (D) is incorrect.** Medicare Part B is deductible as medical insurance.

6.2 Taxes

6. Taxes deductible as an itemized deduction up to $10,000 include all of the following EXCEPT

   A. State and local real estate taxes based on the assessed value of the property and charged uniformly against all property.

   B. State and local income taxes.

   C. Taxes that the taxpayer paid on property owned by his or her parents or children.

   D. Personal property taxes based on the value of the personal property.

Answer (C) is correct.
   REQUIRED: The tax that is not deductible as an itemized deduction.
   DISCUSSION: The taxes that are deductible from adjusted gross income include state and local income taxes withheld, state and local real estate taxes paid, and personal property taxes, all of which are deductible as itemized deductions (Publication 17). However, taxes paid on another person's property are not deductible because the tax liability is the liability of the other person.
   Answer (A) is incorrect. Under Sec. 164(a), state and local real estate taxes based on the assessed value of the property and charged uniformly against all property is a tax that is deductible as an itemized deduction. **Answer (B) is incorrect.** Under Sec. 164(a), state and local income taxes are taxes that are deductible as an itemized deduction. **Answer (D) is incorrect.** Under Sec. 164(a), personal property tax based on the value of the personal property is a tax that is deductible as an itemized deduction.

7. In the current year, Maria paid the following taxes:

Special assessment to provide local benefits	$2,500
County real estate taxes paid on her vacation home	1,250
Sales taxes paid when she purchased a new auto	900
Personal property taxes paid to her local government	350

What amount is allowable as an itemized deduction for the current year?

A. $1,250

B. $2,500

C. $3,750

D. $5,000

Answer (B) is correct.
REQUIRED: The amount of taxes allowable as an itemized deduction.
DISCUSSION: Publication 17 and Sec. 164(a) list the taxes that are deductible from adjusted gross income. The state and local general sales tax (in lieu of state and local income taxes), the county real estate taxes paid on her vacation home, and the personal property taxes are deductible as itemized deductions.
Answer (A) is incorrect. The real estate taxes paid on the vacation home are also deductible. Answer (C) is incorrect. The special assessment is not deductible, but the real estate taxes paid on the vacation home are deductible. Answer (D) is incorrect. The special assessment to provide local benefits is not deductible.

8. During the current year, Ms. Gonzales paid $2,000 for local real estate taxes on property she rents to others and $3,425 real estate taxes on her residence. In addition, she paid gift taxes of $650 and $1,250 for state income taxes to New Jersey. What amount can Ms. Gonzales deduct as an itemized deduction on her tax return for the current year?

A. $4,675

B. $5,325

C. $6,675

D. $7,325

Answer (A) is correct.
REQUIRED: The amount that may be deducted as an itemized deduction.
DISCUSSION: Section 164(a) lists the taxes that are deductible from adjusted gross income. The local real estate taxes on the personal residence ($3,425) and the state income taxes ($1,250) are deductible as itemized deductions for a total of $4,675. The real estate taxes on the rental property may be deductible, but not as an itemized deduction. Gift taxes are not deductible (Publication 17).
Answer (B) is incorrect. Gift taxes are not deductible. Answer (C) is incorrect. The real estate taxes on the rental property are not deductible as an itemized deduction. Answer (D) is incorrect. The real estate taxes on the rental property and the gift taxes are not deductible as itemized deductions.

9. In the current year, Smith paid $6,000 to the tax collector of Big City for realty taxes on a two-family house owned by Smith's mother. Of this amount, $2,800 covered back taxes for the previous year, and $3,200 covered the current-year taxes. Smith resides on the second floor of the house, and his mother resides on the first floor. In Smith's itemized deductions on his current-year return, what amount was Smith entitled to claim for realty taxes?

A. $6,000

B. $3,200

C. $3,000

D. $0

Answer (D) is correct.
REQUIRED: The amount of deductible property taxes paid by a person who does not own the property but resides in half of the property.
DISCUSSION: Taxes may be deducted only by the person on whom they are legally levied. Since Smith does not own the house, none of the taxes paid by Smith can be deducted by Smith. Smith's mother is entitled to the deduction only if she pays the taxes.
Answer (A) is incorrect. Smith paid $6,000 for realty taxes on the home owned by Smith's mother. Deductibility of taxes is affected by ownership. Answer (B) is incorrect. Current-year realty taxes are $3,200 on Smith's mother's home. Deductibility of taxes is affected by ownership. Answer (C) is incorrect. Half of the total amount Smith paid for his mother is $3,000. Deductibility of taxes is affected by ownership.

10. Which of the following types of taxes can be deducted on Schedule A?

A. Transfer taxes on the sale of a residence.

B. A tax on a motor vehicle based on engine horsepower.

C. A tax on a motor vehicle based on vehicle weight.

D. None of the answers are correct.

Answer (D) is correct.
REQUIRED: The type of tax deducted on Schedule A.
DISCUSSION: To deduct a personal property tax on Schedule A, the tax imposed must be determined solely on the value of the property. Transfer taxes incurred on the sale of a residence are not allowed as Schedule A deductions. They are added to the buyer's cost basis of the residence if paid by them. If paid by the seller, transfer taxes serve to lower the realized amount of the sale as sale expenses (Publication 17).
Answer (A) is incorrect. Transfer taxes on the sale of a residence are not deductible on Schedule A. Answer (B) is incorrect. Personal property taxes must be determined by the value of the personal property. Answer (C) is incorrect. Personal property taxes must be determined by the value of the personal property.

11. All of the following taxes are deductible on Schedule A (Form 1040) EXCEPT

A. State or local inheritance tax.

B. State income tax.

C. State real estate tax on a personal residence.

D. Foreign income tax.

Answer (A) is correct.
REQUIRED: The tax not deductible on Schedule A of Form 1040.
DISCUSSION: No deduction is allowed for state or local inheritance taxes. On the federal estate tax return, a credit may be allowed. But for income tax purposes, no deduction is available (Publication 17).
Answer (B) is incorrect. Section 164(a) specifically lists state income taxes as a deduction. Answer (C) is incorrect. Section 164(a) specifically lists state and local real property taxes as a deduction. Answer (D) is incorrect. Section 164(a) provides a deduction for taxes paid or accrued for foreign income, war profits, and excess profits taxes.

6.3 Interest Expense

12. Keith and Margaret had adjusted gross income of $100 000. They had real estate taxes of $4,000 mortgage interest of $12,000, home equity loan interest of $6,000 used to substantially improve the residence, automobile loan interest of $3,000, second home mortgage interest of $4,000, and credit card interest of $2,000. The total allowable interest deduction is

A. $31,000

B. $24,000

C. $22,000

D. $18,000

Answer (C) is correct.
REQUIRED: The total interest deduction allowed.
DISCUSSION: Qualified residence interest is interest paid or accrued during the tax year on acquisition or home equity indebtedness that is used to substantially improve the residence and secured by a qualified residence. The general rule is that no personal interest may be deducted. Personal interest includes interest on credit card debt, revolving charge accounts, lines of credit, car loans, medical fees, and premiums. The real estate taxes are deductible but are not included in the total allowable interest deduction (Publication 17). Thus, only the $4,000 of the second home mortgage interest, $12,000 of mortgage interest, and $6,000 of home equity loan interest are deductible interest expenses.
Answer (A) is incorrect. The amount of $31,000 includes the car loan interest, credit card interest, and real estate taxes. Answer (B) is incorrect. The amount of $24,000 includes the credit card interest. Answer (D) is incorrect. The amount of $18,000 does not include the second home mortgage interest.

13. Which of the following would disqualify points from being fully deductible in the year paid?

  A. The points were computed as a percentage of the amount of the mortgage.

  B. The loan proceeds were used to purchase a second home.

  C. The payment of points is common in your area.

  D. The points are clearly stated on the settlement statement.

Answer (B) is correct.
  REQUIRED: The situation that would disqualify points from being fully deductible in the year paid.
  DISCUSSION: Points paid by the borrower with respect to a home mortgage are prepaid interest, which is typically deductible over the term of the loan. The amount paid as points for a home may only be deducted in the year paid if the points are paid on acquisition indebtedness and the home is the taxpayer's principal place of residence.
  Answer (A) is incorrect. The points were computed as a percentage of the amount of the mortgage would not disqualify points from being fully deductible in the year paid. **Answer (C) is incorrect.** The payment of points is common in your area would not disqualify points from being fully deductible in the year paid. **Answer (D) is incorrect.** The points are clearly stated on the settlement statement would not disqualify points from being fully deductible in the year paid.

14. Johnny has been divorced for 6 years. He failed to make his alimony and support payments. The court ordered him to pay $1,500 as interest on the back alimony and support payments. He paid interest of $1,000 on a car loan, $2,500 on his outstanding credit card balance, $6,000 on a home equity loan that was not used to substantially improve his residence, and $10,000 on his mortgage. Other interest payments amounted to $2,500 on various appliance loan payments. How much is Johnny's deductible interest?

  A. $18,500

  B. $10,000

  C. $23,500

  D. $17,500

Answer (B) is correct.
  REQUIRED: The amount of interest deductible.
  DISCUSSION: Qualified residence interest is interest paid or accrued during the tax year on acquisition or home equity indebtedness that is secured by a qualified residence. The general rule is that no personal interest may be deducted. Personal interest includes interest on credit card debt, revolving charge accounts and lines of credit, car loans, medical fees, and premiums, etc. There is no deduction for "fines and penalties for violations of law, regardless of their nature" (Publication 17).
  Answer (A) is incorrect. The amount of $18,500 includes the $2,500 on appliance loan interest. **Answer (C) is incorrect.** The amount of $23,500 includes the car loan, credit card, and appliance loan interest, as well as court-ordered interest on back alimony and support payments. **Answer (D) is incorrect.** The amount of $17,500 includes the court-ordered interest on back alimony and support payments.

15. Which of the following is treated as personal interest of Individual A?

A. Interest incurred on refinancing A's home if the funds are used to substantially improve the qualified residence.

B. Interest incurred to purchase bonds as an investment.

C. Interest incurred by a limited partnership in which A is a limited partner.

D. Interest incurred on an ordinary bank loan if the funds are used to provide medical care for a dependent of A.

Answer (D) is correct.
REQUIRED: The interest expense treated as personal interest.
DISCUSSION: Personal interest is defined in Sec. 163 as any interest other than qualified residence interest, investment interest, interest taken into account in computing income or loss from a passive activity, interest in connection with a business, student loan interest, and interest during certain extensions of time to pay the estate tax. Interest on an ordinary bank loan incurred for medical care is personal interest. Personal interest is not deductible (Publication 17).
Answer (A) is incorrect. Qualified residence interest is deductible on no more than $750,000 of the sum of acquisition and home equity indebtedness. Home equity debt must be used to buy, build, or substantially improve the qualified residence. **Answer (B) is incorrect.** This is investment interest. **Answer (C) is incorrect.** A limited partnership is generally a passive activity, and the interest is deductible subject to the passive activity loss limitations rules.

6.4 Charitable Contributions

16. Mr. Hardwood has an adjusted gross income of $50,000. In 2020, he donated capital gain property valued at $25,000 to his church and did not choose to reduce the fair market value of the property by the amount that would have been long-term capital gain if he had sold it. His basis in the property was $20,000. In addition, he made the following contributions:

• $500 to upgrade the city public park

• $1,000 to the Hill City Chamber of Commerce

• $5,000 to a charitable organization in Germany

Compute Mr. Hardwood's deduction for charitable contributions in the current year (without regard to any carryover or carryback amounts).

A. $25,000

B. $31,500

C. $16,500

D. $15,500

Answer (D) is correct.
REQUIRED: The contributions that are deductible as a charitable contribution.
DISCUSSION: Charitable contributions are deductible only if they are made to qualified organizations. Donations can be made in the form of cash or noncash property. Qualified organizations include corporations, trusts, community chests, funds, or foundations, created or organized in the U.S. and organized and operated exclusively for religious, charitable, scientific, literary, or educational purposes or for the prevention of cruelty to children or animals. The amount that Hardwood may deduct for the capital gain property donated to the church is $15,000 ($50,000 × 30% special limitation). Hardwood also may deduct the $500 upgrade to the city public park. The donation to the charitable organization in Germany is not deductible, since donations to foreign organizations generally are not considered to be charitable contributions as defined in Sec. 170(c). The total charitable contribution deduction is equal to $15,500 ($15,000 + $500) (Publication 17).
Answer (A) is incorrect. The capital gain property that was donated to the church is limited to 30% of AGI. In addition, the upgrade to the park is also deductible. **Answer (B) is incorrect.** The capital gain property that was donated to the church is limited to 30% of AGI and the contribution to the Chamber of Commerce is not deductible. In addition, the upgrade to the park is also deductible. **Answer (C) is incorrect.** The contribution to the Chamber of Commerce is not deductible.

17. During the current year, John donated $100 to the United Way, $200 to Veterans of Foreign Wars, and $300 to his neighbor whose home was destroyed by a tornado. How much is John's deduction for charitable contributions?

A. $300

B. $400

C. $500

D. $600

Answer (A) is correct.
   REQUIRED: The amount of the charitable contribution deduction.
   DISCUSSION: Charitable contributions are deductible only if they are made to qualified organizations. Qualified organizations can be either public charities or private foundations. (Generally, a public charity is one that derives more than one-third of its support from its members and the general public.) Donations can be made in the form of cash or noncash property. However, any amounts donated to individuals are not allowed as a deduction (Publication 17).
   Answer (B) is incorrect. The amount donated to his neighbor cannot be deducted since the neighbor is an individual. **Answer (C) is incorrect.** The $100 donated to the United Way is deductible as a donation made to a qualified organization, while his $300 donation to his neighbor is disallowed as a donation to an individual. **Answer (D) is incorrect.** The amount donated to his neighbor cannot be deducted since the neighbor is an individual.

18. In 2020, Janice volunteered at her local art museum where she conducted art-education seminars. She was required to wear a blazer that the museum provided, but she paid the dry cleaning costs of $200 for the year. The blazer was not suitable for everyday use. Her travel to and from the museum was 1,000 miles for the year. She estimates the value of the time she contributed during the year at $2,000 ($20/hr × 100 hours). Her Schedule A deduction for charitable contributions is which of the following?

A. $2,340

B. $2,140

C. $140

D. $340

Answer (D) is correct.
   REQUIRED: The amount of the charitable contribution deduction.
   DISCUSSION: The tax code allows for a deduction for expenses and payments made to, or on behalf of, a charitable organization. However, the value of services rendered to an institution is not deductible as contributions. Deductions are allowed for transportation and other travel expenses incurred in the performance of services away from home on behalf of a charitable organization. Individuals who qualify for a deduction for the use of an automobile may use the statutory standard mileage rate of $0.14 per mile. Also, out-of-pocket expenses are included if they involve items that can be used solely for the purpose of volunteer work (Publication 17). Therefore, Janice may deduct $340 of her expenses as a charitable contribution [($200 + (1,000 miles × $0.14)].
   Answer (A) is incorrect. The value of the services is not allowable as a charitable deduction. **Answer (B) is incorrect.** The value of the services is not allowable as a charitable deduction. However, the cleaning and purchase of clothing that can only be used for purposes of the charity can be deducted. **Answer (C) is incorrect.** The cleaning and purchase of clothing that can only be used for purposes of the charity can be deducted.

19. For 2020, Mrs. Lynn had adjusted gross income of $30,000. During the year, she contributed $11,000 to her church, $20,000 to qualified public charities, and a painting she has owned for 8 years with a fair market value of $16,000 and a $4,000 adjusted basis to her city's library. What is the amount of Mrs. Lynn's charitable contributions deduction for the year?

A. $30,000

B. $31,000

C. $35,000

D. $47,000

Answer (A) is correct.

REQUIRED: The taxpayer's allowable charitable contribution deduction.

DISCUSSION: All of Mrs. Lynn's contributions qualify under Sec. 170; thus, the amount of her contribution is $47,000. However, the amount of her allowable charitable contribution deduction for the year is limited to $30,000, accounting first for the 30% AGI limit contribution, and second for the 100% AGI limit contribution of the cash minus the allowed deduction for the painting. The excess $17,000 [($16,000 – $9,000 painting 30% limitation) + $10,000 balance for 100% limit property, i.e., cash] can be carried forward and deducted in the 5 succeeding tax years [Sec. 170(d)]. The amount of the contribution of the painting is its $16,000 FMV. The fair market value is not reduced by what would have been long-term capital gain had Mrs. Lynn sold it because it is presumed that the property is used in connection with the library's tax-exempt purpose. Because no reduction occurs, the 30% limitation on contributions of capital gain property is applicable (Publication 17).

Answer (B) is incorrect. The deduction is limited to 30% of her adjusted gross income for the painting donation plus 100% of her adjusted gross income for the cash donations after reduction for the painting deduction.
Answer (C) is incorrect. The deduction is limited to 30% of her adjusted gross income for the painting donation plus 100% of her adjusted gross income for the cash donations after reduction for the painting deduction.
Answer (D) is incorrect. The amount of $47,000 is the total contributions made during the year and ignores the AGI limitations.

20. The acknowledgment an individual needs from any charitable organization to claim a deduction for any cash contribution of $250 or more in a single donation must include which of the following?

A. The reason for the contribution.

B. The returned check showing the donation amount.

C. A description of past contributions and any plans for future contributions.

D. A contemporaneous written receipt.

Answer (D) is correct.

REQUIRED: The item that is required in an acknowledgment from a donee.

DISCUSSION: Generally, charitable contributions of $250 or more made on or after January 1, 1994, must be substantiated by a contemporaneous written acknowledgment from the donee organization. The acknowledgment must include the amount of cash contributed along with a description and good-faith estimate of the value of any goods or services (other than goods or services with insubstantial value) received for the contributions (Publication 17).

21. Raul and Monika (husband and wife) are both lawyers, and they contribute money to various organizations each year. They file a joint return, and their adjusted gross income for 2020 is $100,000. They contributed to the following organizations in 2020:

- $5,000 to Alta Sierra country club
- $10,000 to prevent cruelty to animals
- $2,000 to state bar association (This state bar association is not a political subdivision of the state, serves both public and private purposes, and the funds used are unrestricted and can be for private purposes.)
- $12,000 to cancer research foundation
- Donated clothing to Salvation Army (Raul purchased the items for $1,000, but the fair market value of the same items at a thrift store is equal to $50.)

How much can Raul and Monika deduct as charitable contributions for 2020?

A. $29,050

B. $25,000

C. $22,050

D. $24,000

Answer (C) is correct.
REQUIRED: The deductibility of charitable contributions.
DISCUSSION: Charitable contributions are deductible only if they are made to qualified organizations. Donations can be made in the form of cash or noncash property. The organizations may be both public and private but should be organized and operated exclusively for religious, charitable, scientific, literary, or educational purposes or for the prevention of cruelty to children or animals. Charitable deductions also are subject to various AGI limitations (Publication 17). Raul and Monika may deduct $22,050 ($10,000 + $12,000 + $50) of their charitable contributions.
Answer (A) is incorrect. The contributions to the country club and the state bar association are not deductible. The country club and state bar association do not qualify under the criteria established for determining a charitable organization. Answer (B) is incorrect. The $2,000 contribution to the state bar is nondeductible. Also, the contribution to the Salvation Army is the FMV at the time of contribution, not the basis in the property. Answer (D) is incorrect. The state bar association contribution is nondeductible.

6.5 Personal Casualty Losses

22. Frank and Melody's home was completely destroyed by fire in a qualified federally declared disaster. They had no insurance. On which of the following forms would they report their loss?

A. Form 4684, *Casualties and Thefts*, and Form 1040, *U.S. Individual Income Tax Return*, as an adjustment to gross income.

B. Schedule A, *Itemized Deductions*, only.

C. Form 4684, *Casualties and Thefts*, and Schedule A, *Itemized Deductions*.

D. Form 4684, *Casualties and Thefts*, only.

Answer (C) is correct.
REQUIRED: The forms on which a casualty loss is reported.
DISCUSSION: Form 4684, Section A, *Personal Use Property*, lists and calculates the amount of the loss. The amount of the loss is then added to Schedule A, *Itemized Deductions* (Publication 547).
Answer (A) is incorrect. Personal casualty losses are reported on Schedule A. Answer (B) is incorrect. Schedule A is used in reporting Frank and Melody's casualty loss. Answer (D) is incorrect. Form 4684 is used in reporting Frank and Melody's casualty loss.

23. Alberta and Archie (wife and husband) had water damage in their home during 2020, which ruined the furniture in their basement. This was in a federal disaster area. The following items were completely destroyed and not salvageable.

Damaged items	Fair market value just prior to damage	Original item cost
Antique bed frame	$5,000	$ 4,000
Pool table	8,000	10,000
Large-screen TV	700	2,500

Their homeowner's insurance policy had a $10,000 deductible for the personal property, which was deducted from their insurance reimbursement of $12,700. Their adjusted gross income for 2020 was $30,000. What is the amount of casualty loss that Alberta and Archie can claim on their joint return for 2020?

A. $10,600

B. $3,400

C. $6,900

D. $0

24. In 2020, the U.S. President declared a qualified federal disaster due to flooding in Minnesota. Lisa lives in that area and lost her home in the flood. What choice does she have regarding when she can claim the loss on her tax return?

A. It must be claimed in 2019 if the return has not been filed by the date of the loss.

B. It must be claimed in 2020 if the loss is greater than the modified adjusted gross income.

C. It may be claimed in 2021 if an election is filed with the 2020 return.

D. It may be claimed in 2019 or 2020.

Answer (C) is correct.
REQUIRED: The amount of casualty loss that can be claimed.
DISCUSSION: The loss is the lesser of the decrease in FMV of the property due to the casualty or the property's adjusted basis. The loss is reduced by any amount recovered by insurance and a $100 floor to any nonbusiness loss. The $100 floor applies only once to a married filing joint return. The loss is also subject to a floor equal to 10% of the AGI. The casualty loss can therefore be calculated as follows: $12,700 loss – $2,700 insurance reimbursement – $100 floor – ($30,000 AGI × 10%) = $6,900. The $12,700 loss is calculated as follows: $4,000 from the antique bed frame (decrease in FMV > original cost); $8,000 from the pool table (original cost > decrease in FMV); $700 from the large-screen TV (original cost > decrease in FMV).
Answer (A) is incorrect. The amount of $10,600 uses the FMV just prior to damage as the basis and fails to reduce the loss by the amount recovered by insurance. **Answer (B) is incorrect.** The amount of $3,400 uses the FMV just prior to damage as the basis and reduces the loss by the $10,000 deductible and only 1% of the AGI, ignoring the floor. **Answer (D) is incorrect.** The amount of $0 fails to account for the deductible.

Answer (D) is correct.
REQUIRED: The correct tax return to claim a loss from a federal disaster.
DISCUSSION: If a taxpayer has a casualty loss from a disaster that occurred in a qualified federally declared disaster area, (s)he can choose to deduct that loss on the current year's tax return or (s)he may amend the return for the tax year immediately preceding the tax year in which the disaster occurred (Publication 547).

25. Alona is a student, and her personal car disappeared during a hurricane in May of 2020 (a federally declared disaster). It was found several days later severely damaged. The decrease in fair market value (less than her adjusted basis) was $3,500. In addition, a personal laptop computer in the car at the time was never recovered (fair market value $500, also less than her adjusted basis). What is the amount and treatment of the casualty loss after considering the $100 minimum floor but before the AGI limitation?

A. Schedule A loss of $3,000 for the car and computer.

B. Schedule D loss of $3,500 for the car and a Schedule A loss of $500 for the computer.

C. Schedule A loss of $3,900 for the car and the computer.

D. Schedule D loss of $4,000 for the car and the computer.

Answer (C) is correct.
    REQUIRED: The amount and treatment of the casualty loss after considering the $100 minimum floor.
    DISCUSSION: Losses incurred from casualty or theft in a qualified federally declared disaster are deductible. The amount of the loss is the lesser of the decrease in fair market value (FMV) of the property due to the casualty or the property's adjusted basis. Thus, the amount of the deduction is the loss in FMV. This, however, is limited to a $100 floor (Publication 547). The computation is illustrated below.

Decrease in FMV of the car	$3,500
Decrease in FMV of the laptop computer	500
	$4,000
Less: $100 minimum floor	(100)
Total loss	$3,900

    This loss is reported on line 15 of Schedule A.
    Answer (A) is incorrect. The total loss is subject to the $100 floor, not each casualty loss. **Answer (B) is incorrect.** The loss for both the car and the computer would be reported on Schedule A. Also, a $100 floor is subtracted from the total. **Answer (D) is incorrect.** The loss for both the car and the computer would be reported on Schedule A. Also, a $100 floor is subtracted from the total.

6.6 Other Itemized Deductions

26. Paula won $5,000 in the lottery in 2020. She also won $200 playing bingo at her lodge hall. She is not a professional gambler. She kept meticulous records of the $6,550 she spent on gambling expenses. How much may she deduct on her Schedule A as an other deduction?

A. $0

B. $200

C. $5,200

D. $6,550

Answer (C) is correct.
    REQUIRED: The amount of gambling expenses that may be deducted by a nonprofessional gambler on Schedule A as an other deduction.
    DISCUSSION: Gambling losses may be deducted, but only to the extent of gambling winnings. In order to deduct these expenses, they must be listed next to line 16 on Schedule A (Publication 17). The type and amount of each expense must be listed (a statement showing these expenses may be attached if there is not enough room). Paula had $5,200 in winnings ($5,000 + $200); thus, $5,200 of the $6,550 of meticulously kept expenses may be deducted.
    Answer (A) is incorrect. Gambling losses may be deducted to the extent of gambling income if good records of the expenses are kept. **Answer (B) is incorrect.** Gambling losses may be deducted to the extent of gambling income. Paula's total gambling income is $5,200 ($5,000 in lottery winnings plus $200 in bingo winnings). **Answer (D) is incorrect.** Gambling losses are only deductible to the extent of gambling income.

27. Which of the following are NOT other itemized deductions?

   A. Federal estate tax on income in respect of a decedent.

   B. Gambling losses up to the amount of gambling winnings.

   C. Impairment-related work expenses of persons with disabilities.

   D. Safety deposit box expenses.

Answer (D) is correct.
   REQUIRED: The expenses that are not other itemized deductions.
   DISCUSSION: According to Publication 17, the following expenses are deductible as other itemized deductions and are reported on line 16 of Schedule A (Form 1040):

1) Amortizable premium on taxable bonds
2) Federal estate tax on income in respect of a decedent
3) Gambling losses up to the amount of gambling winnings
4) Impairment-related work expenses of persons with disabilities
5) Repayment of more than $3,000 under a claim of right
6) Unrecovered investment in a pension

Safety deposit box expenses formerly were second-tier miscellaneous itemized deductions subject to the 2% adjusted gross income limitation. However, those deductions are no longer allowed.

28. Which of the following expenses are deductible on Form 1040 Schedule A in 2020?

   A. Gambling losses up to the amount of gambling winnings.

   B. Fees paid to a broker to collect taxable bond interest or dividends on shares of stock.

   C. Repayment of $3,000 of ordinary income that had been included in taxable income in an earlier year.

   D. Damages paid to a former employer for breach of employment contract, when the damages are attributable to pay received from that employer.

Answer (A) is correct.
   REQUIRED: The itemized deduction.
   DISCUSSION: Gambling losses are deductible to the extent of gambling winnings (Reg. 1.165-10). They are a loss deduction for adjusted gross income if gambling is a trade or business, but in most cases they are an other itemized deduction [Publication 17 and Sec. 67(b)(3)].
   Answer (B) is incorrect. Fees paid to a broker to collect taxable bond interest or dividends on shares of stock are no longer itemized deductions. **Answer (C) is incorrect.** Repayment of $3,000 of ordinary income that had been included in taxable income in an earlier year is no longer an itemized deduction. If the amount had been greater than $3,000, it would be deductible. **Answer (D) is incorrect.** Damages paid to a former employer for breach of employment contract, when the damages are attributable to pay received from that employer, are no longer an itemized deduction.

 Access the **Gleim EA Premium Review System** featuring our SmartAdapt technology from your Gleim Personal Classroom to continue your studies. You will experience a personalized study environment with exam-emulating multiple-choice questions.

STUDY UNIT SEVEN

QUALIFIED BUSINESS INCOME DEDUCTION, AMT, AND OTHER TAXES

(22 pages of outline)

The first subunit explains the last of the below-the-line deductions, the qualified business income deduction (QBID). The last two subunits discuss the alternative minimum tax and other taxes a taxpayer may be subject to, including self-employment taxes.

7.1 QUALIFIED BUSINESS INCOME DEDUCTION (QBID)

NOTE: The following outline is duplicated in EA Part 2, Study Unit 5, Subunit 9.

1.   Calculation

    a.   **Qualified Business Income Deduction (QBID) (Section 199A)**

       1)   When Congress passed the Tax Cuts and Jobs Act (TCJA), it reduced the C corporation tax rate to 21%.

       2)   Congress did not want to disadvantage owners of pass-through entities (sole proprietorships, S corporations, and partnerships) by leaving them with a substantially higher tax liability (potentially 37%) than C corporations (21%). Congress reduced this burden by creating the QBID.

       3)   The QBID is the last deduction before determining a taxpayer's taxable income. It is based on determining qualified business income (QBI).

       4)   For the QBID, Congress divided pass-through entities into two categories: (a) specified service trades or businesses and (b) qualified trades or businesses.

    b.   **Specified Service Trades or Businesses**

       1)   In general, a specified service trade or business (SSTB) is any trade or business in which the principal asset is the reputation or skill of one or more of its employees.

       2)   Specifically, SSTBs include the following types of trades and businesses:

          a)   Health (e.g., physicians, nurses, dentists, and other similar healthcare professionals)

            i)   Health does not include services not directly related to a medical field, such as medical device sales, coding, billing, and payment processing.

          b)   Law

          c)   Accounting

          d)   Actuarial science

          e)   Performing arts

          f)   Consulting

          g)   Athletics

          h)   Financial services (e.g., financial advisors, wealth planners, retirement advisors, investment bankers, and other professionals performing similar services)

            i)   This includes any professional service consisting of investing, investment management, trading or dealing in securities, partnership interests, or commodities.

          i)   Brokerage services

3) Also, an SSTB is any trade or business wherein a principal earns income (e.g., fees, licenses, or compensation) for any of the following activities:

   a) Endorsing products or services
   b) Use of the principal's likeness, image, name, etc.
   c) Appearance fees for an event or media performance (e.g., radio, TV, etc.)

EXAMPLE 7-1	Reputation and Skill

Bill owns Bill's Plumbing, a sole proprietorship. Bill's Plumbing's motto is "Bill is a very skilled plumber with a great reputation." According to the regulations, because Bill's Plumbing does not involve endorsements, compensation for use of one's likeness, or appearance fees, Bill's Plumbing's principal asset is not the reputation or skill of one or more of its employees or owners. Thus, Bill's Plumbing is not considered a specified service business.

4) Trades and businesses that are specifically **not** considered SSTBs include

   a) Architects
   b) Engineers
   c) Real estate agents and brokers
   d) Insurance agents and brokers

EXAMPLE 7-2	SSTB

Danny is a partner at XYZ, LLP, a public accounting firm. Danny is single with taxable income of $500,000. Because Danny's taxable income is above the taxable income threshold, the specified service business limitation applies. Thus, because XYZ is a specified service business (and Danny's taxable income is above the phase-in range), XYZ's business income is not QBI and thus is not eligible for the QBID. However, if Danny's taxable income had instead been $100,000, XYZ's business income would have been eligible for the QBID because the specified service business limitation would not have applied.

c. **Qualified Trades or Businesses**

1) In general, a qualified trade or business is any pass-through entity not considered an SSTB.

2) Specifically, a pass-through entity can be identified as a qualified trade or business if it has QBI.

d.   The QBID on line 13 of Form 1040 is limited due to an **overall limitation**.

    1)   The overall limitation is the **lesser of**

        a)   20% × Qualified business income or

        b)   20% × (Taxable income – Net capital gains).

    2)   Therefore, if a taxpayer has net capital gains, the taxpayer's net capital gains decrease his or her QBID. (For this deduction, net capital gains are long-term gains and qualified dividends, minus short-term losses.)

    3)   Before a taxpayer can apply the overall limitation, (s)he has to determine the combined QBID before the taxable income limitation. Determining the combined QBID is a three-step process. After the three steps have been used to determine the combined QBID, the taxpayer must apply the overall limitation, which becomes Step 4.

e.   To **calculate the combined QBID and ultimately the QBID, the following must be completed**:

    1)   **Step 1** – Every pass-through entity must first determine its QBI.

        a)   This information will be reported on a Schedule K-1 (or a Schedule C if the entity is a sole proprietorship).

        b)   The details of this process are described in Figure 7-1 on the next page.

    2)   **Step 2** – The sum of each pass-through entity's QBI must then be tested against the taxpayer's taxable income.

        a)   If the taxpayer is in the phase-in range (of W-2 wage limit) or upper threshold, the QBID for each respective pass-through entity is reduced or limited by the IRS. This reduction is the allowed amount of QBID for each respective pass-through entity.

            i)   Single taxpayers reach the phase-in range once taxable income exceeds $163,300 and enter the upper threshold at $213,300.

            ii)   Married filing jointly taxpayers reach the phase-in threshold when taxable income exceeds $326,600 and enter the upper threshold at $426,600.

        b)   The details of this process are described in Figure 7-2 on page 198.

    3)   **Step 3** – A taxpayer determines the applicable combined QBID by adding together the allowed QBID amount for each respective entity to arrive at a total (or combined) QBID.

        a)   The details of this process are described in item h. on page 200.

    4)   **Step 4** – The final step is for the taxpayer to apply the overall limitation to total (or combined) QBID to determine the correct amount to deduct. This amount is then reported on line 13 of Form 1040.

        a)   The details of this process are described in item i. on page 200.

Step 1 – Determine What Constitutes QBI[1]
Step 1   Ensure the entity is a relevant pass-through entity (i.e., sole proprietor, S corporation, partnership, estate, or trust).
Step 2   Determine whether the entity is directly owned by the taxpayer (e.g., a K-1 is sent directly to the taxpayer as a direct owner of the pass-through entity or business income is reported on Schedule C).
Step 3   Calculate the net amount of income, gain, deduction, and loss with respect to any trade or business. This includes the sale, exchange, or distribution of unrealized receivables or inventory. Also, post-2017 adjustments from changes to accounting methods or previously disallowed losses or deductions currently allowed are treated as items attributable to the trade or business for computing QBI in the current year.

Limited to Amounts

Effectively connected with the conduct of a trade or business within the United States or Puerto Rico	AND	Included or allowed in determining taxable income for the taxable year

Step 4[2]   Remove the following from the calculation of net income[3]

1) Capital gains and losses
2) Dividends
3) Nonoperating interest income
4) Interest income attributable to working capital
5) Gains or losses relating to transactions in commodities
6) Foreign currency gains[4]
7) Any less-than-reasonable salary payments to owners[5]
8) Any deduction or loss properly allocated to the items above

[1] This is the same methodology for determining income from an SSTB.

[2] Conceptually, Congress is allowing small business owners the ability to deduct income that results from the core operations of a small business because the entrepreneurial spirit of small business can drive domestic employment. Because the overarching goal is to spur growth and, ultimately, employment, Congress hopes to incentivize small business owners to grow their core business rather than speculate on side-ventures unrelated to their main business objectives. Therefore, qualified business income is the ordinary, noninvestment income of a business.

[3] There are more reductions in total, but these are the big-picture items that are most likely to affect most taxpayers.

[4] The IRS lists "excess foreign currency gains." For most taxpayers, this effectively means any foreign currency gains.

[5] If the taxpayer paid himself or herself a salary (or guaranteed payment) less than a reasonable amount to receive a higher QBI deduction, the taxpayer must reduce QBI by the amount of the less-than-reasonable salary payment.

Figure 7-1

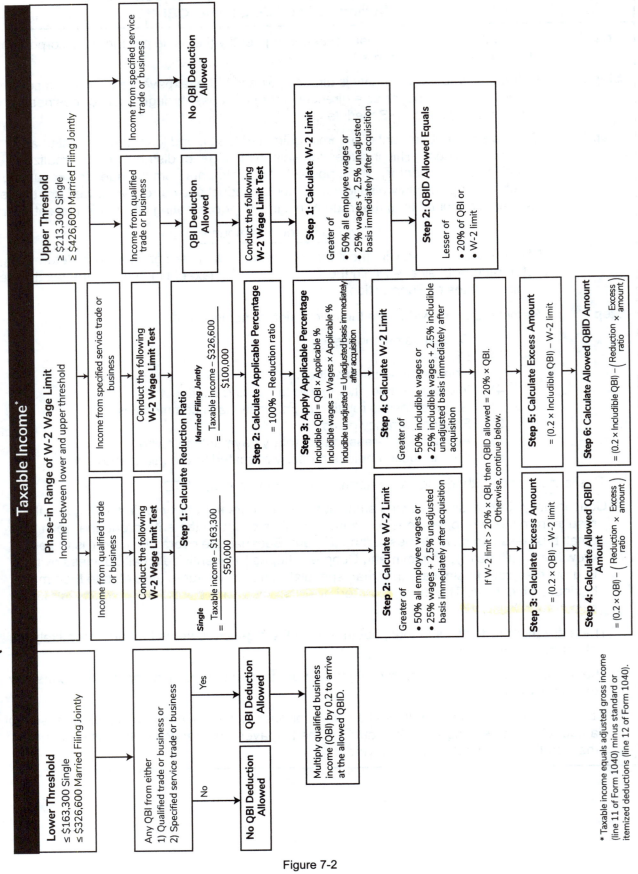

Figure 7-2

f. **Qualified Business Income Deduction Allowed per Entity (Step 2)** is depicted in Figure 7-2 on the previous page.

    1) During this calculation of Step 2, QBID is limited to 20% of QBI. In other words, at best, a taxpayer will be able to ultimately deduct 20% of QBI.

    2) Depending on the taxpayer's taxable income, the QBID may be further reduced beyond 20% of QBI.

    3) A taxpayer's taxable income is divided into three categories: a lower threshold, an upper threshold, and a phase-in range (the range between the two thresholds, i.e., the phase-in of the W-2 wage limit).

        a) Lower threshold (≤ $163,300 single or ≤ $326,600 married filing jointly)
        b) Phase-in range
        c) Upper threshold (≥ $213,300 single or ≥ $426,600 married filing jointly)

    4) If the taxpayer is above the lower threshold, the taxpayer's QBID for each entity begins to be limited. In the case of taxable income being higher than the lower threshold, the QBID allowed from each entity is limited by the amount of the entity's W-2 wages and/or unadjusted basis of assets. If the taxpayer is in the upper threshold, there is no QBID allowed for income from SSTBs.

    5) Figure 7-2 goes into more detail and should be closely reviewed by candidates.

g. **Aggregation Rules**

    1) A business owner may own multiple businesses that are each separate legal entities. For example, a business owner may own multiple gas stations, each of which is a separate S corporation. The IRS will allow a business owner to aggregate these businesses when calculating the allowed QBID if

        a) All aggregated businesses have the same tax year, excluding short years, and

        b) The same person or group of persons owns 50% or more of each trade or business and the businesses to be aggregated satisfy two of the following three criteria:

            i) Products and services of the businesses are the same or customarily offered together.

            ii) Facilities or significant centralized business elements such as HR, accounting, purchasing, IT, etc., are shared.

            iii) The businesses operate in coordination with or reliance upon one or more of the businesses in the aggregated group.

    2) Aggregation is not allowed for SSTBs.

    3) Each individual owner may decide whether to aggregate. The decision need not apply to each entire group of businesses and their owners. For example, Shareholder A could choose to aggregate the businesses on his or her return while Shareholder B may not.

    4) The election to aggregate is a one-time decision, so each subsequent year must be aggregated the same way once aggregation is elected.

5) In terms of meeting the 50% ownership threshold, families are able to aggregate based on their total ownership.

a) Families include spouses, children, grandchildren, and grandparents.

EXAMPLE 7-3	Aggregation Rules			
		Entity A	Entity B	Entity C
Grandfather		60%	20%	
Daughter			30%	40%
Grandson				60%
Total ownership		60%	50%	100%

Grandfather, Daughter, and Grandson can aggregate Entities A, B, and C.

h. **Combined QBID Process (Step 3)**

1) After determining the QBID allowed for each specific company, all of the individual QBIDs are combined (or summed) into one amount.

Combined QBI Process						
Entity Name		**Step 1** **Determine QBI**		**Step 2**		**Step 3** **Sum QBI Allowed**
Entity 1	→	QBI	→	Calculate QBID Allowed	→	QBID Allowed
Entity 2	→	QBI	→	Calculate QBID Allowed	→	QBID Allowed
Entities 3, 4, and 5	→	QBI	→	Calculate QBID Allowed	→	QBID Allowed
Entity 6	→	QBI	→	Calculate QBID Allowed	→	QBID Allowed
				Combined QBID Total		**Sum of QBID Allowed**

i. **Overall Limitation Process (Step 4)**

1) After combining all of the allowed QBIDs, there is one final limitation that determines the amount an individual taxpayer can deduct on line 13 of Form 1040 (i.e., QBID).

Step 4 – QBID Overall Limitation
An individual taxpayer can deduct the lesser of the following: 1) Combined QBID* 2) 20% × (Taxable income – Net capital gains) *Depicted in the previous table as Sum of QBID Allowed

EXAMPLE 7-4	Combined QBI		
		QBI **(Step 1)**	**Allowed QBID per Entity** **(Step 2)**
Entity 1		$100,000	$ 20,000
Entity 2		200,000	30,000
Entities 3, 4, and 5		375,000	75,000
Entity 6		100,000	10,000
		Combined QBID Total	**$135,000** ← (Step 3)

EXAMPLE 7-5	Overall Limitation			

A single taxpayer had net capital gains of $15,000 in the tax year.

		Taxpayer's Taxable Income		
		Scenario A $145,000	Scenario B $175,000	Scenario C $900,000
Step 4	Assumed combined QBID	$135,000	$135,000	$135,000
	20% × (Taxable income – Net capital gains)	$ 26,000	$ 32,000	$177,000
	QBID equals lesser of	$ 26,000	$ 32,000	$135,000

j. **QBI Loss Carryover**

1) If the net QBI (i.e., Step 1 in Figure 7-1 on page 197) for the year from all entities is negative (before any Step 2 calculation), then QBI is treated as a **qualified business loss (QBL)**.

2) If there is more than one positive QBI entity, the losses from the negative entities are allocated to the positive entities in proportion to their QBI amounts to the total of the positive QBIs.

3) A QBL amount is carried forward to the following year (loss cannot be carried back).

a) The W-2 wages and unadjusted basis immediately after acquisition do not carry over to future years; only the QBL carries over.

b) QBL in the subsequent year can be visualized as an entity in the pool of QBI entities and allocated proportionately among that year's QBID per entity.

k. **Other QBID Rules**

1) The deduction does not affect the taxpayer's basis (outside adjusted basis or shareholder's AAA) in the pass-through entity.

2) In addition to SSTBs and qualified trades or businesses, taxpayers can deduct qualified REIT dividends and qualified publicly-traded partnership income.

a) The IRS defines qualified REIT dividend income as neither a capital gain dividend nor a qualified dividend income. Due to these extensive limitations, many tax professionals are waiting for further guidance from the IRS to determine how a REIT dividend could practically be considered a qualified REIT dividend.

b) On the EA exam, candidates could see a conceptual-level question in which qualified REIT dividend income is also a component of the QBID.

EXAMPLE 7-6	Review of QBID for an SSTB

Pam, a married taxpayer, has taxable income of $300,000. For an LLC law firm, her share of income is $200,000, W-2 wages is $60,000, and qualified property is $40,000. Even though Pam is a lawyer, she may take the Sec. 199A deduction because her taxable income is below $426,600. Furthermore, she can take a $40,000 ($200,000 × 20%) deduction because, when taxable income is less than $326,600, the W-2 (wage/qualified property) limit does not apply.

When a married filing jointly taxpayer (who is engaged in an SSTB) has taxable income of more than $326,600 but less than $426,600 ($163,300-$213,300 for single filers), only the "applicable percentage" of qualified items of income, gain, deduction, or loss; the W-2 wages; and the unadjusted basis of qualified property of the taxpayer allocable to such SSTB shall be taken into account in computing the QBI, W-2 wages, and unadjusted basis of qualified property of the taxpayer.

The applicable percentage equals 100% minus the reduction ratio, or {[Taxable income – $163,300 threshold amount ($326,600 for a joint return)] ÷ $50,000 ($100,000 for a joint return)}.

2.   Preparer Reporting Requirements

    a.   Preparers of tax returns qualifying for the QBID are required to report each owner's share of QBI (the determination of QBI is covered in Figure 7-1 on page 197), W-2 wages, unadjusted basis immediately after acquisition of qualified property, and if the entity is an SSTB.

        1)   Separately stating this information is necessary because some partners and shareholders may be eligible to take the deduction while others in the same partnership or S corporation may not because of the taxable incomes of each.

W-2 Wages

    b.   The W-2 wage amounts included and not included on the Schedule C or K-1 for calculating the QBID are presented in the following table:

W-2 Wages

Included	Not Included
Wages paid to employees Elective deferrals to retirement plans Roth contributions W-2 wages taken into account (i.e., as deduction/expense) for calculating QBI	Wages reported in a return filed with the Social Security Administration (SSA) 60 days after due date (including extensions) of that SSA return Payments not reported on a W-2, e.g., amounts on Form 1099 for independent contractor or management fees Payments to statutory employees

Allocation

        1)   In the case of a trade or business conducted by the pass-through entity, a partner's or shareholder's allocable share of wages must be determined in the same manner as the partner's allocable share or a shareholder's pro rata share of wages expense.

Third Party Issued W-2s

        2)   An individual or pass-through entity may take into account wages reported on Forms W-2 issued by a third party provided that the wages reported on the Forms W-2 were paid to employees of the individual or pass-through entity for employment by the individual or pass-through entity.

           a)   The third party paying and reporting the W-2 wages on Form W-2 is precluded from taking into account such wages for the purpose of determining W-2 wages with respect to that third party's reporting for its own QBID.

           b)   The third party payors can include but are not limited to

               i)   Certified professional employer organizations (e.g., ADP, Paychex);

               ii)   Statutory employers (i.e., person/party with control over payment of wages); and

               iii)   Agents, fiduciaries, etc., with control over wage payments and designated (by the Treasury Secretary) to perform employers' duties related to employee wages.

Allocation to Multiple Trades or Businesses

      3) In the case of wages allocable to more than one trade or business, the portion of the W-2 wages allocable to each trade or business is proportional to total W-2 wages as the deductions associated with those wages are allocated among the particular trades or businesses.

          a) The determination of W-2 wages must be made for each trade or business by the individual or the pass-through entity that conducts the trade or business.

               i) In the case of W-2 wages paid by the pass-through entity, the pass-through entity must determine and report W-2 wages for each trade or business conducted by the pass-through entity.

               ii) W-2 wages are presumed to be zero if not determined and reported for each trade or business.

Qualified Property

    c. The qualified property to be reported on the Schedule C or K-1 is defined as depreciable tangible property that is held by and available for use in the qualified trade or business at the close of the tax year, which is used in the production of QBI, and for which the depreciable period has not ended before the close of the tax year.

      1) "Immediately after acquisition" means as of the date the property is placed in service because the IRC provides that "qualified property" must be used in the production of QBI. In order to be used in the production of QBI, the qualified property necessarily must be placed in service.

      2) The unadjusted basis immediately after acquisition (UBIA) of qualified property is not reduced by depreciation, credits, Sec. 179 deductions, or bonus depreciation.

      3) The use of the unadjusted basis of property begins on the date the property is placed in service and ends on the later of

          a) 10 years or

          b) The last day of the last full year in the asset's regular (not ADS) depreciation period.

      4) The UBIA of qualified property is presumed to be zero if not determined and reported for each trade or business.

Allocation

      5) The QBID is applied to partnerships and S corporations at the partner or shareholder level. Thus, a partner's or shareholder's allocable share of the unadjusted basis of qualified property is determined in the same manner as the partner's or shareholder's allocable share of depreciation.

Reporting Specified Service Trade or Business (SSTB)

    d. Each pass-through entity is required to determine whether it conducts an SSTB and disclose that information to its partners, shareholders, or owners on the Schedule C or K-1.

STOP AND REVIEW! **You have completed the outline for this subunit. Study multiple-choice questions 1 through 10 beginning on page 215.**

7.2 ALTERNATIVE MINIMUM TAX (AMT)

Corporations

1. The TCJA repealed the corporate AMT for tax years beginning after December 31, 2017. For tax years beginning in 2018 or 2019 the AMT credit is refundable and can offset regular tax liability. The refundable amount is equal to 50% (2018) or 100% (2019) of the year's available credit less the amount of the credit used to offset the year's regular tax liability.

$$\text{Refundable amount} = \left(\text{Year's available minimum tax credit} - \text{Regular tax liability} \right) \times \text{50\% (2018) or 100\% (2019)}$$

Individuals (Including Sole Proprietors, Partners, and S Corporation Shareholders)

2. The AMT is an income tax in addition to the regular income tax (Form 6251).

   a. The **formula** for computing AMT is below.

AMT FORMULA		
Taxable income		
+ Tax preferences		
+ Standard deduction if taxpayer does not itemize		
+/– Certain other adjustments		
Alternative minimum taxable income (AMTI)		
	2020	25% phaseout for excess over
– Exemption amount		
Single	$ 72,900	$ 518,400
Married filing jointly	$113,400	$1,036,800
Married filing separately	$ 56,700	$ 518,400
Alternative minimum tax base		
× Rate	2020	
AMT base (married filing jointly)		
First $197,900 ($98,950 MFS)	26%	
Excess	28%	
Tentative minimum tax		
– Regular income tax		
Alternative minimum tax		

   1) AMT income (AMTI) is based on taxable income (TI).

      a) AMTI is TI after amounts are added or subtracted for tax preferences, adjustments, and loss limitations.

      b) The AMT base is AMTI reduced by an exemption amount and any AMT NOL carryover.

   2) Tentative AMT is determined by multiplying a rate times the AMT base after a reduction for the AMT Foreign Tax Credit.

      a) For individuals, a two-tiered graduated rate schedule applies.

         i) A 26% rate applies to the first $197,900 ($98,950 if married filing separately) of AMTI (net of the exemption amount).

         ii) A 28% rate applies to any excess.

3) AMT is the excess tentative AMT over regular income tax.

4) AMT must be reported and paid at the same time as regular tax liability. Estimated payments of AMT are required.

5) A credit is allowed for the amount AMT exceeds the regular tax for a tax year. The credit carries forward indefinitely.

b. **Tax preference items.** These items generate tax savings by reducing the taxpayer's taxable income. Therefore, they must be added back to taxable income when computing AMTI.

  1) **Section 1202 stock.** When computing taxable income, noncorporate taxpayers may exclude up to 100% of gain realized on the sale or exchange of qualified small business stock acquired after September 27, 2010, and held more than 5 years.

    a) The exclusion percentage drops to 75% for stock acquired after February 17, 2009, and before September 28, 2010; and to 50% for stock acquired before February 18, 2009. Generally, 7% of the exclusion is a tax preference item for AMT.

    b) However, stock purchased after September 27, 2010, is excluded from tax preference treatment.

  2) **Private activity bonds.** Add any tax-exempt interest minus expenses (including interest) attributable to earning it. Bonds issued in 2009 and 2010 are excluded from tax preference treatment.

  3) **Percentage depletion.** Add any excess of deduction claimed over adjusted basis.

  4) **Intangible drilling costs (IDC).** Add any excess of IDC amortized over 10 years over 65% of net income from oil, gas, and geothermal properties.

c. Usually, **adjustments** eliminate "time value" tax savings from accelerated deductions or deferral of income. An adjustment is an increase or a decrease to TI in computing AMTI and includes the following:

  1) **Installment sales.** The installment method is not allowed for a disposition of stock in trade in the ordinary course of business (e.g., inventory). Add any balance (+ or −) of current-year gain recognized disregarding the installment method, minus gain recognized under the installment method.

  2) **Long-term contracts.** The percentage-of-completion method must be used to determine AMTI. Add any balance (+ or −) if the completed-contract or cash-basis method is normally used.

    a) The same percentage of completion must be used for AMT and regular tax.

    b) Small construction contracts require a simplified method of allocating costs in applying the percentage-of-completion method. The contract's estimated duration must be less than 2 years.

    c) No AMT adjustment is made for home construction contracts.

  3) **Pollution control facilities (certified).** For property placed in service after 1986, the 5-year amortization method for depreciation must be replaced by the alternate depreciation system [Sec. 168(g)]. Add any balance (+ or −).

4) **Mining exploration and development.** If these expenditures were expensed for regular tax purposes, the expenditures must be capitalized and amortized over a 10-year period for AMT. Add any balance (+ or −) for the difference.

   a) Tax loss. If a worthless mine is abandoned, expenditures capitalized but unamortized can be deducted from AMTI.

5) **Net operating loss (NOL) adjustments.** To determine the NOL amount for AMT,

   a) Subtract all amounts added to TI as tax preference amounts to the extent they increased the regular tax NOL.

   b) Tax adjustments made for the AMTI calculation (+ or −) must be made for the NOL calculation.

6) **Distributions from a trust or estate.**

7) In relation to the qualified business income (QBI) deduction, when computing AMTI, the taxpayer determines QBI without taking into consideration any AMT adjustments or preferences.

   a) QBI is the same for AMT as it is for regular tax; thus, the 20% deduction is computed the same way.

   b) The determination of AMTI starts with taxable income, and the amended Code provides no specific add back to AMTI for the 20% deduction.

8) **Research and experimental expenditures.** Add any balance (+ or −) of regular tax deduction claimed for the year (normally expensed), minus expenditures capitalized and amortized over 10 years (beginning in year made).

9) **Standard deduction.** The standard deduction cannot be claimed for AMTI purposes.

10) **Certain itemized deductions.** Some itemized deductions that were claimed for regular tax purposes may not be claimed for AMTI purposes. Disallowed deductions include

    a) State, local, or foreign payments. Likewise, any refunds of these taxes can be excluded from AMTI.

    b) Tax-exempt interest on private activity bonds, which is included in investment income.

    c) **Home equity refinancing.** The TCJA suspended the deduction for interest on home equity indebtedness for the tax years 2018 through 2025 unless the indebtedness is used to buy, build, or substantially improve the taxpayer's home that secures the loan.

11) **Circulation expenditures.** Add any balance (+ or −) of regular tax deduction for the year (normally expensed), minus the expenditures capitalized and amortized over 3 years (beginning in year made).

12) **Incentive stock option (ISO).** Add any balance (+ or −) of the FMV of the stock when exercised, minus the amount paid for stock.

d.   **AMT NOL.** The alternative minimum tax net operating loss (AMT NOL) is technically an adjustment to taxable income (TI).

    1)   After tax preferences have been computed and added to TI and all other adjustments have been computed and made, one of the two AMT NOL adjustment steps is performed.

    2)   **NOL year.** Compute the AMT NOL. It is carried back or forward to another tax year.

        a)   The AMT NOL is modified for each of the tax preferences and other adjustments for the current tax year.

    3)   **Profit year.** An AMT NOL is a final adjustment to TI in computing AMTI in a tax year in which (before reduction by part or all of unused AMT NOLs) there is AMTI.

        a)   Limit: 90% of AMTI. Alternative NOL may not offset more than 90% of the AMT base (computed without the alternative NOL deduction).

e.   **AMT exemption.** An exemption is allowed that reduces AMTI to produce the AMT base. The basic exemption is phased out at $.25 for each dollar of AMTI above a threshold. All members of a controlled group must share the exemption amount.

AMT EXEMPTION AMOUNT (Tax Year 2020)			
Entity/Filing Status	Basic Amount	Threshold	Cap
Married filing jointly	$113,400	$1,036,800	$1,490,400
Surviving spouse	113,400	1,036,800	1,490,400
Head of household	72,900	518,400	810,000
Unmarried and not the previous two	72,900	518,400	810,000
Married filing separately	56,700	518,400	745,200

f.   **AMT FTC.** Only one credit is allowed in computing AMT: the AMT Foreign Tax Credit (FTC). The AMT FTC is the lower of the FTC or 90% of gross tentative AMT computed before any AMT NOL deduction and FTC.

g.   **Minimum Tax Credit (MTC).** A credit is allowed for AMT paid in a tax year against regular tax liability in one or more subsequent tax years.

    1)   **Individuals.** The MTC amount is the AMT that would have been computed if the only adjustments made to TI in computing AMTI were those for (tax-favored) items that result in deferral, as opposed to exclusion, of income.

        a)   To compute the MTC amount, recompute the most recent year's AMT without adjustment for the following (exclusion) items, and add carryover MTC:

            i)   Standard deduction

            ii)   Miscellaneous itemized deductions

            iii)   Tax-exempt interest on private activity bonds

            iv)   Home equity refinancing. The TCJA suspended the deduction for interest on home equity indebtedness for the tax years 2018 through 2025 unless the indebtedness is used to buy, build, or substantially improve the taxpayer's home that secures the loan.

            v)   Depletion

            vi)   Taxes

STOP AND REVIEW! You have completed the outline for this subunit. Study multiple-choice questions 11 through 20 beginning on page 218.

7.3 OTHER TAXES

Employment Taxes and Withholding

1. **Social Security (FICA) tax.** Employers are required to pay tax based on their employee's pay. An employee's wages include all remuneration for employment, including the cash value of all wages paid in a medium other than cash.

    a. The employer must

        1) Pay 6.20% of the first $137,700 (2020) of wages paid for old-age, survivors, and disability insurance (OASDI), plus

        2) Pay 1.45% of all wages for the hospital insurance (Medicare) portion. This tax has no cap.

    b. For 2020, the employer must withhold 6.20% for OASDI and 1.45% for Medicare from the employee's wages.

        1) The employee's contribution (tax) must be withheld upon each payment of wages computed at the same rate up to the same maximum base.

        2) Any overwithholding is taken as a credit against the income tax if the overwithholding resulted from multiple-employer withholding.

    c. Contributions made by the employee are not tax deductible by the employee, while those made by the employer are deductible by the employer.

    d. An employer must pay FICA taxes for all household employees, e.g., babysitters and maids, who are paid more than $2,200 during the year.

        1) Household employees are exempt from withholdings on noncash payments (e.g., goods, lodging, food, or services) made in exchange for household work.

        2) Schedule H is a simplified form that may be used by employers of household workers in private homes. The form is filed, and the employment taxes can be paid with the employer's annual Form 1040.

2. **Additional Medicare Tax**

    NOTE: Throughout our EA Review, "PPACA," instead of "ACA," is used to identify significant topics from the Patient Protection and Affordable Care Act in order to avoid confusion with the Applicable Credit Amount for gift and estate taxes.

    a. PPACA created an additional Medicare tax of 0.9% that applies to wages (cash and noncash), compensation (taxable fringe benefits, bonuses, tips, commissions, etc.), and self-employment income above the specified threshold amount, i.e., the amount of income found in box 5 of the taxpayer's Form W-2 plus net self-employment income on Schedule SE.

Filing Status	Threshold Amount
Married filing jointly	$250,000
Surviving spouse	$200,000
Head of household (with qualifying person)	$200,000
Single	$200,000
Married filing separately	$125,000

1) Withholding by the employer at the additional rate begins at $200,000 regardless of the employee's filing status on Form W-4. If both spouses work for the same employer, the withholding threshold is still applied on an individual basis and not on the combined compensation of both employees.

EXAMPLE 7-7   **No Additional Medicare Tax -- Wages**

One spouse received $220,000 of wages, while the other spouse earned $25,000 of either W-2 wages or net self-employment income. The employer of the first spouse is required to withhold an additional 0.9% additional Medicare tax on the last $20,000 of taxable wages (i.e., $180) even though the couple will not owe the 0.9% additional Medicare tax when they file their 2020 Form 1040 ($220,000 + $25,000 = $245,000, which is less than the $250,000 MFJ threshold). The excess withholding will apply toward any other tax they owe.

---

2) The 0.9% is added to the employer's overall withholding of earned income, as opposed to treating it as a separate item. It is up to the employee to reconcile the total additional Medicare tax at the end of the year when the employee's Form 1040 is filed.

3) Failure by the employer to withhold the additional 0.9% results in the employee being personally responsible for the tax. However, this does not relieve the employer of any penalties associated with failure to withhold the proper amount.

EXAMPLE 7-8   **Additional Medicare Tax -- Wages**

MFJ taxpayers each have box 5 Medicare wages of $170,000 listed on their respective W-2s. The combined $340,000 of earned income will be shown on the form/schedule for calculating the 0.9% additional Medicare tax. The couple will owe a 0.9% additional Medicare tax of $810 [($340,000 − $250,000 threshold) × 0.9%], which will be included as "Other Taxes" on page 2 of Form 1040.

EXAMPLE 7-9   **Additional Medicare Tax -- Self-Employment**

Spouse A has $170,000 of box 5 Medicare wages listed on A's W-2. Spouse B has a K-1 from B's law firm listing box 14 self-employment income of $182,426 ($170,000 net self-employment income). The couple will owe $810 of additional Medicare tax on their collective earned income.

EXAMPLE 7-10   **No Additional Medicare Tax -- Self-Employment**

Spouse X has $170,000 of box 5 Medicare wages listed on X's W-2. Spouse Y has a K-1 from Y's law firm with net self-employment income of $170,000. Y also has a $90,000 loss from the start-up of a new Schedule C business. Since Y's self-employment income is now only $80,000, when it is added to X's $170,000 in W-2 wages, the couple is not above the applicable threshold of $250,000 for married filing jointly taxpayers. Therefore, no additional Medicare tax on their collective earned income is due.

4) The employee portion includes an additional 0.9% for high-income earnings, i.e., earnings in excess of $200,000 ($250,000 MFJ, $125,000 MFS).

    a) Individuals with wages and self-employment income calculate their liabilities in three steps:

        i) Calculate the tax on any wages in excess of the applicable threshold without regard to any withholding;

        ii) Reduce the applicable threshold by the total amount of Medicare wages received, but not below zero; and

        iii) Calculate the tax on any self-employment income in excess of the reduced threshold.

    b) Remember that this tax only applies to the employee's share of Medicare taxes. Therefore, self-employed individuals are not allowed an additional deduction for one-half of the 0.9%, as the deduction is only for the employer's payment of Medicare taxes. Also, a loss from self-employment can only offset self-employment income, i.e., not W-2 income.

EXAMPLE 7-11	Additional Medicare Tax -- Wages and Self-Employment

C, a single filer, has $130,000 in wages and $145,000 in self-employment income. C's wages are not in excess of the $200,000 threshold for single filers, so C is not liable for the surtax on these wages. Before calculating the tax on self-employment income, the $200,000 threshold for single filers is reduced by C's $130,000 in wages, resulting in a reduced self-employment threshold of $70,000. C is liable to pay tax on $75,000 of self-employment income ($145,000 − $70,000).

---

3. **Net investment income tax.** Under PPACA, all investment income in excess of deductions allowable for such income and income from passive activities are subject to a 3.8% tax. This tax essentially applies FICA taxes to income that previously was not subject to the taxes.

    a. The tax is imposed on the lesser of an individual's net investment income or any excess of modified adjusted gross income (MAGI) for the tax year over a specified threshold.

Filing Status	Threshold Amount
Married filing jointly, surviving spouse	$250,000
Single, head of household	$200,000
Married filing separately	$125,000

    b. MAGI is the sum of AGI and excludable foreign earned income/housing costs after any deductions, exclusions, or credits applicable to the foreign earned income.

    c. Net investment income tax does not apply to non-resident aliens.

4. **Self-employment tax.** The FICA tax liability is imposed on net earnings from self-employment at twice the rate that applies to an employer, that is, at the rate of 15.3% [2 × (6.20% + 1.45%)].

    a. In order to figure self-employment tax liability, a self-employed person is entitled to deduct an amount equal to the employer's portion of the tax. This reduced amount of self-employment net income is net earnings from self-employment and is multiplied by the self-employment tax rate to arrive at the amount of self-employment tax.

$$\text{Net earnings from self-employment} = \text{NI from self-employment} - (.0765 \times \text{NI from self-employment})$$

    b. Instead of reducing net income from self-employment by 7.65%, the reduced amount (i.e., net earnings from SE) may be computed by multiplying net income from self-employment by 92.35%.

NI
× .9235%
NI SE
× 15.3%
SE Tax

c. Self-employment income is equal to the net earnings an individual derives from self-employment during any tax year.

d. Net income from self-employment does not include rents, gain (or loss) from disposition of business property, capital gain (or loss), nonbusiness interest, or dividends.

e. An individual who has less than $400 in net earnings from self-employment during the year has no self-employment income.

f. For 2020, the self-employed person is allowed a deduction for the employer portion of the FICA tax paid to arrive at his or her AGI. The deduction is 50% of the FICA tax paid (ignoring any portion subject to the Additional Medicare Tax).

g. The income inclusion for self-employment taxes differs from gross income inclusion in the case of ministers and/or clergymen.

   1) A minister may exclude the rental value of his or her home or parsonage if it is connected with the performance of religious duties.

   2) The rental value is not excluded from the income used to compute self-employment taxes.

   3) Any wages received by ministers and/or clergymen on a W-2 is not subject to Social Security but is included in self-employment income, unless one of the following applies:

      a) The minister and/or clergyman is a member of a religious order who has taken a vow of poverty.

      b) The minister and/or clergyman asks the Internal Revenue Service (IRS) for an exemption from SE tax for his or her services and the IRS approves his or her request.

      c) The minister and/or clergyman is subject only to the Social Security laws of a foreign country under the provisions of a Social Security agreement between the United States and that country.

5. **Unemployment (FUTA) tax.** This tax is imposed on employers. The tax is 6.0% of the first $7,000 of wages paid to each employee. The employee does not pay any portion of FUTA.

   a. Employers are required to pay unemployment taxes for 2020 if they pay wages of $1,500 or more for any quarter in 2019 or 2020.

   b. Up to 5.4% of the 6.0% is allowable as a credit based on state unemployment taxes paid.

6. **Household employee taxes.** An employer is subject to these taxes if (s)he

   a. Paid one household employee cash wages of $2,200 or more during the year (FICA taxes),

   b. Withheld federal income tax at the request of the employee (income tax), or

   c. Paid total cash wages of $1,000 or more in any calendar quarter to household employees (FUTA tax).

7. With regard to income tax withholding and Social Security, Medicare, and federal unemployment, no differences are recognized among full-time employees, part-time employees, and temporary employees.

8. If an individual is required to report employment taxes or give tax statements to employees, (s)he must have an employer identification number (EIN).

   a. The EIN is a nine-digit number the IRS issues to identify the tax accounts of employers.

9.   Penalties are applied when an employer fails to make a required deposit on time.

a.   The penalties do not apply if any failure to make a proper and timely deposit was due to reasonable cause and not to willful neglect.

b.   For amounts not properly or timely deposited, the penalty rates are

1)   2% for deposits made 1 to 5 days late,
2)   5% for deposits made 6 to 15 days late, and
3)   10% for deposits made 16 or more days late.

Special Withholding Deposit Deferrals and Credits for 2020 Only

10. Employers have been provided the following deposit deferral options for and credits against the employer's and employee's portions of Social Security tax as part of COVID-19 relief efforts:

a.   The deposit of the employer's portion of Social Security payroll taxes due from March 27, 2020, through December 31, 2020, can be deferred for eligible employers and self-employed individuals. Fifty percent of the deferred taxes are required to be deposited on or before December 31, 2021, with the remaining 50% required to be deposited on or before December 31, 2022.

b.   The employee's share of Social Security tax liability from September 1, 2020, through December 31, 2020, may be deferred until January 1, 2021, and deposited over the following 4 months (i.e., until April 30, 2021). Qualified employee withholding includes only employees with biweekly pay of less than $4,000.

c.   A refundable employee retention credit is available for 50% of wages paid from March 13, 2020, through December 31, 2020, against the employer's portion of Social Security tax. Each employee's applicable wages are limited to $10,000. The employer must satisfy one of the following conditions to be eligible:

1)   The operation of the trade or business was fully or partially suspended by an appropriate governmental authority due to COVID-19 during any calendar quarter or

2)   The employer suffered a significant decline in gross receipts such that the gross receipts for the calendar quarter are less than 20% of gross receipts for the same calendar quarter in the prior year.

d.   A refundable paid sick leave and family leave credit is available for 100% of leave wages paid from April 1, 2020, through December 31, 2020, against the employer's portion of Social Security tax. To be eligible, the employer must

1)   Have no more than 500 employees and
2)   Be required to pay leave wages under the Families First Coronavirus Response Act.

Farm Optional Method

11. A taxpayer may use this method to figure net earnings from farm self-employment if gross farm income was $8,460 or less or net farm profits were less than $6,107.

Use of the Farm Optional Method

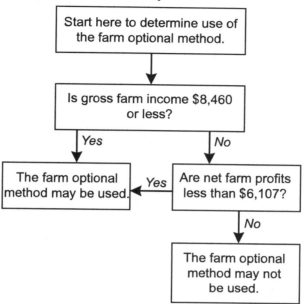

Figure 7-3

a. Net farm profits are the total of the amounts from Schedule F (Form 1040), line 34, and Schedule K-1 (Form 1065), box 14, code A, minus the amount the taxpayer would have entered on Schedule SE, line 1b, had the taxpayer not used the optional method.

b. There is no limit on how many years this method can be used.

c. Under this method, the taxpayer reports in Schedule SE, Part II, line 15, two-thirds of gross farm income, up to $5,640, as net earnings. This method can increase or decrease net earnings from farm self-employment, even if the farming business had a loss.

Figure Farm Net Earnings

IF gross income is . . .	THEN net earnings are equal to . . .
$8,460 or less	two-thirds of gross farm income.
more than $8,460	$5,640.

d. For a farm partnership, figure the taxpayer's share of gross income based on the partnership agreement. With guaranteed payments, the taxpayer's share of the partnership's gross income is the taxpayer's guaranteed payments plus the taxpayer's share of the gross income after it is reduced by all guaranteed payments made by the partnership. If the taxpayer was a limited partner, only guaranteed payments for services the taxpayer actually rendered to or on behalf of the partnership would be included.

Homebuyer Credit Repayment

12. Between April 8, 2008, and May 1, 2010, a credit for qualifying first-time homebuyers was available. Taxpayers who claimed the credit after 2008 did not have to repay the credit once they lived in the home for 3 years. Taxpayers who claimed it in 2008 continue to repay it over 15 years.

    a. The repayment amount each year is 6.67% of the original credit amount. If, at any time during the repayment period, the taxpayer converts the property to nonqualified use (e.g., no longer primary residence), all remaining balance of the credit is due that year.

    b. The repayment is generally reported on Schedule 4 (Form 1040) line 60b; however, some taxpayers may be required to file Form 5405.

FBAR

13. For taxpayers having a financial interest in or signature authority over a foreign financial account (including a bank account, brokerage account, mutual fund, trust, or other type of foreign financial account) exceeding certain thresholds, the Bank Secrecy Act may require them to report the account yearly to the Department of Treasury by electronically filing a Financial Crimes Enforcement Network (FinCEN) 114, *Report of Foreign Bank and Financial Accounts* (FBAR).

    a. Those required to file an FBAR who fail to properly file a complete and correct FBAR may be subject to a civil penalty not to exceed $13,481 per violation for nonwillful violations that are not due to reasonable cause. For willful violations, the penalty may be the greater of $134,806 or 50% of the balance in the account at the time of the violation for each violation.

Specified Foreign Financial Assets

14. Taxpayers with specified foreign financial assets that exceed certain thresholds must report those assets to the IRS on Form 8938, *Statement of Specified Foreign Financial Assets*, which is filed with the taxpayer's tax return. This form is in addition to the FBAR filing requirement, despite the chance of duplication of reported items.

    a. There is a $10,000 penalty for failure to file the form on time. After 90 days of being notified of the failure, an additional $10,000 penalty will be assessed every 30 days, but it is not to exceed $50,000.

STOP AND REVIEW! **You have completed the outline for this subunit. Study multiple-choice questions 21 through 30 beginning on page 222.**

QUESTIONS

7.1 Qualified Business Income Deduction (QBID)

NOTE: The following questions are duplicated in EA Part 2, Study Unit 5, Subunit 9.

1. Which of the following statements about qualified business income (loss) in relation to QBID is correct?

A. If the net amount of qualified income, gain, deduction, and loss is greater than zero, the deduction must be carried over to the next year.

B. If the net amount of qualified income, gain, deduction, and loss is less than zero, the loss must be carried back to the prior year.

C. If the net amount of qualified income, gain, deduction, and loss is less than zero, the loss must be carried over to the next year.

D. The net amount of qualified income, gain, deduction, and loss is always greater than zero.

Answer (C) is correct.
    REQUIRED: The correct statement about QBI.
    DISCUSSION: If the net amount of qualified income, gain, deduction, and loss is less than zero, the loss must be carried over to the next year.
    Answer (A) is incorrect. If the net amount of qualified income, gain, deduction, and loss is greater than zero, the QBI deduction is taken in the current year. **Answer (B) is incorrect.** If the net amount of qualified income, gain, deduction, and loss is less than zero, the loss cannot be carried back. **Answer (D) is incorrect.** The net amount of qualified income, gain, deduction, and loss can be less than zero.

2. Zachary owns 40% of an S corporation that pays him $70,000 of wages and $10,000 of dividends and allocates him $89,000 of income. What is Zachary's qualified business income (QBI)?

A. $70,000

B. $89,000

C. $159,000

D. $99,000

Answer (B) is correct.
    REQUIRED: The QBI amount.
    DISCUSSION: QBI is the net amount of income, gain, deduction, and loss with respect to any qualified trade or business of the taxpayer conducted within the United States and included or allowed in determining taxable income for the taxable year.
    Answer (A) is incorrect. The amount of $70,000 represents employee compensation, which is not QBI. **Answer (C) is incorrect.** QBI does not include employee compensation. **Answer (D) is incorrect.** QBI does not include any dividend or income equivalent to a dividend.

3. Tom owns a domestic sole proprietorship that allocates $55,000 of income to him and pays $30,000 of wages to employees. He also owns 30% of a foreign trust that allocates $60,000 of income to him and pays him $50,000 of wages. Neither the sole proprietorship nor the trust are specified service businesses. What is the total amount of qualified business income (QBI) for Tom?

A. $12,000

B. $110,000

C. $85,000

D. $55,000

Answer (D) is correct.
    REQUIRED: The total QBI amount.
    DISCUSSION: Qualified business income are items of income, gain, deduction, and loss to the extent such items are effectively connected with the conduct of a trade or business within the United States; it does not include wages and foreign income. Thus, Tom has qualified business income of $55,000.
    Answer (A) is incorrect. The amount of $12,000 is 20% of the $60,000 income from the foreign trust. The foreign trust income does not qualify. **Answer (B) is incorrect.** The amount of $110,000 is the total of the $60,000 income from the foreign trust and the $50,000 of wages received from the foreign trust. The foreign trust income does not qualify. **Answer (C) is incorrect.** The amount of $85,000 is the total of the $55,000 income and the $30,000 wages paid from the sole proprietorship. Wages paid to employees factors into the deduction but not the amount of QBI.

4. Lana and Luke are married and have a taxable income of $305,000. Their share of the income from an accounting partnership is $250,000. The accounting partnership pays a total of $90,000 in W-2 wages. What is their allowed qualified business income deduction (QBID) for the partnership?

A. $0

B. $50,000

C. $125,000

D. $61,000

Answer (B) is correct.
REQUIRED: The QBID amount.
DISCUSSION: Lana and Luke's taxable income is less than $326,600, and they can simply deduct 20% of qualified business income, $50,000 ($250,000 × 20%). The limitations and disallowance do not apply at this taxable amount.
Answer (A) is incorrect. Lana and Luke can claim the QBI deduction because the disallowance rule does not apply if the taxpayers have taxable income of less than $426,600 (for a joint return). Answer (C) is incorrect. The amount of $125,000 is 50% of Lana and Luke's share of income from the accounting partnership. Answer (D) is incorrect. The amount of $61,000 is 20% of taxable income.

5. A taxpayer may NOT claim the qualified business income (QBI) deduction if (s)he has qualified business income from which of the following entities?

A. S corporations.

B. C corporations.

C. Sole proprietorships.

D. Trusts.

Answer (B) is correct.
REQUIRED: The non-pass-through entity.
DISCUSSION: The QBI deduction is available to noncorporate taxpayers who have qualified business income from qualified pass-through entities. Qualified pass-through entities include sole proprietorships, S corporations, partnerships, trusts, and estates.

6. Hannah, a single taxpayer, owns 50% of a partnership and has taxable income of $85,000. She has qualified business income (QBI) of $70,000 from the partnership. The partnership paid a total of $27,500 in W-2 wages and does not have any qualified property. Under Sec. 199A, what is Hannah's deductible amount for the partnership (i.e., before applying the taxable income/overall limitation)?

A. $14,000

B. $13,750

C. $35,000

D. $6,875

Answer (A) is correct.
REQUIRED: The deductible QBI amount.
DISCUSSION: Because Hannah's taxable income is less than the $163,300 threshold amount, the W-2 wages/qualified property limit does not apply. Thus, for this partnership, there is a deduction equal to 20% of qualified business income ($70,000), $14,000.
Answer (B) is incorrect. The amount of $13,750 is 50% of the W-2 wages paid by the partnership. Because the taxable income is less than the $163,300 threshold amount, the W-2 wages/qualified property limit does not apply. Answer (C) is incorrect. The amount of $35,000 is 50% of Hannah's qualified business income. Answer (D) is incorrect. The amount of $6,875 is 25% of the W-2 wages paid by the partnership.

7. Robin, Monica, and Rose have a partnership that is a qualified business. In the partnership agreement, each partner has a one-third share in income and expenses. The partnership generated qualified business income (QBI) of $150,000, paid total W-2 wages of $120,000, and purchased qualified property with an unadjusted basis of $60,000. There are no special allocations to partners. What is Robin's allocable share of QBI, W-2 wages, and qualified property, respectively?

	QBI	W-2 Wages	Qualified Property
A.	$150,000	$120,000	$60,000
B.	$50,000	$40,000	$20,000
C.	$50,000	$40,000	$60,000
D.	$450,000	$360,000	$180,000

Answer (B) is correct.
REQUIRED: The allocable share of QBI, wages, and property.
DISCUSSION: The taxpayer should take into account his or her allocable share of each qualified item of income, gain, deduction, and loss; only allocable share of the taxpayer's wages and qualified property should be taken into account to calculate the W-2 wages/qualified property limit. Because Robin is a one-third owner, his allocable share of QBI is $50,000 ($150,000 ÷ 3), his allocable share of W-2 wages is $40,000 ($120,000 ÷ 3), and his allocable share of qualified property is $20,000 ($60,000 ÷ 3).
Answer (A) is incorrect. The amounts of $150,000, $120,000, and $60,000 should be divided by 3 to reach Robin's allocable share of QBI, W-2 wages, and qualified property. **Answer (C) is incorrect.** Robin's allocable share of qualified property is $20,000, not $60,000. **Answer (D) is incorrect.** The amounts of $450,000, $360,000, and $180,000 should be divided by 3, not multiplied by 3, to reach Robin's allocable share of QBI, W-2 wages, and qualified property.

8. Which of the following items are included in qualified business income (QBI)?

A. Pre-2018 previously disallowed losses or deductions that are allowed in the current year.

B. Allocable losses associated with a qualified trade or business.

C. Short-term capital losses.

D. Guaranteed payments paid for services rendered with respect to a qualified trade or business.

Answer (B) is correct.
REQUIRED: The QBI item.
DISCUSSION: QBI includes any items of income, gain, deduction, and loss to the extent that such items are effectively connected with the conduct of a trade or business within the United States and are included or allowed in determining taxable income for the taxable year.
Answer (A) is incorrect. The disallowed losses or deductions have to be from a post-2017 tax year to be included in QBI. **Answer (C) is incorrect.** QBI does not include any item of short-term capital gain, short-term capital loss, long-term capital gain, or long-term capital loss. **Answer (D) is incorrect.** QBI does not include any guaranteed payment described in Sec. 707(c) paid to a partner for services rendered with respect to the trade or business.

9. Robin and Monica are married and filing a joint return. They have a taxable income of $300,000. Robin owns a qualified sole proprietorship that generates qualified business income (QBI) of $50,000, and Monica is the sole owner of a qualified S corporation that generates a QBI of $75,000. How much is Robin and Monica's combined QBI deduction (QBID) amount for the year?

A. $25,000

B. $125,000

C. $300,000

D. $60,000

Answer (A) is correct.
REQUIRED: The combined QBID.
DISCUSSION: The combined QBID allowed amount is the sum of the amount for each qualified trade or business carried on by the taxpayer. Because Robin and Monica's income is less than $326,600, the W-2 wages/qualified property limit does not apply. Thus, their QBID allowed amount for the sole proprietorship is 20% of QBI, $10,000 ($50,000 × 20%), and their QBID allowed amount for the S corporation is 20% of QBI, $15,000 ($75,000 × 20%). Therefore, the combined qualified business income deduction is $25,000 ($10,000 + $15,000).
Answer (B) is incorrect. The amount of $125,000 fails to multiply QBI by 20%. **Answer (C) is incorrect.** The amount of taxable income is $300,000. **Answer (D) is incorrect.** The amount of $60,000 is taxable income multiplied by 20%.

10. John, a single taxpayer, has taxable income of $303,000. He owns a qualified sole proprietorship that generated $100,000 of qualified business income (QBI) and paid no wages. The sole proprietorship has a qualified property with an unadjusted basis of $50,000. What is the QBI deductible amount John can claim for the sole proprietorship?

A. $60,600

B. $1,250

C. $50,000

D. $10,000

Answer (B) is correct.
    REQUIRED: The QBI deduction amount when unadjusted basis is involved.
    DISCUSSION: Because John's taxable income is greater than $213,300, the W-2/qualified property limit applies. Thus, for the sole proprietorship, the deductible amount is limited to the lesser of (1) 20% of QBI, $20,000 ($100,000 × 20%), or (2) 2.5% of the unadjusted basis of qualified property, $1,250 ($50,000 × 2.5%). Thus, John can claim $1,250 under the Sec. 199A deduction for the sole proprietorship.
    Answer (A) is incorrect. The amount of $60,600 is 20% of taxable income. **Answer (C) is incorrect.** The amount of $50,000 is the unadjusted basis of the qualified property. **Answer (D) is incorrect.** The amount of $10,000 is 20% of the qualified property's unadjusted basis.

7.2 Alternative Minimum Tax (AMT)

11. Which of the following would NOT be a part of the computation of alternative minimum tax?

A. Tax-exempt private activity bond interest.

B. Standard deductions.

C. Self-employment tax.

D. Certain itemized deductions.

Answer (C) is correct.
    REQUIRED: The item not included in the computation of alternative minimum tax.
    DISCUSSION: Tax-exempt private activity bond interest is a tax preference item. Self-employment tax is not a part of the computation of alternative minimum tax. Standard deductions and certain itemized deductions also are included in the computation of tentative minimum tax (Publication 17).
    Answer (A) is incorrect. Tax-exempt private activity bond interest is a tax-preference item and is a part of the computation of alternative minimum tax. **Answer (B) is incorrect.** Standard deductions are added back to taxable income in computing alternative minimum tax. **Answer (D) is incorrect.** Certain itemized deductions are added back to taxable income in computing alternative minimum tax.

12. Which of the following is NOT a tax preference item or an adjustment to taxable income for alternative minimum tax purposes?

A. Addition of balance of research and experimental expenditures.

B. Addition of the standard deduction (if claimed).

C. Addition of all itemized deductions (if claimed).

D. Subtraction of any refund of state and local taxes included in gross income.

Answer (C) is correct.
    REQUIRED: The item that is not a tax preference item or an adjustment to taxable income for alternative minimum tax.
    DISCUSSION: To calculate taxable income for alternative minimum tax purposes, tax preferences, balance of research and experimental expenditures, and the standard deduction, if taken, are added back to taxable income. Certain other adjustments are also added to or subtracted from taxable income, including some itemized deductions claimed (Publication 17).
    Answer (A) is incorrect. Addition of balance of research and experimental expenditures is an adjustment to taxable income for the alternative minimum tax. **Answer (B) is incorrect.** The standard deduction is added to taxable income as an adjustment. **Answer (D) is incorrect.** It is a disallowed itemized deduction that is an adjustment to taxable income.

13. In 2019, Ted and Alice had an alternative minimum tax liability of $19,000. This is the first tax year in which they ever paid the alternative minimum tax. They recomputed the alternative minimum tax using only exclusion preferences and adjustments. This resulted in an $8,500 alternative minimum tax liability. In 2020, Ted and Alice have a regular tax liability of $45,000. Their tentative minimum tax liability is $42,000. What is the Minimum Tax Credit carryover to 2021?

A. $19,000

B. $16,000

C. $7,500

D. $0

Answer (C) is correct.

REQUIRED: The taxpayer's MTC carryover.

DISCUSSION: For the first tax year that the AMT is owed, the MTC is the portion of the AMT attributable to deferral preferences or adjustments. Exclusion preferences or adjustments are disallowed itemized deductions or standard deduction, excess percentage depletion, tax-exempt interest from private activity bonds not issued in 2009 or 2010, and excluded gain from the sale of small business stock except for stock purchased after September 27, 2010. In 2019, the deferral preferences and adjustments result in a $10,500 MTC ($19,000 2019 AMT liability – $8,500 2019 recomputed AMT liability). This credit can be carried over to 2020 and used to the extent that the regular tax liability exceeds the tentative minimum tax. This amount is $3,000 ($45,000 2020 regular tax liability – $42,000 2020 TMT liability). Therefore, the $10,500 MTC offsets the $3,000 excess, and a $7,500 MTC is carried forward to 2021 (Publication 17).

Answer (A) is incorrect. This amount is the AMT liability before recomputation. **Answer (B) is incorrect.** Only $7,500 is carried forward to 2021. **Answer (D) is incorrect.** There is a carryforward to 2021.

14. With respect to the alternative minimum tax for individuals, all of the following are tax preference items EXCEPT

A. Casualty (federally declared disaster) loss from Schedule A.

B. Tax-exempt interest on private activity bonds (not issued in 2009 or 2010).

C. Depletion.

D. Intangible drilling costs.

Answer (A) is correct.

REQUIRED: The item that is not considered a tax preference item.

DISCUSSION: A casualty/disaster loss is not an adjustment and is allowed as a deduction for alternative minimum taxable income purposes. Hence, it is not considered a tax preference item (Publication 17).

15. With regard to the alternative minimum tax for individuals, all of the following are adjustments or preferences in the computation of alternative minimum taxable income EXCEPT

A. Adjusted gain from sale of depreciable property.

B. Refund of state income tax.

C. Moving expenses (for military).

D. Research and experimental expenditures.

Answer (C) is correct.

REQUIRED: The item that is not considered an adjustment or tax preference item.

DISCUSSION: Taxable income must be adjusted to arrive at alternative minimum taxable income. The adjustments are described in Secs. 56 and 58, with tax preferences in Sec. 57. The adjustments with respect to itemized deductions of an individual are contained in Sec. 56(b)(1). Moving expenses are not considered as an adjustment or preference in the computation of alternative minimum taxable income (Publication 17).

16. With regard to the alternative minimum tax for individuals, which of the following is always an adjustment or preference in the computation of alternative minimum taxable income?

A. Medical expenses.

B. State income tax payments.

C. Moving expenses (for military).

D. Nonbusiness bad debt.

Answer (B) is correct.
   REQUIRED: The item that is considered an adjustment or tax preference item.
   DISCUSSION: Taxable income must be adjusted to arrive at alternative minimum taxable income (AMTI). The adjustments are described in Secs. 56 and 58, with tax preferences in Sec. 57. The adjustments with respect to itemized deductions of an individual are contained in Sec. 56(b)(1). State income tax payments must be added back into the AMTI calculation (Publication 17).

17. Alternative minimum taxable income is

A. Taxable income increased by tax preferences and increased or decreased by adjustments and other statutory modifications.

B. The sum of all tax preferences.

C. Applicable for both individuals and corporations.

D. Taxable income adjusted by tax preferences and reduced by an exemption amount.

Answer (A) is correct.
   REQUIRED: The definition of alternative minimum taxable income.
   DISCUSSION: Taxable income is adjusted by positive and negative adjustments and various other statutory items to arrive at alternative minimum taxable income. There are numerous adjustments to items taken into account in determining taxable income as well as some additional adjustments. Tax preference items are also added to taxable income to arrive at alternative minimum taxable income (Publication 17).
   Answer (B) is incorrect. The sum of all tax preferences is only one adjustment to taxable income to arrive at alternative minimum taxable income.
   Answer (C) is incorrect. The corporate AMT has been suspended through 2021. **Answer (D) is incorrect.** The exemption amount is subtracted from alternative minimum taxable income to arrive at a tax base before the tax rate is applied.

18. All of the following are considered adjustments for arriving at alternative minimum taxable income EXCEPT

A. Local real property taxes.

B. Local income taxes.

C. Home mortgage interest (debt used to purchase, build, or substantially improve a residence).

D. Standard deduction.

Answer (C) is correct.
   REQUIRED: The item which is not an adjustment for arriving at alternative minimum taxable income.
   DISCUSSION: Taxable income must be adjusted to arrive at alternative minimum taxable income. The adjustments are described in Secs. 56 and 58, with tax preferences in Sec. 57. The adjustments with respect to itemized deductions of an individual are contained in Sec. 56(b)(1). No adjustment is made to taxable income for home mortgage interest in order to arrive at alternative minimum taxable income [Publication 17 and Sec. 56(b)(1)(C)(i)].

19. When determining his alternative minimum tax, Edward had the following adjustments and preference items:

Itemized deduction for state taxes	$1,800
Refund of prior-year state income tax	300
Cash contributions	800
Capital gain	700
Depletion in excess of adjusted basis	700

What are the amounts of tax preference items and adjustments to taxable income for alternative minimum tax purposes on Edward's 2020 tax return?

	Preference	Adjustments
A.	$700	$1,500
B.	$700	$0
C.	$1,400	$1,800
D.	$2,200	$2,200

Answer (A) is correct.
REQUIRED: The amounts of tax preference items and adjustments.
DISCUSSION: The depletion is a tax preference item that must be added back for alternative minimum tax purposes. The adjustments, on the other hand, include the itemized deduction reduced by the refund of prior-year state income tax (Publication 17). Thus, the tax preference item totals $700, and the adjustments equal $1,500 ($1,800 itemized deduction – $300 refund).
Answer (B) is incorrect. The preferences include the depletion, and the adjustments include the itemized deduction reduced by the refund. **Answer (C) is incorrect.** The adjustments are reduced for the state refund. **Answer (D) is incorrect.** The preferences include the depletion, and the adjustments do not include the capital gain.

20. Alternative minimum tax for individuals adjustments and preferences. Which of the following is a preference or adjustment item for noncorporate taxpayers?

A. Standard deduction.

B. Incentive stock options.

C. Tax-exempt interest on certain private activity bonds (not issued in 2009 or 2010).

D. All of the answers are correct.

Answer (D) is correct.
REQUIRED: The item that is a preference or adjustment item for noncorporate taxpayers.
DISCUSSION: Several adjustments affect only noncorporate taxpayers. The standard deduction, tax-exempt interest on private activity bonds (not issued in 2009 or 2010) (which is included in investment income), and incentive stock options are examples of these adjustments (Publication 17).
Answer (A) is incorrect. Incentive stock options and tax-exempt interest on certain private activity bonds (not issued in 2009 or 2010) are also preference or adjustment items for noncorporate taxpayers when determining the alternative minimum tax. **Answer (B) is incorrect.** The standard deduction and tax-exempt interest on certain private activity bonds (not issued in 2009 or 2010) are also preference or adjustment items for noncorporate taxpayers when determining the alternative minimum tax. **Answer (C) is incorrect.** The standard deduction and incentive stock options are also preference or adjustment items for noncorporate taxpayers when determining the alternative minimum tax.

7.3 Other Taxes

21. Taxpayers A and B, filing a joint return, earned box 5 Medicare wages of $190,000 and $110,000, respectively. Determine the amount of additional Medicare tax they owe on their final Form 1040.

A. $0

B. $450

C. $2,700

D. $25,650

Answer (B) is correct.
REQUIRED: The applicable amount of additional Medicare tax for this couple filing a joint return.
DISCUSSION: Married filing joint taxpayers owe the additional Medicare tax of 0.9% of excess income when combined income exceeds $250,000. Taxpayers A and B have a combined income of $300,000 ($190,000 + $110,000) and additional Medicare tax liability of $450 [($300,000 – $250,000) × 0.9%].
Answer (A) is incorrect. Neither taxpayer individually exceeds the threshold, but together they do. Therefore, they owe the additional tax. Answer (C) is incorrect. The additional Medicare tax has a floor threshold of $250,000 for MFJ taxpayers. The amount of $2,700 ignores the floor. Answer (D) is incorrect. The total of all three FICA taxes is $25,650 if both the OASDI ceiling and additional Medicare tax floor were ignored.

22. Rev. Janice Burton is a full-time minister at the Downtown Missionary Church. The church allows her to use the parsonage that has an annual fair rental value of $4,800. The church pays an annual salary of $13,200, of which $1,200 is designated for utility costs. Her utility costs during the year were $1,000. What is Rev. Burton's income for self-employment tax purposes?

A. $18,000

B. $13,200

C. $12,200

D. $13,400

Answer (A) is correct.
REQUIRED: The computation of a minister's income for self-employment tax purposes.
DISCUSSION: In the case of a minister, net earnings from self-employment in connection with the performance of religious duties are computed without regard to the exclusion of rental value of home or parsonage (Publication 517 and Sec. 107). Therefore, the $13,200 annual salary plus the $4,800 rental value is used to determine Rev. Burton's self-employment taxes.
Answer (B) is incorrect. The annual salary and rental value of the parsonage are combined to determine the self-employment tax. Answer (C) is incorrect. The rental value of the parsonage is included in income for self-employment tax purposes. Answer (D) is incorrect. The rental value of the parsonage and the utility costs are included in income for self-employment tax purposes.

23. In which situation would Janice NOT be required to file Schedule H, *Household Employment Taxes*, for the year 2020?

A. Paid $2,200 wages to Cynthia for babysitting in Janice's home.

B. Withheld $100 federal income tax from payments to her yard worker.

C. Paid $2,200 to her mother for housekeeping.

D. Paid household help, other than her mother, $1,000 for the period July, August, and September.

Answer (C) is correct.
REQUIRED: The situation that does not require the taxpayer to file Schedule H.
DISCUSSION: A taxpayer should file Schedule H if (s)he has paid cash wages of $2,200 or more to any single household employee during the year 2020 (FICA tax liability) or paid $1,000 or more to household employees in any quarter of the year (FUTA tax liability). However, wages that a taxpayer pays to a parent are not counted for purposes of determining Social Security and Medicare wages, even if the amount paid exceeds $2,200 for the year 2020 (Publication 926).
Answer (A) is incorrect. Schedule H should be filed when payments of $2,200 or more are made to a single household employee during the year. Answer (B) is incorrect. Schedule H should be filed to reflect the employee's wages withheld. Answer (D) is incorrect. Schedule H should be filed when employees earn $1,000 or more in a quarter year (Publication 926).

24. A single taxpayer has $130,000 in wages and $200,000 in net self-employment income. What is the amount of additional Medicare tax that would be due on Form 1040 for the year?

A. $0

B. $720

C. $1,170

D. $1,845

Answer (C) is correct.
REQUIRED: The additional Medicare tax for a single taxpayer.
DISCUSSION: A single taxpayer with income in excess of $200,000 is taxed an additional 0.9% on the excess as a Medicare tax. The taxpayer had total income of $330,000 ($130,000 + $200,000). The additional Medicare tax due is $1,170 [($330,000 – $200,000) × 0.9%].
Answer (A) is incorrect. A single taxpayer with income in excess of $200,000 is subject to a 0.9% tax on the excess income. **Answer (B) is incorrect.** The taxpayer is single, not MFJ. **Answer (D) is incorrect.** The taxpayer is single, not MFS.

25. Randy Lee is an ordained minister of a tax-exempt church. Randy receives a salary plus a housing allowance for rent and utilities. Which of the following statements is correct?

A. Randy must claim as income on his return all of his salary and all of his housing allowance. The salary is subject to income tax and self-employment tax, but his housing allowance is subject to income tax only.

B. Randy does not have to report any income received from the church because the church is tax exempt.

C. Randy has to pay both income tax and self-employment tax on his salary, but only self-employment tax for the housing allowance. The housing allowance is not subject to income tax.

D. Randy only has to pay the self-employment tax on both his salary and the housing allowance. Neither is subject to income tax.

Answer (C) is correct.
REQUIRED: The ordained minister's housing allowance for federal tax and self-employment tax purposes.
DISCUSSION: Under the gross income inclusion rules, a minister may exclude the rental value of his or her home or parsonage if it is connected with the performance of religious duties. However, the rental value is not excluded from the income used to compute self-employment taxes. Thus, Randy must include the housing allowance for self-employment tax purposes. He may exclude the housing allowance for federal income tax purposes (Publication 517).
Answer (A) is incorrect. The housing allowance is specifically excluded for federal income tax purposes by Sec. 107. **Answer (B) is incorrect.** Randy must include wages earned for federal income tax purposes. The tax status of the entity is irrelevant when determining the tax status of the individual. **Answer (D) is incorrect.** Randy's wages are subject to federal income tax.

26. All investment income in excess of deductions allowable for such income and income from passive activities are subject to an additional tax, the net investment income tax. Which of the following individuals are NOT subject to this tax?

A. Taxpayers over the age of 65.

B. Non-resident aliens.

C. U.S. citizens.

D. Spouses filing separately.

Answer (B) is correct.
REQUIRED: The individuals who do not need to pay net investment income tax.
DISCUSSION: Non-resident aliens are not subject to the net investment income tax.

27. The Social Security tax does NOT apply to which of the following?

A. Medical and hospital reimbursements by the employer that are excluded from gross income.

B. Compensation paid in forms other than cash.

C. Self-employment income of $1,000.

D. Bonuses and vacation time pay.

Answer (A) is correct.

REQUIRED: The payment to which the Social Security tax does not apply.

DISCUSSION: The Social Security tax imposed by the Federal Insurance Contribution Act (FICA) applies to virtually all compensation received for employment, including money or other forms of wages, bonuses, commissions, vacation pay, severance allowances, and tips. Reimbursements by one's employers for medical and hospital expenses that are not included in gross income are not subject to FICA [Sec. 3121(a)(2)]. However, sick pay, which is a wage payment paid when unable to work, is subject to FICA (Publication 15).

Answer (B) is incorrect. Compensation paid in forms other than cash is subject to FICA. **Answer (C) is incorrect.** Self-employment income is taxed for the same Social Security benefits, although the tax is imposed by Sec. 1401 rather than Secs. 3101 and 3111. **Answer (D) is incorrect.** Bonuses and vacation time pay are subject to FICA.

28. Rev. Elvin Snider is the ordained minister at Crossroads United Methodist Church. His salary on his Form W-2 is $20,000. He also receives a $12,000 housing allowance. His housing costs for the year are $14,000. What is Rev. Snider's self-employment income?

A. $34,000.

B. $32,000.

C. $20,000.

D. None of the answers are correct.

Answer (B) is correct.

REQUIRED: The self-employment income to be reported by an ordained minister.

DISCUSSION: Ministers may exclude from gross income the rental value of a home or a rental allowance to the extent the allowance is used to provide a home, even if deductions are taken for home expenses paid with the allowance. However, a minister should include any offerings given directly to him or her for church-related functions (e.g., marriages). The income inclusion for self-employment taxes differs from gross income inclusion in the case of ministers and/or clergymen. Under the gross income inclusion rules, a minister may exclude the rental value of his or her home or parsonage if it is connected with the performance of religious duties. However, the rental value is not excluded from the income used to compute self-employment taxes. Therefore, the minister's self-employment income is $32,000 ($20,000 salary plus $12,000 housing allowance) (Publication 517).

Answer (A) is incorrect. This amount includes $14,000 of the minister's housing costs, which are not included in income. The housing allowance of $12,000 is included in self-employment income. **Answer (C) is incorrect.** This amount does not include the housing allowance. To compute self-employment income, a minister must include rental value or housing allowances in the calculation. **Answer (D) is incorrect.** A correct answer is given.

29. The net investment income tax may apply to which of the following?

A. Alimony.

B. Taxable mutual fund distribution.

C. Tax-exempt municipal bond interest.

D. Traditional IRA distribution.

Answer (B) is correct.
REQUIRED: The income that falls under the net investment income tax bracket.
DISCUSSION: The net investment income tax is applied to all investment income in excess of deductions. In order for the investment to be subject to the net investment income tax, it must be taxable and must fall under the proper investment category. A taxable mutual fund distribution satisfies both needs.
Answer (A) is incorrect. Regardless of the effective date of the divorce, alimony is not investment income and therefore is not subject to this tax. If the divorce is pre-2019, the receiving spouse reports the alimony as income, subject to the ordinary tax rate of the spouse. If the divorce is post-2018, alimony is not any type of income. **Answer (C) is incorrect.** Tax-exempt municipal bond interest is not taxable. Therefore, it is not subject to the net investment income tax. **Answer (D) is incorrect.** A traditional IRA distribution is excluded from net investment income.

30. A couple filed their 2008 return as married filing jointly and claimed $7,500 for the First-Time Homebuyer Credit. The couple used this home as a primary residence. In 2020, they converted the home into rental property. What, if any, is the tax obligation of the taxpayers regarding the First-Time Homebuyer Credit?

A. They must pay the unpaid balance of the credit.

B. They must pro-rate the credit received over 15 years and repay 50% of the original credit.

C. They must reduce their depreciable basis in the property by 50% of the unpaid balance of the credit.

D. Since they used this home as a primary residence for 5 years, there is no requirement to repay.

Answer (A) is correct.
REQUIRED: The First-Time Homebuyer Credit repayment requirement when a primary residence is turned into a rental property.
DISCUSSION: A taxpayer who claimed the First-Time Homebuyer Credit for 2008 must repay it over 15 years, in amounts equal to 6.67% of the original credit. Only 12 years have passed. When the home is converted to rental property, the taxpayer must repay the unpaid balance on the credit.
Answer (B) is incorrect. A taxpayer who claimed the First-Time Homebuyer Credit for 2008 must repay it over 15 years, in amounts equal to 6.67% of the original credit. The taxpayer must repay the balance on the credit when converting the property to a rental. **Answer (C) is incorrect.** The taxpayer must repay the balance on the credit when converting the property to a rental. **Answer (D) is incorrect.** Taxpayers who claimed the credit after 2008 do not have to repay the credit once they have lived in the home for 3 years.

Access the **Gleim EA Premium Review System** featuring our SmartAdapt technology from your Gleim Personal Classroom to continue your studies. You will experience a personalized study environment with exam-emulating multiple-choice questions.

STUDY UNIT EIGHT

TAX CREDITS AND PAYMENTS

(26 pages of outline)

The first subunit discusses tax credits, which are used to achieve policy objectives such as encouraging energy conservation or providing tax relief to low-income taxpayers. A $1 credit reduces gross tax liability by $1. Various nonrefundable and refundable tax credits are available. Most credits are nonrefundable, meaning that once the tax liability reaches zero, no more credits can be taken to produce refunds. Nonrefundable personal credits include the

- Foreign Tax Credit
- Child and Dependent Care Credit
- Lifetime Learning Credit
- Retirement Savings Contribution Credit
- Child Tax Credit
- Credit for Other Dependents
- Credit for the Elderly or Disabled
- Adoption Credit
- Residential Mortgage Interest Credit
- Minimum Tax Credit
- Family and Medical Leave Credit

Refundable credits are treated as payments and can result in refunds for the taxpayer. Refundable credits include the

- American Opportunity Tax Credit
- Additional Child Tax Credit
- Earned Income Credit
- Health Insurance Premium Tax Credit

In the last subunit, we discuss payment requirements, claims for refunds, and the statute of limitations.

8.1 TAX CREDITS

Foreign Tax Credit (FTC)

1. A taxpayer may elect either a credit or a deduction for taxes paid to other countries or U.S. possessions.

    a. Generally, the FTC is applied against gross tax liability after nonrefundable personal credits and before all other credits.

    b. The FTC, as modified, may offset AMT liability.

        1) The FTC is not creditable against the accumulated earnings tax (AET) or the personal holding company (PHC) tax.

    c. **Pass-through entities** apportion the foreign taxes among the partners, shareholders (of an S corporation), or beneficiaries (of an estate).

        1) The taxpayers then elect and compute a credit or deduction on their personal returns.

    d. For a **non-U.S. person**, the FTC is allowed only for foreign taxes paid on income effectively connected with conduct of a trade or business in the U.S. and against U.S. tax on the effectively connected income.

        1) Nonresident aliens and foreign corporations are included under this provision.

    e. **Qualified foreign taxes (QFTs)** include foreign taxes on income, war profits, and excess profits.

        1) QFTs must be analogous to the U.S. income tax.

            a) They must be based on a form of net annual income, including gains.
            b) Concepts such as realization should be incorporated into the tax structure.

        2) Foreign taxes paid on foreign earned income or housing costs excluded as excessive may neither be credited nor deducted.

        3) Deemed QFT. A domestic corporation that owns at least 10% (voting) of a foreign corporation is deemed to have paid the foreign taxes paid by the foreign corporation on income that it distributed to the domestic corporation as a dividend.

    f. **FTC limit.** The maximum amount of tax that may be credited is computed using the following formula:

$$FTC = \frac{\text{U.S. income}}{\text{tax before FTC}} \times \frac{\text{Foreign source taxable income}}{\text{Worldwide taxable income}}$$

        1) The limit must be applied separately to nonbusiness interest income and all other income.

        2) The amount used for TI in the numerator and denominator is regular TI with adjustments.

    g. The FTC is claimed on Form 1116, *Foreign Tax Credit*, unless the taxpayer meets all of the following conditions and elects to claim the credit on Schedule 3 (Form 1040), line 1:

        1) The taxpayer is an individual,

        2) The only foreign source income for the year is passive income that is reported on a payee statement, and

        3) The QFTs for the year do not exceed $300 ($600 for a joint return).

h. **Carryover.** Foreign tax paid in excess of the FTC limit may be carried back 1 year and forward 10, in chronological order. The carryover is treated as foreign tax paid subject to the FTC limit.

   1) The carryover may not be applied in any year when a deduction for foreign taxes is taken (in lieu of the FTC).

i. A credit (or deduction) cannot be taken for foreign income taxes paid on income that is excluded from U.S. tax under the foreign earned income exclusion.

j. A choice must be made to take either a credit or a deduction for all qualified foreign taxes.

EXAMPLE 8-1   Foreign Tax Credit

Maria had an AGI of $100,000 in 2020, of which $80,000 was wages earned in the United States and $20,000 was unqualified foreign dividend income. She paid $4,000 of foreign taxes on the dividend income. Maria's 2020 tax liability before the FTC is $15,000. The portion of U.S. tax liability assigned to foreign income is $3,000 ($15,000 × $20,000 ÷ $100,000). Maria is able to claim a $3,000 Foreign Tax Credit on Form 1116 and has $1,000 ($4,000 taxes paid – $3,000 allowed credit) of unused Foreign Tax Credit that can be carried back to 2019 or forward through 2030.

Child and Dependent Care Credit

2. The Child and Dependent Care Credit is nonrefundable.

   a. A taxpayer is eligible for this credit only if items b. and c. below are satisfied.

   b. **Employment.** Child and dependent care expenses are incurred to enable the taxpayer to be gainfully employed.

      1) The expenses may be incurred when the claimant is employed or actively seeking employment.

   c. **Household cost.** The taxpayer provides more than half the cost of maintaining a household for a dependent under age 13 or a physically or mentally incapacitated spouse or dependent. *fully incapacitated*

      1) To be a qualifying person, the person must have lived with the taxpayer for more than half of 2020.

      2) **Special rule for children of divorced or separated parents.** Even if the taxpayer cannot claim his or her child as a dependent, the child is treated as the taxpayer's qualifying person if

         a) The child was under age 13 or was not physically or mentally able to care for himself or herself and

         b) The taxpayer was the child's custodial parent.

            i) The custodial parent is the parent with whom the child lived for the greater number of nights in 2020. If the child was with the parent for an equal number of nights, the custodial parent is the parent with the higher adjusted gross income.

3) Qualifying Expenses

    a) Household services, such as babysitting, housekeeping, and nursery.

    b) Outside services, such as day care.

        i) Qualified individuals over the age of 13 must spend more than 8 hours a day in the taxpayer's home.

    c) The cost of sending a child to school if the child is in a grade below kindergarten.

    d) Payments to a relative for the care of a qualifying individual.

        i) These payments do not qualify for the credit if the taxpayer claims a dependent exemption for the relative or if the relative is the taxpayer's child and is under age 19.

4) The cost of transporting a qualifying person from the home to the care location and back is a nonqualified expense.

5) Total child and dependent care expenses cannot exceed the taxpayer's earned income. For married taxpayers, the income for this limitation is the smaller income of the two.

    a) If one of the spouses is a full-time student at an educational institution or is unable to care for himself or herself, (s)he is considered to have earned $250 per month if there is one qualifying individual and $500 per month if there are two or more qualifying individuals.

6) Child and dependent care expenses are limited to $3,000 for one qualifying individual and $6,000 for two or more individuals, less excludable employer dependent-care assistance program payments.

7) The credit is equal to 35% of the child and dependent care expenses.

    a) This rate is reduced by 1% (but not below 20%) for each $2,000 (or part thereof) by which AGI exceeds $15,000.

    b) Taxpayers with AGI over $43,000 will have a credit of 20% (Form 2441).

EXAMPLE 8-2	Child and Dependent Care Credit

Kimberly is a head of household taxpayer with twin 2-year-old daughters. Kimberly has an AGI of $40,000. Claiming the standard deduction results in $2,280 {[($40,000 – $18,650 – $14,100) × 12%] + $1,410} of tax liability on taxable income of $21,350 ($40,000 AGI – $18,650 standard deduction). Kimberly is eligible for a 22% credit on the first $6,000 of dependent care expenses. Kimberly spent $5,500 on childcare, allowing her to claim a $1,210 Dependent Care Credit ($5,500 × 22%). Her net tax liability is $1,070 ($2,280 tax – $1,210 credit).

d. Taxpayers must provide each dependent's **taxpayer identification number** in order to claim the credit, as well as the identifying number of the service provider.

e. The figure below is a general guide for determining if the taxpayer qualifies for the credit:

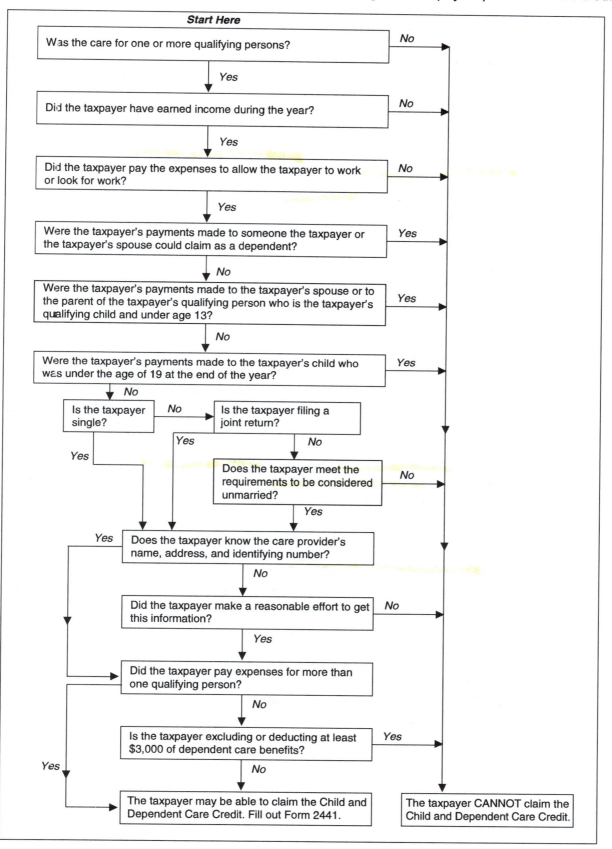

Figure 8-1

Education Credits

3.   Two tax credits may be elected by low- and middle-income individuals for education expenses incurred by students pursuing higher education or vocational training.

    a.   The American Opportunity Tax Credit is partially refundable, and the Lifetime Learning Credit is nonrefundable. In addition, neither credit is allowed by married taxpayers who file separately; i.e., they must file a joint return.

    b.   **American Opportunity Tax Credit (AOTC).** The AOTC provides a maximum credit of $2,500 per student for each of the first 4 years of post-secondary education.

        1)   The $2,500 per year is the sum of 100% of the first $2,000 of qualified expenses and 25% of the next $2,000 of qualified expenses.

        2)   The credit applies to the first 4 years of higher education received by the taxpayer, the taxpayer's spouse, and/or the taxpayer's dependents.

        3)   The credit applies to tuition and tuition-related fees, books, and other required course materials.

        4)   Qualified education expenses paid in 2020 for an academic period that begins in the first 3 months of 2021 can be used in figuring an education credit for 2020.

        5)   The credit cannot be claimed if

            a)   An exclusion for an education IRA or a state tuition program is claimed for the same expenses

            b)   The student has been convicted of a federal or state felony offense consisting of the possession or distribution of a controlled substance

            c)   The student is not taking at least one-half of the normal full-time workload for at least one academic period that begins during the calendar year in which the credit is claimed

        6)   The credit phases out for AGI between $80,000 and $90,000 for single taxpayers and between $160,000 and $180,000 on a joint return. The calculation of the maximum allowable credit is

$$\$2,500 \ \times \ \frac{\textbf{\$90,000 (if single) or \$180,000 (if joint return)} - \textbf{MAGI}}{\textbf{\$10,000 (if single) or \$20,000 (if joint return)}}$$

        7)   Up to 40% of the credit is refundable.

            a)   When the original tax equals or exceeds $2,500, the entire $2,500 is used to lower the tax bill. Thus, no credit will be refunded.

            b)   When the original tax is less than $2,500 and the tax is lowered to zero, the remaining credit is partially (40%) refundable. For example, the original tax is $1,500. After $1,500 of the credit is used to lower the tax to zero, 40% (i.e., $400) of the remaining $1,000 credit is refundable.

            c)   No refund of the credit is allowed if the student is a child subject to the "kiddie tax" (covered in Study Unit 1, Subunit 5).

EXAMPLE 8-3	American Opportunity Tax Credit

Jack and Jill Smith, married taxpayers who file a joint return, have a combined modified AGI of $172,000. They paid $3,000 in tuition expenses for their dependent daughter, who is in her second year of college, and $8,000 in tuition expenses for their dependent son, who is in his fifth calendar year of college (the spring semester of his senior year). The tuition expenses the Smiths paid for their son do not qualify for the AOTC because he is not in his first 4 years of post-secondary education.

The $3,000 of tuition expenses paid for their daughter's education qualifies for the credit. The tentative credit allowed is $2,250 [($2,000 × 100%) + ($1,000 × 25%)]. However, the Smiths' AGI is within the phase-out range and their credit must be reduced accordingly. The reduction is calculated as follows:

$$\$2,250 \times [(\$180,000 - \$172,000) \div \$20,000] = \$900$$

The Smiths may claim an AOTC of $1,350 ($2,250 − $900).

c. **Lifetime Learning Credit.** The Lifetime Learning Credit provides a credit of 20% of qualified tuition expenses paid by the taxpayer for any year the AOTC is not claimed.

1) The maximum credit allowed per year is $2,000.

2) This is based on 20% of up to $10,000 of qualified tuition and fees paid for the taxpayer, the taxpayer's spouse, and/or the taxpayer's dependents.

3) The credit is figured on a per-taxpayer basis.

4) It applies to any number of years of higher education.

5) Eligible expenses for this credit include tuition and fees required for enrollment.

6) The Lifetime Learning Credit phases out for AGI between $59,000 and $69,000 for single filers and between $118,000 and $138,000 for those filing a joint return.

d. The credits may not be used for room and board, activity fees, athletic fees, insurance expense, or transportation.

e. The tuition statement (1098-T) provided to the taxpayer/student is required to include the name, address, and TIN of the taxpayer/student.

EXAMPLE 8-4	Lifetime Learning Credit

Barney is a single taxpayer with a modified AGI of $52,000. Barney has two dependent daughters in graduate school. He pays $6,000 in tuition expenses for each of his daughters, for a total of $12,000. The first $10,000 of these expenses qualifies for the Lifetime Learning Credit. Thus, Barney may claim a credit of $2,000 ($10,000 × 20%).

EXAMPLE 8-5	Lifetime Learning Credit

Weasley and Brandy Kat, who file a joint tax return, have an adjusted gross income (AGI) of $116,000 for 2020. Their daughter Honey began her first year of graduate school on July 21, 2019. Weasley and Brandy incurred tuition expenses of $12,000 in 2020.

A Lifetime Learning Credit is limited to 20% of the first $10,000 of tuition paid. The Lifetime Learning Credit is available in years the American Opportunity Tax Credit is not claimed. The Kats' credit for 2020 will be $2,000 ($10,000 × 20%). There is no phaseout of the Lifetime Learning Credit for the Kats because the credit phaseout for married taxpayers filing jointly commences when modified AGI is $118,000 and ends at $138,000.

Child Tax Credit, Additional Child Tax Credit, and Credit for Other Dependents

4.   The Child Tax Credit (CTC) is for taxpayers who have a qualifying child. It is in addition to the Child and Dependent Care Credit and the Earned Income Credit.

   a.   The TCJA increased the credit from $1,000 to $2,000 for the tax years 2018 to 2025.

   b.   The CTC is nonrefundable.

5.   The Additional Child Tax Credit (ACTC) is for certain individuals who get less than the full amount of the CTC. The ACTC may give the taxpayer a refund even if the taxpayer does not owe any tax.

   a.   The ACTC is refundable up to 15% of earned income in excess of $2,500. Special for 2020 tax year only, a taxpayer may use the prior-year (i.e., 2019) earned income if greater than 2020 earned income, for calculating this credit.

   b.   The refund is capped at the per child amount of $1,400.

   c.   This refundable credit is calculated on Schedule 8812.

6.   A qualifying child for purposes of the CTC is a child who

   a.   Is the taxpayer's son, daughter, stepchild, foster child, brother, sister, stepbrother, stepsister, half brother, half sister, or a descendant of any of them (for example, the taxpayer's grandchild, niece, or nephew);

   b.   Was under age 17 at the end of 2020;

   c.   Did not provide over half of his or her own support for 2020;

   d.   Lived with the taxpayer for more than half of 2020;

      1)   A child is considered to have lived with the taxpayer for more than half of 2020

         a)   If the child was born or died in 2020 and the taxpayer's home was the child's home for more than half the time (s)he was alive during the year.

         b)   Temporary absences by the taxpayer or the child for special circumstances, such as school, vacation, business, medical care, military service, or detention in a juvenile facility, count as time the child lived with the taxpayer.

         c)   Exceptions exist for kidnapped children and children of divorced or separated parents.

   e.   Is claimed as a dependent on the taxpayer's return;

   f.   Does not file a joint return for the year (or files it only to claim a refund of withheld income tax or estimated tax paid);

   g.   Was a U.S. citizen, a U.S. national, or a U.S. resident alien; and

   h.   Has a Social Security number (SSN) issued before the due date of the return.

   NOTE: An adopted child is always treated as the taxpayer's own child. An adopted child includes a child lawfully placed with the taxpayer for legal adoption.

EXAMPLE 8-6   CTC Age Test

The taxpayer's son turned 17 on December 30, 2020. He is a citizen of the United States, and the taxpayer claimed him as a dependent on the taxpayer's return. He is not a qualifying child for the CTC because he was not under age 17 at the end of 2020.

EXAMPLE 8-7   CTC Citizenship Test

Your 10-year-old nephew lives in Mexico and qualifies as your dependent. Because he is not a U.S. citizen, U.S. national, or U.S. resident alien, he is not a qualifying child for the CTC.

7. The credit is phased out when AGI reaches $400,000 for married taxpayers filing jointly ($200,000 for all other taxpayers).

   a. The credit is reduced by $50 for each $1,000 (rounded up to the next multiple of $1,000 if not one already) by which the taxpayer's AGI exceeds the threshold.

8. The credit is allowed only for tax years consisting of 12 months.

9. The Credit for Other Dependents is a $500 nonrefundable credit for dependents other than a qualifying child or for a qualifying child without the required SSN. Nonrefundable means that any Credit for Other Dependents is not included with the CTC when calculating the ACTC.

10. The worksheet below and on the next page walks through the steps for determining the credit.

Part 1

1. Number of qualifying children under 17 with the required social security number: _____ × $2,000. Enter the result. | **1** ☐

2. Number of other dependents, including qualifying children who are not under 17 or who do not have the required social security number: _____ × $500. Enter the result. | **2** ☐

   Caution: Do not include yourself, your spouse, or anyone who is not a U.S. citizen, U.S. national, or U.S. resident alien. Also, do not include anyone you included on line 1.

3. Add lines 1 and 2. | **3** ☐

4. Enter the amount from line 11 of your Form 1040, 1040-SR, or 1040-NR. | **4** ☐

5. **1040 and 1040-SR filers.** Enter the total of any—
   • Exclusion of income from Puerto Rico; and
   • Amounts from Form 2555, lines 45 and 50, and Form 4563, line 15.
   1040-NR filers. Enter -0-. | **5** ☐

6. Add lines 4 and 5. Enter the total. | **6** ☐

7. Enter the amount shown below for your filing status.
   • Married filing jointly—$400,000
   • All other filing statuses—$200,000 | **7** ☐

8. Is the amount on line 6 more than the amount on line 7?
   ☐ **No.** Leave line 8 blank. Enter -0- on line 9.
   ☐ **Yes.** Subtract line 7 from line 6. | **8** ☐
   If the result is not a multiple of $1,000, increase it to the next multiple of $1,000. For example, increase $425 to $1,000, increase $1,025 to $2,000, etc.

9. Multiply the amount on line 8 by 5% (0.05). Enter the result. | **9** ☐

10. Is the amount on line 3 more than the amount on line 9?
    ☐ **No.** (STOP) You cannot take the child tax credit or credit for other dependents on line 19 of your Form 1040, 1040-SR, or 1040-NR. You also cannot take the additional child tax credit on line 28 of your Form 1040, 1040-SR, or 1040-NR. Complete the rest of your Form 1040, 1040-SR, or 1040-NR.
    ☐ **Yes.** Subtract line 9 from line 3. Enter the result. | **10** ☐
    Go to Part 2 on the next page.

Figure 8-2

Part 2

11. Enter the amount from line 18 of your Form 1040, 1040-SR, or 1040-NR.   **11** [   ]

12. Add the following amounts (if applicable) from:

        Schedule 3, line 1 . . . . + _____
        Schedule 3, line 2 . . . . + _____
        Schedule 3, line 3 . . . . + _____
        Schedule 3, line 4 . . . . + _____
        Form 5695, line 30 . . . . + _____
        Form 8910, line 15 . . . . + _____
        Form 8936, line 23 . . . . + _____
        Schedule R, line 22 . . . . + _____

                          Enter the total.   **12** [   ]

13. Subtract line 12 from line 11.   **13** [   ]

14. Are you claiming any of the following credits?
  • Mortgage interest credit, Form 8396.
  • Adoption credit, Form 8839.
  • Residential energy efficient property credit, Form 5695, Part I.
  • District of Columbia first-time homebuyer credit, Form 8859.

  ☐ **No.** Enter -0-.

  ☐ **Yes.** If you are filing Form 2555, enter -0-.
     Otherwise, complete the Line 14 Worksheet, later, to figure
     the amount to enter here.   **14** [   ]

15. Subtract line 14 from line 13. Enter the result.   **15** [   ]

16. Is the amount on line 10 of this worksheet more than the amount on line 15?

  ☐ **No.** Enter the amount from line 10.

  ☐ **Yes.** Enter the amount from line 15.
     See the **TIP** below.

    This is your child tax credit and credit for other dependents.   **16** [   ]

*Enter this amount on
Form 1040, line 19;
Form 1040-SR, line 19;
or Form 1040-NR, line 19.*

1040
1040-SR
1040-NR

TIP *You may be able to take the **additional child tax** credit on line 28
of your Form 1040, 1040-SR, or 1040-NR, only if you answered
"Yes" on line 16 and line 1 is more than zero.*

  • *First, complete your Form 1040, 1040-SR, or 1040-NR
through line 27 (also complete Schedule 3, line 10).*

  • *Then, use Schedule 8812 to figure any additional
child tax credit.*

Figure 8-2 (continued)

Retirement Savings Contributions Credit (Saver's Credit)

11. The Saver's Credit can be taken for the taxpayer's contributions to a traditional or Roth IRA, 401(k), SIMPLE IRA, SARSEP, 403(b), 501(c)(18), or governmental 457(b) plan and for voluntary after-tax employee contributions to qualified retirement and 403(b) plans.

12. Rollover contributions (money that the taxpayer moved from another retirement plan or IRA) are not eligible for the Saver's Credit. Additionally, eligible contributions may be reduced by any recent distributions the taxpayer received from a retirement plan or IRA.

13. The taxpayer is eligible for the credit if the taxpayer is (a) age 18 or older, (b) not claimed as a dependent on another person's return, and (c) not a full-time student.

    a.   A taxpayer is a student if, during any part of 5 calendar months of 2020, the taxpayer was

        1)   Enrolled as a full-time student at a school

            a)   A school includes technical, trade, and mechanical schools. It does not include on-the-job training courses, correspondence schools, or schools offering courses only through the Internet.

        2)   Took a full-time, on-farm training course given by a school or a state, county, or local government agency

14. The amount of the credit is 50%, 20%, or 10% of the taxpayer's retirement plan or IRA contributions, up to $2,000 ($4,000 if married filing jointly), depending on the taxpayer's adjusted gross income.

    a.   The chart below has the Saver's Credit AGI limits for 2020.

2020 Saver's Credit

Credit Rate	Married Filing Jointly	Head of Household	All Other Filers
50% of contribution	AGI ≤ $39,000	AGI ≤ $29,250	AGI ≤ $19,500
20% of contribution	$39,001-$42,500	$29,251-$31,875	$19,501-$21,250
10% of contribution	$42,501-$65,000	$31,876-$48,750	$21,251-$32,500
0% of contribution	more than $65,000	more than $48,750	more than $32,500

EXAMPLE 8-8	Retirement Savings Contribution Credit

Stephanie, who works at a retail store, is married and earned $39,000 in 2020. Stephanie's husband was unemployed in 2020 and did not have any earnings. Stephanie contributed $1,000 to her IRA in 2020. After deducting her IRA contribution, Stephanie's adjusted gross income on her joint return is $38,000. Stephanie may claim a 50% credit, $500, for her $1,000 IRA contribution.

Credit for the Elderly or Disabled

15. The Credit for the Elderly or Disabled is nonrefundable.

   a.   An individual may be eligible for this credit if (s)he was age 65 before the close of the tax year or retired before the close of the tax year due to a total and permanent disability.

Qualified Individual for the Credit for the Elderly or Disabled

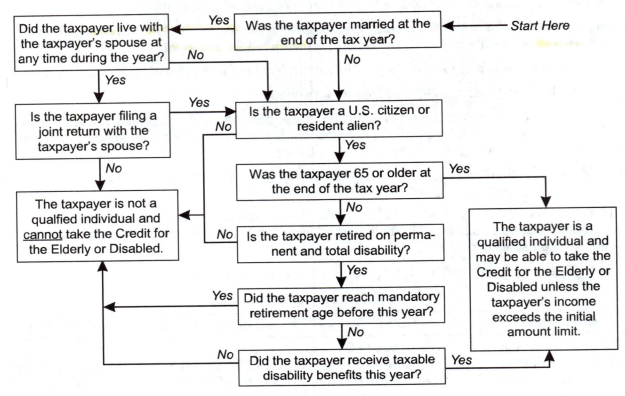

Figure 8-3

   b.   The credit is equal to 15% times an initial base amount, which is $5,000 ($7,500 for married filing joint return with both spouses age 65 or older, $3,750 MFS), and limited to disability income if under age 65. This initial base amount is reduced by the following:

   1) Tax-exempt Social Security benefits,

   2) Pension or annuity benefits excluded from gross income, and

   3) One-half the excess of AGI over $7,500 ($10,000 for married filing jointly, $5,000 MFS).

EXAMPLE 8-9   Elderly Credit

Virginia is 66 and unmarried, claims the standard deduction, and has not started to receive any retirement income. In 2020, Virginia's AGI is $15,000 and her taxable income is $950 ($15,000 AGI – $12,400 standard deduction – $1,650 additional standard deduction), creating a $95 ($950 × 10%) tax liability. Virginia's remaining base amount for the elderly credit is $1,250 {$5,000 – [($15,000 – $7,500) × 50%]}, creating a $188 credit ($1,250 × 15%). Virginia's $95 tax liability is less than the $188 credit, so she can only claim $95 of the credit.

---

   c.   A married person filing separately who lives with the spouse at any time during the year may not claim the credit.

d. The credit is claimed/reported on Schedule R. The following table provides the initial credit amounts:

Initial Amounts

IF the taxpayer's filing status is . . .	THEN entered on line 10 of Schedule R is . . .
single, head of household, or **qualifying widow(er)** with dependent child and, by the end of 2020, the taxpayer was	
• 65 or older	$5,000
• under 65 and retired on permanent and total disability	$5,000
married filing a joint return and by the end of 2020	
• both spouses were 65 or older	$7,500
• both spouses were under 65 and one spouse retired on permanent and total disability	$5,000
• both spouses were under 65 and both spouses retired on permanent and total disability	$7,500
• one spouse was 65 or older, and the other was under 65 and retired on permanent and total disability	$7,500
• one spouse was 65 or older, and the other was under 65 and **not** retired on permanent and total disability	$5,000
married filing a separate return and the taxpayer did not live with the taxpayer's spouse at any time during the year and, by the end of 2020, the taxpayer was	
• 65 or older	$3,750
• under 65 and retired on permanent and total disability	$3,750

IF the taxpayer's filing status is . . .	THEN, even if the taxpayer qualifies, the taxpayer CANNOT take credit if . . .	
	The taxpayer's adjusted gross income (AGI) is equal to or more than . . .	OR the total of the taxpayer's nontaxable Social Security and other nontaxable pension(s), annuities, or disability income is equal to or more than . . .
single, head of household, or qualifying widow(er) with dependent child	$17,500	$5,000
married filing jointly **and** only one spouse qualifies	$20,000	$5,000
married filing jointly **and** both spouses qualify	$25,000	$7,500
married filing separately and the taxpayer lived apart from the taxpayer's spouse for all of 2020	$12,500	$3,750

Adoption Credit

16. A nonrefundable Adoption Credit is allowed for qualified adoption expenses.

    a. An eligible child must be under 18 years of age or must be physically or mentally incapable of self-care.

    b. Qualified adoption expenses are reasonable and necessary adoption expenses, including adoption fees, court costs, attorney fees, and other directly related expenses.

        1) Expenses that are not eligible for the Adoption Credit include

            a) Costs associated with a surrogate parenting arrangement,

            b) Expenses incurred in violation of state or federal law,

            c) Expenses incurred in connection with the adoption of a child of the taxpayer's spouse, and

            d) Infant care supplies.

EXAMPLE 8-10   Adoption Credit

A taxpayer with modified AGI of $80,000 pays $15,000 of qualified adoption expenses to adopt a 10-year-old girl. As part of the taxpayer's employee benefit program, the employer reimburses the taxpayer for $5,000. This amount reduces the taxpayer's qualified adoption expenses to $10,000. Thus, the taxpayer can only claim a $10,000 credit for qualified adoption expenses.

---

    c. The maximum credit is $14,300 per child, including a special-needs domestic adoption.

        1) The amount of the credit allowable for any tax year is phased out for taxpayers with modified adjusted gross income (MAGI) in excess of $214,520 and is fully eliminated when MAGI reaches $254,520.

$$\text{Adoption Credit} = \$14,300 \times \left[1 - \left(\frac{\text{MAGI} - \$214,520}{\$40,000} \right) \right]$$

        2) The credit is also reduced if the taxpayer receives excludable adoption assistance from an employer.

    d. Unused credit may be carried forward for up to 5 years and is not subject to the AGI phaseout.

Residential Mortgage Interest Credit

17. The Residential Mortgage Interest Credit is nonrefundable.

    a. State and local governments can elect to issue qualified mortgage bonds (QMBs) in lieu of certain tax-exempt bonds.

        1) The QMBs finance mortgage credit certificates (MCCs) issued to qualified individuals who use the MCCs when privately financing their first purchase of a principal residence.

        2) The interest on the home mortgage is the base.

        3) The MCC rate is between 10% and 50% (assumption is 25%).

        4) If the rate exceeds 20%, the credit is limited to $2,000 per year.

        5) MCC credit disallowed by the overall limit may be carried forward 3 years.

EXAMPLE 8-11   Residential Mortgage Interest Credit

David and Lydia paid $4,800 of interest in 2020 on the mortgage given upon acquiring their first home. They received a mortgage credit certificate that specifies a 20% credit rate. They are entitled to a credit of $960 ($4,800 × 20%). The amount of mortgage interest they may use as an itemized deduction is reduced by the amount of the credit to $3,840 ($4,800 − $960).

Minimum Tax Credit (MTC)

18. The Minimum Tax Credit is nonrefundable.

   a.   A credit is allowed for alternative minimum tax (AMT) paid in a tax year against regular tax liability in one or more subsequent tax years (Form 8801).

   b.   **Individuals.** The MTC amount is the AMT that would have been computed if the only adjustments made to taxable income in computing AMTI were those for (tax-favored) items that result in deferral, as opposed to exclusion, of income.

   1)   To compute the MTC amount, recompute the most recent year's AMT without adjustment for the following (exclusion) items, and add carryover MTC:

   a)   Standard deduction,

   b)   Tax-exempt interest on private activity bonds (except ones issued in 2009 or 2010),

   c)   Interest expense (e.g., investment interest),

   d)   Depletion, and

   e)   Taxes.

   c.   **Limits.** The MTC allowable is limited to current-year gross regular tax (reduced by certain credits) minus current-year tentative minimum tax.

   Gross regular tax
   − Credits
   − Tentative minimum tax (for current year)
   = MTC maximum allowable

   1)   The current-year gross regular tax amount is reduced by the amount currently allowable for each of the following:

   a)   Refundable credits
   b)   Nonrefundable personal credits
   c)   Foreign tax, drug testing, nonconventional source fuel credits
   d)   General Business Credit

   d.   **Carryover.** Any MTC amount beyond the current limit may be carried forward indefinitely.

Earned Income Credit (EIC)

19. The Earned Income Credit is refundable.

   a. Under Sec. 32(a), the EIC is available to individuals who have earned income and gross income below certain thresholds.

      1) An individual is not eligible for the EIC if (s)he does not include his or her correct SSN on the return claiming the credit.

      2) Individual taxpayer identification numbers (ITINs) disqualify the taxpayer and/or the otherwise qualifying child (QC) from the credit.

      3) Married individuals who file separately are not eligible for the EIC.

      4) The EIC increases for individuals having at least one QC. Schedule EIC must be attached to the return; it lists relevant information about each QC.

      5) The credit is not available for taxpayers who fraudulently claim the EIC.

      6) The IRS may request birth certificates, medical records, school records, etc., to verify eligibility for the credit.

   b. An individual without a QC must have his or her principal residence in the U.S. for more than half of the tax year, be at least 25 but not over 64 years old, and not be a dependent of another.

   c. **QC tests.** In order for a child to be a QC, three tests must be met:

      1) **Relationship.** The child must be related by birth or adoption or be an eligible foster child or stepchild.

      2) **Residency.** The child must have lived with the taxpayer in the United States for more than half of the year.

      3) **Age.** The child must be under age 19 at the close of the tax year, be permanently disabled, or be a student under the age of 24.

Tests for Qualifying Child

Relationship

A qualifying child who is the taxpayer's . . .

Son, daughter, stepchild, foster child, or a descendant of any of them (for example, the taxpayer's grandchild)

OR

Brother, sister, half brother, half sister, stepbrother, stepsister, or a descendant of any of them (for example, the taxpayer's niece or nephew)

AND

Age

was . . .

Under age 19 at the end of the tax year and younger than the taxpayer (or taxpayer's spouse, if filing jointly)

OR

Under age 24 at the end of the tax year, a student, and younger than the taxpayer (or the taxpayer's spouse, if filing jointly)

OR

Permanently and totally disabled at any time during the year, regardless of age

AND

Residency

Who lived with the taxpayer in the United States for more than half of the tax year

Figure 8-4

d. **Child claimed by both parents.** In the event that two or more taxpayers claim the same child in the same calendar year, the child will be the qualifying child for the parents first and then for the taxpayer with the highest AGI.

   1) If both of a qualifying child's parents seek to claim the credit, but do not file jointly, then the parent with whom the child resides the longest period of time during the year may claim the child.

   2) The parent with the highest AGI will be able to claim the child as a qualifying child in the event the child spends an equal amount of time with each parent during the year (Publication 504).

e. **QC of another person.** A taxpayer (or spouse if filing a joint return) who is a qualifying child of another person cannot claim the EIC.

1) This applies even if the person for whom the taxpayer is the qualifying child does not claim the EIC or meet the criteria in order to claim the EIC.

f. **Earned income** includes wages, salaries, tips, and net earnings from self-employment. For the 2020 tax year only, a taxpayer may use the prior-year (i.e., 2019) earned income, if greater than 2020 earned income, for calculating this credit.

1) It does not include nontaxable compensation (e.g., military allowances), welfare benefits (e.g., AFDC), veteran's benefits, pensions, annuities, unemployment compensation, and scholarships.

2) Disqualified income includes interest, dividends, capital gain net income, positive passive income, nonbusiness rents, or royalties.

3) For 2020, the amount of disqualified income that causes a taxpayer to become ineligible for the EIC is $3,650.

g. **Calculation of EIC.** Multiply the individual's earned income by the applicable percentage.

EIC: Maximum Amounts, 2020			
Type of Taxpayer	Applicable Percentage	Earned Income Amount	Maximum EIC
0 QC	7.65%	$ 7,030	$ 538
1 QC	34.00%	$10,540	$3,584
2 QC	40.00%	$14,800	$5,920
3 or more QC	45.00%	$14,800	$6,660

h. **Phaseout of EIC.** Decrease the maximum EIC by any phaseout, which is determined by multiplying the applicable phaseout percentage by the excess of the amount of the individual's AGI (or earned income, if greater) over the beginning amount.

1) No EIC is available when AGI or earned income exceeds the completed phaseout amount.

EIC: Phaseout Amounts, 2020					
Type of Taxpayer	Applicable Phaseout Percentage	Beginning Phaseout Amount	Beginning Phaseout Amount for Joint Filers	Completed Phaseout Amount	Completed Phaseout Amount for Joint Filers
0 QC	7.65%	$ 8,790	$14,680	$15,820	$21,710
1 QC	15.98%	$19,330	$25,220	$41,756	$47,646
2 QC	21.06%	$19,330	$25,220	$47,440	$53,330
3 or more QC	21.06%	$19,330	$25,220	$50,954	$56,844

EXAMPLE 8-12   Earned Income Credit

Joe is a 50-year-old single taxpayer with wages of $12,300 and $8,000 of AGI. Joe does not have any qualifying children and is eligible for the EIC. With no qualifying children, Joe's applicable percentage for the EIC is 7.65%. Joe's earned income of $12,300 is greater than the amount required for the maximum credit of $7,030. The higher of his earned income or AGI is $12,300, which is greater than the beginning phaseout amount of $8,790. Therefore, Joe's earned income credit is $269 {$538 − [($12,300 − $8,790) × 7.65%]}.

Due Diligence Requirement

    i.   **Penalty.** Section 6695(g) imposes a $540 penalty with respect to any return or claim for refund for each failure to comply with the four due diligence requirements imposed by regulations with respect to determining a taxpayer's eligibility for the EIC or the amount of any allowable EIC.

        1)   New expanded regulations clarify these requirements and set a performance standard for the "knowledge" requirement (i.e., what a reasonable and well-informed tax return preparer, knowledgeable in the law, would do). The four due diligence requirements are discussed below and on the next page.

Completion of Form 8867

    a)   Complete Form 8867, *Paid Preparer's Due Diligence Checklist*, truthfully and accurately and any actions described on Form 8867 for applicable credit(s) claimed.

        i)   Determine that this taxpayer is eligible to claim the EIC for the number of children for whom the EIC is being claimed or to claim the EIC if the taxpayer has no qualifying children.

        ii)   Determine that the child lived with the taxpayer for over half of the year.

        iii)   Explain the tiebreaker rules as described in item d. on page 243.

Computation of the Credit

    b)   Complete the applicable EIC worksheet associated with Form 1040, 1040-SS, 1040-PR, or 1040-NR or an equivalent and all related forms and schedules.

Knowledge

    c)   Interview the taxpayer, ask questions, and document the taxpayer's responses and review the information to determine that the taxpayer is eligible to claim the credit.

        i)   Do not ignore the implications of information furnished or known.

        ii)   Make reasonable inquiries in such a manner that another well-informed tax preparer would conclude that the information furnished appears to be correct, consistent, and complete.

        iii)   Document any additional inquiries made and the client's responses.

Record Retention

    d) Satisfy the document retention requirement by retaining the following five records:

        i) Form 8867;

        ii) The EIC worksheet(s) or the preparer's own worksheet(s);

        iii) Copies of any taxpayer documents relied on to determine eligibility for or amount of EIC;

        iv) A record of how, when, and from whom the information used to prepare the form and worksheet(s) was obtained; and

        v) A record of any additional questions the preparer asked and the client's answers.

    e) These records must be kept for 3 years from the latest of the following due dates:

        i) The due date of the tax return (not including extensions)

        ii) The date the return was filed (if a signing tax return preparer electronically filed the return)

        iii) The date the return was presented to the taxpayer for signature (if the signing tax preparer is not electronically filing the return)

        iv) The date a preparer submitted the part of the return for which they were responsible to the signing tax return preparer (if that preparer is a nonsigning tax return preparer)

    f) The retention of a copy of the Social Security cards of the taxpayer and each qualifying child is not required.

Residential Energy Credits

20. There are two credits available for individuals to improve the energy consumption of their residence. The first is for installing alternative energy property, and the second is for installing energy-efficient improvement property.

    a. The residential energy efficient property credit for 2020 is 26% of the cost of qualified property, which includes the following:

        1) Solar electric
        2) Solar water heating
        3) Small wind energy
        4) Geothermal heat pump
        5) Fuel cell property

    b. The nonbusiness energy property credit is 10% of the cost of some qualified property, and a fixed limit for other property.

10% Property	Fixed Limit Property	
Insulation	Energy-efficient building property	$300
Exterior doors	Natural gas, propane, oil furnace,	
Metal and asphalt roof	hot water boiler	$150
Exterior windows and skylights	Advanced main air circulating fan	$50

Premium Tax Credit (PTC)

21. Taxpayers who obtain health insurance coverage through the Health Insurance Marketplace may be eligible for the Health Insurance Premium Tax Credit. The Premium Tax Credit is a refundable credit.

    a. The credit is a subsidy for households that made less than four times (i.e., 400%) the federal poverty line in 2019 (the prior year).

        1) $49,960 for household size of one
        2) $67,640 for household size of two
        3) $85,320 for household size of three
        4) $103,000 for household size of four
        5) $120,680 for household size of five

22. The cost of insurance is capped at 9.78% of income. The percentage decreases as their income decreases.

23. Taxpayers may be eligible for the credit if they meet all of the following requirements:

    a. Buy health insurance through the Marketplace;
    b. Are ineligible for coverage through an employer or government plan;
    c. Are within certain income limits;
    d. Do not file a separate return, if married[1]; and
    e. Cannot be claimed as a dependent by another person.

    [1]There is an exception for MFS if the taxpayer is a victim of domestic violence.

24. Eligible taxpayers may either receive advance payments toward their health insurance premiums or receive a regular credit at the end of the year.

25. Taxpayers who claim the Advanced Premium Tax Credit must file a tax return regardless of whether the taxpayer's income is below the filing threshold.

    a. The return must include Form 8962, *Premium Tax Credit (PTC)*, to compare the amount the taxpayer received for the Advanced Premium Tax Credit to the amount the taxpayer is actually eligible for based on the taxpayer's actual income.

        1) If the taxpayer earns more income than was used for determining the Advanced Premium Tax Credit, the taxpayer may be required to repay some or all of the excess credit received.

        2) A taxpayer who does not complete the reconciliation will not be eligible for the Advanced Premium Tax Credit in future years.

26. A refund is available for eligible taxpayers who did not receive any advance payments. All taxpayers who received advanced payments must deduct the total of any advanced payments received during the year from the amount of the premium tax credit calculated on the return. This may affect the tax refund or balance due.

27. Taxpayers must claim the credit by filing a federal income tax return regardless of which method is used to receive the tax credit.

28. Taxpayers with insurance coverage will receive one of three tax forms showing their insurance coverage status. All Forms 1095 show information about the coverage, who is included in the coverage, and for what months the coverage was applied.

    a. Form 1095-A, *Health Insurance Marketplace Statement*, is received by individuals who purchased health insurance through a state or federal health insurance marketplace.

    b. Form 1095-B, *Health Coverage*, is received by individuals from their health insurance provider (e.g., a health insurance company).

    c. Form 1095-C, *Employer-Provided Health Insurance Offer and Coverage*, is received by certain employees with information about what coverage the employer offered.

    d. Only taxpayers who receive health insurance through a state or federal health insurance marketplace are required to wait to file until they receive Form 1095-A, as this impacts the calculation of the premium tax credits.

    e. Taxpayers who expect to receive Form 1095-B or 1095-C may file their federal income tax return before their form is received by confirming how many months they were covered by qualifying health insurance.

    f. Taxpayers should store these forms like any other tax document for recordkeeping purposes.

    g. Taxpayers can receive multiple Forms 1095 if their health insurance coverage changed during the year.

Health Coverage Tax Credit

29. The Health Coverage Tax Credit (HCTC) is a refundable tax credit that pays 72.5% of qualified health insurance premiums for eligible individuals and their families through 2020.

    a. The following individuals may elect to take the HCTC:

        1) An eligible trade adjustment assistance (TAA) recipient, alternative trade adjustment assistance (ATAA) recipient, reemployment trade adjustment assistance (RTAA) recipient

        2) An eligible Pension Benefit Guaranty Corporation (PBGC) pension payee

        3) The family member of a TAA, ATAA, or RTAA recipient or PBGC pension payee who is deceased or who finalized a divorce with the taxpayer

    b. An individual is not eligible if (s)he could have been claimed as a dependent on another person's federal income tax return.

    c. Health Insurance Marketplace coverage is no longer qualified coverage for the HCTC.

    d. Once the taxpayer makes the election to take the HCTC for an eligible coverage month, (s)he cannot take the premium tax credit (PTC) for the same coverage in that coverage month and for all subsequent eligible coverage months during the tax year in which the taxpayer is eligible to take the HCTC.

***STOP AND REVIEW!* You have completed the outline for this subunit. Study multiple-choice questions 1 through 22 beginning on page 253.**

8.2 PAYMENTS

Estimated Tax Payments

1. The IRC is structured to obtain at least 90% of the final income tax through withholding and estimated tax payments. Individuals who earn income not subject to withholding must pay estimated tax on that income in quarterly installments.

    a. **Calendar-year due dates.** For a calendar-year taxpayer, the installments are due by
    1) April 15 (January-March),
    2) June 15 (April-May),
    3) September 15 (June-August), and
    4) January 15 (September-December) of the following year.

    NOTE: Dates are adjusted for weekends and holidays.

    b. Underpayment of the fourth installment does not result in penalty if, on or before January 31 of the following tax year, an individual both files a return and pays the amount computed payable on that return.
    1) Any underpayment penalties from the first three quarterly installments will not increase any further.

    c. Each of the following is treated as payment of estimated tax:
    1) The election to apply an overpayment of tax in a prior tax year, which has not been refunded, to the following year's tax return
        a) It is applied to the first required installment due.
    2) Amount of federal income tax (FIT) withheld (by an employer) from wages
        a) The aggregate amount is treated as if an equal part was paid on each due date, unless the individual establishes the actual payment dates.
    3) Direct payment by the individual (or another on his or her behalf)
        a) It is applied to the first estimated tax payment due.
    4) Excess FICA withheld when an employee has two or more employers during a tax year who withheld (in the aggregate) more than the ceiling on FICA taxes

    d. **Installment percentage.** Each installment must be 25% of the least of the following amounts:
    1) 100% of the prior year's tax (if a return was filed)
    2) 90% of the current year's tax
    3) 90% of the annualized current year's tax (applies when income is uneven)

    e. **Safe harbor rule.** Taxpayers whose 2019 tax returns showed AGI in excess of $150,000 ($75,000 for married filing separately) must apply the safe harbor rule. This rule requires the taxpayer to make estimated payments of the lesser of 110% of the 2019 tax liability or 90% of the 2020 tax liability.

    f. A taxpayer is not required to make a payment until the first period in which there is income.

    g. Tax refers to the sum of the regular tax, AMT, self-employment tax, and household employee tax.

h.   **Penalty.** A penalty is imposed if, by the quarterly payment date, the total of estimated tax payments and income tax withheld is less than 25% of the required minimum payment for the year.

   1)   The penalty is determined each quarter.
   2)   The penalty is the federal short-term rate plus 3% times the underpayment.
   3)   The penalty is not allowed as an interest deduction.

i.   The penalty will not be imposed if any of the following apply:

   1)   Actual tax liability shown on the return for the tax year (after reduction for amounts withheld by employers) is less than $1,000.
   2)   No tax liability was incurred in the prior tax year.
   3)   The IRS waives it for reasonable cause shown.

j.   **Farmers or fishermen** who expect to receive at least two-thirds of their gross income from farming or fishing activities (or did in the prior tax year) may pay estimated tax in one installment.

   1)   For 2020, the installment can be made as late as January 15, 2021, without penalty. The installment must be for the entire amount of estimated tax.

   2)   Alternatively, the farmer or fisherman does not need to make an installment payment if (s)he files his or her tax return for 2020 and pays the entire amount due by March 1, 2021.

   3)   Wages received as a farm employee are not farm income.

   4)   S corporation distributions from farming are farm income to the shareholder.

k.   To avoid underpayment penalties, taxpayers may review their withholding and estimated tax payment situation throughout the year. A mid-year review allows the taxpayer to look back at the recently filed prior-year return and know if too much or too little was withheld last year.

   1)   Any need for correction can be accomplished by having an employer adjust the amount being withheld for the rest of the year or by the taxpayer calculating any deficiency and making appropriate estimated quarterly payments. Items taxpayers should consider include life events (e.g., marriages and births) and financial changes (e.g., a raise or bonus, change in employment, or a significant capital gain from the sale of property).

l.   The following chart explains in general who is and is not subject to estimated payments:

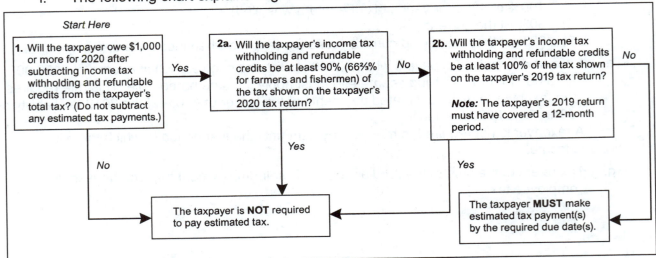

Figure 8-5

Exemption from Withholding on Form W-4

2. Some taxpayers are exempt from withholding requirements. The following chart explains the exemptions:

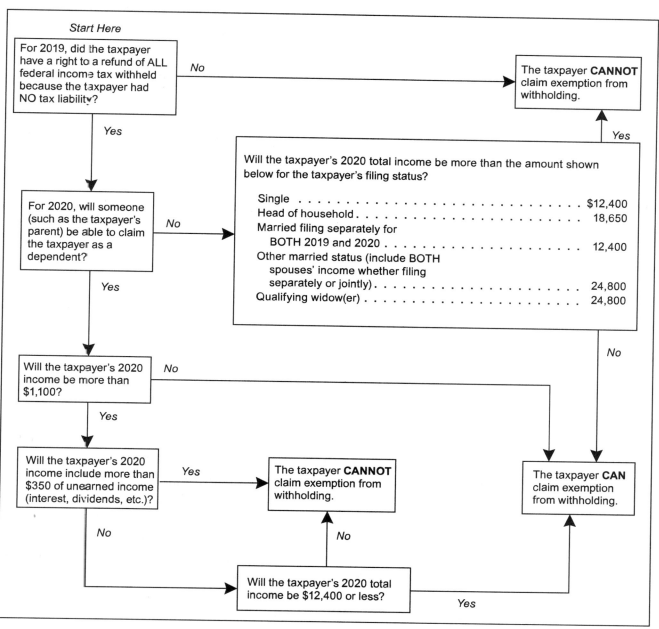

Figure 8-6

NOTE: This chart does not apply if the taxpayers are 65 or older or blind or if the taxpayers will itemize deductions or claim tax credits.

Excess Social Security Credit

3. An employer must deduct and withhold Social Security tax on an employee's first $137,700 of wages. For 2020, the withholding rate is 6.2%.

    a. When the maximum withholding is exceeded due to the correct withholding of two or more employers, a special refund of the excess amount may be obtained only by claiming a credit for the amount.

        1) The credit must be claimed in the same manner as if such special refund were an amount deducted and withheld as income tax at the source.

        2) The credit is computed separately for each spouse on a joint return.

    b. When an employer incorrectly withholds Social Security taxes on more than the maximum amount, a credit may not be claimed for the excess.

        1) The employer should refund the overcollection to the employee.

Claims for Refund

4. Taxpayers have a limited amount of time in which to file a claim for a credit or refund. Taxpayers encountering trouble obtaining a refund or other tax issues may request assistance from the Taxpayer Advocate Service by submitting Form 911.

    a. **Form 1040-X.** Taxpayers file a claim for refund on Form 1040-X with the Internal Revenue Service Center where the original return was filed.

        1) A separate form for each year or period involved is filed.

        2) An explanation of each item of income, deduction, or credit on which the refund claim is based is included.

    b. **Statute of limitations.** Generally, taxpayers must file a claim for credit or refund within 3 years from the date the return was filed or 2 years from the date the tax was paid, whichever is later.

        1) The Tax Court can consider taxes paid during the 3-year period preceding the date of a notice of deficiency for determining any refund due to a nonfiler.

        2) If a claim is made within 3 years after the filing of the return, the credit or refund cannot be more than the part of the tax paid within the 3 years (plus the length of any extension of time granted for filing the return) before the claim was filed.

            a) If a claim is filed after the 3-year period but within the 2 years from the time a tax was paid, the credit or refund cannot be more than the tax paid within the 2 years immediately before the filed claim.

        3) The period of limitations on credits and refunds can be suspended for individuals during periods in which they are unable to manage their financial affairs because of physical or mental impairment that is medically determinable and either

            a) Has lasted or can be expected to last continuously for at least 12 months or
            b) Can be expected to result in death.

STOP AND REVIEW! **You have completed the outline for this subunit. Study multiple-choice questions 23 through 30 beginning on page 262.**

QUESTIONS

8.1 Tax Credits

1. Ruth had wages of $34,000, and her husband John s wages were $27,000. They have three children ages 3, 6, and 9. They paid a total of $7,200 to Creative Child Care School, Inc. Assuming a 20% credit rate, what will be their Child Care Credit?

A. $1,440

B. $1,200

C. $6,000

D. $7,200

Answer (B) is correct.
 REQUIRED: The amount of the Child Care Credit.
 DISCUSSION: The maximum amount of employment-related expenses to which the credit may be applied is $3,000 if one qualifying child or dependent is involved, or $6,000 if two or more are involved. The maximum credit that can be claimed in this situation is $1,200 (20% of $6,000 limit) (Publication 17).

2. For the current year, Gannon Corporation has U.S. taxable income of $500,000, which includes $100,000 from a foreign division. Gannon paid $45,000 of foreign income taxes on the income of the foreign division. Assuming Gannon's U.S. income tax for the current year before credits is $170,000, its maximum Foreign Tax Credit for the current year is

A. $9,000

B. $45,000

C. $34,000

D. $136,000

Answer (C) is correct.
 REQUIRED: The Foreign Tax Credit that can be claimed in the current year.
 DISCUSSION: The Foreign Tax Credit is allowed under Sec. 27 and Sec. 901 for foreign income taxes paid or accrued during the year and is limited by Sec. 904(a). The limitation is the proportion of the taxpayer's tentative U.S. income tax (before the Foreign Tax Credit) that the taxpayer's foreign source taxable income bears to his or her worldwide taxable income for the year (Publication 514). The following calculation should be made:

$$\frac{\text{Foreign source taxable income}}{\text{Worldwide taxable income}} \times \text{U.S. income tax} = \frac{\text{Foreign tax}}{\text{credit limitation}}$$

The unused credit of $11,000 ($45,000 − $34,000) may be carried back 1 year and then forward to the following 10 taxable years [Sec. 904(c)].
 Answer (A) is incorrect. The credit is limited to 20% of the U.S. tax, not 20% of the foreign tax. **Answer (B) is incorrect.** The maximum Foreign Tax Credit for the current year is limited and does not equal foreign income taxes paid. **Answer (D) is incorrect.** This amount is Gannon's liability after subtracting the Foreign Tax Credit.

3. Carol, an individual taxpayer, received a Form 1099-Div from her global mutual fund that showed dividend income of $500 and foreign taxes withheld of $70. This is the only foreign source income she received for the year. Her income tax before any credits is $4,320. On which of the following forms may Carol elect to claim a credit for the foreign tax paid?

  A. Schedule 3 (Form 1040), line 12, "Other...refundable credits:"

  B. Schedule 3 (Form 1040), line 1, "Foreign tax credit."

  C. Form 1040, Schedule A, *Itemized Deductions*, line 6, "Other taxes."

  D. Form 1040, Schedule B, by electing to reduce the dividend income by $140 ($70 × 2).

Answer (B) is correct.
  REQUIRED: The correct form to claim a credit for the foreign tax paid.
  DISCUSSION: Line 1 on Schedule 3 (Form 1040) is labeled "Foreign tax credit." This is where a taxpayer would claim a credit on foreign tax paid.
  Answer (A) is incorrect. A taxpayer claims a Foreign Tax Credit on line 1 of Schedule 3 (Form 1040). **Answer (C) is incorrect.** Form 1040, Schedule A, *Itemized Deductions*, line 6, "Other taxes," is the line used to deduct a foreign tax paid, not receive a credit. **Answer (D) is incorrect.** A taxpayer claims a Foreign Tax Credit on line 1 of Schedule 3 (Form 1040).

4. Which of the following is NOT a qualifying student for purposes of the Lifetime Learning Credit?

  A. A student in a graduate program.

  B. A part-time student (less than half-time).

  C. A student in a vocational program.

  D. All are qualifying students for the Lifetime Learning Credit.

Answer (D) is correct.
  REQUIRED: The individual who is not eligible for the Lifetime Learning Credit.
  DISCUSSION: Generally, students who qualify for the AOTC also qualify for the Lifetime Learning Credit. Additionally, graduate students, students enrolled part-time, and students enrolled in a vocational program qualify for the Lifetime Learning Credit (Publication 17 and Sec. 25A).

5. All of the following child and dependent care expenses may qualify as work-related for purposes of the Child and Dependent Care Credit EXCEPT

  A. The cost of care provided to a qualifying person outside the home.

  B. The cost of getting a qualifying person from the home to the care location and back.

  C. The cost of household services that are partly for the well-being of a qualifying person.

  D. The cost of sending a child to school if the child is in a grade below kindergarten and the cost is incident to and cannot be separated from the cost of care.

Answer (B) is correct.
  REQUIRED: The child or dependent care expense that does not qualify as employment-related.
  DISCUSSION: Employment-related expenses are paid for household services and for the care of a qualifying individual [Sec. 21(b)(2)]. Expenses are only classified as work-related if they are incurred to enable the taxpayer to be gainfully employed. The cost of transporting a qualifying individual to a place where care is provided is not considered to be incurred for the individual's care [Publication 17 and Reg. 1.44A-1(c)(3)].
  Answer (A) is incorrect. The cost of care provided outside the home qualifies as long as the dependent regularly spends at least 8 hours a day in the taxpayer's home. **Answer (C) is incorrect.** The cost of household services for the care of a qualifying individual is included as qualified expenses. **Answer (D) is incorrect.** Expenses incurred in sending a child to school before (s)he enters kindergarten are included as qualified expenses.

6. Virginia's earned income for 2020 was $24,000. She paid $3,000 to a qualifying child care center for the care of her 2-year-old son while she worked. She received $2,000 from Social Services to assist with her child care expenses. Compute Virginia's Child Care Credit for 2020 from the following excerpt from the child and dependent care table:

IF your adjusted gross income is:		THEN the percentage is:
Over:	But not over:	
$ 0	$15,000	35%
$15,000	$17,000	34%
$17,000	$19,000	33%
$19,000	$21,000	32%
$21,000	$23,000	31%
$23,000	$25,000	30%
$25,000	$27,000	29%

A. $300

B. $900

C. $930

D. $310

Answer (A) is correct.
   REQUIRED: The amount of the Child Care Credit.
   DISCUSSION: The Child Care Credit is limited to $3,000 for one qualifying child. Virginia received $2,000 from Social Services to assist with her child care expenses; however, she must deduct this amount from the expenses that she paid for child care. The amount of expense that she must use for calculating her credit is $1,000 ($3,000 – $2,000). You must find the income bracket that Virginia is in (over $23,000, but not over $25,000) and multiply the expenses that she paid during the year for child care by the applicable percentage (30%). Thus, the credit for Virginia for 2020 is $300 ($1,000 × 30%) (Publication 503).
   Answer (B) is incorrect. The expenses paid by Virginia must be reduced by the amount she received from Social Services to assist with her child-care expenses. **Answer (C) is incorrect.** The expenses paid by Virginia must be reduced by the amount she received from Social Services to assist with her child-care expenses. In addition, Virginia's income is over $23,000, but not over $25,000. **Answer (D) is incorrect.** Virginia's income is over $23,000, but not over $25,000.

7. Which one of the following could prevent an individual from qualifying for the Child and Dependent Care Credit?

A. Unearned income of more than $400.

B. Paying for care for more than one qualifying person.

C. Not identifying the care provider on the tax return.

D. Paying for child care while looking for work.

Answer (C) is correct.
   REQUIRED: The event that could cause an individual to be disqualified for the Child and Dependent Care Credit.
   DISCUSSION: Taxpayers must provide each dependent's taxpayer identification number in order to claim the credit, as well as the identifying number of the service provider [Publication 17, Secs. 21(e)(9) and 21(e)(10), and Notice 89-71].

8. Jerry has two dependent children, Greg and Mandy, who are attending an accredited college in 2020. Greg, a fifth-year senior since January 1, spent $7,000 for tuition and fees. Mandy, a freshman with no prior post-secondary education, had tuition expenses of $4,000. Jerry meets all the income and filing status requirements for the education credits. There is no tax-free assistance to pay these expenses. Jerry's tax liability before credits equals $14,000. What is the maximum credit that Jerry may claim on his 2020 tax return?

A. $2,200 Lifetime Learning Credit.

B. $5,000 AOTC.

C. $2,500 AOTC and $1,000 Lifetime Learning Credit.

D. $2,500 AOTC and $1,400 Lifetime Learning Credit.

Answer (D) is correct.
   REQUIRED: The maximum credit that Jerry may claim on his 2020 tax return.
   DISCUSSION: There are two education-related credits: the AOTC and the Lifetime Learning Credit. These credits may be claimed by the individuals for tuition, fee, and book expenses incurred by students pursuing college or graduate degrees or vocational training. In 2020, the AOTC provides a maximum allowable credit of $2,500 per student for each of the first 4 years of post-secondary education. The calculation is the sum of 100% of the first $2,000 and 25% of the second $2,000 paid. The Lifetime Learning Credit allows a credit of 20% of the amount of tuition paid by the taxpayer and is available for the first $10,000 of tuition (Publication 17).
   Answer (A) is incorrect. Jerry is entitled to the Lifetime Learning Credit as well as the AOTC. **Answer (B) is incorrect.** In 2020, the AOTC is only available for individuals who are in their first 4 years of post-secondary education. **Answer (C) is incorrect.** Twenty percent of the first $10,000 of tuition is eligible for the Lifetime Learning Credit.

9. In 2020, Jonathan Smith paid his educational expenses at a community college where he completed his freshman year and began his sophomore year. His father, John Smith, provides more than half of the support for Jonathan and claims an exemption for him on his tax return. Which of the following is true?

A. Jonathan is eligible to take the AOTC on his 2020 tax return.

B. John is eligible to take the AOTC on his 2020 tax return.

C. Jonathan and John may split the AOTC between their 2020 tax returns.

D. Neither may take the AOTC.

Answer (B) is correct.
   REQUIRED: The true answer regarding the AOTC.
   DISCUSSION: The AOTC may be taken by a taxpayer who claims a dependent exemption for an eligible student on his tax return. The student claimed as a dependent is not eligible to take the credit (Publication 17).

10. For which of the following dependent children will a parent NOT be allowed a Child Tax Credit?

A. 15-year-old daughter.

B. 12-year-old foster child.

C. 19-year-old stepchild.

D. 16-year-old grandchild.

Answer (C) is correct.
   REQUIRED: The child who does not qualify for the Child Tax Credit.
   DISCUSSION: A "qualifying child" is a child, descendant, stepchild, eligible foster child, sibling, or descendant of siblings. The child must also be under 17 years of age and be claimed as a dependent by the taxpayer (Publication 17 or 972).

11. Which of the following statements is NOT true regarding tax benefits for education?

- A. The AOTC may be claimed for tuition expenses incurred in the first 4 years of post-secondary education.
- B. The dollar limitations for the AOTC are calculated on a per-student basis.
- C. The Lifetime Learning Credit is allowed for tuition paid for graduate program studies.
- D. Room and board are qualifying expenses for the AOTC.

Answer (D) is correct.

REQUIRED: The incorrect statement regarding tax benefits for education.

DISCUSSION: The AOTC provides a maximum tax credit of $2,500 per student for each of the first 4 years of post-secondary education. The $2,500 per year is the sum of 100% of the first $2,000 of qualified expenses and 25% of the next $2,000 of qualified expenses. The Lifetime Learning Credit provides a credit of 20% of qualified tuition expenses paid by the taxpayer for any year the AOTC is not claimed. The maximum credit allowed per year is 20% of $10,000 of qualified tuition and fees paid for the taxpayer, the taxpayer's spouse, and/or the taxpayer's dependents. Eligible expenses for both of these credits include tuition and fees required for enrollment. Books and required course materials are allowed for the AOTC but not the Lifetime Learning Credit. However, the credits may not be used for room and board, activity fees, athletic fees, insurance expense, or transportation (Publication 970).

Answer (A) is incorrect. The AOTC can be claimed for tuition expenses incurred in the first 4 years of post-secondary education. **Answer (B) is incorrect.** The dollar limitations for the AOTC are calculated on a per-student basis. **Answer (C) is incorrect.** The Lifetime Learning Credit is allowed for tuition paid for graduate program studies.

12. For purposes of claiming the Child Tax Credit, which of the following is NOT true for a qualifying child?

- A. Child must be under age 16 at the end of the year.
- B. Child must be a citizen or resident of the United States.
- C. Child must be claimed as your dependent.
- D. Child may be an eligible foster child.

Answer (A) is correct.

REQUIRED: The false statement regarding requirements for a qualifying child for the Child Tax Credit.

DISCUSSION: A qualifying child for the purposes of the Child Tax Credit is defined as a child, descendant, stepchild, eligible foster child, sibling, or descendant of a sibling (1) who is a U.S. citizen, (2) for whom the taxpayer may claim a dependency exemption, and (3) who is less than 17 years old at the close of the tax year. Accordingly, a child is not required to be under the age of 16 at the end of the year to receive the Child Tax Credit; (s)he must be under the age of 17 (Publication 17 or 972).

Answer (B) is incorrect. The child is required to be a citizen or resident of the U.S. in order to be a qualifying child for the purposes of the Child Tax Credit. **Answer (C) is incorrect.** The child is required to be the taxpayer's dependent in order to be a qualifying child for the purposes of the Child Tax Credit. **Answer (D) is incorrect.** The child is required to be a child, descendant, stepchild, eligible foster child, sibling, or descendant of a sibling in order to be a qualifying child for the purposes of the Child Tax Credit.

13. Mr. and Mrs. Robinson are both over age 65 and file a joint return. During the current year, they received $4,000 in nontaxable benefits from Social Security. This was their only nontaxable income. Their adjusted gross income was $12,000. How much can they claim as tentative credit for the elderly?

A. $0

B. $225

C. $375

D. $525

Answer (C) is correct.
REQUIRED: The amount the taxpayers may claim as a credit for the elderly.
DISCUSSION: In the case of an individual who has attained age 65 before the close of the taxable year, the credit for the elderly or disabled allows a credit equal to 15% of the individual's applicable base amount. On a joint return when both spouses are eligible for the credit, the applicable base amount is equal to an initial amount of $7,500 reduced by any amounts received as Social Security benefits or otherwise excluded from gross income [Sec. 22(c)(3)]. The base amount is also reduced by one-half of the excess of adjusted gross income over $10,000 (in the case of a joint return), which is $1,000 [($12,000 AGI – $10,000 phaseout threshold) × 50%] for the Robinsons (Publication 524).

Initial base amount	$ 7,500
Less: Social Security	(4,000)
Less: AGI limitation	(1,000)
Adjusted amount	$ 2,500
	× .15
Robinsons' tentative credit for the elderly	$ 375

Authors' note: The actual credit received would be $0 because there would be no taxable income after subtracting the basic standard deduction, the additional standard deduction.
Answer (A) is incorrect. A credit is available to qualified elderly people. The question asked for the tentative amount. Answer (B) is incorrect. The AGI limitation is only 50% of the excess of AGI over $10,000. Answer (D) is incorrect. The initial Sec. 22 amount must be reduced by an AGI limitation.

14. Liz incurred qualified adoption expenses of $15,000 in 2020. Liz's AGI for 2020 was $60,000. What is the amount of the credit Liz can take in 2020 for the adoption expenses she incurred?

A. $0

B. $7,500

C. $14,300

D. $15,000

Answer (C) is correct.
REQUIRED: The amount of the credit for adoption expenses.
DISCUSSION: A credit is allowed for qualified adoption expenses incurred after 1996 (Sec. 23). The maximum credit for 2020 is $14,300 per child (Publication 17). Liz's AGI is well below the threshold of $214,520.
Answer (A) is incorrect. A credit is allowed for qualified adoption expenses incurred (Sec. 23), and it is not fully eliminated until the taxpayer's AGI reaches $254,520. Answer (B) is incorrect. The maximum credit is $14,300 for a child. Answer (D) is incorrect. The maximum credit is $14,300 for a child.

15. A taxpayer paid $7,000 of interest in 2020 on the mortgage given upon acquiring her first home. The taxpayer received a mortgage credit certificate (MCC), which specifies a 30% credit rate. How much of a credit is the taxpayer entitled to in 2020?

A. $2,000

B. $2,100

C. $5,000

D. $7,000

Answer (A) is correct.
   REQUIRED: The calculation of Residential Mortgage Interest Credit and applicable limits.
   DISCUSSION: Under Sec. 25, MCCs are issued to qualified individuals when privately financing their first purchase of a principal residence (Publication 530). If the specified rate exceeds 20%, the credit is limited to $2,000.
   Answer (B) is incorrect. This amount ignores the $2,000 limit when the rate exceeds 20%. The remaining $100 may be carried forward. **Answer (C) is incorrect.** This amount is the maximum interest deduction allowed when the credit is taken. **Answer (D) is incorrect.** The credit is the applicable percentage of the interest paid, subject to a limit when the rate exceeds 20%.

16. The Minimum Tax Credit (MTC) allocable for the current year is limited to

A. Current-year gross regular tax (reduced by certain credits) minus current-year tentative minimum tax.

B. Current-year gross regular tax (without regard to any credits) minus current-year tentative minimum tax.

C. Current-year gross regular tax (reduced by certain credits) plus current-year tentative minimum tax.

D. Current-year gross regular tax (reduced by certain credits) minus previous-year tentative minimum tax.

Answer (A) is correct.
   REQUIRED: The true statement regarding the Minimum Tax Credit.
   DISCUSSION: The MTC allowable is limited to current-year gross regular tax (reduced by certain credits) minus current-year tentative minimum tax.
   Answer (B) is incorrect. The current-year gross regular tax is reduced by certain credits. **Answer (C) is incorrect.** Current-year tentative minimum tax is subtracted from current-year gross regular tax. **Answer (D) is incorrect.** Current-year, not previous-year, tentative minimum tax is subtracted from current-year gross regular tax.

17. Which of the following is earned income for Earned Income Credit purposes?

A. Unemployment compensation.

B. Alimony.

C. The wages of a minister who has an exemption from self-employment tax.

D. The wages of an inmate working in the prison laundry.

Answer (C) is correct.
   REQUIRED: The qualifications for earned income.
   DISCUSSION: The Earned Income Credit is based on all earned income, which includes wages, salaries, tips, other employee compensation, and net earnings from self employment. Earned income does not include interest and dividends, welfare benefits, veterans' benefits, pensions or annuities, alimony, Social Security benefits, workers' compensation, unemployment compensation, taxable scholarships or fellowships that are not reported on the taxpayer's W-2 form, amounts received for services performed by prison inmates while in prison, amounts that are subject to Code Sec. 871(a), or payments received from work activities if sufficient private sector employment is not available and from community service programs.
   Answer (A) is incorrect. Unemployment compensation is not earned income. **Answer (B) is incorrect.** Alimony is not earned income if per a pre-2019 divorce. It is not even income at all (i.e., unearned) if per a post-2018 divorce. **Answer (D) is incorrect.** Wages of an inmate working in the prison laundry are not earned income.

18. Which of the following is NOT a test to determine if a child is a qualifying child for the Earned Income Credit (EIC)?

    A. Relationship.

    B. Age.

    C. Residency.

    D. Support.

Answer (D) is correct.
    REQUIRED: The item that is not a test to determine if a child qualifies under the EIC.
    DISCUSSION: In order for a child to be a qualifying child, three tests must be met: (1) The child must be related by birth or adoption or be an eligible foster child or stepchild; (2) the taxpayer must provide the child's principal place of abode for more than half of the year; and (3) the child must be under age 19 at the close of the tax year, be permanently disabled, or be a student under the age of 24.

19. The Earned Income Credit is available to

    A. Persons with a qualifying child.

    B. Persons without a qualifying child.

    C. Persons who are age 40.

    D. All of the answers are correct.

Answer (D) is correct.
    REQUIRED: The individuals who qualify for the Earned Income Credit.
    DISCUSSION: A taxpayer can be eligible for the Earned Income Credit by having a qualifying child or meeting three qualifications: (1) The individual must have his or her principal place of abode in the United States for more than one-half of the taxable year, (2) the individual must be at least 25 years old and not more than 64 years old at the end of the taxable year, and (3) the individual cannot be claimed as a dependent of another taxpayer for any tax year beginning in the year the credit is being claimed.

20. For the current year, for purposes of the Earned Income Credit, which of the following amounts qualifies as earned income?

    A. Earnings from self-employment.

    B. Excluded combat-zone pay.

    C. Unemployment compensation.

    D. Value of meals or lodging provided by an employer for the convenience of the employer.

Answer (A) is correct.
    REQUIRED: The item that qualifies as earned income.
    DISCUSSION: Earned income includes all wages, salaries, tips, and other employee compensation (including union strike benefits), plus the amount of the taxpayer's net earnings from self-employment. For purposes of the Earned Income Credit, earned income does not include nontaxable compensation such as the basic quarters and subsistence allowances for the military, parsonage allowances, the value of meals and lodging furnished for the convenience of the employer, and excludable employer-provided dependent care benefits. Earned income does not include interest and dividends, welfare benefits, veterans' benefits, pensions or annuities, alimony, Social Security benefits, workers' compensation, unemployment compensation, and taxable scholarships or fellowships.

21. Which of the following is NOT required for a taxpayer to be eligible for the Premium Tax Credit?

    A. The taxpayer's health insurance is purchased through the Marketplace.

    B. The taxpayer is not eligible to be claimed as a dependent by another taxpayer.

    C. The taxpayer's income is within certain income limits.

    D. The taxpayer is eligible for coverage through an employer plan.

Answer (D) is correct.
    REQUIRED: The item not required for a taxpayer to be eligible for the Premium Tax Credit.
    DISCUSSION: Taxpayers may be eligible for the Premium Tax Credit if they

1. Buy health insurance through the Marketplace;
2. Are ineligible for coverage through an employer or government plan;
3. Are within certain income limits;
4. Do not file a separate return, if married (though exceptions exist if the taxpayer is a victim of domestic violence); and
5. Cannot be claimed as a dependent by another taxpayer.

Thus, to be eligible for the Premium Tax Credit, the taxpayer must be ineligible for coverage through an employer or government plan.
    Answer (A) is incorrect. In order to be eligible for the Premium Tax Credit, the taxpayer must purchase his or her health insurance plan through the Marketplace. **Answer (B) is incorrect.** A taxpayer must not be eligible to be claimed as a dependent by another taxpayer in order to qualify for the Premium Tax Credit. **Answer (C) is incorrect.** The Premium Tax Credit is a subsidy for households that make less than four times the federal poverty line. Therefore, the taxpayer must be within certain income limits in order to qualify.

22. Brad, age 19, is a full-time student in 2020. Brad works a part-time job and contributes $500 to his IRA account. He has AGI of $15,000 for the year and cannot be claimed as a dependent by another taxpayer. Assuming that Brad files as a single taxpayer, what amount of Retirement Savings Contributions Credit may Brad claim in 2020?

    A. $250

    B. $0

    C. $100

    D. $50

Answer (B) is correct.
    REQUIRED: The amount of Retirement Savings Contributions Credit that can be claimed.
    DISCUSSION: A taxpayer is eligible for the Retirement Savings Contributions Credit if the taxpayer is

1. Age 18 or older,
2. Not claimed as a dependent on another person's return, and
3. Not a full-time student.

Because Brad is a full-time student, he is ineligible for the credit.
    Answer (A) is incorrect. Based on his tax status and AGI, Brad would be eligible for a credit that is equal to 50% of his $500 contribution. However, as a full-time student, Brad is not eligible for the Retirement Savings Contributions Credit. **Answer (C) is incorrect.** The amount of $100 is 20% of Brad's contributions. However, Brad is not eligible for the credit as a full-time student. **Answer (D) is incorrect.** The amount of $50 is 10% of Brad's contributions. However, Brad cannot claim the credit because he is a full-time student.

8.2 Payments

23. Marge Godfrey sold her investment property March 30, 2020, at a gain of $50,000. Marge expects to owe $10,000 in additional income taxes on this sale. She had a tax liability of $900 for 2019 and will have no withholding for 2020. Marge's first estimated tax payment is due on what date?

A. April 30, 2020.

B. April 15, 2020.

C. January 31, 2021.

D. June 15, 2020.

Answer (B) is correct.
REQUIRED: The date the first payment of estimated tax is due.
DISCUSSION: Marge must make estimated payments because she had a tax liability in the previous year. Estimated tax payments are not required until the first period in which there is income (IRS Pub. 505). If income subject to estimated tax occurs in the first payment period, then the first payment is due by the due date of the first payment period, April 15, 2020. Marge has estimated income in the first period.
Answer (A) is incorrect. Estimated tax is due on April 15 for income made in the first payment period. **Answer (C) is incorrect.** Estimated tax is due on April 15 for income made in the first payment period. **Answer (D) is incorrect.** Marge had income in the first payment period.

24. For 2020, Mike and Denise, calendar-year taxpayers, had gross income comprised of the following:

Wages received as a farm employee	$26,000
Gross income from Schedule F dairy operations	40,000
Distributable share of an S corporation's gross income from farming	12,000
Long-term capital gains from stock sales	18,000
Short-term capital losses from stock sales	(21,000)

They have made no estimated tax payments as of December 31, 2020, and the withholding from wages is not sufficient to relieve them from the estimated tax penalty. Which of the following statements is true if they make an estimated tax payment by January 15, 2021?

A. They will avoid the estimated tax penalty since they are qualified farmers.

B. They will avoid the estimated tax penalty since all of their earned income is from farming activities.

C. They will not avoid the estimated tax penalty since their farm income does not comprise two-thirds of their gross income.

D. They can avoid the estimated tax penalty only by filing their return by March 1, 2021, and paying all the tax due.

Answer (C) is correct.
REQUIRED: The true statement regarding estimated tax payments.
DISCUSSION: Section 6654(i) allows farmers or fishermen who expect to receive at least two-thirds of their gross income from farming or fishing activities, or who received at least two-thirds of their gross income for the prior tax year from farming or fishing, to pay estimated tax for the year in one installment. If Mike and Denise had received two-thirds of their gross income from farming, they could have waited until January 15, 2021, to make their 2020 estimated tax payment without penalty. They would have been required to pay the entire estimated tax for the year at that time. Mike and Denise's gross income for the year was $96,000 ($26,000 + $40,000 + $12,000 + $18,000). Losses are not included in the calculation of gross income. Their gross income from farming was $52,000 ($40,000 Schedule F + $12,000 S corp.). Wages received as a farm employee or capital gains are not included in farm income. Therefore, 54% of their gross income came from farming. At least 67% of their gross income must come from farming activities in order to avoid the penalty (Publication 505).
Answer (A) is incorrect. Two-thirds of their gross income must come from farming for them to qualify as farmers. **Answer (B) is incorrect.** Wages, distributive share of an S corporation, and capital gains are not included as farm income. **Answer (D) is incorrect.** They cannot avoid the estimated tax penalty.

25. All of the following individuals file their income tax returns as single. Which one is required to make estimated tax payments for 2020?

   A. Ms. Kirkland, who had no tax liability for 2019, expects to owe $2,500 self-employment tax for 2020 (she has no withholding tax or credits).

   B. Mr. Brady, who had a $2,000 tax liability for 2019, expects a $2,100 tax liability for 2020 and withholding of $1,900.

   C. Ms. Evans, who had no tax liability for 2019, expects a tax liability of $4,900 for 2020, with $3,500 withholding.

   D. Mr. Jones, who had a 2019 tax liability of $9,500, expects a tax liability of $12,400 for 2020, with $8,500 withholding.

Answer (D) is correct.
   REQUIRED: The individual who must make estimated tax payments.
   DISCUSSION: In general, individuals must make estimated tax payments or be subject to a penalty (Sec. 6654). Amounts withheld from wages are treated as estimated tax payments. The annual estimated payment that must be made is equal to the lesser of (1) 90% of the tax for the current year or (2) 100% of the tax for the prior year (Publication 17). Also, no penalty will apply to an individual whose tax for the year, after credit for withheld tax, is less than $1,000. Mr. Jones does not meet either the 90% or the 100% test, and his tax after credit for withholding is not less than $1,000. Therefore, he will have to make estimated tax payments.
   Answer (A) is incorrect. Ms. Kirkland had no tax liability in the prior year. **Answer (B) is incorrect.** The difference between Mr. Brady's withholding and his tax liability is less than $1,000. **Answer (C) is incorrect.** Ms. Evans had no tax liability in the prior year.

26. Violet made no estimated tax payments for 2020 because she thought she had enough tax withheld from her wages. In January 2021, she realized that her withholding was $2,000 less than the amount needed to avoid a penalty for the underpayment of estimated tax so she made an estimated tax payment of $2,500 on January 10. Violet filed her 2020 return on March 1, 2021, showing a refund due her of $100. Which of the following statements is NOT true regarding the estimated tax penalty?

   A. Violet will not owe a penalty for the quarter ending December 31, 2020, because she made sufficient payment before January 15, 2021.

   B. Violet will not owe a penalty for any quarter because her total payments exceed her tax liability.

   C. Violet could owe a penalty for one or all of the first three quarters even though she is due a refund for the year.

   D. If Violet owes a penalty for any quarter, the underpayment will be computed from the date the amount was due to the date the payment is made.

Answer (B) is correct.
   REQUIRED: The false statement regarding the estimated tax penalty.
   DISCUSSION: A penalty may be imposed if, by the quarterly payment date, the total of estimated tax payments and income tax withheld is less than 25% of the required minimum payment for the year. The penalty is determined each quarter. In addition, it is calculated by adding 3 percentage points to the federal short-term rate and multiplying this percent by the amount of the underpayment. Finally, the penalty is not allowed as an interest deduction. Although Violet paid her tax liability by the due date for the last quarter, she may still be assessed a penalty for not making estimated tax payments in the first three quarters of the year (Publication 505).
   Answer (A) is incorrect. Violet will not owe a penalty on the last quarter because she paid the balance of her estimated tax liability by the due date of the last quarter. **Answer (C) is incorrect.** Violet could owe a penalty on one or all of the first three quarters of the year because she did not make quarterly payments of estimated tax. **Answer (D) is incorrect.** The penalties on estimated tax are computed as of the due date for the quarter in which the estimated tax was due and will be assessed for the period between that due date and the date in which the payment was made.

27. Ms. W, who is single, determined that her total tax liability for Year 2 would be $10,000. W is required to make estimated tax payments if

A. Her Year 1 tax liability was $12,000 and her Year 2 income tax withholding will be $9,750.

B. Her Year 1 tax liability was $12,000 and her Year 2 income tax withholding will be $9,000.

C. Her Year 1 tax liability was $5,000 and her Year 2 income tax withholding will be $6,000.

D. Her Year 1 tax liability was $9,000 and her Year 2 income tax withholding will be $8,500.

28. An employee who has had Social Security tax withheld in an amount greater than the maximum for a particular year may claim

A. Such excess as either a credit or an itemized deduction, at the election of the employee, if that excess resulted from correct withholding by two or more employers.

B. Reimbursement of such excess from his or her employers if that excess resulted from correct withholding by two or more employers.

C. The excess as a credit against income tax, if that excess resulted from correct withholding by two or more employers.

D. The excess as a credit against income tax, if that excess was withheld by one employer.

Answer (D) is correct.
   REQUIRED: The circumstances under which the taxpayer would be required to make estimated tax payments.
   DISCUSSION: In general, individuals must make estimated tax payments or be subject to a penalty (Sec. 6654). Amounts withheld from wages are treated as estimated tax payments. The annual estimated payment that must be made is equal to the lesser of (1) 90% of the tax for the current year or (2) 100% of the tax for the prior year (Publication 17). Assuming Ms. W's tax liability for Year 2 is $10,000 and her Year 1 tax liability was $9,000, the $8,500 withheld from her Year 2 wages does not meet the required annual estimated payment.
   Answer (A) is incorrect. The amount of $9,750 is greater than 90% of the Year 2 tax liability. **Answer (B) is incorrect.** The amount of $9,000 equals 90% of the Year 2 tax liability. **Answer (C) is incorrect.** The amount of $6,000 is greater than 100% of the Year 1 tax liability.

Answer (C) is correct.
   REQUIRED: The proper treatment when a taxpayer overpays the Social Security tax.
   DISCUSSION: When an employee overpays the Social Security tax, proper adjustments must be made. If the overpayment cannot be adjusted, the amount must be refunded. If the overpayment resulted from correct withholding by two or more employers, the extra Social Security tax may be used to reduce income taxes.
   Answer (A) is incorrect. The overpayment is not available as a deduction. **Answer (B) is incorrect.** It is not the employer's responsibility to refund the tax (the employer turned it over to the government). **Answer (D) is incorrect.** The extra Social Security tax may be used to reduce income taxes only when an employee has worked for two or more employers.

29. Ms. B filed her Year 1 Form 1040 on April 15, Year 2, but did not pay her tax liability of $3,000. On June 15, Year 3, she paid the tax in full. In Year 4, Ms. B discovered additional deductions for Year 1 that will result in a refund of $1,000. To receive her refund, Ms. B must file an amended income tax return by (assuming no relevant days are Saturdays, Sundays, or holidays)

   A. April 15, Year 5.

   B. June 15, Year 5.

   C. April 15, Year 6.

   D. June 15, Year 6.

Answer (B) is correct.
   REQUIRED: The date for filing a refund claim for taxes paid after the related return was filed.
   DISCUSSION: Section 6511(b) states that a claim for a refund must be filed within the time limits established in the statute of limitations on refunds. Section 6511(a) provides that refunds may be made 3 years from the time the return was due or 2 years from the time the tax was paid, whichever is later (Publication 17). Here, 2 years from the time the tax was paid is the later date, so Ms. B must file a claim before June 15, Year 5.

30. If an individual paid income taxes in the current year through withholding but did not file a current-year return because his or her income was insufficient to require the filing of a return, the deadline for filing a refund claim is

   A. 2 years from the date the tax was paid.

   B. 2 years from the date a return would have been due.

   C. 3 years from the date the tax was paid.

   D. 3 years from the date a return would have been due.

Answer (A) is correct.
   REQUIRED: The deadline for filing a refund claim when no return is filed.
   DISCUSSION: Section 6511(a) and (b) state that a claim for refund must be filed within 3 years from the time the return was filed or 2 years from the time the tax was paid, whichever is later. Section 6511(a) further states that, if no return was filed, the claim for refund is due within 2 years from the time the tax was paid. For tax years ending after August 5, 1997, taxpayers who initially fail to file a return, but who receive a notice of deficiency and file suit to contest in Tax Court during the third year after the return due date, are permitted to obtain a refund of excessive amounts paid within the 3-year period prior to the deficiency notice (Publication 17).

 Access the **Gleim EA Premium Review System** featuring our SmartAdapt technology from your Gleim Personal Classroom to continue your studies. You will experience a personalized study environment with exam-emulating multiple-choice questions.

STUDY UNIT NINE

PROPERTY TRANSACTIONS: BASIS AND DISPOSITIONS

(19 pages of outline)

The concept of basis is important in federal income taxation. Generally, basis is the measurement of a taxpayer's investment in property, which the taxpayer is entitled to have returned without tax consequences. The property basis is generally used in determining the gain or loss associated with the property.

The basis of an asset is generally its cost, but it may be adjusted over the course of time due to various events. The basis of property must be increased by capital expenditures and decreased by capital returns.

- Increases in basis have the effect of reducing the amount of gain realized or increasing the amount of realized loss.

- Decreases in basis have the effect of increasing the amount of realized gain or decreasing the amount of loss.

9.1 COST BASIS

When a taxpayer acquires property, his or her basis in the property is initially cost, substituted, transferred, exchanged, or converted basis.

1. **Cost basis** is the sum of capitalized acquisition costs.
2. **Substituted basis** is computed by reference to basis in other property.
3. **Transferred basis** is computed by reference to basis in the same property in the hands of another.
4. **Exchanged basis** is computed by reference to basis in other property previously held by the person.
5. **Converted basis** is when personal-use property is converted to business use; the basis of the property is the lower of its basis or the FMV on the date of conversion.

Capitalized Acquisition Costs

6. Initial basis in purchased property is the cost of acquiring it. Only capital costs are included, i.e., those for acquisition, title acquisition, and major improvements.

Common Capitalized Costs (for Sec. 1012)

Purchase Price (Stated)	Miscellaneous Costs
Includes liability to which property is subject NOTE: Not unstated interest	Appraisal fees Freight Installation Testing
Closing Costs	**Major Improvements**
Brokerage commissions Pre-purchase taxes Sales tax on purchase Title transfer taxes Title insurance Recording fees Attorney fees Document review, preparation	New roof New gutters Extending water line to property Demolition costs and losses New electrical wiring

Expenses Not Properly Chargeable to a Capital Account

a. Costs of maintaining and operating property are not added to basis, e.g., interest on credit related to the property, insurance (e.g., casualty), and ordinary maintenance or repairs (e.g., painting).

Uniform Capitalization Rules

7. Costs for construction of real or tangible personal property to be used in trade or business are capitalized.

   a. All costs necessary to prepare the property for its intended use are capitalized, including both direct and most allocable indirect costs, e.g., for permits, materials, equipment rent, compensation for services (minus any work opportunity credit), and architect fees.

   b. Construction-period interest and taxes must be capitalized as part of building costs.

8. Cost basis includes the FMV of property given up. If it is not determinable with reasonable certainty, use FMV of property received.

   a. Capital acquisition expenditures may be made by cash, by cash equivalent, in property, with liability, or by services.

   b. A rebate to the purchaser is treated as a reduction of the purchase price. It is not included in basis or in gross income.

9. Uniform capitalization rules do not apply if property is acquired for resale and the company's annual gross receipts (for the past 3 years) do not exceed $26 million.

Liabilities

10. Acquisition basis is

    a. Increased for notes to the seller (minus unstated interest)
    b. Increased for liabilities to which the acquired property is subject

EXAMPLE 9-1	Tax Basis -- Building with a Mortgage

If an individual buys a building for $30,000 cash and assumes a mortgage on it of $190,000, the individual's basis is $220,000.

11. The FMV of property received in exchange for services is income (compensation) to the provider when it is not subject to a substantial risk of forfeiture and not restricted as to transfer. The property acquired has a tax cost basis equal to the FMV of the property.

    a. Sale of stock to an employee is treated as gross income (bonus compensation) to the extent any price paid is less than the stock's FMV.

       1) The basis of restricted stock is the price paid other than by services.

       2) Upon lapse of the restriction, the recipient has ordinary gross income of the spread between FMV on that date and any amounts otherwise paid.

       3) Basis is increased by that same amount.

       4) The transferee may elect to include the FMV minus the cost spread in gross income when the stock is purchased.

          a) Basis includes tax cost, but no subsequent deduction (recovery of tax cost) is allowed if the stock is forfeited by operation of the restriction.

Lump Sum Purchase

12. When more than one asset is purchased for a lump sum, the basis of each is computed by apportioning the total cost based on the relative FMV of each asset.

$$\text{Allocable cost (basis)} = \frac{\text{FMV of asset}}{\text{FMV of all assets purchased}} \times \text{Lump sum purchase price}$$

    a.   Alternatively, the transferor and transferee may agree in writing as to the allocation of consideration or the FMV of any assets.

        1)   The agreement is binding on the parties unless the IRS deems it improper.

           a)   If improper, the residual method may be applied.

    b.   The residual method, particularly relevant to goodwill and going-concern value when a transferor-transferee agreement is not applicable, allocates purchase price for both transferor and transferee to asset categories up to FMV in the following order:

        1)   Cash and cash equivalents

        2)   Near-cash items, such as CDs, U.S. government securities, foreign currency, and other marketable securities

        3)   Accounts receivable and other debt instruments, as well as other assets marked to market at least annually

    NOTE: Regulation 1.338-6(b)(2)(iii) created exceptions applicable to certain specific debt instruments.

        4)   Property held primarily for sale to customers in the ordinary course of a trade or business or stocks that are part of dealer inventory

        5)   All other assets, excluding Sec. 197 intangibles

        6)   Section 197 intangibles, such as patents and covenants not to compete except goodwill and going-concern value

        7)   Goodwill and going-concern value

    NOTE: When the purchase price is lower than the aggregate FMV of the assets other than goodwill and going-concern value, the price is allocated first to the face amount of cash and then to assets listed in 2) through 6) above according to relative FMVs.

Sale of Stock

13. To compute gain realized on the sale of stock, specific identification of the stock sold is used if possible. Otherwise, FIFO is assumed.

Demolition

14. Costs and losses associated with demolishing a structure are allocated to the land. The costs include the remaining basis (not FMV) of the structure and demolition costs.

STOP AND REVIEW! **You have completed the outline for this subunit. Study multiple-choice questions 1 through 4 beginning on page 286.**

9.2 PROPERTY RECEIVED BY GIFT

The donee's basis in property acquired by gift is the donor's basis, increased for any gift tax paid attributable to appreciation. The donor's basis is increased by

$$\text{Gift tax paid} \times \left[\frac{\text{FMV (at time of gift)} - \text{Donor's basis}}{\text{FMV (at time of gift)} - \text{Annual exclusion}} \right]$$

NOTE: The 2020 annual exclusion for gift tax is $15,000.

1. If the FMV on the date of the gift is less than the donor's basis, the donee has a dual basis for the property, which minimizes the gain (loss) recognized on a subsequent transfer.

    a. **Loss basis.** The FMV at the date of the gift is used if the property is later transferred at a loss.

    b. **Gain basis.** The donor's basis is used if the property is later transferred at a gain.

    c. If the property is later transferred for more than FMV at the date of the gift but for less than the donor's basis at the date of the gift, no gain (loss) is recognized.

Depreciable Basis

2. If gift property is immediately used as business property, the basis for depreciation is the donor's AB.

3. If gift property is later converted from personal to business use, the AB is the lower of the transferor's AB or the FMV on the date of conversion.

STOP AND REVIEW! You have completed the outline for this subunit. Study multiple-choice questions 5 through 9 beginning on page 288.

9.3 PROPERTY RECEIVED FOR SERVICES

All compensation for personal services is gross income. The form of payment is irrelevant. If property is received for services, gross income is the fair market value of the property received minus any cash or other property given.

1. Basis in property received is the amount included in income plus any cash or other property given.

2. Gross income of an employee includes any amount paid by an employer for a liability (including taxes) or an expense of the employee.

STOP AND REVIEW! You have completed the outline for this subunit. Study multiple-choice question 10 on page 290.

9.4 INHERITED PROPERTY

Basis is the FMV on the date of death.

1. If the executor elects the alternate valuation date, the basis of the assets is the FMV 6 months after the decedent's death.

    a. If the assets are sold or distributed within the first 6 months after death, basis equals FMV on the sale or distribution date.

2. The FMV basis rule also applies to the following property:

    a. One-half of community property interests

    b. Property acquired by form of ownership, e.g., right of survivorship, except if consideration was paid to acquire the property from a nonspouse

    c. Property received prior to death without full and adequate consideration (if a life estate was retained in it) or subject to a right of revocation

        1) Reduce basis by depreciation deductions allowed the donee.

    NOTE: The FMV rule does not apply to (1) income in respect of a decedent or (2) appreciated property given to the decedent within 1 year of death (use adjusted basis in the property immediately prior to death).

    A shareholder must report his or her ratable share of any income that is income in respect to a decedent as if (s)he had received it directly from the decedent. *FMV – ratable share of income*

EXAMPLE 9-2	Tax Basis -- Inherited S Corporation Stock

The shareholder's basis in the inherited S corporation stock is its FMV on the date of death minus the ratable share of any S corporation income attributable to those shares.

---

3. If no federal estate tax return is required to be filed, the value as appraised for state inheritance tax purposes is used.

STOP AND REVIEW! **You have completed the outline for this subunit. Study multiple-choice questions 11 through 13 beginning on page 290.**

9.5 STOCK DIVIDENDS

A corporation recognizes no gain or loss on transactions involving its own stock.

1. A proportionate distribution of stock issued by the corporation is generally not gross income to the shareholders.

    a. A shareholder allocates the aggregate adjusted basis (AB) in the old stock to the old and new stock in proportion to the FMV of the old and new stock.

        1) Basis is apportioned by relative FMV to different classes of stock if applicable.

    b. The holding period of the distributed stock includes that of the old stock.

    c. E&P are not altered for a tax-free stock dividend.

Stock Rights

2. A distribution of stock rights is treated as a distribution of the stock.

    a. Basis is allocated based on the FMV of the rights.

        1) Basis in the stock rights is zero if their aggregate FMV is less than 15% of the FMV of the stock on which they were distributed, unless the shareholder elects to allocate.

    b. Basis in the stock, if the right is exercised, is any basis allocated to the right plus the exercise price.

    c. Holding period of the stock begins on the exercise date.

    d. No deduction is allowed for basis allocated to stock rights that lapse.

        1) Basis otherwise allocated remains in the underlying stock.

Taxable Stock Distribution

3. Distributions of stock, described in a. through g. below, are subject to tax. The amount of a distribution subject to tax is the FMV of distributed stock or stock rights.

    a. If a shareholder has an option to choose between a distribution of stock or a distribution of other property, the amount of the distribution is the greater of the FMV of stock or the cash or FMV of other property.

        1) For example, some shareholders receive property, and other shareholders receive stock; or some common shareholders receive common stock, and others receive preferred.

    b. Distribution of preferred stock is made with respect to preferred stock.

        1) Limited change in conversion ratios, by itself, does not trigger taxability.

    c. Convertible preferred stock is distributed, and the effect is to change the shareholder's proportionate stock ownership.

    d. Constructive stock distributions change proportionate interests, resulting from a transaction such as a change in conversion ratio or redemption price.

    e. E&P are reduced by the FMV of stock and stock rights distributed.

    f. Basis in the underlying stock does not change. Basis in the new stock or stock rights is their FMV.

    g. Holding period for the new stock begins on the day after the distribution date.

Stock Split

4. A stock split is not a taxable distribution.

    a. The basis of the old stock is divided by the number of new shares.
    b. Holding period of the new stock includes that of the old stock.

STOP AND REVIEW! **You have completed the outline for this subunit. Study multiple-choice questions 14 and 15 on page 292.**

9.6 ADJUSTMENTS TO ASSET BASIS

Initial basis is adjusted consistent with tax-relevant events. Adjustments include the following.

Subsequent to Acquisition

1. Certain expenditures subsequent to acquisition are property costs, and they increase basis, e.g., legal fees to defend title or title insurance premiums.

Prolong Life

2. Basis must be increased for expenditures that substantially prolong the life of the property by at least 1 year or materially increase its value.

    a. Examples include major improvements (e.g., new roof, addition to building) and zoning changes.

    b. Generally, maintenance, repair, and operating costs are not capitalized.

3. An increase to basis may result from a liability to the extent it is secured by real property and applied to extend its life.

Depreciation

4. Depreciation taken on business property will decrease the basis.

    a. The base for MACRS depreciation is the cost.

    b. All assets depreciated under the General Depreciation System (GDS) under MACRS must be included in a class of depreciation, such as 5-, 7-, or 20-year property.

    c. A few of the depreciation classes follow:

        1) Five-year property includes automobiles; computers and peripheral equipment; office machinery (such as typewriters, calculators, and copiers); any property used in research and experimentation; and appliances, carpets, furniture, etc., used in a residential real estate activity.

        2) Seven-year property includes office furniture and fixtures (such as desks, files, and safes), agricultural machinery and equipment, and any property that does not have a class life and has not been designated by law as being in any other class.

        3) Residential real property is any property from which 80% or more of its gross rental income comes from dwelling units. This property has a recovery period of 27 1/2 years.

        4) Nonresidential real property is Sec. 1250 property.

            a) It includes office buildings, stores, or warehouses that are not classified as residential real property and are not otherwise specified to have a life less than 27 1/2 years.

            b) The recovery period of this property is 39 years.

5. Basis must be reduced by the larger of the amount of depreciation allowed or allowable (even if not claimed). Unimproved land is not depreciated.

    a. Section 179 expense is treated as a depreciation deduction. (The Sec. 179 amount is $1,040,000 for 2020.)

Contributed Property

6. A shareholder does not recognize gain on the voluntary contribution of capital to a corporation.

    a. The shareholder's stock basis is increased by the basis in the contributed property.

    b. The corporation has a transferred basis in the property.

Dividends

7. Distributions out of earnings and profits (E&P) are taxable as dividends.

    a. Dividends are taxable and therefore do not reduce basis.

Return of Capital

8. When a corporation makes a distribution that is not out of E&P, it is a nontaxable return of capital (until basis is reduced to zero).

    a. Distributions in excess of basis are treated as capital gain.

    b. When a shareholder has purchased several stocks, the distribution is applied on a specific identification method, if applicable.

        1) The FIFO method is used when specific identification is impossible.

        2) If a shareholder purchases stock in different lots and at different times and it is impossible to definitely identify the shares subject to a return of capital, the basis of the earliest shares purchased is reduced first [Reg. 1.1012-1(c)].

Stock Rights

9. The basis of stock acquired in a nontaxable distribution (e.g., stock rights) is allocated a portion of the basis of the stock upon which the distribution was made.

    a. The basis is allocated in proportion to the FMV of the original stock and the distribution as of the date of distribution.

    b. If the FMV of the stock rights is less than 15% of the FMV of the stock upon which it was issued, the rights have a zero basis (unless an election is made to allocate basis).

Tax Benefits

10. Basis adjustment is required for certain specific items that represent a tax benefit. Three examples follow:

Casualty Losses

    a. Basis is reduced by the amount of the casualty loss allowed as a deduction and by any amounts recovered by insurance. Generally, the itemized deduction for personal casualty and theft losses for tax years 2018 through 2025 has been limited. The limitations include

        1) Loss attributed to a federally declared disaster and

        2) Non-federally declared disaster losses limited to casualty gains.

Debt Discharge

    b. Specific exclusion from gross income is allowed to certain insolvent persons for debt discharged. Reduction in basis is required for certain amounts excluded.

Credit on Asset Purchases

    c. Credits are allowed on certain asset purchases, such as building rehabilitation, energy equipment, and low-income housing.

        1) A partial or full amount of the credit must be deducted from the basis.

Partial Disposition of Property

11. The basis of the whole property must be equitably apportioned among the parts; relative FMV is generally used.

Personal Use Converted to Business Use

12. Basis for depreciation is the lesser of the FMV of the property at the conversion date or the adjusted basis at conversion.

Leasehold Improvements

13. Generally, lessors do not report income when a lessee makes leasehold improvements or when the leasehold improvements revert to the lessor at the termination of the lease.

   a. Thus, the lessor has a zero basis in the leasehold improvements.

STOP AND REVIEW! **You have completed the outline for this subunit. Study multiple-choice questions 16 and 17 on page 293.**

9.7 HOLDING PERIOD (HP)

1. The holding period of an asset is measured in calendar months, beginning on the date after acquisition and including the disposal date.

   a. The holding period may include that of the transferor.
   b. If the property is held for 1 year or less, it is considered short-term.
   c. If it is held for more than 1 year, it is long-term.

Acquisition by or of	Holding Period - Starts or by reference to
Sale or exchange	Acquisition*
Gift: for gain	Donor's acquisition
for loss	Acquisition
Inheritance	Automatic LT
Nontaxable exchanges	
Like-kind (Sec. 1031)	Include HP of exchanged asset**
Corporate stock (Sec. 351)	Include HP of contributed asset**
Property in entity	Include transferor's HP
Stock dividend (307)	Include HP of "old stock"
Partnership interest (Sec. 721)	Include HP of contributed asset**
Property in entity	Include transferor's HP**
Ordinary income property	Exchange
Involuntary conversion (Sec. 1033)	Include HP of converted asset
Residence	Acquisition
Use conversion (T/B & personal)	Include period of prior use
Optioned property	Exclude option period
Securities	Trading date
Short sales (Ss)	Earlier of Ss closing or property sale date
Commodity futures	LT after 6-month HP
Capital gain dividend	Automatic LT

* Always start computation using day after date of applicable acquisition.
** If capital asset or Sec. 1231 property; otherwise, the holding period starts the day after date of exchange

STOP AND REVIEW! **You have completed the outline for this subunit. Study multiple-choice questions 18 and 19 on page 294.**

9.8 CAPITAL GAINS AND LOSSES

A capital gain or loss is realized on the sale or exchange of a capital asset.

Capital Assets

1. All property is characterized as a capital asset, unless expressly excluded.

   a. The following types of property are not capital assets:

      1) Inventory (or stock-in-trade): property held primarily for sale to customers in the ordinary course of a trade or business (e.g., homes held by a builder)

      2) Real or depreciable property used in a trade or business

      3) Accounts or notes receivable acquired in the ordinary course of trade or business for services rendered or for item 1) above

      4) Copyrights and artistic compositions held by the person who composed them, including letters

      5) Certain U.S. government publications acquired at reduced cost

   b. Property held either for personal use or for the production of income is a capital asset, but dealer property is not.

   c. Examples of capital assets are

      1) Personal homes,
      2) Furnishings,
      3) Automobiles,
      4) Stocks,
      5) Bonds,
      6) Commodities,
      7) Partnership interests,
      8) Land,
      9) Internally generated goodwill,
      10) Contract rights,
      11) Patents,
      12) Trade secrets, and
      13) Collectibles.

   d. Examples of collectibles are

      1) Works of art,
      2) Rugs,
      3) Antiques,
      4) Metals,
      5) Gems,
      6) Stamps,
      7) Coins, and
      8) Alcoholic beverages.

Goodwill

e. Goodwill is a capital asset when generated within the business.

  1) Goodwill acquired with the purchase of a trade or business is an amortizable intangible asset under Sec. 197.

    a) This ability to amortize characterizes acquired goodwill as a Sec. 1231 asset rather than as a capital asset.

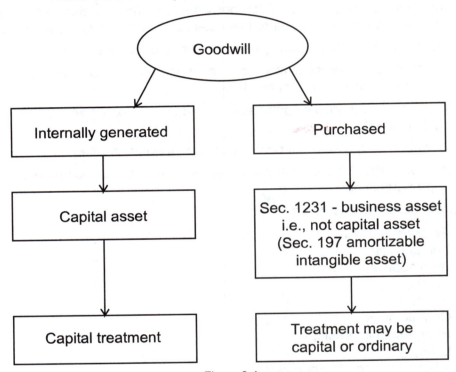

Figure 9-1

Option

f. An option is treated the same as the underlying property.

Stocks, Bonds, Commodities

g. Stocks, bonds, commodities, and the like are capital assets for investors and traders but not dealers.

  1) A dealer holds an asset primarily for sale to customers in the ordinary course of his or her trade or business.

  2) A dealer may identify particular assets as held for investment by the close of the business day of acquisition.

    a) Such assets are capital.

    b) A trader buys and sells assets for his or her own account. They are capital assets in that they are not considered held for sale to customers.

c) To be engaged in business as a trader in securities, all of the following conditions must be met:

    i) The taxpayer must seek to profit from daily market movements in the prices of securities and not from dividends, interest, or capital appreciation;

    ii) The activity must be substantial; and

    iii) The taxpayer must carry on the activity with continuity and regularity.

d) If the nature of the trading activities does not qualify as a business, the taxpayer is considered an investor and not a trader.

e) Investors typically buy and sell securities and expect income from dividends, interest, or capital appreciation. They buy and sell these securities and hold them for personal investment; they are not conducting a trade or business. Most investors are individuals and hold these securities for a substantial period of time.

Land Investment

h. Land held primarily for investment (capital asset) that is then subdivided may be treated as converted to property held for sale in a trade or business.

    1) Mere subdivision for sale of land held by other than a C corporation does not establish that it is held for sale in a trade or business.

    2) The subdivided land is treated as a capital asset if particular conditions are satisfied, e.g., if no substantial improvements have been made to the land while held by the person.

Sale or Exchange

2. Generally, under Sec. 1001, all gains are realized on the "sale or other disposition of property." This includes sales or exchanges that are required in characterizing a realized gain or loss as capital.

    a. A sale is a transfer of property in exchange for money or a promise to pay money, while an exchange is a transfer of property in return for other properties or services.

    b. For real property, a sale or exchange occurs on the earlier of the date of conveyance or the date that the burdens of ownership pass to the buyer.

    c. Also, liquidating distributions and losses on worthless securities are treated as sales or exchanges.

Gain (Loss) Recognized

3.   All realized gains must be recognized unless the IRC expressly provides otherwise. Conversely, no deduction is allowed for a realized loss unless the IRC expressly provides for it. The following formula shows computation of gain or loss realized:

How to Figure a Gain or Loss	
IF the taxpayer's . . .	THEN the taxpayer has a . . .
Adjusted basis is more than the amount realized	Loss
Amount realized is more than the adjusted basis	Gain

Money received (or to be received)
+   FMV of other property received[1]
+   Liability relief[2]
−   Money or other property given up
−   Selling expenses[3]
−   Liabilities assumed[2]
=   **Amount realized**

Amount realized
−   Adjusted basis
=   **Gain (loss) realized**

1 If the FMV of other property received is not determinable with reasonable certainty, FMV of the property given up is used.
2 Whether recourse or nonrecourse.
3 Selling expenses are subtracted from gross receivables to yield the amount realized.

a.   Long-term capital gain or loss (LTCG or LTCL) is realized from a capital asset held for more than 1 year. Short-term capital gain or loss (STCG or STCL) is realized if the asset was held 1 year or less.

Short-Term or Long-Term Gain or Loss	
IF property is held . . .	THEN it is a . . .
1 year or less	Short-term capital gain or loss
More than 1 year	Long-term capital gain or loss

b.   For individuals, net capital gain (NCG) is the excess of net LTCG over net STCL. Net STCG is not included in NCG.

c.   Net STCG is treated as ordinary income for individuals. NCG rates do not apply to net STCG.

   1)   Net STCG = STCG − STCL
   2)   But net STCG may be offset by net LTCL.

Capital Gains Rates

    d.   For individuals, net short-term capital gain is taxed as ordinary income.

    e.   For individuals, capital transactions involving **long-term holding periods** (assets held for over 12 months) are grouped by tax rates. The maximum capital gains rates are 0%, 15%, 20%, 25%, or 28%.

        1)   The TCJA does not change the current tax treatment of qualified dividends and capital gains. The thresholds for the application of the capital gains rates are adjusted for inflation. The 2020 thresholds are listed below.

Filing Status	0% Breakpoint	15% Breakpoint	20% Breakpoint
Married Filing Jointly	Under $80,000	$80,000	$496,600
Head of Household	Under 53,600	53,600	469,050
Single	Under 40,000	40,000	441,450
Married Filing Separately	Under 40,000	40,000	248,300
Estates and Trusts	Under 2,650	2,650	13,150

        2)   The capital gains rate is **25%** on unrecaptured Sec. 1250 gains (discussed further in Study Unit 10, Subunit 2).

        3)   The capital gains rate is **28%** on gains and losses from the sale of collectibles and gains from Sec. 1202 stock (certain small business stock).

        NOTE: The 0%, 15%, 20%, 25%, and 28% capital gains rate outline content above will be referenced as "baskets" in the following outline content for simplicity.

    f.   After gains and losses are classified in the appropriate baskets, losses for each long-term basket are first used to offset any gains within that basket.

    g.   If a long-term basket has a net loss, the loss will be used first to offset net gain for the highest long-term rate basket, then to offset the next highest rate basket, and so on.

EXAMPLE 9-3   **Capital Gains (Losses) and Grouping by Tax Rates**

A taxpayer realizes a $10,000 net loss in the 15% basket, a $5,000 net gain in the 25% basket, and an $8,000 net gain in the 28% basket. The taxpayer will first apply the net loss against the gain in the 28% basket, reducing the gain in this basket to zero. Then, the remaining $2,000 loss is applied against the gain in the 25% basket, leaving a $3,000 net capital gain in the 25% basket.

Carryover of NLTCL

    h.   A carryover of a net long-term capital loss from a prior year is used first to offset any net gain in the 28% basket, then to offset any net gain in the 25% basket, and finally to offset any net gain in the 15% basket. Likewise, net STCL is also used first to offset net gain for the highest long-term basket and so on.

EXAMPLE 9-4   **Long-Term Capital Loss Carryover and Net STCL**

A taxpayer has a $1,000 long-term capital loss carryover, a net short-term capital loss of $2,000, a $1,000 net gain in the 28% basket, and a $5,000 net gain in the 15% basket. Both losses are first applied to offset the 28% rate gain, using the $1,000 loss carryover first until completely exhausted. Since no gain exists in the 28% basket after applying the carryover, the net STCL is then applied against the next highest gain in the 15% basket. As a result, only a $3,000 net capital gain remains in the 15% basket.

Corporations

    i.   For corporations, all capital gains (ST or LT) are taxed at the corporation's regular tax rate.

Loss Limits

    j.   An individual may offset a net capital gain with a net capital loss. If the individual does not have net capital gains, (s)he recognizes a net capital loss in the current year up to the lesser of $3,000 ($1,500 for married filing separately) or ordinary income. An individual may carry forward any excess CLs indefinitely.

        1)   The carryforward is treated as a CL incurred in the subsequent year.

        2)   Net STCL is treated as having been deductible in the preceding year before net LTCL.

        3)   There can be no carryover from a decedent to his or her estate.

    k.   A corporation may use CLs only to offset CGs each year. A corporation must carry the excess CL back 3 years and forward 5 years and characterize all carryovers as STCLs (regardless of character).

Schedule D

    l.   Schedule D (Form 1040) is used to compute and summarize total capital gains and/or losses on the sale or disposition of capital assets listed on Form 8949, and the summary combines the long-term gains (losses) with the short-term gains (losses).

        1)   When these capital gains and losses all net to a gain, it is called "capital gain net income" [Sec. 1222(a)].

        2)   If a taxpayer has capital gain distributions and no other capital gains or losses, the capital gains distributions may be reported directly on Schedule 1 (Form 1040) (without using Schedule D), provided that the following conditions are met:

            a)   (S)he only has capital gains from box 2a from Form 1099-DIV to report.

            b)   No amounts appear in box 2b (unrecaptured Sec. 1250 gain), box 2c (Sec.1202 gain), or box 2d [collectibles (28%) gain].

            c)   Form 4952, *Investment Interest Expense Deduction*, is not being filed, or, if the amount on line 4g of that form includes any qualified dividends, it also includes all net capital gains from the disposition of property held for investment.

    m.   Liabilities discharged in bankruptcy are treated as a short-term capital loss on Schedule D to a creditor who is an individual.

        1)   The loss is short-term capital loss regardless of how long the debt was in the hands of the creditor.

STOP AND REVIEW! You have completed the outline for this subunit. Study multiple-choice questions 20 through 23 beginning on page 294.

9.9 CAPITAL GAINS ON SALES OF STOCK

Gains and Losses

1. Gains and losses from the disposition of securities are generally determined and taxed like gains and losses from the disposition of other property.

    a. Securities held by investors are capital assets.

Return of Capital

2. A return of capital distribution reduces basis and becomes a capital gain when the shareholder's basis in the stock reaches zero.

Undistributed Gains

3. Undistributed capital gains earned in a mutual fund are taxed as capital gains in the current period.

    a. A credit is allowed for any tax paid by the mutual fund on behalf of the taxpayer.

60/40 Rule

4. Generally, positions in regulated futures contracts, foreign currency contracts, nonequity options, and dealer equity options in an exchange using the mark-to-market system are treated as if they were sold on the last day of the year.

    a. Any capital gains or losses arising under this rule are treated as if they were 60% long-term and 40% short-term without regard to the holding period.

STOP AND REVIEW! **You have completed the outline for this subunit. Study multiple-choice questions 24 through 29 beginning on page 296.**

9.10 SECTIONS 1202 AND 1244 STOCK

50% Exclusion

1. Taxpayers may exclude 50% of the gain from the sale or exchange of qualified small business stock (QSB stock).

    a. The stock must have been issued after August 10, 1993, and held for more than 5 years.

    b. For Sec. 1202 stock acquired after February 17, 2009, and before September 28, 2010, the exclusion increases to 75%.

    c. For Sec. 1202 stock acquired after September 27, 2010, the exclusion increases to 100%.

Asset Limits

2. Qualified small business stock must be that of a domestic C corporation with aggregate gross assets not exceeding $50 million.

3. The corporation must have at least 80%, by value, of its assets used in the active conduct of a qualified business.

    a. A qualified business is any business other than

        1) The performance of personal services (e.g., banking, financing, and leasing),
        2) Any farming business,
        3) Any extractive industry, and
        4) Hospitality businesses (e.g., hotels and restaurants).

Annual Gain Limit

4. The aggregate annual gain for which a taxpayer may qualify under Sec. 1202 is limited to the greater of $10 million or 10 times the adjusted tax basis of qualified stock disposed of by the taxpayer during the year.

Rate

5. Section 1202 stock qualifying for the 50% or 75% exclusions are taxed at the 28% rate.

AMT Preference

6. An alternative minimum tax (AMT) preference is equal to 7% of the excluded gain. Since this is an exclusion preference, there is no minimum tax credit allowed.

    a. For stock acquired after September 27, 2010, there is no AMT preference.

Gain Rollover

7. Individuals are allowed to roll over capital gains from the sale of Sec. 1202 stock if other small business stock is purchased within 60 days after the date of sale.

   a. The small business stock being sold must have been held for more than 6 months.

   b. The normal rules of nontaxable exchange apply to the gain being deferred, the basis of the small business stock acquired, and the holding period for the acquired stock.

   c. Qualified small business (QSB) stock held through pass-through entities qualifies for the rollover rules (Rev. Proc. 98-48, 1998-38 IRB 7).

      1) A pass-through entity may make the election if the entity sells QSB stock held more than 6 months and purchases replacement QSB stock during the 60-day period beginning on the date of sale.

         a) The benefit of deferral will flow through to the taxpayers (other than C corporations) that held interests in the entity during the entire period in which the entity held the QSB stock.

      2) If a pass-through entity sells QSB stock held for more than 6 months, an individual who has held an interest in the entity and who purchases replacement QSB stock may make the rollover election with respect to the individual's share of any gain on the sale that the entity does not defer under Sec. 1045.

         a) The individual's interest in the entity must be held during the entire period in which the entity held the QSB stock.

         b) The purchase of replacement QSB stock must take place during the 60-day period beginning on the date of the sale of the QSB stock.

   d. If a person has more than one sale of QSB stock in a tax year that qualifies for the rollover election, the person may make the rollover election for any one or more of those sales.

Section 1244

8. An individual may deduct, as an ordinary loss, a loss from the sale or exchange or from worthlessness of "small business stock" (Sec. 1244 stock) issued by a qualifying small business corporation.

   a. A corporation qualifies if the amount of money and other property it receives as a contribution to capital does not exceed $1 million.

      1) This determination is to be made at the time the stock is issued.

   b. The shareholder must be the original owner of the stock.

   c. The maximum amount deductible as an ordinary loss in any one year is $50,000 ($100,000 on a joint return).

   d. If a taxpayer makes capital investments in the corporation without receiving stock, the loss must be allocated between the investments where stock was received and investments where stock was not received.

      1) Losses from investments without receiving stock are not eligible for Sec. 1244.

   e. The loss is shown on Form 4797.

STOP AND REVIEW! **You have completed the outline for this subunit. Study multiple-choice question 30 on page 298.**

QUESTIONS

9.1 Cost Basis

1. Mr. Rabbitt purchased a home for $200,000. He incurred the following additional expenses:

- $200 fire insurance premiums
- $500 mortgage insurance premiums
- $400 recording fees
- $250 owner's title insurance

Compute his basis in the property.

A. $201,350

B. $200,000

C. $200,650

D. $201,150

Answer (C) is correct.
    REQUIRED: The costs included in the basis of the property.
    DISCUSSION: When a taxpayer purchases property, his or her basis in the property is initially cost. Cost basis is the sum of capitalized acquisition costs. Initial basis in purchased property is the cost of acquiring it. Only capital costs are included. One component of capital costs is closing costs, which include brokerage commissions, prepurchase taxes, sales tax on purchase, title transfer taxes, title insurance, recording fees, attorney fees, and document review preparation. Expenses not properly chargeable to a capital account include costs of maintaining and operating the property (e.g., interest on credit related to the property), insurance (e.g., casualty), and ordinary maintenance or repairs (e.g., painting). Mr. Rabbitt should include the cost of the home ($200,000), the recording fees ($400), and the cost of the owner's title insurance ($250) in the basis of his new home. Thus, his basis in his new home is $200,650 ($200,000 cost of home + $400 recording fees + $250 title insurance).
    Answer (A) is incorrect. Insurance is not chargeable to the basis of the property. **Answer (B) is incorrect.** The basis should also include the recording fees ($400) and the cost of the owner's title insurance ($250). **Answer (D) is incorrect.** The mortgage insurance premiums are not chargeable to the basis of the property.

2. In March 2020, Jesse traded in a 2017 van for a new 2020 model. He used both the old van and the new van 75% for business. Jesse has claimed actual expenses for the business use of the old van since 2017. He did not claim a Sec. 179 deduction of the old or new van. Jesse paid $12,800 for the old van in June 2017. Depreciation claimed on the 2017 van was $7,388, which included 6 months for 2020. Jesse paid $9,800 cash in addition to a trade-in allowance of $2,200 to acquire the new van. What is Jesse's depreciable basis in the new van?

A. $11,409

B. $9,562

C. $9,009

D. $9,000

Answer (B) is correct.
    REQUIRED: The depreciable basis of property acquired in an exchange.
    DISCUSSION: The basis of property is generally its cost (Sec. 1012). In the case of a taxable exchange of property, the cost is the value of the property given up plus any additional cash paid. The basis for figuring depreciation for the new van is the adjusted basis of the old van, $5,412 ($12,800 original cost – $7,388 depreciation), plus any additional cash paid, $9,800, minus the excess of the total amount of depreciation that would have been allowable before the trade if the old van had been used 100% for business. The depreciation under 100% business assumption, $9,850 ($7,388 ÷ .75), is reduced by the actual depreciation, $7,388, to obtain the excess total of $2,462. The total depreciable basis for the new van is $12,750 ($5,412 adjusted basis of van + $9,800 additional cash paid – $2,462 excess total). This total must be reduced by the amount of personal use (25%) to determine the new depreciable basis of $9,562 ($12,750 new van's basis × 75%).

3. Charles, the landlord, made several repairs and improvements to his rental house. He spent $1,500 to add carpeting in the hallway, $550 for a stove, $750 for a refrigerator, $170 to replace the broken faucet in the bathroom, and $590 to replace damaged shingles on the roof. How much of these costs must he depreciate?

A. $3,560

B. $2,800

C. $1,300

D. $3,390

Answer (B) is correct.
  REQUIRED: The expenditures that require capitalization.
  DISCUSSION: Generally, expenses that add to the value of the property, substantially prolong the useful life of the property, or adapt the property to a new or different use are considered capital expenditures and are not currently deductible. Thus, capital expenditures include the cost of acquiring or constructing buildings, machinery, equipment, furniture, and any similar property that has a useful life that extends substantially beyond the end of the tax year. Maintenance and repair expenditures that only keep an asset in a normal operating condition are deductible if they do not increase the value or prolong the useful life of the asset. Distinguishing between a currently deductible expenditure and a capital expenditure can be difficult because expenditures for normal maintenance and repair can cost more than a capital improvement. Normal maintenance and repair may also increase the value of an asset. The amount of costs that can be depreciated is $2,800 ($1,500 carpeting + $550 stove + $750 refrigerator).
  Answer (A) is incorrect. The $170 bathroom repair and $590 roof repair are not capital expenditures. **Answer (C) is incorrect.** The $1,500 expense of adding carpet in the hallway is considered a capital expenditure. **Answer (D) is incorrect.** The $590 roof repair is not a capital expenditure.

4. Mr. Pine purchased a small office building during the year. Included in his costs were the following:

Cash down payment	$ 50,000
Mortgage on property assumed	300,000
Title insurance	2,000
Fire insurance premiums	2,000
Attorney fees	1,000
Rent to former owner to allow Mr. Pine to occupy the office building prior to closing	4,000

What is Mr. Pine's basis in the property?

A. $359,000

B. $355,000

C. $353,000

D. $350,000

Answer (C) is correct.
  REQUIRED: The basis of purchased property subject to a mortgage.
  DISCUSSION: The basis of property is its original cost (Sec. 1012). The cost of property includes debt to which the property is subject (*Crane*, 331 U.S. 1, 1947). Further, the cost of property includes necessary expenses paid in connection with the acquisition of the property. The attorney fees and title insurance are included in the cost of the property. The fire insurance premiums and rent expense, however, are not paid in connection with the acquisition of the property. Thus, the basis is $353,000 ($50,000 cash payment + $300,000 mortgage assumed + $2,000 title insurance + $1,000 attorney fees).
  Answer (A) is incorrect. The fire insurance premiums and the rent are not paid in connection with the acquisition of the property. **Answer (B) is incorrect.** The fire insurance premiums are not paid in connection with the acquisition of the property. **Answer (D) is incorrect.** Necessary expenses paid in connection with the acquisition of the property are included in basis.

9.2 Property Received by Gift

5. Which of the following is the depreciable basis in rental property that is placed in service immediately upon receiving it as a gift if the donor's basis was more than the fair market value of the property?

A. The fair market value on the date of the gift plus or minus any required adjustments to basis.

B. The fair market value of the property on the date of conversion to rental property.

C. The donor's basis of the property plus or minus any required adjustments to basis.

D. All of the answers are correct.

Answer (C) is correct.
    REQUIRED: The basis of property that is placed in service immediately upon receiving it as a gift.
    DISCUSSION: If gift property is immediately used as business property, the basis for depreciation is the donor's AB (plus or minus any required adjustments).
    Answer (A) is incorrect. The adjustments are made to the donor's basis, not FMV. **Answer (B) is incorrect.** The property FMV is less than AB. **Answer (D) is incorrect.** Adjustments are made to the donor's basis, not FMV.

6. Jane acquired an acre of land as a gift. At the time of the gift, the acre had a fair market value (FMV) of $20,000. The donor's adjusted basis in the land was $15,000. No gift tax was paid on the gift. No events occurred to increase or decrease her basis in the property. Jane later sold the acre for $10,000. What is Jane's gain or loss on the sale?

A. $5,000 loss.

B. $10,000 loss.

C. $0 (no gain or loss).

D. $10,000 gain.

Answer (A) is correct.
    REQUIRED: The gain or loss recognized on the sale of property received by gift.
    DISCUSSION: The basis of property acquired by gift is generally the donor's adjusted basis [Sec. 1015(a)]. When computing a loss, the donee assumes the lesser of the FMV at the date of transfer or the donor's adjusted basis. Therefore, Jane assumes the lesser adjusted basis of $15,000 and subtracts her $10,000 amount realized to yield a $5,000 loss.
    Answer (B) is incorrect. The loss is limited by the adjusted basis of the property at the time of transfer. **Answer (C) is incorrect.** A loss is realized. **Answer (D) is incorrect.** No gain is realized on the sale.

7. In 2019, Tony received a gift of 200 shares of mutual funds stock. The stock was worth $20,000 when Tony received it. The donor had originally paid $10,000 for the stock when he bought it in 2015. Tony sold the stock for $15,000 in 2020. What is Tony's basis in the stock, disregarding gift tax?

A. $0

B. $20,000

C. $10,000

D. $15,000

Answer (C) is correct.
    REQUIRED: The donee's basis in mutual funds stock received by gift.
    DISCUSSION: The basis of the gift Tony received equals $10,000. The FMV at the date of the gift equals $20,000. Since the FMV exceeds the donor's basis in the stock, Tony must use the basis of the donor, $10,000.
    Answer (A) is incorrect. The donee must use either the donor's basis or the FMV on the date of transfer. **Answer (B) is incorrect.** The FMV is greater than the donor's basis in the stock. Thus, Tony must use the donor's basis. **Answer (D) is incorrect.** The FMV is greater than the donor's basis in the stock. Thus, Tony must use the donor's basis.

8. In 2018, Paul received a boat as a gift from his father. At the time of the gift, the boat had a fair market value of $60,000 and an adjusted basis of $80,000 to Paul's father. After Paul received the boat, nothing occurred affecting Paul's basis in the boat. In 2020, Paul sold the boat for $75,000. What is the amount and character of Paul's gain?

   A. Ordinary income of $15,000.

   B. Long-term capital gain of $15,000.

   C. Long-term capital loss of $5,000.

   D. Neither a gain nor a loss.

9. Juan received a gift of property from his uncle. When the gift was made in 2020, the property had a fair market value of $100,000 and an adjusted basis to his uncle of $40,000. Gift tax on the transfer, completely paid by Juan's uncle, was $14,500. What is Juan's basis in the property?

   A. $40,000

   B. $50,235

   C. $60,000

   D. $110,235

Answer (D) is correct.
   REQUIRED: The amount and character of a gain to be reported upon the sale of property acquired by gift.
   DISCUSSION: For determining gain on the sale of property acquired by gift, the basis is the donor's adjusted basis. Paul's sale results in no gain ($75,000 sales price – $80,000 basis). For determining loss on the sale of property acquired by gift, the basis may not exceed the fair market value of the property at the date of the gift. Hence, there is no loss ($75,000 sales price – $60,000 basis).
   Answer (A) is incorrect. None of the proceeds will be characterized as ordinary income. **Answer (B) is incorrect.** In determining gain on the sale of property acquired by gift, the basis is the donor's adjusted basis. For determining loss on the sale of property acquired by gift, the basis may not exceed the fair market value of the property at the date of the gift. Paul has neither a gain nor a loss. **Answer (C) is incorrect.** In determining gain on the sale of property acquired by gift, the basis is the donor's adjusted basis. For determining loss on the sale of property acquired by gift, the basis may not exceed the fair market value of the property at the date of the gift. Paul has neither a gain nor a loss.

Answer (B) is correct.
   REQUIRED: The donee's basis in property on which gift tax was paid.
   DISCUSSION: The basis of property acquired by gift is generally the donor's adjusted basis [Sec. 1015(a)], increased by a gift tax paid applicable to appreciation [Sec. 1015(d)]. The gift tax applicable to appreciation is the appreciation divided by the taxable gift times the gift tax.

Donor's adjusted basis	$40,000
Gift tax*	10,235
Donee's basis	$50,235

$$*\frac{\$100,000 - \$40,000}{\$100,000 - \$15,000} \times \$14,500 = \$10,235$$

   Answer (A) is incorrect. The basis must be increased by a portion of the gift tax. **Answer (C) is incorrect.** The basis is determined by adding the applicable gift tax to the donor's adjusted basis. **Answer (D) is incorrect.** The basis is determined by adding the applicable gift tax to the donor's adjusted basis.

9.3 Property Received for Services

10. All of the following statements concerning the basis of property received for services are true EXCEPT

A. If you receive property for services, your basis is equal to the fair market value of the property received.

B. If your employer allows you to purchase property at less than fair market value, include the fair market value of the property in income.

C. If you receive property for services and the property is subject to restrictions, your basis in the property is its fair market value when it becomes substantially vested.

D. If your employer allows you to purchase property at less than fair market value, your basis in the property is its fair market value.

Answer (B) is correct.
REQUIRED: The false statement regarding the basis of property received for services.
DISCUSSION: In general, the basis for property received for services is its fair market value. However, the basis used by an employee who received property from an employer at less than its fair market value is the purchase price plus the amount included in the employee's income. The amount included in the employee's income is the difference between the fair market value and the price paid. Thus, even in such a case, the basis is the property's fair market value.
Answer (A) is incorrect. The basis of property received for services is its FMV. **Answer (C) is incorrect.** The basis of property that is received for services and is subject to restrictions is not included in income until the restrictions are lifted, and then the basis is its FMV. **Answer (D) is incorrect.** The basis of property purchased from an employer is the purchase price plus the income recognized, which, in effect, is the FMV.

9.4 Inherited Property

11. Mr. Apple and Ms. Melon purchased a small apartment house at the beginning of 2013 for $400,000, which they held for investment. Each furnished one-half of the purchase price, and each had a half interest in the income from the property. They held the apartment in joint tenancy with the right of survivorship (i.e., a tenancy in which the interest of the first tenant to die passes to the survivor on the death of the first tenant to die). They depreciated the apartment house at the rate of $10,000 per year. On December 31, 2020, Mr. Apple died. At the date of Mr. Apple's death, the apartment house had an adjusted basis (cost minus depreciation) of $320,000 and a fair market value of $550,000. What is Ms. Melon's basis as of the date of Mr. Apple's death?

A. $500,000

B. $435,000

C. $400,000

D. $320,000

Answer (B) is correct.
REQUIRED: The basis of jointly held property that is inherited.
DISCUSSION: The basis of property received from a decedent is generally the fair market value of the property on the date of the decedent's death [Sec. 1014(a)]. Under Sec. 2040, the general rule is that the gross estate of a decedent includes the entire value of property held jointly at the time of death except that portion of the property that was acquired by the other joint owner for adequate and full consideration. In this question, each investor contributed one-half of the purchase price. Therefore, when Mr. Apple died, his gross estate included only one-half of the apartment house. Accordingly, Ms. Melon will receive only a step-up in basis for that one-half of property included in Mr. Apple's estate. Ms. Melon's basis in the apartment house is $435,000 [$275,000 (1/2 of $550,000 FMV that represents Mr. Apple's portion) + $160,000 (Ms. Melon's original one-half basis in the property of $200,000 minus her share of depreciation of $40,000)].
Answer (A) is incorrect. The amount of $500,000 cannot be the basis. **Answer (C) is incorrect.** The amount of $400,000 is the total original basis for both investors. **Answer (D) is incorrect.** The amount of $320,000 is the total original basis reduced by depreciation.

12. The basis in property inherited from a decedent may be determined as follows:

   A. The decedent's basis plus any inheritance tax paid on the increased value.

   B. The fair market value at the date of death.

   C. The fair market value at an alternate valuation date.

   D. The fair market value at the date of death or the fair market value at an alternative valuation date.

Answer (D) is correct.

   REQUIRED: The item that determines basis of property inherited from a decedent.

   DISCUSSION: The basis of property received from a decedent is generally the fair market value of the property on the date of the decedent's death [Sec. 1014(a)]. If the executor elects the alternate valuation date for the estate tax return, the basis of the assets is their fair market value 6 months after death or the date of sale or distribution, if earlier.

13. Mr. More inherited 2,000 shares of Corporation Zero stock from his father, who died on March 4, 2020. His father paid $10 per share for the stock on September 4, 1993. The fair market value of the stock on the date of death was $50 per share. On September 4, 2020, the fair market value of the stock was $60 per share. Mr. More sold the stock for $75 per share on July 3, 2020. The estate qualified for, and the executor elected, the alternate valuation date. An estate tax return was filed. What was Mr. More's basis in the stock on the date of the sale?

   A. $100,000

   B. $120,000

   C. $130,000

   D. $150,000

Answer (D) is correct.

   REQUIRED: The basis of inherited property when the alternate valuation date is elected.

   DISCUSSION: The basis of property received from a decedent is generally the fair market value of the property on the date of the decedent's death [Sec. 1014(a)]. If the executor elects the alternate valuation date for the estate tax return, the basis of the assets is their fair market value 6 months after death or the date of sale or distribution if earlier. Mr. More's basis in the stock is $150,000, the fair market value on the date of sale (2,000 shares × $75 per share).

   Answer (A) is incorrect. The amount of $100,000 was the value on the date of death, not on the date of sale. **Answer (B) is incorrect.** The 6-month alternate valuation date is not used if the property is sold after the decedent's death but within the 6 months after the decedent's death. **Answer (C) is incorrect.** The correct per-share value of the stock is $75, not $65.

9.5 Stock Dividends

14. Alex bought four shares of common stock for $200. Later the corporation distributed a share of preferred stock for every two shares of common. At the date of distribution, the common stock had a FMV of $60 and preferred stock had a FMV of $40. What is Alex's basis in the common stock and the preferred stock after the nontaxable stock dividend?

A. $200 common; $80 preferred.

B. $150 common; $50 preferred.

C. $60 common; $40 preferred.

D. $240 common; $80 preferred.

Answer (B) is correct.
    REQUIRED: The basis in common stock and preferred stock after a nontaxable stock dividend.
    DISCUSSION: Since the preferred stock dividend was nontaxable, the original basis of the common stock would be allocated between the common stock and the preferred stock based on the relative fair market values of each on the date of the stock dividend (Reg. 1.307-1). The market values of Alex's common and preferred stock on the date of the dividend were $240 and $80, respectively. Alex's tax basis in the common stock after the receipt of the dividend is $150 [($240 FMV of common stock ÷ $320 total FMV) × $200 original cost of stock]. Alex's tax basis in the preferred stock is $50 [($80 FMV of preferred stock ÷ $320 total FMV) × $200 original cost of stock].

15. In 2018, Mary purchased 10 shares of Acorn Corporation common stock for $100 per share. In 2019, Mary purchased an additional 10 shares of Acorn Corporation common stock for $200 per share. At the end of 2020, Acorn Corporation declared a 2-for-1 common-stock split. What is Mary's total basis in her Acorn Corporation common stock?

A. $3,000

B. $4,000

C. $5,000

D. $6,000

Answer (A) is correct.
    REQUIRED: The total basis of common stock after a 2-for-1 split.
    DISCUSSION: A stock split results in an increase in the number of shares held by the taxpayer but no change in the total basis. The basis can therefore be calculated as follows: (10 shares × $100) + (10 shares × $200) = $3,000.

9.6 Adjustments to Asset Basis

16. Which of the following will decrease the basis of property?

A. Depreciation.

B. Return of capital.

C. Recognized losses on involuntary conversions.

D. All of the answers are correct.

Answer (D) is correct.
    REQUIRED: The item that will decrease the basis of property.
    DISCUSSION: Basis must be reduced by the larger of the amount of depreciation allowed or allowable (even if not claimed). A return of capital is a tax-free distribution that reduces a stock's basis by the amount of the distribution. If a shareholder's basis has been reduced to zero because of a tax-free return of capital, any excess amounts received are treated as a capital gain. Under Sec. 1033(b), the basis of the replacement property from an involuntary conversion is reduced by any gain not recognized.
    Answer (A) is incorrect. Return of capital and recognized losses on involuntary conversions will also reduce the basis of property. **Answer (B) is incorrect.** Depreciation and recognized losses on involuntary conversions will also reduce the basis of property. **Answer (C) is incorrect.** Depreciation and return of capital will also reduce the basis of property.

17. All of the following statements regarding a return of capital distribution based on your stock are true EXCEPT

A. A return of capital reduces the basis of your stock.

B. When the basis of your stock has been reduced to zero, you should report any additiona return of capital as a capital loss.

C. Any liquicating distribution you receive is not taxable to you until you have recovered the basis of your stock.

D. If the tota liquidating distributions you receive are less than the basis of your stock, you may have a capital loss.

Answer (B) is correct.
    REQUIRED: The false statement regarding a return of capital distribution based on stock.
    DISCUSSION: A return of capital is a tax-free distribution that reduces a stock's basis by the amount of the distribution. If a shareholder's basis has been reduced to zero because of a tax-free return of capital, any excess amounts received are treated as a capital gain.

9.7 Holding Period (HP)

18. The holding period for determining short-term and long-term gains and losses includes which of the following?

A. The day you acquired the property.

B. In the case of a bank that repossessed real property, the time between the original sale and the date of repossession.

C. The donor's holding period in the case of a gift if your basis is the donor's adjusted basis.

D. All of the answers are correct.

Answer (C) is correct.
REQUIRED: The true statement regarding holding periods.
DISCUSSION: In the case of property received as a gift, the basis of the property is generally the same as the donor's basis. The basis may be increased by a portion or all of the gift tax paid on the transfers. When this occurs, the holding period is carried over from the donor.
Answer (A) is incorrect. The holding period generally begins the day following the acquisition date. **Answer (B) is incorrect.** The holding period does not include the time between the original sale and the date of repossession. **Answer (D) is incorrect.** Not all of the statements are correct.

19. On June 1, 2018, Mr. Smart purchased investment land. On January 31, 2019, Mr. Smart traded the land plus cash for some other investment land in a nontaxable exchange. On August 15, 2020, he sold the land received in the nontaxable exchange for a gain. What is the character of Mr. Smart's gain for 2020?

A. Short-term capital gain.

B. Long-term capital gain.

C. Part short-term capital gain and part long-term capital gain.

D. Ordinary income.

Answer (B) is correct.
REQUIRED: The character of gain from the sale of land received in a nontaxable exchange.
DISCUSSION: If property received in an exchange has the same basis in whole or in part as that of the property given (and if the property given is a capital asset or a Sec. 1231 asset), the holding period of the property received includes the period for which the property given was held [Sec. 1223(1)]. Thus, when the property is sold, the holding period includes the holding period of the property exchanged. And, under Sec. 1222, capital assets held more than 1 year are treated as long-term.
Answer (A) is incorrect. The gain is long-term. Nontaxable transactions normally give rise to a carryover of basis; thus, Mr. Smart held the land for more than 1 year. **Answer (C) is incorrect.** All of the gain is long-term. **Answer (D) is incorrect.** The asset is a capital asset. Thus, the gain is characterized as a capital gain.

9.8 Capital Gains and Losses

20. Mark sold a building for $100,000 cash plus property with a fair market value (FMV) of $10,000. He had purchased the building 5 years ago for $85,000. He made $30,000 worth of improvements and deducted $25,000 for depreciation. The buyer assumed Mark's real estate taxes of $12,000 and mortgage of $20,000 on the building. What is the amount realized on the sale of the building?

A. $110,000

B. $142,000

C. $130,000

D. $145,500

Answer (B) is correct.
REQUIRED: The amount realized on the sale of real property.
DISCUSSION: The amount realized under Sec. 1001 includes money received, fair market value of other property received, and any liabilities of which the seller is relieved. Mark's amount realized is $142,000 ($100,000 cash + $10,000 fair market value property + $32,000 liabilities relieved).
Answer (A) is incorrect. Any liabilities of which the seller is relieved is included in their amount realized. **Answer (C) is incorrect.** The $12,000 of real estate taxes assumed by the buyer count as a liability of which the seller is relieved. **Answer (D) is incorrect.** The amount realized under Sec. 1001 includes money received, FMV of other property received, and any liabilities of which the seller is relieved.

21. A married couple has a $40,000 short-term capital loss, a $20,000 collectible long-term capital gain, and a $25,000 long-term capital gain subject to the 15% rate. What are the amount and the character of their capital gain (loss) after netting the gains and losses?

A. $5,000 long-term gain taxed at 28%.

B. $5,000 long-term gain taxed at 15%.

C. $(20,000) short-term loss and $25,000 long-term gain taxed at 15%.

D. $0

Answer (B) is correct.
    REQUIRED: The netting process of capital gains and losses.
    DISCUSSION: The short-term capital loss is first used to offset the $20,000 collectible long-term capital gain that would be taxed at 28%. The remaining $20,000 of the short-term capital loss is then offset against the $25,000 long-term capital gain taxed at 15%. The $5,000 remaining long-term capital gain taxed at 15% is reported on the return and is subject to tax.
    Answer (A) is incorrect. The loss is first netted against the 28% gain, not the 15% gain. **Answer (C) is incorrect.** The remaining $20,000 short-term loss is then applied against the $25,000 gain taxed at 15%. **Answer (D) is incorrect.** The short-term capital loss does not completely eliminate the gain.

22. Elton declared bankruptcy in the current year. Included in the liabilities discharged in the bankruptcy was a $15,000 personal loan Elton had received from his friend, Edward, 2 years ago. How would Edward treat this for tax purposes?

A. Ordinary loss on Form 4797.

B. Long-term capital loss on Schedule D.

C. Short-term capital loss on Schedule D.

D. Investment expense.

Answer (C) is correct.
    REQUIRED: The tax treatment of a $15,000 bad debt from a loan to a friend.
    DISCUSSION: If a nonbusiness bad debt becomes totally worthless within the tax year, it is treated as a short-term capital loss. Short-term capital losses are reported on Schedule D of Form 1040.
    Answer (A) is incorrect. This bad debt is not related to a business and is a short-term capital loss. Thus, it would not be reported on Form 4797, *Sales of Business Property*. **Answer (B) is incorrect.** Bad debt acquired through nonbusiness activities is always a short-term loss, regardless of the length of the loan. **Answer (D) is incorrect.** Bad debt from a loan is not an investment expense; it is a short-term capital loss.

23. In computing the gain or loss from a sale or trade of property, which statement below best describes the amount you realize?

A. The money you actually receive.

B. The fair market value of the property on the transaction date.

C. Everything you receive for the property.

D. The value of any services you received.

Answer (C) is correct.
    REQUIRED: The amount realized from a transaction.
    DISCUSSION: When computing the gain or loss from a transaction, the taxpayer must compute the amount realized from the transaction. The amount realized equals the sum of money received, the FMV of property received, and liability relief, less selling expenses and liabilities assumed.
    Answer (A) is incorrect. The amount realized is more than actual cash money received. **Answer (B) is incorrect.** The amount realized does not necessarily equal the FMV of the property on the transaction date. **Answer (D) is incorrect.** The value of services received does not necessarily equal the amount realized.

9.9 Capital Gains on Sales of Stock

24. Maggie trades stock in ABC Company with an adjusted basis of $7,000 for DEF Company stock with a fair market value of $10,000. She had no other transactions during the year. What is the amount realized and what is her gain or loss on this transaction?

A. The amount realized is $10,000, and the amount of gain is $3,000.

B. The amount realized is $10,000, and the amount of loss is $3,000.

C. The amount realized is $7,000, and the amount of gain is $4,000.

D. The amount realized is $17,000, and the amount of gain is $3,000.

Answer (A) is correct.
REQUIRED: The amount realized and gain recognized in the exchange of stock.
DISCUSSION: All realized gains must be recognized unless the IRC expressly provides otherwise. Conversely, no deduction is allowed for a realized loss unless the IRC expressly provides for it. The amount realized in most cases is the money received, plus the FMV of other property received, and liability relief, minus money or other property given up, selling expenses, and liabilities assumed. The gain (loss) realized is the amount realized less the adjusted basis. Thus, Maggie has realized $10,000 on this exchange, of which her gain is $3,000 ($10,000 – $7,000).
Answer (B) is incorrect. Maggie realized a gain on the exchange of stock. **Answer (C) is incorrect.** The amount realized is equal to the FMV of the property she received, and the gain is only $3,000 ($10,000 – $7,000). **Answer (D) is incorrect.** The amount realized is equal to the FMV of the property she received.

25. Larry purchased stock in 2015 for $100. During 2018, he received a return of capital of $80 on this stock. During 2020, he received another return of capital of $30. Larry had no other stock transactions in 2020. What amount should he report on his 2020 income tax return, and what is his basis in the stock at the end of 2020?

A. $30 capital gain, $100 stock basis.

B. $30 dividend income, $100 stock basis.

C. $10 capital gain, zero stock basis.

D. $10 dividend income, zero stock basis.

Answer (C) is correct.
REQUIRED: The amount and type of gain and the basis in the stock.
DISCUSSION: A return of capital is a tax-free distribution that reduces a stock's basis by the amount of the distribution. If a shareholder's basis is reduced to zero because of a tax-free return of capital, any excess amounts received are treated as a capital gain.
Answer (A) is incorrect. A return of capital reduces basis, and a capital gain is not recognized until basis is reduced to zero. **Answer (B) is incorrect.** A return of capital reduces basis, and any gain, after basis is reduced to zero, is a capital gain. **Answer (D) is incorrect.** A capital gain is recognized when a return of capital distribution exceeds the stock's remaining basis.

26. Kiran bought stock in the Big Bang Corporation in 2015 for $2,000. In 2019, Kiran received a return of capital distribution of $100 as a partial return on her investment. In 2020, Kiran sold the stock for $3,000. Her basis in the stock is

A. $3,000

B. $2,100

C. $1,900

D. $2,000

Answer (C) is correct.
REQUIRED: The basis in stock after receiving a return of capital distribution.
DISCUSSION: The original basis in Kiran's stock is $2,000, the original purchase. Kiran must adjust the basis for the return of capital distribution of $100. Therefore, Kiran's basis at the time of disposition equals $1,900 ($2,000 – $100).
Answer (A) is incorrect. The basis in the stock must not necessarily equal the selling price of the stock. **Answer (B) is incorrect.** The $100 return of capital distribution decreases the basis of the stock. **Answer (D) is incorrect.** The $100 return of capital distribution decreases the basis of the stock.

27. Vanessa inherited 100 shares of stock from her grandmother when her grandmother died on December 10, 2019. At that time, the fair market value of the stock was $50 per share. Vanessa's grandmother paid $40 per share when she purchased the stock July 1, 2019. If Vanessa sells all 100 shares for $60 per share on June 30, 2020, how should she report the sale on her return for 2020?

A. $1,000 short-term capital gain.

B. $2,000 short-term capital gain.

C. $1,000 long-term capital gain.

D. $2,000 long-term capital gain.

Answer (C) is correct.
REQUIRED: The correct treatment of the disposition of stock acquired from a decedent.
DISCUSSION: The basis of property received from a decedent is generally the fair market value of the property on the date of the decedent's death. Basis in the stock is the fair market value (the date of her grandmother's death). Any asset received from a decedent is considered held long-term no matter how long it is held. Thus, Vanessa has a long-term capital gain of $1,000 (100 × $60 – 100 × $50).
Answer (A) is incorrect. Assets received from a decedent are considered long-term no matter how long they are held. **Answer (B) is incorrect.** The basis of property received from a decedent is generally the fair market value of the property at the date of the decedent's death. Also, assets received from a decedent are considered long-term no matter how long they are held. **Answer (D) is incorrect.** The basis of property received from a decedent is generally the fair market value of the property at the date of the decedent's death.

28. Mr. and Mrs. Able are investors in a mutual fund that is not part of a qualified retirement plan. For 2020, the fund notified them that it had allocated a $9,500 long-term capital gain to their account. Of this total, only $4,500 was distributed in 2020. In addition, the fund paid $500 federal tax on their behalf. What is the correct amount of long-term capital gain that the Ables should report on their 2020 tax return?

A. $10,000

B. $9,500

C. $5,000

D. $4,500

Answer (B) is correct.
REQUIRED: The amount of long-term capital gain to be included in gross income.
DISCUSSION: A mutual fund is a regulated investment company, the taxation of which is determined by Sec. 852. Dividends paid by the mutual fund to shareholders are taxed. Undistributed capital gains must be included in income by shareholders, but a credit is allowed for their proportionate share of any tax on the capital gain paid by the mutual fund. Therefore, the Ables must report the full $9,500 as a long-term capital gain.
Answer (A) is incorrect. The $500 of federal income taxes paid is not reported as capital gain but is taken by the Ables as a credit. **Answer (C) is incorrect.** Both the distributed and the undistributed amounts of capital gain must be reported as income. **Answer (D) is incorrect.** The actual amount of the gain, not only the amount distributed, must be reported.

29. Karen Smith bought stock for $475 on March 31, 2020. On November 15, 2020, Karen received a non-taxable distribution of $155 on the 50 shares of stock she owned. She sold the stock for $300 on December 22, 2020. What is her gain or loss on the sale?

A. $175 gain.

B. $175 loss.

C. $20 gain.

D. $20 loss.

Answer (D) is correct.
REQUIRED: The amount of loss on the sale of stock following a nontaxable stock distribution.
DISCUSSION: Since the distribution is nontaxable, it is considered a return of capital that reduces the basis of the stock. The basis of the stock cannot be decreased below zero. Karen's basis in the stock is reduced because of the distribution from $475 to $320 ($475 – $155 distribution). When it is sold for $300, the recognition of a $20 loss occurs ($300 realized – $320 adjusted basis).

9.10 Sections 1202 and 1244 Stock

30. Shannon and Dan Smith (wife and husband) purchased Section 1244 (small business) stock in 2020. Which of the following statements is true?

A. If they incurred a loss on Section 1244 stock, they can deduct the loss as a capital loss rather than as an ordinary loss.

B. If the stock becomes worthless, they can claim an ordinary loss limited to $50,000 individually or $100,000 together on a joint return, per year.

C. If the loss is $60,000 and Shannon does not have any other losses, Dan can only deduct $50,000 as ordinary loss on the joint return.

D. If they incurred a gain on Section 1244 stock, they should treat it as ordinary gain.

Answer (B) is correct.
   REQUIRED: The true statement regarding Sec. 1244 stock.
   DISCUSSION: Taxpayers may deduct losses on Sec. 1244 stock as ordinary up to $50,000 in any 1 year ($100,000 on a joint return).
   Answer (A) is incorrect. The loss is treated as ordinary rather than as capital. **Answer (C) is incorrect.** Up to $100,000 may be deducted on a joint return. **Answer (D) is incorrect.** The gain is treated as a capital gain rather than as ordinary income.

STUDY UNIT TEN

RELATED PARTIES, BUSINESS PROPERTY, AND INSTALLMENT SALES

(13 pages of outline)

This study unit involves a discussion of related party sales, the sale of business property, and installment sales. Special rules prevent taxpayers from receiving unwarranted tax benefits. Losses on sales to related parties are disallowed, except for sales in corporate liquidation rules. Depreciation is recaptured on the sale of business property in order to prevent taxpayers from taking ordinary depreciation deductions and then receiving capital gain treatment at the time of sale of the property. When payments from the sale of property are received after the year of sale, gain recognition is deferred for each payment until the payment's corresponding tax year.

10.1 RELATED PARTY SALES

These rules limit tax avoidance between related parties.

1. Gain recognized on sale of an asset is ordinary income when an asset is transferred to a related person in whose hands the asset is depreciable.

    a. For this unique situation, "related" means

    1) A person and the person's controlled entity(ies),

    2) A taxpayer and any trust in which the taxpayer (or spouse) is a beneficiary,

    3) An executor and a beneficiary of an estate, and

    4) An employer and a welfare benefit fund controlled directly or indirectly by the employer (or related person).

Loss Nonrecognition

2. Loss realized on sale or exchange of property to a related person is not recognized.

    a. The transferee takes a cost basis.

    b. There is no adding of holding periods.

    c. Gain realized on a subsequent sale to an unrelated party is recognized only to the extent it exceeds the previously disallowed loss.

EXAMPLE 10-1   Disallowed Loss on Sale to Related Person

Taxpayer A sells stock with a basis of $100,000 to a related person, Taxpayer B, for $80,000, creating a $20,000 disallowed loss for Taxpayer A. If Taxpayer B in turn sells the stock to an unrelated party for $130,000, creating a realized gain of $50,000 ($130,000 sales price − $80,000 basis), Taxpayer B only has to recognize $30,000 of gain ($50,000 realized gain − $20,000 disallowed loss from original transaction between A and B). In addition, if the unrelated sale had been for only $90,000, resulting in $10,000 gain ($90,000 sale price − $80,000 basis), Taxpayer B would not recognize any gain as the $10,000 gain is offset by $10,000 of the prior $20,000 disallowed loss. Finally, if the unrelated sale had been for only $65,000, creating an additional $15,000 loss, Taxpayer B could only recognize the $15,000 loss and not a $35,000 loss ($20,000 disallowed loss + $15,000 unrelated sale loss).

---

    d. Loss realized on a subsequent sale to a third party is recognized, but the previously disallowed loss is not added to it.

3. For property purchased on or after January 1, 2016, a new rule precludes the previously discussed recognition of the disallowed loss when later sold to an unrelated party, if the original transferor (e.g., Taxpayer A in the prior example) is a tax-indifferent party.

    a. Tax-indifferent parties are those not subject to federal income tax or to whom an item would have no substantial impact on its income tax. Examples of tax-indifferent parties include non-U.S. persons, tax-exempt organizations, and government entities.

EXAMPLE 10-2   Disallowed Loss -- Tax-Indifferent Party

Going back to Example 10-1 but changing A to a tax-indifferent party, the disallowed loss is still $20,000 when sold for $80,000; however, on the sale from Taxpayer B to an unrelated party for $130,000, the realized and recognized gain is $50,000 ($130,000 − $80,000). The $50,000 gain is not offset by the disallowed loss.

Related Parties

4. Related parties under Sec. 267(b) and (c) for purposes of these provisions include

    a. Ancestors, lineal descendants, spouses, and siblings (nephews and nieces are not descendants) *∗ or uncle, aunt, cousins*

    b. Trusts and beneficiaries thereof

    c. Controlled entities (50% ownership)

    NOTE: Constructive ownership rules between family members apply.

5. Loss on sale or exchange of property between a partnership and a person owning more than 50% of the capital or profit interests in the partnership is not recognized.

Employer-Employee Transactions

6.   An employee is not a related party to the employer for purposes of the related-party sale rules.

   a.   When an employer sells assets to an employee at less than FMV, the difference between FMV and the sales price is considered compensation to the employee.

      1)   Since the employee pays tax on the compensation, his or her basis in the new property will be FMV.

Interspousal Transfer

7.   No gain or loss is recognized on the transfer of property between spouses or, incident to a divorce, on transfers of property to a former spouse.

   a.   The transferee takes a carryover basis in the property.
   b.   These rules apply whether the transfer is a gift, a sale, or an exchange.

STOP AND REVIEW! You have completed the outline for this subunit. Study multiple-choice questions 1 through 7 beginning on page 312.

10.2 BUSINESS PROPERTY

   Sections 1231, 1245, and 1250 recharacterize gain or loss. Sections 1245 and 1250 also accelerate recognition of certain installment gain that would otherwise be deferred.

   Because the concepts in this subunit are challenging, we have included Examples 10-7 to 10-9, beginning on page 306, to provide additional context.

Overview of Business Property Recharacterization

(i.e., depreciation recapture)

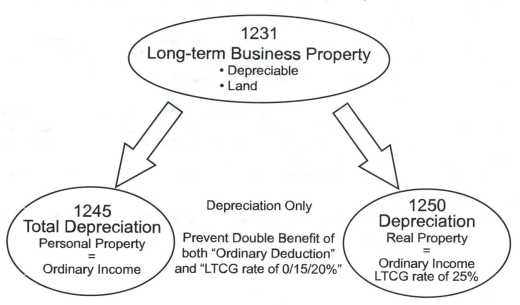

Figure 10-1

Section 1245 Property

1. A realized gain on the disposition of Sec. 1245 property is ordinary income to the extent of all depreciation or amortization taken.

    a. Amounts expensed under Sec. 179 are considered depreciation deductions. Depreciation deductions may be taken for the taxable year the business property is placed in service.

    b. Property is considered placed in service when it is ready and available for a specific use.

    c. The downward basis adjustment for a general business credit is considered a deduction allowed for depreciation and is subject to recapture.

    d. The realized gain in excess of the depreciation taken may be treated as a gain from the sale or exchange of Sec. 1231 property.

2. Section 1245 property generally is depreciable personal property.

    a. It is tangible (intangible), depreciable (amortizable) personal property (e.g., equipment, patent); recovery property, including specified real property; and tax benefit property (e.g., qualified Sec. 179 expense property).

    b. Other tangible property (excluding a building or its structural components) includes property used as an integral part of a trade or business, e.g., manufacturing or production equipment.

    c. Intangible, amortizable (Sec. 197) personal Sec. 1245 property examples include

        1) Leaseholds of Sec. 1245 property

        2) Professional athletic contracts, e.g., major league baseball

        3) Patents

        4) Livestock

        5) Goodwill acquired after August 10, 1993, in connection with the acquisition of a trade or business

    d. Particular types of property are treated as Sec. 1245 property due to an attributable tax benefit. An example is amortized pollution control facilities.

EXAMPLE 10-3   Section 1245 Ordinary Income and Section 1231 Gain

Paige owns a patent with a cost of $300,000 and an adjusted basis of $260,000. On January 2 of this year, Paige sold the patent for $345,000.

Total amortization taken previously equals $40,000 ($300,000 – $260,000). Paige's realized gain is $85,000 ($345,000 sales price – $260,000 adjusted basis). Section 1245 requires the gain to be recognized as ordinary income to the extent of the amortization taken. Therefore, $40,000 of the $85,000 gain is Sec. 1245 gain and the remaining $45,000 is Sec. 1231 gain.

Section 1250 Ordinary Income

3. Section 1250 property is all depreciable real property, held for more than 1 year, that is not Sec. 1245 property, such as a building or its structural components.

a. Section 1250 property is subject to its own recapture rules. For the three items listed below, the aggregate gain recognized on the sale or disposition of Sec. 1250 property is ordinary income (OI).

1) The excess of accelerated depreciation taken over S-L depreciation is OI.

   a) Partial reduction of excess depreciation is provided for under Sec. 1250 for low-income housing and rehabilitated structures.

2) For corporations, the gain must be computed under both Secs. 1245 and 1250. If Sec. 1245 gain is larger than Sec. 1250 gain, 20% of the difference is characterized as OI.

3) For property held 1 year or less, any depreciation is recaptured as OI.

b. Section 1250 property includes depreciable real property not listed in Sec. 1245 acquired

1) Prior to 1981 or after 1986 or

2) During 1981 through 1986 and either residential property or property depreciated using the S-L method.

c. Examples of Sec. 1250 property include shopping malls, an apartment or office building, low-income housing, rented portions of residences, and escalators or elevators (placed in service after 1986).

d. Income received or accrued for more than one asset is allocated to each asset by agreement, by FMV, or by the residual method.

1) To compute Sec. 1245 and Sec. 1250 OI, an amount realized allocable to an asset must be further allocated to each use of a mixed-use asset for each tax year.

2) Apportionment is on the basis of relative time or amount of asset usage, e.g., 5% of automobile usage for business or one-half of a house used as rental property.

e. Recapture of depreciation as OI of post-1986 real property is not required because post-1986 property must be depreciated under the S-L method.

Unrecaptured Section 1250 Depreciation

4. Only applies to individual taxpayers and only if there is a gain on the sale of the asset. In the case of multiple Sec. 1231 assets, this rule applies only if there is a net Sec. 1231 gain on the sale of all the assets bundled together. If multiple Sec. 1231 sales net to a loss, then the loss is simply ordinary.

a. The lesser of the following is taxed at a maximum capital gains rate of 25%:

1) Gain on the sale of the asset less any depreciation recognized as OI.

2) Accumulated depreciation on the asset less any depreciation recognized as OI (straight-line depreciation taken).

b. Any excess gain is allocated to net Sec. 1231 gain to be taxed at a 0%, 15%, or 20% rate.

EXAMPLE 10-4	Section 1250 Unrecaptured Gain Taxed as Sec. 1231 Gain

Annie sold a building used in her trade or business for $110,000. This is her only Sec. 1231 property sale for the year. Annie purchased the building several years ago for $100,000. At the time of the sale, the building has accumulated depreciation of $20,000. Because the building was acquired after 1986, it has been depreciated using the straight-line method; therefore, Sec. 1250 recapture does not apply, and Annie has a Sec. 1231 gain of $30,000 ($110,000 amount realized – $80,000 adjusted basis). Of the $30,000 gain, $20,000 is attributable to straight-line depreciation and is classified as Sec. 1250 unrecaptured gain, which is subject to a maximum rate of 25%. The remaining $10,000 gain is taxed at a maximum rate of 0/15/20%.

Section 1231 Property

5. Unlike the recapture provisions in Secs. 1245 and 1250, Sec. 1231 is beneficial to the taxpayer.

    a. When Sec. 1231 property gains exceed losses (a net Sec. 1231 gain), each gain or loss is treated as being from the sale of a long-term capital asset.

    b. If Sec. 1231 property losses exceed gains (a net Sec. 1231 loss), each gain or loss is considered ordinary.

    c. Section 1231 property is property held for more than 1 year and includes

        1) All real or depreciable property used in a trade or business or

        2) Involuntarily converted capital assets held in connection with a trade or business or in a transaction entered into for a profit.

    d. Examples of Sec. 1231 property include apartment buildings, parking lots, manufacturing equipment, and involuntarily converted investment artwork.

    e. Examples that are not Sec. 1231 property include personal-use property and inventory.

    f. Section 1231 has a two-step test.

        1) Step 1: Determine net gain or loss from all casualties or thefts of Sec. 1231 property for the tax year. Gain or loss from involuntary conversions by other than casualty or theft is included in Step 2 but not Step 1.

            a) If the result is a net loss, each gain or loss is treated as ordinary income or loss.

            b) If the result is a net gain, each gain or loss is included in Step 2.

        2) Step 2: Determine net gain or loss from all dispositions of Sec. 1231 property for the year, including the property included in Step 1 only if Step 1 resulted in a net gain.

            a) If the result is a net loss, each gain or loss is treated as ordinary income or loss.

            b) If the result is a net gain, each gain or loss is treated as a long-term capital gain or loss, subject to the recapture rules under i. below.

Allocation

    g. Allocation is required when Sec. 1245 or Sec. 1250 property is also Sec. 1231 property and only a portion of gain recognized is Sec. 1245 or Sec. 1250 OI.

    h. The installment method can apply to Sec. 1231 property.

    i. Recapture. Net gain on Sec. 1231 property is treated as OI to the extent of unrecaptured net Sec. 1231 losses from preceding tax years.

        1) Unrecaptured net Sec. 1231 losses are the total of net Sec. 1231 losses for the last 5 tax years, reduced by net Sec. 1231 gains characterized as OI under Sec. 1231(c).

EXAMPLE 10-5   Section 1231 Recapture

Eric has unrecaptured Sec. 1231 losses of $4,500 from 2 years ago. This year, he has a net Sec. 1231 gain of $7,600. Of this gain, $4,500 will be recharacterized as ordinary, and the remaining $3,100 will be classified as long-term capital gain.

2) Sections 1245 and 1250 recapture is computed before Sec. 1231 recapture, but Sec. 1231 recapture is computed before Steps 1 and 2 on the previous page.

3) Section 1231 merely characterizes gain or loss. Any Sec. 1231 gain that is recharacterized as ordinary income will first consist of 28% gain, then 25% gain, and finally 15/20% gain.

   a) When sales price is above the cost of the asset and no losses exist (current year and preceding tax years), the Sec. 1231 gain is characterized as follows:

      i) Ordinary income as depreciation is recaptured up to the cost of the asset and then as

      ii) Capital gain for sales price amount in excess of cost.

EXAMPLE 10-6   Section 1231 Gain

ZP Enterprises purchased a delivery truck for $100,000 more than 1 year ago and fully depreciated the truck. ZP Enterprises sold the truck for $120,000 this year resulting in a $120,000 Sec. 1231 gain. The character of the $120,000 gain is as follows:

$100,000	Ordinary income
20,000	Section 1231 long-term capital gain
$120,000	Total gain

Installment Sales

6. All gain realized from a disposal of recapture property in an installment sale is characterized as OI by Sec. 1245 or Sec. 1250 and must be recognized in the period of sale. Excess gain over Sec. 1245 or Sec. 1250 OI is accounted for by the installment method.

Gift Property

7. Neither Sec. 1245 nor Sec. 1250 applies to a gift disposition. Any gain realized by the donee upon a subsequent taxable disposition is subject to Sec. 1245 and Sec. 1250 characterization up to the sum of any potential Sec. 1245 and Sec. 1250 OI at the time of the gift and any Sec. 1245 and Sec. 1250 OI potential arising between gift and subsequent disposition.

Inherited Property

8. Neither Sec. 1245 nor Sec. 1250 applies to a disposition by bequest, devise, or intestate succession. Exceptions include the following:

   a. Section 1245 and Sec. 1250 OI is recognized for a transfer at death to the extent of any income in respect of a decedent (IRD).

   b. Section 1245 OI potential also results from depreciation allowed to a decedent because the depreciation does not carry over to the transferee.

Section 351 Exchange for Stock

9. Generally, no gain is recognized upon an exchange of property for all the stock of a newly formed corporation. Section 1245 and Sec. 1250 OI is limited to any amount of gain recognized in a Sec. 351 transaction.

10. Section 1245 applies to the amount of gain recognized plus the FMV of non-Sec. 1245 property received (e.g., boot) that is not already taken into account in calculating the recognized gain.

EXAMPLE 10-7   Section 1245 Recapture

On January 17, Year 1, Relief Corp. purchased and placed into service 7-year MACRS tangible property costing $100,000. On December 21, Year 4, Relief Corp. sold the property for $105,000 after taking $60,000 in MACRS depreciation deductions.

The adjusted basis of the property is $40,000 ($100,000 historical cost – $60,000 depreciation); therefore, Relief recognizes a gain of $65,000 ($105,000 selling price – $40,000 adjusted basis). Since this property qualifies for Sec. 1245 recapture, the gain is recaptured as ordinary income to the extent of the lesser of all depreciation taken or gain realized. Thus, Relief has $60,000 of Sec. 1245 (ordinary) gain. The remaining $5,000 of gain is Sec. 1231 (capital) gain.

EXAMPLE 10-8   Section 1245 Recapture

The facts from Example 10-7 apply, except Relief sold the property for $95,000.

Relief recognizes a gain of $55,000 ($95,000 selling price – $40,000 adjusted basis). Since this property qualifies for Sec. 1245 recapture, the gain is recaptured as ordinary income to the extent of the lesser of all depreciation taken or gain realized. Thus, Relief has $55,000 of Sec. 1245 (ordinary) gain.

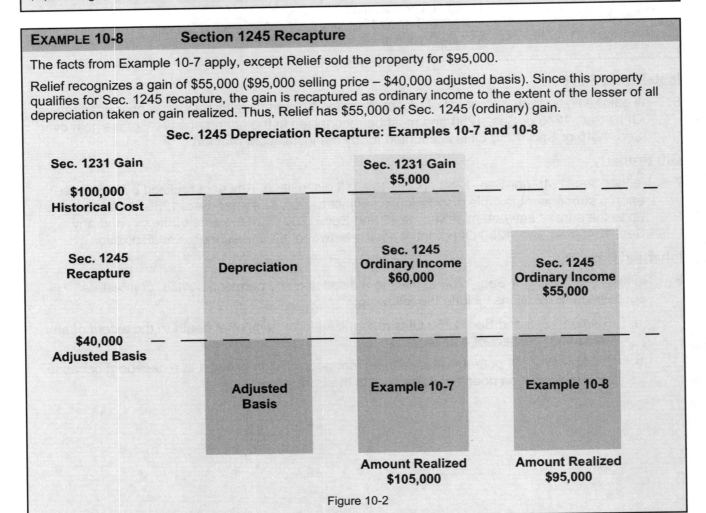

Sec. 1245 Depreciation Recapture: Examples 10-7 and 10-8

Figure 10-2

EXAMPLE 10-9   Section 1250 Recapture

Martha purchased and placed into service Sec. 1250 property for $600,000 on January 1, 1984. Depreciation was taken using the 150% declining-balance method. On January 1, 2020, the property was sold for $650,000 after taking $546,000 in depreciation. Straight-line depreciation would have been $540,000.

The adjusted basis of the property is $54,000 ($600,000 historical cost – $546,000 depreciation); therefore, Martha recognizes a gain of $596,000 ($650,000 selling price – $54,000 adjusted basis). The recaptured depreciation (excess of depreciation taken over the straight-line depreciation) is $6,000 ($546,000 depreciation taken – $540,000 straight-line depreciation) and is taxed at ordinary income rates. The Sec. 1250 unrecaptured depreciation is $540,000 and taxed at a maximum capital gains rate of 25%. The remaining $50,000 gain ($596,000 gain recognized – $6,000 ordinary income – $540,000 Sec. 1250 gain) is Sec. 1231 gain. If this is Martha's only Sec. 1231 transaction for the year, the $50,000 is taxed at a maximum capital gains rate of 15/20%.

Sale of Business-Use Assets Held **One Year or Less**

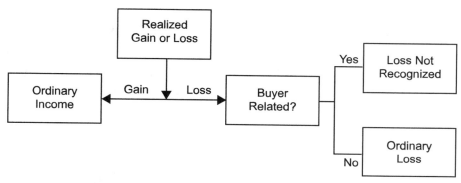

Figure 10-3

Sale of Business-Use Assets Held **More than One Year**

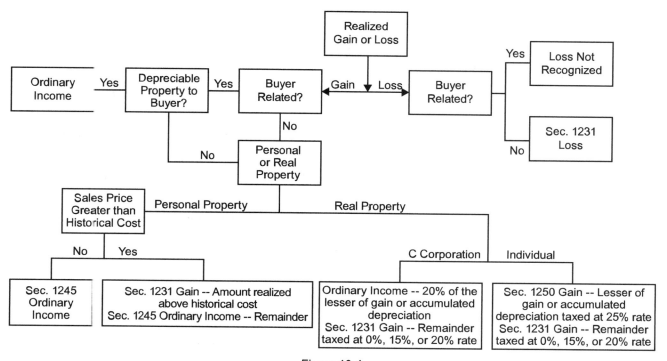

Figure 10-4

STOP AND REVIEW! **You have completed the outline for this subunit. Study multiple-choice questions 8 through 15 beginning on page 315.**

10.3 INSTALLMENT SALES

The installment method must be used to report installment sales unless election is made not to apply the method. An installment sale is a disposition of property in which at least one payment is to be received after the close of the tax year in which the disposition occurs.

1.   Installment sales do not apply to the following dispositions:

    a.   Inventory personal property sales

    b.   Revolving credit personal property sales

    c.   Dealer dispositions, including dispositions of

        1)   Personal property of a type regularly sold by the person on the installment plan
        2)   Real property held for sale to customers in the ordinary course of trade or business

    d.   Securities, generally, if publicly traded

    e.   Sales with agreement to establish an irrevocable escrow account

2.   Not excluded from installment sale deferral are

    a.   Certain sales of residential lots or timeshares subject to interest on the deferred tax
    b.   Property used or produced in a farming business

Recognized Gain

3.   The amount of realized gain to be recognized in a tax year is equal to the gross profit multiplied by the ratio of payments received in the current year divided by the total contract price.

    a.   Recognize, as income, payments received multiplied by the gross profit percentage.

Recognized gain = Gross profit percentage × Payments received

        1)   Excess of liability assumed over adjusted basis (AB) and selling expenses is treated as part of the down payment.

        2)   A payment is considered paid in full if the balance is placed into an irrevocable escrow account (i.e., amounts that cannot revert to the purchaser) at a later date.

    b.   The gross profit percentage is the ratio of the gross profit to the total contract price.

$$\textbf{Gross profit percentage} = \frac{\textbf{Gross profit}}{\textbf{Contract price}} = \frac{\textbf{Selling price} - \textbf{Selling expenses} - \textbf{Adjusted basis}}{\textbf{Amount to be collected}}$$

        1)   The gross profit is the sales price reduced by any selling expenses (including debt cancellation) and adjusted basis.

           a)   When the selling price is reduced in a future year, the gross profit on the sale will also be reduced.

              i)   The gross profit percentage must be recalculated for the remaining periods by using the reduced sales price and subtracting the gross profit already recognized.

EXAMPLE 10-10   **Gain Recognition on Installment Sale**

In Year 1, Harry sold land with an adjusted basis to him of $120,000 to Joe for $200,000. Joe made a down payment of $80,000 in Year 1, and agreed to pay $30,000 per year plus interest for the next 4 years beginning January Year 2. After Joe made the payment in Year 2, Harry and Joe agreed to reduce the overall sales price to $185,000 and the yearly payments to $25,000. Since the selling price is reduced at a later date, the gross profit on the sale will also change. The gross profit percentage must be recalculated for the remaining periods by using the reduced sales price and subtracting the gross profit already recognized. The amount includible in Year 3 is determined as follows:

Gross profit ($185,000 sales price – $120,000 basis)	$65,000
Less: Gain recognized to date [$110,000 payments ×	
($80,000 original gross profit ÷ $200,000 original sales price)]	(44,000)
Remaining gain	$21,000
Adjusted gross profit ratio ($21,000 remaining gain ÷	
$75,000 remaining payments)	28%
Multiplied by: Payment received in Year 3	25,000
Gain recognized in Year 3	$ 7,000

---

       b)   Gross profit includes the unrecognized gain on sale of a personal residence.

   2)   The sales price is the sum of any cash received, liability relief, and installment notes from the buyer. It does not include imputed interest.

   3)   The total contract price is the amount that will be collected.

       a)   An existing mortgage assumed is not collected by the seller.

EXAMPLE 10-11   **Installment Sale with Mortgage Assumption**

John owns a piece of land with a basis of $100,000 and a mortgage attached of $50,000. He sells the land for $300,000 plus interest, with the buyer taking over the mortgage, paying $20,000, and issuing a promissory note for $230,000. The sales price is $300,000 ($250,000 + $50,000). The contract price is $250,000 ($300,000 amount realized – $50,000 mortgage assumed). John incurs selling expenses of $10,000.

---

       b)   The contract price and the amount received in the span of sale includes the excess of liability assumed over AB and selling expenses.

EXAMPLE 10-12   **Installment Sale with Mortgage Assumption**

If the mortgage attached in Example 10-11 were $140,000, the selling price would be $390,000 ($250,000 + 140,000). The contract price would be $280,000 ($390,000 – 140,000 + 30,000) excess of mortgage assumed over the basis plus selling expenses.

---

       i)   When the liability exceeds the AB and selling expenses, the gross profit percentage is 100%.

   4)   The adjusted basis for installment sale purposes is the total of the following three items:

       a)   Adjusted basis

       b)   Selling expenses

       c)   Depreciation recapture

Character of Gain

4. Character of gain recognized depends on the nature of the property in the transferor's hands.

5. The full amount of Sec. 1245 and Sec. 1250 ordinary gain ("depreciation recapture") must be recognized in the year of sale, even if it exceeds payments received.

    a. If a taxpayer sells property for which a depreciation deduction was claimed, any depreciation recapture income in the year of sale must be reported, whether or not an installment payment was received that year.

    b. The gain is added to basis before further applying the installment method.

Anti-Avoidance Rule

6. An anti-avoidance rule applies to an installment sale of property to a related party. On a second disposition (by the related party transferee in the first sale), payments received must be treated as a payment received by the person who made the first (installment) sale to a related party.

    a. A second disposition by gift is included. The FMV is treated as the payment.
    b. Death of the first disposition seller or buyer does not accelerate recognition.

Repossession

7. The seller of personal property recognizes as gain or loss any difference between the FMV of repossessed property and the AB of an installment sale obligation satisfied by the repossession. If real property, recognize the lesser of

    a. Cash and other property (FMV) received in excess of gain already recognized or
    b. Gross profit in remaining installments less repossession costs.

Example Calculations for Gain (Loss) on Repossession (Per Publication 537)		
Basis of Repossessed Personal Property		
1) The unpaid balance of the installment obligation	$160,000	
2) Gross profit percentage for the installment sale	20%	
3) Unrealized profit (multiply line 1 by line 2)	$32,000	
4) Basis of the obligation (subtract line 3 from line 1)		$128,000
5) Taxable gain on the repossession..		27,000
6) Cost of repossessing the property..		5,000
7) Add lines 4, 5, and 6. This is the basis in the repossessed real property.		160,000
Taxable Gain on Repossession of Real Property		
1) Total payments received before repossession		$90,000
2) Gain already reported as income		18,000
3) Gain on Repossession (subtract line 2 from line 1)		72,000
4) Gross profit on the original sale		50,000
5) Repossession costs		5,000
6) Add line 2 and line 5		23,000
7) Subtract line 6 from line 4		27,000
8) Taxable gain (lesser of line 3 or line 7)		27,000

Interest

8. Interest is imposed on deferred tax on obligations from nondealer installment sales (of more than $150,000) outstanding at the close of the tax year.

   a. This interest is applied if the taxpayer has nondealer installment receivables of over $5 million at the close of the tax year from installment sales of over $150,000 that occurred during the year.

   b. This interest is not applied to
      1) Personal-use property,
      2) Residential lots and time shares, and
      3) Property produced or used in the farming business.

Disposition of Installment Obligations

9. Excess of the FMV over the AB of an installment obligation is generally recognized as income if it is transferred.

   a. FMV is generally the amount realized.

   b. If a gift, use the face value of the obligation.

   c. The adjusted basis is generally determined by the following formula:

   Face value × (100% – Gross profit percentage)

EXAMPLE 10-13   Disposition of Installment Obligation

In Year 1, Bob sold land to Ann for $80,000. He reported the sale using the installment method. At the time of the sale, the land had an adjusted basis of $20,000. Ann made a down payment of $25,000 in Year 1 and agreed to pay $11,000 per year plus interest for the next 5 years. Before the Year 3 payment was made, Bob sold the installment obligation for $30,000. The face amount of the obligation is $44,000 ($11,000 annual payments × 4 years). The basis of the obligation is $11,000 [$44,000 face amount × (100% – 75% gross profit percentage)]. The gain is $19,000 ($30,000 amount realized – $11,000 basis).

---

   d. Characterize as if the property for which the installment obligation was received was sold.

   e. A disposition of the installment obligation is deemed to occur when the obligation is transferred by gift, is forgiven, or becomes unenforceable.

   f. Exceptions. Disposition of obligations by the following events can result in the transferee treating payments as the transferor would have:
      1) Transfers to a controlled corporation
      2) Corporate reorganizations and liquidations
      3) Contributions to capital of, or distributions from, partnerships
      4) Transfer between spouses incident to divorce
      5) Transfer upon death of the obligee

STOP AND REVIEW! **You have completed the outline for this subunit. Study multiple-choice questions 16 through 30 beginning on page 318.**

QUESTIONS

10.1 Related Party Sales

1. Larry sold stock with a cost basis of $10,500 to his son for $8,500. Larry cannot deduct the $2,000 loss. His son sold the same stock to an unrelated party for $15,000, realizing a gain. What is his son's reportable gain?

   A. $6,500.

   B. $4,500.

   C. $2,000.

   D. No gain.

Answer (B) is correct.
   REQUIRED: The amount of gain recognized when property is sold after acquisition from a related party in a loss transaction.
   DISCUSSION: Under Sec. 267(a)(1), losses are not allowed on sales or exchanges of property between related parties. Related parties include a father and a son. Larry realized a $2,000 loss on the sale but may not deduct it. On the subsequent sale, his son realized a $6,500 gain. However, he recognizes only a $4,500 reportable gain. The disallowed loss is used to offset the subsequent gain on the sale of the property ($6,500 realized gain – $2,000 disallowed loss).
   Answer (A) is incorrect. The gain must be offset by the disallowed loss. **Answer (C) is incorrect.** This is the amount by which the gain will be offset. **Answer (D) is incorrect.** A gain must be reported.

2. Jim sells stock that he purchased in 2007 to his brother John for a $500 loss. He also sells a truck purchased in 2018 to ABC Corporation, his 100%-owned C corporation, for a profit of $800, including $500 of depreciation recapture. What is the effect of these transactions on Jim's 2020 tax return?

   A. A loss of $500 on the stock and no gain on the truck.

   B. A disallowed loss on the stock, $500 ordinary gain, and $300 long-term capital gain on the truck.

   C. A loss of $500 on the stock and $800 ordinary gain on the truck.

   D. A disallowed loss on the stock and $800 ordinary gain on the truck.

Answer (D) is correct.
   REQUIRED: The effect of the sale of assets to related parties on a tax return.
   DISCUSSION: The loss on the sale of a capital asset (such as stock) is not allowed when sold to a member of the individual's family [Sec. 267(b)]. Capital gain treatment is denied when depreciable property is sold between related taxpayers [Sec. 1239(a)]. This rule pertains to sales or exchanges between the following:

1. A person and all entities controlled by such person
2. A taxpayer and any trust of which the taxpayer is a beneficiary unless the beneficiary's interest is because of a remote possibility to a contingency
3. An executor of an estate and a beneficiary of the estate, unless the sale or exchange is in satisfaction of a monetary value bequeathed to the beneficiary (Sec. 1293)

   Answer (A) is incorrect. A loss is disallowed when property is sold to one's brother, and an ordinary gain of $800 may be recognized for the truck. **Answer (B) is incorrect.** A capital gain is disallowed when a taxpayer sells depreciable property to an entity that (s)he controls. **Answer (C) is incorrect.** A loss is disallowed on property sold to one's brother.

3. Robert sold his Lebec Corporation stock to his sister Karen for $8,000. Robert's cost basis in the stock was $15,000. Karen later sold this stock to Dana, an unrelated party, for $15,500. What is Karen's realized gain?

A. $500

B. $7,000

C. $7,500

D. $0

Answer (C) is correct.
REQUIRED: The amount of realized gain when stock is sold after acquisition from a related party in a loss transaction.
DISCUSSION: Under Sec. 267, losses are not allowed on sales or exchanges of property between related parties. Brothers and sisters are related parties. Robert realized a $7,000 ($15,000 cost basis in stock – $8,000 sales price to Karen) loss on the sale but may not deduct it. On the subsequent sale, Karen realized a $7,500 gain ($15,500 sales price – $8,000 basis). However, she does not have to recognize the entire gain because the Sec. 267(d) disallowed loss is used to offset the subsequent gain on the sale of the property. Karen would recognize a $500 gain.
Answer (A) is incorrect. Karen's basis in the stock for computing a realized gain is $8,000, not $15,000. **Answer (B) is incorrect.** This amount represents Robert's nondeductible loss. **Answer (D) is incorrect.** This is the amount of Karen's recognized gain if sold for $15,000.

4. Geena paid $10,000 for stock in a start-up company. A few months after she bought it, she sold the stock to her brother Henry for $8,000, its current value. Later, he sold the stock to an unrelated party for $15,000. What gain or loss should Geena and Henry recognize on their tax returns in the year of sale?

A. Geena recognizes $2,000 loss; Henry recognizes $7,000 gain.

B. Geena recognizes $2,000 loss; Henry recognizes $5,000 gain.

C. Geena recognizes $0 loss; Henry recognizes $7,000 gain.

D. Geena recognizes $0 loss; Henry recognizes $5,000 gain.

Answer (D) is correct.
REQUIRED: The treatment of a loss on the sale of stock to a related party and the amount recognized on a subsequent sale to an unrelated party.
DISCUSSION: Under Sec. 267, losses are not allowed on sales or exchanges of property between related parties. Siblings are related parties for this purpose. Thus, Geena's loss of $2,000 ($10,000 stock – $8,000 sales price to Henry) on the sale of the stock is disallowed. On the subsequent sale, Henry realized a $7,000 gain ($15,000 sales price – $8,000 basis). However, he recognizes only a $5,000 gain [Sec. 257(d)]. The disallowed loss is used to offset the subsequent gain on the sale of the property ($7,000 realized gain – $2,000 disallowed loss).
Answer (A) is incorrect. Geena's loss is disallowed under Sec. 267. **Answer (B) is incorrect.** Geena's loss is disallowed under Sec. 267. **Answer (C) is incorrect.** Geena's disallowed loss reduces her brother Henry's realized gain on the sale of the property to $5,000.

5. In May of the current year, Automatic, Inc., sold land with a basis to Automatic of $10,000 to Jack, its 60% shareholder, for $8,000. In July, Jack sold the land to an unrelated party for $11,000. What is the amount of Jack's recognized gain?

A. $0

B. $1,000

C. $2,000

D. $3,000

Answer (B) is correct.
REQUIRED: The amount of recognized gain when property is sold after acquisition from a related party in a loss transaction.
DISCUSSION: Under Sec. 267, losses are not allowed on sales or exchanges of property between related parties. Related parties include an individual and a corporation in which the individual owns more than 50% of the outstanding stock. Automatic, Inc., realized a $2,000 loss ($10,000 basis – $8,000 sales price to Jack) on the sale but may not deduct it. On the subsequent sale, Jack realized a $3,000 gain ($11,000 sales price – $8,000 basis). However, he recognizes only a $1,000 capital gain [Sec. 267(d)]. The disallowed loss is used to offset the subsequent gain on the sale of the property ($3,000 realized gain – $2,000 disallowed loss).
   Answer (A) is incorrect. Jack must recognize a $1,000 capital gain. **Answer (C) is incorrect.** Jack's recognized gain is only $1,000. **Answer (D) is incorrect.** The disallowed loss offsets the realized gain.

6. Mark owned 100% of the stock in Gathers Corporation. In 2020, Gathers Corporation sold a computer with an adjusted basis of $5,000 and a fair market value of $8,000 to Mark's Uncle Seth for $4,000. What is the amount of Gathers Corporation's deductible loss on the sale of this computer in 2020?

A. $(4,000)

B. $(3,000)

C. $(1,000)

D. $0

Answer (C) is correct.
REQUIRED: Realization of losses from sales with related parties.
DISCUSSION: Tax laws limit tax avoidance between related parties. Losses realized on sale or exchange of property to a related person is not recognized. The transferee takes a cost basis. Uncles, however, are not considered related parties for federal income tax purposes. Gathers may recognize a loss on the sale of $1,000 ($4,000 selling price – $5,000 basis).
   Answer (A) is incorrect. Gathers cannot subtract the selling price from the FMV to arrive at the recognizable loss. **Answer (B) is incorrect.** Gathers cannot subtract the adjusted basis from the FMV to arrive at the recognizable loss. **Answer (D) is incorrect.** Mark's Uncle Seth is not a related party for federal income tax purposes. Therefore, Gathers is allowed to recognize a loss on this transaction.

7. Mr. Smith decided to retire from his business in 2020. Included in his assets was a large delivery truck for which he had paid $35,000 in 2016. Mr. Smith had offers to buy his truck for $25,000 from two local truck dealers. He decided instead to sell his truck for $15,000 to his long-time employee, John Pine, as partial compensation for John's helping Mr. Smith wind up his business. What is John's basis in the truck?

A. $35,000.

B. $25,000.

C. $15,000.

D. None of the answers are correct.

Answer (B) is correct.
REQUIRED: The amount of basis in an employee bargain purchase.
DISCUSSION: If an employer transfers property to an employee at less than its fair market value, whether or not the transfer is in the form of a sale or exchange, the difference may be income to the purchaser as compensation for personal services (Reg. Sec. 1.61-2). The basis of the property will be the amount paid increased by the amount previously included in income. John will recognize $10,000 ($25,000 FMV – $15,000 paid) of income on the employee bargain purchase. His basis will be $25,000 ($15,000 cash paid + $10,000 income recognized).
   Answer (A) is incorrect. The original basis of the truck is not carried over in an employee bargain purchase. **Answer (C) is incorrect.** The basis is the amount paid plus the amount of previously recognized income on the purchase. **Answer (D) is incorrect.** John's basis in the truck is $25,000.

10.2 Business Property

8. Allen purchased a trademark on January 1 of last year for $150,000 and began amortizing it over the required 15-year period. On January 2 of this year, Allen sold the trademark for $200,000. How much of Allen's gain on the sale of the trademark is Sec. 1245 gain?

A. $5,000

B. $10,000

C. $50,000

D. $60,000

Answer (B) is correct.
    REQUIRED: The amount of Sec. 1245 gain.
    DISCUSSION: Under Sec. 197, a trademark is an intangible asset that is amortizable over a 15-year period, beginning in the month of acquisition. Total amortization for the period January 1 of last year through January 2 of this year equals $10,000 ($150,000 ÷ 15). Allen's realized gain is $60,000 [$200,000 sales price – ($150,000 cost – $10,000 amortization)]. Section 1245 requires the gain to be recognized as ordinary income to the extent of the amortization taken. Therefore, $10,000 of the $60,000 gain is Sec. 1245 gain [Sec. 1245(a)(3)].
    Answer (A) is incorrect. A trademark is amortized on a straight-line method over a 15-year period.
Answer (C) is incorrect. Section 1245 gain is recognized only to the extent of the amortization taken. **Answer (D) is incorrect.** Section 1245 gain is recognized only to the extent of the amortization taken.

9. In July, Tommy Tromboni sold for $10,000 a printing press used in his business that originally cost him $10,000. His adjusted basis at the time of the sale was $1,000, and Tommy paid $1,000 in selling expenses. What is the amount of the gain that would be ordinary income under Sec. 1245?

A. $0

B. $8,000

C. $9,000

D. $10,000

Answer (B) is correct.
    REQUIRED: The amount of gain classified as ordinary income under Sec. 1245.
    DISCUSSION: Under Sec. 1001, the gain realized and recognized on the sale of property is the excess of the amount realized over its adjusted basis. Selling expenses also reduce the gain recognized. Thus, Tommy recognizes

Money received	$10,000
Less: Adjusted basis of printing press	(1,000)
Selling expenses	(1,000)
Realized and recognized gain	$ 8,000

Section 1245 requires the recapture of ordinary income up to the amount of depreciation taken. Thus, the full $8,000 recognized gain must be recaptured as ordinary income since $9,000 of depreciation expense was incurred ($10,000 original basis – $1,000 ending basis).
    Answer (A) is incorrect. A portion of the recognized gain is classified as ordinary income. **Answer (C) is incorrect.** Selling expenses and the adjusted basis both reduce the amount realized. **Answer (D) is incorrect.** Selling expenses and the adjusted basis both reduce the amount realized.

10. Which of the following assets will NOT qualify for gain or loss treatment under Sec. 1231?

   A. Factory machine acquired March 1, 2019; sold August 1, 2020.

   B. Land used as a parking lot acquired August 1, 2019; sold September 1, 2020.

   C. Sculpture acquired August 1, 2019, by an investor for the purpose of making a profit on it; destroyed in a fire on September 1, 2020.

   D. Personal automobile acquired August 1, 2019; destroyed in a collision on September 1, 2020.

Answer (D) is correct.
   REQUIRED: The asset that is not Sec. 1231 property.
   DISCUSSION: Section 1231 property is depreciable or real property used in a trade or business and held for more than 1 year or an involuntarily converted nonpersonal capital asset (i.e., held in connection with a trade or business or a transaction entered into for profit) held for more than 1 year. The personal automobile is a personal-use capital asset and does not qualify for treatment under Sec. 1231.

---

11. If the fair market value of Sec. 1245 property is greater than its basis, which of the following transactions will give rise to Sec. 1245 income?

   A. Disposition at death.

   B. Disposition by gift.

   C. A Sec. 351 exchange with a newly formed corporation for all of its stock.

   D. None of the answers are correct.

Answer (D) is correct.
   REQUIRED: The transaction to which Sec. 1245 applies.
   DISCUSSION: The general rule of Sec. 1245(a) is that it applies notwithstanding any other section of the Code.
   Answer (A) is incorrect. Section 1245(b) provides that it will not apply to dispositions by death. **Answer (B) is incorrect.** Section 1245(b) provides that it will not apply to dispositions by gift. **Answer (C) is incorrect.** Section 1245(b) provides that depreciation will be recaptured on a Sec. 351 exchange only to the extent that gain is recognized under Sec. 351. Generally, no gain is recognized upon the transfer of assets to a new corporation solely for stock.

---

12. The Quick Torch Insurance Agency owns the land and building in which its offices are located. The agency also owns its office furniture, company cars, office equipment, and client files. Which of the following is NOT Sec. 1245 property?

   A. The office equipment.

   B. The office furniture.

   C. The company cars.

   D. The client files.

Answer (D) is correct.
   REQUIRED: The asset that is not Sec. 1245 property.
   DISCUSSION: Section 1245 property includes property depreciable under Sec. 167, which is either personal property or specified real property, and most recovery property under Sec. 168. Client files are not Sec. 1245 property because they are neither depreciable nor recovery property.
   Answer (A) is incorrect. Office equipment used in a trade or business is Sec. 1245 property. **Answer (B) is incorrect.** Office furniture used in a trade or business is Sec. 1245 property. **Answer (C) is incorrect.** Company cars used in a trade or business are Sec. 1245 property.

13. You purchased a heating, ventilating, and air conditioning (HVAC) unit for your rental property on December 15. It was delivered on December 28 and was installed and ready for use on January 2. When should the HVAC unit be considered placed in service?

A. December 15.

B. December 28.

C. December 31.

D. January 2.

Answer (D) is correct.
    REQUIRED: The date a depreciable business asset is placed in service.
    DISCUSSION: Publication 946 states, "You place property in service when it is ready and available for a specific use, whether in a business activity, an income-producing activity, a tax-exempt activity, or a personal activity."

14. Mary Brown purchased an apartment building on January 1, 1986, for $200,000. The building was depreciated using the straight-line method. On December 31 of the current year, the building was sold for $210,000 when the asset basis net of accumulated depreciation was $140,000. On her current-year tax return, Brown should report

A. Section 1231 gain of $70,000.

B. Ordinary income of $70,000.

C. Section 1231 gain of $60,000 and ordinary income of $10,000.

D. Section 1231 gain of $10,000 and ordinary income of $60,000.

Answer (A) is correct.
    REQUIRED: The amount and character of gain that must be recognized.
    DISCUSSION: When depreciable property used in a trade or business is sold by a noncorporate owner at a gain, first Sec. 1245 and Sec. 1250 are applied; then the balance of the gain not recaptured as ordinary income is Sec. 1231 gain. In this case, Sec. 1245 does not apply (the building is residential rental property acquired before 1987), and Sec. 1250 recapture is limited to the excess of accelerated depreciation taken by the taxpayer over straight-line depreciation. Since the building was depreciated on the straight-line method, the entire $70,000 gain ($210,000 sales price – $140,000 asset basis) is Sec. 1231 gain. In addition, the straight-line depreciation of $60,000 ($200,000 purchase price – $140,000 basis net of accumulated depreciation) is unrecaptured Sec. 1250 gain and is taxed at the capital gains rate of 25% as opposed to the lower capital gain rates for the other $10,000 LTCG.

15. A gain on the disposition of Sec. 1245 property is treated as ordinary income to the extent of

A. Depreciation allowed or allowable.

B. Excess of the accelerated depreciation allowed or allowable over the depreciation figured for the same period using the straight-line method.

C. Excess of the appreciated value over depreciation allowed or allowable using the straight-line method.

D. The difference between the amount realized over the cost of the property.

Answer (A) is correct.
    REQUIRED: The maximum amount of gain on the disposition of Sec. 1245 property that can be characterized as ordinary income.
    DISCUSSION: A gain on the disposition of Sec. 1245 property is treated as ordinary income to the extent of the total amount of depreciation allowed or allowable. The recaptured gain cannot exceed the amount of the realized gain.
    Answer (B) is incorrect. The method of depreciation used makes no difference in the calculation of ordinary income. Answer (C) is incorrect. The excess of the appreciated value over depreciation allowed under any method receives Sec. 1231 treatment. Answer (D) is incorrect. The amount realized in excess of the asset's original cost is Sec. 1231 gain.

10.3 Installment Sales

16. Arlene sold property with an adjusted basis of $35,000 to Sandy for $50,000. Sandy paid cash of $5,000 and assumed an existing mortgage of $20,000. Sandy signed an installment note for the $25,000 balance at 8% interest. Payments on the note were to be made at the rate of $5,000 a year plus interest beginning 1 year after the date of the contract. Arlene did not elect out of the installment method. What is the amount of gain that Arlene should include in the first year after the date of the contract?

A. $5,000

B. $2,500

C. $1,500

D. $4,500

Answer (B) is correct.
REQUIRED: The amount of gain a taxpayer should include in the first year of an installment sales contract.
DISCUSSION: The installment method is a special method of reporting gains (not losses) from sales of property for which at least one payment is received in a tax year after the year of sale. Under the installment method, gain from an installment sale is prorated and recognized over the years in which payments are received. The amount of gain from an installment sale that is taxable in a given year is calculated by multiplying the payments received in that year by the gross profit ratio for the sale. The gross profit ratio is equal to the anticipated gross profit divided by the total contract price. The gross profit is equal to the selling price of the property minus its adjusted basis. The total contract price is equal to the selling price minus that portion of qualifying indebtedness assumed by, or taken subject to, the buyer that does not exceed the seller's basis in the property (adjusted to reflect commissions and other selling expenses). Arlene realized a $15,000 gain ($50,000 sale price – $35,000 adjusted basis) on the sale, and this amount serves as the anticipated gross profit in the gross profit ratio. The total contract price is $30,000 ($50,000 selling price – $20,000 mortgage assumed by buyer). Accordingly, the gross profit ratio is 50% ($15,000 gain on the sale ÷ $30,000 contract price), and a $2,500 gain is recognized ($5,000 payment × 50%).
Answer (A) is incorrect. A portion of the payment constitutes a return of capital. Answer (C) is incorrect. The gross profit ratio is not 30%. Answer (D) is incorrect. Interest on the outstanding debt is not added to the amount of gain recognized.

17. Mildred and John purchased 40 acres of undeveloped land 40 years ago for $120,000. They paid personal real estate taxes of $50,000, which they elected to add to the property's basis. They sold the property for $600,000, having total settlement costs of $70,000. The settlement costs are allowable as an expense of sale. Mildred and John received a down payment of $100,000 with the balance to be paid over 15 years. What is their gross profit percentage?

A. 60%

B. 72%

C. 68.33%

D. 82%

Answer (A) is correct.
REQUIRED: The gross profit percentage.
DISCUSSION: The gross profit percentage is the ratio of the gross profit to the total contract price. The gross profit is the sales price reduced by any selling expenses and adjusted basis ($600,000 sales price – $70,000 selling expenses – $170,000 adjusted basis = $360,000 gross profit). The total contract price is the amount that will be collected, $600,000. The gross profit percentage is then calculated as follows:

$$\frac{\$360,000 \text{ gross profit}}{\$600,000 \text{ contract price}} = .60 \text{ or } 60\%$$

Answer (B) is incorrect. The $100,000 down payment is not taken into consideration when calculating the gross profit percentage. Answer (C) is incorrect. The $50,000 of real estate taxes must be added back to the basis of the property. Answer (D) is incorrect. The real estate taxes must be added back to the basis of the property, and the $70,000 settlement costs should be subtracted from the selling price when calculating the gross profit percentage.

18. Mr. Pickle purchased property from Mr. Apple by assuming an existing mortgage of $12,000 and agreeing to pay an additional $6,000, plus interest, over the next 3 years. Mr. Apple had an adjusted basis of $8,800 in the building and paid selling expenses totaling $1,200. What were the sales price and the contract price in this transaction?

	Sales Price	Contract Price
A.	$6,000	$12,000
B.	$18,000	$9,200
C.	$18,000	$8,000
D.	$18,000	$6,000

Answer (C) is correct.
REQUIRED: The sales price and contract price in an installment sale transaction.
DISCUSSION: The sales price includes any cash paid, relief of seller's liability by buyer, and any installment note given by the buyer. Here, the sales price is $18,000 ($12,000 relief of liability + $6,000 installment note). The contract price is the total amount the seller will ultimately collect from the buyer. However, if an existing mortgage assumed by the buyer exceeds the adjusted basis of the property, such excess (reduced by selling expenses) is treated as a payment and must be included both in the contract price and in the first year's payment received. The contract price is $8,000 ($6,000 note + $3,200 mortgage in excess of basis – $1,200 selling expenses).
Answer (A) is incorrect. The sales price includes the $12,000 relief of liabilities, and the contract price is not the value of the existing mortgage. **Answer (B) is incorrect.** The contract price is reduced by the selling expenses. **Answer (D) is incorrect.** The contract price is increased by the $3,200 mortgage in excess of basis and reduced by the selling expenses.

19. You sold a residential lot 2 years ago and reported the $20,000 capital gain on the installment method. In the third year of payments, the buyer defaulted and you had to repossess the lot. In the first year you reported $5,000 ($10,000 × 50%) and $3,000 ($6,000 × 50%) in the second year. No payments were received in the third year, and you spent $2,500 in legal fees to repossess the property. What is the taxable gain you must report on the repossession?

A. $0

B. $9,500

C. $8,000

D. $4,000

Answer (C) is correct.
REQUIRED: The amount of taxable gain to be reported for a repossession.
DISCUSSION: If you repossess your property after making an installment sale, you must figure the following amounts: (1) Your gain (or loss) on the repossession and (2) your basis in the repossessed property. The rules for figuring these amounts depend on the kind of property you repossess. The rules for repossessions of personal property differ from those for real property. The taxable gain for the repossession of real property is figured using the following schedule.

1) Payments received before repossession		$16,000
2) Minus: Gain reported		8,000
3) Gain on repossession		$ 8,000
4) Gross profit on sale		$20,000
5) Gain reported (line 2)	$8,000	
6) Plus: Repossession costs	2,500	10,500
7) Subtract line 6 from line 4		$ 9,500
8) Taxable gain (lesser of line 3 or 7)		$ 8,000

Answer (A) is incorrect. A gain exists on the repossession of this property. **Answer (B) is incorrect.** The lesser of the two methods of computing the capital gain must be chosen. **Answer (D) is incorrect.** This property is real property, and the gain must be computed using the schedule for real property.

20. During 2020, Judy sold a pleasure boat that had an adjusted basis to her of $60,000 to Terry for $100,000. Terry paid $20,000 as a down payment and agreed to pay $20,000 per year plus interest for the next 4 years. What is the amount of gain to be included in Judy's gross income for 2020?

A. $8,000

B. $16,000

C. $20,000

D. $24,000

Answer (A) is correct.
REQUIRED: The amount of gain in the year of an installment sale.
DISCUSSION: The amount of gain under Sec. 453 is the proportion of the payments received in the year that the gross profit bears to the total amount the seller will ultimately collect from the buyer. Judy's gross profit is $40,000 ($100,000 sales price – $60,000 adjusted basis). Since $20,000 was received in the year of sale, the gain is $8,000.

$$\frac{\$40,000 \text{ gross profit}}{\$100,000 \text{ contract price}} \times \$20,000 = \$8,000$$

Answer (B) is incorrect. The gross profit is not $80,000. Answer (C) is incorrect. The gain is limited to the gross profit percentage. Answer (D) is incorrect. The gross profit percentage must be used to determine the amount of gain.

21. In Year 1, Ray sold land with a basis of $40,000 for $100,000. He received a $20,000 down payment and the buyer's note for $80,000. In Year 2, he received the first of four annual payments of $20,000 each, plus 12% interest. What is the gain to be reported in Year 2?

A. None.

B. $8,000

C. $12,000

D. $20,000

Answer (C) is correct.
REQUIRED: The amount of gain reported on an installment sale.
DISCUSSION: The transaction qualifies for treatment as an installment sale. The amount of gain under Sec. 453 is the proportion of the payments received in the year that the gross profit bears to the total contract price. The contract price is the total amount the seller will ultimately collect from the buyer. Ray's gross profit is $60,000 ($100,000 sales price – $40,000 adjusted basis). Since $20,000 was received in Year 2, the gain is $12,000.

$$\frac{\$60,000 \text{ gross profit}}{\$100,000 \text{ contract price}} \times \$20,000 = \$12,000$$

Answer (A) is incorrect. A gain must be reported on the sale. Answer (B) is incorrect. It is the amount of the payment that is considered a return of capital. Answer (D) is incorrect. Only the portion that is not a return of capital must be reported as a gain. This portion is determined by calculating the gross profit percentage.

22. Jim and Jean purchased a vacation home in 2013 for $100,000. They sold the property for $500,000 in 2020 and received a down payment of $200,000. They took a mortgage from the purchaser for the remaining $300,000. What is Jim and Jean's gross profit percentage on this sale?

A. 40%.

B. 60%.

C. 80%.

D. None of the answers are correct.

Answer (C) is correct.
REQUIRED: The calculation of the gross profit percentage.
DISCUSSION: The gross profit percent is the difference between the price the property was sold for and the price the property was purchased at, divided by the price for which the property was sold, multiplied by 100. The gross profit percent for Jim and Jean is calculated below.

$$\frac{\$500,000 - \$100,000}{\$500,000} \times 100 = 80\%$$

SU 10. Related Parties, Business Property, and Installment Sales

23. Dennis and Martha sell their lake house (which they have owned for 10 years and spend each summer in) for $250,000. Their original cost was $175,000, and they had improvements of $25,000. They have never used the house as a business or rental property. They agreed to take $50,000 down and finance the balance. Monthly payments are to begin next year. How much capital gain must they report in the year of sale?

A. $10,000

B. $50,000

C. $15,000

D. $0

Answer (A) is correct.
REQUIRED: The amount of capital gain to be reported.
DISCUSSION: The amount of gain under Sec. 453 is the proportion of the payments received in the year that the gross profit bears the total amount to the seller. Gross profit, $50,000, is found by subtracting the adjusted basis, $200,000 ($175,000 original cost + $25,000 improvements) from the sales price, $250,000. Next, the gross profit percentage, 20%, is found by dividing the gross profit, $50,000, by the sales price ($250,000). The capital gain is found by multiplying the gross profit percentage, 20%, by the down payment, $50,000. The capital gain is $10,000.
Answer (B) is incorrect. The amount of $50,000 is the gross profit, not the reported capital gain. **Answer (C) is incorrect.** The capital gain is the gross profit percentage multiplied by the gross profit. **Answer (D) is incorrect.** There is a capital gain which must be reported when the gross profit can be foreseen by the seller.

24. Ethel and George sold an investment property they purchased 10 years ago for $300,000. The property was sold for $700,000 with a down payment of $140,000. What is the gross profit percentage?

A. 57.14%.

B. 22.86%.

C. 28.57%.

D. None of the answers are correct.

Answer (A) is correct.
REQUIRED: The amount of gross profit percentage.
DISCUSSION: The amount of gain under Sec. 453 is the proportion of the payments received in the year that the gross profit bears to the total contract price. The contract price is the total amount the seller will ultimately collect from the buyer (Publication 537). Ethel and George's gross profit is $400,000 ($700,000 sales price – $300,000 adjusted basis). Therefore, their gross profit percentage is 57.14% ($400,000 ÷ $700,000).
Answer (B) is incorrect. A 22.86% gross profit is found by dividing $160,000 by $700,000. **Answer (C) is incorrect.** A 28.57% gross profit is found by dividing $200,000 by $700,000. **Answer (D) is incorrect.** The correct gross profit percentage is 57.14%.

25. In an installment sale, if the buyer assumes a mortgage that is greater than the installment sale basis of the property sold,

A. There is never a profit or a loss.

B. The transaction is disqualified as an installment sale.

C. The gross profit percentage is always 100%.

D. The gain is treated as short-term capital gain.

Answer (C) is correct.
REQUIRED: The statement that applies when a buyer assumes a mortgage greater than the installment sale basis of the property sold.
DISCUSSION: In an installment sale when the buyer assumes a mortgage that is greater than the basis of the asset, the seller is required to recognize the excess mortgage as a payment in year of sale and also increase the contract price by the amount of the excess. If the contract price was not increased, the gross profit percentage would be greater than 100%. The amount of increase in the contract price will make the contract price equal to the gross profit, thus giving a gross profit percentage of 100%.
Answer (A) is incorrect. The installment sale may give rise to a profit or loss. **Answer (B) is incorrect.** The presented circumstance does not prevent the sale from qualifying as an installment sale. **Answer (D) is incorrect.** Any gain realized from a disposal of recaptured property in an installment sale is characterized as ordinary income by Secs. 1245 and 1250.

26. Cheryl sold a boat, which had cost her $3,600, for $6,000. The boat was not used in a trade or business or held for rent. Cheryl accepted a $1,800 down payment and an installment obligation calling for 30 monthly payments of $140, plus interest. After receiving 8 months' payments, Cheryl sold the installment obligation for $2,500. What was Cheryl's gain or loss on the disposition of the installment obligation?

A. $820

B. $(420)

C. $2,192

D. $652

Answer (D) is correct.
REQUIRED: The income recognized on the disposition of an installment obligation.
DISCUSSION: Section 453B provides that, when an installment obligation is disposed of, gain or loss is recognized to the extent of the difference between the basis of the obligation and the amount realized (or the fair market value of the obligation if disposed of other than by sale or exchange). The adjusted basis of the obligation is equal to the face amount of the obligation reduced by the gross profit that would be realized if the holder collected the face amount [Sec. 453B(b)]. The face amount is $3,080 [($140 × 30) – ($140 × 8)]. The basis is $1,848 [$3,080 face amount × (100% – 40% gross profit percentage)].
Since Cheryl sold the installment obligation, the excess of the amount realized over Cheryl's basis in the obligation is recognized as income on the transfer. This amount of income is $652 ($2,500 amount realized – $1,848 basis). The gain is treated as resulting from the sale or exchange of the property in respect of which the installment obligation was originally held.

27. In 2011, Sally sold a personal residence on the installment method. She needed cash in 2020, so she sold the note for $7,500 when the balance due her was $9,000. Her gross profit percentage was 47.5%. How much profit must Sally report on the disposition of the obligation?

A. $2,775

B. $7,500

C. $0

D. $3,225

Answer (A) is correct.
REQUIRED: The amount of profit recognized on the disposition of an installment obligation.
DISCUSSION: The balance due to Sally was $9,000. The basis of the receivable is $4,725 [$9,000 × (1 – 47.5%)]. The amount realized is $7,500, and therefore Sally recognizes a profit of $2,775 ($7,500 – $4,725).
Answer (B) is incorrect. The receivable has a basis of $4,725. Answer (C) is incorrect. The amount realized exceeds the basis of the receivable by $2,775. Answer (D) is incorrect. The basis of the receivable is 52.5% of $9,000, not 47.5%.

28. Each of the following situations would be considered a disposition of an installment obligation EXCEPT

A. An installment obligation that you give as a gift.

B. An installment obligation for which you accept part payment on the balance of the buyer's installment debt to you and forgive the rest of the debt.

C. An installment obligation assumed by a new buyer at a rate of interest higher than the rate paid by the original buyer.

D. An installment obligation that has become unenforceable.

Answer (C) is correct.
REQUIRED: The situation that is not considered a disposition of an installment obligation.
DISCUSSION: Section 453B provides that, when an installment obligation is disposed of, gain or loss is recognized to the extent of the difference between the basis of the obligation and the amount realized (or the fair market value of the obligation if disposed of other than by sale or exchange). The main purpose of Sec. 453B is to prevent the shifting of income between taxpayers. Section 453B(a) expressly requires recognition whether the obligation is sold or otherwise disposed of. An installment obligation assumed by a new buyer does not cause a shift in income and is therefore not a disposition of an installment obligation.
Answer (A) is incorrect. The transfer of an installment obligation by gift is treated as a disposition. Answer (B) is incorrect. The cancellation of an installment obligation is treated as a disposition. Answer (D) is incorrect. An unenforceable installment obligation is treated as a disposition.

29. With respect to the disposition of an installment obligation, which of the following is false?

A. No gain or loss is recognized on the transfer of an installment obligation between a husband and wife if incident to a divorce.

B. If the obligation is sold, the gain or loss is the difference between the basis in the obligation and the amount realized.

C. A gift of an installment obligation is considered a disposition.

D. If an installment obligation is canceled, it is not treated as a disposition.

Answer (D) is correct.
    REQUIRED: The false statement with respect to the disposition of an installment obligation.
    DISCUSSION: Section 453B provides that, when an installment obligation is disposed of, gain or loss is recognized to the extent of the difference between the basis of the obligation and the amount realized (or the fair market value of the obligation if disposed of other than by sale or exchange). The main purpose of Sec. 453B is to prevent the shifting of income between taxpayers. Section 453B(a) expressly requires recognition whether the obligation is sold or otherwise disposed of. Cancellation of an installment obligation is a disposition of the obligation.
    Answer (A) is incorrect. Section 453B(g) excludes from the definition of a disposition a transfer between husband and wife incident to a divorce. The same tax treatment with respect to the obligation that would have applied to the transferor then applies to the transferee.
    Answer (B) is incorrect. The gain or loss on sale of an installment obligation is the difference between the amount realized and the basis in the obligation.
    Answer (C) is incorrect. A gift is a disposition for purposes of Sec. 453B.

30. The owner of unimproved land with a basis of $40,000 sold the property for $100,000 in 2015. The seller accepted a note for the entire $100,000 sales price. In 2020, when the buyer still owed $10,000, the note was sold for $9,000 cash. How should the disposition of the note be reported on the seller's 2020 return?

A. $5,000 capital gain.

B. $5,000 ordinary income.

C. $2,000 capital gain.

D. $1,000 capital loss.

Answer (A) is correct.
    REQUIRED: The amount and character of income to be reported from the disposition of a note.
    DISCUSSION: Section 453B provides that, when an installment obligation is disposed of, gain or loss is recognized to the extent of the difference between the basis of the obligation and the amount realized (or the fair market value of the obligation if disposed of other than by sale or exchange). The adjusted basis of the obligation is equal to the face amount of the obligation reduced by the gross profit that would be realized if the holder collected the face amount [Sec. 453B(b)]. The basis is $4,000 [$10,000 face amount × (100% − 60% gross profit percentage)]. Since the seller sold the installment obligation, the excess of the amount realized over the seller's basis in the obligation is recognized as income on the transfer. This amount of income is $5,000 ($9,000 amount realized − $4,000 basis). The gain is treated as resulting from the sale or exchange of the property in respect of which the installment obligation was originally held. If the original sale resulted in a capital gain or loss, the disposition of the obligation will result in a capital gain or loss.
    Answer (B) is incorrect. If the original sale resulted in a capital gain or loss, the disposition of the obligation will result in a capital gain or loss. The original sale of land resulted in a capital gain. **Answer (C) is incorrect.** The gain is the excess sale price over the basis. The basis is the face amount multiplied by the basis percentage of the original note. **Answer (D) is incorrect.** A gain based on the sale price of the note in excess of the basis is reported.

STUDY UNIT ELEVEN

NONRECOGNITION PROPERTY TRANSACTIONS

(8 pages of outline)

Generally, a taxpayer recognizes a gain when the fair market value of the property received is greater than the adjusted basis of the property given up. This study unit deals with situations in which there may be nonrecognition of the gain or loss. This nonrecognition can be temporary, as in the deferral of gain on a like-kind exchange of real property, or it can be permanent, as in the exclusion of the gain on a sale of a principal residence.

11.1 SALE OF A PRINCIPAL RESIDENCE

Section 121 provides an exclusion upon the sale of a principal residence. No loss may be recognized on the sale of a personal residence.

Ownership and Occupancy

1. The exclusion is available if the individual owned and occupied the residence for an aggregate of at least 2 of the 5 years before the sale.

2. Nonqualified use after 2008 requires the gain to be reduced for the period of nonqualified use.

3. The exclusion may be used only once every 2 years.

Exclusion Amount

4. A taxpayer may exclude up to $250,000 ($500,000 for married taxpayers filing jointly) of realized gain on the sale of a principal residence.

    a. The exclusion is increased to $500,000 for married individuals filing jointly if

        1) Either spouse meets the ownership test,

        2) Both spouses meet the use test, and

        3) Neither spouse is ineligible for the exclusion by virtue of a sale or an exchange of a residence within the last 2 years.

    b. A surviving spouse can qualify for the $500,000 exclusion if the residence is sold within 2 years of the other spouse's death.

5. The exclusion is determined on an individual basis. Therefore, for married couples who do not share a principal residence but file joint returns, a $250,000 exclusion is available for a qualifying sale or exchange of each spouse's principal residence.

6. If a single individual eligible for the exclusion marries a person who used the exclusion within 2 years before marriage, the individual is entitled to a $250,000 exclusion. Even though the individual's spouse used the exclusion within the past 2 years, an individual may not be prevented from claiming the $250,000 exclusion.

Divorce Transfer

7. If a residence is transferred to a taxpayer incident to a divorce, the time during which the taxpayer's spouse or former spouse owned the residence is added to the taxpayer's period of ownership.

    a. A taxpayer who owns a residence is deemed to use it as a principal residence while the taxpayer's spouse or former spouse is given use of the residence under the terms of a divorce or separation.

Widowed Taxpayer

8. A widowed taxpayer's period of ownership of residence includes the period during which the taxpayer's deceased spouse owned the residence.

Physically or Mentally Incapable Individuals

9. If an individual becomes physically or mentally incapable of self-care, the individual is deemed to use a residence as a principal residence during the time in which the individual owns the residence and resides in a licensed care facility.

    a. The individual must have owned and used the residence as a principal residence for an aggregate period of at least 1 year during the 5 years preceding the sale or exchange.

Prorating the Exclusion

10. The exclusion amount may be prorated if the use, ownership, or prior sale tests are not met.

    a. The exclusion is based on the ratio of months used to 24 months and is a proportion of the total exclusion.

    b. The pro rata exclusion is allowed only if the sale is due to a change in place of employment, health, or unforeseen circumstances.

EXAMPLE 11-1	Prorating the Section 121 Exclusion

A taxpayer purchased and moved into a house. Then, 18 months later, he sold the residence because of a change of job location. He must prorate any gain exclusion by 18/24, the number of months used as a principal residence to 24 months.

Nonqualified Use

11. The exclusion on the sale of the residence must be prorated between qualified and nonqualified use.

    a. Nonqualified use includes periods that the residence was not used as the principal residence of the taxpayer, prior to the last day the homeowner lived in the house.

EXAMPLE 11-2	Nonqualified Use Reduction of the Section 121 Exclusion

During the 5 years prior to the sale of the house, the taxpayer lived in the house for Years 1, 2, and 4. The absence during the third year is nonqualified use, causing a reduction (prorated based on 1 year of nonqualified use) in the allowed exclusion. The absence during the fifth year does not affect the allowed exclusion since the taxpayer did not return to live in the house prior to the sale. Therefore, only $200,000 of the $250,000 exclusion is available ($250,000 × 4/5).

    b. Nonqualified use does not include use before 2009.

    c. Members of the military are allowed up to a 10-year suspension of the 5-year test period for extended duty away from home. Together this gives a 15-year test period.

Principal Residence Requirement

12. Section 121 excludes realized gain on the sale of a principal residence only. Therefore, gain may need to be recognized on the portion of the property that is not considered a personal residence (e.g., use of a guest facility as rental property).

    a. The portion of the principal residence that is business-use property (e.g., a home office for the taxpayer's business and not as an employee) may not qualify for gain exclusion.

        1) If the business-use property is within the taxpayer's home, such as a room used as a home office for a business, the part of any gain equal to any depreciation allowed or allowable after May 6, 1997, is included in income.

        2) If the business-use property is a separate part of the property (e.g., a rental suite not attached to the principal residence, a working farm on which the house was located, etc.), the basis of the property and the amount realized upon its sale must be allocated between the business rental part and the part used as a home. Any gain associated with the business-use property is not eligible for the principal residence exclusion and must be reported on Form 4797.

    b. Realized gain may qualify for exclusion even though the entire property is used as rental property or business-use property at the time of sale.

        1) For example, the entire property is subject to gain exclusion as long as the individual owned and occupied the entire residence (as a principal residence) for an aggregate of at least 2 of the 5 years before the sale (as noted in item 1. on page 325). The full exclusion amount would be reduced by the nonqualified use.

    c. Deductions (other than depreciation) that relate solely to the rental or business-use portion of the property do not reduce the basis of the principal residence portion.

    d. Any selling expenses incurred in selling the personal residence reduce the amount realized by the seller.

    e. Any gain equal to depreciation allowed or allowable may not be excluded.

    f. Any capital improvements made to the personal residence are added to the adjusted basis of the house.

    g. Any amount of gain not excludable is reported on Schedule D, *Capital Gains*.

Basis

13. Basis in a new home is its cost.

Like-Kind Exchange

14. If the residence was acquired in a Sec. 1031 like-kind exchange in which any gain was not recognized in the prior 5 years, then the Sec. 121 exclusion for gain on sale or exchange of a principal residence does not apply.

Reporting

15. If the amount of the realized gain is less than the maximum exclusion amount, the gain need not be reported on the individual's income tax return.

Stop and Review! **You have completed the outline for this subunit. Study multiple-choice questions 1 through 15 beginning on page 333.**

11.2 LIKE-KIND EXCHANGES

NOTE: The following outline is duplicated in EA Part 2, Study Unit 6, Subunit 3.

Section 1031 defers recognizing gain or loss to the extent that **real** property productively used in a trade or business or held for the production of income (investment) is exchanged (commonly referred to as relinquished) for property of like-kind. Realized gain (loss) is the gain (loss) from the sale or exchange. Recognized gain (loss) is the amount reported on the tax return.

Like-Kind Property

1. Only real property qualifies for like-kind treatment for transfers after 2017. Like-kind real property is alike in nature or character but not necessarily in grade or quality.

   a. Properties are of like kind if each is within a class of like nature or character, without regard to differences in use (e.g., business or investment), improvements (e.g., bare land or house), location (e.g., city or rural), or proximity.

      1) A real estate lease that runs 30 years or more is treated as real property, and the exchange of it for other real estate qualifies under Sec. 1031 as long as the parties to the exchange are not dealers in real estate.

   b. Real property located within the United States is like-kind with all other real property in the U.S. Foreign real estate is like-kind with other foreign real estate. But, U.S. real estate and foreign real estate are not like-kind.

Boot

2. Boot is all nonqualified property transferred in an exchange transaction.

   a. Gain is recognized equal to the lesser of gain realized or boot received.
   b. Boot received includes cash, net liability relief, and other nonqualified property (its FMV).

EXAMPLE 11-3   Like-Kind Exchange with Boot

Scott owned a parcel of real estate that he was holding for investment. It had an adjusted basis of $50,000. Scott exchanged the real estate for a piece of land with a fair market value of $60,000, a boat for personal use that had a fair market value of $3,000, and $2,000 cash. Scott's basis in the land received is equal to the adjusted basis of the real estate transferred ($50,000), less the boot received of the boat ($3,000) and the cash ($2,000), plus the gain recognized on the transaction. Gain is recognized to the extent of boot received. Here, the boat and the cash are boot; therefore, a gain of $5,000 must be recognized. This recognized gain increases basis of the land to $50,000.

EXAMPLE 11-4   Like-Kind Exchange

Real property with an adjusted basis of $50,000 is exchanged for $20,000 cash and like-kind property with a FMV of $40,000. The recognized gain is $10,000 ($40,000 + $20,000 – $50,000), the lesser of the gain realized ($10,000) and the boot received ($20,000).

EXAMPLE 11-5   Like-Kind Qualified Property

Alan exchanged real property with a basis of $60,000 plus $5,000 cash for like-kind property with a FMV of $63,000. Alan's $2,000 loss [$63,000 – ($60,000 + $5,000)] is not deductible.

Liabilities

3. Liabilities are treated as money paid or received.

   a. If each party assumes a liability of the other, only the net liability given or received is treated as boot.

   b. Liabilities include mortgages on property.

Basis

4. Qualified property received in a like-kind exchange has an exchanged basis adjusted for boot and gain recognized.

    AB of property given
    + Gain recognized
    + Boot given (cash, liability incurred, other property)
    − Boot received (cash, liability relief, other property) + Exchange fees incurred
    − Loss recognized (boot given)
    _____
    = Basis in acquired property

NOTE: The IRS has ruled that exchange expenses can be deducted to compute gain or loss realized, offset against cash payments received in determining recognized gain, or included in the basis of the property received.

Realized Gain

5. Under Sec. 1031, realized gain is usually recognized only to the extent of boot received (Cash + FMV of other property + Net liability relief).

   a. **Section 1245** ordinary income is limited to the sum of the following:

      1) Gain recognized and

      2) FMV of property acquired that is not Sec. 1245 property and is not included in computing the recognized gain.

   b. **Section 1250** ordinary income is limited to the greater of the following:

      1) Recognized gain or

      2) Excess of the potential Sec. 1250 ordinary income over the FMV of Sec. 1250 property received.

   c. Basis in property acquired is increased for gain recognized.

Loss

6. If some qualified property is exchanged, loss realized with respect to qualified property is not recognized, but loss on boot given may be recognized.

Deferred Like-Kind Exchanges

7. If a taxpayer sells property and buys similar property in two mutually dependent transactions, the taxpayer may have to treat the sale and purchase as a single nontaxable exchange.

Qualified Exchange Accommodation Arrangement or Agreement

8. With a qualified exchange accommodation agreement, the property given up or the replacement property is transferred to a qualified intermediary (QI), also referred to as exchange accommodation titleholder (EAT) or facilitator. The QI is considered the beneficial owner of the property.

    a. This arrangement allows a transfer in which a taxpayer acquires replacement property before transferring relinquished property to qualify as a tax-free exchange.

    b. The following requirements must be met:

        1) Time limits for identifying and transferring the property are satisfied.

        2) A written agreement exists.

        3) The exchange accommodation titleholder has the qualified indications of ownership of the property.

Deadlines

    c. An exchange of like-kind real properties must be completed within the earlier of

        1) 180 days after the transfer of the exchanged property or

        2) The due date (including extensions) for the transferor's tax return for the taxable year in which the exchange took place.

    d. The taxpayer has 45 days from the date of the transfer to identify the like-kind real property received in the exchange.

        1) The replacement property must be clearly described in a signed, written document. The document then must be delivered to the other person involved in the exchange.

            a) The identification of multiple replacement real properties is permitted.

                i)   The replacement property must be received within 180 days from the date of transfer.

Exchange Expenses

9. Any exchange expenses are subtracted from the total of the following (but not below zero):

    a. Any cash paid to the taxpayer by the other party;

    b. The FMV of other (not like-kind) property received by the taxpayer, if any; and

    c. Net liabilities assumed by the other party–the excess, if any, of liabilities (including mortgages) assumed by the other party over the total of (1) any liabilities assumed, (2) cash paid by the taxpayer to the other party, and (3) the FMV of the other (not like-kind) property given up by the taxpayer. If the exchange expenses exceed (1), (2), and (3), the excess is added to the basis of the like-kind property.

Related Parties

10. Like-kind exchanges between related parties are subject to special restrictions.

    a. In a related-party exchange, the taxpayer cannot dispose of the property within 2 years after the date of the last transfer which was part of the exchange in order not to recognize any gain on the initial exchange.

    b. Related parties include members of a family, a grantor of a trust, a corporation in which the taxpayer has more than 50% ownership, or a partnership in which the taxpayer directly or indirectly owns more than 50% interest in the capital or profits.

Multiple Parties

    c.   There is no exception in Sec. 1031 that prohibits multiple-party transactions from qualifying as like-kind exchanges.

    d.   The trade of like-kind real property is reported on IRS Form 8824.

Reporting

11. A taxpayer must substantiate the existence of a like-kind exchange.

12. Section 1031 like-kind exchanges are reported annually on Form 8824 and include the following:

    a.   Description of property exchanged
    b.   Dates of acquisition, transfer, property identification, and actual receipt
    c.   Related party exchange information
    d.   Realized gain (loss) and basis in property received

Depreciation

13. Generally, a taxpayer must depreciate MACRS (Modified Accelerated Cost Recovery System) property that was acquired in a like-kind exchange of other MACRS property over the remaining period of the exchanged property and continue to use the same depreciation method.

    a.   Any excess basis of the acquired property is treated as newly purchased separate property.

Holding Period

14. If property received in an exchange has the same basis in whole or in part as that of the property given and if the property given is a capital asset or a Sec. 1231 asset, the holding period of the property received includes the period for which the property given was held.

Like-Kind Exchange Process Flowchart

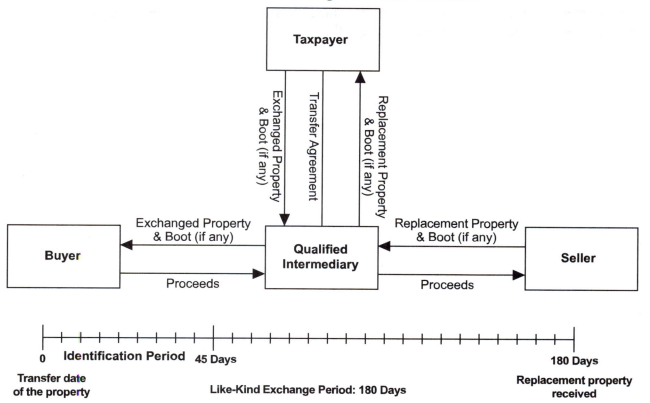

Figure 11-1

Realized Gain or (Loss), Recognized Gain, and Basis of Like-Kind Property Received

Not Like-Kind Property

1. Fair market value (FMV) of other property given up	$XXX,XXX	
2. **Less:** Adjusted basis of other property given up	(XX,XXX)	
3. **Gain or (loss) recognized on other property given up**		**$XX,XXX**

Realized Gain or (Loss)

4. Boot Received: Cash received, FMV of other property received, plus net liabilities assumed by other party, reduced (but not below zero) by any exchange expenses	$ XX,XXX	
5. **Plus:** FMV of acquired like-kind property	XX,XXX	
6. **Less:** Adjusted basis of like-kind property given up, net amounts paid to other party, plus any exchange expenses not used above	(XX,XXX)	
7. **Realized gain or (loss)**		**XX,XXX**

Recognized Gain

8. Lesser of boot received or realized gain or (loss), but not less than zero	$ XX,XXX	
9. **Less:** Ordinary income under recapture rules	(XX,XXX)	
10. Subtract line 9 from line 8 (if zero or less, enter -0-)	X,XXX	
11. **Recognized gain** (add lines 9 and 10)		**XX,XXX**

Deferred Gain or (Loss)

12. Subtract line 11 from line 7 (see related party restrictions on page 330)		**$XX,XXX**

Basis of Acquired Like-Kind Property

13. Subtract line 4 from the sum of lines 6 and 11		**$XX,XXX**

STOP AND REVIEW! **You have completed the outline for this subunit. Study multiple-choice questions 16 through 28 beginning on page 339.**

QUESTIONS

11.1 Sale of a Principal Residence

1. Anne, who is single, owned and used her house as her main home from January 2014 until January 2019. She then moved away and rented her home from February 2019 until she sold it in August 2020. Her home sold for $240,000, which included $20,000 of depreciation and $12,000 of selling expenses. Using a zero basis, compute the amount that is excludable from income.

A. $208,000

B. $220,000

C. $228,000

D. $240,000

Answer (A) is correct.
   REQUIRED: The portion of the gain that may be excluded on the sale of a personal residence that was used as rental property before the sale.
   DISCUSSION: The taxpayer may exclude $250,000 ($500,000 for married taxpayers filing jointly) of a realized gain on the sale of a principal residence. The exclusion is available if the individual owned and occupied the residence for an aggregate of at least 2 of the 5 years before the sale. The gain on sale must be prorated between qualified and nonqualified use. Nonqualified use includes periods that the residence was not used as the principal residence of the taxpayer, prior to the last day the homeowner lived in the house. Since all of Anne's nonqualified use occurred after the last day she lived in the house, there are zero periods of nonqualified use. Any selling expenses incurred reduce the amount realized, therefore Anne's amount realized is $228,000 ($240,000 − $12,000). Also, any gain equal to depreciation allowed or allowable may not be excluded. The amount that is excludable is therefore $208,000 ($228,000 amount realized − $20,000 depreciation).
   Answer (B) is incorrect. The selling expenses must also be deducted to arrive at the amount of the gain that may be excluded from income. **Answer (C) is incorrect.** The depreciation attributable to renting the property must be deducted from the gain to arrive at the excludable portion of the gain. **Answer (D) is incorrect.** The selling expenses and the depreciation attributable to renting the property must be deducted from the gain to arrive at the excludable portion of the gain.

2. Which of the following statements is NOT a requirement that must be met before married taxpayers filing jointly can elect to exclude up to $500,000 of the gain on the sale of a personal residence?

A. Either taxpayer must be age 55 or over at the date of the sale.

B. Either spouse must have owned the home as a principal residence for 2 of the 5 previous years.

C. Both spouses must have used the home as a principal residence for 2 of the 5 previous years.

D. Neither spouse is ineligible for the exclusion by virtue of a sale or exchange of a residence within the last 2 years.

Answer (A) is correct.
   REQUIRED: The statement that is not required for the exclusion of a gain on the sale of a personal residence.
   DISCUSSION: Certain married individuals filing jointly may exclude up to $500,000 on the sale of a principal residence. Married individuals are eligible for a $500,000 exclusion if (1) either spouse owned the home as a principal residence for 2 of the 5 previous years, (2) both spouses used the home as a principal residence for 2 of the 5 previous years, and (3) neither spouse is ineligible for the exclusion by virtue of a sale or an exchange of a residence within the last 2 years. But even if one spouse does not meet the use test, a $250,000 exclusion may still be available for the sale. The age limitation of 55, however, is no longer applicable to the exclusion.

3. Which of following does NOT qualify for exclusion from income of all or part of the gain from the sale of their main home in 2020?

A. You sold a personal residence January 1, 2019, and excluded all the gain. You sold another personal residence December 30, 2020. You did not sell because of health problems or a change in employment.

B. You owned and lived in your house from January 1, 2016, until February 15, 2017, when you moved out and lived with your friend. You moved back into your house July 12, 2018, and then sold it October 20, 2020. The sale was not due to health problems or a change of employment.

C. Betty sells her house (that she had owned and lived in since 2010) in February 2020 and gets married 1 month later. Her husband had excluded the gain on the sale of his residence on his 2019 return.

D. You and your spouse are divorced in 2015, and your spouse is allowed to live in the house until sold. The house sells on July 15, 2020.

Answer (A) is correct.
REQUIRED: The false statement regarding the exclusion of gain recognized on the sale of a principal residence.
DISCUSSION: The exclusion of gain provided by Sec. 121 may be used only once every 2 years.
Answer (B) is incorrect. The exclusion is available if the individual owned and occupied the residence for an aggregate of at least 2 of the 5 years before the sale. Answer (C) is incorrect. If a single individual eligible for the exclusion marries a person who used the exclusion within 2 years before marriage, the individual is entitled to a $250,000 exclusion. Even though the individual's spouse used the exclusion within the past 2 years, an individual may not be prevented from claiming the $250,000 exclusion. Answer (D) is incorrect. If a residence is transferred to a taxpayer incident to a divorce, the time during which the taxpayer's spouse or former spouse owned the residence is added to the taxpayer's period of ownership. Also, a taxpayer who owns a residence is deemed to use it as a principal residence while the taxpayer's spouse or former spouse is given use of the residence under the terms of a divorce or separation.

4. Karen, who is single, paid $150,000 for her residence in January 2016 and lived in it until January 2018. She then moved away and rented her home from February 2018 until she moved back in February 2019. She sold it in August 2020 for $240,000. What amount of gain on the sale of her residence is excludable from income?

A. $250,000

B. $70,380

C. $90,000

D. $240,000

Answer (B) is correct.
REQUIRED: The portion of the gain that may be excluded on the sale of a personal residence.
DISCUSSION: The taxpayer may exclude $250,000 ($500,000 for married taxpayers filing jointly) of a realized gain on the sale of a principal residence. The exclusion is available if the individual owned and occupied the residence for an aggregate of at least 2 of the 5 years before the sale. The exclusion may be used only once every 2 years. The gain on the sale of the residence must be prorated between qualified and nonqualified use. Nonqualified use includes periods that the residence was not used as the principal residence of the taxpayer prior to the last day the homeowner lived in the house. The period when Karen is renting her home is nonqualified use because she moved back in. Karen owned the property for 55 months (January 2016-July 2020), but 12 months is nonqualified use. Thus, the percentage of gain that can be excluded is 78.2% (43 qualified use months ÷ 55 total months). Karen's gain is $90,000 and she can exclude $70,380.
Answer (A) is incorrect. The amount of $250,000 is the maximum amount that may be excluded from the gain on a principal residence by a single individual. Answer (C) is incorrect. The amount of $90,000 does not prorate the gain for nonqualified use. Answer (D) is incorrect. The amount of $240,000 is the amount the principal residence was sold for, not the gain on the principal residence.

5. Steve and Karen, a married couple, purchased a new residence on May 1, 2018. They sold their prior home on July 1, 2019, and realized a gain of $250,000, all of which they excluded. They sold the new home on August 1, 2020, because they wanted to live in a condo. What is the maximum amount of the gain they may exclude in 2020?

A. $0

B. $135,417

C. $270,833

D. $500,000

6. Joe and Jean, a married couple, purchased their primary residence in 1994 for $100,000. While they lived there, they made renovations at a cost of $125,000. They lived there until July 1, 2017. On June 15, 2020, the residence was sold for $800,000. From July 1, 2017, until June 15, 2020, the home was unoccupied. Joe and Jean file a joint return, and they have never excluded a gain from the sale of another home. What is their taxable gain?

A. $575,000

B. $0

C. $75,000

D. $200,000

Answer (A) is correct.
REQUIRED: The maximum amount of gain that may be excluded when a personal residence is sold within 2 years.
DISCUSSION: Since the taxpayers sold another residence within 2 years of the 2020 sale, the exclusion is not allowed.

Answer (C) is correct.
REQUIRED: The maximum taxable gain on sale of a primary residence.
DISCUSSION: Publication 523 states that you can exclude the entire gain on the sale of your main home up to

1. $250,000 or
2. $500,000 if all of the following are true:

  a. You are married and file a joint return for the year.
  b. Either you or your spouse meets the ownership test.
  c. Both you and your spouse meet the use test.
  d. During the 2-year period ending on the date of the sale, neither you nor your spouse excluded gain from the sale of another home.

In addition, Publication 523 states that, in order to claim the exclusion, you must meet the ownership and use tests. This means that, during the 5-year period ending on the date of the sale, you must have

1. Owned the home for at least 2 years (the ownership test) and
2. Lived in the home as your main home for at least 2 years (the use test).

The required 2 years of ownership and use during the 5-year period ending on the date of the sale do not have to be continuous.
You meet the tests if you can show that you owned and lived in the property as your main home for either 24 full months or 730 days (365 × 2) during the 5-year period ending on the date of sale.
The taxpayers have a gain of $575,000, of which $75,000 is taxable after the $500,000 exclusion.
Answer (A) is incorrect. The couple meets the requirements to take the $500,000 exclusion. **Answer (B) is incorrect.** Even after taking the $500,000 exclusion, Joe and Jean have a $75,000 taxable gain. **Answer (D) is incorrect.** The renovations cost of $125,000 should be added to the adjusted basis.

7. Bill purchased a home for his principal residence January 1, 2016. However, from January 1, 2018, to December 31, 2019, another location served as Bill's principal residence. Bill's basis in the home was $300,000, and he sold the home for $600,000 on December 31, 2020. What is Bill's recognized gain on the sale of the home?

A. $150,000

B. $250,000

C. $300,000

D. $50,000

Answer (A) is correct.
    REQUIRED: The recognized gain on the sale of a principal residence not used for 2 consecutive years.
    DISCUSSION: The $250,000 exclusion is available to an individual if (s)he owned and occupied the residence as a principal residence for an aggregate of at least 2 of the 5 years before the sale. The gain on the sale of the principal residence must be prorated between qualified and nonqualified use. Nonqualified use includes periods of time that the residence was not used as the principal residence. The period when Bill uses another location for his principal residence is nonqualified use. Bill's nonqualified use is thus 2 years (January 1, 2018-December 31, 2019). The percentage of the exclusion that can be claimed is 60% (3 years ÷ 5 years). Therefore, Bill can exclude gain of $150,000 ($250,000 × 60%), and his recognized gain is $150,000 ($300,000 gain − $150,000).
    Answer (B) is incorrect. The amount of $250,000 is the maximum exclusion, not the recognized gain. **Answer (C) is incorrect.** The amount of $300,000 is the realized gain. **Answer (D) is incorrect.** The amount of $50,000 does not prorate the gain for nonqualified use.

8. When Amelia bought her first home in 2017, she paid $100,000 plus $1,000 closing costs. In 2018, she added a deck that cost $5,000. Then, in July of 2020, a real estate dealer accepted her house as a trade-in and allowed her $125,000 toward a new house priced at $200,000. How should Amelia report this transaction on her 2020 return?

A. $19,000 long-term capital gain.

B. No reporting because the trade is not a sale.

C. $0 taxable gain and reduce her basis in her new house by $19,000.

D. No reporting required.

Answer (D) is correct.
    REQUIRED: The amount and character of the disposition of a principal residence.
    DISCUSSION: Amelia has a $19,000 [$125,000 trade-in − ($100,000 purchase price + $1,000 closing cost + $5,000 deck)] long-term capital gain on the disposition of her house. However, a taxpayer may exclude up to $250,000 of gain on the sale of a principal residence. The exclusion is available if the individual owned and occupied the residence as a principal residence for an aggregate of at least 2 of the 5 years before the sale.
    Answer (A) is incorrect. Capital gains on the sale of a qualifying principal residence is excludable up to $250,000. **Answer (B) is incorrect.** This transaction is classified as a sale. **Answer (C) is incorrect.** There is no effect on her basis from the sale of her principal residence.

9. Joe had a taxable gain on the sale of his main home, which could not be excluded on his 2020 tax return. He had no business use of the home. Which schedule does he need to submit to report the gain?

A. Schedule C, for sole proprietors.

B. Schedule A, for itemized deductions.

C. Schedule D, for capital gains.

D. Schedule SE, for self-employment income.

Answer (C) is correct.
    REQUIRED: Where to report the gain on sale of principal residence that cannot be excluded.
    DISCUSSION: A personal residence is a capital asset. When the taxpayer cannot exclude a portion or all of the gain from the sale of principal residence, the gain is reported on Schedule D.

10. Pete purchased his home on June 1, 2011. On June 1, 2016, Pete became physically incapable of self-care and entered a licensed care facility. Pete sold the residence on April 15, 2020. Pete was residing in the facility at the time of sale. Pete had purchased the home for $150,000, and he sold the home for $300,000. What is Pete's recognized gain for 2020?

A. $300,000

B. $250,000

C. $150,000

D. $0

Answer (D) is correct.
   REQUIRED: The recognized gain on the sale of a personal residence when the resident enters a licensed care facility.
   DISCUSSION: If an individual becomes physically or mentally incapable of self-care, the individual is deemed to use a residence as a principal residence during the time when the individual owns the residence and resides in a licensed care facility. To apply, the individual must have owned and used the residence as a principal residence for an aggregate period of at least 1 year during the 5 years preceding the sale or exchange. Pete met these requirements, so the gain is excluded.
   Answer (A) is incorrect. The amount of $300,000 is the proceeds from the sale. **Answer (B) is incorrect.** The amount of $250,000 is the maximum amount excluded. **Answer (C) is incorrect.** The amount of $150,000 is the realized gain.

11. Roy and Joyce were single, and each owned a home as a separate principal residence for a number of years. In August 2019, Roy sold his home and had a gain of $130,000, which he entirely excluded. Roy and Joyce were married in October 2020. Joyce then decided to sell her principal residence for a $350,000 realized gain. They plan on filing a joint return for 2020. How much of the gain from the sale of Joyce's home can be excluded on their joint tax return for 2020?

A. $0

B. $100,000

C. $250,000

D. $350,000

Answer (C) is correct.
   REQUIRED: The amount of the exclusion when one spouse does not qualify for the exclusion.
   DISCUSSION: An individual may be able to exclude up to $250,000 of gain on the sale of a personal residence. This exclusion amount is $500,000 for married taxpayers filing jointly if the use and ownership requirements are met and if neither spouse has used the exclusion in the previous 2 years. But even if a single individual marries someone who has used the exclusion within 2 years before marriage, the qualifying individual is not precluded from claiming the $250,000 exclusion to which (s)he is entitled. Thus, Joyce may still claim the exclusion of $250,000 on the joint return and must recognize only $100,000.
   Answer (A) is incorrect. A portion of the gain may be excluded. **Answer (B) is incorrect.** The amount of the gain that may be recognized is $100,000. **Answer (D) is incorrect.** The entire gain may not be excluded.

12. John bought his principal residence for $250,000 on May 3, 2019. He sold it on May 3, 2020, for $400,000. What is the amount and character of his gain?

A. Long-term, ordinary gain of $650,000.

B. Long-term, capital gain of $150,000.

C. Short-term, ordinary gain of $650,000.

D. Short-term, capital gain of $150,000.

Answer (D) is correct.
   REQUIRED: The amount and character of a gain on the sale of principal residence.
   DISCUSSION: Real property not used in trade or business is a capital asset (e.g., principal residence). Short-term capital is any capital held for 12 months or less starting with the day after acquisition and ending on the day of the sale. Because this sale took place within the prescribed 12-month period, it is classified as a sale of short-term capital property.
   Answer (A) is incorrect. The gain on the sale of a residence owned for 1 year is a short-term capital gain, and the gain cannot exceed the selling price. **Answer (B) is incorrect.** The gain on the sale of a residence owned for 1 year is a short-term capital gain. **Answer (C) is incorrect.** The gain on the sale of a residence owned for 1 year is a short-term capital gain, and the gain cannot exceed the selling price.

13. Clyde, a single person, sold his principal residence for $700,000. He purchased his home 10 years ago for $150,000 and lived there until he sold it. He paid for capital improvements of $75,000, real estate commissions of $36,000, and other settlement costs of $4,000. How much taxable gain must Clyde report?

A. $0

B. $185,000

C. $435,000

D. $225,000

Answer (B) is correct.
   REQUIRED: The gain that must be reported on the sale of a principal residence.
   DISCUSSION: A taxpayer may exclude up to $250,000 ($500,000 for a joint return) of a gain on the sale of a principal residence if (s)he primarily resided in this home for 2 years of a 5-year period before the sale of the home. The gain is determined by subtracting the adjusted basis of $225,000 ($150,000 purchase price + $75,000 capital improvements) from the amount realized of $660,000 ($700,000 sale price – $36,000 commissions – $4,000 settlement cost). This yields a gain of $435,000. Clyde only has to claim $185,000 ($435,000 – $250,000 exclusion) as a gain (Sec. 121).
   Answer (A) is incorrect. Clyde must report a taxable gain. **Answer (C) is incorrect.** The amount of $435,000 is the gain before deducting the $250,000 exclusion. **Answer (D) is incorrect.** The amount of $225,000 is the sum of the purchase price ($150,000) and the capital improvements ($75,000). This is the adjusted basis of the residence.

14. Robert purchased his home for $150,000 in 2010. He sold it for $350,000 (including $100,000 for the land) in 2020. This was his primary residence until it was sold. However, Robert claimed one-fifth of his home as an office for his self-employed business. He claimed a total of $6,000 depreciation over the years. The $150,000 purchase was assessed at $90,000 building and $60,000 land. What is Robert's taxable income as a result of the sale of this primary residence?

A. $6,000

B. $38,000

C. $200,000

D. $0

Answer (A) is correct.
   REQUIRED: The taxable income from sale of principal residence.
   DISCUSSION: Under Reg. 1.121-1(e)(i), no allocation of gain is required if both the residential and nonresidential portions of the property are within the same dwelling unit. However, Sec. 121 will not apply to the gain to the extent of any post-May 6, 1997, depreciation adjustments. Thus, the $6,000 depreciation taken must be reported as income and is taxed at a maximum rate of 25%.
   Answer (B) is incorrect. The office is within the same dwelling unit. **Answer (C) is incorrect.** The entire gain is not taxed. **Answer (D) is incorrect.** The depreciation must be included in income.

15. Martha, filing single, purchased her home on July 7, 2018, and lived in it continuously until its sale on January 7, 2020. The sale is due to a change in place of employment. Her gain on the sale of the home is $300,000. She did not exclude any gain on any other home sale during this time. What is the maximum amount of gain she may exclude on this sale?

A. $125,000

B. $250,000

C. $300,000

D. $187,500

Answer (D) is correct.
REQUIRED: The maximum amount of gain a taxpayer may exclude on the sale of a principal residence.
DISCUSSION: An individual may exclude $250,000 ($500,000 for married individuals filing jointly) on the sale of a principal residence provided (s)he lived there for at least 2 years. Additionally, a pro rata exclusion is available if the sale occurred prior to 2 years if the sale was a result of a change in job locations, health reasons, or other unforeseen circumstances. Therefore, Martha may exclude $187,500 [$250,000 exclusion × (18 months resided ÷ 24 months in 2 years)].
Answer (A) is incorrect. Martha resided in her home for 18, not 12, months. **Answer (B) is incorrect.** Martha cannot exclude the full $250,000 exemption because she did not reside at the house for at least 2 years. **Answer (C) is incorrect.** Martha cannot exclude the full amount of the realized gain.

11.2 Like-Kind Exchanges

16. Jarel transferred an apartment building held for investment to Ron, an unrelated party, in exchange for an office building. At the time of the exchange, the apartment building had a fair market value of $60,000 and an adjusted basis to Jarel of $50,000. The apartment building was subject to a liability of $15,000, which Ron assumed for legitimate business purposes. The office building had an adjusted basis to Ron of $30,000 and a fair market value of $40,000. In addition, Jarel received $5,000 cash in exchange. What is Jarel's recognized gain on this exchange?

A. $5,000

B. $15,000

C. $20,000

D. $10,000

Answer (D) is correct.
REQUIRED: The recognized gain on a like-kind exchange of property.
DISCUSSION: Since the transaction qualifies as a like-kind exchange of real property, Sec. 1031(b) requires the realized gain to be recognized only to the extent of boot received. Regulation 1.1031(d)-2 provides that liabilities assumed by the other party are to be treated as money received by the taxpayer. Jarel's realized gain equals $10,000 ($40,000 FMV of property received + $15,000 liabilities assumed + $5,000 cash received − $50,000 adjusted basis of property given up). Jarel received boot equaling $20,000 ($5,000 cash + $15,000 liabilities). Therefore, the $20,000 of boot received is recognized only to the extent of realized gain (or $10,000).
Answer (A) is incorrect. The liabilities assumed by the other party are also treated as boot. **Answer (B) is incorrect.** The cash received is boot. **Answer (C) is incorrect.** The amount of $20,000 is the total boot received, and the realized gain is only $10,000.

17. Which of the following statements is false with respect to the identification requirement of like-kind real property?

A. You can identify more than one replacement property.

B. Money or unlike property received in full payment for property transferred will still qualify as a nontaxable exchange as long as you receive replacement property within 180 days.

C. The property to be received must be identified on or before the day that is 45 days after the date you transfer the property given up in the exchange.

D. You must clearly describe the replacement property in a signed written document and deliver it to the other person involved in the exchange.

Answer (B) is correct.
REQUIRED: The false statement regarding like-kind property.
DISCUSSION: For purposes of Sec. 1031, a deferred exchange is defined as an exchange of real property in which, pursuant to an agreement, the taxpayer transfers property held for productive use in a trade or business or for investment (the relinquished property) and subsequently receives real property to be held either for productive use in a trade or business or for investment (the replacement property). Failure to satisfy one or more of the requirements for a deferred exchange results in part or all of the replacement property received being treated as property that is not of a like kind to the property relinquished [Reg. 1.1031(k)-1(a)]. In a like-kind exchange, any unlike property or money received in full amount of consideration results in part or all of the realized gain being recognized. This result does not change merely because a deferred exchange is taking place since money and unlike property are not qualifying replacement properties [Reg. 1.1031(k)-1(f)]. Thus, money or unlike property received in full payment for property transferred will not qualify as a nontaxable exchange even though you receive replacement property within 180 days.
Answer (A) is incorrect. Regulation 1.1031(k)-1(c)(4) permits the identification of multiple replacement properties. **Answer (C) is incorrect.** This is one of the requirements of a deferred exchange under Sec. 1031(a)(3)(A). **Answer (D) is incorrect.** Regulation 1.1031(k)-1(c) requires the replacement to be unambiguously described in a written document or agreement that is delivered to the other party.

18. Clark uses a lot in his landscaping business. Clark's sister Lois is a home decorator who uses a similar lot in her business. On December 27, 2019, Clark and Lois exchanged lots. The fair market value of Clark's lot was $7,000 with an adjusted basis of $6,000. The fair market value of Lois's lot was $7,200 with an adjusted basis of $1,000. On December 28, 2020, Clark sold the lot to a third party for $7,200. What is the amount of gain, if any, that Clark has to report on his 2020 return?

A. $6,200

B. $1,200

C. $0

D. $1,000

Answer (B) is correct.
REQUIRED: The amount of gain recognized when like-kind properties are exchanged between related parties.
DISCUSSION: Since the like-kind exchange is between related parties, and a subsequent sale to a third party occurred within 2 years of the exchange, then the gains deferred at the original exchange must be recognized at the date of the subsequent sale. The gain recognized is the amount realized (at the original exchange date) less the adjusted basis (at the original exchange date). In Clark's case, the amount realized is the fair market value of the lot ($7,200). Since boot was neither given nor received, Clark's adjusted basis in the received lot equals his adjusted basis in the traded lot ($6,000). Therefore, when Clark sells the lot, he must report a gain of $1,200 ($7,200 FMV − $6,000 basis).
Answer (A) is incorrect. The amount of $6,200 is the gain if the basis is $1,000. **Answer (C) is incorrect.** A gain is recognized. **Answer (D) is incorrect.** The recognized gain is $1,200.

19. A nontaxable exchange is an exchange in which any gain is not taxed and any loss cannot be deducted. To be nontaxable, the exchange must meet all of the following conditions EXCEPT

A. The property must be business or investment property.

B. The property must be "like-kind" or "like-class" property.

C. The property must be intangible property.

D. The property must not be property held for sale.

Answer (C) is correct.
REQUIRED: The item that is not a requirement for a transaction to qualify as a tax-free like-kind exchange of real property.
DISCUSSION: Section 1031(a)(1) requires that real property qualifying for tax-free treatment must be held for productive use in a trade or business or investment. Only real property, not intangible property, qualifies. Section 1031(a) requires that real property exchanged tax-free must be of like-kind. Hence, real property exchanged for similar real property would qualify for tax-free treatment.

20. Rochelle transferred an apartment building she held for investment to Mona in exchange for land moving equipment. The apartment building was subject to a liability of $20,000, which Mona assumed for legitimate business purposes. The land moving equipment had an adjusted basis of $40,000 and a fair market value of $70,000. The apartment building had a fair market value of $100,000 and an adjusted basis of $60,000. Rochelle received $8,000 cash in addition to receiving the land moving equipment. What is Rochelle's recognized gain on this exchange?

A. $0

B. $8,000

C. $28,000

D. $38,000

Answer (D) is correct.
REQUIRED: The recognized gain on an exchange of property that is not a like-kind exchange.
DISCUSSION: Since the transaction does not qualify as a like-kind exchange, the entire realized gain must be recognized. The realized gain equals $38,000 ($70,000 FMV of property received + $8,000 cash + $20,000 liabilities assumed – $60,000 adjusted basis of property sold).

21. Mr. Almond farmed a total of 200 acres of land, comprised of two parcels of land located about one-half mile apart. One parcel was 120 acres, and the second parcel was 80 acres. Mr. Almond found moving his workers and equipment between the two parcels to be very expensive. He approached the ABC farming partnership, which owned 80 acres next to Mr. Almond's 120-acre parcel, about entering into a nontaxable exchange of his 80 acres for the 80 acres owned by the partnership. Mr. Almond has a cost basis of $100,000 in his 80 acres. The fair market value of his 80 acres at the time of the proposed exchange was $400,000, and the fair market value of the ABC partnership's 80 acres was $350,000. The ABC partnership agreed to an exchange. In 2020, Mr. Almond transferred his 80 acres to the ABC partnership in exchange for ABC's 80 acres and $50,000 cash. What was the amount of Mr. Almond's recognized gain in 2020?

A. $400,000

B. $300,000

C. $50,000

D. No gain.

Answer (C) is correct.
REQUIRED: The amount of recognized gain in an exchange in which boot is received.
DISCUSSION: The transfer qualifies for nonrecognition under Sec. 1031. Mr. Almond must recognize a gain equal to the lesser of gain realized or boot received. Therefore, he must recognize a $50,000 gain, which is less than his realized gain.
Answer (A) is incorrect. The amount of $400,000 is the total value of the property received. **Answer (B) is incorrect.** The amount of $300,000 is the gain realized. **Answer (D) is incorrect.** A gain is recognized.

22. Emmett transferred an apartment building he held for investment to Ray, an unrelated party, in exchange for an office building. At the time of the exchange, the apartment building had a fair market value of $90,000 and an adjusted basis to Emmett of $70,000. The apartment building was subject to a liability of $30,000, which Ray assumed for legitimate business purposes. The office building had an adjusted basis to Ray of $30,000 and a fair market value of $80,000. In addition, Emmett received $10,000 cash in exchange. What is Emmett's recognized gain on this exchange?

A. $10,000

B. $30,000

C. $40,000

D. $50,000

Answer (C) is correct.
REQUIRED: The recognized gain on a like-kind exchange of real property.
DISCUSSION: Since the transaction qualifies as a like-kind exchange of real property, Sec. 1031(b) requires the realized gain to be recognized only to the extent of boot received. Regulation 1.1031(d)-2 provides that liabilities assumed by the other party are to be treated as money received by the taxpayer. The amount realized equals $120,000 ($80,000 FMV of property received + $30,000 relief of mortgage + $10,000 cash received). The adjusted basis of the property is $70,000. The realized gain is $50,000 ($120,000 amount realized − $70,000 adjusted basis). However, boot received is less than the gain realized. Since boot received equals $40,000, only $40,000 is recognized.
Answer (A) is incorrect. The liabilities assumed by the other part are also treated as boot. **Answer (B) is incorrect.** The cash received is boot. **Answer (D) is incorrect.** The $50,000 is the realized gain.

23. Ernie had an adjusted basis of $15,000 in real estate he held for investment. Ernie exchanged it for other real estate to be held for investment with a fair market value of $12,500, a truck with a fair market value of $3,000, and $1,000 cash. What is the total basis of the real estate and the truck?

A. $15,500

B. $14,000

C. $15,000

D. $16,500

Answer (A) is correct.
REQUIRED: The total basis of property after a like-kind exchange.
DISCUSSION: The basis of property acquired in a like-kind exchange is equal to the adjusted basis of property surrendered, decreased by any boot received or loss recognized, and increased by any gain recognized or boot given [Sec. 1031(d)]. Thus, the basis of the real estate received is equal to the adjusted basis of the real estate transferred ($15,000), less the boot received of the cash ($1,000) and the truck ($3,000), plus the gain recognized on the transaction. Section 1031(b) requires that gain be recognized only to the extent of the lesser of boot received or gain realized. The truck and cash are boot, so the boot received is $4,000. However, the gain realized is $1,500 ($12,500 FMV of real estate + $3,000 FMV of truck + $1,000 cash – $15,000 AB of truck), so only a $1,500 gain is recognized. Therefore, the adjusted basis of the real estate received is $12,500 ($15,000 adjusted basis of real estate – $4,000 boot received + $1,500 gain recognized). The total basis of the real estate and the truck is $15,500.
Answer (B) is incorrect. The basis of the properties will include the $1,500 of gain that must be recognized. **Answer (C) is incorrect.** The basis of property that qualifies for a like-kind exchange must be adjusted when boot property is involved. **Answer (D) is incorrect.** The transaction qualifies as an exchange of like-kind property.

24. Which of the following examples of property may qualify for a like-kind exchange?

A. Inventories.

B. Rental house.

C. Accounts receivable.

D. Raw materials.

Answer (B) is correct.
REQUIRED: The type of property that qualifies for a like-kind exchange.
DISCUSSION: Only real property qualifies for like-kind treatment for transfers after December 31, 2017. Therefore, the rental house qualifies for like-kind treatment because it is real property.
Answer (A) is incorrect. Inventories are not real property. **Answer (C) is incorrect.** Accounts receivable do not fall within the definition of real property. **Answer (D) is incorrect.** Raw materials are the components of inventory, not real property.

25. Matt Carlsen owned an office building for investment purposes on the south side of Chicago. Matt's adjusted basis in the building was $75,000 and the fair market value (FMV) was $90,000. He exchanged his investment for other real estate held for investment with a FMV of $80,000. What is Matt's basis in the new building?

A. $80,000

B. $90,000

C. $95,000

D. $75,000

Answer (D) is correct.
REQUIRED: The basis of newly acquired property following a like-kind exchange.
DISCUSSION: Section 1031(a) provides for the nonrecognition of gain or loss on the exchange of like-kind real property held for productive use in a trade or business for investment. Like-kind refers to the nature or character of property and not to its grade or quality [Reg. 1.1031(a)-1(b)]. The parcels of real property are like-kind property regardless of whether they are improved, unimproved, or used for different purposes. The basis in the new building is the adjusted basis the taxpayer had in the old building, since no gain is recognized.

26. Mr. McCarthy exchanged real estate that he held for investment purposes for other real estate that he will hold for investment purposes. The real estate that he gave up had an adjusted basis of $8,000. The real estate that he received in the exchange had a fair market value of $10,000, and he also received cash of $1,000. Mr. McCarthy paid $500 in exchange expenses. What is the amount of gain recognized by Mr. McCarthy?

A. $1,000

B. $2,500

C. $500

D. None of the answers are correct.

Answer (C) is correct.
    REQUIRED: The gain recognized on the like-kind exchange of real property when boot is also received.
    DISCUSSION: The basis of real property acquired in a like-kind exchange is equal to the adjusted basis of property surrendered, decreased by any boot received or loss recognized, and increased by any gain recognized or boot given [Sec. 1031(d)]. The gain recognized equals the lesser of the realized gain ($10,000 FMV of land + $1,000 boot received – $8,000 basis – $500 boot given) or the boot received ($1,000). The IRS has ruled that exchange expenses may be deducted in computing the amount of gain or loss realized, offset against cash payments received in determining gain to be recognized, or included in the basis of the property received (Rev. Ruling 72-456). The best action would be to offset the cash received. Therefore, Mr. McCarthy will recognize a $500 gain ($1,000 – $500).
    Answer (A) is incorrect. The $1,000 boot received has not been reduced by the $500 of expenses. **Answer (B) is incorrect.** The $2,500 equals the realized gain. **Answer (D) is incorrect.** A gain of $500 is recognized.

27. Mr. Monty owned an office building that he had purchased at a cost of $600,000 and that later had an adjusted basis of $400,000. This year, he traded it to a person who was not related to him for an apartment house having a fair market value of $500,000. The apartment house has 50 units and rents to individuals. The office building has 25 units and rents to Monty's businesses. What is Mr. Monty's recognized gain or loss on this exchange?

A. $100,000 long-term capital gain.

B. $100,000 long-term capital loss.

C. $100,000 ordinary gain.

D. $0

Answer (D) is correct.
    REQUIRED: The recognized gain or loss on the exchange of an office building for an apartment building.
    DISCUSSION: Section 1031(a) provides for the nonrecognition of gain or loss on the exchange of like-kind real property held for productive use in a trade or business for investment. Like-kind refers to the nature or character of real property and not to its grade or quality [Reg. 1.1031(a)-1(b)]. The parcels of real property are like-kind property regardless of whether they are improved, unimproved, or used for different purposes.
    Mr. Monty has a realized gain of $100,000 ($500,000 amount realized – $400,000 adjusted basis). However, none of this gain is recognized under Sec. 1031 since no boot property was received.

28. During the current year, James exchanged a warehouse he used in his business for a storage facility his sister Donna used in her legal practice. For this to be treated as a nontaxable exchange, how long must James and Donna each hold the property exchanged?

A. 6 months.

B. 1 year.

C. 2 years.

D. May be sold at any time.

Answer (C) is correct.
    REQUIRED: The waiting period to dispose of the property in a like-kind exchange between related parties.
    DISCUSSION: Section 1031(f) outlines special rules for like-kind exchanges between related parties. Neither party can dispose of the property within 2 years after the date of the last transfer that was part of the exchange in order to avoid recognizing any gain on the initial exchange.

STUDY UNIT TWELVE

INDIVIDUAL RETIREMENT ACCOUNTS

(12 pages of outline)

An individual retirement account (IRA) is a personal savings plan that offers tax advantages to individuals who set aside money for retirement. Two advantages include

1) The deductibility of contributions and
2) The tax exemption of IRA earnings until they are distributed.

An IRA can be set up with most banks and similar savings institutions, mutual funds, stock brokerage firms, and insurance companies.

Included in this coverage are the rules applicable to employees for employer-established IRA plans. These plans include SEPs and SIMPLE plans.

12.1 IRAs DEFINED

Taxable Compensation

1. Any individual who receives taxable compensation during the year may set up an IRA.

    a. An individual may set up a spousal IRA for a spouse, provided a joint return is filed.

Compensation

2. Compensation is defined as earned income. It includes

    a. Wages and salaries
    b. Commissions
    c. Self-employment income
    d. Taxable alimony and separate maintenance payments (i.e., pre-2018 divorce decree)

3. Compensation does not include earnings and profits from property, such as rental income, interest income, dividend income or pension and annuity income, S corporation income, and deferred compensation distributions.

Types of IRAs

4. There are five kinds of individual retirement accounts:

    a. Individual retirement account
    b. Individual retirement annuity
    c. Employer and employee association trust accounts
    d. Simplified employee pension (SEP)
    e. Savings Incentive Match Plans for Employees (SIMPLE)

5. Publications 590-A and 590-B also list individual retirement bonds, but not individual savings bonds, as permitted individual retirement accounts.

Fully Vested

6. Under Secs. 219(d) and 408, an IRA must be fully vested at all times, the assets of the trust cannot be commingled with other property except in a common trust fund or common investment fund, and no part of the trust funds can be used to purchase life insurance contracts.

Shareholder Status

7. Generally, IRAs and Roth IRAs are not permitted as S corporation shareholders. However, if the IRA or Roth IRA held bank stock on or after October 22, 2004, the IRA or Roth IRA is permitted to hold this stock, and the owner of the plan is considered the shareholder.

    a. Prohibited transaction rules do not apply to the sale of stock by an IRA or Roth IRA to the individual beneficiary of the trust if the following are true:

        1) The stock is stock in a bank.

        2) The stock is held by the IRA or Roth IRA on or after October 22, 2004.

        3) The sale is pursuant to an S election by the bank.

        4) The sale is for FMV at the time of the sale, and the terms of the sale are otherwise at least as favorable to the IRA or Roth IRA as the terms that would apply for a sale to an unrelated party.

        5) The IRA or Roth IRA does not pay any commissions, costs, or other expenses in connection with the sale.

        6) The stock is sold in a single transaction for cash not later than 120 days after the S election is made.

STOP AND REVIEW! **You have completed the outline for this subunit. Study multiple-choice questions 1 through 5 beginning on page 357.**

12.2 CONTRIBUTIONS

1. Once an IRA is set up, a taxpayer may make contributions each year in which (s)he is qualified.

    a. To qualify to make contributions, a taxpayer must have received compensation.
    b. However, contributions are not required to be made each year.
    c. Contributions must be made by the due date of the return (not including extensions).

Contribution Limits

2. The maximum contribution that can be made during any year to a traditional IRA is the lesser of

    a. Compensation received or
    b. $6,000.

        1) Individuals age 50 and older at the end of the year can contribute an additional $1,000 (i.e., total contribution limit is $7,000).

    NOTE: For 401(k) plans, the limit is $19,500 ($26,000 if 50 or older). For 415(c) plans, the limit is $57,000 or 100% of includible compensation if less (an additional $6,500 is allowed for those 50 or older).

3. SIMPLE plans allow small employers to make matching contributions to employees' traditional IRAs.

    a. The maximum employee contribution to a SIMPLE plan is $13,500. For employees age 50 and over, an additional $3,000 may be contributed.

4. SEP plans allow employers to contribute to employees' traditional IRAs as well, though the employer contributions are not matching contributions like those of SIMPLE plans.

    a. The maximum contribution allowed is up to 25% of the employee's income, limited to an annual ceiling of $57,000 in 2020.

Inherited IRAs

5. A person may deduct contributions made to an inherited IRA only if the IRA was inherited from a spouse. Contributions or rollovers cannot be made to an IRA inherited from someone who died after December 31, 1983, and who was not a spouse. An IRA is included in the estate of the decedent who owned it.

    a. When an IRA is inherited from a person other than a spouse, the IRA cannot be treated as though it was owned by the taxpayer who inherited the IRA.

Spousal IRA Limit

6. If a joint return is filed and a taxpayer makes less than his or her spouse, the taxpayer may still contribute the lesser of

    a. The sum of his or her compensation and the taxable compensation of the spouse, reduced by the amount of the spouse's IRA contribution and contributions to a Roth IRA, or
    b. $6,000 ($7,000 if over age 50).

    NOTE: Thus, the total combined contributions to an IRA and a spouse's IRA can be as much as $12,000 for the year (plus an additional $1,000 for each spouse age 50 or older).

7. If a taxpayer has more than one IRA, the limit applies to the total contributions made to the IRAs for the year.

Deductible Contributions

8. Generally, a deduction is allowed for contributions that are made to an IRA.

    a. If neither spouse was covered for any part of the year by an employer retirement plan, the entire contribution may be deducted.

    b. If a taxpayer is not covered by an employer plan but the taxpayer's spouse is, the taxpayer may still deduct the full amount of the contribution. However, the deduction is reduced if the adjusted gross income on the joint return is greater than $196,000 but less than $206,000. The deduction is eliminated if the income is greater than $206,000.

    c. If a taxpayer is covered by a retirement plan at work, the IRA deduction will be phased out or eliminated if the taxpayer's modified AGI is between

        1) $65,000 and $75,000 for a single individual
        2) $104,000 and $124,000 for a married couple filing a joint return
        3) $0 and $10,000 for a married individual filing a separate return

    d. If a taxpayer did not live with his or her spouse at any time during the year and the taxpayer's filing status is married filing separately, the taxpayer's filing status is considered single for the purpose of computing the phaseout.

    e. Deductible contributions to an IRA have to be made in cash and not any other property.

9. For an individual whose modified AGI falls within one of the phaseout ranges above, the amount that must be reduced from the IRA deduction is determined by the following equation:

$$\frac{\text{Modified AGI} - \text{Applicable minimum phaseout amount}}{\text{Maximum phaseout amount} - \text{Minimum phaseout amount}} \times \$6,000$$

    a. This amount is subtracted from the maximum allowable deduction to arrive at the allowable deductible amount.

    b. Round it up to the next multiple of $10 to find the allowable deduction.

        1) If a deduction is allowed, $200 or more is allowed.
        2) However, the deduction may not exceed the contributions made.

10. Unlike contributions to traditional IRAs, contributions to SEP-IRAs are excluded from an employee's income rather than deducted from it. Any excess employer contributions must be included in income without any offsetting deduction.

Rollovers

11. Generally, a rollover is a tax-free distribution of cash or other assets from one retirement plan to another retirement plan. There are two types of rollovers: direct and indirect.

    a. A **direct** rollover is a direct transfer of assets from one qualified plan to another qualified plan.

    b. An **indirect** rollover is a rollover in which the taxpayer takes physical possession of the assets (e.g., a check).

        1) The taxpayer must deposit the assets into another qualified plan within 60 days of the withdrawal to avoid taxes and penalties.

    c. A rollover cannot be deducted.

   d.   Distributions that are not qualified distributions eligible for the rollover include the following:

     1) Required minimum distributions
     2) Hardship distributions
     3) Any series of substantially periodic distributions
     4) Corrective distributions due to excess contributions
     5) A loan treated as a distribution
     6) Dividends on employer securities
     7) The cost of life insurance coverage
     8) A distribution to the plan participant's beneficiary

   e.   If a taxpayer withdraws assets from an IRA, rolls over part of it tax-free, and keeps the rest, ordinary income must be recognized, and (s)he may be subject to the 10% tax on premature distributions.

   f.   The same property that was received from an old IRA may be rolled over into a new IRA.

   g.   If an individual inherits a traditional IRA from anyone other than a deceased spouse (as previously discussed in item 5. on page 347), the person is not permitted to treat the inherited IRA as his or her own, making direct contributions.

     1) The inherited IRA will generally not have tax assessed on the IRA assets until distributions are received.

   h.   The basis of a traditional IRA because of nondeductible contributions remains with the IRA.

   i.   For distributions from an inherited IRA, either

     1) The distributions must begin by the end of the year following the death of the original IRA holder or

     2) The IRA must be completely distributed by the end of the fifth year following death.

   j.   When transferring an IRA account to a spouse (or an ex-spouse pursuant to a domestic relations order), taxes and penalties may be avoided by

     1) Changing the name on the IRA account or
     2) Transferring the IRA assets into another qualified plan.

   k.   Distributions from a SIMPLE IRA can be rolled over to another IRA 2 years after the first contribution is made.

   l.   Rollovers to tax-sheltered annuities are not tax-free.

Collectibles

12. Generally, an IRA is prohibited from investing in collectibles. However, an IRA may hold platinum coins as well as gold, silver, or platinum bullion.

Prohibited Transactions

13. A taxpayer may not engage in any of the transactions listed below with a traditional IRA. The tax consequence for engaging in any of these acts is that the account ceases to be an IRA and all assets are treated as if distributed that same year.

   a.   Sell property to it
   b.   Use it as security for a loan
   c.   Buy property with it for the taxpayer's personal use

Basis in a Traditional IRA (Form 8606)

14. A taxpayer will have a cost basis in a traditional IRA if any nondeductible contributions were made.

    a. Cost basis is the sum of the nondeductible contributions to the IRA minus any withdrawals or distributions of nondeductible contributions.

    b. The difference between the taxpayer's total permitted contributions and the taxpayer's IRA deduction, if any, is the nondeductible contribution.

        1) To designate contributions as nondeductible, Form 8606 must be filed.

        2) A taxpayer must file Form 8606 to report nondeductible contributions even if (s)he does not have to file a tax return for the year.

    c. For distributions from IRAs having a cost basis, only the part of the distribution that represents nondeductible contributions is tax-free. While basis exists, each distribution is partly taxable and partly nontaxable.

15. A taxpayer may be able to treat a contribution made to one type of IRA as having been made to a different type of IRA. This is called recharacterizing the contribution.

    a. A trustee-to-trustee transfer between the accounts must be made. The net income allocable to the contribution must also be included in the transfer.

    b. The transfer must be made by the due date for the tax return for the tax year during which the contribution was made.

    c. The contribution is treated as having been made to the second IRA on the date that it was actually made to the first IRA.

Qualified Charitable Distributions (QCDs)

16. Up to $100,000 of distributions may be excluded from income if distributed directly by the trustees of the IRA to a qualified charitable organization (following the same rules as charitable itemized deductions). The only other requirements for this exclusion of income are that the taxpayer must

    a. Be at least age 70 1/2 and

    b. Retain the same acknowledgment of charitable contribution as for a charitable contribution deduction.

17. Only otherwise includible portions of the distribution are considered QCDs.

> **EXAMPLE 12-1   Qualified Charitable Distributions**
>
> On December 23, 2020, Jeff, age 75, directed the trustee of his IRA to make a distribution of $25,000 directly to a qualified 501(c)(3) organization (i.e., a charitable organization eligible to receive tax-deductible contributions). The total value of Jeff's IRA is $30,000 and consists of $20,000 of deductible contributions and earnings and $10,000 of nondeductible contributions (basis). Since Jeff is at least age 70 1/2 and the distribution is made directly by the trustee to a qualified organization, the part of the distribution that would otherwise be includible in Jeff's income ($20,000) is a QCD.
>
> The remaining $5,000 of the $25,000 distribution to the charity may be deducted as an itemized charitable deduction on Jeff's Schedule A since that portion was taxed originally on contribution to the IRA, i.e., not double-dipping with both exclusion and deduction.

Retirement Savings Contributions Credit (Saver's Credit)

18. The Saver's Credit can be taken for the taxpayer's contributions to a traditional or Roth IRA, 401(k), SIMPLE IRA, SARSEP, 403(b), 501(c)(18), or governmental 457(b) plan and for voluntary after-tax employee contributions to qualified retirement and 403(b) plans.

19. Rollover contributions (money that the taxpayer moved from another retirement plan or IRA) are not eligible for the Saver's Credit. Additionally, eligible contributions may be reduced by any recent distributions the taxpayer received from a retirement plan or IRA.

20. The taxpayer is eligible for the credit if the taxpayer is (a) age 18 or older, (b) not claimed as a dependent on another person's return, and (c) not a full-time student.

    a.   A taxpayer is a student if, during any part of 5 calendar months of 2020, the taxpayer was

        1)   Enrolled as a full-time student at a school

            a)   A school includes technical, trade, and mechanical schools. It does not include on-the-job training courses, correspondence schools, or schools offering courses only through the Internet.

        2)   Took a full-time, on-farm training course given by a school or a state, county, or local government agency

21. The amount of the credit is 50%, 20%, or 10% of the taxpayer's retirement plan or IRA contributions, up to $2,000 ($4,000 if married filing jointly), depending on the taxpayer's adjusted gross income.

    a.   The chart below has the Saver's Credit AGI limits for 2020.

	2020 Saver's Credit		
Credit Rate	Married Filing Jointly	Head of Household	All Other Filers
50% of your contribution	AGI ≤ $39,000	AGI ≤ $29,250	AGI ≤ $19,500
20% of your contribution	$39,001-$42,500	$29,251-$31,875	$19,501-$21,250
10% of your contribution	$42,501-$65,000	$31,876-$48,750	$21,251-$32,500
0% of your contribution	more than $65,000	more than $48,750	more than $32,500

EXAMPLE 12-2   **Retirement Savings Contribution Credit**

Stephanie, who works at a retail store, is married and earned $39,000 in 2020. Stephanie's husband was unemployed in 2020 and did not have any earnings. Stephanie contributed $1,000 to her IRA in 2020. After deducting her IRA contribution, Stephanie's adjusted gross income on her joint return is $38,000. Stephanie may claim a 50% credit, $500, for her $1,000 IRA contribution.

Unrelated Business Income (UBI)

22. An IRA is subject to tax on UBI if it carries on an unrelated trade or business.

    a.   An unrelated trade or business means any trade or business regularly carried on by the IRA, or by a partnership of which it is a member, that is not substantially related to performance of its exempt purpose or function.

        1)   If the IRA has $1,000 or more of unrelated trade or business gross income, the IRA trustee is required to file a Form 990-T, *Exempt Organization Business Income Tax Return*.

            a)   The Form 990-T must be filed by the 15th day of the 4th month after the end of the IRA's tax year.

STOP AND REVIEW! You have completed the outline for this subunit. Study multiple-choice questions 6 through 19 beginning on page 359.

12.3 PENALTIES

Excess Contributions

1. Generally, an excess contribution is the amount contributed to an IRA that is more than the lesser of

    a. The taxpayer's compensation received or

    b. $6,000 ($7,000 for taxpayers age 50 and older).

        1) For SIMPLE plans, the limit is $13,500 ($16,500 for taxpayers age 50 and older).

        2) For SEP plans, the limit is the lesser of 25% of the employee's income or $57,000.

2. An excess contribution could be the result of a taxpayer's contribution, a spouse's contribution, an employer's contribution, or an improper rollover contribution.

3. A 6% excise tax (10% to employers contributing to SEP-IRAs) is imposed each year on excess contribution amounts that remain in an IRA at the end of each tax year. Distribution of excess contributions is reported on Form 1099-R in box 2a and coded in box 7.

4. The tax can be avoided if the excess contribution and the interest earned on it are withdrawn by the due date (including extensions) of the tax return.

    a. The interest earned on the excess contribution qualifies as a premature distribution and is subject to an additional tax of 10% on that distribution.

5. Under Sec. 219(f)(6), the taxpayer may treat the unused (excess) contributions from a previous year as having been made in the current year to the extent that the allowable contribution limit exceeds the actual contributions for the current year.

Premature Distributions

6. Premature distributions are amounts withdrawn from an IRA or annuity before a taxpayer reaches age 59 1/2.

    a. The additional tax on premature distributions is equal to 10% of the amount of the premature distribution that must be included in gross income. This tax is in addition to any regular income tax that is due.

    b. In certain circumstances, the additional tax does not apply to distributions from an IRA, even if they are made before a taxpayer reaches age 59 1/2 [Sec. 72(f)]. The exceptions are for when the distributions

        1) Are made to a beneficiary (or to the estate of the employee) on or after the death of the employee

        2) Result from the employee having a qualifying disability

3) Are part of a series of substantially equal periodic payments beginning after separation from service and made at least annually for the life or life expectancy of the employee or the joint lives or life expectancies of the employee and his or her designated beneficiary

4) Are made to an employee after (s)he separated from service if the separation occurred during or after the calendar year in which the employee reached age 55 (not applicable to SEP or traditional IRAs)

5) Are made to an employee for medical care up to the amount allowable as a medical expense deduction (determined without regard to whether the employee itemizes deductions)

6) Are made to an alternate payee under a qualified domestic relations order (QDRO)

7) Are made because of an IRS levy on the plan

8) Are made as a qualified U.S. reservist distribution (those called to active duty)

9) Are from dividends on employer securities

10) Are from federal retirement funds of a phased program

11) Are hurricane or wildfire distributions

12) Are qualified higher education expenses, including those related to graduate-level courses (IRAs only)

   a) However, the amount of qualified higher education expenses is reduced by the amount of any qualified scholarship, educational assistance allowance, or payment (other than by gift, bequest, device, or inheritance) for an individual's educational enrollment, which is excludable from gross income.

13) Are used to pay medical insurance premiums of an unemployed individual (IRAs only)

14) Are used to pay first-time homebuyer expenses (IRAs only)

15) Are timely made to reduce excess contributions or excess deferrals (IRAs only)

16) Are qualified COVID-19-related distributions and are no more than $100,000

17) Are made as a permissible withdrawal from an eligible automatic contribution arrangement (EACA)

c. If a taxpayer borrows money against an IRA, the fair market value of the IRA as of the first day of the tax year must be included in gross income. The taxpayer may also be subject to the 10% penalty tax. An individual may withdraw all or part of the assets of a traditional IRA and exclude the withdrawal from income if the individual transfers it to another traditional IRA or returns it to the same IRA within 60 days after the withdrawal.

d. A distribution from a SIMPLE IRA within 2 years after the first contribution is made is subject to a 25% tax.

Excess Accumulations

7.   Generally, a taxpayer must begin receiving distributions by April 1 of the year following the year in which (s)he reaches age 72 (70 1/2 for years before 2020).

   a.   If distributions are less than the required minimum distribution (RMD) for the year, a 50% excise tax will be imposed on the amount not distributed.

   b.   Under the CARES Act, no minimum distribution is required for calendar year 2020 from an IRA. The provision waives the 2020 minimum distribution requirement for lifetime distributions to IRA owners. The next required minimum distributions for these plans will be for calendar year 2021.

   c.   In the case of an individual whose required beginning date is April 1, 2020, because the individual attained age 70 1/2 in 2019, the provision waives the minimum distribution requirement with respect to a distribution that would have been required to be made in 2020 on account of the distribution not having been made in 2019.

   d.   In the case of an individual whose required beginning date is April 1, 2021, because the individual attains age 72 in 2020, the first year for which a minimum distribution would have been required is 2020. Under the provision, no distribution is required for 2020; thus, no distribution will be required to be made by April 1, 2021.

   e.   However, the provision does not change the individual's required beginning date for purposes of determining the required minimum distribution for calendar years after 2020. Thus, for an individual whose required beginning date is April 1, 2021, the required minimum distribution for 2021 will be required to be made no later than December 31, 2021.

Borrowing from the Plan

8.   The terms of a qualified plan [i.e., 401(k)] may permit the plan to lend money to participants without adverse income or excise tax results, if certain requirements are met.

   a.   Section 72(p) basically treats loans as distributions.

      1)   A loan will not be treated as a distribution to the extent loans to the employee do not exceed the lesser of

         a) $50,000 ($100,000 for qualified COVID-19-related distributions) or

         b)   The greater of one-half (100% for qualified COVID-19-related distributions) of the present value of the employee's vested accrued benefit under such plans or $10,000.

      2)   The $50,000 ($100,000) maximum sum is reduced by the participant's highest outstanding loan balance during the preceding 12-month period.

   b.   Plan loans generally have to be repaid within 5 years unless the funds are to acquire a principal residence for the participant.

   c.   Plan loans must be amortized in level payments, made no less frequently than quarterly over the term of the loan.

   d.   A pledge of the participant's interest under the plan or an agreement to pledge such interest as security for a loan by a third party, as well as a direct or indirect loan from the plan itself, is treated as a loan.

   e.   Plan loan repayments due March 27-December 31, 2020, may be delayed 1 year.

STOP AND REVIEW! **You have completed the outline for this subunit. Study multiple-choice questions 20 through 24 beginning on page 364.**

12.4 ROTH IRAs

Exempt Distributions

1. A tax-free IRA (referred to as a Roth IRA) has been available since the beginning of 1998.

   a. Contributions to a Roth IRA are nondeductible, but income can be accumulated tax-free.

   b. To be treated as a Roth IRA, the account must be designated as such when it is established.

Income Limits

   c. Roth IRAs are subject to income limits. The maximum yearly contribution that can be made to a Roth IRA is phased out for

      1) Single taxpayers with a modified AGI between $124,000 and $139,000,
      2) Joint filers with a modified AGI between $196,000 and $206,000, and
      3) A married taxpayer filing separately with a modified AGI between $0 and $10,000.

   d. Modified AGI is determined by subtracting any income resulting from a conversion of a traditional IRA to a Roth IRA and any minimum required distributions from a qualified retirement plan, including an IRA, from adjusted gross income. The following items are added to adjusted gross income:

      1) Traditional IRA deduction
      2) Student loan interest deduction
      3) Foreign earned income and/or housing exclusion
      4) Foreign housing deduction
      5) Exclusion of bond interest
      6) Exclusion of employer-provided adoption benefits

Contribution Limit

2. The contribution amount is the same as the amount for a deductible IRA, and the total contribution to both deductible and nondeductible IRAs cannot exceed $6,000 per taxpayer ($7,000 for individuals who will be at least 50 years old by the end of the year).

No Age Limit

3. Like deductible IRAs, individuals are allowed to make contributions to the Roth IRA at any age.

Qualified Distribution

4. Qualified distributions from a Roth IRA are not included in the taxpayer's gross income and are not subject to the additional 10% early withdrawal tax.

   a. To be a qualified distribution, the distribution must satisfy a 5-year holding period and must meet one of four additional requirements.

      1) To satisfy the 5-year holding period, the Roth IRA distribution may not be made before the end of the 5-tax-year period beginning with the first tax year for which the individual made a contribution to the Roth IRA.

         a) The 5-year holding period begins to run with the tax year to which the contribution relates, not the year in which the contribution is actually made; thus, a contribution made in April 2016, designated as a 2015 contribution, may be withdrawn tax free in 2020, if it is otherwise a qualified distribution.

      2)   Taxpayers must meet one of four other requirements for a tax-free distribution. The distribution must be

           a)   Made on or after the date on which the individual attains age 59 1/2,

           b)   Made to a beneficiary (or the individual's estate) on or after the individual's death,

           c)   Attributed to the individual's being disabled, or

           d)   Distributed to pay for "qualified first-time homebuyer expenses."

5.   Distributions are treated as made from contributions first; thus, no portion of a distribution is treated as attributable to earnings or includible in gross income until the total of all distributions from the Roth IRA exceeds the amount of contributions. Nonqualified distributions are included in income after recovery of contribution, and they are subject to the 10% early withdrawal penalty.

Rollover

6.   Distributions from one Roth IRA can be rolled over or "converted" tax-free to another Roth IRA.

7.   Amounts in a traditional IRA that was not inherited from a person other than a spouse can be rolled into a Roth IRA.

      a.   If a taxpayer has both deductible and nondeductible IRAs and only a portion of the IRAs are converted into a Roth IRA, any amount rolled into a Roth IRA will be considered to have been drawn proportionately from both the deductible and nondeductible IRAs and will be taxed accordingly.

      b.   Once a taxpayer has begun periodic distributions of a traditional IRA, (s)he is able to convert his or her traditional IRA into a Roth IRA and resume the periodic payments. In addition, the 10% penalty on early distributions will not apply to unqualified distributions.

      c.   Hardship distributions are not directly convertible.

      d.   Required minimum distributions are not permissible conversions.

      e.   Once amounts from a traditional IRA have been rolled over or converted into a Roth IRA, the amounts may not be recharacterized back into a traditional IRA. However, recharacterization is still permitted with respect to other contributions. For example, an individual may make a contribution for a year to a Roth IRA and, before the due date for the individual's income tax return for that year (including extensions), recharacterize it as a contribution to a traditional IRA.

8.   Amounts carried in a SIMPLE IRA may be converted to a Roth IRA, assuming the required 2-year participation period has been met.

Required Distribution

9.   Distributions from Roth IRAs are required only upon death.

***STOP AND REVIEW!* You have completed the outline for this subunit. Study multiple-choice questions 25 through 27 on page 367.**

QUESTIONS

12.1 IRAs Defined

1. Which of the following is compensation for the purpose of contributions to individual retirement accounts?

    A. Deferred compensation received.

    B. Foreign earned income excluded from income.

    C. Pension or annuity income.

    D. Taxable alimony and separate maintenance.

Answer (D) is correct.
    REQUIRED: The item that is compensation for the purpose of contributions to IRAs.
    DISCUSSION: Publication 590-A states that compensation is defined as earned income. It includes wages and salaries, commissions, self-employment income, and taxable alimony and separate maintenance payments. Compensation does not include earnings and profits from property, such as rental income, interest income, and dividend income or pension and annuity income.
    Answer (A) is incorrect. Deferred compensation received is not considered compensation but is includible in modified adjusted gross income for the purpose of contributions to IRAs. **Answer (B) is incorrect.** Foreign earned income excluded from income is not considered compensation but is includible in modified adjusted gross income for the purpose of contributions to IRAs. **Answer (C) is incorrect.** Pension or annuity income is not considered compensation but is includible in modified adjusted gross income for the purpose of contributions to IRAs.

2. When figuring compensation for purposes of determining the amount of an allowable contribution to a traditional IRA, which of the following is an incorrect statement?

    A. Pension or annuity income is not considered compensation for an IRA plan.

    B. Earnings and profits from property, such as rental income, are considered compensation.

    C. Interest and dividends are not considered compensation for an IRA plan.

    D. Generally, amounts excluded from income are not considered compensation for an IRA plan.

Answer (B) is correct.
    REQUIRED: The incorrect statement about figuring compensation for purposes of determining the amount of an allowable contribution to a traditional IRA.
    DISCUSSION: Compensation is defined as earned income. It includes

1) Wages and salaries,
2) Commissions,
3) Self-employment income, and
4) Taxable alimony and separate maintenance payments.

    Compensation does not include earnings and profits from property such as rental income, interest income, dividend income, or pension and annuity income, the share of S corporation income, and deferred compensation distributions.

3. Generally, an IRA contribution is limited to the lesser of $6,000 in 2020 or the taxpayer's compensation. However, which of the following items is NOT treated as compensation for this limitation?

    A. Wages earned by an individual under the age of 18.

    B. Taxable alimony.

    C. Self-employment loss.

    D. Commissions.

Answer (C) is correct.
    REQUIRED: The item that is not considered to be earned compensation for IRA contribution purposes.
    DISCUSSION: Compensation is defined as earned income. It includes

1) Wages and salaries,
2) Commissions,
3) Self-employment income, and
4) Taxable alimony and separate maintenance payments.

    Self-employment loss is not considered income for the purposes of contributing to an IRA.
    Answer (A) is incorrect. Wages earned are considered income even if the individual is under the age of 18. **Answer (B) is incorrect.** Taxable alimony is treated as earned income and is treated as compensation for the IRA limit. **Answer (D) is incorrect.** Commissions are earned income and treated as compensation for the IRA limit.

4. Which one of the following types of individual retirement accounts (IRAs) cannot be established?

    A. An individual retirement annuity that is purchased from a life insurance company.

    B. An individual retirement account with a trustee who invests one's money in 1-ounce U.S. gold coins.

    C. A simplified employee pension account.

    D. An individual retirement account with a trustee who invests one's money in life insurance contracts.

Answer (D) is correct.
    REQUIRED: The type of IRA that cannot be established.
    DISCUSSION: An individual retirement account must be either a trust or a custodial account established in the United States for the exclusive benefit of the owner and the owner's beneficiaries. It must be established by a written document and meet the requirements of Sec. 408(a). Section 408(a)(4) states that no part of the amount in the account may be used to buy life insurance.

5. All of the following types of income would be considered compensation in determining if an individual retirement account could be set up and contributions could be made EXCEPT

    A. Tip income.

    B. Net rental income.

    C. Partnership income of an active partner providing services to the partnership.

    D. Commissions.

Answer (B) is correct.
    REQUIRED: The item not treated as compensation with respect to contributions to an IRA.
    DISCUSSION: Section 219(f) defines compensation as earned income. Rental income is not generally considered earned income; rather, it is treated as a passive form of income.
    Answer (A) is incorrect. Tip income is a common example of earned income. **Answer (C) is incorrect.** Partnership income of an active partner providing services to the partnership is a common example of earned income. **Answer (D) is incorrect.** Commission is a common example of earned income.

12.2 Contributions

6. Gary and Mabel have been married for many years and file jointly. Gary was born February 21, 1947. Mabel was born April 10, 1951. They each received Social Security benefit payments throughout 2020. Gary earned $7,200 as a part-time security guard in 2020; he was not covered by any type of retirement plan. Mabel has been retired for many years. Gary and Mabel expect their 2020 adjusted gross income not to exceed $104,000. What is the amount of Gary and Mabel's largest allowable IRA deduction for 2020 (assume the proper amount claimed as a deduction was paid timely)?

A. $14,000

B. $12,000

C. $7,000

D. $6,000

Answer (A) is correct.
REQUIRED: The maximum allowable IRA deduction.
DISCUSSION: An individual may make contributions to an IRA regardless of their age. In addition, if the individual has received compensation, a spouse may also deduct up to $6,000 of contributions, plus $1,000 if age 50 or older. Therefore, the total allowable deduction is $14,000 [($6,000 + $1,000) × 2].
Answer (B) is incorrect. Gary and Mabel are both over 50 and therefore eligible for the $1,000 catch-up contribution. **Answer (C) is incorrect.** They are both allowed the $6,000 and an extra $1,000 because they are over 50 years old. **Answer (D) is incorrect.** They are both allowed the $6,000 and an extra $1,000 because they are over 50 years old.

7. Which of the following would be an allowable investment for a traditional IRA?

A. Stamps that have been issued by the United States Postal Service.

B. An oil painting certified by an art expert as being an authentic original by a Dutch master artist.

C. One-ounce silver coins minted by the U.S. Treasury Department.

D. All of the answers are correct.

Answer (C) is correct.
REQUIRED: The allowed investment for a traditional IRA.
DISCUSSION: Generally, an IRA is prohibited from investing in collectibles. However, an IRA may hold platinum coins as well as gold, silver, or platinum bullion. Thus, 1-ounce silver coins minted by the U.S. Treasury Department are considered an allowable investment for a traditional IRA.
Answer (A) is incorrect. Stamps are considered collectible items, which are not an allowable investment. **Answer (B) is incorrect.** An oil painting certified by an art expert as being an authentic original by a Dutch master artist is considered a collectible item, which is not an allowable investment. **Answer (D) is incorrect.** Neither the stamps nor the oil painting are allowable contributions because they are collectibles.

8. Alice and Mike file a joint return for 2020 on April 15, 2021. Alice, who is a nonworking spouse, is 49. Both Alice and Mike contributed $2,000 each to a traditional IRA, although they qualified to contribute the maximum amount. They filed their return timely. On June 1, 2021, Mike's mother gave each of them $1,000. What additional amount of the gift may Alice and Mike contribute to each of their IRAs for the year 2020?

A. $0

B. $1,000

C. $500

D. $4,000

Answer (A) is correct.
REQUIRED: The maximum amount of money that can be contributed to a traditional IRA for 2020.
DISCUSSION: Contributions to Alice and Mike's IRA must be made during the 2020 tax year or made before the filing deadline in 2021. Therefore, Alice and Mike's 2020 tax year deadline for an IRA contribution for the 2020 tax year was April 15, 2021. Any contributions made after April 15, 2021, are treated as contributed in the 2021 tax year [Sec. 219 (f)(3)].

9. Morris, a single taxpayer, is not covered by a qualified plan at his place of employment. He wishes to establish an IRA and contribute $6,000 for 2020. An IRA may be invested in all of the following accounts EXCEPT

    A. Bank CD.

    B. Mutual fund.

    C. Annuity.

    D. Artwork.

Answer (D) is correct.
    REQUIRED: The item an IRA may not be invested in.
    DISCUSSION: Generally, an IRA is prohibited from investing in collectibles. Artwork would be considered a collectible. However, an IRA may hold platinum coins as well as gold, silver, or platinum bullion.

10. In 2020, MaryAnn, a nonworking spouse, files a joint return with Jack, who is not covered by a pension plan at work. Their AGI is $50,000, and Jack plans to contribute $5,500 to a traditional IRA. MaryAnn, who is 51, wishes to contribute to an IRA. What is the maximum amount she can contribute?

    A. $6,000

    B. $5,500

    C. $7,000

    D. $0

Answer (C) is correct.
    REQUIRED: The maximum amount of contributions to an IRA.
    DISCUSSION: Under Sec. 408(a)(1), the maximum contribution to an IRA that can be made every year is the lesser of the compensation received or $6,000. Individuals age 50 and older at the end of the year can contribute an additional $1,000. If Jack and MaryAnn file a joint return, they are eligible to contribute the $6,000 on MaryAnn's behalf and the additional $1,000 for being over 50 years of age. The total amount that MaryAnn can contribute is $7,000.
    Answer (A) is incorrect. The $6,000 limit does not take into account the extra $1,000 MaryAnn is allowed to contribute for being over 50 years of age. **Answer (B) is incorrect.** The $5,500 limit was the 2018 limit on IRA contributions and does not take into account the $1,000 contribution for being over 50 years of age. **Answer (D) is incorrect.** MaryAnn is allowed to contribute to an IRA.

11. A contribution to a traditional individual retirement plan (IRA) is deductible for tax year 2020 in which of the following situations?

    A. The individual's employer does not have a retirement plan at any time during 2020.

    B. The contribution is made on August 15, 2021, under a properly filed and accepted extension.

    C. The individual is covered by a retirement plan but does not have any compensation in 2020.

    D. All of the answers are correct.

Answer (A) is correct.
    REQUIRED: The situation that permits a contribution to a traditional IRA to be deductible for the tax year.
    DISCUSSION: All traditional IRA contributions made by employees for a particular year must be made no later than the due date for filing that year's tax return without regard to any filing extensions that may have been granted [Sec. 219(f)(3)]. Several other restrictions apply. Individuals may only make deductible contributions equal to the lesser of $6,000 ($7,000 if aged 50 or older) or 100% of compensation. Also, the amount of the deduction is phased out, based on modified AGI, if the individual is an active participant in an employer-sponsored retirement plan. Only traditional IRAs qualify for the deduction.
    Answer (B) is incorrect. Contributions must be made prior to the due date of the return, regardless of extensions. **Answer (C) is incorrect.** Individuals may only make deductible contributions equal to the lesser of $6,000 ($7,000 if aged 50 or older) or 100% of compensation. **Answer (D) is incorrect.** Traditional IRA contributions made by employees must be made prior to the due date of the return, regardless of extensions, and individuals may only make deductible contributions equal to the lesser of $6,000 ($7,000 if aged 50 or older) or 100% of compensation.

12. Sam received a total distribution of $40,000 from his employer's 401(k) plan consisting of $25,000 in cash and land with a fair market value of $15,000. If Sam decides to keep the land, what is the total amount that he can roll over to his traditional IRA?

A. Sam may substitute $15,000 of his own funds for the property and consider his rollover to be $40,000 in cash.

B. Sam can roll over only $15,000, the value of the land he received.

C. Sam can roll over the $25,000 cash received into his IRA.

D. Sam is required to sell the land before any part of the distribution can be rolled over.

Answer (C) is correct.
REQUIRED: The amount of a retirement distribution that can be rolled over to a traditional IRA.
DISCUSSION: Generally, a rollover is a tax-free distribution of cash or other assets from one retirement plan to another retirement plan. If the taxpayer does not make a direct transfer of assets from one retirement plan to another but instead withdraws assets from the plan, the taxpayer must deposit the assets into another qualified plan within 60 days of the withdrawal in order to avoid taxes and penalties. A rollover cannot be deducted. The taxpayer may not substitute assets in the transfer between retirement plans (Publication 590-A).
Answer (A) is incorrect. Sam is not allowed to substitute his own funds for keeping the land. **Answer (B) is incorrect.** Sam is not allowed to roll over the $15,000 value of the land he received if he is keeping the land. **Answer (D) is incorrect.** Sam can still roll over the $25,000 in cash regardless of whether he sells the land.

13. Margaret is fully vested. She will receive Social Security benefits at retirement but has no other retirement plan coverage. Her present and past employers have not had retirement plans available. In 2020, she files as single, and her earnings are $68,000. Also in 2020, she contributes $6,000 to a traditional IRA. How much of the $6,000 contribution may she deduct?

A. $0

B. $4,200

C. $6,000

D. $1,800

Answer (C) is correct.
REQUIRED: The deduction a taxpayer may take for his or her traditional IRA contribution.
DISCUSSION: Margaret is able to take a full $6,000 deduction for her contribution to an IRA. She is not a member of a retirement plan; thus, her deduction is not reduced.
Answer (A) is incorrect. Margaret is entitled to a deduction. **Answer (B) is incorrect.** The amount of $4,200 ($6,000 – $1,800) would be the allowed deduction if Margaret was a member of a retirement plan. **Answer (D) is incorrect.** The amount of $1,800 [($68,000 – $65,000) ÷ ($75,000 – $65,000) × $6,000] is the reduction Margaret would be required to make if she were a member of a retirement plan.

14. Which of the following statements is false with respect to setting up a traditional individual retirement account (IRA)?

A. An IRA cannot be set up with joint ownership of husband and wife.

B. A taxpayer cannot roll over assets from his IRA to his spouse's IRA.

C. A taxpayer may be eligible to set up an IRA for a spouse regardless of whether the spouse received compensation.

D. An individual who files a joint return and is not covered by an employer retirement plan can deduct the entire contribution to an IRA, regardless of the amount of his or her adjusted gross income, even if the spouse is covered by an employer's plan.

Answer (D) is correct.
REQUIRED: The false statement regarding setting up an IRA.
DISCUSSION: An individual may deduct the contributions to an IRA even if his or her spouse is covered by an employer plan. However, the deduction is phased out if the couple's AGI is more than $196,000 but less than $206,000. The deduction is eliminated if the AGI on the joint return is $206,000 or more.

15. Kimberly, age 30, a full-time student with no taxable compensation, married Michael, age 30, during 2020. For the year, Michael had taxable compensation of $35,000. He plans to contribute and deduct $6,000 to his traditional IRA. If he and Kimberly file a joint return, how much may each deduct in 2020 for contributions to their individual traditional IRAs and what is the compensation Kimberly uses to figure her contribution limit?

	IRA Deduction	Compensation for Kimberly to Figure IRA Contribution Limit
A.	$6,000	$29,000
B.	$6,000	$35,000
C.	$4,000	$35,000
D.	$2,000	$35,000

Answer (A) is correct.

REQUIRED: The maximum deductible amount that can be contributed to a traditional IRA and the amount of compensation that should be used to figure an IRA contribution limit.

DISCUSSION: Under Sec. 219(c), if a joint return is filed and a taxpayer makes less than his or her spouse, the taxpayer may still contribute the lesser of

1) The sum of his or her compensation and the taxable compensation of the spouse, reduced by the amount of the spouse's IRA contribution and contributions to a Roth IRA, or

2) $6,000 ($7,000 if over age 50).

Kimberly is still eligible to deduct the full $6,000 for her IRA contribution. However, the income is based upon Michael's $35,000 income reduced by his $6,000 IRA contribution.

Answer (B) is incorrect. The $35,000 of compensation is reduced by Michael's IRA contribution. Answer (C) is incorrect. The limit on IRA deductions is $6,000. Answer (D) is incorrect. The limit on IRA deductions is $6,000, and Michael's compensation limit is reduced by his $6,000 contribution for a total compensation limit of $29,000.

16. Dave, age 40, had a traditional IRA with a $40,000 balance at the beginning of 2020. All of Dave's contributions have been tax deductible. On July 1, 2020, Dave borrowed $20,000 from the IRA account. Which of the following would be a correct statement regarding the tax consequences of this transaction?

A. This would not be a prohibited transaction, provided that the loan called for periodic payments and an interest rate at least equal to the applicable federal rate (AFR).

B. Dave would be required to include $20,000 in income as a distribution in 2020.

C. Dave would be required to include $40,000 in income as a distribution in 2020.

D. Dave would not have to include the $20,000 in income if it were used for qualified higher education expenses.

Answer (C) is correct.

REQUIRED: The tax consequence of borrowing from a traditional IRA.

DISCUSSION: Publications 590-A and 590-B state, "Generally, a prohibited transaction is any improper use of your traditional IRA account . . . by any disqualified person." Examples of prohibited transactions include

- Borrowing money from it
- Selling property to it
- Receiving unreasonable compensation for managing it
- Using it as security for a loan
- Buying property for personal use (present or future) with IRA funds

These transactions stop the account from being an IRA. "If you borrow money against your traditional IRA annuity contract, you must include in your gross income the fair market value of the annuity contract as of the first day of your tax year."

Answer (A) is incorrect. Borrowing money from a traditional IRA is a prohibited transaction regardless of payment plan. Answer (B) is incorrect. The amount that Dave would have to include in income is not $20,000. Answer (D) is incorrect. If an individual withdraws funds from an IRA prematurely for higher education expenses, the individual is not subject to the 10% early withdrawal penalty; however, the withdrawn amount must be included in gross income as long as the IRA contributions were tax deductible.

17. In December 2017, Gail worked for ABC Co. and participated in its retirement plan. On February 1, 2020, Gail was employed by XYZ Corp., which has a qualified retirement plan. On March 1, 2020, the ABC Co. plan administrator distributed to Gail her vested share of the plan. Gail was 42 years old at the time of distribution. Which of the following will allow Gail to avoid paying taxes and penalties on her withdrawal?

    A. Deposit the plan funds in a local bank.

    B. Contribute the distribution to the XYZ Corp. plan within 60 days.

    C. Donate the plan funds to a charity.

    D. None of the answers are correct.

Answer (B) is correct.
    REQUIRED: The qualifying distribution rollover.
    DISCUSSION: A taxpayer can avoid taxes and penalties on a distribution of assets from a qualified retirement plan if the assets are deposited into another qualified plan within 60 days (Publication 575). Section 408(d)(3)(A) allows an eligible rollover distribution from an individual retirement account to be rolled over into a qualified employer plan, a 403(b) tax-sheltered annuity, or a Sec. 457 deferred compensation plan.
    Answer (A) is incorrect. The only way for Gail to avoid taxes and penalties is to transfer the retirement plan assets into another qualified plan within 60 days of the withdrawal. **Answer (C) is incorrect.** The only way for Gail to avoid taxes and penalties is to transfer the retirement plan assets into another qualified plan within 60 days of the withdrawal. **Answer (D) is incorrect.** A correct answer choice is provided.

18. Joe Smith never married and had no children. When he died, he left all of his assets, including his traditional IRA, to his nephew, David. What is David allowed to do with the inherited IRA?

    A. He could make additional direct contributions to the IRA, treating it as his own.

    B. He could roll over amounts out of the inherited IRA to another IRA tax-free.

    C. He could make additional contributions, which were rollovers from Roth IRAs.

    D. None of the answers are correct.

Answer (D) is correct.
    REQUIRED: The allowable treatment of an inherited IRA.
    DISCUSSION: If an individual inherits a traditional IRA from anyone other than a deceased spouse, the person is not permitted to treat the inherited IRA as his or her own, making direct contributions. The inherited IRA will generally not have tax assessed on the IRA assets until distributions are received (Publication 590-A).
    Answer (A) is incorrect. The inherited IRA cannot have additional direct contributions made as if it were the heir's own. **Answer (B) is incorrect.** Rolling over amounts to another IRA tax-free are only permitted if inherited from a spouse. **Answer (C) is incorrect.** Additional contributions that were rollovers from Roth IRAs are not permitted.

19. Edwin and Donna were married. Edwin had established a traditional IRA to which he made contributions and had taken no distributions. The total value of the IRA was $50,000, of which $20,000 was nondeductible contributions. As the spousal beneficiary, which of the following applies to Donna?

    A. Edwin's $20,000 basis in the IRA may be treated as basis to Donna.

    B. When Donna receives the distribution, she may not roll it over to her own traditional IRA.

    C. Donna must begin receiving periodic distributions by December 31 of the fifth year following Edwin's death.

    D. Donna must pay a 10% penalty on the funds in the IRA if she receives an immediate distribution after Edwin's death.

Answer (A) is correct.
    REQUIRED: The statement applicable to a spousal beneficiary of an inherited traditional IRA.
    DISCUSSION: The basis attached to a traditional IRA because of non-deductible contributions remains with the IRA. If it is inherited to a spouse, the basis received is considered to belong to the spousal beneficiary (Publication 590).
    Answer (B) is incorrect. Donna is permitted to roll the distribution over to her own traditional IRA. **Answer (C) is incorrect.** Donna may roll the distribution into her IRA. **Answer (D) is incorrect.** The 10% penalty is not assessed if immediate distribution occurs after the spouse's death.

12.3 Penalties

20. Generally, which of the following is a prohibited transaction concerning your traditional IRA?

A. Withdraw funds for qualified higher education expenses.

B. Pledge your IRA account as security for your mortgage.

C. Withdraw funds for qualified medical expenses.

D. Withdraw funds to purchase your first home.

Answer (B) is correct.
REQUIRED: The transaction concerning a traditional IRA that is prohibited.
DISCUSSION: A taxpayer may not engage in the following transactions with a traditional IRA: sell property to it, use it as security for a loan, or buy property with it for the taxpayer's personal use. Amounts withdrawn in qualified transactions require the amount withdrawn to be included in income but do not incur the 10% early withdrawal penalty.

21. Sunnie is single and does not actively participate in her employer's pension plan. She received taxable compensation of $3,500 in Year 1 and $4,500 in Year 2. Her modified adjusted gross income was $26,000 in both years. For Year 1, she contributed $6,000 to her IRA but deducted only $3,500 on her income tax return. For Year 2, she contributed $2,000 but deducted $4,500 on her income tax return. Based on this information, which of the following statements is true?

A. Sunnie must pay an excise tax on the excess contribution for Year 1 and also for Year 2 since she did not withdraw the excess.

B. Sunnie must pay an excise tax for Year 1 on the $2,500 excess contribution made in Year 1, but since she properly treated the Year 1 excess contribution as part of her Year 2 deduction, she does not owe the excise tax for Year 2.

C. Sunnie will be assessed a 10% tax for early withdrawals when she withdraws the excess contribution.

D. Sunnie should claim an IRA deduction of only $1,500 for Year 2.

Answer (B) is correct.
REQUIRED: The true statement regarding deductions and contributions to an IRA.
DISCUSSION: Section 408 limits contributions to an IRA to the lesser of $6,000 ($7,000 if aged 50 or older) or the amount of compensation includible in the taxpayer's gross income. Sunnie's Year 1 contributions should have been limited to $3,500. She therefore had $2,500 of excess contributions in Year 1 ($6,000 – $3,500). Under Sec. 4973, a nondeductible 6% excise tax is imposed on excess contributions to an IRA. Under Sec. 219(b), the deduction for contributions to an IRA is limited to the lesser of $6,000 or the amount of compensation that must be included in gross income. Sunnie's $3,500 deduction in Year 1 was correct. In Year 2, Sunnie contributed only $2,000 but deducted $4,500. Under Sec. 219(f)(6), Sunnie may treat the $2,500 unused contributions from Year 1 as having been made in Year 2. Therefore, her allowable deduction for IRA contributions in Year 2 is $4,500.
Answer (A) is incorrect. Sunnie did not make excess contributions in Year 2. **Answer (C) is incorrect.** A 6% excise tax is assessed when the excess contributions are made. **Answer (D) is incorrect.** Sunnie can claim an IRA deduction of $4,500 for Year 2.

22. Gina, who is single, received taxable compensation of $1,700 in 2019 and $2,500 in 2020. She did not actively participate in a pension plan. She contributed $2,000 in 2019 and $2,000 in 2020 to her IRA. On March 18, 2020, she withdrew $300 of her 2019 contribution plus the interest accumulated on it from her IRA and did not deduct that amount on her 2019 tax return. Based on this information, what is the amount of her excess contributions subject to the 6% tax?

A. $0

B. $300

C. $500

D. $800

Answer (A) is correct.
REQUIRED: The amount of excess contributions subject to the 6% tax.
DISCUSSION: In general, an individual who withdraws an excess contribution made during a tax year and the interest earned on it before the return due date will not be subject to the excess contributions tax. This rule is available only for individuals who did not take a deduction for the amount of the excess contribution.

23. Martin, age 35, made an excess contribution to his traditional IRA in 2020 of $1,000, which he withdrew by April 15, 2021. Also in 2020, he withdrew the $50 income that was earned on the $1,000. Which of the following statements is true?

I. Martin must include the $50 in his gross income in 2020.

II. Martin would have to pay the 6% excise tax on the $1,050.

III. Martin would have to pay the 10% additional tax on the $50 as an early distribution.

IV. Martin would have to pay the 10% additional tax on the $1,000 because he made a withdrawal.

A. I only.

B. I, II, and III only.

C. III and IV only.

D. I and III only.

Answer (D) is correct.
REQUIRED: The true statement regarding an excess contribution and the tax that will be assessed.
DISCUSSION: Premature distributions are amounts withdrawn from an IRA or annuity before a taxpayer reaches age 59 1/2. The additional tax on premature distributions is equal to 10% of the amount of premature distribution that must be included in gross income. Therefore, both I and III are true statements, making this the best choice of the listed options.
Answer (A) is incorrect. Martin must also pay the 10% additional tax on the $50 as an early distribution. **Answer (B) is incorrect.** Martin is not required to pay the 6% excise tax on the $1,050 because it was withdrawn by the due date of the return (i.e., April 15). **Answer (C) is incorrect.** Martin must include the $50 in his gross income for 2020. Furthermore, the 10% additional tax only applies to the funds that are distributed; therefore, the $1,000 will not incur any additional penalty.

24. With regard to excess contributions to a traditional IRA, which of the following statements is false?

A. A taxpayer may deduct from gross income, in the first year available, the amount of the excess contribution in the IRA, from the preceding years up to the difference between the maximum amount that is deductible in the year and the amount actually contributed during the year.

B. If a taxpayer has an excess contribution in his or her IRA as a result of a rollover, and the excess occurred because the taxpayer had incorrect information required to be supplied by the plan, the taxpayer can withdraw the excess contribution.

C. If the excess contribution for a year is not withdrawn by the date a taxpayer's return is due, the taxpayer is subject to an 8% tax.

D. Generally, an excess contribution is the amount contributed to an IRA that is more than the smaller of the following amounts: (1) a taxpayer's taxable compensation or (2) $6,000 ($7,000 if age 50 or older).

Answer (C) is correct.
REQUIRED: The false statement regarding excess contributions to a traditional IRA.
DISCUSSION: In general, if the excess contribution for a year and any earnings on it are not withdrawn by the due date of the return, the taxpayer is subject to a 6% tax.

12.4 Roth IRAs

25. Which of the following is true regarding contributions to a Roth IRA?

A. Contributions may be made regardless of age, provided other requirements are met.

B. Contributions may be deducted if you are within certain income limits.

C. Contributions may be deducted if you are not covered under a retirement plan.

D. Contributions may not be deducted, but earnings are taxable when distributed.

Answer (A) is correct.
    REQUIRED: The true statement regarding contributions to a Roth IRA.
    DISCUSSION: Publication 590-A states that contributions can be made to a Roth IRA regardless of age. Also, amounts can be left in the Roth IRA as long as the taxpayer lives.
    Answer (B) is incorrect. Contributions to a Roth IRA cannot be deducted. **Answer (C) is incorrect.** Contributions to a Roth IRA cannot be deducted. **Answer (D) is incorrect.** Qualified distributions from a Roth IRA are not included in the taxpayer's gross income.

26. Which of the following amounts may be converted directly to a Roth IRA, provided all requirements are met?

A. Amounts in a SIMPLE IRA, and the 2-year participation period has been met.

B. Amounts in a traditional IRA inherited from a person other than a spouse.

C. Hardship distribution from a 401(k) plan.

D. Required minimum distributions from a traditional IRA.

Answer (A) is correct.
    REQUIRED: The amount permitted to be converted to a Roth IRA, provided all requirements are met.
    DISCUSSION: Amounts carried in a SIMPLE IRA may be converted assuming the required 2-year participation period has been met (Publication 590-A).
    Answer (B) is incorrect. A traditional IRA inherited from a person other than a spouse is not convertible. **Answer (C) is incorrect.** Hardship distributions are not directly convertible. **Answer (D) is incorrect.** Required minimum distributions from a traditional IRA are not permissible conversions.

27. In general, a taxpayer over age 50 may make which of the following in a given tax year?

I. A $7,000 contribution to a Roth IRA.

II. A $7,000 contribution to a traditional IRA.

A. I only.

B. II only.

C. I and II.

D. I or II.

Answer (D) is correct.
    REQUIRED: The rules regarding allowed contributions to IRAs.
    DISCUSSION: In total, a taxpayer over the age of 50 may make contributions to either Roth IRAs or traditional IRAs, provided the total contributions do not exceed $7,000. For instance, $2,500 could be contributed to a Roth IRA, allowing a maximum $4,500 contribution to a traditional IRA for the year.
    Answer (A) is incorrect. A taxpayer may make contributions to traditional IRAs after reaching the age of 50. **Answer (B) is incorrect.** A taxpayer may make contributions to Roth IRAs after reaching the age of 50. **Answer (C) is incorrect.** Only $7,000 may be contributed per year for a taxpayer over the age of 50.

STUDY UNIT THIRTEEN

GIFT TAX

(6 pages of outline)

The gift tax is a wealth transfer tax that applies if a property transfer occurs during a person's lifetime. The property transferred may be real, personal, tangible, or intangible. Both the gift tax and the estate tax are part of a unified transfer tax system under which gratuitous transfers of property between persons are subject to taxation.

13.1 GIFT TAX RETURN

A donor is required to file a gift tax return, Form 709, for any gift(s) made unless all gifts are excluded by the following:

1. The annual $15,000 exclusion,
2. The deduction for qualified charitable gifts, or
3. The deduction for qualified transfers to the donor's spouse.

These exclusions apply for gifts of present interests only. Any gift of a future interest requires the filing of Form 709. Gift splitting does not excuse the donor from the requirement to file.

Due Date

1. A gift tax return is due on the 15th of April following the calendar year in which a gift was made. But a gift tax return for a year of death is due no later than the estate tax return due date.

    a. A calendar-year taxpayer who receives an extension of time for filing his or her income tax return automatically receives an extension to that same extended due date for filing his or her gift tax return for that same year.

Marital Exclusion

2. A taxpayer does not have to file a gift tax return to report gifts to his or her spouse. This rule does not apply if either

    a. The spouse is not a U.S. citizen and the total gifts exceed $157,000 or

    b. The taxpayer makes any gift of a terminable interest that does not meet the power of appointment exception.

Charitable Gifts

3. If the only gifts a taxpayer makes during the year are deductible as gifts to charities, the taxpayer is not required to file a return.

    a. The entire interest in the property must be transferred to the qualified charity.

    b. If only a partial interest was transferred, a return must be filed.

    c. If a taxpayer made both charitable and noncharitable gifts, all gifts must be included on the return.

Filing Requirement

4. If the total value of gifts of present interests to any donee is $15,000 or less, the taxpayer need not report on Form 709, Schedule A, any gifts (except gifts of future interests) that were made to that donee.

5. If the total value of the gifts of present interests to any donee is more than $15,000, the taxpayer must report all such gifts that were made during the year to or on behalf of that donee.

    a. This includes those gifts that will be excluded under the annual exclusion.

Form 709

6. Publication 559 excludes the following from taxable gifts:

    a. The annual exclusion ($15,000 for 2020)
    b. Gifts to a spouse
    c. Charitable gifts
    d. Political contributions
    e. Qualified tuition payments
    f. Medical costs

7. Subunit 13.2 contains definitions of qualified tuition and medical costs.

STOP AND REVIEW! **You have completed the outline for this subunit. Study multiple-choice questions 1 through 12 beginning on page 375.**

13.2 GIFT TAX

Gift tax is a tax of the transfer, imposed on the donor. The table below presents the basic tax formula, modified for the gift tax.

```
       Gift Amount
            FMV on date of gift, for
            all gifts in the calendar year
    −   Exclusions
            Annual exclusion
                $15,000 per donee
                Gift splitting between spouses
            Paid on behalf of another for
                Medical care
                Education tuition
    −   Deductions
            Marital
            Charitable
    =   Taxable gifts for current year
    +   Taxable gifts for prior years
    =   Taxable gifts to date
    ×   Tax rate
    =   Tentative gift tax
    −   [Prior year's gifts × Current tax rates]
    −   Applicable credit amount
    =   Gift tax liability
```

Amount of Gift

1. Any excess of FMV of transferred property over the FMV of consideration for it is a gift.

```
        FMV of transferred property: Given
    −   FMV of consideration (property, money, etc.):
        Received
        Gift amount
```

   a. A gift is complete when the giver has given over dominion and control such that (s)he is without legal power to change its disposition.

EXAMPLE 13-1	Joint Bank Account -- Completion of Gift

R opens a joint bank account with A, I, and H, with R as the only depositor to the account. R, A, I, and H may each withdraw money. A gift is complete only when A, I, or H withdraws money.

b.   Gifts completed when the donor is alive **(inter vivos gifts)** are the only ones subject to gift tax. Transfers made in trust are included.

1)   Property passing by will or inheritance is not included.

c.   To the extent credit is extended with less than sufficient stated interest, the Code imputes that interest is charged. If the parties are related, the lender is treated as having made a gift of the imputed interest to the borrower each year the loan is outstanding.

1)   Gift loans are excluded if the aggregate outstanding principal is not more than $10,000.

d.   Basis in a gift is basis in the hands of the donor plus gift tax attributable to appreciation.

EXAMPLE 13-2   Basis of a Gift of Land

Thomas made a gift to his daughter of a piece of land with a FMV of $95,000. The land had a basis to Thomas of $60,000. He made a taxable gift of $80,000 ($95,000 FMV – $15,000 annual exclusion) and paid a gift tax of $32,000 ($80,000 × 40%). The basis of the land to the daughter is carryover basis of $60,000 plus the gift tax attributable to the appreciation.

$$\$60,000 \ + \ \left(\frac{\$35,000 \text{ increase in value}}{\$80,000 \text{ taxable gift}} \ \times \ \$32,000 \right) \ = \ \$74,000$$

Annual Exclusion

2.   The first $15,000 of gifts of present interest to each donee is excluded from taxable gift amounts. The annual exclusion is indexed to reflect inflation.

a.   The $15,000 exclusion applies only to gifts of present interests.

b.   A present interest in property includes an unrestricted right to the immediate possession or enjoyment of property or to the income from property (such as a life estate or a term for years). Gifts of future interest in property (such as remainders or reversions) do not qualify for the annual exclusion.

EXAMPLE 13-3   Gift of a Present Interest and a Future Interest

Edward sets up a trust with the income going to his daughter for her life and the remainder to his granddaughter. Edward has made a gift of a present interest to his daughter and a future interest to his granddaughter.

Medical or Tuition Costs

3.   Excluded from taxable gifts are amounts paid on behalf of another individual as tuition to an educational organization or for medical care.

a.   The payment must be made directly to the third party, i.e., the medical provider or the educational organization.

b.   Amounts paid for room, board, and books are not excluded.

Support

4.   Transfers that represent support of a former spouse or a child are not gifts. Generally, child support payments end at age 18.

Political Contributions

5.   Political contributions are not subject to gift tax and are not reported on the return.

Marital Deduction

6. The amount of a gift transfer to a spouse is deducted in computing taxable gifts. Donor and donee must be married at the time of the gift, and the donee must be a U.S. citizen.

   a. The deduction may not exceed the amount includible as taxable gifts. Otherwise, the amount of the deduction is not limited.

EXAMPLE 13-4   Marital Deduction

Sid Smith gave his wife, Mary, a diamond ring valued at $20,000 and cash gifts of $30,000 during 2020. Sid is entitled to a $15,000 exclusion with respect to the gifts to Mary. His marital deduction is $35,000 ($20,000 + $30,000 – $15,000).

Charitable Deduction

7. The FMV of property donated to a qualified charitable organization is deductible. Like the marital deduction, the amount of the deduction is the amount of the gift reduced by the $15,000 exclusion with respect to the donee.

Qualified Tuition Program

8. Payments to a qualified tuition program (QTP), also known as a 529 plan, are not to be confused with qualified tuition costs (explained on the previous page).

   a. A taxpayer may elect to treat up to $75,000 of a contribution to a QTP as if made ratably over a 5-year period.

   b. By making the election, the contribution will be excluded each year under the $15,000 annual limit.

   c. Any contribution in excess of the $75,000 limit is reported for the year of contribution (as opposed to being apportioned over the 5 years).

   d. Contributions to QTPs do not qualify for the education exclusion.

Computing the Gift Tax

9. Tentative tax is the sum of taxable gifts to each person for the current year and for each preceding year times the gift tax rate. Taxable gifts to a person is the total of gift amounts (FMV) in excess of exclusions and the marital and charitable deductions for a calendar year.

   a. The unified transfer tax rates are used.

      1) Current-year applicable rates are applied to both current and preceding years' taxable gifts.

      2) The rate is 18% for taxable gifts up to $10,000.

      3) The rates increase in small steps (e.g., 2%, 3%) over numerous brackets.

      4) The maximum rate is 40% on cumulative gifts in excess of $1,000,000 in 2020.

   b. The tentative gift tax is reduced by the product of prior years' taxable gifts and the current-year rates.

   c. Applicable credit amount (ACA). Tentative tax may also be reduced by any ACA (also referred to as unified credit). The ACA is a base amount ($4,577,800) reduced by amounts allowable as credits for all preceding tax years. This excludes the first $11,580,000 of taxable gifts.

   Gift tax liability for a current year = Tentative tax – (Prior-year gifts × Current rates) – ACA

STOP AND REVIEW! **You have completed the outline for this subunit. Study multiple-choice questions 13 through 25 beginning on page 379.**

13.3 GIFT SPLITTING

If both spouses consent, married couples may consider a gift made by one spouse to any person other than the other spouse as made one-half by each spouse.

1. A married couple is not allowed gift splitting if

    a. The couple is not married at the time of the gift;

    b. The couple divorces after the gift, and either spouse remarries before the end of the calendar year; or

    c. One of the spouses is a nonresident alien.

2. A joint gift tax return does not exist.

    a. Each spouse must file his or her own gift return.

    b. A spouse may simply give his or her consent to gift splitting by signing the donor spouse's return if all the requirements of one of the following exceptions are met:

        1) Only one spouse made any gifts, and the total value of these gifts did not exceed $30,000.

        2) One spouse made gifts of more than $15,000 but less than $30,000, and the only gifts made by the other spouse were gifts of not more than $15,000.

3. If taxpayers elect to split gifts, all gifts made by both spouses to third-party donees must be split. The only exception is if the taxpayer gives the spouse a general power of appointment over a gift the taxpayer made.

4. If spouses elect to split gifts, both spouses are jointly and severally liable.

5. Gift-splitting couples are not required to file a joint return.

STOP AND REVIEW! **You have completed the outline for this subunit. Study multiple-choice questions 26 through 30 beginning on page 384.**

QUESTIONS

13.1 Gift Tax Return

1. Nancy's books and records reflect the following for the year. Which transaction would require filing Form 709, *United States Gift (and Generation-Skipping Transfer) Tax Return*?

A. Gratuitously transferred a vehicle with a fair market value of $22,000 to her fiance a month before they were married.

B. Donated $16,000 to a qualified political organization.

C. Paid $22 000 to St. Francis Hospital for her aunt's unreimbursed medical expenses.

D. Paid $16 000 to State University for her brother's tuition.

Answer (A) is correct.
   REQUIRED: The transaction that requires the filing of a gift tax return.
   DISCUSSION: Section 6019 provides that a gift tax return must be filed unless all gifts may be excluded under the $15,000 exclusion of Sec. 2503(b), or the charitable gifts provision of Sec. 6019(3), or unless they may be deducted under the marital deduction rules of Sec. 2523(a). The gift to the fiance must be reported since he does not qualify for the marital deduction at the time of the gift.
   Answer (B) is incorrect. Donations to political organizations do not require a gift tax return to be filed. They are not "gifts." **Answer (C) is incorrect.** The expenses qualify for the medical payment exclusion of 2503(e). They are not "gifts." **Answer (D) is incorrect.** The expense qualifies for the educational payment exclusion of 2503(e). It is not a "gift."

2. Generally, in which of the following scenarios must a gift tax return be filed?

A. You gave gifts to an individual (other than your spouse) totaling more than $15,000.

B. You gave a gift of a future interest that was less than $15,000.

C. You wish to split gifts with your spouse.

D. All of the answers are correct.

Answer (D) is correct.
   REQUIRED: The situation(s) in which a gift tax return must be filed.
   DISCUSSION: A donor is required to file a gift tax return, Form 709, for any gift(s), unless all gifts are excluded under the annual $15,000 exclusion, the exclusion for qualified charitable gifts, or the deduction for qualified transfers to the donor's spouse. These exclusions apply for gifts of present interest only. Any gift of a future interest requires the filing of Form 709 since the exclusion does not apply. Gift splitting does not excuse the donor from the requirement to file.

3. Form 709, *United States Gift (and Generation-Skipping Transfer) Tax Return*, is required to be filed for

A. A transfer of a present interest that is not more than the annual exclusion ($15,000).

B. A qualified transfer for educational or medical expenses.

C. A transfer of a future interest that is not more than the annual exclusion ($15,000).

D. A transfer to your spouse that qualifies for the unlimited marital deduction.

Answer (C) is correct.
   REQUIRED: The transfer that requires the filing of Form 709.
   DISCUSSION: In general, Form 709, *United States Gift (and Generation-Skipping Transfer) Tax Return*, is required for any gift of a future interest.
   Answer (A) is incorrect. Present interest gifts are excluded from gift taxation if they are less than the annual exclusion. **Answer (B) is incorrect.** Transfers for qualified educational or medical needs of the recipient are not gifts. **Answer (D) is incorrect.** Transfers to a spouse that qualify for the marital deduction do not require the filing of a return.

4. Which of the following situations would require the filing of Form 709?

    A. You and your spouse agree to split your gifts, which total $20,000.

    B. You gave more than $15,000 during the year to any one donee.

    C. Any of the gifts you made were of a future interest.

    D. All of the answers are correct.

Answer (D) is correct.
    REQUIRED: The situation(s) requiring the filing of Form 709.
    DISCUSSION: A gift tax return must be filed for gifts that exceed $15,000 and were split with a spouse. Additionally, a return is required to be filed if more than $15,000 is gifted to any one donee or if any of the gifts were of a future interest.
    Answer (A) is incorrect. Along with the requirement to file split gifts, Form 709 is required when $15,000 is given to any one donee or for any gifts of a future interest. **Answer (B) is incorrect.** Along with the requirement to file for gifts exceeding $15,000 to any one donee, Form 709 is required for gift splitting or gifts of a future interest. **Answer (C) is incorrect.** Along with the requirement to file if the gift is of a future interest, Form 709 is required for gift splitting or gifts that exceed $15,000 to any one donee.

5. Tom, who is married, gave a vase worth $40,000 to his sister, Julie. Tom's basis in the vase is $10,000. What amount will Tom report as the value of the gift on Form 709?

    A. $10,000

    B. $20,000

    C. $30,000

    D. $40,000

Answer (D) is correct.
    REQUIRED: The value of the gift.
    DISCUSSION: The amount of a gift is the fair market value of what was given. In this situation, the fair market value is $40,000, which is what Tom will report as the value of the gift on Form 709.
    Answer (A) is incorrect. The basis of the vase is $10,000. **Answer (B) is incorrect.** The value of the gift is $40,000. **Answer (C) is incorrect.** The difference between the fair market value of the vase and the basis of the vase is $30,000.

6. John made the following transfers during tax year 2020:

- To his neighbor in the amount of $19,000
- To his nephew in the amount of $16,000
- To his uncle in the amount of $17,000

All of the transfers are gifts that qualify for the annual exclusion. John files one Form 709 for tax year end December 31, 2020. What is the total annual exclusion amount for gifts listed on John's 2020 Form 709 filing?

    A. $52,000

    B. $45,000

    C. $15,000

    D. $14,000

Answer (B) is correct.
    REQUIRED: The annual exclusion amount.
    DISCUSSION: Section 2503(b) authorizes a $15,000 exclusion from gross income for income tax purposes and is available to an unlimited number of donees. Therefore, the total annual exclusion amount for gifts listed on John's 2019 Form 709 filing is $45,000 ($15,000 annual-exclusion per donee × 3 donees).
    Answer (A) is incorrect. The amount of $52,000 is the total value of the gifts. **Answer (C) is incorrect.** John is allowed more than one exclusion. **Answer (D) is incorrect.** The exclusion amount for tax year 2017 is $14,000.

7. The following transfers were made by Ed during 2020. What is the gross amount of gifts to be included on Ed's 2020 Form 709 filing?

- $17,000 to the United Way
- $15,000 to a political organization
- $21,000 paid directly to his nephew's college for tuition
- $16,000 paid directly to his niece for her college tuition

    A. $37,000

    B. $16,000

    C. $33,000

    D. $54,000

Answer (C) is correct.
    REQUIRED: The gross amount of gifts required on Form 709.
    DISCUSSION: If a taxpayer is required to file a return to report noncharitable gifts and made gifts to charities, all of the gifts to charities must be included on the return. The $21,000 and the $15,000 are not considered gifts and are not included in total gifts. Therefore, Ed must only include the $17,000 contribution to the United Way and the $16,000 paid directly to his niece.
    Answer (A) is incorrect. The $21,000 is exempted as a gift, and the contribution to the United Way is included as a charitable contribution. **Answer (B) is incorrect.** Ed was required to file a return to report his noncharitable gifts, and this fact requires him to include all gifts to charities (the United Way) on the return. Thus, he also must include the $17,000 contribution to the United Way. **Answer (D) is incorrect.** The $21,000 is exempted as a gift and is not included on the gift tax return.

8. In which of the following circumstances would a gift tax return be due?

    A. Check for $25,000 to son.

    B. Transfer of stock valued at $30,000 to spouse.

    C. Payment of a friend's $16,000 tuition expense.

    D. None of the answers are correct.

Answer (A) is correct.
    REQUIRED: Filing requirements of a gift tax return.
    DISCUSSION: A donor is required to file a gift tax return, Form 709, for any gift(s), unless all gifts are excluded under the annual $15,000 exclusion and the deduction for qualified transfers to the donor's spouse. These exclusions apply for gifts of present interests only. Any gift of a future interest requires the filing of Form 709. The tuition expense is not a "gift." Gift splitting does not excuse the donor from the requirement to file. A check for $25,000 to a son exceeds the amount of the exclusion.
    Answer (B) is incorrect. The deduction for qualified transfers to the donor's spouse is permitted. **Answer (C) is incorrect.** An exclusion exists for payment of tuition. It is not considered a "gift." **Answer (D) is incorrect.** A check for $25,000 to a son does not qualify for an exclusion.

9. For calendar year 2020, if a gift tax return is required to be filed and the donor is not deceased, what is the due date of the return excluding extensions?

    A. Within 75 days of making the gift.

    B. On or before December 31, 2020.

    C. No earlier than January 1, 2021, and no later than April 15, 2021.

    D. Within 130 days of making the gift.

Answer (C) is correct.
    REQUIRED: The due date of a gift tax return if the donor is not deceased.
    DISCUSSION: Form 709 must generally be filed for the year 2020 after January 1, but not later than April 15, 2021.
    Answer (A) is incorrect. The filing date is not dependent on the gift date, but rather the calendar year. **Answer (B) is incorrect.** The filing does not occur before the end of the year 2020. **Answer (D) is incorrect.** The filing date is not dependent on the gift date, but rather the calendar year.

10. On June 15, 2020, Marlo made a transfer by gift in an amount sufficient to require the filing of a gift tax return. If Marlo did not request an extension of time for filing the 2020 gift tax return, the due date for filing was

   A. December 31, 2020.

   B. March 15, 2021.

   C. April 15, 2021.

   D. June 17, 2021.

Answer (C) is correct.
   REQUIRED: The date that a gift tax return is due.
   DISCUSSION: Under Sec. 6075, gift tax returns are due on or before the 15th day of April following the close of the calendar year in which a gift was made. Since Marlo made a gift in 2020, Form 709 is due by April 15, 2021.

11. Which of the following entities are required to file Form 709, *United States Gift Tax Return*?

   A. An individual.

   B. An estate or trust.

   C. A corporation.

   D. An individual, an estate or trust, and a corporation.

Answer (A) is correct.
   REQUIRED: The entity required to file Form 709, *United States Gift Tax Return*.
   DISCUSSION: The only entity required to file Form 709 is an individual taxpayer.
   Answer (B) is incorrect. An estate or trust is not required to file Form 709. **Answer (C) is incorrect.** A corporation is not required to file Form 709. **Answer (D) is incorrect.** Neither an estate or trust nor a corporation is required to file Form 709.

12. On February 4, Year 1, Mr. Smith made a gift in an amount sufficient to require the filing of a federal gift tax return. On October 5, Year 1, Mr. Smith died. No estate tax return will need to be filed for Mr. Smith. Assuming extensions have not been obtained, the gift tax return, Form 709, must be filed by (assuming none of the dates are Saturdays, Sundays, or holidays)

   A. April 15, Year 1.

   B. March 15, Year 2.

   C. April 15, Year 2.

   D. July 5, Year 2.

Answer (C) is correct.
   REQUIRED: The date that Form 709, *United States Gift Tax Return*, is due.
   DISCUSSION: Under Sec. 6075, gift tax returns are due on or before the 15th day of April following the close of the calendar year in which a gift was made. Since Mr. Smith made a gift in Year 1, Form 709 is generally due by April 15, Year 2. If the date falls on a weekend or holiday, the return is due the next business day.
   If an estate tax return were required of Mr. Smith's estate, this return would be due no later than 9 months after the date of death unless an extension was obtained [Sec. 6075(a)]. The due date for the gift tax return for the year of death is no later than the estate tax return due date [Sec. 6075(b)(3)]. Since an estate tax return is not being filed, the due date does not change.
   Answer (A) is incorrect. The return is due on April 15 following the calendar year in which the gift is made. **Answer (B) is incorrect.** The return is due on April 15 following the calendar year in which the gift is made. **Answer (D) is incorrect.** An estate return was not required to be filed.

13.2 Gift Tax

13. During 2020, Sadie made the following transfers:

- She deeded her personal residence to her daughter and herself to be held in joint tenancy. The fair market value of the residence at the time of transfer was $150,000.

- She placed a $30,000 bank account in joint tenancy with her daughter. Neither she nor her daughter made any withdrawals in 2020.

- She placed a $20,000 bank account in joint tenancy with her daughter. During 2020, Sadie withdrew $2,000, and her daughter withdrew $5,000 from the account.

- She bought $10,000 in U.S. savings bonds registered as payable to herself or her daughter. Neither she nor her daughter cashed any of the bonds during 2020.

What is the gross amount of gifts given by Sadie in 2020?

- A. $105,000

- B. $90,000

- C. $80,000

- D. $5,000

Answer (C) is correct.
    REQUIRED: The gross amount of gifts given during the year.
    DISCUSSION: If a donor buys property with his or her own funds and the title to such property is held by the donor and the donee as joint tenants with right of survivorship and, if either the donor or the donee may give up those rights by severing his or her interest, the donor has made a gift to the donee in the amount of half the value of the property. Thus, $75,000 should be included in the gross amount of gifts ($150,000 FMV of residence ÷ 2 = $75,000).
    If the donor creates a joint bank account for himself or herself and the donee [or a similar kind of ownership by which (s)he can get back the entire fund without the donee's consent], the donor has made a gift to the donee when the donee draws on the account for his or her own benefit. The amount of the gift is the amount that the donee took out without any obligation to repay the donor. Thus, the daughter's $5,000 withdrawal should be included in the gross amount of gifts. If the donor buys a U.S. savings bond registered as payable to himself or herself or the donee, there is a gift to the donee when (s)he cashes the bond without any obligation to account to the donor. Therefore, Sadie's gross amount of gifts given is $80,000 ($75,000 for the house + $5,000 for the amount withdrawn).
    Answer (A) is incorrect. One-half of all the gifts is not the proper treatment of bank accounts in joint tenancy or savings bonds. **Answer (B) is incorrect.** The savings bonds are not considered a gift until they are cashed. **Answer (D) is incorrect.** One-half the value of the personal residence is treated as a gift.

14. Lanny won $10 million at a casino in 2018 and invested in mutual funds. When he married Judy in 2019, they signed prenuptial agreements. Then, in 2020, Lanny decided to give away some of his money. He made the following gifts:

- $100,000 cash to Judy
- $50,000 to each of his three adult children
- $50,000 to the Republican Party

What are the total taxable gifts that Lanny made in 2020? (Assume no gift splitting was elected.)

- A. $200,000

- B. $300,000

- C. $105,000

- D. $150,000

Answer (C) is correct.
    REQUIRED: The total amount of taxable gifts assuming no gift splitting was elected.
    DISCUSSION: The total of the taxable gifts is the total gift amount of $250,000 minus exclusions for each gift and the marital deduction. The $50,000 transfer to the Republican Party is not subject to gift tax, and it is not included in the total taxable gifts.

	Total Gifts	Exclusions and Deductions	Taxable Gifts
Judy	$100,000	$(100,000)	$ 0
Child 1	50,000	(15,000)	35,000
Child 2	50,000	(15,000)	35,000
Child 3	50,000	(15,000)	35,000
Total	$250,000	$(145,000)	$105,000

    Answer (A) is incorrect. The $50,000 transfer to the Republican Party is not subject to gift tax. Gifts are reduced by annual exclusion. **Answer (B) is incorrect.** The total amount of money Lanny gave away is $300,000. **Answer (D) is incorrect.** The total amount of gifts is reduced by the $15,000 exclusion for each child.

15. During the current year, Mr. and Mrs. X made joint gifts to their son of the following items:

- A painting with an adjusted basis of $15,000 and a fair market value of $45,000.

- Stock with an adjusted basis of $27,000 and a fair market value of $30,000.

- An auto with an adjusted basis of $15,000 and a fair market value of $17,000.

- An interest-free loan of $8,000 for a boat (for the son's personal use) on January 1 of the current year, which was repaid by their son on December 31 of the current year. Assume the applicable federal rate was 11% per annum.

What is the gross amount of gifts includible in Mr. and Mrs. X's gift tax return?

A. $92,880

B. $92,000

C. $57,880

D. $57,000

Answer (B) is correct.
REQUIRED: The gross amount of gifts including an interest-free loan.
DISCUSSION: The amount of a gift made in property is the fair market value of the property on the date of the gift [Sec. 2512(a)]. The auto, painting, and stock have a combined fair market value of $92,000.
In general, an interest-free loan results in deemed transfers of interest between the borrower and lender. When the two parties are related, the lender is deemed to have made a gift of the interest amount to the borrower [Sec. 7872(a)(1)]. However, Sec. 7872(c)(2) excludes gift loans between individuals from this provision if the aggregate outstanding principal does not exceed $10,000. Accordingly, the $8,000 interest-free loan does not result in a gift.
Answer (A) is incorrect. The amount of $92,880 includes $880 worth of interest from the loan. Loans under $10,000 are excluded from gift taxation.
Answer (C) is incorrect. The amount of $57,880 includes $880 worth of interest, and the other properties are valued at their adjusted-basis amounts. Loans under $10,000 are excluded from gift taxation. Answer (D) is incorrect. The amount of $57,000 values the properties at their adjusted-basis amounts.

16. Ralph gave his aunt an antique clock during tax year 2020. He had purchased the clock for $17,000 in 2016. The fair market value at the date of the transfer was $23,000. What amount should be recorded on Form 709 as the value of this gift?

A. $17,000

B. $8,000

C. $23,000

D. $2,000

Answer (C) is correct.
REQUIRED: The amount of gifts given when the FMV and basis differ.
DISCUSSION: Regulation 25.2512-1 states that the amount of a gift made in property is the fair market value of the property at the date of the gift. Therefore, the value of the gift is $23,000.
Answer (A) is incorrect. The adjusted basis of the gift is $17,000. Answer (B) is incorrect. The annual exclusion reduces the taxable gift, not the value. Answer (D) is incorrect. The annual exclusion is not deducted from the adjusted basis.

17. During 2020, Dave gave his daughter Joan the following items: stock with a fair market value of $42,000 and an adjusted basis of $45,000, a boat with a fair market value of $5,000 and an adjusted basis of $3,000, and a print with a fair market value of $12,000 and an adjusted basis of $5,000. What is the gross amount of gifts includible in Dave's gift tax return for 2020?

A. $50,000

B. $53,000

C. $59,000

D. $62,000

Answer (C) is correct.
REQUIRED: The gross amount of includible gifts.
DISCUSSION: The amount of a gift made in property is the fair market value of the property at the date of the gift (Reg. 25.2512-1). The fair market value is that which would occur in an arm's-length transaction between a willing buyer and a willing seller in the normal market. Therefore, Dave must include $59,000 of gifts on his 2020 tax return ($42,000 + $5,000 + $12,000).
Answer (A) is incorrect. The lesser of the FMV or adjusted basis is not used to determine the gross amount of gifts. Answer (B) is incorrect. The gross amount of gifts is not the total of the adjusted bases of the distributed properties. Answer (D) is incorrect. The greater of the FMV or adjusted basis is not used to determine the gross amount of gifts.

18. All of the following are deductions allowed in determining the gift tax EXCEPT

   A. A gift to the state of Pennsylvania for exclusively public purposes.

   B. The value of any gift made to one's spouse who is not a United States citizen.

   C. A gift made to one's spouse, a United States citizen, in excess of $157,000.

   D. A gift of a copyrightable work of art to a qualified organization if the copyright is not transferred to the charity.

Answer (B) is correct.
   REQUIRED: The deduction that is not allowed in determining the gift tax.
   DISCUSSION: Although a full marital deduction is available for a gift to a spouse who is a U.S. citizen, regardless of the citizenship or residence of the donor, the marital deduction for a gift made to a spouse who is not a U.S. citizen is limited to $157,000 for 2020.

19. Listed below are gifts Joan made during 2020:

- $25,000 gift to a nonprofit home for the underprivileged
- $15,000 gift to her daughter
- $15,000 in contributions to a historical museum
- $40,000 gift to her spouse

What is the amount of taxable gifts to be reported on Form 709 for 2020?

   A. $0

   B. $40,000

   C. $55,000

   D. $80,000

Answer (A) is correct.
   REQUIRED: The donor's taxable gifts for the current year.
   DISCUSSION: "Taxable gifts" means the total amount of gifts made during the calendar year reduced by the charitable and marital deductions [Sec. 2503(a)]. The first $15,000 of gifts of present interests made to each donee during the year is excluded [Sec. 2503(b)]. All of Joan's transfers qualify for exclusion from gift taxation.

20. Which of the following statements regarding the annual exclusion for gift taxes is true?

   A. The gift of a present interest to more than one donee as joint tenants qualifies for only one annual exclusion.

   B. A gift of a future interest cannot be excluded under the annual exclusion.

   C. The annual exclusion amount for 2020 is $16,000.

   D. None of the answers are correct.

Answer (B) is correct.
   REQUIRED: The true statement regarding the annual exclusion for gift taxes.
   DISCUSSION: The first $15,000 of gifts of present interest to each donee is excluded from taxable gift amounts. The $15,000 exclusion applies only to gifts of present interests.
   Answer (A) is incorrect. Each donee would qualify for the annual exclusion. **Answer (C) is incorrect.** The annual exclusion for 2020 is $15,000. **Answer (D) is incorrect.** A gift of a future interest cannot be excluded under the annual exclusion.

21. During the calendar year, John made the following payments:

- $16,000 to a qualified political party
- $20,000 to a local hospital for his mother's recent operation
- $25,000 to the state university for his nephew's tuition expense
- $16,000 to his favorite qualified charity

What is the gross amount that John must report on his gift tax return (Form 709)?

A. John does not have to file a gift tax return for the calendar year.

B. $77,000

C. $61,000

D. $16,000

Answer (A) is correct.
REQUIRED: The gross amount to be reported on the gift tax return (Form 709).
DISCUSSION: Not all transfers of money are subject to gift tax. Included in those excluded transfers are those to political organizations [defined in Sec. 527(e)(1)], amounts paid for qualified education expenses, and amounts paid for providing medical care. Additionally, the $16,000 transfer to the charity qualifies for exclusion when no other items are taxable.
Answer (B) is incorrect. The amounts paid to the political organization, the hospital, the qualified charity, and the university for tuition are excluded transfers.
Answer (C) is incorrect. No gift return must be filed for the political, educational, and medical payments.
Answer (D) is incorrect. The charitable contribution qualifies for exclusion when no other items are taxable.

22. Donald is a tax return preparer. His client, Jody Black, told him that she had made several gifts during 2020. She asked whether she should file a gift tax return and, if so, how much tax she would owe. Jody has never given a taxable gift before. Donald reviewed Jody's gift transactions as follows:

1. Paid her parents' medical bills, $15,000 for her father and $10,000 for her mother
2. Bought a sports car for her son at a cost of $39,000
3. Gave $17,000 cash to her church
4. Prepared her will, leaving her vacation cabin, valued at $75,000, to her sister
5. Sent a wedding gift of $1,000 to her niece

What is Donald's best answer to Jody's questions?

A. No return is due because gifts to family are excluded.

B. Jody must file a gift tax return and will owe tax on $24,000.

C. Jody must file a gift tax return, but she will not owe tax because of the unified credit.

D. None of the answers are correct.

Answer (C) is correct.
REQUIRED: The determination for filing a gift tax return and the amount of gift tax due.
DISCUSSION: A tax return must be filed if there are any taxable gifts. After the $15,000 exclusion, Jody will have a taxable gift of $24,000 to her son. For gifts made in 2020, the applicable credit amount is $4,577,800, reduced by the amount allowable as an applicable credit amount for all preceding calendar years [Sec. 2505(a)].
Answer (A) is incorrect. A return must be filed if there are any taxable gifts. Only gifts to spouses are allowed with no limit. The gift to her son is taxable in excess of the annual exclusion. **Answer (B) is incorrect.** Due to the applicable credit, no tax will be owed.
Answer (D) is incorrect. A gift tax return must be filed, but no tax will be owed because of the applicable credit amount (unified credit).

23. In 2020, Linda gave her daughter a gift of land that had a fair market value of $12,000,000. She made no gifts from 1992 through 2020 In 1991, she used $1,506,800 of her applicable credit to offset gift tax otherwise due. What amount of applicable credit can Linda use to offset gift tax due on the 2020 gift?

A. $4,577,800

B. $3,071,000

C. $15,000

D. $0

Answer (B) is correct.
    REQUIRED: The calculation of allowable applicable credit.
    DISCUSSION: For gifts made in 2020, the applicable credit amount is $4,577,800 reduced by the amount allowable as an applicable credit amount for all preceding calendar years [Sec. 2505(a)]. Since Linda used $1,506,800 of applicable credit amount in previous years, the amount of applicable credit she may use in 2020 is $3,071,000 ($4,577,800 – $1,506,800).
    Answer (A) is incorrect. The full amount of the applicable credit amount may not be taken when the credit was used in a prior year. **Answer (C) is incorrect.** This amount is the annual exclusion. **Answer (D) is incorrect.** The applicable credit amount has increased since 1991, and the excess may be used to offset current gift tax.

24. Margaret's 2020 Form 709, page 1, has the following entries:

- $1,785,000 tax of current-year gifts
- $4,577,800 maximum unified credit
- $3,530,800 credit used in prior years

Based on this information, what is the balance due on Margaret's Form 709 Gift Tax Return this year?

A. $0

B. $1,785,000

C. $738,000

D. $1,745,800

Answer (C) is correct.
    REQUIRED: The deductible amount of unified credit.
    DISCUSSION: The applicable credit amount available to offset tax due on the current year's gifts is equal to the statutory credit for the current year reduced by the sum of the amounts allowable as a credit to the individual for all preceding calendar years [Sec. 2505(a)]. The credit may not exceed the tax for the calendar year. For 2020, the statutory credit is $4,577,800. Therefore, Margaret's balance on Form 709 is $738,000 [$1,785,000 – ($4,577,800 – $3,530,800)].
    Answer (A) is incorrect. Margaret's tax on current year gifts exceed her available unified credit. **Answer (B) is incorrect.** Margaret should deduct her maximum unified credit reduced by any credit used in prior years. **Answer (D) is incorrect.** Margaret should deduct her maximum unified credit reduced by any credit used in prior years.

25. Which of the following statements is true in respect to determining the amount of net gift tax?

A. There is a one-time marital deduction of $600,000.

B. The annual exclusion is limited to a total of $15,000 per year per donor.

C. The applicable credit amount may be used to reduce up to $4,577,800 of gift tax liability per year.

D. The applicable credit amount claimed may not exceed the tax for the calendar year.

Answer (D) is correct.
    REQUIRED: The true statement regarding net gift tax.
    DISCUSSION: The applicable credit amount available to offset tax due on the current year's gifts is equal to the statutory credit for the current year reduced by the sum of the amounts allowable as a credit to the individual for all preceding calendar years [Sec. 2505(a)]. The credit may not exceed the tax for the calendar year. For 2020, the statutory credit is $4,577,800.
    Answer (A) is incorrect. There is an unlimited marital deduction. **Answer (B) is incorrect.** The annual exclusion is available to each individual recipient. **Answer (C) is incorrect.** The applicable credit amount of $4,577,800 is a one-time credit and is eliminated when it is used up.

13.3 Gift Splitting

26. Mr. Fred Wall bought a house that cost $50,000 for an unrelated friend, Gloria Wilson, in 2020. Mrs. Wall made no gifts in 2020. In filing their gift tax returns for 2020, Mr. and Mrs. Wall should file Form 709, *United States Gift Tax Return*, as follows:

A. Mr. Wall should file a gift tax return reporting the $50,000 gift and taking a $15,000 annual exclusion.

B. File one joint gift tax return reporting the $50,000 gift and taking a $15,000 annual exclusion for each spouse, or a $30,000 exclusion.

C. File two gift tax returns, one for Mr. Wall and one for Mrs. Wall, with each spouse signing the consent section of the other's gift tax return signifying that the spouse agrees to treat all gifts as made one-half by each spouse. A $15,000 annual exclusion may be taken on each return.

D. Either Mr. Wall should file a gift tax return reporting the $50,000 gift and taking a $15,000 annual exclusion or Mr. and Mrs. Wall should file two gift tax returns, one for Mr. Wall and one for Mrs. Wall, with each spouse signing the consent section of the other's gift tax return signifying that the spouse agrees to treat all gifts as made one-half by each spouse. A $15,000 annual exclusion may be taken on each return.

Answer (D) is correct.
    REQUIRED: The proper methods of gift splitting.
    DISCUSSION: A gift tax return must be filed for a transfer that exceeds the annual exclusion. Fred may either report the entire gift on his gift tax return and take the $15,000 exclusion or elect to split the gift between his wife and himself. Gift splitting allows spouses to treat each gift as made one-half by each. This allows each spouse to exclude the first $15,000 of each gift of a present interest to a third person in a calendar year, for a total exclusion of $30,000 per donee. Gift splitting is not available to a couple if they legally divorce after the gift and one of the spouses remarries before the end of the calendar year.
    Answer (A) is incorrect. Fred may also choose to split the gift between his wife and himself. **Answer (B) is incorrect.** There is no such thing as a joint gift tax return. **Answer (C) is incorrect.** Fred may also choose to include the entire gift on his gift tax return.

27. Valerie and Dino, who were married in 2013, made a gift to their son Michael on January 2, 2020. In July 2020, Valerie and Dino were legally divorced. Valerie married Scott on December 20, 2020. Which answer below best describes this situation?

A. The gift splitting benefits are available to Valerie and Dino if Valerie consents.

B. The gift splitting benefits are not available to Valerie and Dino because they were divorced in 2020.

C. The gift splitting benefits are not available to Valerie and Dino because Valerie remarried in 2020.

D. The gift splitting benefits are available to Valerie and Dino because they were married at the time the gift was made.

Answer (C) is correct.
    REQUIRED: The proper gift splitting treatment when a couple divorces and one of the spouses remarries.
    DISCUSSION: Gift splitting allows spouses to treat each gift as made one-half by each. This allows each spouse to exclude the first $15,000 of each gift of a present interest to a third person in a calendar year, for a total exclusion of $30,000 per donee. Gift splitting is not available to a couple if they legally divorce after the gift and one of the spouses remarries before the end of the calendar year.
    Answer (A) is incorrect. Valerie and Dino were divorced and Valerie remarried. **Answer (B) is incorrect.** Valerie remarried before the end of the year. **Answer (D) is incorrect.** Valerie and Dino were divorced and Valerie remarried.

28. George and Helen are husband and wife. During 2020, George gave $36,000 to his brother and Helen gave $30,000 to her niece. George and Helen both agree to split the gifts they made during the year. What is the taxable amount of gifts, after the annual exclusion, each must report on Form 709?

    A. George and Helen each have taxable gifts of $19,000.

    B. George has a taxable gift of $21,000 and Helen has a taxable gift of $15,000.

    C. George and Helen each have taxable gifts of $3,000.

    D. George has a taxable gift of $6,000 and Helen has a taxable gift of zero.

Answer (C) is correct.
    REQUIRED: The total amount of taxable gifts to be reported by a spouse who elects gift splitting.
    DISCUSSION: Gift splitting allows spouses to treat each gift as made one-half by each. This allows each spouse to exclude the first $15,000 of each gift of a present interest to a third person in a calendar year, for a total exclusion of $30,000 per donee. The $36,000 gift to George's brother is treated as half given by George, the other half given by Helen. The same rule applies for the gift to Helen's niece. Since half of the gift to Helen's niece is $15,000 ($30,000 ÷ 2 spouses), the annual exclusion applies and neither George nor Helen must report the gift to the niece. George and Helen, for tax purposes, are considered to have given $18,000 each ($36,000 ÷ 2 spouses) to George's brother. This amount is reduced by the $15,000 annual exclusion. Thus, George and Helen each have taxable gifts of $3,000 ($18,000 − $15,000 annual exclusion).
    Answer (A) is incorrect. This answer disregards the $15,000 annual exclusion for each donee. **Answer (B) is incorrect.** Helen and George have elected to split gifts. Moreover, the $15,000 annual exclusion applies to both the gift to George's brother and the gift to Helen's niece. **Answer (D) is incorrect.** The couple has agreed to gift splitting. Therefore, Helen and George would split the gift and each would report $3,000 of taxable gifts.

29. Which of the following statements concerning gift splitting is false?

    A. To qualify for gift splitting, a couple must be married at the time the gift is made to a third party.

    B. Both spouses must consent to the use of gift splitting.

    C. For gift tax purposes, a husband and wife must file a joint income tax return to qualify for the gift splitting benefits.

    D. The annual gift tax exclusion allows spouses who consent to split their gifts to transfer up to $30,000 to any one person during any calendar year without gift tax liability, if the gift qualifies as a present interest.

Answer (C) is correct.
    REQUIRED: The false statement concerning gift splitting.
    DISCUSSION: Section 2513 allows a gift to be treated as made one-half by the donor and one-half by the donor's spouse. There are marriage and residency status requirements. The spouses are not required to file a joint gift tax return.
    Answer (A) is incorrect. The donor must be married at the time of the gift to qualify for gift splitting. **Answer (B) is incorrect.** Both spouses must consent to the use of gift splitting. **Answer (D) is incorrect.** Gift splitting allows spouses who consent to split their gifts to exclude the first $30,000 of each gift of a present interest.

30. Which of the following statements regarding gift splitting is true?

    A. The couple must have been married at the time the gift was given, but either or both spouses may be remarried during the year.

    B. The couple must have been married at the time the gift was given, and neither spouse may remarry during the year.

    C. The couple need not be married at the time of the gift, but must be married by the end of the year.

    D. The couple must be married at all times during the year.

Answer (B) is correct.
    REQUIRED: The true statement regarding gift splitting.
    DISCUSSION: Publication 950 states, "If you or your spouse make a gift to a third party, the gift can be considered as made one-half by you and one-half by your spouse." Furthermore, Instructions for Form 709 state that if a taxpayer is divorced or widowed after the gift, neither spouse may remarry during the rest of the calendar year to qualify for gift splitting.
    Answer (A) is incorrect. A married couple is not allowed gift splitting if the couple divorces after the gift, and one of the spouses remarries before the end of the calendar year. **Answer (C) is incorrect.** A married couple is not allowed gift splitting if the couple is not married at the time of the gift. **Answer (D) is incorrect.** The couple can divorce after the gift, but neither spouse can remarry before the end of the calendar year.

 Access the **Gleim EA Premium Review System** featuring our SmartAdapt technology from your Gleim Personal Classroom to continue your studies. You will experience a personalized study environment with exam-emulating multiple-choice questions.

STUDY UNIT FOURTEEN

ESTATE TAX

(9 pages of outline)

Estate taxes are wealth transfer taxes that apply to dispositions of property that occur as a result of the transferor's death. The tax base for the federal estate tax is the total of the decedent's taxable estate and adjusted taxable gifts. The taxable estate is the gross estate minus allowable deductions. Current-year applicable rates are applied to both current and preceding years' taxable gifts. The rate is 18% for taxable gifts up to $10,000. The rates increase in small steps (e.g., 2%, 3%) over numerous brackets. The maximum rate is 40% on cumulative taxable gifts and estates in excess of $11.58 million in 2020.

14.1 THE GROSS ESTATE (GE)

A decedent's gross estate includes the FMV of all property, real or personal, tangible or intangible, wherever situated, to the extent the decedent owned a beneficial interest at the time of death.

1. Included in the GE are such items as cash, personal residence and effects, securities, other investments (e.g., real estate, collector items), and other personal assets such as notes and claims (e.g., dividends declared prior to death if the record date had passed), and business interests (e.g., interest in a sole proprietorship, partnership interest).

    a. Special tax-avoidance rules are established for U.S. citizens or residents who surrender their U.S. citizenship or long-term U.S. residency.

Decedent's Liabilities

2. Liabilities of the decedent generally do not affect the amount of the GE unless the estate actually pays them.

Dower/Curtesy

3. The GE includes the value of the surviving spouse's interest in property as dower or curtesy.

    a. Dower and curtesy are common-law rights recognized in some states, usually in modified form.

        1) **Dower** entitles a surviving wife to a portion of lands her husband owned and possessed during their marriage.

        2) **Curtesy** entitles a surviving husband to a life estate in all of his wife's land if they had children.

Joint Tenants with the Right of Survivorship

4. The GE includes the full value of property held as joint tenants with the right of survivorship, except to the extent of any part shown to have originally belonged to the other person and for which adequate and full consideration was not provided by the decedent (i.e., the other tenant provided consideration).

    a. The GE includes 50% of property held as joint tenants by spouses or as tenants by the entirety regardless of the amount of consideration provided by each spouse.

Power of Appointment

5.   The value of property interests over which the decedent had a general power of appointment (POA) is included in the GE. A POA is a power exercisable in favor of the decedent, his or her estate, his or her creditors, or the creditors of his or her estate.

Government Obligations

6.   Bonds, notes, bills, and certificates of indebtedness of the federal, state, and local governments are included in the GE, even if interest on them is exempt from income tax.

Insurance Proceeds

7.   The GE includes insurance proceeds on the decedent's life in certain situations.

   a.   The insurance proceeds are payable to or for the estate (including if payable to the executor).

   b.   The decedent had any incident of ownership in the policy at death, e.g.,

   1)   Right to change beneficiaries
   2)   Right to terminate the policy

   c.   The proceeds of insurance policies given to others by the decedent within 3 years of death are included in the estate. This is an exception to the "gifts within 3 years of death rules."

   d.   The proceeds included under c. above are allocated proportionately if the premiums are partially paid by the insured and partially paid by someone else.

EXAMPLE 14-1	GE and Life Insurance Proceeds

Twenty years before her death, Joanna bought a $200,000 term life insurance policy. One year before her death, she irrevocably transferred the policy and all incidents of ownership to a trust that paid the last year's premiums. Joanna's GE included $190,000 of proceeds since Joanna paid 95% of the premiums.

Annuities and Survivor Benefits

8.   The GE includes the value of any annuity receivable by a beneficiary by reason of surviving the decedent if either of the following statements applies:

   a.   The annuity was payable to the decedent
   b.   The decedent had the right to receive the annuity or payment

   1)   Either alone or in conjunction with another
   2)   For his or her life or for any period not ascertainable without reference to his or her death, or for any period that does not end before his or her death

Medical Insurance

9.   Medical insurance reimbursements due to the decedent at death are treated as property in which the decedent had an interest.

Gifts within 3 Years of Death

10.   Gifts made within 3 years of death are not included in the GE of a decedent except for certain transfers, such as transfers of life insurance and property in which a life estate was retained.

   a.   The GE does include gift taxes paid on gifts within 3 years before death.

Inter Vivos Transfer

11. The GE includes assets transferred during life in which the decedent retained, at death, any of the following interests:

    a.   A life estate, an income interest, possession or enjoyment of assets, or the right to designate who will enjoy the property

    b.   A 5% or greater reversionary interest if possession was conditioned on surviving the decedent

    c.   The power to alter, amend, revoke, or terminate the transfer

    d.   An interest in a qualified terminable interest property (QTIP) trust

Valuing the Gross Estate

12. Value is the FMV of the property unless a special valuation rule is used.

    a.   Real property is usually valued at its highest and best use.

    b.   A transfer of interests in a corporation or partnership to a family member is subject to estate tax-freeze rules.

        1)   Generally, the retained interest is valued at zero.

    c.   Valuing property at FMV is referred to as stepped-up basis. Of course, if an asset declined in value, it would be a stepped-down basis.

13. The executor may elect to value the estate at either the date of death or the alternate valuation date. An alternate valuation date election is irrevocable.

    a.   The election can be made only if it results in a reduction in both the value of the gross estate and the sum of the federal estate tax and the generation-skipping transfer tax (reduced by allowable credits).

    b.   The alternate valuation date is 6 months after the decedent's death.

        1)   Assets sold or distributed before the alternate valuation date are valued on the date of sale or distribution.

        2)   Assets, the value of which is affected by mere lapse of time, are valued as of the date of the decedent's death, but adjustment is made for value change from other than mere lapse of time.

            a)   Examples of such assets are patents, life estates, reversions, and remainders.

            b)   The value of such assets is based on years.

            c)   Changes due to time value of money are treated as from more than mere lapse of time.

EXAMPLE 14-2   **Election of Alternate Valuation Date**

Jenny died on January 1, Year 1. On the date of death, her estate was valued at $15,000,000, of which $10,000,000 was in her stock portfolio. On July 1, Year 1, the value of her portfolio decreased to $7,000,000, and the changes in value of the remaining assets were negligible. In order to minimize the estate's tax liability, the executor of Jenny's estate should elect to use the alternate valuation date of July 1, Year 1.

STOP AND REVIEW! You have completed the outline for this subunit. Study multiple-choice questions 1 through 11 beginning on page 396.

14.2 DEDUCTIONS AND CREDITS

Deductions from the Gross Estate

1. Deductions from the GE in computing the taxable estate (TE) include ones with respect to expenses, claims, and taxes.

NOTE: A deductible amount is allowed against gross income on the decedent's final income tax return only if the right to deduct them from the GE is waived.

    a.   Expenses for selling property of an estate are deductible if the sale is necessary to

        1) Pay the decedent's debts
        2) Pay expenses of administration
        3) Pay taxes
        4) Preserve the estate
        5) Effect distribution

    b.   Administration and funeral expenses are deductible.

    c.   Claims against the estate (including debts of the decedent) are deductible.

        1) Medical expenses paid within 1 year of death may be deducted on either the estate tax return or the income tax return for the year incurred (not both).

    d.   Unpaid mortgages on property are deductible if the value of the decedent's interest is included in the GE.

    e.   State inheritance taxes are deductible from the gross estate. Federal estate taxes and income tax paid on income earned and received after the decedent's death are not deductible.

    f.   Casualty or theft losses (deemed deductible) incurred during the settlement of the estate are deductible if they were not deducted on the estate's income tax return.

Charitable Contributions

    g.   Bequests to qualified charitable organizations are deductible.

        1) The entire interest of the decedent in the underlying property generally must be donated.

        2) Trust interests may enable deductible transfer of partial interests in underlying property.

        3) An inter vivos contribution (vs. a bequest) may result in exclusion from the GE and a current deduction for regular taxable income.

Marital Transfers

    h.   Outright transfers to a surviving spouse are deductible from the GE to the extent the interest is included in the gross estate.

        1) The surviving spouse generally must be a U.S. citizen when the estate tax return is filed.

        2) A marital deduction is allowed for transfers of QTIP. These transfers allow a marital deduction where the recipient spouse is not entitled to designate which parties will eventually receive the property.

3) QTIP is defined as property that passes from the decedent in which the surviving spouse has a qualifying income interest for life and to which an election applies.

4) A spouse has a qualifying income interest for life if (s)he is entitled to all the income from the property that is paid at least annually, and no person has a power to appoint any portion of the property to anyone other than the surviving spouse unless the power cannot be exercised during the spouse's lifetime.

Credits

2. Four credits are available to offset federal estate tax liability:

   a. **Applicable credit amount** (ACA). The ACA is a base amount ($4,577,800 in 2020) not reduced by amounts allowable as credits for gift tax for all preceding tax years.

      1) The ACA offsets the estate tax liability that would be imposed on a taxable estate of up to $11.58 million, per spouse, computed at current rates (2020).

      2) The ACA was formerly called the unified credit.

      3) Any unused amount by a deceased spouse may be used by the surviving spouse in addition to the surviving spouse's own exclusion amount. Under this portability election, the surviving spouse could potentially have an available exclusion amount of $23.16 million.

EXAMPLE 14-3	Surviving Spouse's ACA

The deceased spouse only used $5.58 million of the allowed exclusion in 2020. The surviving spouse, who died later in 2020, is allowed a $17.58 million exclusion ($11.58 million surviving spouse original amount + $6 million unused by the deceased spouse).

   b. A credit is allowable for death taxes paid to foreign governments.

   c. A credit is allowable on gift tax paid on gifts made before 1977 and included in the gross estate.

   d. **Prior transfers.** A credit is allowed for taxes paid on transfers by or from a person who died within 10 years before, or 2 years after, the decedent's death.

      1) Amounts creditable are the lesser of the following:

         a) Estate tax paid by the (prior) transferor
         b) Amount by which the assets increase the estate tax

      2) Adjustment is made to the credit for transfers more than 2 years prior to the decedent's death.

Income in Respect of a Decedent

3. Beneficiaries may take a deduction for the estate tax paid on income earned before death but received after the decedent's death (income in respect of a decedent).

   a. The deduction is taken by individuals on Schedule A.

STOP AND REVIEW! You have completed the outline for this subunit. Study multiple-choice questions 12 through 18 beginning on page 401.

14.3 ESTATE TAX PAYMENT AND RETURN

The executor is required to file Form 706, *United States Estate Tax Return*, if the gross estate at the decedent's death exceeds $11.58 million in 2020. Adjusted taxable gifts made by the decedent during his or her lifetime reduce the threshold.

Return Due Date

1. The estate tax return is due within 9 months after the date of the decedent's death. An extension of up to 6 months may be granted.

Payment Due Date

2. Time for payment may be extended for a period of 1 year past the due date. For reasonable cause, the time for payment may be extended for up to 10 years.

Assessment Period

3. The general period for assessment of estate tax is 3 years after the due date for a timely filed Form 706.

    a. The assessment period is extended an additional (fourth) year on transferees for transfers from an estate.

Tax Charged to Property

4. Estate tax is charged to estate property.

    a. If the tax on part of the estate distributed is paid out of other estate property, equitable contribution from the distributee beneficiary is recoverable.

    b. The executor is ultimately liable for payment of the taxes.

Closely Held Business

5. An estate that includes a substantial interest in a closely held business may be allowed to delay payment of part of the estate tax, if that interest exceeds 35% of the gross estate.

    a. A closely held business includes the following if carrying on a trade or business:

        1) A corporation, if it has 45 or fewer shareholders or if 20% or more in value of the voting stock is included in the gross estate

        2) A partnership, if it has 45 or fewer partners or if 20% or more of the capital interests in the partnership is included in the gross estate

6. Consistent Basis Reporting for Estate Tax and Income Tax

    a. Those who file a Form 706, *United States Estate Tax Return*, after July 2015 are required to report the final estate tax value of property distributed from the estate.

        1) Form 8971, *Information Regarding Beneficiaries Acquiring Property From a Decedent*, along with a copy of every Schedule A (Form 8971), is used to report values to the IRS. Each beneficiary receiving the property is only provided their corresponding Schedule A.

        2) This filing requirement ties beneficiaries to the value the estate put on an asset for when the asset is later sold.

EXAMPLE 14-4   Beneficiary's Basis

Peter died in 2020 and left his son Victor a tract of land worth $6 million, which Peter had originally purchased for $1 million. The value of the land listed on Peter's estate tax return is $6 million, the stepped-up basis that Victor will have in the land. Victor cannot use a different appraisal amount to give himself a higher basis in the land.

   b. If the decedent has no estate tax filing requirement (for example, if the gross estate is valued less than the basic exclusion amount, which is $11,580,000 in 2020) but for whom a return is filed for the sole purpose of making an allocation or election respecting the generation-skipping transfer tax, a Form 8971 is not required.

   c. The Form 8971 due date is 30 days after the due date of the estate tax return.

   d. Form 8971 is subject to both the $280 failure to file penalty and the accuracy related 20% of underpayment penalty.

       1) The latter (i.e., 20% penalty) applies to a beneficiary overstating his or her basis in an asset upon a subsequent sale. This prevents an individual from using both a low basis to avoid estate tax and a high basis to prevent a gain on the subsequent sale.

STOP AND REVIEW! **You have completed the outline for this subunit. Study multiple-choice questions 19 through 22 beginning on page 403.**

14.4 GENERATION-SKIPPING TRANSFERS

1. The generation-skipping transfer tax (GSTT) is imposed separately and in addition to gift and estate taxes on transfers directly to or in trust for the sole benefit of a person at least two generations younger than the transferor.

    a. GSTT is generally imposed on each generation-skipping transfer (GST).

Transfer Types

    b. There are three types of GSTs:

        1) Direct skips
        2) Taxable distributions
        3) Taxable terminations

Direct Skip

2. A direct skip is a transfer of an interest in property, subject to estate tax or gift tax, to a skip person. The transferor is liable for the tax.

    a. A **skip person** is either a natural person assigned to a generation that is two or more generations below the transferor or a trust, all interests of which are held by skip persons.

    b. In the case of related persons, a skip person is identified by reference to the family tree.

        1) For example, a grandchild is two generations below the grandparent.

    c. In the case of nonrelated persons, a skip person is identified by reference to age differences.

        1) For example, an individual born between 37 1/2 years and 62 1/2 years after the transferor is two generations below the transferor.

EXAMPLE 14-5   GSTT

Darlene, age 95, left a large estate of property to her neighbor Tom, age 35, in her will. The lawyers managing the estate found that this transfer was subject to estate tax. In addition to the estate tax, Darlene's estate is responsible for the GSTT because Tom is two generations below Darlene and is a skip person.

Taxable Distribution

3. A taxable distribution is a distribution from a trust to a skip person of income or principal, other than a distribution that is a direct skip or taxable termination. The transferee is liable for the tax.

Taxable Termination

4.   A taxable termination is a termination of an interest in property held in trust. A taxable termination has not occurred if, immediately after the termination, a nonskip person has an interest in the property or if distributions are not permitted to be made to a skip person at any time following the termination.

    a.   Termination may be by lapse of time, release of power, death, or otherwise.

    b.   The trustee is liable to pay the tax.

5.   The GSTT approximates the maximum federal estate tax that would have applied to the transfer on the date of the transfer.

Exemption

6.   Each individual is allowed an $11.58 million exemption in 2020 that (s)he, or his or her executor, may allocate to GST property. The exemption is indexed for inflation.

    a.   Gift splitting applies to GSTTs; $23.16 million is allocable.

EXAMPLE 14-6	GST Exemption

Parent dies, leaving $3.5 million in trust to a child and the remainder to grandchildren. The entire $3.5 million is allocated to property held in trust. The child dies 25 years later, and the property held in trust is now worth $10 million. No GSTT is imposed.

7.   Inter vivos gifts are exempt from the GSTT if they are not subject to gift tax due to the $15,000 annual exclusion or the medical or tuition exclusion.

Computation

8.   The GSTT is computed by multiplying the taxable amount by the applicable rate.

    a.   The applicable rate is the maximum federal rate multiplied by the inclusion ratio.

        1)   The maximum federal rate is 40% (for 2020).

        2)   The inclusion ratio is

$$1 - \left(\frac{\text{Transferor's exemption allocable to property transferred}}{\text{FMV property transferred} - (\text{Estate tax} + \text{Charitable deduction})} \right)$$

9.   The GSTT does not apply when neither the federal estate tax nor the federal gift tax applies.

    a.   General power of appointment includes the trust in the estate; thus, it is not subject to GSTT.

Termination Tax

10.   Generation-Skipping Termination Tax

    a.   The interest of a non-skip person terminates by reason of death, expiration of time, or another reason, and a skip person becomes the recipient of the trust property.

EXAMPLE 14-7	Generation-Skipping Termination Tax

Under a parent's will, a trust is created with income to a child for life and corpus to a grandchild. The child's death is an event that terminates the child's interest in the trust, causing a taxable termination.

The grandchild is a skip person two generations below the parent.

    b.   The trustee files and pays the tax.

Distribution Tax

11. Generation-Skipping Distribution Tax (GSDT)

    a.   GSDT applies to trust distributions out of income or corpus to a beneficiary at least two generations below the grantor, while an older generation beneficiary has an interest in the trust.

> **EXAMPLE 14-8**   **Generation-Skipping Distribution Tax**
>
> A trust is created by a parent for a child. The trust allows for distributions to the grandchild during the child's lifetime. A taxable distribution occurs when a distribution is made from the trust to the grandchild.

    b.   The distributee is entitled to a federal income tax deduction for GSDT imposed on current distributions of trust income.

    c.   The basis of property received is increased by the proportion of GSDT imposed.

    d.   The distributee reports and pays GSDT.

        1)   A trustee's payment of GSDT is deemed an additional distribution to a beneficiary.

Direct Skips

12. A direct skip occurs when one or more generations are bypassed altogether, and property is transferred directly to or in trust for a skip person.

    a.   Direct Skip Gift Tax (DSGT)

        1)   The tax is imposed on gifts by an individual to a third generation or below beneficiary.

        2)   The tax applies only to the FMV of the property given.

        3)   Only the gift tax annual exclusion and the generation-skipping tax exemption apply.

        4)   The donor is liable for both the gift tax and the DSGT.

            a)   The donor trustor is liable if the transfer is in trust.

            b)   The donee can add a proportion of the DSGT to his or her income tax basis in property received.

            c)   The DSGT is added to federal taxable gifts, and it increases the federal gift tax.

    b.   Direct Skip Estate Tax (DSET)

        1)   The DSET applies when there is a bequest by an individual to a third generation or below beneficiary.

        2)   The donor estate is liable for the estate tax and the DSET.

        3)   Any unallocated $11.58 million generation-skipping tax exemptions are used to reduce taxable direct skip bequests.

        4)   The basis is FMV at date of death.

            a)   It is not increased by DSET.

STOP AND REVIEW! **You have completed the outline for this subunit. Study multiple-choice questions 23 through 30 beginning on page 405.**

QUESTIONS

14.1 The Gross Estate (GE)

1. Chester is preparing the estate tax return, Form 706, for his deceased brother John. John died December 15 of the current year. Which of the following will NOT be included in John's gross estate?

- A. Real estate that will be passed to John when his parents die.
- B. Stocks and bonds owned by John at his death.
- C. Land that John had signed a contract to sell, but the sale of which was not completed.
- D. Property jointly owned by John and his spouse.

Answer (A) is correct.
    REQUIRED: The item not included in a decedent's GE.
    DISCUSSION: A decedent's gross estate includes the FMV of all property, real or personal, tangible or intangible, wherever situated, to the extent the decedent owned a beneficial interest at the time of death. Special tax-avoidance rules are established for U.S. citizens or residents who surrender their U.S. citizenship or long-term U.S. residency. Included in the GE are such items as cash, personal residence and effects, securities, other investments (e.g., real estate, collector items), and other personal assets, such as notes and claims (e.g., dividends declared prior to death if the record date had passed) and business interests (e.g., partnership interest). The GE includes the value of the surviving spouse's interest in property as dower or curtesy. John does not include the real estate in his gross estate since he does not own the real estate. However, the discounted value of his remainder interest in the real estate would be included in his gross estate. John is still the owner of the land that is under contract.

2. Candace died on January 20, 2020. The assets included in her estate were valued as follows:

	1/20/20	7/20/20	10/20/20
House	$13,000,000	$12,900,000	$12,700,000
Stocks	12,850,000	12,700,000	13,000,000

The executor sold the house on October 20, 2020, for $12,700,000. The alternate valuation date was properly elected. What is the value of Candace's estate?

- A. $25,850,000
- B. $25,700,000
- C. $25,600,000
- D. $25,400,000

Answer (C) is correct.
    REQUIRED: The true value of the decedent's estate if the alternate valuation date is elected.
    DISCUSSION: Under Sec. 2032, if the executor elects to use the alternate valuation date, the estate's assets are valued as of the date 6 months after the decedent's death. Assets that are sold or distributed within that 6-month period are valued as of the date of sale or distribution. Any asset sold after the 6-month period is valued at the alternate valuation date.
    Because the home was sold after the 6-month period following the decedent's death, it is valued as of the alternate valuation date. Its value for estate tax purposes is therefore $12,900,000. The stocks are included in the estate at their alternate-valuation-date value. Thus, the value of Candace's estate is $25,600,000 ($12,900,000 house + $12,700,000 stocks).
    Answer (A) is incorrect. The alternate valuation date allows the property to be valued 6 months from the date of death. **Answer (B) is incorrect.** The alternate valuation date allows the property to be valued 6 months from the date of death. **Answer (D) is incorrect.** The property was sold after the 6-month period.

3. John, who was not married, died on October 12, 2020. He did not leave any of his assets to charity. Given the following information, may the executor of the estate make the alternate valuation election and, if so, what is the value of the gross estate on the alternate valuation date?

	FMV Date of Death	FMV Alternate Valuation
Residence	$16,000,000	$16,010,000
Installment note	5,000	500
Stock	600,000	350,000
Expenses	(450,000)	(300,000)

A. No, the election cannot be made.

B. Yes, the election can be made. The alternate value of the gross estate is $16,350,500.

C. Yes, the election can be made. The alternate value of the gross estate is $16,360,500.

D. Yes, the election can be made. The alternate value of the gross estate is $16,365,000.

Answer (C) is correct.
   REQUIRED: The value of the gross estate under the alternate valuation election.
   DISCUSSION: The election can be made only if it results in a reduction in the value of the gross estate and the sum (reduced by allowable credits) of the estate and GST taxes payable. The assets are valued on the date 6 months after the date of the decedent's death. Expenses are not included in the gross estate. Therefore, the gross estate includes the value of the residence, the stock, and the value of the installment note on the alternate valuation date (Instructions for Form 706), i.e., $16,360,500 ($16,010,000 + $500 + $350,000). It is assumed that the installment note declined in value. Any payments made on the installment note between the date of death and the alternative date are added to the estate value on the alternative date.
   Answer (A) is incorrect. The election can be made since it reduces the value of the gross estate. **Answer (B) is incorrect.** The residence is valued on the alternate valuation date. The installment note is valued on the alternative date. **Answer (D) is incorrect.** The installment note is valued on the alternative date.

4. Which of the following items are included in a decedent's gross estate?

- The decedent's IRA, where the decedent's spouse is the named beneficiary.

- A checking account with the decedent's daughter as a joint tenant. The daughter's funds were used to set up the account.

- Assets held in the decedent's revocable grantor trust.

A. All of the assets are included in the decedent's estate.

B. The IRA and checking account are included in the decedent's estate.

C. The IRA and the assets in the revocable grantor trust are included in the decedent's estate.

D. None of the assets are included in the decedent's estate.

Answer (C) is correct.
   REQUIRED: The items included in a decedent's gross estate.
   DISCUSSION: Instructions for Form 706 state that the gross estate includes all property in which the decedent had an interest, and also includes annuities, the includible portion of joint estates with right of survivorship, and property over which the decedent possessed a general power of appointment. Schedule E states, "Generally, you must include the full value of the jointly owned property in the gross estate. However, the full value should not be included if you can show . . . that any part of the property was acquired with consideration originally belonging to the surviving joint tenant or tenants. In this case, you may exclude from the value of the property any amount proportionate to the consideration furnished by the other tenant or tenants."
   Answer (A) is incorrect. The checking account is not included in the decedent's estate. **Answer (B) is incorrect.** The checking account is not included in the decedent's estate. **Answer (D) is incorrect.** The IRA and the assets in the revocable grantor trust are included in the decedent's estate.

5. Following are the fair market values of Wald's assets at the date of death:

Personal effects and jewelry	$ 2,298,000
Land bought by Wald with Wald's funds 5 years prior to death and held with Wald's sister as joint tenants with right of survivorship	11,490,000

The executor of Wald's estate did not elect the alternate valuation date. The amount includible as Wald's gross estate in the federal estate tax return is

A. $2,298,000

B. $7,660,000

C. $11,490,000

D. $13,788,000

Answer (D) is correct.
   REQUIRED: The amount includible on the estate tax return.
   DISCUSSION: The gross estate includes the value of all property in which the decedent had an interest at the time of death. Therefore, the value of the personal effects and jewelry is included in the gross estate. A decedent's gross estate includes property held jointly at the time of the decedent's death by the decedent and another person with right of survivorship. Since the decedent furnished the entire purchase price of the jointly-held property, the value of the entire property is included in the gross estate.
   Answer (A) is incorrect. The gross estate includes property the decedent held jointly with another. **Answer (B) is incorrect.** Wald furnished the entire purchase price of the jointly-held property. **Answer (C) is incorrect.** The decedent had an interest in the personal effects and jewelry.

6. Mrs. Flame passed away on March 15, 2020. The assets included in her estate were properly valued as follows:

	3/15/20	7/15/20	9/15/20
Personal residence	$14,500,000	$14,600,000	$14,700,000
Stocks held	2,000,000	1,700,000	1,750,000

The executor sold the home on July 15, 2020, for $14,600,000. The alternate valuation date was properly elected. What is the value of the estate reported for estate tax purposes?

A. $16,450,000

B. $16,500,000

C. $16,350,000

D. $16,300,000

Answer (C) is correct.
   REQUIRED: The true value of the decedent's estate if the alternate valuation date is elected.
   DISCUSSION: Under Sec. 2032, if the executor elects to use the alternate valuation date, the estate's assets are valued as of the date 6 months after the decedent's death. Assets that are sold or distributed within that 6-month period are valued as of the date of sale or distribution. Because the home was sold within the 6-month period after the decedent's death, it is valued as of the date of sale. Its value for estate tax purposes is therefore $14,600,000. The stocks are included in the estate at their alternate-valuation-date value. Therefore, the value of the estate is $16,350,000 ($14,600,000 personal residence + $1,750,000 stocks).
   Answer (A) is incorrect. The house was sold within the 6-month period. **Answer (B) is incorrect.** The home is not valued at the date of death. **Answer (D) is incorrect.** The stocks are not valued at the date the home was sold.

7. After Mary died on June 30 of the current year, her executor identified the following items belonging to her estate:

- Personal residence with a fair market value of $400,000 and an existing mortgage of $100,000
- Certificate of deposit in the amount of $150,000 of which $10,000 was accrued interest payable at maturity on August 1
- Stock portfolio with a value at date of death of $2,000,000 and a basis of $500,000
- Life insurance policy, with her daughter named as an irrevocable beneficiary, in the amount of $150,000

Assuming that no alternate valuation date is elected, what is the gross value of Mary's estate?

- A. $2,700,000
- B. $2,090,000
- C. $2,550,000
- D. $2,450,000

Answer (C) is correct.
    REQUIRED: The gross value of decedent's estate.
    DISCUSSION: The gross value of Mary's estate includes items valued at their gross amount. The $100,000 mortgage is deducted after the gross valuation of the estate. Therefore, the gross value is $2,550,000 ($400,000 personal residence + $150,000 CD + $2,000,000 stock portfolio). The life insurance is excluded under Sec. 2042 because there is no incidence of ownership of the decedent.
    Answer (A) is incorrect. The life insurance proceeds are excluded. **Answer (B) is incorrect.** The portfolio is valued at its FMV at the date of death, not her basis, and the CD's accrued interest is not deducted. **Answer (D) is incorrect.** The mortgage is not subtracted from the gross value of the estate.

8. Mr. Park died on December 1 of the current year. The alternate valuation method was not elected. The assets in his estate were valued as of the date of death as follows:

Home	$5,400,000
Car	30,000
Stocks, bonds, and savings	350,000
Jewelry	25,000
Dividends date of record November 15, not paid as of December 1	5,000
Accrued interest on savings as of December 1	2,500
Life insurance (proceeds receivable by the estate)	300,000

What is the amount of Mr. Park's gross estate?

- A. $6,112,500
- B. $6,110,000
- C. $6,105,000
- D. $5,812,500

Answer (A) is correct.
    REQUIRED: The amount of the gross estate.
    DISCUSSION: Under Sec. 2033, the value of the gross estate includes the value of all property in which the decedent had an interest at the time of death. Therefore, the value of the home, stocks, car, accrued interest, and jewelry is included in the gross estate. Section 2042 requires the inclusion of proceeds from life insurance policies when the proceeds are receivable by, or for the benefit of, the estate. A dividend is includible in the decedent's gross estate only if the decedent died after the record date of the dividend; the record date is the date when the shareholder of record becomes entitled to receive the dividend. Therefore, all of the items are included in the gross estate.
    Answer (B) is incorrect. The accrued interest is included in the gross estate. **Answer (C) is incorrect.** The accrued interest and dividends declared are included in the gross estate. **Answer (D) is incorrect.** The life insurance proceeds are included in the gross estate.

9. Laura's gross estate equals $16,000,000. Given the following information, determine Laura's taxable estate:

Charitable contribution specified in Laura's will	$100,000
Funeral expenses	10,000
Medical expenses claimed on Laura's Form 1040	20,000

A. $15,870,000

B. $15,880,000

C. $15,890,000

D. $16,000,000

Answer (C) is correct.
    REQUIRED: The amount of Laura's taxable estate.
    DISCUSSION: The estate is allowed to take a deduction for the charitable contribution and the funeral expenses. The medical expenses are not allowed to be deducted on Laura's gross estate because the expenses were already claimed on Laura's Form 1040. Medical expenses paid within 1 year of death may be deducted on either the estate tax return or the final income tax return, but not both. Therefore, the taxable estate is $15,890,000 ($16,000,000 gross estate – $100,000 charitable contribution – $10,000 funeral expenses).
    Answer (A) is incorrect. The estate is not allowed to take a deduction for the medical expenses because the expenses were already deducted on Laura's final Form 1040. **Answer (B) is incorrect.** The estate is entitled to a deduction for the charitable contribution and the funeral expenses. No deduction is allowed for the medical expenses because the expenses were already deducted on Laura's final Form 1040. **Answer (D) is incorrect.** The estate is entitled to a deduction for the charitable contribution and the funeral expenses.

10. Carl died on June 1, 2020. After determining that an estate tax return will be required, his executor decided to use the alternate valuation date for valuing the gross estate. Which of the following dates will be the alternate valuation date?

A. April 15, 2021.

B. December 31, 2020.

C. December 1, 2020.

D. On or before the due date of the *United States Estate Tax Return.*

Answer (C) is correct.
    REQUIRED: The date if the alternate valuation date is selected to value the gross estate.
    DISCUSSION: Under Sec. 2032, if the executor elects to use the alternate valuation date, the estate's assets are valued as of the date 6 months after the decedent's death.

11. When Lisa's husband died in 2017, a qualified terminable interest property (QTIP) trust he had set up, named Lisa as the beneficiary for her life. Lisa died in 2020. Given the following information, determine the value of Lisa's gross estate:

	FMV at Date of Death
Lisa's revocable grantor trust	$ 750,000
QTIP trust	1,000,000

A. $0

B. $750,000

C. $1,000,000

D. $1,750,000

Answer (D) is correct.
    REQUIRED: The value of the decedent's gross estate.
    DISCUSSION: The value of both the trusts must be included in Lisa's gross estate. Lisa is the owner at her death of a revocable grantor trust. The QTIP trust allowed her husband to take a marital deduction at his death and must be included in Lisa's estate.
    Answer (A) is incorrect. The amount of both trusts must be included when valuing Lisa's gross estate. **Answer (B) is incorrect.** The amount of $750,000 does not include the value of the QTIP trust. **Answer (C) is incorrect.** The amount of $1,000,000 does not include the value of the revocable grantor trust.

14.2 Deductions and Credits

12. Which of the following amounts paid may be claimed as a credit on the estate tax return?

A. Charitable contributions.

B. Generation-skipping transfer tax.

C. State death taxes paid.

D. None of the answers are correct.

Answer (D) is correct.
REQUIRED: The amount that may be claimed as a credit on an estate tax return.
DISCUSSION: None of the credits may be taken on the estate tax return.
Answer (A) is incorrect. Charitable contributions are a deduction from the gross estate, not a credit against the estate tax liability. **Answer (B) is incorrect.** The generation-skipping transfer tax is imposed as a separate tax, in addition to the gift and estate taxes, on generation-skipping transfers that are taxable distributions or terminations with respect to a generation-skipping trust or direct skips. **Answer (C) is incorrect.** The credit for state death taxes paid was repealed in 2005 and replaced with a deduction.

13. Which of the following tax credits are allowed on an estate tax return (Form 706)?

A. Credit for foreign death taxes.

B. Credit for federal gift taxes (pre-1977).

C. Credit for tax on prior transfers.

D. All of the answers are correct.

Answer (D) is correct.
REQUIRED: The allowed tax credits on an estate tax return.
DISCUSSION: Section 2013 allows a credit for taxes paid on prior transfers. The credit applies to a transfer of property by or from a person who died within 10 years before, or within 2 years after, the decedent's death. Section 2014 allows a credit for death taxes paid to foreign governments, and Sec. 2012 allows for a credit for gift taxes paid on federal gift taxes (pre-1977).

14. What amount of a decedent's taxable estate is effectively tax-free if the maximum applicable credit amount is taken?

A. $0

B. $15,000

C. $4,577,800

D. $11,580,000

Answer (D) is correct.
REQUIRED: The amount of a decedent's taxable estate that is effectively tax-free.
DISCUSSION: The $4,577,800 ACA for 2020 offsets the estate tax liability that would be imposed on a taxable estate of $11.58 million computed at current tax rates.
Answer (A) is incorrect. Some of the taxable estate will be effectively tax-free. **Answer (B) is incorrect.** Although $15,000 is the annual amount of gifts excluded per donee, it does not directly affect the tax-free portion of a decedent's estate. **Answer (C) is incorrect.** This amount is the ACA that offsets the estate tax liability that would be imposed on a taxable estate of $11.58 million.

15. Which of the following statements is true regarding allowable deductions on Form 706, *United States Estate Tax Return*?

A. Penalties incurred as the result of a federal estate tax deficiency are deductible administrative expenses.

B. Attorney fees paid incidental to litigation incurred by the beneficiaries are a deductible administrative expense.

C. Executor's commissions may be deducted if they have actually been paid or if it is expected that they will be paid.

D. Funeral expenses are not an allowable expense.

Answer (C) is correct.
　　REQUIRED: The true statement regarding allowable deductions on Form 706.
　　DISCUSSION: Executor's commissions may be deducted if they have actually been paid or if it is expected that they will be paid.
　　Answer (A) is incorrect. Penalties imposed by the IRS for deficiencies are not deductible on Form 706. **Answer (B) is incorrect.** Attorney fees paid incidental to litigation incurred by the beneficiaries are not deductible on Form 706. They may be deductible on the beneficiaries' Form 1040. **Answer (D) is incorrect.** Funeral expenses are deductible on Form 706.

16. Form 706, *United States Estate (and Generation-Skipping Transfer) Tax Return*, was filed for the estate of John Doe. The gross estate tax was $250,000. Which of the following items cannot be credited against the gross estate tax to determine the net estate tax payable?

A. Credit for marital deduction.

B. Credit for gift taxes (gift made pre-1977).

C. Credit for foreign death taxes.

D. Credit for tax on prior transfers.

Answer (A) is correct.
　　REQUIRED: The credit that is not deductible in the determination of the estate tax payable.
　　DISCUSSION: There is no credit for a marital deduction. Instead, the marital deduction is deductible in arriving at the taxable estate. The estate tax is then computed on the taxable estate.
　　Answer (B) is incorrect. Indirectly there is a credit for gift taxes. This reduction occurs because the gross estate tax is computed on the taxable estate and all prior transfers. Subtracted from that is the amount of tax paid on prior transfers (gifts) based on current rates to arrive at the net estate tax. **Answer (C) is incorrect.** There is a credit for death taxes paid to foreign governments. **Answer (D) is incorrect.** Section 2013 allows a credit for taxes paid on prior transfers.

17. All of the following items can be claimed as deductions against a decedent's estate EXCEPT

A. Specific bequest to son.

B. Executor's fees.

C. Legal fees to settle estate.

D. Charitable bequests.

Answer (A) is correct.
　　REQUIRED: The item that cannot be claimed as a deduction against a decedent's estate.
　　DISCUSSION: Publication 559 states, "Expenses of administering an estate can be deducted either from the gross estate in figuring the federal estate tax on Form 706 or from the estate's gross income in figuring the estate's income tax on Form 1041." Bequests to qualified charitable organizations are deductible. Publication 559 excludes a deduction for a bequest when: "It is required by the terms of the will, . . . it is a gift or bequest of a specific sum of money or property . . . [and] it is paid out in three or fewer installments under the terms of the will."

18. Which of the following items is NOT an allowable deduction on a decedent's estate tax return?

    A. Bequest to a surviving ex-spouse.

    B. Property taxes accrued before death but not paid until after death.

    C. Executor's fees for administering the estate.

    D. None of the items is allowed as a deduction against the decedent's estate.

Answer (A) is correct.

    REQUIRED: The item that is not an allowable deduction on a decedent's estate tax return.

    DISCUSSION: Publication 559 states that accrued taxes "are allowable as a deduction for estate tax purposes as claims against the estate and also are allowable as deductions in respect of a decedent for income tax purposes."

    In addition, Publication 559 states, "Expenses of administering an estate can be deducted either from the gross estate in figuring the federal estate tax on Form 706 or from the estate's gross income in figuring the estate's income tax on Form 1041."

    Publication 559 excludes a deduction for a bequest when: "It is required by the terms of the will, . . . it is a gift or bequest of a specific sum of money or property . . . [and] it is paid out in three or fewer installments under the terms of the will." A bequest to a spouse qualifies for a deduction, but not a bequest to an ex-spouse.

    Answer (B) is incorrect. Accrued taxes are allowable as a deduction for estate tax purposes. **Answer (C) is incorrect.** Expenses of administering an estate can be deducted for estate tax purposes. **Answer (D) is incorrect.** A deduction is not allowed for a bequest when it is required by the terms of the will, it is a bequest of a specific sum of money or property, and it is paid out in three or fewer installments under the terms of the will.

14.3 Estate Tax Payment and Return

19. If a person died in 2020, an estate tax return must be filed if the value of the gross estate at the date of death was more than

    A. $11,580,000

    B. $11,400,000

    C. $11,180,000

    D. $5,490,000

Answer (A) is correct.

    REQUIRED: The amount of the gross estate that requires filing an estate tax return.

    DISCUSSION: In 2020, Sec. 6018 provides that, when the gross estate of a decedent exceeds $11,580,000, the personal representative must file an estate tax return.

    Answer (B) is incorrect. The exemption amount in 2019 was $11,400,000. **Answer (C) is incorrect.** The exemption amount in 2018 was $11,180,000. **Answer (D) is incorrect.** The exemption amount in 2017 was $5,490,000.

20. On June 30, 2020, Rita died with a taxable estate of $12,340,000 and estate taxes payable of $304,000. Victor, the executor, filed the estate tax return on December 31, 2020. He distributed all the assets of the estate without paying the estate tax liability. Dustin (one of several beneficiaries) received $35,000. What are the possible tax assessments against Victor and/or Dustin?

	Victor	Dustin
A.	$304,000	$0
B.	$152,000	$152,000
C.	$304,000	$35,000
D.	$304,000	$304,000

Answer (C) is correct.
    REQUIRED: The liability of an executor and a beneficiary for estate tax due.
    DISCUSSION: An executor is personally liable for unpaid estate taxes. An estate beneficiary is also personally liable but only to the extent of the value of assets (s)he received from the estate.

21. Mr. Brown died on September 30, 2020. His gross estate was valued at $10,480,000. Unless an extension is granted, a *United States Estate Tax Return* (Form 706) must be filed on or before

A. April 15, 2021.

B. January 15, 2021.

C. June 30, 2021.

D. A *United States Estate Tax Return* does not have to be filed.

Answer (D) is correct.
    REQUIRED: The filing date of the *United States Estate Tax Return* (Form 706).
    DISCUSSION: Normally, Form 706 must be filed within 9 months after the decedent's death unless an extension is filed with Form 4768. However, no *United States Estate Tax Return* has to be filed because the value of $10,480,000 of the gross estate is below the $11,580,000 exemption amount for 2020.

22. Anna died January 20, 2020. John, the executor, filed Form 706, *United States Estate (and Generation-Skipping Transfer) Tax Return*, on June 30, 2020. John paid the tax due and distributed the assets on September 30, 2020. The assets were properly valued at $14 million on the date of death. The alternate valuation method was not elected. Generally, what is the last day that estate tax may be assessed upon recipients of property?

A. September 30, 2023.

B. October 20, 2023.

C. June 30, 2024.

D. October 20, 2024.

Answer (D) is correct.
    REQUIRED: The period for assessment of estate tax when transfers from an estate are made.
    DISCUSSION: Although the general period for assessment of estate tax is 3 years after the due date for a timely filed Form 706, the assessment period is extended an additional (fourth) year for transfers from an estate. The due date is 9 months after the date of the decedent's death.

14.4 Generation-Skipping Transfers

23. Kramer (age 63) established a trust and named his second wife, Theresa (age 50), as income beneficiary for 20 years. After 20 years, Kramer's son Trevor (age 40) and nephew Bob (age 25) are to receive lifetime income interests. Trevor died 22 years after the trust was established, and Bob died 34 years after the trust was established. After the death of both Trevor and Bob, the remainder passes equally to Kramer's granddaughter Sara (age 20) and great-granddaughter Hope (age 1). Assuming both Sara and Hope were alive when Bob died, how many times is the generation-skipping transfer tax levied?

  A. Never.

  B. Once.

  C. Twice.

  D. Three times.

Answer (B) is correct.
  REQUIRED: The number of times the generation-skipping transfer tax is levied.
  DISCUSSION: The generation-skipping transfer tax (GSTT) is imposed on generation-skipping transfers, which are any taxable distributions or terminations with respect to a generation-skipping trust or direct skips [Sec. 2611(a)]. A taxable termination means the termination of an interest held in trust unless (1) immediately after the termination a non-skip person has an interest in the trust, or (2) at no time after the termination may a distribution be made to a skip person [Sec. 2612(a)(1)]. A skip person is a natural person assigned to a generation that is two or more generations below the transferor or a trust, all interests of which are held by skip persons. A non-skip person is any person who is not a skip person [Sec. 2613(b)].
  Trevor and Bob are one generation below the transferor and are non-skip persons. There is no taxable termination on Trevor's death since Bob, a non-skip person, has an interest in the trust. Both Sara and Hope are skip persons, so there is a taxable termination on Bob's death.
  Answer (A) is incorrect. The generation-skipping transfer tax must be levied after Bob's death. **Answer (C) is incorrect.** The generation-skipping transfer tax must be levied only once after Bob's death. **Answer (D) is incorrect.** The generation-skipping transfer tax must be levied only once after Bob's death.

24. Which of the following is NOT a characteristic of a skip person as it pertains to the GSTT tax?

  A. A natural person.

  B. A person only one generation below the generation of the donor.

  C. A person two or more generations below the generation of the donor.

  D. A donee of a gift.

Answer (B) is correct.
  REQUIRED: The definition of a skip person.
  DISCUSSION: A skip person is defined in Sec. 2613(a) as a natural person assigned to a generation that is two or more generations below the generation assignment of the transferor.

25. Pearl gave $11.58 million in securities to her granddaughter Ruby in 2020. Pearl, a widow, had never made any gift to Ruby prior to the 2020 transfer. Pearl allocated $1,158,000 of her GST exemption to this direct skip. What is the generation-skipping transfer tax amount, and who must pay it?

	Tax	Payor
A.	$4,168,800	Pearl
B.	$4,168,800	Ruby
C.	$4,632,000	Pearl
D.	$4,632,000	Ruby

Answer (A) is correct.
REQUIRED: The calculation of the generation-skipping transfer tax on a direct skip in 2020.
DISCUSSION: The GSTT is the product of the taxable amount of the transfer times the applicable rate (Sec. 2602). The applicable rate is the maximum federal estate tax rate for the date of the direct skip (40% for 2020) times the inclusion ratio (Sec. 2641). The taxable amount of the transfer is $11.58 million. The inclusion ratio is one minus the fraction whose numerator is the GST exemption allocated to the property transferred, and whose denominator is the value of the transfer involved in the direct skip reduced by federal estate tax, state death taxes, and charitable deductions related to the property. The inclusion ratio in this case is

$$1 - \frac{\$1,158,000}{\$11,580,000} = 0.90$$

The generation-skipping transfer tax is the product of the taxable amount (i.e., amount transferred times the inclusion ratio) times the applicable rate (Sec. 2602). The applicable rate is the maximum federal estate tax rate for decedents dying on the date of the direct skip (40% for 2020). The tax on this transfer is $4,168,800 ($11,580,000 × 40% × 0.90). The transferor, Pearl, is liable for the tax on the direct skip [Sec. 2603(a)(3)].
Answer (B) is incorrect. Section 2603 states that the transferor (Pearl), not the transferee (Ruby), is responsible for the GSTT. **Answer (C) is incorrect.** The amount transferred multiplied by the maximum federal estate tax rate is $4,632,000. It should also be multiplied by the 0.90 inclusion ratio. **Answer (D) is incorrect.** The amount transferred multiplied by the maximum federal estate tax rate is $4,632,000. It should also be multiplied by the 0.90 inclusion ratio, and Ruby is not responsible for the GSTT.

26. Edwin gave his grandson Todd $30,000. Todd is 15 years old and lives with his parents. Which of the following statements regarding the generation-skipping transfer tax is true?

A. Because the gift is subject to the generation-skipping transfer tax, it is not subject to the regular gift tax.

B. The gift is subject to both the regular gift tax and the generation-skipping transfer tax.

C. The gift is not subject to the generation-skipping transfer tax because Todd's parents are still alive.

D. If Edwin had transferred the funds into a trust solely for his grandson's benefit, the gift would not be subject to the generation-skipping transfer tax.

Answer (B) is correct.
REQUIRED: The true statement regarding generation-skipping transfer tax.
DISCUSSION: The generation-skipping transfer tax (GSTT) is imposed, separately and in addition to gift and estate taxes, on transfers directly or in trust for the sole benefit of a person at least two generations younger than the transferor. Instructions for Form 709 specify requirements for gifts that are subject to both regular gift tax and the GSTT.
Answer (A) is incorrect. The gift is subject to gift tax in addition to the GSTT. **Answer (C) is incorrect.** The gift is subject to both gift tax and GSTT. **Answer (D) is incorrect.** Direct transfers as well as transfers in trust are subject to GSTT.

27. In 2020, Jim's will established a trust for his son Kevin and his grandsons. In 2021, a taxable termination occurred when Kevin died, and trust assets were distributed to grandsons Mark and John. Jim's executor allocated $1,500,000 of his exemption to the trust, which had a value of $6,500,000 at that time. When the taxable termination occurred in 2021, trust assets had a value of $9,000,000. State death taxes attributable to trust property were $500,000. What is the generation-skipping transfer tax due on the taxable termination?

A. $1,800,000

B. $1,950,000

C. $2,550,000

D. $2,700,000

Answer (D) is correct.
    REQUIRED: The calculation of the generation-skipping transfer tax on a taxable termination.
    DISCUSSION: The generation-skipping transfer tax is the product of the taxable amount times the applicable rate (Sec. 2602). The applicable rate is the maximum federal estate tax rate for the date of the taxable termination, taxable distribution, or direct skip (40%) times the inclusion ratio, which is 3/4 {1 − [$1,500,000 exemption ÷ ($6,500,000 trust FMV − $500,000 state death taxes)]} (Sec. 2641). The inclusion ratio is 1 minus a fraction whose numerator is the GST exemption allocated to the trust and whose denominator is generally the value of the property transferred into the trust reduced by the sum of federal estate taxes or state death taxes attributable to the property and paid by the trust and charitable deductions with respect to the trust property [Sec. 2642(a)]. The taxable amount of a taxable termination is the value of all property with respect to which the taxable termination has occurred ($9,000,000) reduced by expenses, deductions, and taxes that would be allowable under Sec. 2053 if this were an estate. State death taxes are not allowable deductions under Sec. 2053(c)(1)(B), so the taxable amount is $9,000,000. The generation-skipping transfer tax is $2,700,000 ($9,000,000 × 40% × 3/4), and the tax will be paid by the trustee from trust assets.
    Answer (A) is incorrect. It uses the initial value of the trust reduced by the state death taxes as the tax base. **Answer (B) is incorrect.** It uses the initial value of the trust ($6,500,000) as the tax base. **Answer (C) is incorrect.** It deducts the state death taxes from the 2021 value of the trust property as the tax base.

28. The generation-skipping transfer tax is imposed

A. Instead of the gift tax.

B. Instead of the estate tax.

C. As a separate tax in addition to the gift and estate taxes.

D. On transfers of future interest to beneficiaries who are more than one generation above the donor's generation.

Answer (C) is correct.
    REQUIRED: The applicability of the GSTT.
    DISCUSSION: The generation-skipping transfer tax (GSTT) is imposed, as a separate tax in addition to the gift and estate taxes, on generation-skipping transfers that are any taxable distributions or terminations with respect to a generation-skipping trust or direct skips [Sec. 2611(a)]. A taxable termination means the termination of an interest held in trust unless (1) immediately after the termination, a non-skip person has an interest in the trust or (2) at no time after the termination may a distribution be made to a skip person [Sec. 2612(a)(1)]. A skip person is a natural person assigned to a generation that is two or more generations below the transferor or a trust, all interests of which are held by skip persons.
    Answer (A) is incorrect. The GSTT is a separate tax in addition to the gift tax. **Answer (B) is incorrect.** The GSTT is a separate tax in addition to the estate tax. **Answer (D) is incorrect.** The GSTT prevents tax avoidance by transferring property directly to a person more than one generation below the donor.

29. Which of the following is a correct statement of the events that may trigger a generation-skipping transfer tax?

   A. A taxable termination only.

   B. A taxable distribution only.

   C. A taxable termination or a taxable distribution but not a direct skip.

   D. A taxable termination, a taxable distribution, or a direct skip.

Answer (D) is correct.

   REQUIRED: The event which may trigger a generation-skipping transfer tax.

   DISCUSSION: A generation-skipping transfer is defined as a taxable termination, a taxable distribution, or a direct skip [Sec. 2611(a)]. A taxable termination is a termination (by death, lapse of time, release of power, or otherwise) of an interest in property held in trust, unless immediately after the termination, a non-skip person has an interest in the property or if at no time after the termination may a distribution be made to a skip person [Sec. 2612(a)]. A taxable distribution is any distribution from a trust to a skip person if it is not a taxable termination or a direct skip [Sec. 2612(b)]. A direct skip is a transfer subject to the estate tax or the gift tax of an interest in property to a skip person. A skip person is a natural person assigned to a generation that is two or more generations below the generation assignment of the transferor or a trust where all interests are held by skip persons [Sec. 2613(a)].

   Answer (A) is incorrect. It is not the only event that may trigger a generation-skipping transfer tax. **Answer (B) is incorrect.** It is not the only event that may trigger a generation-skipping transfer tax. **Answer (C) is incorrect.** A direct skip may trigger a generation-skipping transfer tax.

30. Which of the following is a true statement about the taxable amount of a generation-skipping transfer?

   A. The taxable amount for a direct skip and a taxable termination are the same.

   B. The taxable amount for a taxable termination is the value of the property received by the transferee reduced by expenses incurred by the transferee in connection with the determination, collection, or refund of the GSTT.

   C. The taxable amount for a taxable distribution is the value of all property distributed less allowable expenses, debt, and taxes.

   D. If a generation-skipping transfer tax on a taxable distribution is paid by the generation-skipping trust, an amount equal to the taxes paid by the trust will be treated as a taxable distribution.

Answer (D) is correct.

   REQUIRED: The true statement about the taxable amount of a generation-skipping transfer.

   DISCUSSION: Under Sec. 2603, the transferee is liable for the GSTT on a taxable distribution. Therefore, if the GSTT on a taxable distribution is paid by the trust, the transferee is deemed to have received an additional taxable distribution equal to the amount of taxes paid by the trust [Sec. 2621(b)].

   Answer (A) is incorrect. The taxable amount of a direct skip is the amount received by the transferee before taxes (Sec. 2623), but the taxable amount of a taxable termination (Sec. 2622) is the value of all property, with respect to which the termination occurred, reduced by deductions similar to those deductible against a gross estate under Sec. 2053 (taxes, debt, certain expenses). **Answer (B) is incorrect.** It describes the taxable amount of a taxable distribution (Sec. 2621) but not a taxable termination. **Answer (C) is incorrect.** The taxable amount of a taxable distribution is the value of property received by the transferee less any expense incurred by the transferee in connection with the determination, collection, or refund of the GSTT.

Access the **Gleim EA Premium Review System** featuring our SmartAdapt technology from your Gleim Personal Classroom to continue your studies. You will experience a personalized study environment with exam-emulating multiple-choice questions.

APPENDIX A
CALCULATING PHASEOUTS

The EA exam topics include several items (exclusions, deductions, credits, exemptions, etc.) that are phased out based on the amount of the taxpayer's income. In this appendix, we present the general formulas required for calculating the appropriate amounts subject to a phaseout. The details specific to each exam topic are presented in the related Knowledge Transfer Outline material.

The income limits are most often based on adjusted gross income or a modification of such. A taxpayer with income at or below the minimum amount of the phaseout range (i.e., lower threshold) will not have any reduction to the maximum amount of the exclusion, deduction, etc. (i.e., 100% is allowed). A taxpayer with income at or above the maximum amount of the phaseout range (i.e., upper threshold) will not be allowed any of the exclusion, deduction, etc. (i.e., 100% is disallowed).

The most common method/formula simply multiplies the maximum amount of the exclusion, deduction, etc., by the difference of the taxpayer's AGI and the lower threshold over the difference of the upper threshold and the lower threshold. This is referred to as a **proportionate** reduction.

$$\text{Amount (exclusion, deduction, etc.)} \times \frac{\text{AGI} - \text{Applicable minimum phaseout amount}}{\text{Maximum phaseout amount} - \text{Minimum phaseout amount}}$$

EXAMPLE A-1

A $2,500 deduction of interest paid on qualified education loans begins to be phased out for joint filers when AGI exceeds $140,000 and is completely phased out when AGI reaches $170,000. Assume for this example that the couple's AGI is $150,000. The $2,500 deduction would be reduced by $833 for a total allowed deduction of $1,667.

$$\$2,500 \times \frac{\$150,000 - \$140,000}{\$170,000 - \$140,000} = \$833 \quad \text{Alternative calculation: } \$2,500 \times \left[1 - \left(\frac{\$150,000 - \$140,000}{\$170,000 - \$140,000}\right)\right]$$

Other phaseouts are based on a percentage and are calculated as follows:

$$(\text{AGI} - \text{Applicable minimum phaseout amount}) \times \text{Applicable percentage}$$

EXAMPLE A-2

A single taxpayer who otherwise qualifies for a $538 Earned Income Credit with no qualifying child has AGI of $11,770. The taxpayer's allowed credit would be reduced by $228 for a total credit allowed of $310. The applicable phaseout percentage for a single taxpayer with no qualifying child is 7.65%.

$(\$11,770 - \$8,790) \times 7.65\% = \$228$ Alternative calculation: $\$538 - [(\$11,770 - \$8,790) \times 7.65\%]$

Finally, other phaseouts are performed in steps (i.e., not proportionate over the applicable income range).

1. (AGI – Applicable minimum phaseout amount) ÷ Step amount = Step designator (always round up)
2. Step designator × Designated amount = Reduction amount
3. Maximum credit – Reduction amount = Allowable credit

EXAMPLE A-3

Taxpayers filing jointly with a $6,000 Child Tax Credit and AGI of $404,400 are allowed a credit of only $5,750.

1) ($404,400 – $400,000) ÷ $1,000 = 4.4, which rounds up to 5
2) 5 × $50 = $250
3) $6,000 – $250 = $5,750

APPENDIX B
EXAM CONTENT OUTLINES WITH
GLEIM CROSS-REFERENCES

This section contains the Part 1 Exam Content Outlines (ECOs) for 2021/2022.

The ECOs are subdivided into sections, and each section has one or more topics, which are further divided into specific items. According to the IRS's *Candidate Information Bulletin* (available at www.prometric.com/irs), not every topic in the ECOs will appear on the exam, and the list of topics may not be all-inclusive. However, the ECOs are meant to reflect the knowledge needed for tasks performed by EAs.

Next to each topic, we have provided a cross-reference to the most relevant Gleim study unit(s) or subunit(s).

Section 1: Preliminary Work with Taxpayer Data (14 Questions)

a. **Preliminary Work to Prepare Tax Returns**

1) Use of prior years' returns for comparison, accuracy, and carryovers for current year's return – 1.1

2) Taxpayer personal information (e.g., date of birth, marital status, dependents, identity protection PIN, state issued photo ID) – 1.1, 1.3

3) Residency status and/or citizenship (e.g., visas, green cards, resident alien or non-resident alien, ITIN) – 1.1, 1.6

4) Filing requirements and due date – 1.3

5) Taxpayer filing status – 1.2

6) Sources of worldwide taxable and non-taxable income (e.g., interest, wages, business, sales of property, dividends, rental income, flow-through entities, alimony received) – 1.1, 2, 3

7) Sources of applicable exclusions and adjustments to gross income (e.g., foreign earned income exclusion, retirement plans, HSAs, alimony paid, health insurance, self-employment tax) – 2, 3, 5.2-5.5

8) Sources of applicable deductions (e.g., itemized, standard) – 1.2, 6, 7.1

9) Qualification for dependency – 1.4

10) Sources of applicable credits (e.g., education, foreign tax, child and dependent care, credit for other dependents, child tax credit) – 8.1

11) Sources of tax payments and refundable credits – 8

12) Previous IRS correspondence with taxpayer – 1.1

13) Additional required returns to be filed, and taxes paid (e.g., employment, gifts, international information returns, and other information returns) – 1.1, 7.2-7.3, 13, 14

14) Special filing requirements (e.g., foreign income, presidentially declared disaster areas, injured spouse) – 1.1, 1.3, 2, 6.5, 8

15) Foreign account and asset reporting (e.g., FBAR, Form 8938) – 1.1, 7.3

16) Minor children's unearned income ("Kiddie" tax) – 1.5

17) ACA requirements (e.g., total household income, premium tax credit, household size) – 6.1, 7.3, 8.1

Section 2: Income and Assets (17 Questions)

a.   **Income**

    1)   Taxability of wages, salaries and other earnings – 2

    2)   Interest Income (e.g., taxable and non-taxable) – 3.1

    3)   Dividends and other distributions from mutual funds, corporations, and other entities – 3.2

    4)   Personal property rental – 2

    5)   Gambling income and allowable deductions (e.g., Form W-2G, documentation) – 2, 6.6

    6)   Tax treatment of cancellation of debt (e.g., Form 1099C, foreclosures, insolvency) – 2

    7)   Tax treatment of a U.S. citizen/resident with foreign income (e.g., tax treaties, Form 1116, Form 2555, Form 3520, Form 5471) – 1.1, 2, 8.1

    8)   Other income (e.g., scholarships, barter income, hobby income, alimony, non-taxable combat pay, unearned income, taxable recoveries, NOL, illegal income) – 2, 4.1, 6.5, 7.2

    9)   Constructive receipt of income – 2

    10)   Constructive dividends (e.g., payments of personal expenses from a business entity) – 3.2

    11)   Passive income and loss – 5.8

    12)   Pass-through income (e.g., Schedule K-1, income, deductions, basis, qualified business income (QBI) items) – 5.8, 7.1

    13)   Royalties and related expenses – 2

    14)   State/local income tax refund and other itemized deduction recoveries – 2

    15)   1099 MISC, 1099 NEC, 1099 K reporting, irregularities, and corrections – 2, 4.1

b.   **Retirement Income**

    1)   Basis in a traditional IRA (Form 8606) – 12.2

    2)   Comparison of and distributions from traditional and Roth IRAs – 5.5, 12.3-12.4

    3)   Distributions from qualified and non-qualified plans (e.g., pre-tax, after-tax, rollovers, Form 1099R, qualified charitable distribution) – 5.5, 12

    4)   Excess contributions and tax treatment (e.g., penalties) – 12.3

    5)   Penalties and exceptions on premature distributions from qualified retirement plans and IRAs – 12.3

    6)   Prohibited transactions and tax consequences – 12.1-12.3

    7)   IRA conversions and recharacterization (Form 8606) – 12.4

    8)   Required minimum distributions – 12.3

    9)   Loans from qualified plans – 12.3

    10)   Taxability of Social Security and Railroad Retirement benefits – 1.3, 2

    11)   Inherited retirement accounts – 12.2

    12)   Foreign pensions and retirement income – 2

c.   **Property, Real and Personal**

    1)   Sale or disposition of property including depreciation recapture rules and 1099A – 2, 7.2, 10-11

    2)   Capital gains and losses (e.g., netting effect, short-term, long-term, mark-to-market, virtual currency) – 2, 9.8-9.9

    3)   Basis of assets (e.g., purchased, gifted or inherited) – 9.1-9.6

    4)   Basis of stock after stock splits and/or stock dividends (e.g., research, schedules, brokerage records) – 9.5

5) Publicly traded partnerships (PTP) (e.g., sales, dispositions, losses) – 1.1

6) Sale of a personal residence (e.g., IRC sec 121 exclusions) – 11.1

7) Installment sales (e.g., related parties, original cost, date of acquisition, possible recalculations and recharacterization) – 10.3

8) Options (e.g., stock, commodity, ISO, ESPP) – 3.2

9) Like-kind exchange – 11.2

10) Non-business bad debts – 4.1

11) Investor versus trader – 9.8

d. **Adjustments to Income**

1) Self-employment tax – 5.3, 7.3

2) Retirement contribution limits and deductibility (e.g., earned compensation requirements) – 5.3, 5.5

3) Health savings accounts – 5.2

4) Other adjustments to income (e.g., student loan interest, alimony, moving expenses for active military, write-in adjustments) – 5.3-5.7

5) Self-Employed Health Insurance – 5.3

Section 3: Deductions and Credits (17 Questions)

a. **Itemized Deductions and QBI**

1) Medical, dental, vision, long-term care expenses – 6.1

2) Various taxes (e.g., state and local, personal property, real estate) – 6.2

3) Interest expense (e.g., mortgage interest, investment interest, tracing rules, points, indebtedness limitations) – 6.3

4) Charitable contributions (e.g., cash, non-cash, limitations, documentation required) – 6.4

5) Nonbusiness casualty and theft losses – 6.5

6) Other itemized deductions – 6.6

7) Itemized deductions for Form 1040-NR – 1.6

8) Qualified Business Income (QBI) deduction – 7.1

b. **Credits**

1) Child and dependent care credit – 8.1

2) Child tax credit and credit for other dependents – 8.1

3) Education credits – 8.1

4) Foreign tax credit – 8.1

5) Earned income tax credit (e.g., paid preparer's earned income credit checklist, eligibility and disallowance) – 8.1

6) Adoption credits (e.g., carryovers, limitations, special needs) – 8.1

7) ACA premium tax credit – 8.1

8) Other credits (refundable and non-refundable) (e.g., health coverage tax credit, energy credits, Retirement savings contribution credit) – 8.1

Section 4: Taxation (15 Questions)

a.   **Taxation**

1)   Alternative minimum tax and credit for prior year – 7.2, 8.1
2)   Household employees – 7.3
3)   Underpayment penalties and interest – 8.2
4)   Self-employment tax – 5.3, 7.3
5)   Excess Social Security withholding – 8.2
6)   Tax provisions for members of the clergy – 7.3
7)   Tax provisions for members of the military – 1.1, 1.3, 2, 5.7, 6.3
8)   Income in respect of decedent – 2, 3.3, 6.6, 9.4, 10.2, 14.2
9)   Net investment income tax – 7.3
10)   Additional Medicare tax – 7.3
11)   Uncollected Social Security and Medicare tax – 7.3
12)   Other taxes (e.g., first time homebuyer credit repayment) – 7.3, 8.1

Section 5: Advising the Individual Taxpayer (11 Questions)

a.   **Advising the Individual Taxpayer**

1)   Reporting obligations for individuals (e.g., 1099, bartering, cash) – 1-14

2)   Property sales (e.g., homes, stock, businesses, antiques, collectibles) – 10-11

3)   Education planning (e.g., lifetime learning credit, IRC section 529 plans) – 8.1, 13.2

4)   Estate planning (e.g., gift versus inheritance, trusts, family partnerships, charitable giving, long-term care, life insurance) – 14

5)   Retirement planning (e.g., annuities, IRAs, employer plans, early retirement rules, required minimum distribution, beneficiary ownership, charitable distributions from an IRA) – 12

6)   Marriage and divorce (e.g., divorce settlement, common-law, community property, alimony) – 2, 5.4

7)   Items that will affect future/past returns (e.g., carryovers, net operating loss, Schedule D, Form 8801, negative QBI carryover) – 1.1, 5.8, 7.1

8)   Injured spouse – 1.2

9)   Innocent spouse – 1.2

10)   Estimated tax and penalty avoidance (e.g., mid-year estimated tax planning) – 8.2

11)   Adjustments, deductions, and credits for tax planning (e.g., timing of income and expenses) – 4-7

12)   Character of transaction (e.g., use of capital gain rates versus ordinary income rates) – 2, 9.8

13)   Advantages and disadvantages of MFJ/MFS/HOH filing statuses in various scenarios (e.g., joint and several liability) – 1.2

14)   Conditions for filing a claim of refund (e.g., amended returns) – 8.2

15)   Penalty of perjury – 1.3

Section 6: Specialized Returns for Individuals (11 Questions)

a.   **Estate Tax**

    1)   Gross estate, taxable estate (calculations and payments), unified credit – 14.1
    2)   Jointly held property – 14.1
    3)   Marital deduction and other marital issues (e.g., portability election) – 14.2
    4)   Life insurance, IRAs, and retirement plans – 14.1
    5)   Estate filing requirements and due dates (e.g., Form 706; Form 1041) – 14.3

b.   **Gift Tax**

    1)   Gift-splitting – 13.3
    2)   Annual exclusion – 13.2
    3)   Unified credit – 13.2
    4)   Effect on estate tax (e.g., Generation skipping transfer tax) – 14.1, 14.4
    5)   Filing requirements (e.g., Form 709) – 13.1

c.   **International Information Reporting**

    1)   Filing and reporting requirements and due dates (e.g., FBAR, Form 8938, Form 8865, Form 5471, Form 3520) – 1.1, 7.3

    2)   Covered accounts (e.g., FBAR, Form 8938) – 1.1

    3)   Potential penalties (e.g., failure to file, underreporting, substantially incomplete, statute of limitations, reduction of tax attributes) – 1.1, 8.2

    4)   Distinctions between FBAR and Form 8938 requirements – 1.1

INDEX